HORNGREN'S

10TH CANADIAN EDITION

ACCOUNTING

D0536225

VOLUME TWO

HORNGREN'S 10TH CANADIAN EDITION
ACCOUNTING

TRACIE L. MILLER-NOBLES
Austin Community College

BRENDA MATTISON
Tri-County Technical College

ELLA MAE MATSUMURA
University of Wisconsin–Madison

CAROL A. MEISSNER
Georgian College

JO-ANN L. JOHNSTON
British Columbia Institute of Technology

PETER R. NORWOOD
Langara College

VOLUME TWO

Toronto

Editorial Director: Claudine O'Donnell
Senior Acquisitions Editor: Megan Farrell
Senior Marketing Manager: Loula March
Program Manager: Patricia Ciardullo
Project Manager: Sarah Lukaweski
Manager of Content Development: Suzanne Schaan
Developmental Editor: Suzanne Simpson Millar
Production Editor: Leanne Rancourt
Media Editor: Anita Smale
Media Developer: Olga Avdyeyeva

Copyeditor: Leanne Rancourt
Proofreaders: Susan Broadhurst and
    Bradley T. Smith
Permissions Project Manager: Joanne Tang
Photo and Text Permissions Research: Integra
    Publishing Services
Compositor: Cenveo® Publisher Service
Interior and Cover Designer: Anthony Leung
Cover Image: © John Kuczala / Getty Images

Vice-President, Cross Media and Publishing Services: Gary Bennett

Credits and acknowledgments for material borrowed from other sources and reproduced, with permission, in this textbook appear on the appropriate page within the text.

5   17

Library and Archives Canada Cataloguing in Publication

Miller-Nobles, Tracie L., author
    Horngren's accounting / Tracie Nobles (Texas State University-San
Marcos), Brenda Mattison (Tri-County Technical College), Ella Mae
Matsumura (University of Wisconsin-Madison), Carol A. Meissner (Georgian
College), Jo-Ann L. Johnston (British Columbia Institute of Technology), Peter
R. Norwood (Langara College). – Tenth Canadian edition.

Includes indexes.
Issued in print and electronic formats.
ISBN 978-0-13-385537-1 (volume 1 : paperback).—ISBN 978-0-13-414064-3
(volume 1 : loose leaf).—ISBN 978-0-13-385538-8 (volume 2 : paperback).—
ISBN 978-0-13-418293-3 (volume 2 : loose leaf).—ISBN 978-0-13-418033-5
(volume 1 : html).—ISBN 978-0-13-418140-0 (volume 2 : html)

    1. Accounting—Textbooks. I. Norwood, Peter R., author
II. Matsumura, Ella Mae, 1952-, author III. Johnston, Jo-Ann L., author
IV. Mattison, Brenda, author V. Meissner, Carol A., author VI. Title.
VII. Title: Accounting.

HF5636.M54 2016   657   C2015-904630-0
C2015-904631-9

ISBN 978-0-13-385538-8

In memory of *Charles T. Horngren* 1926–2011

Whose vast contributions to the teaching and learning of accounting impacted and will continue to impact generations of accounting students and professionals.

I would like to thank my students for keeping me on my toes. Hearing their new ideas and how they think about accounting makes teaching such a wonderful job.

Carol A. Meissner

I would like to thank my husband, Bill, and my family for their encouragement and support.

Jo-Ann L. Johnston

I would like to thank my wife, Helen, and my family very much for their support and encouragement.

Peter R. Norwood

BRIEF CONTENTS

Part 1 The Basic Structure of Accounting

1 Accounting and the Business Environment *2*
2 Recording Business Transactions *58*
3 Measuring Business Income: The Adjusting Process *116*
4 Completing the Accounting Cycle *174*
5 Merchandising Operations *244*
6 Accounting for Merchandise Inventory *324*
7 Accounting Information Systems *376*

Part 2 Accounting for Assets and Liabilities

8 Internal Control and Cash *444*
9 Receivables *504*
10 Property, Plant, and Equipment; and Goodwill and Intangible Assets *558*
11 Current Liabilities and Payroll *612*

Part 3 Accounting for Partnerships and Corporate Transactions

12 Partnerships *672*
13 Corporations: Share Capital and the Balance Sheet *728*
14 Corporations: Retained Earnings and the Income Statement *780*
15 Long-Term Liabilities *836*
16 Investments and International Operations *910*

Part 4 Analysis of Accounting Information

17 The Cash Flow Statement *974*
18 Financial Statement Analysis *1054*

CONTENTS

Part 3 Accounting for Partnerships and Corporate Transactions 672

12 Partnerships 672

Characteristics of a Partnership 675
Types of Partnerships 677
Partnership Financial Statements 678
Forming a Partnership 679
Sharing Partnership Profits and Losses 681
Partner Withdrawals (Drawings) 686
Admission of a Partner 688
Withdrawal of a Partner from the Business 693
Liquidation of a Partnership 696

Summary Problem for Your Review 700

Summary 702

Assignment Material 705

Extending Your Knowledge 725

13 Corporations: Share Capital and the Balance Sheet 728

Corporations 730
Shareholders' Equity 733
Issuing Shares 736
Ethical Considerations in Accounting for the Issuance of Shares 742
Organization Costs 742
Accounting for Cash Dividends 743
Different Values of Shares 746
Evaluating Operations 748
The Impact of IFRS on Share Capital 750

Summary Problem for Your Review 751

Summary 753

Assignment Material 757

Extending Your Knowledge 776

14 Corporations: Retained Earnings and the Income Statement 780

Retained Earnings 782
Stock Dividends 783
Stock Splits 785
Repurchase of Its Shares by a Corporation 788
Ethical and Legal Issues for Share Transactions 791
The Corporate Income Statement 792
Statement of Retained Earnings 798
Statement of Shareholders' Equity 799
Accounting for Errors and Changes in Accounting Policy and Circumstances 800
Restrictions on Retained Earnings 802
The Impact of IFRS on the Income Statement and the Statement of Shareholders' Equity 803

Summary Problem for Your Review 806

Summary 808

Assignment Material 811

Extending Your Knowledge 832

15 Long-Term Liabilities 836

Bonds: An Introduction 838
Bond Prices 841
Issuing Bonds to Borrow Money 843
Amortization of a Bond Discount and a Bond Premium 849
Reporting Liabilities and Bonds Payable 855
Adjusting Entries for Interest Expense 855
Retirement of Bonds 858
Convertible Bonds and Notes 859
Advantages and Disadvantages of Issuing Bonds versus Shares 860
Mortgages and Other Long-Term Liabilities 862
Lease Liabilities 863
The Effects on Long-Term Liabilities of IFRS 867

Summary Problem for Your Review 868

Summary 870

Assignment Material 874

Extending Your Knowledge 895

Chapter 15 Appendix: Time Value of Money: Future Value and Present Value 897

16 Investments and International Operations 910

Share Investments **912**
Accounting for Short-Term Investments **914**
Accounting for Long-Term Share Investments **917**
Long-Term Share Investments Accounted for by the Equity Method **920**
Long-Term Share Investments Accounted for by the Consolidation Method **923**
Consolidated Financial Statements **925**
Investments in Bonds **931**
Foreign-Currency Transactions **935**
The Impact of IFRS on Accounting for Investments and International Transactions **940**

Summary Problems for Your Review **941**

Summary **944**

Assignment Material **947**

Extending Your Knowledge **968**

Comprehensive Problem for Part 3 972

Part 4 Analysis of Accounting Information 974

17 The Cash Flow Statement 974

The Cash Flow Statement: Basic Concepts **978**
Purpose of the Cash Flow Statement **979**
Operating, Investing, and Financing Activities **981**
Measuring Cash Adequacy: Free Cash Flow **984**
Format of the Cash Flow Statement **985**
The Cash Flow Statement: The Direct Method **986**
Computing Individual Amounts for the Cash Flow Statement **991**
The Cash Flow Statement: The Indirect Method **1000**
The Impact of IFRS on the Cash Flow Statement **1005**

Summary Problem for Your Review **1006**

Summary **1012**

Assignment Material **1014**

Extending Your Knowledge **1048**

18 Financial Statement Analysis 1054

Objectives of Financial Statement Analysis **1056**
Methods of Analysis **1057**
Horizontal Analysis **1057**
Vertical Analysis **1061**
Common-Size Statements **1063**
Using Ratios to Make Decisions **1066**
Limitations of Financial Analysis **1076**
Investor Decisions **1077**
The Impact of IFRS on Financial Statement Analysis **1081**

Summary Problem for Your Review **1081**

Summary **1083**

Assignment Material **1087**

Extending Your Knowledge **1117**

Comprehensive Problem for Part 4 1123

Appendix A: Indigo Books and Music Inc. 2014 Annual Report **A-1**

Appendix B: Typical Chart of Accounts for Service Proprietorships and Partnerships (ASPE), and Merchandising Corporations (IFRS) **B-1**

Glossary G-1
Index I-1

ABOUT THE AUTHORS

TRACIE L. MILLER-NOBLES, CPA, received her bachelor's and master's degrees in accounting from Texas A&M University. She is an associate professor at Austin Community College. Previously she served as a senior lecturer at Texas State University, San Marcos, Texas, and has served as department chair of the Accounting, Business, Computer Information Systems, and Marketing/Management Department at Aims Community College, Greeley, Colorado. In addition, Tracie has taught as an adjunct professor at University of Texas and has public accounting experience with Deloitte Tax LLP and Sample & Bailey, CPAs.

Tracie is a recipient of the Texas Society of CPAs Outstanding Accounting Educator Award, NISOD Teaching Excellence Award, and the Aims Community College Excellence in Teaching Award. She is a member of the Teachers of Accounting at Two Year Colleges, the American Accounting Association, the American Institute of Certified Public Accountants, and the Texas State Society of Certified Public Accountants. She is currently serving on the board of directors as secretary/webmaster of Teachers of Accounting at Two Year Colleges, as chair of the American Institute of Certified Public Accountants Pre-certification Executive Education committee, and as program chair for the Teaching, Learning and Curriculum section of the American Accounting Association. In addition, Tracie served on the Commission on Accounting Higher Education: Pathways to a Profession.

Tracie has spoken on such topics as using technology in the classroom, motivating nonbusiness majors to learn accounting, and incorporating active learning in the classroom at numerous conferences. In her spare time she enjoys spending time with her friends and family, and camping, fishing, and quilting.

BRENDA L. MATTISON has a bachelor's degree in education and a master's degree in accounting, both from Clemson University. She is currently an accounting instructor at Tri-County Technical College (TCTC) in Pendleton, South Carolina. Brenda previously served as Accounting Program Coordinator at TCTC and has prior experience teaching accounting at Robeson Community College, Lumberton, North Carolina; University of South Carolina Upstate, Spartanburg, South Carolina; and Rasmussen Business College, Eagan, Minnesota. She also has accounting work experience in retail and manufacturing businesses.

Brenda is a member of Teachers of Accounting at Two Year Colleges and the American Accounting Association. She is currently serving on the board of directors as vice-president of registration of Teachers of Accounting at Two Year Colleges.

Brenda engages in the scholarship of teaching and learning (SOTL). While serving as Faculty Fellow at TCTC, her research project was Using Applied Linguistics in Teaching Accounting, the Language of Business. Brenda has presented her research findings. Other presentations include using active learning and manipulatives, such as building blocks and poker chips, in teaching accounting concepts.

In her spare time, Brenda enjoys reading and spending time with her family, especially touring the United States in their motorhome. She is also an active volunteer in the community, serving her church, local Girl Scouts, and other organizations.

ELLA MAE MATSUMURA is a professor in the Department of Accounting and Information Systems in the School of Business at the University of Wisconsin—Madison, and is affiliated with the university's Center for Quick Response Manufacturing. She received a Bachelor of Arts degree in mathematics from the University of California, Berkeley, and a Master of Science and PhD degree from the University of British Columbia. Ella Mae has won two teaching excellence awards at the University of Wisconsin–Madison and was elected as a lifetime fellow of the university's Teaching Academy, formed to promote effective teaching. She is a member of the university team awarded an IBM Total Quality Management Partnership grant to develop curriculum for total quality management education.

Ella Mae was a co-winner of the 2010 Notable Contributions to Management Accounting Literature Award. She has served in numerous leadership positions in the American Accounting Association (AAA). She was co-editor of *Accounting Horizons* and has chaired and served on numerous AAA committees. She has been secretary–treasurer and president of the AAA's Management Accounting Section. Her past and current research articles focus on decision making, performance evaluation, compensation, supply chain relationships, and sustainability. She co-authored a monograph on customer profitability analysis in credit unions.

CAROL A. MEISSNER is a professor in both the School of Business and the Automotive Business School of Canada at Georgian College in Barrie, Ontario. She teaches in the Accounting Diploma,

Automotive Business Diploma, and Bachelor of Business (Automotive Management) programs. Her favourite courses are introductory financial accounting and dealership financial statement analysis.

In 2014, Carol was awarded the Georgian College Board of Governors' Award of Excellence Academic for outstanding contributions to the college and an ongoing commitment to excellence.

Carol has broad experience in curriculum development. She has been a curriculum chair, program coordinator, member of several curriculum committees, and has been involved in writing and renewing degree, diploma, and graduate certificate programs. She is currently helping to launch the new Automotive Dealership Management graduate certificate program for automotive industry executives.

A self-professed "learning junkie," Carol holds a Bachelor of Commerce degree, a Master of Business Administration degree, a Master of Arts degree in Education (Community College concentration), and a CPA designation. She has also earned Georgian College's Professional Development Teaching Practice Credential and is a graduate of Georgian's Aspiring Leaders program. She is a regular attendee at conferences related to teaching, accounting, and the automotive industry.

Carol has always been a teacher. She started as a part-time college instructor when she completed her first degree and has taught full time since 2005. Her "real world" experience includes car dealership controllership and self-employment as a part-time controller and consultant for a wide variety of businesses. Carol recently worked on several online projects for publishers and OMVIC as a subject matter expert. She is a trustee for OPSEU Local 35 and a member of the Secretary Treasurers Association of Ontario.

JO-ANN JOHNSTON is an instructor in the Accounting, Finance and Insurance Department at the British Columbia Institute of Technology (BCIT). She obtained her Diploma of Technology in Financial Management from BCIT, her Bachelor in Administrative Studies degree from British Columbia Open University, and her Master of Business Administration degree from Simon Fraser University. She is also a certified general accountant and completed the Canadian securities course.

Prior to entering the field of education, Jo-Ann worked in public practice and industry for over 10 years. She is a past member of the board of governors of the Certified General Accountants Association of British Columbia and has served on various committees for the association. She was also a member of the board of directors for the BCIT Faculty and Staff Association, and served as treasurer during that tenure.

In addition to teaching duties and committee work for BCIT, Jo-Ann is the financial officer for a family-owned business.

PETER R. NORWOOD is an instructor in accounting and coordinator of the Accounting program at Langara College in Vancouver. A graduate of the University of Alberta, he received his Master of Business Administration from the University of Western Ontario. He is a CPA, a fellow of the Institute of Chartered Accountants of British Columbia, a certified management accountant, and a fellow of the Society of Management Accountants of Canada.

Before entering the academic community, Peter worked in public practice and industry for over 15 years. He is a past president of the Institute of Chartered Accountants of British Columbia and chair of the Chartered Accountants School of Business (CASB). He is also the chair of the Chartered Accountants Education Foundation for the British Columbia Institute of Chartered Accountants and has been active on many provincial and national committees, including the Board of Evaluators of the Canadian Institute of Chartered Accountants. Peter is also a sessional lecturer in the Sauder School of Business at the University of British Columbia.

HORNGREN'S ACCOUNTING ... REDEFINING TRADITION

MAKING CONNECTIONS

CONNECTING CHAPTER boxes appear at the beginning of each chapter. These features combine the chapter outline with the learning objectives, key questions, and page references.

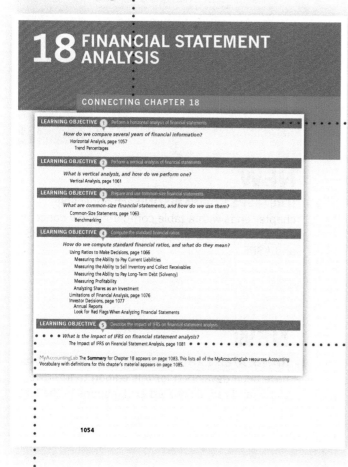

LEARNING OBJECTIVES provide a roadmap showing what will be covered and what is especially important in each chapter.

PAGE REFERENCES give students the ability to quickly connect to the topic they are seeking within the chapter.

KEY QUESTIONS are questions about the important concepts in the chapter, expressed in everyday language.

CHAPTER OPENERS set up the concepts to be covered in the chapter using stories students can relate to. They show why the topics in the chapter are important in the business world. These vignettes are now 100 percent Canadian content.

NEW

INSTRUCTOR TIPS RIGHT IN THE CHAPTER

Found throughout the text, these handwritten notes mimic the experience of having an experienced teacher walk a student through concepts on the board. Many include mnemonic devices or examples to help students remember the rules of accounting.

Many companies have needed to seek protection from their creditors due to mismanagement of the cash needed to sustain a business. This chapter focuses on the management or summarized changes in a company's cash account. An example of a company that has faced tough competition in the Canadian home and garden sector as well as stagnant economic conditions is RONA Inc.

RONA Inc. is a major Canadian retailer and distributor of hardware, building materials, and home renovation products. Major US retailers have been interested in RONA in recent years, but the company remains solid. RONA has over 530 franchises and affiliate stores under several different names or banners and in a number of strategically aligned formats. It has 13 distribution centres, and its specialized TruServ Canada wholesaler serves RONA's network as well as many other independent dealers operating under other names. Roughly 25,000 employees work at RONA, and the company has annual consolidated sales of $4.2 billion.

Fiscal 2013 was a rough year for Rona. Store closures and lower housing starts across the country led to a decline in consolidated revenue of 5.7 percent. However, strong capital management and the sale of one of its divisions for $214 million enabled RONA to generate cash flows of about $31 million. These funds were used to purchase shares as well as reduce corporate debt. Changes in RONA's cash position can be seen in the 2013 annual report.[1]

[1] RONA Inc., 2013 Annual Report. Retrieved from www.rona.ca/corporate/financial-documents.

975

NEW

IFRS/ASPE COMPARISON

Each applicable chapter ends with a table comparing how concepts in that chapter are dealt with for those using IFRS and ASPE.

NEW

ANNOTATED EXHIBITS

More annotated exhibits have been developed for this edition to improve clarity and reduce related explanations in the text.

NEW

TRY IT! BOXES

Found at the end of each learning objective section in the text, **Try It!** features (formerly Just Checking) give students the opportunity to apply the concepts they just learned to an accounting problem. For this edition, care was taken to streamline this feature to include fewer questions to avoid interrupting the flow of student learning. Deep linking in the eText will allow students to practise in MyAccountingLab without interrupting their interaction with the eText. **Try It! Solutions** are provided at the end of each chapter.

Why is it important to consolidate the financial results of companies under common control? The consolidated financial statements *communicate useful information* to interested users to help them assess the success of the company—this is the primary objective of the accounting framework. If the parent company provided financial information on each of its subsidiaries on a company-by-company basis only, users would find it difficult to pull all the pieces together on their own. Intercompany transactions would be difficult to identify unless a user had direct access to the same information as internal managers.

In the accounting framework, the *economic entity assumption* directs us to eliminate intercompany transactions because these occur *within the larger economic entity* (which is the consolidated group of companies)

and would cause double-counting errors if they were not eliminated.

The framework's characteristic of *understandability* promotes disclosure in the notes to the financial statements. The parent company's notes to the financial statements must list the subsidiary companies and the parent's percentage of ownership of each. GAAP also require that companies provide **segmented information** in their financial statement notes. This segmented information is either by industry or by geography, and it is reported by companies that operate in different industries or regions of the world, including parent and subsidiary companies.

By presenting details about a parent company's subsidiaries and segmented information in the notes, consolidated financial statements communicate even *more useful information* to users to help them assess the success of the company.

• • • • • **REVISED WHY IT'S DONE THIS WAY BOXES**
Descriptions in these boxes have been shortened to focus on the key new points in the chapter, without referencing levels. For instructors who want longer and more technical notes, these are included in the instructor's material.

REVISED END-OF-CHAPTER MATERIAL

The number of Starters and Exercises provided in each chapter has been increased, while maintaining both A and B Problem sets.

All learning objectives now have consistent coverage in end-of-chapter questions.

There is now more variety of questions provided.

ENGAGING REDESIGN The redesign of this text throughout includes clean and consistent art for T-accounts, journal entries, financial statements, and the accounting equation.

New art types include clear explanations and connection arrows to help students follow the transaction process. Illustrations are updated to be more modern and clean.

Margins have been decluttered, ensuring a smoother, more open and approachable look, while keeping the most important content visible.

Closing entry ❸ would then credit Income Summary to close its debit balance and transfer the net loss to Lisa Hunter, Capital:

❸ May 31	Lisa Hunter, Capital	1,000	
	Income Summary		1,000
	To close the Income Summary account and transfer net loss to the Capital account.		

After posting, these two accounts would appear as follows:

Income Summary			
Clo. ❷ 27,500	Clo. ❶ 26,500
Bal. 1,000	Clo. ❸ 1,000

Lisa Hunter, Capital		
Clo. ❸ 1,000	120,100
	Bal. 119,100

Changes to the Tenth Canadian Edition

Additional Starters and Exercises have been added to most chapters in Volume 2. Instructors wanted more of these types of questions and more variety in the questions, so the Tenth Canadian Edition has been updated to reflect this.

Chapter 12—Partnerships
- Coverage of a death of a partner has been reduced, since it is similar to other withdrawals from a partnership.
- Added more T-accounts to clarify how balances are calculated.

Chapter 13—Corporations: Share Capital and the Balance Sheet
- Streamlined coverage of the concepts of corporations to emphasize material that students need to know at this level.

Chapter 15—Long-Term Liabilities
- Included more calculator instructions to assist students who struggle with the math.
- Added shareholder loans as a topic to improve coverage of other important liabilities.
- Removed off-balance-sheet financing to keep focus of the chapter on the most important transactions.

Chapter 16—Investments and International Operations
- New exhibit added to clarify the accounting methods and financial statement effects of investments.
- Updated exchange rates to what was current at the time of writing.

Chapter 17—The Cash Flow Statement
- Added a Summary Problem to illustrate the direct method so that both methods are fully demonstrated.

Chapter 18—Financial Statement Analysis
- Reduced the number of comparative companies in ratio analyses.
- Reduced text to let the formulas speak for themselves.

Student and Instructor Resources

The primary goal of the supplements that accompany *Horngren's Accounting,* Tenth Canadian Edition, is to help instructors deliver their course with ease using any delivery method—traditional, self-paced, or online—and for students to learn and practise accounting in a variety of ways that meet their learning needs and study preferences.

MyAccountingLab

MyAccountingLab delivers proven results in helping individual students succeed. It provides engaging experiences that personalize, stimulate, and measure learning for each student, including a personalized study plan, mini-cases, and videos. MyAccountingLab is the portal to an array of learning tools for all learning styles—algorithmic practice questions with guided solutions are only the beginning!

For Students

The following features are **NEW** to MyAccountingLab for the Tenth Canadian Edition:

Assignable Accounting Cycle Tutorial—MyAccountingLab's new interactive tutorial helps students master the accounting cycle for early and continued success in the introduction to accounting course. The tutorial, accessed by computer, smartphone, or tablet, provides students with brief explanations of each concept of the accounting cycle through engaging videos and/or animations. Students are immediately assessed on their understanding, and their performance is recorded in the MyAccountingLab gradebook. Whether the Accounting Cycle Tutorial is used as a remediation self-study tool or course assignment, students have yet another resource within MyAccountingLab to help them be successful with the accounting cycle.

Enhanced Pearson eText—The Enhanced eText keeps students engaged in learning on their own time, while helping them achieve greater conceptual understanding of course material. The worked examples bring learning to life, and algorithmic practice allows students to apply the concepts they are reading about. Combining resources that illuminate content with accessible self-assessment, MyAccountingLab with Enhanced eText provides students with a complete digital learning experience—all in one place.

The Pearson eText gives students access to the text whenever and wherever they have online access to the Internet. eText pages look exactly like the printed text, offering powerful new functionality for students and instructors. Users can create notes, highlight text in different colours, create bookmarks, zoom, click hyperlinked words and phrases to view definitions, and view in single-page or two-page view.

Dynamic Study Modules—Canadian study modules allow students to work through groups of questions and check their understanding of foundational accounting topics. As students work through questions, the Dynamic Study Modules assess their knowledge and only show questions that still require practice. Fully Assignable, flowing through the Gradebook, or Self-Directed Dynamic Study Modules can be completed online using a computer, tablet, or mobile device.

Learning Catalytics—A "bring your own device" assessment and classroom activity system that expands the possibilities for student engagement. Using Learning Catalytics, you can deliver a wide range of auto-gradable or open-ended questions that test content knowledge and build critical thinking skills. Eighteen different answer types provide great flexibility, including graphical, numerical, textual input, and more.

Audio Lecture Videos—These pre-class learning aids are available for every learning objective and are professor-narrated PowerPoint summaries that will help students prepare for class. These can be used in an online or flipped classroom experience or simply to get students ready for the lecture.

Adaptive Assessment—Integrated directly into the MyAccountingLab Study Plan, Pearson's adaptive assessment is the latest technology for individualized learning and mastery. As students work through each question, they are provided with a custom learning path tailored specifically to the concepts they need to practise and master.

In addition, students will find the following assets to help improve their learning experience:

- Help Me Solve This Guides
- Worked Solutions
- Videos
- DemoDocs
- Check Figures
- Student PowerPoint Presentations
- Audio Chapter Summaries
- Accounting Cycle Tutorial Animations
- Excel Spreadsheet Templates
- General Ledger **(NEW!)**
- Open-Response Questions **(NEW!)**

For Instructors

Additional Resources
The following resources are available for Instructors at the Instructor's Resource Centre on the catalogue, at catalogue.pearsoned.ca:

- **Instructor's Solutions Manual.** This manual provides instructors with a complete set of solutions to all the end-of-chapter material in the text. Available in both Word and PDF formats.
- **Computerized Testbank.** The Testbank for *Horngren's Accounting* offers a comprehensive suite of tools for testing and assessment. TestGen allows educators to easily create and distribute tests for their courses, either by printing and distributing through traditional methods or by online delivery. The more than 100 questions per chapter can be sorted by the chapter's Learning Objectives, difficulty ranking, Bloom's Taxonomy, and—new to this edition—applicable Canadian Professional Accounting Standards. Types of questions included are Multiple Choice, True/False, Short Answer, and Essay. One NEW Essay question has been created for each chapter, building on cumulative learning across all previous chapters.

- **Test Item File.** All the test questions from the TestGen testbank are available in Microsoft Word format.
- **Instructor's Teaching Tips in Digital eText Resource:** Instructors can easily locate useful teaching tips and resources throughout the eText, which is annotated by apple icons throughout the chapters. This eText is located in MyAccountingLab.
- **PowerPoint Presentations.** Prepared for each chapter of the text, these presentations offer helpful graphics that illustrate key figures and concepts from the text.
- **Image Library.** We are pleased to provide the exhibits from the text in .jpg format for use in the classroom or for building your own lectures or PowerPoint presentations.

Learning Solutions Managers

Pearson's Learning Solutions Managers work with faculty and campus course designers to ensure that Pearson technology products, assessment tools, and online course materials are tailored to meet your specific needs. This highly qualified team is dedicated to helping schools take full advantage of a wide range of educational resources by assisting in the integration of a variety of instructional materials and media formats. Your local Pearson sales representative can provide you with more details on this service program.

Acknowledgements for *Horngren's Accounting*, Tenth Canadian Edition

Horngren's Accounting, Tenth Canadian Edition, is the product of a rigorous research process that included multiple reviews in the various stages of development to ensure the revision meets the needs of Canadian students and instructors. The extensive feedback from the following reviewers helped shape this edition into a clearer, more readable and streamlined textbook in both the chapter content and assignment material:

- Bharat Aggarwal, Seneca College
- Ionela Bacain, Humber College
- Maria Belanger, Algonquin College
- Robin Day, British Columbia Institute of Technology
- Meredith Delaney, Seneca College
- Denise Dodson, Nova Scotia Community College
- Stanley Faria, Humber College
- Carol Fearon, Seneca College
- Darla Lutness, Northern Alberta Institute of Technology
- Michael Malkoun, St. Clair College
- Vnit Nath, British Columbia Institute of Technology
- Dal Pirot, MacEwan University
- Raymond Sungaila, Humber College
- Selina Tang, Douglas College
- Dan Wong, Southern Alberta Institute of Technology

Special thanks to Brad Witt at Humber College for being a "super reviewer" of this manuscript—his comments helped us improve the end-of-chapter material.

We would also like to thank the late Charles Horngren and Tom Harrison for their support in writing the original material.

We would like to give special thanks to Chris Deresh, CPA, Manager, Curriculum Content, at Chartered Professional Accountants of Canada for his guidance and technical support. His willingness to review and discuss portions of the manuscript was generous and insightful, and it is gratefully acknowledged.

The Chartered Professional Accountants, as the official administrator of generally accepted accounting principles in Canada, and the *CPA Canada Handbook*, are vital to the conduct of business and accounting in Canada. We have made every effort to incorporate the most current *Handbook* recommendations in this new edition of *Accounting* for both private enterprises (ASPE) and for publicly accountable enterprises subject to International Financial Reporting Standards (IFRS).

Thanks are extended to Indigo Books & Music Inc. and TELUS Corporation for permission to use their annual reports in Volumes I and II of this text and on MyAccountingLab. We acknowledge the support provided by the websites of various news organizations and by the annual reports of a large number of public companies.

We would like to acknowledge the people of Pearson Canada, in particular Senior Acquisitions Editor Megan Farrell, who put together a great team for this project, and Marketing Manager Loula March. Special thanks to Suzanne Simpson Millar, Queen Bee at Simpson Editorial Services, who was an awesome Developmental Editor on this edition. Leanne Rancourt as Production Editor also added her many talents as the project neared completion.

We would like to thank Media Editor Anita Smale for her excellent work on the MyAccountingLab that accompanies this textbook.

Our task is to provide educational material in the area of accounting to instructors and students to aid in the understanding of this subject area. We welcome your suggestions and comments on how to serve you better.

12 PARTNERSHIPS

CONNECTING CHAPTER 12

LEARNING OBJECTIVE 1   Identify the characteristics of a partnership

What are the characteristics of a partnership?

Characteristics of a Partnership, page 675
   The Written Partnership Agreement
   Limited Life
   Mutual Agency
   Unlimited Liability
   Co-ownership of Property
   No Partnership Income Tax
   Advantages/Disadvantages
Type of Partnerships, page 677
   General Partnerships
   Limited Partnerships
Partnership Financial Statements, page 678

LEARNING OBJECTIVE 2   Account for partners' initial investments in a partnership

How do we account for partners' investments in a partnership?

Forming a Partnership, page 679

LEARNING OBJECTIVE 3   Allocate profits and losses to the partners by different methods

How can we allocate profits and losses to the partners?

Sharing Partnership Profits and Losses, page 681
   Sharing Based on a Stated Fraction
   Sharing Based on Capital Investments
   Sharing Based on Capital Investments and on Service
   Sharing Based on Service and Interest
   Allocation of a Net Loss
Partnership Withdrawals (Drawings), page 686

LEARNING OBJECTIVE 4   Account for the admission of a new partner

How do we account for a new partner?

Admission of a Partner, page 688
   Admission by Purchasing a Partner's Interest
   Admission by Investing in the Partnership

LEARNING OBJECTIVE 5   Account for the withdrawal of a partner

How do we account for the withdrawal of a partner?

Withdrawal of a Partner from the Business, page 693
   Withdrawal at Book Value
   Withdrawal at Less than Book Value
   Withdrawal at More than Book Value
   Death of a Partner

LEARNING OBJECTIVE 6 Account for the liquidation of a partnership

How do we account for the ending of a partnership?

Liquidation of a Partnership, page 696
Sale of Assets at a Gain
Sale of Assets at a Loss
Capital Deficiencies

MyAccountingLab The **Summary** for Chapter 12 appears on page 702. This lists all of the MyAccountingLab resources. **Accounting Vocabulary** with definitions for this chapter's material appears on page 704.

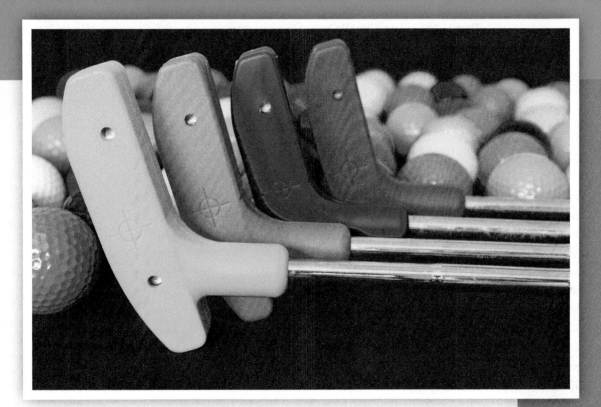

Jenny Lo and Sam Lachlan are considering opening a miniature golf course in Wasaga Beach, Ontario. The golf course will have 18 holes with dinosaurs, windmills, water features, and more. Jenny has been carefully evaluating the tourism industry in the town and believes that the golf course will be busy enough during the summer tourist season to close during the winter months, allowing Jenny and Sam plenty of time to ski and snowboard in the off season.

Jenny and Sam are considering organizing the business as a partnership. Jenny is willing to contribute a piece of property in the prime downtown area that she just inherited. She is also interested in managing the day-to-day operations of the business. Sam, with his degree in accounting, has agreed to handle the accounting and business aspects of the golf course.

Now all Jenny and Sam need to decide is how the partnership will be organized. Some questions they are considering include, What are the specific responsibilities of each partner? How should profits and losses be shared between the partners? What if one of the partners wants out of the partnership in the future? How would the partnership add a new partner?

partnership is an association of two or more persons who co-own a business for profit. This definition is common to the various provincial partnership acts, which tend to prescribe similar rules with respect to the organization and operation of partnerships in their jurisdictions.

Forming a partnership is easy. It requires no permission from government authorities and involves no legal procedures, with the exception that most provinces require partnerships to register information such as the names of the partners and the name under which the business will be conducted.[1] When two people decide to go into business together, a partnership is automatically formed.

A partnership combines the assets, talents, and experience of the partners. Business opportunities closed to an individual may open up to a partnership. As the chapter-opening story illustrates, this is an important characteristic of a partnership. The miniature golf course will likely be successful because it is able to combine the skills of its two owners. It is unlikely that Jenny or Sam would be able to operate the business as well if either tried to do it on his or her own.

Partnerships come in all sizes. Many partnerships have fewer than 10 partners. Some medical practices may have 10 or more partners, while some of the largest law firms in Canada have more than 500 partners. The largest accounting firm in Canada has more than 800 partners. Exhibit 12–1 lists the 10 largest public accounting firms in Canada. The majority of them are partnerships.

EXHIBIT 12–1 | The 10 Largest Accounting Firms in Canada (by Revenue)

Rank 2013	Firm	Partners	Professional Staff	Offices
1	Deloitte LLP	865	5,316	55
2	PricewaterhouseCoopers LLP	513	4,263	25
3	KPMG LLP	696	3,795	37
4	Ernst & Young LLP	358	2,992	17
5	Grant Thornton Canada	404	2,983	135
6	MNP LLP	357	1,026	58
7	BDO Canada LLP	392	2,229	111
8	Collins Barrow	207	541	41
9	Richter	58	415	2
10	Mallette	66	472	24

Source: "Canada's Accounting Top 30," *The Bottom Line*, April 2014, www.thebottomlinenews.ca/documents/Canadas_Accounting_Top_30.pdf, accessed August 1, 2014.

 Beginning with this chapter, you will learn more about the different types of organization structures that were first introduced in Chapter 1. So far, we have only really looked at accounting for proprietorships.

The good news is that the principles and concepts in the accounting framework apply equally to all types of organizations, including partnerships. Accounting differences among types of organizations only relate to the equity section of the balance sheet.

---

[1] Smyth, J.E., D.A. Soberman, A.J. Easson, and S.S. McGill, *The Law and Business Administration in Canada*, 13th ed. (Toronto: Pearson Canada Inc., 2013), 598–602.

CHARACTERISTICS OF A PARTNERSHIP

LO 1

What are the characteristics of a partnership?

Starting a partnership is voluntary. A person cannot be forced to join a partnership, and partners cannot be forced to accept another person as a partner (unless existing partners vote and the majority accept the new partner). The following characteristics distinguish partnerships from proprietorships and from corporations.

The Written Partnership Agreement

A business partnership is somewhat like a marriage. To be successful, the partners must cooperate. However, business partners do not vow to remain together for life. To make certain that each partner fully understands how the partnership operates, partners should draw up a **partnership agreement**. Although the partnership agreement may be oral, a written agreement between the partners reduces the chance of a misunderstanding. This agreement is a contract between the partners, so transactions under the agreement are governed by contract law. The provincial legislatures in Canada have passed their respective versions of a partnership act, the terms of which apply in the absence of a partnership agreement or in the absence of particular matters in the partnership agreement.[2]

The partnership agreement should specify the following points:

- Name, location, and nature of the business
- Name, capital investment, and duties of each partner
- Procedures for admitting a new partner
- Method of sharing profits and losses among the partners
- Withdrawals of assets allowed to the partners
- Procedures for settling disputes among the partners
- Procedures for settling with a partner who withdraws from the firm
- Procedures for removing a partner who will not withdraw or retire from the partnership voluntarily
- Procedures for liquidating the partnership—selling the assets, paying the liabilities, and giving any remaining cash to the partners

KEY POINTS

A partnership is not required to have a formal written agreement. But a written agreement prevents confusion as to the sharing of profits and losses, partners' responsibilities, admission of new partners, how the partnership will be liquidated, and so on. However, there can still be disagreements even when there is a written agreement.

Limited Life

A partnership has a limited life. If one partner withdraws from the business or dies, the partnership dissolves and its books are closed. If the remaining partners want to continue as partners in the same business, they form a new partnership with a new set of financial records and a new partnership agreement. **Dissolution** is the ending of a partnership and does not require liquidation; that is, the assets need not be sold to outside parties for a new partnership to be created. Often the new partnership continues the former partnership's business, and the new partnership may choose to continue to use the dissolved partnership's name. Some types of large partnerships, such as PricewaterhouseCoopers LLP (PwC), retain the firm name even after partners resign from the firm.

Mutual Agency

Mutual agency means that every partner is a mutual agent of the firm. Any partner can bind the business to a contract within the scope of the partnership's regular business operations. If a partner enters into a contract with a person or another business to provide a service, then the firm—not just the partner who signed the contract—is bound to provide that service. If the partner signs a contract to buy her

---

[2] Ibid., 598–618.

LEARNING TIPS

Chapter 1 introduced these concepts for a sole proprietorship. You may want to go back and review them now.

own car, however, the partnership is not liable because the car is a personal matter; it is not within the scope of the regular business operations of the partnership.

The following example shows the impact mutual agency can have on a partnership. Richard Harding and Simon Davis formed a partnership to deal in lumber and other building materials. The partners agreed that their company should not handle brick or any stone materials and that neither partner had the right to purchase these commodities. While Harding was away during the summer, Davis purchased a quantity of these materials for the company because he could buy them at a cheap price. Two months later, when Harding returned, business was very slow, and brick and stone were selling at a price lower than Davis had paid for them. Harding, therefore, refused to accept any more deliveries under the contract. Harding argued that Davis had no authority to buy these goods since the partnership was not organized to deal in brick and stone. The supplier of the brick and stone said that he did not know the partnership was not in the brick and stone business. In fact, he believed that it did handle these goods since all of the other lumber companies in the area bought or sold brick and stone. Because the supplier acted in good faith, he claimed that Harding and Davis should accept the remaining deliveries of brick and stone according to the agreement that was made. Who is correct? Under normal circumstances, the brick and stone supplier is correct because the mutual agency characteristic of a partnership allows partners to bind each other in business contracts. The agreements made within the partnership would not be known by an outside party like the supplier, so the supplier would have a solid case and could sue the partnership to abide by the contract.[3]

Unlimited Liability

Each partner has **unlimited personal liability** for the debts of the business. When a partnership cannot pay its debts with business assets, the partners must pay with their personal assets. (There are exceptions, which are described in the next section, Types of Partnerships.) If either partner is unable to pay his or her part of the debt, the other partner (or partners) must make payment.

Unlimited liability and mutual agency are closely related. A dishonest partner or a partner with poor judgment may commit the partnership to a contract under which the business loses money. In turn, creditors may force *all* the partners to pay the debt from their personal assets. Hence, a business partner should be chosen with great care.

Co-ownership of Property

Any asset—cash, inventory, machinery, computers, and so on—that a partner invests into the partnership becomes the joint property of all the partners. The partner who invested the asset is no longer its sole owner.

No Partnership Income Tax

The partnership *reports* its income to the government tax authority (the Canada Revenue Agency), but the partnership pays *no* income tax. The net income of the partnership is divided and flows through the business to the partners, who pay personal income tax on their share.

For example, suppose that the Willis & Jones partnership earned net income of $150,000, shared equally by the two partners. The partnership would pay no income tax *as a business entity*. However, each partner would pay income tax *as an individual* on his or her $75,000 share of partnership income.

---

[3] This case is based on the scenario described at ChestofBooks.com, "B. Apparent Scope of Authority," http://chestofbooks.com/business/law/Case-Method/B-Apparent-Scope-Of-Authority.html#ixzz1qimHxY2o, accessed August 14, 2012.

Advantages/Disadvantages

Exhibit 12–2 lists the advantages and disadvantages of partnerships (compared with proprietorships and corporations). Most features of a proprietorship also apply to a partnership, most importantly:

- Limited life
- Unlimited liability
- No business income tax

EXHIBIT 12–2 | Advantages and Disadvantages of Partnerships

Partnership Advantages

Versus Proprietorships:
- A partnership can raise more capital since capital comes from more than one person.
- A partnership brings together the abilities of more than one person.
- Partners working well together can achieve more than by working alone: 1 + 1 > in a good partnership.

Versus Corporations:
- A partnership is less expensive to organize than a corporation, which requires articles of incorporation from a province or the federal government.
- A partnership is subject to fewer governmental regulations and restrictions than is a corporation.

Partnership Disadvantages
- A partnership agreement may be difficult to formulate. Each time a new partner is admitted or a partner leaves the partnership, the business needs a new partnership agreement.
- Relationships among partners may be fragile. It is hard to find the right partner.
- Mutual agency and unlimited liability create personal obligations for each partner.
- Lack of continuity of the business is faced by a partnership but not a corporation.

TYPES OF PARTNERSHIPS

There are two basic types of partnerships: general and limited.

General Partnerships

A **general partnership** is the basic form of partnership organization. Each partner is a co-owner of the business with all the privileges and risks of ownership. The general partners share the profits, losses, and the risks of the business.

Limited Partnerships

Partners can avoid unlimited personal liability for partnership obligations by forming a *limited partnership*. A **limited partnership** has at least two classes of partners:

- There must be at least one *general partner*, who takes primary responsibility for the management of the business. The general partner also takes most of the risk of failure if the partnership goes bankrupt (liabilities exceed assets). In some limited partnerships, such as real estate limited partnerships, the general partner often invests little cash in the business. Instead, the general partner's contribution is her or his skill in managing the organization. Usually, the general partner is the last owner to receive a share of partnership profits and losses. But the general partner may earn all excess profits after the limited partners get their share of the income.

- The *limited partners* are so named because their personal obligation for the partnership's liabilities is limited to the amount they have invested in the business. Limited partners have limited liability similar to the limited liability that shareholders in a corporation have. Usually, the limited partners have invested the bulk of the partnership's assets and capital. They, therefore, usually have the first claim

KEY POINTS

Since all partners are personally liable for any debt of the business, it is extremely important to choose a partner carefully. This is one reason some investors/partners prefer the *limited partnership* form of business organization.

to partnership profits and losses, but only up to a specified limit. In exchange for their limited liability, their potential for profits usually has a limit as well.

Limited Liability Partnerships Many professionals, such as doctors, lawyers, and most public accounting firms in Canada—including most of those in Exhibit 12–1—are now organized as **limited liability partnerships (LLPs)**. An LLP can only be used by eligible professions (such as accounting) and is designed to protect innocent partners from negligence damages that result from another partner's actions. This means that each partner's personal liability for other partners' negligence is limited to a certain dollar amount, although liability for a partner's own negligence is still unlimited. The LLP must carry an adequate amount of malpractice insurance or liability insurance to protect the public.

PARTNERSHIP FINANCIAL STATEMENTS

Partnership financial statements are much like those of a proprietorship. Exhibit 12–3 compares partnership statements (in Panel A) against the same reports for a sole proprietorship (in Panel B).

EXHIBIT 12–3 | Financial Statements of a Partnership and a Proprietorship (all amounts in thousands of dollars)

PANEL A—PARTNERSHIP

WILLIS & JONES		
Income Statement		
For the Year Ended December 31, 2017		
Revenues		$460
Expenses		(270)
Net income		$190
Allocation of net income:		
To Leslie Willis	$114	
To Andrew Jones	76	$190

WILLIS & JONES		
Statement of Partners' Equity		
For the Year Ended December 31, 2017		
	Willis	Jones
Capital, January 1, 2017	$50	$40
Additional investments	10	—
Net income	114	76
Subtotal	174	116
Withdrawals	(72)	(48)
Capital, December 31, 2017	$102	$68

WILLIS & JONES	
Balance Sheet	
December 31, 2017	
Assets	
Cash and other assets	$170
Partners' Equity	
Leslie Willis, capital	$102
Andrew Jones, capital	68
Total equity	$170

PANEL B—PROPRIETORSHIP

WILLIS CONSULTING	
Income Statement	
For the Year Ended December 31, 2017	
Revenues	$460
Expenses	(270)
Net income	$190

WILLIS CONSULTING	
Statement of Owner's Equity	
For the Year Ended December 31, 2017	
Capital, January 1, 2017	$90
Additional investments	10
Net income	190
Subtotal	290
Withdrawals	(120)
Capital, December 31, 2017	$170

WILLIS CONSULTING	
Balance Sheet	
December 31, 2017	
Assets	
Cash and other assets	$170
Owner's Equity	
Leslie Willis, capital	$170

The key differences between a proprietorship's and a partnership's financial statements are as follows:

- A partnership income statement includes a section showing the division of net income to the partners.

- A partnership balance sheet reports a separate Capital account for each partner in the section now called Partners' Equity. Large partnerships may show one balance, the total for all partners, and provide the details in a separate report.

1. John Richards and Patricia Quinn would like to form a partnership to open up a night club—Endelay's. They each have $100,000 and have decided that since they have been lifelong friends they do not need a written partnership agreement. Detail the contents of a partnership agreement and explain the importance of a written agreement to Richards and Quinn.

2. Suppose you were giving the friends in the previous question advice on their decision to form a partnership. Detail the advantages and disadvantages of their decision.

3. Richards and Quinn may, at some point, want to bring in a partner who does not want any day-to-day responsibility for managing the operations; he or she may simply want to receive a return on his or her investment. Describe the type of partner this person would be.

Solutions appear at the end of this chapter and on MyAccountingLab

FORMING A PARTNERSHIP

Let's examine the start up of a partnership. Partners in a new partnership may invest assets and their related liabilities in the business. These contributions are journalized in the same way as for proprietorships, by debiting the assets and crediting the liabilities at their agreed-upon values. Each person's net contribution—assets minus liabilities—is credited to the equity account for that person. Often the partners hire an independent firm to *appraise* their assets and liabilities at current market value at the time a partnership is formed. This outside evaluation assures an objective valuation for what each partner brings into the business.

Suppose Katie Zheng and Dan Chao form a partnership on June 1, 2017, to develop and sell computer software. The partners agree on the following values based on an independent appraisal:

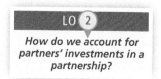

LO 2

How do we account for partners' investments in a partnership?

REAL WORLD EXAMPLE

There is a way for a partner to allow the partnership to use a personal asset, such as a car or money, without losing his or her claim to that asset: The partner could lease the car to the partnership. If the partnership were liquidated, the car would have to be returned to its owner. The partner could also lend money to the partnership instead of investing it. Upon liquidation, the partnership would have to repay the loan to the lending partner before any distribution of capital to the partners.

Zheng's contributions

- Cash, $10,000; inventory, $40,000; and accounts payable, $80,000
- Computer equipment: cost, $800,000; accumulated amortization, $200,000; current market value, $450,000

Chao's contributions

- Cash, $5,000
- Computer software: cost, $50,000; current market value, $100,000

The partnership entries are as follows:

<table>
<tr><th colspan="4">Zheng's investment</th></tr>
<tr><td>2017</td><td></td><td></td><td></td></tr>
<tr><td>Jun. 1</td><td>Cash</td><td>10,000</td><td></td></tr>
<tr><td></td><td>Inventory</td><td>40,000*</td><td></td></tr>
<tr><td></td><td>Computer Equipment</td><td>450,000*</td><td></td></tr>
<tr><td></td><td>   Accounts Payable</td><td></td><td>80,000*</td></tr>
<tr><td></td><td>   Katie Zheng, Capital</td><td></td><td>420,000</td></tr>
<tr><td></td><td>To record Zheng's investment in the partnership ($500,000 − $80,000).</td><td></td><td></td></tr>
<tr><th colspan="4">Chao's investment</th></tr>
<tr><td>2017</td><td></td><td></td><td></td></tr>
<tr><td>Jun. 1</td><td>Cash</td><td>5,000</td><td></td></tr>
<tr><td></td><td>Computer Software</td><td>100,000*</td><td></td></tr>
<tr><td></td><td>   Dan Chao, Capital</td><td></td><td>105,000</td></tr>
<tr><td></td><td>To record Chao's investment in the partnership.</td><td></td><td></td></tr>
</table>

*Current market values are used.

> The partnership records receipts of the partners' initial investments at the current market values of the assets and liabilities because, in effect, the partnership is buying the assets and assuming the liabilities at their current market values.

The initial partnership balance sheet appears in Exhibit 12–4.

EXHIBIT 12–4 | Partnership Balance Sheet

ZHENG AND CHAO			
Balance Sheet			
June 1, 2017			
Assets		**Liabilities**	
Cash	$ 15,000	Accounts payable	$ 80,000
Inventory	40,000	**Partners' Equity**	
Computer equipment	450,000	Katie Zheng, capital	420,000
Computer software	100,000	Dan Chao, capital	105,000
		Total partners' equity	525,000
Total assets	$605,000	Total liabilities and equity	$605,000

> Try It!

4. Marty Kaur invests land in a partnership with Lee Manors. Kaur purchased the land in 2011 for $20,000. Three independent real estate appraisers now value the land at $50,000. Kaur wants $50,000 capital in the new partnership, but Manors objects. Manors believes that Kaur's capital investment should be measured by the book value of his land. Manors and Kaur seek your advice.

   a. Which value of the land is appropriate for measuring Kaur's capital: book value or current market value?

   b. Give the partnership's journal entry to record Kaur's investment in the business on September 1.

Solutions appear at the end of this chapter and on MyAccountingLab

SHARING PARTNERSHIP PROFITS AND LOSSES

LO 3

How can we allocate profits and losses to the partners?

Allocating profits and losses among partners can be challenging and can be a major source of disputes. Any division of profits and losses is allowed as long as the partners agree and it is in the partnership agreement. Typical arrangements include the following:

- Sharing profits and losses based on a stated fraction for each partner, such as 50/50, or 2/3 and 1/3, or 4:3:3 (which means 40 percent to Partner A, 30 percent to Partner B, and 30 percent to Partner C)
- Sharing based on each partner's capital investment
- Sharing based on each partner's service
- Sharing based on a combination of stated fractions, investments, service, and other items

If the partners have not drawn up an agreement, or if the agreement does not state how the partners will divide profits and losses, then, by law, the partners must share profits and losses equally. If the agreement specifies a method for sharing profits but not losses, then losses are shared in the same proportion as profits. For example, a partner receiving 75 percent of the profits would likewise absorb 75 percent of any losses.

In some cases an equal division is not fair. One partner may perform more work for the business than the other partner, or one partner may make a larger capital contribution. In the preceding example, Dan Chao might agree to work longer hours for the partnership than Katie Zheng in order to earn a greater share of profits. Zheng could argue that she should receive more of the profits because she contributed more net assets ($420,000) than Chao did ($105,000). Chao might contend that his computer software program is the partnership's most important asset, and that his share of the profits should be greater than Zheng's share. Arriving at fair sharing of profits and losses in a partnership may be difficult. We now demonstrate how to account for some options available in determining partners' shares of profits and losses.

Sharing Based on a Stated Fraction

The partnership agreement may state each partner's fraction of the total profits and losses. Suppose the partnership agreement of Shannon Kerry and Raoul Calder allocates two-thirds of the business profits and losses to Kerry and one-third to Calder. This sharing rule can also be expressed as 2:1. If net income for the year is $60,000, and all revenue and expense accounts have been closed, the Income Summary account has a credit balance of $60,000 prior to its closing:

LEARNING TIPS

The ratio of 2:1 is equal to fractions of 2/3 and 1/3, where the denominator of the fraction is the sum of the numbers in the ratio. The ratio of 2:1 is also a 66.7 percent: 33.3 percent sharing ratio.

Income Summary

	Bal. 60,000

The entry to close this account and allocate the net income to the partners' Capital accounts is as follows:

Dec. 31	Income Summary	60,000	
	Shannon Kerry, Capital		40,000
	Raoul Calder, Capital		20,000
	To allocate net income to partners.		
	(Kerry: $60,000 $\times$ $^2/_3$; Calder: $60,000 $\times$ $^1/_3$)		

Suppose Kerry's beginning Capital balance was $50,000 and Calder's was $10,000. After posting, the accounts appear as follows:

Income Summary		Shannon Kerry, Capital		Raoul Calder, Capital	
Clo. 60,000	Beg. 60,000		Beg. 50,000		Beg. 10,000
			Clo. 40,000		Clo. 20,000
			End. 90,000		End. 30,000

If the partnership had a net loss of $15,000, the Income Summary account would have a debit balance of $15,000. In that case, the closing entry to allocate the loss to the partners' Capital accounts would be:

Dec. 31	Shannon Kerry, Capital	10,000	
	Raoul Calder, Capital	5,000	
	Income Summary		15,000
	To allocate net loss to partners. (Kerry: $15,000 × $^2/_3$; Calder: $15,000 × $^1/_3$)		

> *A profit or loss will increase or decrease each partner's Capital account, but cash will not change hands. The Withdrawals account records the cash each partner takes from the partnership.*

Sharing Based on Capital Investments

Profits and losses are often allocated in proportion to the partners' capital investments in the business. Suppose John Abbot, Erica Baxter, and Tony Craven are partners in ABC Company. Their Capital accounts at the end of the first year of business have the following balances, before closing entries. These amounts are equal to the original capital investments for each of the partners, since no earnings or withdrawals have yet been posted to these accounts.

John Abbot, Capital	$120,000
Erica Baxter, Capital	180,000
Tony Craven, Capital	150,000
Total Capital balances	$450,000

LEARNING TIPS

Do not round the interim percentages. For this chapter, round only the final dollar amount to the nearest whole dollar.

Assume that the partnership earned a profit of $300,000 for the year. To allocate this amount based on capital investments, each partner's percentage share of the partnership's total capital investment amount must be computed.

We divide each partner's investment by the total capital investment amount:

Abbot:	($120,000 ÷ $450,000)	= 26.6667%
Baxter:	($180,000 ÷ $450,000)	= 40%
Craven:	($150,000 ÷ $450,000)	= 33.3333%

These figures, multiplied by the $300,000 profit amount, yield each partner's share of the year's profits:

Abbot:	$300,000 × 26.6667%	= $80,000.10, round to $80,000
Baxter:	$300,000 × 40%	= $120,000
Craven:	$300,000 × 33.3333%	= $99,999.90, round to $100,000

Or it can be calculated in one step as follows:

Abbot:	($120,000 ÷ $450,000) × $300,000	=	$ 80,000
Baxter:	($180,000 ÷ $450,000) × $300,000	=	120,000
Craven:	($150,000 ÷ $450,000) × $300,000	=	100,000
	Net income allocated to partners	=	$300,000

The closing entry to allocate the profit to the partners' Capital accounts is:

Dec. 31	Income Summary	300,000	
	John Abbot, Capital		80,000
	Erica Baxter, Capital		120,000
	Tony Craven, Capital		100,000
	To allocate net income to partners.		

After this closing entry, the partners' Capital balances are:

John Abbot, Capital	($120,000 + $80,000)	$200,000
Erica Baxter, Capital	($180,000 + $120,000)	300,000
Tony Craven, Capital	($150,000 + $100,000)	250,000
Total Capital balances after allocation of net income		$750,000

Sharing Based on Capital Investments and on Service

One partner, regardless of his or her capital investment, may put more work into the business than the other partners. Even among partners who log equal service time, one person's superior experience and knowledge may be worth more to the firm. To reward the harder-working or more valuable person, the profit-and-loss-sharing method may be based on a combination of partner capital investments *and* **service** to the business. In this case, the partners are allocated predetermined sums to be withdrawn. These are *not* employee salaries but they are sometimes referred to as a **salary allowance**.

Assume Michelle Wallas and Carolyn Borugian formed a partnership in which Wallas invested $50,000 and Borugian invested $50,000, a total of $100,000. Borugian devotes more time to the partnership and earns the larger income allocation from the partnership. Accordingly, the two partners have agreed to share profit as follows:

1. The first $40,000 of partnership profit is to be allocated based on the partners' capital investments in the business.

2. The next $60,000 of profit is to be allocated based on service (Borugian works 60 percent of the time and Wallas 40 percent of the time), with Borugian receiving $36,000 and Wallas receiving $24,000.

3. Any remaining profit is allocated equally.

If net income for the first year is $125,000, the partners' shares of this profit are computed as follows:

	Wallas	Borugian	Total
Total net income			$125,000
① Sharing the first $40,000 of net income, based on capital investments:			
Wallas ($50,000 ÷ $100,000 × $40,000)	$20,000		
Borugian ($50,000 ÷ $100,000 × $40,000)		$20,000	
Total			40,000
Net income remaining for allocation			85,000
② Sharing of next $60,000, based on service:			
Wallas	24,000		
Borugian		36,000	
Total			60,000
Net income left for allocation			25,000
③ Remainder shared equally:			
Wallas ($25,000 × 1/2)	12,500		
Borugian ($25,000 × 1/2)		12,500	
Total			25,000
Net income left for allocation			$ 0
Net income allocated to the partners	$56,500	$68,500	$125,000

On the basis of this allocation, the closing entry is as follows:

Dec. 31	Income Summary	125,000	
	Michelle Wallas, Capital		56,500
	Carolyn Borugian, Capital		68,500
	To allocate net income to partners.		

Sharing Based on Service and Interest

Partners may be rewarded for their service and their capital investments to the business in other ways. In the sharing plan we just saw, the capital investment was recognized with a lump-sum payment. Another option is to allocate an **interest allowance** calculated as a percentage of their Capital balances. It is important to remember that the service (salaries) and interest amounts discussed above are not the business expenses for salaries and interest in the usual sense. Service and interest in partnership agreements are ways of expressing the allocation of profits and losses to the partners. The service component rewards work done for the partnership. The interest component rewards a partner's investment of cash or other assets in the business. But the partners' service and interest amounts are *not* salary expense and interest expense in the partnership's accounting or tax records.

Allocation of Profit Assume Edward Meyers and Pierre Zrilladich form an oil-exploration partnership. Their partnership agreement outlines the following income allocation:

① The partnership agreement allocates an annual "salary" of $107,000 to Meyers and $88,000 to Zrilladich.

② After these amounts are allocated, each partner earns 8 percent interest on his beginning Capital balance. At the beginning of the year, their Capital balances are $200,000 and $250,000, respectively.

③ Any remaining net income is divided equally.

Partnership profit of $240,000 for 2017 will be allocated as follows:

	Meyers	Zrilladich	Total
Total net income			$240,000
❶ Allocation for service:			
Meyers	$107,000		
Zrilladich		$ 88,000	
Total			195,000
Net income remaining for allocation			45,000
❷ Interest on beginning capital balances:			
Meyers ($200,000 × 0.08)	16,000		
Zrilladich ($250,000 × 0.08)		20,000	
Total			36,000
Net income remaining for allocation			9,000
❸ Remainder shared equally:			
Meyers ($9,000 × $\frac{1}{2}$)	4,500		
Zrilladich ($9,000 × $\frac{1}{2}$)		4,500	
Total			9,000
Net income remaining for allocation			$ 0
Net income allocated to the partners	$127,500	$112,500	$240,000

Allocation of a negative remainder   In the preceding illustration, net income exceeded the sum of service and interest. If the partnership profit is less than the allocated sum of service and interest, a negative remainder will occur at some stage in the allocation process. Even so, the partners use the same method for allocation purposes. For example, assume that Meyers and Zrilladich Partnership earned only $205,000 in 2017.

	Meyers	Zrilladich	Total
Total net income			$205,000
❶ Allocation for service:			
Meyers	$107,000		
Zrilladich		$88,000	
Total			195,000
Net income remaining for allocation			10,000
❷ Interest on beginning capital balances:			
Meyers ($200,000 × 0.08)	16,000		
Zrilladich ($250,000 × 0.08)		20,000	
Total			36,000
Net income remaining for allocation			(26,000)
❸ Remainder shared equally:			
Meyers [($26,000) × $\frac{1}{2}$]	(13,000)		
Zrilladich [($26,000) × $\frac{1}{2}$]		(13,000)	
Total			(26,000)
Net income remaining for allocation			$ 0
Net income allocated to the partners	$110,000	$95,000	$205,000

Allocation of a Net Loss

A net loss would be allocated to Meyers and Zrilladich in the same manner outlined for net income. The sharing procedure would begin with the net loss and then allocate service interest and any other specified amounts to the partners.

For example, assume that Meyers and Zrilladich Partnership had a loss of $30,000 in 2017.

	Meyers	Zrilladich	Total
Total net income (loss)			($ 30,000)
① Allocation for service:			
Meyers	$107,000		
Zrilladich		$ 88,000	
Total			195,000
Net income (loss) remaining for allocation			(225,000)
② Interest on beginning Capital balances:			
Meyers ($200,000 × 0.08)	16,000		
Zrilladich ($250,000 × 0.08)		20,000	
Total			36,000
Net income (loss) remaining for allocation			(261,000)
③ Remainder shared equally:			
Meyers [($261,000) × ½]	(130,500)		
Zrilladich [($261,000) × ½]		(130,500)	
Total			(261,000)
Net income remaining for allocation			$ 0
Net income (loss) allocated to the partners	($ 7,500)	($ 22,500)	($ 30,000)

In this case, Zrilladich might be surprised to be allocated such a large share of the loss. It is important for partners to understand the partnership agreement and what it might mean in case of a loss.

PARTNER WITHDRAWALS (DRAWINGS)

REAL WORLD EXAMPLE

According to the Income Tax Act, partners are taxed on their share of partnership income, not on the amount of their withdrawals.

Partners need cash for personal living expenses like anyone else. Partnership agreements usually allow partners to withdraw cash or other assets from the business. These withdrawals are sometimes called *drawings* and are recorded in a separate Withdrawals or Drawings account for each partner. (Drawings from a partnership are recorded exactly as they are for a proprietorship.) Assume that both Edward Meyers and Pierre Zrilladich are allowed a monthly withdrawal of $12,500. The partnership records the March 2017 withdrawal with this entry:

Mar. 31	Edward Meyers, Withdrawals	12,500	
	Cash		12,500
	Monthly partner withdrawal of cash—cheque #101.		
Mar. 31	Pierre Zrilladich, Withdrawals	12,500	
	Cash		12,500
	Monthly partner withdrawal of cash—cheque #102.		

During the year, each partner's Withdrawal account accumulates 12 such amounts, a total of $150,000 ($12,500 × 12). At the end of the year, the general ledger shows the following account balances immediately after net income has been closed to the partners' Capital accounts. Assume the January 1, 2017, balances for Meyers and Zrilladich are shown below, and that $205,000 of profit has been allocated on the basis of the illustration on page 685.

Edward Meyers, Capital

Jan. 1, 2017 Bal.	200,000
Dec. 31, 2017	
Net income	110,000

Pierre Zrilladich, Capital

Jan. 1, 2017 Bal.	250,000
Dec. 31, 2017	
Net income	95,000

Edward Meyers, Withdrawals

Dec. 31, 2017 Bal. 150,000	

Pierre Zrilladich, Withdrawals

Dec. 31, 2017 Bal. 150,000	

$12,500 per month for 12 months

The Withdrawals accounts must be closed at the end of the period:

2017			
Dec. 31	Edward Meyers, Capital	150,000	
	Edward Meyers, Withdrawals		150,000
	To close the Withdrawals account to Capital.		
Dec. 31	Pierre Zrilladich, Capital	150,000	
	Pierre Zrilladich, Withdrawals		150,000
	To close the Withdrawals account to Capital.		

After posting the final closing entry, the balances in the capital accounts for each partner are as follows:

Edward Meyers, Capital

		Jan. 1, 2017 Bal.	200,000
		Dec. 31, 2017	
		Net income	110,000
Dec. 31, 2017			
Withdrawals	150,000		
		Balance	160,000

Pierre Zrilladich, Capital

		Jan. 1, 2017 Bal.	250,000
		Dec. 31, 2017	
		Net income	95,000
Dec. 31, 2017			
Withdrawals	150,000		
		Balance	195,000

The amount of the withdrawal does not depend on the partnership's income or loss for the year. In fact, it is possible for a partner to withdraw more than the balance in the Capital account if, for example, profits were expected to be higher than they proved to be and withdrawals were made in anticipation of these high profits. This situation can only occur if the partnership has the cash required for the withdrawal and the other partners agree with the withdrawal and the ending Capital balance.

5. Calculate the net income or net loss to be allocated to each partner under the following partnership agreements:

  a. Burns and White share profits and losses 60/40. Net partnership income was $50,000.

  b. Betty, Luella, and Pius share profits and losses 3:4:3. Net partnership loss was $200,000.

  c. Locke and Barnel share profits 1/3 and 2/3. The partnership agreement does not address the sharing of losses. Net partnership loss was $60,000.

  d. Hampton and Kirk do not have a partnership agreement. Hampton does one-third of the work and Kirk does two-thirds of the work. Partnership net income was $90,000.

Solutions appear at the end of this chapter and on MyAccountingLab

ADMISSION OF A PARTNER

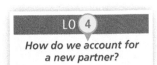

LO 4

How do we account for a new partner?

A partnership lasts only as long as its current set of partners remain in the business. Admitting a new partner dissolves the old partnership and begins a new one.

Often the new partnership continues the former partnership's business. In fact, the new partnership may choose to retain the dissolved partnership's name, as is the case with accounting firms. PricewaterhouseCoopers LLP, for example, is an accounting firm that retires and admits many partners during the year. Thus the former partnership dissolves and a new partnership begins many times. The business, however, retains the name and continues operations. Other partnerships may dissolve and then re-form under a new name. Let's look at the ways that a new owner can be added to a partnership.

Admission by Purchasing a Partner's Interest

A person can become a member of a partnership by purchasing an existing partner's interest in the business. First, however, the new person must gain the approval of the other partners.

Let's assume that Stephanie Spelacy and Carlo Lowes have a partnership with the following account balances:

Cash	$ 40,000	Total liabilities	$120,000
Other assets	360,000	Stephanie Spelacy, capital	170,000
		Carlo Lowes, capital	110,000
Total assets	$400,000	Total liabilities and equity	$400,000

Business is so successful that Spelacy receives an offer from Linda Drake, an outside party, to buy her $170,000 interest in the business for $200,000. Lowes approves Drake as a new partner, and Spelacy agrees to accept $200,000. The firm records the transfer of capital with this entry:

Apr. 16	Stephanie Spelacy, Capital	170,000	
	Linda Drake, Capital		170,000
	To transfer Spelacy's equity to Drake.		

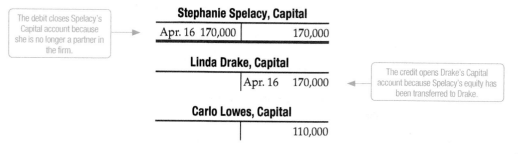

Stephanie Spelacy, Capital

Apr. 16 170,000	170,000

The debit closes Spelacy's Capital account because she is no longer a partner in the firm.

Linda Drake, Capital

	Apr. 16 170,000

The credit opens Drake's Capital account because Spelacy's equity has been transferred to Drake.

Carlo Lowes, Capital

	110,000

The entry amount is Spelacy's Capital balance ($170,000) and not the $200,000 price that Drake paid Spelacy to buy into the business. The full $200,000 goes to Spelacy because the partnership does not receive cash. The transaction was between Drake and Spelacy, not between Drake and the partnership. Suppose Drake pays Spelacy less than Spelacy's Capital balance. The entry on the partnership books is not affected. Spelacy's equity is transferred to Drake at book value ($170,000).

Admission by Investing in the Partnership

A person may be admitted as a partner by investing directly in the partnership rather than by purchasing an existing partner's interest. The new partner invests assets—for example, cash, inventory, equipment, or a patent—in the business. Let's consider several possible independent investment scenarios for a new partner.

Admission by Investing in the Partnership at Book Value—No Bonus   Assume that the partnership of Robin Hardy and Michael May has the following assets, liabilities, and capital:

Cash	$ 20,000	Total liabilities	$ 60,000
Other assets	200,000	Robin Hardy, capital	70,000
		Michael May, capital	90,000
Total assets	$220,000	Total liabilities and equity	$220,000

Devan Mann wants to join the Hardy and May partnership. Mann can invest equipment with a market value of $80,000. Hardy and May agree to dissolve their partnership and to start up a new one, giving Mann one-third interest in exchange for the contributed asset, as follows:

Partnership capital before Mann is admitted ($70,000 + $90,000)	$160,000
Mann's investment in the partnership	80,000
Partnership capital after Mann is admitted	$240,000
One-third interest is ($240,000 × $^1/_3$). Share to Mann.	$ 80,000

Notice that Mann is buying into the partnership at book value because her one-third investment ($80,000) equals one-third of the new partnership's total capital ($240,000).

LEARNING TIPS

Always add the new partner's investment to the existing partners' capital total *first* before calculating the new partner's ownership interest amount in the partnership.

The partnership's entry to record Mann's investment is:

Jul. 18	Equipment	80,000	
	Devan Mann, Capital		80,000
	To admit D. Mann as a partner with a one-third interest in the business.		

After this entry, the partnership books show the following:

Cash	$ 20,000	Total liabilities	$ 60,000
Equipment	80,000	Robin Hardy, capital	70,000
Other assets	200,000	Michael May, capital	90,000
		Devan Mann, capital	80,000
Total assets	$300,000	Total liabilities and equity	$300,000

Mann's one-third interest in the partnership does not necessarily entitle her to one-third of the profits. The sharing of profits and losses is a separate element in the partnership agreement.

Admission by Investing in the Partnership—Bonus to the Old Partners   If the partnership is successful, a new partner may be required to make a higher payment to enter the business. The old partners may demand a bonus, which will increase their Capital accounts.

Suppose that Hiro Nagasawa and Lisa Wendt's partnership has earned above-average profits for 10 years. The two partners share profits and losses equally. The balance sheet carries these figures:

Cash	$ 40,000	Total liabilities	$100,000
Other assets	210,000	Hiro Nagasawa, capital	70,000
		Lisa Wendt, capital	80,000
Total assets	$250,000	Total liabilities and equity	$250,000

Nagasawa and Wendt agree to admit Alana Moor to a one-fourth interest in return for Moor's cash investment of $90,000. Moor's Capital balance on the new partnership books is only $60,000, computed as follows:

Partnership capital before Moor is admitted ($70,000 + $80,000)	$150,000
Moor's investment in the partnership	90,000
Partnership capital after Moor is admitted	$240,000
One-quarter interest ($240,000 × $\frac{1}{4}$). Share to Moor.	$ 60,000
Bonus to the old partners ($90,000 − $60,000)	$ 30,000

In effect, Moor had to buy into the partnership at a price ($90,000) above the book value of her one-fourth interest ($60,000). Moor's greater-than-book-value investment of $30,000 creates a *bonus* for Nagasawa and Wendt.

The entry on the partnership books to record Moor's investment is:

Mar. 1	Cash	90,000	
	Alana Moor, Capital		60,000
	Hiro Nagasawa, Capital		15,000
	Lisa Wendt, Capital		15,000
	To admit A. Moor as a partner with a one-fourth interest in the business. Nagasawa and Wendt each receive a bonus of $15,000 ($30,000 × $\frac{1}{2}$).		

KEY POINTS

Notice in the March 1 journal entry that Nagasawa's and Wendt's Capital accounts increased because of Moor's investment, but that Nagasawa and Wendt have not received cash. All the cash went into the partnership. Their increased Capital accounts include the bonus amount contributed by Moor, calculated according to the original partners' profit-and-loss ratio.

Moor's Capital account is credited for her one-fourth interest in the partnership. The bonus is allocated to the original partners (Nagasawa and Wendt) based on their profit-and-loss ratio.

The new partnership's balance sheet reports these amounts:

Cash*	$130,000	Total liabilities	$100,000
Other assets	210,000	Hiro Nagasawa, capital**	85,000
		Lisa Wendt, capital†	95,000
		Alana Moor, capital	60,000
Total assets	$340,000	Total liabilities and equity	$340,000

*($40,000 + $90,000)
**($70,000 + $15,000)
†($80,000 + $15,000)

Admission by Investing in the Partnership—Bonus to the New Partner A potential new partner may be so important that the old partners offer a partnership share that includes a bonus to the new partner. A law firm may strongly desire a former premier, cabinet minister, or other official as a partner because of the person's reputation. A restaurant owner may want to go into partnership with a famous sports personality like Sidney Crosby or a musician like Deadmau5.

Suppose Jan Page and Miko Goh have a restaurant. Their partnership balance sheet appears as follows:

Cash	$140,000	Total liabilities	$120,000	
Other assets	360,000	Jan Page, capital	230,000	} $380,000
		Miko Goh, capital	150,000	
Total assets	$500,000	Total liabilities and equity	$500,000	

The partners admit Martin Santiago, a famous hockey player, as a partner with a one-third interest in exchange for Santiago's cash investment of $100,000. At the time of Santiago's admission, the firm's capital is $380,000. Page and Goh share profits and losses in the ratio of two-thirds to Page and one-third to Goh. The computation of Santiago's equity in the new partnership is as follows:

Partnership capital before Santiago is admitted ($230,000 + $150,000)		$380,000
Santiago's investment in the partnership		100,000
Partnership capital after Santiago is admitted		$480,000
One-third interest ($480,000 × $^1/_3$). Share to Santiago.		$160,000
Bonus to new partner ($160,000 − $100,000)		$ 60,000

In this case, Santiago entered the partnership at a price ($100,000) below the book value of his equity ($160,000). The Capital accounts of Page and Goh are debited for the $60,000 difference between the new partner's equity ($160,000) and his investment ($100,000). The old partners share this decrease in capital, which is accounted for as though it were a loss, based on their profit-and-loss ratio. The entry to record Santiago's investment is:

Aug. 24	Cash	100,000	
	Jan Page, Capital	40,000	
	Miko Goh, Capital	20,000	
	Martin Santiago, Capital		160,000
	To admit M. Santiago as a partner with a one-third interest in the business.		
	Split loss according to profit-and-loss ratio: Page = $60,000 × 2/3 and Goh = $60,000 × 1/3		

The new partnership's balance sheet reports these amounts:

Cash*	$240,000	Total liabilities	$120,000
Other assets	360,000	Jan Page, capital**	190,000
		Miko Goh, capital†	130,000
		Martin Santiago, capital	160,000
Total assets	$600,000	Total liabilities and equity	$600,000

*($140,000 + $100,000)
**($230,000 − $40,000)
†($150,000 − $20,000)

In the next section we will see how to account for the withdrawal of a partner from a business.

> Try It!

6. Tina and Jean are partners with Capital balances of $25,000 and $75,000, respectively. They share profits and losses in a 30:70 ratio. Tina and Jean admit Phyllis to a 10 percent interest in a new partnership when Phyllis invests $20,000 in the business.

   a. Compute the bonus to Tina and Jean.

   b. Journalize the partnership's receipt of Phyllis's investment on June 12.

   c. What is each partner's Capital in the new partnership?

7. Refer to the data in the previous question. If Phyllis had invested only $10,000 into the partnership for a 10 percent interest, journalize the partnership's receipt of Phyllis's investment.

Solutions appear at the end of this chapter and on MyAccountingLab

WITHDRAWAL OF A PARTNER FROM THE BUSINESS

A partner may leave the business for many reasons, including retirement or a dispute with the other partners. The withdrawal of a partner dissolves the old partnership. The partnership agreement should specify how to split the partnership assets and liabilities with a withdrawing partner.

In the simplest case, a partner may withdraw by selling his or her interest to another party in a personal transaction. This is the same as admitting a new person who purchases an old partner's interest, as we saw earlier. The journal entry simply debits the withdrawing partner's Capital account and credits the new partner's Capital account. The dollar amount of the entry is the old partner's Capital balance, regardless of the price paid by the purchaser, as illustrated for Spelacy and Drake on page 688.

Another option would be for a current partner to buy a second partner's interest. This is recorded the same way as when an outside party buys a current partner's interest.

The two main steps that must be completed prior to identifying how much is owed to the withdrawing partner are as follows:

1. Close the books. If the partner withdraws in the middle of the accounting period, the partnership books should be updated to determine the withdrawing partner's Capital balance. The business must measure net income or net loss for the fraction of the year up to the withdrawal date and allocate profit or loss according to the existing ratio.
2. If it is in the partnership agreement, the settlement procedure may specify an independent appraisal of the assets to determine their current market value of the assets. In that case, the partnership must update the value of the assets in the accounting records. This is known as an **asset revaluation**. The partners share any market value changes according to their profit-and-loss ratio.

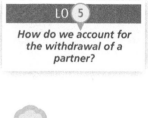

LO 5

How do we account for the withdrawal of a partner?

LEARNING TIPS

Terminology alert! Notice that here the term "withdrawal" refers to a partner who is leaving and not the "drawings" that were discussed earlier.

REAL WORLD EXAMPLE

When a partner leaves a partnership, she or he ceases to be an agent and no longer has the authority to bind the business to contracts. Third parties with whom the partnership has dealt should be notified that the exiting partner can no longer bind the partnership. All others can be informed with a newspaper advertisement.

Withdrawal at Book Value

Suppose Ben Wolfe is retiring in the middle of the year from the partnership of Sheldon, Greis, and Wolfe. After the books have been adjusted for partial-period income but before the asset appraisal, revaluation, and closing entries are recorded, the balance sheet reports the following:

Cash		$ 70,000	Total liabilities	$ 80,000
Inventory		40,000	Joan Sheldon, capital	50,000
Land		50,000	George Greis, capital	40,000
Building	$90,000		Ben Wolfe, capital	20,000
Less: Accumulated amortization	60,000	30,000		
Total assets		$190,000	Total liabilities and equity	$190,000

An independent appraiser revalues the inventory at $34,000 (down from $40,000) and the land at $100,000 (up from $50,000). The partners share the differences between market value and book value based on their profit-and-loss ratio of 1:2:1.

We identify what share each partner has for the revaluation:

The ratios of 1:2:1 is the same as a ¼, ½, ¼ fraction. It is also the same as a 25 percent, 50 percent, 25 percent sharing ratio.

These figures, multiplied by the gain or loss in value from the revaluation, yield each partner's share to be recorded:

The inventory has a $6,000 decrease ($40,000 – $34,000) to allocate:

Sheldon:	$6,000 × ¼ = $1,500
Greis:	$6,000 × ½ = $3,000
Wolfe:	$6,000 × ¼ = $1,500

The land has a $50,000 increase ($100,000 – $50,000) to allocate:

Sheldon:	$50,000 × ¼ = $12,500
Greis:	$50,000 × ½ = $25,000
Wolfe:	$50,000 × ¼ = $12,500

The entries to record the revaluation of the inventory and land are as follows:

Jun. 30	Joan Sheldon, Capital	1,500	
	George Greis, Capital	3,000	
	Ben Wolfe, Capital	1,500	
	Inventory		6,000
	To revalue the inventory and allocate the loss in value to the partners.		

Jun. 30	Land	50,000	
	Joan Sheldon, Capital		12,500
	George Greis, Capital		25,000
	Ben Wolfe, Capital		12,500
	To revalue the land and allocate the gain in value to the partners.		

After the revaluations, the partnership balance sheet reports the following:

Cash		$ 70,000	Total liabilities	$ 80,000
Inventory		34,000		
Land		100,000		
Building	$90,000		Joan Sheldon, capital*	61,000
Less: Accumulated			George Greis, capital**	62,000
amortization	60,000	30,000	Ben Wolfe, capital†	31,000
Total assets		$234,000	Total liabilities and equity	$234,000

*($50,000 – $1,500 + $12,500)
**($40,000 – $3,000 + $25,000)
†($20,000 – $1,500 + $12,500)

As the balance sheet shows, Wolfe has a claim to $31,000 in partnership assets. Now we can account for Wolfe's withdrawal from the business.

If Ben Wolfe withdraws by taking cash equal to the book value of his owner's equity, the entry would be:

Jun. 30	Ben Wolfe, Capital	31,000	
	Cash		31,000
	To record the withdrawal of B. Wolfe from the partnership.		

This entry records the payment of partnership cash to Wolfe and the closing of his Capital account upon his withdrawal from the business.

Withdrawal at Less than Book Value

The withdrawing partner may be so eager to depart that she or he is willing to take less than her or his equity. Assume Ben Wolfe withdraws from the business and agrees to receive cash of $10,000 and a $15,000 note payable from the new partnership. This $25,000 settlement is $6,000 less than Wolfe's $31,000 equity in the business. The remaining partners share this $6,000 difference—which is a bonus to them—according to their profit-and-loss ratio.

Because Wolfe has withdrawn from the partnership, Wolfe's capital account is closed, and Greis and Sheldon may or may not continue the partnership. Assuming they agree to form a new partnership, a new agreement—and a new profit-and-loss ratio—is needed. In forming a new partnership, Greis and Sheldon may decide on any ratio they wish. Assume Greis and Sheldon agree on a profit-and-loss ratio of ⅔ for Greis and ⅓ for Sheldon.

The entry to record Wolfe's withdrawal at less than book value is as follows:

KEY POINTS
Whenever a new partnership is formed, a new partnership agreement and a new profit-and-loss ratio are needed and should be created.

Jun. 30	Ben Wolfe, Capital	31,000	
	Cash		10,000
	Note Payable to Ben Wolfe		15,000
	Joan Sheldon, Capital		2,000
	George Greis, Capital		4,000
	To record withdrawal of B. Wolfe from the partnership. Sheldon's bonus is $2,000 ($6,000 × $\frac{1}{3}$) and Greis's bonus is $4,000 ($6,000 × $\frac{2}{3}$).		

Withdrawal at More than Book Value

A withdrawing partner may receive assets worth more than the book value of her or his equity. This situation creates:

• A bonus to the withdrawing partner
• A decrease in the remaining partners' Capital accounts, shared in their profit-and-loss ratio

The accounting for this situation follows the pattern illustrated previously for withdrawal at less than book value—with one exception. In this situation, the remaining partners' Capital accounts are debited because they are paying a bonus to the withdrawing partner.

Refer back to our previous example. Suppose Wolfe withdraws from the partnership and agrees to receive $40,000 cash. Greis and Sheldon agree that Greis will get two-thirds of the new partnership's profits and losses and Sheldon one-third. The entry to record Wolfe's withdrawal at more than book value is:

Jun. 30	Ben Wolfe, Capital	31,000	
	Joan Sheldon, Capital	3,000	
	George Greis, Capital	6,000	
	Cash		40,000
	To record withdrawal of B. Wolfe from the partnership. Sheldon's Capital is reduced by $3,000 ($9,000 \times \frac{1}{3}$) and Greis's Capital is reduced by $6,000 ($9,000 \times \frac{2}{3}$).		

Death of a Partner

REAL WORLD EXAMPLE

Partners commonly carry life insurance on themselves, with the partners as beneficiaries. In the event of a death, the partners receive the cash flow necessary to settle with the deceased partner's estate, without putting the partnership into financial jeopardy.

As with any other form of partnership withdrawal, the death of a partner dissolves a partnership. The partnership accounts are adjusted to measure net income or loss for the fraction of the year up to the date of death. The accounts are then closed to determine all partners' Capital balances on that date. Settlement with the deceased partner's estate is based on the partnership agreement. There may or may not be an asset revaluation. The estate commonly receives partnership assets equal to the partner's Capital balance.

Alternatively, a remaining partner may purchase the deceased partner's equity. The deceased partner's Capital account is debited and the purchaser's Capital account is credited. The amount of this entry is the ending Capital balance of the deceased partner.

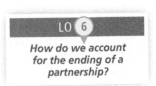

8. Suppose Ruth is withdrawing from the partnership of Ruth, Nick, and Adriana. The partners share profits and losses in a 1:2:3 ratio for Ruth, Nick, and Adriana, respectively. After the revaluation of assets, Ruth's Capital balance is $40,000, and the other partners agree to pay her $50,000. Nick and Adriana agree to a new profit-and-loss ratio of 2:3 for Nick and Adriana, respectively. Journalize the payment to Ruth for her withdrawal from the partnership on August 31.

9. Refer to the previous question. Suppose the situation is the same except that the other partners agree to pay Ruth $30,000. Journalize the payment to Ruth for her withdrawal from the partnership.

Solutions appear at the end of this chapter and on MyAccountingLab

LIQUIDATION OF A PARTNERSHIP

LO 6

How do we account for the ending of a partnership?

As we have seen, the admission or withdrawal of a partner dissolves the partnership. However, the business may continue operating with no apparent change to outsiders such as customers and creditors. In contrast, business **liquidation** is the process of going out of business by selling the entity's assets and paying its liabilities. The business shuts down. Before the business is liquidated, the books should be adjusted and closed.

Liquidation of a partnership includes three basic steps:

1. Sell the assets. Allocate the gain or loss to the partners' Capital accounts based on the profit-and-loss ratio.
2. Pay all the partnership's liabilities.
3. Pay the remaining cash to the partners in proportion to their Capital balances.

The liquidation of a business can stretch over weeks or months, even years for a large company. Selling every asset and paying every liability of the entity takes time. For example, in early 2014 the law firm of Heenan Blaikie, which had over 500 lawyers at one time, failed and the firm estimated it would take a team of five lawyers "several months" to close.[4] In early 2015, the work still wasn't completed.

To avoid excessive detail in our illustrations, we include only two asset categories—Cash and Noncash Assets—and a single liability category—Liabilities. Our examples also assume that the business sells the assets in a single transaction and then pays the liabilities at once. (In actual practice, each asset and its related amortization would be accounted for separately when it is sold, and each liability would be accounted for separately when it is paid.)

Assume that Ryan Lauren, Alexis Andrews, and Scott Benroudi have shared profits and losses in the ratio of 3:1:1. The partners decide to liquidate their partnership. After the books are adjusted and closed, these accounts remain:

LEARNING TIPS

The ratio of 3:1:1 is equal to 3/5, 1/5, 1/5, or a 60 percent, 20 percent, 20 percent sharing ratio.

Cash	$ 10,000	Liabilities	$ 30,000
Noncash assets	90,000	Ryan Lauren, capital	40,000
		Alexis Andrews, capital	20,000
		Scott Benroudi, capital	10,000
Total assets	$100,000	Total liabilities and equity	$100,000

Sale of Assets at a Gain

① Sell the Assets Assume the Lauren, Andrews, and Benroudi partnership sells its noncash assets for $150,000 (book value, $90,000). The partnership realizes a gain of $60,000, which is allocated to the partners based on their profit-and-loss-sharing ratio.

This could be broken down into two steps: recording the gain or loss on liquidation, and recording the allocation of the gain or loss to the partners. The journal entries would be:

Oct. 31	Cash	150,000	
	Noncash Assets		90,000
	Gain on Liquidation		60,000
	To sell noncash assets in liquidation.		
31	Gain on Liquidation	60,000	
	Ryan Lauren, Capital		36,000
	Alexis Andrews, Capital		12,000
	Scott Benroudi, Capital		12,000
	To allocate gain to partners. Lauren's share of the gain is $36,000 ($60,000 × 0.60), Andrew's and Benroudi's are $12,000 each ($60,000 × 0.20).		

Now the partners' Capital accounts have the following balances:

Ryan Lauren, Capital		Alexis Andrews, Capital		Scott Benroudi, Capital	
	40,000		20,000		10,000
Oct. 31	36,000	Oct. 31	12,000	Oct. 31	12,000
Bal.	76,000	Bal.	32,000	Bal.	22,000

---

[4] Janet McFarland, Jeff Gray, Kathryn Blaze Carlson, and Sean Fine, "Storied Law Firm Heenan Blaikie Sunk by a Shifting Legal Landscape," *Globe and Mail*, February 5, 2014, accessed August 4, 2014, www.theglobeandmail.com/report-on-business/industry-news/the-law-page/pace-of-departures-from-struggling-heenan-blaikie-continues-to-escalate/article16708371.

2 Pay All the Partnership Liabilities

Oct. 31	Liabilities	30,000	
	Cash		30,000
	To pay liabilities in liquidation.		

3 **Pay the Remaining Cash to the Partners in Proportion to Their Capital Balances** (By contrast, *gains* and *losses* on the sale of assets are shared by the partners based on their profit-and-loss ratio.) The amount of cash left in the partnership is $130,000, as follows:

Cash

Beg. bal.	10,000	Payment of liabilities	30,000
Sale of assets	150,000		
End. bal.	130,000		

The partners divide the remaining cash according to their Capital balances:

Oct. 31	Ryan Lauren, Capital	76,000	
	Alexis Andrews, Capital	32,000	
	Scott Benroudi, Capital	22,000	
	Cash		130,000
	To disburse cash to partners in liquidation.		

A convenient way to summarize the transactions in a partnership liquidation is given in Exhibit 12–5. Remember:

- Upon liquidation, gains and losses on the sale of assets are divided according to the *profit-and-loss ratio.*
- The final cash payment to the partners is based on *Capital balances.*

EXHIBIT 12–5 | Partnership Liquidation—Sale of Assets at a Gain

					Capital		
					Lauren	Andrews	Benroudi
	Cash	+ Noncash Assets	= Liabilities	+	(60%) +	(20%) +	(20%)
Balances before sale of assets	$10,000	$90,000	$30,000		$40,000	$20,000	$10,000
1 Sale of assets and sharing of gain	150,000	(90,000)	—		36,000	12,000	12,000
Balances	160,000	0	30,000		76,000	32,000	22,000
2 Payment of liabilities	(30,000)		(30,000)				
Balances	130,000	0	0		76,000	32,000	22,000
3 Disbursement of cash to partners	(130,000)				(76,000)	(32,000)	(22,000)
Balances	$ 0	$ 0	$ 0		$ 0	$ 0	$ 0

After the disbursement of cash to the partners, the business has no assets, liabilities, or equity. All final balances are zero.

Sale of Assets at a Loss

Liquidation of a business often includes the sale of assets at a loss. When a loss occurs, the partners' Capital accounts are debited based on the profit-and-loss ratio. Otherwise, the accounting follows the pattern illustrated for the sale of assets at a gain.

Suppose the Lauren, Andrews, and Benroudi partnership sold its noncash assets for $30,000 and all other details in Exhibit 12–5 remained the same. This creates a loss of $60,000 on the sale of the noncash assets. Exhibit 12–6 summarizes the transactions in a partnership liquidation when the assets are sold at a loss.

EXHIBIT 12–6 | Partnership Liquidation—Sale of Assets at a Loss

	Cash	+ Noncash Assets	= Liabilities	+	Lauren (60%)	+	Andrews (20%)	+	Benroudi (20%)
Balances before sale of assets	$10,000	$90,000	$30,000		$40,000		$20,000		$10,000
① Sale of assets and sharing of loss	30,000	(90,000)			(36,000)		(12,000)		(12,000)
Balances	40,000	0	30,000		4,000		8,000		(2,000)
② Payment of liabilities	(30,000)		(30,000)						
Balances	10,000	0	0		4,000		8,000		(2,000) ◂
③ Disbursement of cash to partners	(10,000)				(4,000)		(8,000)		2,000
Balances	$ 0	$ 0	$ 0		$ 0		$ 0		$ 0

Capital Deficiencies

Notice that Benroudi's Capital account has a negative balance (follow the arrow). This is known as a **capital deficiency**. The capital deficiency must be dealt with *before* the ending cash is distributed. One way of dealing with the $2,000 capital deficiency in Benroudi's Capital account is for Benroudi to contribute $2,000 of assets to the partnership to erase his capital deficiency. If Benroudi contributes cash, the journal entry to record this is:

Oct. 31	Cash	2,000	
	Scott Benroudi, Capital		2,000
	Contributed cash to erase capital deficiency on liquidation.		

Another option for dealing with Benroudi's $2,000 capital deficiency is for Benroudi's partners, Lauren and Andrews, to agree to absorb Benroudi's capital deficiency by decreasing their own Capital balances in proportion to their remaining profit-sharing percentages: Lauren, 60/80; Andrews, 20/80. The journal entry to record this is:

Oct. 31	Ryan Lauren, Capital	1,500	
	Alexis Andrews, Capital	500	
	Scott Benroudi, Capital		2,000
	To absorb the Benroudi capital deficiency by decreasing remaining partners' Capital balances. Lauren $1,500 ($2,000 × 60/80) and Andrews $500 ($2,000 × 20/80)		

How do partners deal with a situation where two of the three partners have capital deficiencies? Both partners could contribute assets in the amount of their deficiencies to the third partner. However, if the deficient partners cannot contribute personal assets, then the deficits must be absorbed by the remaining partner. If the remaining partner then still has a balance in his or her Capital account, any remaining cash balance would be paid to that partner.

When a business liquidates, there may not be enough cash from the sale of the assets to pay the liabilities. The partners (who are personally liable for the partnership debts) must contribute cash on the basis of their profit-and-loss ratio to cover unpaid debts.

> Try It!

10. Refer to the Lauren, Andrews, and Benroudi partnership on page 697. Suppose the partnership sold its noncash assets for $20,000 and all other details in Exhibit 12–5 remained the same.

   a. What is the profit or loss created on the sale of the noncash assets?

   b. Allocate the profit or loss calculated in part (a) to the partners.

   c. How can the partnership deal with any capital deficiencies in this situation?

Solutions appear at the end of this chapter and on MyAccountingLab

SUMMARY PROBLEM FOR YOUR REVIEW

The partnership of Anderssen and Wang admits Sony Pappachan as a partner on January 2, 2017. The partnership has these balances on that date:

Cash	$ 9,000	Total liabilities	$ 50,000
Other assets	110,000	Magnus Anderssen, capital	45,000
		Songyao Wang, capital	24,000
Total assets	$119,000	Total liabilities and equity	$119,000

Magnus Anderssen's share of profits and losses is 60 percent and Songyao Wang's share is 40 percent.

Required

(Requirements 1 and 2 are independent.)

1. Suppose Pappachan pays Wang $30,000 to acquire Wang interest in the business after Anderssen approves Pappachan as a partner.

   a. Record the transfer of owner's equity on the partnership books.

   b. Prepare the partnership balance sheet immediately after Pappachan is admitted as a partner.

2. Suppose Pappachan becomes a partner by investing $31,000 cash to acquire a one-fourth interest in the business.

    a. Compute Pappachan's Capital balance and determine whether there is any bonus. If so, who gets the bonus?

    b. Record Pappachan's investment in the business.

    c. Prepare the partnership balance sheet immediately after Pappachan is admitted as a partner. Include the appropriate heading.

3. Which way of admitting Pappachan to the partnership increases its total assets? Give your reason.

SOLUTION

Requirement 1

a.

Jan. 2	Songyao Wang, Capital	24,000	
	Sony Pappachan, Capital		24,000
	To transfer Wang equity in the partnership to Pappachan.		

When a new partner acquires an old partner's interest, the new partner purchases the old partner's equity balance on the books and *replaces* the old partner. Any amount paid in excess goes to the old partner personally.

b. The balance sheet for the partnership of Anderssen and Pappachan is identical to the balance sheet given for Anderssen and Wang in the problem, except Sony Pappachan's name replaces Songyao Wang's name in the title and in the listing of Capital accounts.

Requirement 2

a. Computation of Pappachan's Capital balance:

Partnership capital before Pappachan is admitted ($45,000 + $24,000)	$ 69,000
Pappachan's investment in the partnership	31,000
Partnership capital after Pappachan is admitted	$100,000
Pappachan's capital in the partnership ($100,000 × $^1/_4$)	$ 25,000
Bonus to the old partners ($31,000 − $25,000)	$ 6,000

When a new partner acquires an interest in a partnership, the new partner *joins the existing partners* by adding cash to the pool of capital, then dividing the pool among the old and new partners. Any amount paid in excess increases the old partners' Capital balances.

b.

Jan. 2	Cash	31,000	
	Sony Pappachan, Capital		25,000
	Magnus Anderssen, Capital		3,600
	Songyao Wang, Capital		2,400
	To admit Pappachan as a partner with a one-fourth interest in the business. Anderssen's bonus is $3,600 [($31,000 − $25,000) × 0.60] and Wang bonus is $2,400 [($31,000 − $25,000) × 0.40].		

Any amount paid in excess increases the old partners' Capital balances by giving each old partner a bonus. The bonus is based on the profit-and-loss-sharing percentage in place before the new partner joined.

The Cash and Capital accounts will change when a new partner joins existing partners. Add the bonus to each of the old partners' Capital balances and add the new partner's Capital balance, all from the January 2, 2017, journal entry.

ANDERSSEN, WANG, AND PAPPACHAN
Balance Sheet
January 2, 2017

Cash*	$ 40,000	Total liabilities	$ 50,000
Other assets	110,000	Magnus Anderssen, capital**	48,600
		Songyao Wang, capital***	26,400
		Sony Pappachan, capital	25,000
Total assets	$150,000	Total liabilities and equity	$150,000

*$9,000 + $31,000 = $40,000

**$45,000 + $3,600 = $48,600

***$24,000 + $2,400 = $26,400

Requirement 3

A partnership's total assets are increased only when a new partner joins existing partners, not when a new partner "replaces" an old partner by purchasing the old partner's Capital.

Pappachan's investment in the partnership increases its total assets by the amount of his contribution. Total assets of the business are $150,000 after his investment, compared with $119,000 before. By contrast, Pappachan's purchase of Wang's interest in the business is a personal transaction between the two individuals. It does not affect the assets of the partnership, regardless of the amount Pappachan pays Wang.

SUMMARY

LEARNING OBJECTIVE ❶ Identify the characteristics of a partnership

What are the characteristics of a partnership? Pg. 675

- A *partnership* is a business co-owned by two or more persons for profit.
- The characteristics of partnerships are:
  - Ease of formation
  - Limited life
  - Mutual agency
  - Unlimited liability
  - No partnership income taxes
- In a *limited partnership*, the limited partners have limited personal liability for the obligations of the business.
- A written *partnership agreement* establishes procedures for admission of a new partner, withdrawal of a partner, and the sharing of profits and losses among the partners.
- When a new partner is admitted to the firm or an existing partner withdraws, the old partnership is *dissolved*, or ceases to exist. A new partnership may or may not emerge to continue the business.

LEARNING OBJECTIVE ❷ Account for partners' initial investments in a partnership

How do we account for partners' investments in a partnership? Pg. 679

- Accounting for a partnership is similar to accounting for a proprietorship. However, a partnership has more than one owner.
- Each partner has an individual Capital account and a Withdrawal account; the Capital accounts for each partner are shown on the balance sheet.
- The partnership income statement includes a section showing the division of net income to the partners.

LEARNING OBJECTIVE 3 — Allocate profits and losses to the partners by different methods

How can we allocate profits and losses to the partners?   Pg. 681

- Partners share net income or loss in any manner they choose.
- Common sharing agreements base the *profit-and-loss ratio* on:
  - A stated fraction
  - Partners' capital investments
  - Other methods, including a combination of service and interest, which, despite their name, are not expenses of the business.
- Partner withdrawals reduce the partner capital accounts but are not a form of net income allocation.

LEARNING OBJECTIVE 4 — Account for the admission of a new partner

How do we account for a new partner?   Pg. 688

- If the old partners agree to admit a new partner to the partnership, the old partnership is dissolved and a new partnership is created.
- An outside person may become a partner by:
  - Purchasing a current partner's interest (the transaction is between the partners and does not increase the total partnership equity)
  - Investing in the partnership (the transaction increases the total partnership equity by the amount of the investment)
- In some cases, the new partner must pay the current partners a bonus to join. In other situations, the new partner may receive a bonus to join.

LEARNING OBJECTIVE 5 — Account for the withdrawal of a partner

How do we account for the withdrawal of a partner?   Pg. 693

- The two steps prior to accounting for the withdrawal of a partner are:
  1. Adjust and close the books up to the date of the partner's withdrawal from the business.
  2. Appraise the assets and the liabilities to determine their current market value. Allocate the gain or loss in value to the partners' Capital accounts based on their profit-and-loss ratio.
- Then account for the partner's withdrawal
  a. At book value (no change in remaining partners' Capital balances)
  b. At less than book value (increase the remaining partners' Capital balances)
  c. At greater than book value (decrease the remaining partners' Capital balances)

LEARNING OBJECTIVE 6 — Account for the liquidation of a partnership

How do we account for the ending of a partnership?   Pg. 696

- In *liquidation*, a partnership goes out of business by:
  1. Selling the assets
  2. Paying the liabilities
  3. Paying any remaining cash to the partners based on their capital balances.

Check **Accounting Vocabulary** on page 704 for all key terms used in Chapter 12 and the Glossary at the back of the book for all key terms used in the textbook.

MORE CHAPTER REVIEW MATERIAL

MyAccountingLab

DemoDoc covering Partnerships

Student PowerPoint Slides

Audio Chapter Summary

Note: All MyAccountingLab resources can be found in the Chapter Resources section and the Multimedia Library.

ACCOUNTING VOCABULARY

Asset revaluation   Adjusting asset values to reflect current market values, usually based on an independent appraisal of the assets *(p. 693)*.

Capital deficiency   A partnership's claim against a partner. Occurs when a partner's Capital account has a debit balance *(p. 699)*.

Dissolution   Ending a partnership *(p. 675)*.

General partnership   A form of partnership in which each partner is an owner of the business, with all the privileges and risks of ownership *(p. 677)*.

Interest allowance   An interest component that rewards a partner with an allocation because of his or her investment in the business. This is not the same as interest expense paid on a loan *(p. 684)*.

Limited liability partnership (LLP)   A partnership in which each partner's personal liability for the business's debts is limited to a certain dollar amount *(p. 678)*.

Limited partnership   A partnership with at least two classes of partners: a general partner and limited partners *(p. 677)*.

Liquidation   The process of going out of business by selling the entity's assets and paying its liabilities. The final step in liquidation of a business is the distribution of any remaining cash to the owners *(p. 696)*.

Mutual agency   Every partner can bind the business to a contract within the scope of the partnership's regular business operations *(p. 675)*.

Partnership   An unincorporated business with two or more owners *(p. 674)*.

Partnership agreement   An agreement that is the contract between partners specifying such items as the name, location, and nature of the business; the name, capital investment, and duties of each partner; and the method of sharing profits and losses by the partners *(p. 675)*.

Salary allowance   Another term for *service* *(p. 683)*.

Service   An allocation to a partner based on his or her service to the partnership. This is not the same as salary expense for an employee *(p. 683)*.

Unlimited personal liability   When a partnership (or a proprietorship) cannot pay its debts with business assets, the partners (or the proprietor) must use personal assets to meet the debt *(p. 676)*.

SIMILAR ACCOUNTING TERMS

Limited liability partnership	LLP
Liquidation	Shutting down the business; going out of business
Partners' equity	Partners' capital; Capital
Service	Salary allowance
Withdrawals	Drawings

SELF-STUDY QUESTIONS

Test your understanding of the chapter by marking the correct answer for each of the following questions:

1. Which of these characteristics identifies a partnership? *(pp. 675–676)*
   a. Unlimited life
   b. No income tax paid by the business entity
   c. Limited personal liability
   d. All of the above

2. A partnership records a partner's investment of assets in the business at *(p. 679)*
   a. The partner's book value of the assets invested
   b. The market value of the assets invested
   c. A special value set by the partners
   d. Any of the above, depending upon the partnership agreement

3. The partnership of Hungerford, LaPlante, and Egly divides profits in the ratio of 4:5:3. There is no provision for losses. During 2017, the business earned $40,000. Egly's share of this income is *(pp. 681–682)*
   a. $10,000
   b. $13,333
   c. $16,000
   d. $16,667

4. Suppose the partnership of Hungerford, LaPlante, and Egly in the preceding question lost $40,000 during 2017. LaPlante's share of this loss is *(p. 681–682)*
   a. Not determinable because the ratio applies only to profits
   b. $13,333
   c. $10,000
   d. $16,667

5. The partners of Martin, Short, and Chase share profits and losses 1/5, 1/6, and 19/30. During 2017, the first year of their partnership, the business earned $120,000, and each partner withdrew $50,000 for personal use. What is the balance in Chase's Capital account after all closing entries? (p. 682)
   a. Not determinable because Chase's beginning Capital balance is not given
   b. Minus $10,000
   c. Minus $50,000
   d. $26,000

6. Elaine Robinson buys into the partnership of Quantz and Goodwin by purchasing a one-third interest for $55,000. Prior to Robinson's entry, Edward Quantz's Capital balance was $46,000 and Louisa Goodwin's balance was $52,000; profits and losses were shared equally. The entry to record Robinson's buying into the business is (pp. 689–692)

a.	Cash	55,000	
	Elaine Robinson, Capital		55,000
b.	Edward Quantz, Capital	27,500	
	Louisa Goodwin, Capital	27,500	
	Elaine Robinson, Capital		55,000
c.	Cash	55,000	
	Elaine Robinson, Capital		51,000
	Edward Quantz, Capital		2,000
	Louisa Goodwin, Capital		2,000
d.	Cash	51,000	
	Edward Quantz, Capital	2,000	
	Louisa Goodwin, Capital	2,000	
	Elaine Robinson, Capital		55,000

7. The partners of Tsui, Valik, and Wollenberg share profits and losses equally. Their Capital balances are $40,000, $50,000, and $60,000, respectively, when Wollenberg sells her interest in the partnership to Valik for $90,000. Tsui and Valik continue the business. Immediately after Wollenberg's retirement, the total assets of the partnership are (pp. 693–695)
   a. Increased by $30,000
   b. Increased by $90,000
   c. Decreased by $60,000
   d. The same as before Wollenberg sold her interest to Valik

8. Prior to Bill Ching's withdrawal from the partnership of Ching, Han, and Lee, the partners' Capital balances were $140,000, $110,000 and $250,000, respectively. The partners share profits and losses 1/3, 1/4, and 5/12. The appraisal indicates that assets should be written down by $36,000. Arthur Han's share of the write-down is (pp. 693–695)
   a. $7,920   c. $12,000
   b. $9,000   d. $18,000

9. The process of closing the business, selling the assets, paying the liabilities, and disbursing remaining cash to the owners is called (p. 696)
   a. Dissolution
   b. Forming a new partnership
   c. Withdrawal
   d. Liquidation

10. Mike Marr and Pamela Coombs have shared profits and losses equally. Immediately prior to the final cash disbursement in a liquidation of their partnership, the books show:
    Cash $100,000 = Liabilities $0 + Mike Marr, Capital $60,000 + Pamela Coombs, Capital $40,000
    How much cash should Marr receive? (p. 697)
    a. $40,000   c. $60,000
    b. $50,000   d. None of the above

ASSIGNMENT MATERIAL

QUESTIONS

1. List at least five items that the partnership agreement should specify.

2. Ron Montgomery, who is a partner in M&N Associates, commits the firm to a contract for a job within the scope of its regular business operations. What term describes Montgomery's ability to obligate the partnership?

3. If a partnership cannot pay a debt, who must make payment? What term describes this obligation of the partners?

4. How is income of a partnership taxed?

5. Identify the advantages and disadvantages of the partnership form of business organization.

6. Most professionals in Canada, such as doctors, lawyers, and public accounting firms, are organized as limited liability partnerships (LLPs). Explain the fundamental concept that governs an LLP.

7. Chris Higgins and Taylor Pyett's partnership agreement states that Higgins gets 60 percent of profits and Pyett gets 40 percent. If the agreement does not discuss the treatment of losses, how are losses shared? How do the partners share profits and losses if the agreement specifies no profit-and-loss-sharing ratio?

8. What determines the amount of the credit to a partner's Capital account when the partner contributes assets other than cash to the business?

9. Do partner withdrawals of cash for personal use affect the sharing of profits and losses by the partner? If so, explain how. If not, explain why not.

10. Name two events that can cause the dissolution of a partnership.

11. Briefly describe how to account for the purchase of an existing partner's interest in the business.

12. Jeff Malcolm purchases Sheila Wilson's interest in the Wilson & Conners partnership. What right does Malcolm obtain from the purchase? What is required for Malcolm to become Paula Conners' partner?

13. Sal Assissi and Hamza Zahari each have capital of $150,000 in their business. They share profits in the ratio of 55:45. Sheetal Kaur acquires a one-fifth share in the partnership by investing cash of $100,000. What are the Capital balances of the three partners immediately after Kaur is admitted?

14. When a partner resigns from the partnership and receives assets greater than her or his Capital balance, how is the difference shared by the other partners?

15. Distinguish between dissolution and liquidation of a partnership.

16. Name the three steps in liquidating a partnership.

17. The partnership of Ralls and Sauls is in the process of liquidation. How do the partners share (a) gains and losses on the sale of noncash assets, and (b) the final cash disbursement?

18. Compare and contrast the financial statements of a proprietorship and a partnership.

19. Summarize the situations in which partnership allocations are based on (a) the profit-and-loss ratio, and (b) the partners' Capital balances.

MyAccountingLab

Make the grade with MyAccountingLab: Most of the Starters, Exercises, and Problems marked in red can be found on MyAccountingLab. You can practise them as often as you want, and most feature step-by-step guided instructions to help you find the right answer.

STARTERS

The partnership form of business
①

Starter 12–1 For each of the three independent situations below, indicate if you would recommend the partnership form of business organization. State the reasons for your recommendation.

1. Sarah, Alisha, and Connie just graduated from a two-year college program and would like to start a bookkeeping business called SAC Bookkeeping. They each have equivalent assets to bring to the business.

2. Philip Harcourt just joined the law practice of Osler and Hoskins. He thinks he will be making a huge salary and is worried about the tax effects of this income. He thinks the partners should incorporate the partnership and avoid the tax bill.

3. Fred Klaus and Felix Cadeau would like to form a construction company. Fred has the contacts, cash, and estimating skills, while Felix has equipment and field experience. There will be minimal profits until the business has a few projects.

Statement of equity
①

Asanti, $76,900

Starter 12–2 Asanti and Quall are partners. Using the following information, prepare a statement of equity on December 31, 2017, for the A&Q Partnership:

	Capital Jan. 1, 2017	Capital Contributions	Net Income Allocated	Partner Drawings
Asanti	$45,000	$10,000	$33,900	$12,000
Quall	$60,000	$10,000	$22,100	$12,000

Starter 12-3 Susan Knoll and Emerson Wyndon are forming a partnership to develop a craft beer brewing company. Knoll contributes cash of $300,000 and land appraised at $80,000 with a building that has a current market value of $200,000. When Knoll purchased the land and building in 2014, its cost was $250,000. The partnership will assume Knoll's mortgage on the property in the amount of $110,000. Wyndon contributes cash of $500,000 and equipment with a current market value of $90,000.

Partnership formation
(2)
2. Total assets, $1,170,000

1. Journalize the partnership's receipt of assets and liabilities on October 15. Record this as a compound journal entry for both partners.
2. Compute the partnership's total assets, total liabilities, and total partners' equity immediately after organizing.

Starter 12-4 On June 30, 2016, Rick Reeves, Jason Bateman, and Oliver Morali started a partnership called RJO Enterprises. Prepare an opening balance sheet showing their investments:

Partnership balance sheet
(2)
Total partners' equity, $400,000

R. Reeves	Land appraised at $150,000
J. Bateman	Cash, $175,000
O. Morali	Inventory, $105,000; accounts payable $30,000

Starter 12-5 Abel and Baker decided to form a partnership. Abel contributed equipment (book value $65,000), inventory (paid $20,000), and $10,000 cash. The equipment and inventory have a current market value of $40,000 and $15,000, respectively. Abel also had a debt of $20,000 for the equipment. Baker contributed office equipment (book value $20,000) and cash of $50,000. The current market value of the office equipment is $10,000. The two partners fail to agree on a profit-and-loss-sharing ratio. For the first month (June 2017), the partnership lost $4,000.

Partners' profits, losses, and Capital balances
(3)
2. Abe Capital, $43,000

1. How much of this loss goes to Abel? How much goes to Baker?
2. The partners withdrew no assets during June. What is each partner's Capital balance at June 30? Prepare a T-account for each partner's Capital.

Starter 12-6 Friesen, Walters, and Onley have Capital balances of $12,000, $6,000, and $6,000, respectively. The partners share profits and losses as follows:

Dividing partnership profits based on capital contributions and service
(3)
Friesen, $43,000

a. The first $40,000 is divided based on the partners' capital investments.
b. The next $30,000 is based on service, shared equally by Friesen and Onley.
c. The remainder is divided equally.

Compute each partner's share of the $94,000 net income for the year.

Starter 12-7 The partnership of Bosch and Cutler had these balances at September 30, 2017:

Partnership income statement
(1)(2)(3)
Net income for Bosch, $36,000

Cash	$ 20,000	Service Revenue	$145,000
Liabilities	40,000	Bosch, Capital	30,000
Cutler, Capital	10,000	Total expenses	85,000
Other assets	120,000		

Bosch gets 60 percent of profits and losses, and Cutler gets 40 percent. Prepare the partnership's income statement and ending Capital balances for the year ended September 30, 2017.

Starter 12-8 Todd has a Capital balance of $60,000; Carlson's balance is $50,000. Reynaldo pays $200,000 to purchase Carlson's interest in the Todd & Carlson partnership. Carlson gets the full $200,000.

Admitting a partner who purchases an existing partner's interest
(4)

Journalize the partnership's transaction to admit Reynaldo to the partnership on August 1.

Admitting a partner who invests in the business ④ 1. No bonus	**Starter 12-9** The partnership of Evans and Falconi has these Capital balances:

Admitting a partner who invests in the business
④
1. No bonus

Starter 12-9 The partnership of Evans and Falconi has these Capital balances:

- Judy Evans $60,000
- Julie Falconi $80,000

Joan Gray invests cash of $70,000 to acquire a one-third interest in the partnership.

1. Does Gray's investment in the firm provide a bonus to the partners? Show your work.
2. Journalize the partnership's receipt of the $70,000 from Gray on February 1.

Admitting a new partner; bonus to the old partners
④
Bonus, $5,000

Starter 12-10 Bo and Go have partner Capital balances of $115,000 and $75,000, respectively. Bo gets 60 percent of profits and losses, and Go gets 40 percent. Assume Mo invests $70,000 to acquire a 25 percent interest in the new partnership of Bogomo. Is there a bonus? If so, who gets it? Journalize the partnership's receipt of cash from Mo on May 21.

Withdrawal of a partner
⑤

Starter 12-11 Adams, Everett, and Chapman each have a $75,000 Capital balance. They share profits and losses as follows: 25 percent to Adams, 50 percent to Everett, and 25 percent to Chapman. Suppose Chapman is withdrawing from the business, and the partners agree that no appraisal of assets is needed. How much in assets can Chapman take from the partnership? Give the reason for your answer. What role does the profit-and-loss ratio play in this situation?

Withdrawal of a partner; asset revaluation
⑤
(a) Debit Land, $20,000

Starter 12-12 Simpson, Locke, and Job each have a $27,000 Capital balance. Simpson is retiring from the business. The partners agree to revalue the assets at current market value. A real estate appraiser values the land at $70,000 (book value is $50,000). The profit-and-loss ratio is 1:2:1. Journalize (a) the revaluation of the land on July 31, and (b) a payment of $32,000 to Simpson upon his retirement the same day.

Liquidation of a partnership at a loss
⑥
Lauren, $34,000

Starter 12-13 Use the data in Exhibit 12-5. Suppose the partnership of Lauren, Andrews, and Benroudi liquidates by selling all noncash assets for $80,000. Complete the liquidation schedule as shown in Exhibit 12-6.

Liquidation of a partnership
⑥

Starter 12-14 This Starter builds on the solution to Starter 12-13. After completing the liquidation schedule in Starter 12-13, journalize the partnership's (a) sale of noncash assets for $80,000 (use a single account for Noncash Assets), (b) payment of liabilities, and (c) payment of cash to the partners on October 31. Include an explanation with each entry.

Capital deficit upon liquidation of a partnership
⑥

Starter 12-15 This Starter builds on the solution to Starter 12-13. After completing the liquidation schedule in Starter 12-13, you notice that Benroudi has a final balance of negative $8,000. What are the options for dealing with this capital deficit?

EXERCISES

MyAccountingLab

Exercise 12-1

Partnership characteristics
①

Mark Giltrow and Denise Chan are forming a business to imprint T-shirts. Giltrow suggests that they organize as a partnership to avoid the unlimited liability of a proprietorship. According to Giltrow, partnerships are not very risky.

Giltrow explains to Chan that if the business does not succeed, each partner can withdraw from the business, taking the same assets that she or he invested at its beginning. Giltrow states that the main disadvantage of the partnership form of organization is double taxation: First, the partnership pays a business income tax; second, each partner also pays personal income tax on her or his share of the business's profits.

Correct the errors in Giltrow's explanation.

Exercise 12–2

Joanna Volescu, a friend from college, approaches you about forming a partnership to export software. Since graduation, Joanna has worked for the World Bank, developing important contacts among government officials and business leaders in Poland and Hungary. Joanna believes she is in a unique position to capitalize on expanding markets. With your expertise in finance, you would have responsibility for accounting and finance in the partnership.

Required Discuss the advantages and disadvantages of organizing the export business as a partnership rather than a proprietorship. Comment on the way partnership income is taxed.

Organizing a business as a partnership
(1)

Exercise 12–3

Jackson Cooke and Julia Bamber are forming a partnership to develop an amusement park near Ottawa. Cooke contributes cash of $3 million and land valued at $30 million. When Cooke purchased the land, its cost was $16 million. The partnership will assume Cooke's $6 million note payable on the land. Bamber invests cash of $15 million and construction equipment that she purchased for $14 million (accumulated amortization to date is $6 million). The equipment's market value is equal to its book value.

Investments by partners
(2)
2. Total assets, $56 mil.

Required

1. Journalize the partnership's receipt of assets and liabilities from Cooke and Bamber on November 10. Record each asset at its current market value with no entry to accumulated amortization.

2. Compute the partnership's total assets, total liabilities, and total owners' equity immediately after organizing.

Exercise 12–4

On January 1, 2016, Chris Hunts and Carol Lo formed the Chris and Carol Partnership by investing the following assets and liabilities in the business:

Recording a partner's investment
(2)
Total capital, $350,000

	Chris's Book value	Carol's Book value
Cash	$12,000	$18,500
Equipment	38,000	53,500
Accumulated amort.—equipment	8,200	9,900
Buildings	84,000	95,000
Accumulated amort.—buildings	25,000	35,000
Land	60,000	66,000
Accounts payable	35,000	35,000
Note payable	17,000	28,000

An independent appraiser believes that Chris's equipment has a market value of $29,000 and Carol's equipment has a market value of $47,500. The appraiser indicates Chris's building has a current value of $90,000 and Carol's building has a current value of $110,000. The appraiser further indicates that Chris's land has a current value of $78,000 and Carol's land has a current value of $80,000. Chris and Carol agree to share profits and losses in a 60:40 ratio. During the first year of operations, the business net income is $74,000. Each partner withdrew $30,000 cash.

Required

1. Prepare the journal entries to record the initial investments in the business by Chris and Carol.

2. Prepare a balance sheet dated January 1, 2016, after the completion of the initial journal entries.

Excel Spreadsheet
Template
Computing partners' shares of
net income and net loss
(3)
c. Danolo, $104,000

Exercise 12–5

Ken Danolo and Jim Goldman form a partnership, investing $96,000 and $168,000, respectively. Determine their shares of net income or net loss for each of the following situations:

a. Net loss is $124,800 and the partners have no written partnership agreement.

b. Net income is $105,600 and the partnership agreement states that the partners share profits and losses based on their capital investments.

c. Net income is $264,000. The first $132,000 is shared based on the partner's capital investments. The next $100,000 is shared based on partner service, with Danolo receiving 40 percent and Goldman receiving 60 percent. The remainder is shared equally.

Exercise 12–6

Harper, Cheves, and Calderon have capital investments of $20,000, $30,000, and $50,000, respectively. The partners share profits and losses as follows:

a. The first $40,000 is divided based on the partner's capital investments.

b. The next $40,000 is based on service, shared equally by Harper and Cheves.

c. The remainder is divided equally.

Compute each partner's share of the $92,000 net income for the year.

Exercise 12–7

Oscar and Elmo have formed a partnership and invested $50,000 and $70,000, respectively. They have agreed to share profits as follows:

a. Oscar is to receive a payment of $25,000 for his service and Elmo is to receive a payment of $15,000 for his service.

b. $12,000 is to be allocated according to their original capital contributions to the partnership.

c. The remainder is to be allocated 5:4 respectively.

Assuming that the business had a loss of $11,000, allocate the loss to Oscar and Elmo.

Exercise 12–8

Ken Danolo withdrew cash of $148,000 for personal use, and Jim Goldman withdrew cash of $120,000 during the year. Using the data from situation (c) in Exercise 12–5, journalize the entries to close to each Capital account (a) the net income to the partners, and (b) the partners' Withdrawal accounts. Explanations are not required. Indicate the amount of increase or decrease in each partner's Capital balance. What was the overall effect on partnership capital?

Exercise 12–9

Goertz Accounting Services has a capital balance of $30,000 after adjusting assets to the fair market value. Leonard Goertz wants to form a partnership with Morley Neilson, who will receive a 30 percent interest in the new partnership. Neilson contributes $17,000 for his 30 percent interest. Determine Neilson's equity after admission and any bonus if applicable.

Exercise 12–10

Joanna Wang is admitted to a partnership. Prior to the admission of Wang, the partnership books show Tanya Wird's Capital balance at $79,000 and Alan Bales's Capital balance at $39,500. Wird and Bales share profits and losses equally.

Required

1. Compute the amount of each partner's equity on the books of the new partnership under each of the following plans:

a. Wang purchases Bales's interest in the business, paying $47,250 directly to Bales.

b. Wang invests $39,500 to acquire a one-fourth interest in the partnership.

c. Wang invests $71,500 to acquire a one-fourth interest in the partnership.

2. Make the partnership journal entry to record the admission of Wang under plans (a), (b), and (c) in Requirement 1. Explanations are not required.

Using a partnership financial
statement, admitting a new
partner
(1) (3) (4)
1. Harry Simra 40%;
Sunny Simra 60%

Exercise 12–11

The Simra Brothers Partnership had the following statement of partners' equity for the years ended December 31, 2016, and 2017. (This is similar to the statement of partners' equity shown in Exhibit 12–3 on page 678.)

	Simra Brothers Partnership			
	Statement of Partners' Equity			
	For the Years Ended December 31, 2016 and 2017			
	Harry Simra, Capital	Sunny Simra, Capital	Amin Simra, Capital	Total Partnership Capital
Balance, Jan. 1, 2016	$75,000	$ 50,000		$125,000
Net income for 2016	20,000	30,000		50,000
Balance, Dec. 31, 2016	95,000	80,000		175,000
Amin's contribution	2,000	3,000	$45,000	50,000
Net income for 2017	8,000	56,000	16,000	80,000
Less partner withdrawals	(12,000)	(16,000)	(10,000)	(38,000)
Balance, Dec. 31, 2017	$93,000	$123,000	$51,000	$267,000

Required

1. What was the profit-and-loss-sharing ratio in 2016?
2. Refer to Amin's contribution, which was made in cash. How much cash did Amin contribute to the partnership?
3. What percentage of interest did Amin obtain?
4. Why do Harry and Sunny have additions to their balances as a result of Amin's contribution?
5. What was the profit-and-loss-sharing ratio in 2017?

Exercise 12–12

After closing the books, Stihl & Laksa's partnership balance sheet reports owner's equity of $40,500 for Stihl and $54,000 for Laksa. Stihl is withdrawing from (leaving) the firm. He and Laksa agree to write down partnership assets by $18,000. They have shared profits and losses in the ratio of one-third to Stihl and two-thirds to Laksa. The partnership agreement states that a partner withdrawing from the firm will receive assets equal to the book value of his owner's equity.

Withdrawal of a partner from a business
⑤
2. $42,000

Required

1. How much will Stihl receive?
2. Laksa will continue to operate the business as a proprietorship. What is Laksa's beginning Capital on the proprietorship books?

Exercise 12–13

Alana Bruno is retiring from the partnership of Bruno, Teale, and White on May 31. The partner Capital balances are Bruno, $108,000; Teale, $153,000; and White, $66,000. The partners agree to have the partnership assets revalued to current market values. The independent appraiser reports that the book value of the inventory should be decreased by $24,000, and the book value of the land should be increased by $96,000. The partners agree to these revaluations. The profit-and-loss ratio has been 2:4:4 for Bruno, Teale, and White, respectively. In retiring from the firm, Bruno received $150,000 cash.

Withdrawal of a partner
⑤
b. Debit Bruno, Capital, $122,400

Required Journalize (a) the asset revaluations and (b) Bruno's withdrawal from the firm.

Exercise 12–14

Jonas, Teese, and Moyer are liquidating their partnership. Before selling the noncash assets and paying the liabilities, the Capital balances are Jonas, $57,500; Teese, $34,500; and Moyer, $23,000. The partnership agreement divides profits and losses equally.

Liquidation of a partnership
⑥
2. Jonas, $53,500

Required

1. After selling the noncash assets and paying the liabilities, suppose the partnership has cash of $115,000. How much cash will each partner receive in final liquidation?
2. After selling the noncash assets and paying the liabilities, suppose the partnership has cash of $103,000. How much cash will each partner receive in final liquidation?

Exercise 12-15

Liquidation of a partnership
(6)
Payment of cash:
Garcia, $26,400

Prior to liquidation, the accounting records of Garcia, Woods, and Mickelson included the following balances and profit-and-loss-sharing percentages:

		Noncash						Capital				
								Garcia		Woods		Mickelson
	Cash	+	Assets	=	Liabilities	+		(40%)	+	(30%)	+	(30%)
Balances before sale of assets	$10,000		$62,500		$26,500			$20,000		$15,000		$11,000

The partnership sold the noncash assets for $78,500, paid the liabilities, and disbursed the remaining cash to the partners. Complete the summary of transactions in the liquidation of the partnership. Use the format illustrated in Exhibit 12-5.

Exercise 12-16

Liquidation of a partnership
(6)
Shelly Linus, Capital,
$29,600

The partnership of Linus, Lebrun, and Beale is liquidating. Business assets, liabilities, and partners' Capital balances prior to dissolution are shown below. The partners share profits and losses as follows: Shelly Linus, 20 percent; Peter Lebrun, 30 percent; and Cathy Beale, 50 percent.

Required Create a spreadsheet or solve manually—as directed by your instructor—to show the ending balances in all accounts after the noncash assets are sold for $280,000. Determine the unknown amounts, represented by (?).

	A	B	C	D	E	F
1	LINUS, LEBRUN, AND BEALE					
2	Sale of Noncash Assets					
3	(For $280,000)					
4				Shelly	Peter	Cathy
5		Noncash		Linus,	Lebrun,	Beale,
6	Cash	Assets	Liabilities	Capital	Capital	Capital
7						
8	$ 12,000	$252,000	$154,000	$24,000	$74,000	$12,000
9	280,000	(252,000)		? †	?	?
10						
11	$292,000	$ 0	$154,000	$?	$?	$?
12						

† ($A9 − $B8) * .2

SERIAL EXERCISE

This exercise continues following the Lee Management Consulting business from earlier chapters. If you did not complete any Serial Exercises in earlier chapters, you can still complete Exercise 12-17 as it is presented because we are starting with a new set of accounting assumptions for a new set of business decisions.

Exercise 12-17

Preparing a partnership balance sheet
(2)
Total assets, $211,021

Michael Lee has been running Lee Management Consulting as a proprietorship but is planning to expand operations in the near future. The revised Lee Management Consulting July 31, 2016, balance sheet appears on the next page, with all amounts adjusted to current market values so they can be used for the start of a partnership. Michael Lee is considering forming a partnership with Jill Monroe, who provides the market value financial information shown on the next page. Create the Lee and Monroe Consulting partnership balance sheet at July 31, 2016, assuming there are no payables or receivables between Lee and Monroe.

	Lee Management Consulting	Monroe's Business
Assets		
Cash	$21,650	$100,000
Accounts receivable	5,900	50,000
Inventory	2,713	5,000
Supplies	100	1,000
Prepaid rent	6,000	0
Equipment	1,000	10,000
Accumulated amortization—equipment	(75)	(100)
Furniture	5,000	4,000
Accumulated amortization—furniture	(267)	(900)
Total assets	$42,021	$169,000
Liabilities and Equity		
Accounts payable	$9,600	$ 20,000
Salary payable	1,000	0
Unearned service revenue	1,200	0
Notes payable	0	50,000
Michael Lee, capital	30,221	—
Jill Monroe, capital	—	99,000
Total liabilities and equity	$42,021	$169,000

CHALLENGE EXERCISE

Exercise 12–18

On December 31, 2017, Jim Austin and Mike Mundy agree to combine their proprietorships as a partnership. Their balance sheets on December 31 are as follows:

Preparing a partnership balance sheet

②

Total assets, $1,425,000

	Austin's Business		Mundy's Business	
	Book Value	Current Market Value	Book Value	Current Market Value
Assets				
Cash.................................	$ 30,000	$ 30,000	$ 25,000	$ 25,000
Accounts receivable (net)............	110,000	100,000	40,000	35,000
Inventory.............................	255,000	230,000	170,000	180,000
Capital assets (net)......................	610,000	525,000	270,000	300,000
Total assets.............................	$1,005,000	$885,000	$505,000	$540,000
Liabilities and Equity				
Accounts payable........................	$ 120,000	$120,000	$ 50,000	$ 50,000
Accrued expenses payable.........	10,000	10,000	10,000	10,000
Notes payable.............................	275,000	275,000		
Jim Austin, capital......................	600,000	480,000		
Mike Mundy, capital..................			445,000	480,000
Total liabilities and equity..........	$1,005,000	$885,000	$505,000	$540,000

Required

1. Prepare the partnership balance sheet at December 31, 2017.

2. Assume John Allen wants to join the partnership by paying $212,000 for a 1/4 interest. The partnership equity before John joins is $960,000, and Jim Austin and Mike Mundy shared profits 60 percent for Austin and 40 percent for Mundy. Prepare the journal entry to record Allen's admission to the partnership on January 1, 2018.

3. What percent of the profits will John Allen receive after becoming a partner?

BEYOND THE NUMBERS

Beyond the Numbers 12–1

Partnership issues

① ⑤

The following questions relate to issues faced by partnerships:

1. The text suggests that a written partnership agreement should be drawn up between the partners in a partnership. One benefit of an agreement is that it provides a mechanism for resolving disputes between the partners. What are five areas of dispute that might be resolved by a partnership agreement?

2. The statement has been made that "If you must take on a partner, make sure the partner is richer than you are." Why is this statement valid?

3. Frizzell, Clamath, & Legree is a partnership of lawyers. Clamath is planning to move to Australia. What are the options open to her to convert her share of the partnership assets to cash?

ETHICAL ISSUE

Feng Li and Tanya Ng operate The Party Centre, a party supply store in Red Deer, Alberta. The partners split profits and losses equally, and each takes an annual withdrawal of $90,000. To even out the workload, Ng does the buying and Li serves as the accountant. From time to time, they use small amounts of store merchandise for personal use. In preparing for a large private party, Li took engraved invitations, napkins, place mats, and other goods that cost $3,000. She recorded the transaction as follows:

Cost of Goods Sold	3,000	
Inventory		3,000

Required

1. How should Li have recorded this transaction?
2. Discuss the ethical dimension of Li's action.

PROBLEMS (GROUP A)   MyAccountingLab

Problem 12–1A

Investments by partners

②

2. Total assets, $252,000

Vince Sharma and Klaus Warsteiner formed a partnership on January 1, 2017. The partners agreed to invest equal amounts of capital. Sharma invested his proprietorship's assets and liabilities (all accounts have normal balances):

	Sharma's Book Value	Current Market Value
Accounts receivable..	$24,000	$20,000
Inventory...	86,000	62,000
Prepaid expenses...	13,000	12,000
Store equipment...	72,000	52,000
Accounts payable..	40,000	40,000

On January 1, Warsteiner invested cash in an amount equal to the current market value of Sharma's partnership capital. The partners decided that Sharma would earn 70 percent of partnership profits because he would manage the business. Warsteiner agreed to accept 30 percent of profits. During the period ended December 31, 2017, the partnership earned $432,000. Warsteiner's withdrawals were $128,000 and Sharma's withdrawals were $172,800.

Required

1. Journalize the partners' initial investments.
2. Prepare the partnership balance sheet immediately after its formation on January 1, 2017.
3. Calculate the partners' Capital balances on December 31, 2017.

Problem 12–2A

Sheila Sasso, Karen Schwimmer, and Jim Perry have formed a partnership. Sasso invested $60,000, Schwimmer $120,000, and Perry $180,000. Sasso will manage the store, Schwimmer will work in the store three-quarters of the time, and Perry will not work in the business.

Excel Spreadsheet Template
Computing partners' shares of net income and net loss
(3)

1. b. Net income allocated to Sasso, $58,000

Required

1. Compute the partners' shares of profits and losses under each of the following plans:
   a. Net loss is $70,500, and the partnership agreement allocates 45 percent of profits to Sasso, 35 percent to Schwimmer, and 20 percent to Perry. The agreement does not discuss the sharing of losses.
   b. Net income for the year is $136,500. The first $45,000 is allocated on the basis of partners' Capital investments. The next $75,000 is based on service, with $45,000 going to Sasso and $30,000 going to Schwimmer. Any remainder is shared equally.
   c. Net loss for the year is $136,500. The first $45,000 is allocated on the basis of partners' Capital investments. The next $75,000 is based on service, with $45,000 going to Sasso and $30,000 going to Schwimmer. Any remainder is shared equally.

2. Revenues for the year were $858,000 and expenses were $721,500. Under plan (b), prepare the partnership income statement for the year. Assume a year end of September 30, 2017.
3. How will what you have learned in this problem help you manage a partnership?

Problem 12–3A

SAC & Company is a partnership owned by K. Santiago, R. Astorga, and J. Camino, who share profits and losses in the ratio of 1:3:4. The adjusted trial balance of the partnership (in condensed form) at June 30, 2017, follows:

Capital amounts for the balance sheet of a partnership
(2) (3)

2. K. Santiago, Capital, $41,500

SAC & COMPANY		
Adjusted Trial Balance		
June 30, 2017		
Cash	$ 166,000	
Noncash assets	800,000	
Liabilities		$ 690,000
K. Santiago, capital		152,000
R. Astorga, capital		282,000
J. Camino, capital		428,000
K. Santiago, withdrawals	126,000	
R. Astorga, withdrawals	272,000	
J. Camino, withdrawals	312,000	
Revenues		748,000
Expenses	624,000	
Totals	$2,300,000	$2,300,000

Required

1. Prepare the June 30, 2017, entries to close the Revenue, Expense, Income Summary, and Withdrawals accounts.
2. Using T-accounts, insert the opening balances in the partners' Capital accounts, post the closing entries to the Capital accounts, and determine each partner's ending Capital balance.

Problem 12–4A

Admitting a new partner

④

c. B. Peller, Capital, $20,000

Sudden Valley Resort is a partnership, and its owners are considering admitting Ben Peller as a new partner. On July 31, 2017, the Capital accounts of the three existing partners and their shares of profits and losses are as follows:

	Capital	Profit-and-Loss Percentage
Eleanor Craven...............	$20,000	20%
Amy Osler.......................	30,000	30
Brian Harmon.................	40,000	50

Required Journalize the admission of Peller as a partner on July 31, 2017, for each of the following independent situations:

a. Peller pays Harmon $55,000 cash to purchase Harmon's interest.

b. Peller invests $30,000 in the partnership, acquiring a one-quarter interest in the business.

c. Peller invests $30,000 in the partnership, acquiring a one-sixth interest in the business.

Problem 12–5A

Recording changes in partnership Capital

④ ⑤

c. Debit Karen Tenne, Capital, $248,000

Trail Equipment is a partnership owned by three individuals. The partners share profits and losses in the ratio of 30 percent to Karen Tenne, 40 percent to Frank Durn, and 30 percent to Erin Hana. At December 31, 2017, the firm has the following balance sheet amounts:

Cash		$ 354,000	Total liabilities		$ 520,000
Accounts receivable	$ 88,000				
Less: Allowance					
for uncollectibles	4,000	84,000			
Inventory		432,000	Karen Tenne, capital		248,000
Equipment	460,000		Frank Durn, capital		160,000
Less: Accumulated			Erin Hana, capital		270,000
amortization	132,000	328,000	Total liabilities		
Total assets		$1,198,000	and capital		$1,198,000

Karen Tenne withdraws from the partnership on December 31.

Required Record Tenne's withdrawal from the partnership under the following independent plans:

a. In a personal transaction, Tenne sells her equity in the partnership to Michael Adams, who pays Tenne $176,000 for her interest. Durn and Hana agree to accept Adams as a partner.

b. The partnership pays Tenne cash of $72,000 and gives her a note payable for the remainder of her book equity in settlement of her partnership interest.

c. The partnership pays Tenne $260,000 cash for her equity in the partnership.

d. The partners agree that the equipment is worth $548,000 (net). After the revaluation, the partnership settles with Tenne by giving her cash of $44,000 and inventory for the remainder of her book equity.

Problem 12–6A

Liquidation of a partnership

⑥

1. b. Cash distributed to partners, $228,000

The partnership of Malkin, Neale, & Staal has experienced operating losses for three consecutive years. The partners, who have shared profits and losses in the ratio of Lisa Malkin, 20 percent, John Neale, 40 percent, and Brian Staal, 40 percent, are considering liquidating the business. They ask you to analyze the effects of liquidation under various assumptions about the sale of the noncash assets. They present the following partnership balance sheet amounts at December 31, 2017:

Cash	$ 41,000	Liabilities	$151,000
Noncash assets	367,000	Lisa Malkin, capital	57,500
		John Neale, capital	158,500
		Brian Staal, capital	41,000
Total assets	$408,000	Total liabilities and capital	$408,000

Required

1. Prepare a summary of liquidation transactions (as illustrated in the chapter) for each of the following situations:
   a. The noncash assets are sold for $420,000.
   b. The noncash assets are sold for $338,000.
2. Make the journal entries to record the liquidation transactions in Requirement 1(b).

Problem 12–7A

The partnership of Telliher, Bachra, and Lang has experienced operating losses for three consecutive years. The partners, who have shared profits and losses in the ratio of Thea Telliher, 60 percent, Denis Bachra, 20 percent, and Alan Lang, 20 percent, are considering liquidating of the business. They ask you to analyze the effects of liquidation under various possibilities about the sale of the noncash assets. *None of the partners have personal assets if they go into a deficit financial position.* They present the following partnership balance sheet amounts at December 31, 2017:

Liquidation of a partnership (deficits)

⑥

1. a. Loss allocated to Telliher, $49,500

Cash	$ 6,750	Liabilities	$ 28,350
Noncash assets	118,800	Thea Telliher, capital	46,600
		Denis Bachra, capital	30,000
		Alan Lang, capital	20,600
Total assets	$125,550	Total liabilities and capital	$125,550

Required

1. Prepare a summary of liquidation transactions (as illustrated in Exhibits 12–5 or 12–6) for each of the following situations:
   a. The noncash assets are sold for $36,300.
   b. The noncash assets are sold for $27,600.
2. What legal recourse do the remaining partners have to be reimbursed for deficit balances?
3. Suppose, after allocating Telliher's deficit balance, Lang now has a deficit balance. How would the partnership deal with this deficiency?

Problem 12–8A

2014

Jun. 10 Adam Buckner and Amber Kwan have agreed to pool their assets and form a partnership to be called B&K Consulting. They agree to share all profits equally and make the following initial investments:

Accounting for partners' investments; allocating profits and losses; accounting for the admission of a new partner; accounting for the withdrawal of a partner; preparing a partnership balance sheet

② ③ ④ ⑤

2. A. Buckner, Capital, $387,209

	Buckner	Kwan
Cash..	$15,000	$30,000
Accounts receivable (net)................	33,000	27,000
Office furniture.................................	36,000	24,000

Dec. 31 The partnership's reported net income was $195,000 for the year ended December 31, 2014.

2015

Jan. 1 Buckner and Kwan agree to accept Heidi Nguen into the partnership with a $180,000 investment for 30 percent of the business. The partnership agreement is amended to provide for the following sharing of profits and losses:

	Buckner	Kwan	Nguen
Service..	$90,000	$120,000	$75,000
Interest on capital balance.................	5%	5%	5%
Balance in ratio of................................	3 :	2 :	5

Dec. 31 The partnership's reported net income was $480,000.

2016

Oct. 10 Buckner withdrew $84,000 cash from the partnership and Kwan withdrew $57,000 (Nguen did not make any withdrawals).

Dec. 31 The partnership's reported net income was $255,000.

2017

Jan. 2 After a disagreement as to the direction in which the partnership should be moving, Nguen decided to withdraw from the partnership. The three partners agreed that Nguen could take cash of $300,000 in exchange for her equity in the partnership.

Required

1. Journalize all of the transactions for the partnership.
2. Prepare the partners' equity section of the B&K Consulting balance sheet as of January 2, 2017.

Problem 12–9A

Accounting for partners' investments; allocating profits and losses; accounting for the admission of a new partner; accounting for the liquidation of a partnership

② ③ ④ ⑤ ⑥

Dec. 31, 2016,
Debit Dennis Devlin,
Capital, $90,000

Dennis Devlin, Gary Freemont, and Jean London started a partnership to operate a management consulting business. The partnership (DFL Partners) had the following transactions:

2015

Jan. 2 Devlin, Freemont, and London formed the partnership by signing an agreement that stated that all profits would be shared in a 3:2:5 ratio and by making the following investments:

	Devlin	Freemont	London
Cash..	$ 24,000	$ 42,000	$138,000
Accounts receivable (net)................	84,000	126,000	180,000
Office furniture.................................	0	66,000	0
Computer equipment........................	156,000	0	54,000

Dec. 31 The partnership reported net income of $252,000 for the year.

2016

Jun. 7 Devlin and London agreed that Freemont could sell his share of the partnership to André Hughes for $390,000. The new partners agreed to keep the same profit-sharing arrangement (3:2:5 for Devlin:Hughes:London).

Dec. 31 The partnership reported a net loss of $300,000 for the year.

2017

Jan. 3 The partners agreed to liquidate the partnership. On this date the balance sheet showed the following items, all at their normal balances:

Cash..	$ 78,000
Accounts receivable...	1,476,000
Allowance for uncollectible accounts.....................................	72,000
Office furniture..	360,000

Computer equipment	600,000
Accumulated amortization (total)	180,000
Accounts payable	1,440,000

The assets were sold for the following amounts:

Accounts receivable	$ 720,000
Office furniture	390,000
Computer equipment	360,000

Devlin and Hughes both have personal assets, but London does not.

Required Journalize all the transactions for the partnership.

PROBLEMS (GROUP B)
MyAccountingLab

Problem 12–1B

On January 1, 2017, Svitlana Yaeger and Val Havlac formed a partnership. The partners agreed to invest equal amounts of capital. Havlac invested her proprietorship's assets and liabilities (all accounts have normal balances) as follows:

Investments by partners
②

	Havlac's Book Value	Current Market Value
Accounts receivable	$20,200	$20,000
Inventory	44,000	48,000
Prepaid expenses...	4,800	4,000
Office equipment..	92,000	56,000
Accounts payable...	48,000	48,000

On January 1, 2017, Yaeger invested cash in an amount equal to the current market value of Havlac's partnership capital. The partners decided that Havlac would earn two-thirds of partnership profits because she would manage the business. Yaeger agreed to accept one-third of profits. During the remainder of the year, the partnership earned $276,000. Havlac's withdrawals were $76,000, and Yaeger's withdrawals were $56,000.

Required

1. Journalize the partners' initial investments.
2. Prepare the partnership balance sheet immediately after its formation on January 1, 2017.
3. Calculate the partners' Capital balances at December 31, 2017.

Problem 12–2B

Sav Berlo, Silvio Felini, and Louis Valente have formed a partnership. Berlo invested $30,000, Felini $40,000, and Valente $50,000. Berlo will manage the store, Felini will work in the store half time, and Valente will not work in the business.

Required

1. Compute the partners' shares of profits and losses under each of the following plans:
   a. Net loss is $200,000, and the partnership agreement allocates 40 percent of profits to Berlo, 25 percent to Felini, and 35 percent to Valente. The agreement does not discuss the sharing of losses.

Excel Spreadsheet Template
Computing partners' shares of net income and net loss

b. Net income for the year is $354,000. The first $150,000 is allocated based on partner capital investments. The next $72,000 is based on service, with Berlo receiving $56,000 and Felini receiving $16,000. Any remainder is shared equally.

2. Revenues for the year were $1,014,000 and expenses were $660,000. Under plan (b), prepare the partnership income statement for the year. Assume a January 31, 2017, year end.

3. How will what you learned in this problem help you manage a partnership?

Problem 12–3B

Capital amounts for the balance sheet of a partnership

(2) (3)

SY&I is a partnership owned by T. Shitang, D. Yamamoto, and J. Ishikawa, who share profits and losses in the ratio of 2:3:5. The adjusted trial balance of the partnership (in condensed form) at September 30, 2017, follows:

SY&I		
Adjusted Trial Balance		
September 30, 2017		
Cash	$ 110,000	
Noncash assets	389,000	
Liabilities		$ 319,000
T. Shitang, capital		125,000
D. Yamamoto, capital		97,000
J. Ishikawa, capital		46,000
T. Shitang, withdrawals	99,000	
D. Yamamoto, withdrawals	81,000	
J. Ishikawa, withdrawals	40,000	
Revenues		928,000
Expenses	796,000	
Totals	$1,515,000	$1,515,000

Required

1. Prepare the September 30, 2017, entries to close the Revenue, Expense, Income Summary, and Withdrawals accounts.

2. Using T-accounts, insert the opening Capital balances in the partner Capital accounts, post the closing entries to the Capital accounts and determine each partner's ending Capital balance.

Problem 12–4B

Admitting a new partner

(4)

Pineridge Consulting Associates is a partnership, and its owners are considering admitting Helen Fluery as a new partner. On March 31, 2017, the Capital accounts of the three existing partners and their shares of profits and losses are as follows:

	Capital	Profit-and-Loss Ratio
Jim Zook..	$ 50,000	40%
Richard Land.............................	100,000	20
Jennifer Lowe.............................	150,000	40

Required Journalize the admission of Fluery as a partner on March 31, 2017, for each of the following independent situations:

a. Fluery pays Lowe $200,000 cash to purchase Lowe's interest in the partnership.

b. Fluery invests $100,000 in the partnership, acquiring a one-fourth interest in the business.

c. Fluery invests $80,000 in the partnership, acquiring a one-fourth interest in the business.

Problem 12–5B

Vector Financial Planning is a partnership owned by three individuals. The partners share profits and losses in the ratio of 20 percent to Katherine Depatie, 40 percent to Sam Seamus, and 40 percent to Emily Hudson. At December 31, 2017, the firm has the following balance sheet amounts:

Recording changes in partnership capital ④ ⑤

Cash		$ 350,400	Total liabilities		$ 573,000
Accounts receivable	$ 92,400				
Less: Allowance					
for uncollectibles	16,800	75,600			
Building	1,102,000		Katherine Depatie, capital		390,600
Less: Accumulated			Sam Seamus, capital		210,000
amortization	294,000	808,000	Emily Hudson, capital		260,400
Land		200,000	Total liabilities		
Total assets		$1,434,000	and capital		$1,434,000

Seamus withdraws from the partnership on December 31, 2017, to establish his own consulting practice.

Required Record Seamus's withdrawal from the partnership under the following independent plans:

a. In a personal transaction, Seamus sells his equity in the partnership to Rea Pearlman, who pays Seamus $120,000 for one-half of his interest. Depatie and Hudson agree to accept Pearlman as a partner.

b. The partnership pays Seamus cash of $163,000 and gives him a note payable for the remainder of his book equity in settlement of his partnership interest.

c. The partnership pays Seamus cash of $336,000.

d. The partners agree that the building is worth $682,000 (net). After the revaluation, the partnership settles with Seamus by giving him cash of $82,000 and a note payable for the remainder of his book equity.

Problem 12–6B

The partnership of Du, Chong, and Quing has experienced operating losses for three consecutive years. The partners, who have shared profits and losses in the ratio of Jia Du, 10 percent, Denis Chong, 30 percent, and Alan Quing, 60 percent, are considering liquidating the business. They ask you to analyze the effects of liquidation under various possibilities about the sale of the noncash assets. They present the following partnership balance sheet amounts at December 31, 2017:

Liquidation of a partnership ⑥

Cash	$ 70,000	Liabilities	$316,000
Noncash assets	526,000	Jia Du, capital	80,000
		Denis Chong, capital	102,000
		Alan Quing, capital	98,000
Total assets	$596,000	Total liabilities and capital	$596,000

Required

1. Prepare a summary of liquidation transactions (as illustrated in the chapter) for each of the following situations:
   a. The noncash assets are sold for $552,000.
   b. The noncash assets are sold for $448,000.
2. Make the journal entries to record the liquidation transactions in Requirement 1(b).

Problem 12-7B

Liquidation of a partnership (deficit)

(6)

The partnership of Pavelski, Ovechin, and Oh has experienced operating losses for three consecutive years. The partners, who have shared profits and losses in the ratio of Steven Pavelski, 60 percent, Eddie Ovechin, 20 percent, and Kwan Oh, 20 percent, are considering liquidating the business. They ask you to analyze the effects of liquidation under various possibilities about the sale of the noncash assets. *None of the partners has personal assets if they go into a deficit financial position.* They present the following partnership balance sheet amounts at December 31, 2017:

Cash	$ 27,000	Liabilities	$113,400
Noncash assets	475,200	Steven Pavelski, capital	186,400
		Eddie Ovechin, capital	120,000
		Kwan Oh, capital	82,400
Total assets	$502,200	Total liabilities and capital	$502,200

Required

1. Prepare a summary of liquidation transactions (as illustrated in Exhibits 12–5 or 12–6) for each of the following situations:

   a. The noncash assets are sold for $145,200.

   b. The noncash assets are sold for $110,400.

2. What legal recourse do the remaining partners have to be reimbursed for deficit balances?

Problem 12-8B

2014

Accounting for partners' investments; allocating profits and losses; accounting for the admission of a new partner; accounting for the withdrawal of a partner; preparing a partnership balance sheet

(2)(3)(4)(5)

Jun. 10   Steven Hodgson and Sarah Asham have agreed to pool their assets and form a partnership to be called H&A Distributors. They agree to share all profits equally and make the following initial investments:

	Hodgson	Asham
Cash..	$21,000	$36,000
Accounts receivable (net)................	42,000	21,000
Office furniture (net)........................	48,000	27,000

Dec. 31   The partnership's reported net income was $228,000 for the year.

2015

Jan. 1   Hodgson and Asham agree to accept Myra Sirroca into the partnership with a $210,000 investment for 40 percent of the business. The partnership agreement is amended to provide for the following sharing of profits and losses:

	Hodgson	Asham	Sirroca
Service..	$120,000	$90,000	$80,000
Interest on end-of-period			
capitial balance	10%	10%	10%
Balance in ratio of..............................	2 :	3 :	5

Dec. 31   The partnership's reported net income is $570,000.

2016

Oct. 10   Hodgson withdrew $90,000 cash from the partnership and Asham withdrew $60,000 (Sirroca did not make any withdrawals).

Dec. 31   The partnership's reported net income is $225,000.

2017

Jan. 2   After a disagreement as to the direction in which the partnership should be moving, Sirroca decided to withdraw from the partnership. The three partners agreed that Sirroca could take cash of $510,000 in exchange for her equity in the partnership.

Required

1. Journalize all of the transactions for the partnership.
2. Prepare the partners' equity section of the balance sheet as of January 2, 2017.

Problem 12–9B

William Dione, Julie Porter, and Regina Westlake started a partnership to operate a courier service. The partnership (DP&W Couriers) had the following transactions:

Accounting for partners' investments; allocating profits and losses; accounting for the admission of a new partner; accounting for the liquidation of a partnership
② ③ ④ ⑤ ⑥

2015

Jan.　2　Dione, Porter, and Westlake formed the partnership by signing an agreement that stated that all profits would be shared in a 2:3:5 ratio and by making the following investments:

	Dione	Porter	Westlake
Cash	$12,000	$ 8,000	$14,000
Accounts receivable (net)	20,000	14,500	60,000
Office furniture (net)	0	0	15,000
Vehicles (net)	21,000	38,500	0

Dec.　31　The partnership reported net income of $53,500 for the year.

2016

Jun.　7　Dione and Westlake agreed that Porter could sell her share of the partnership to Ray Ewing for $82,500. The new partners agreed to keep the same profit-sharing arrangement (2:3:5 for Dione:Ewing:Westlake).

Dec.　31　The partnership reported a net loss of $67,000 for the year.

2017

Jan.　3　The partners agreed to liquidate the partnership. On this date, the balance sheet showed the following items (all accounts have their normal balances):

Cash	$ 17,500
Accounts receivable	316,000
Allowance for uncollectible accounts	22,500
Office furniture	74,500
Vehicles	240,000
Accumulated amortization (total)	49,500
Accounts payable	386,500

The assets were sold for the following amounts:

Accounts receivable	$190,000
Office furniture	82,500
Vehicles	106,000

Dione and Ewing both have personal assets, but Westlake does not.

Required Journalize all of the transactions for the partnership.

CHALLENGE PROBLEMS

Problem 12–1C

Nancy Wesla and Jordon Dugger have been in a partnership for five years. The principal business of the partnership is systems design for financial institutions. Gross revenues have increased from $330,000 in 2013 to $3,800,000 in 2017, the year just ended. The number of

Deciding on a capital structure
① ②

employees has increased from two in the first year to nine in the most recent year. Wesla and Dugger realized that they had to build up the partnership's capital and have withdrawn only part of the annual profits. As a result, their Capital accounts have increased from $200,000 (Wesla, $140,000; Dugger, $60,000) in 2010 to $2,000,000 (Wesla, $1,080,000; Dugger, $920,000) in 2017.

The two partners realize that they must expand their capital base to expand their operations in order to meet the increasing demand for their systems designs. At the same time, they wish to take personal advantage of the partnership's earnings. They have been trying to determine whether they should continue the partnership and borrow the necessary funds, take on one or more partners (several of their employees have expressed interest and have capital to invest), or incorporate and sell a portion of the business to outsiders. With respect to incorporation, Faisal Jamal, a former classmate of Wesla's who works for a stockbroker, has indicated he knows of investors who would be interested in buying a share of the business.

Required Wesla and Dugger have come to you to ask for advice. Provide an analysis of the situation and make a recommendation. In response to your questions, they indicate they will need additional capital of $1,600,000 to $2,000,000.

Problem 12–2C

The effects of accounting decisions on profits
③

Simone Perrier, Mary Salter, and Sean Patten have been partners in a systems design business for the past eight years. Perrier and Patten work full time in the business; Salter has a public accounting practice and works about 5 to 10 hours per week on the administrative side of the business. The business has been successful and the partners are considering expansion.

The partnership agreement states that profits will be distributed as follows:

1. Partners will get 6 percent interest on their average Capital balances.
2. Perrier will get a payment of $75,000 for her service; Salter will get a payment of $9,375 for her service; and Patten will get a payment of $75,000 for his service.
3. The balance remaining will be distributed on the basis of Perrier, 40 percent; Salter, 20 percent; and Patten, 40 percent.

The agreement also stipulates that the distributions outlined in parts 1 and 2 of the agreement will be made even if there are not sufficient profits and that any deficiency will be shared on the basis of part 3.

The capital structure was as follows at December 31, 2017, and reflects the average Capital balances for 2017:

Perrier...	$ 228,750
Salter..	1,091,250
Patten...	491,250
Total...	$1,811,250

There has been some stress in the partnership of late because Perrier believes that she is contributing a major part of the effort but is earning much less than Patten; Salter is upset because she believes that she is earning the least even though her capital is essentially funding the partnership.

Required Perrier, Salter, and Patten have come to you to ask for advice as to how they might amicably settle the present dispute. Analyze the situation and make a recommendation. Assume net income in 2017 was $400,000.

EXTENDING YOUR KNOWLEDGE

DECISION PROBLEM

Lori Barclay invested $30,000 and Vanesa Resultan invested $15,000 in a public relations firm that has operated for 10 years. Neither partner has made an additional investment. They have shared profits and losses in the ratio of 2:1, which is the ratio of their investments in the business. Barclay manages the office, supervises the 16 employees, and does the accounting. Resultan, the moderator of a television talk show, is responsible for marketing. Her high profile generates important revenue for the business. During the year ended December 2017, the partnership earned net income of $75,000, shared in the 2:1 ratio. On December 31, 2017, Barclay's Capital balance was $152,500 and Resultan's Capital balance was $105,000.

Settling disagreements among partners

③

Required

Respond to each of the following situations:

1. What explains the difference between the ratio of partner Capital balances at December 31, 2017, and the 2:1 ratio of partner investments and profit sharing?

2. Resultan believes the profit-and-loss-sharing ratio is unfair. She proposes a change, but Barclay insists on keeping the 2:1 ratio. What two factors may underlie Resultan's unhappiness?

3. During January 2017, Barclay learned that revenues of $24,000 were omitted from the reported 2016 income. She brings this to Resultan's attention, pointing out that her share of this added income is two-thirds, or $16,000, and Resultan's share is one-third, or $8,000. Resultan believes they should share this added income based on their Capital balances: 60 percent (or $14,400) to Barclay, and 40 percent (or $9,600) to Resultan. Which partner is correct? Why?

4. Assume that an account payable of $18,000 for an operating expense in 2016 was omitted from 2016 reported income. On what basis would the partners share this amount?

FINANCIAL STATEMENT CASE

Lisogar, Philip, & Walters (LPW) is a regional accounting firm with four offices. Summary data from the partnership's annual report follow:

| | Years Ended June 30 | | | | |
| | (Dollars in thousands, except where indicated) | | | | |
	2017	**2016**	**2015**	**2014**	**2013**
Revenues					
Assurance services	$1,234	$1,122	$1,064	$1,093	$1,070
Consulting services	1,007	775	658	473	349
Tax services	743	628	567	515	557
Total Revenues	$2,984	$2,525	$2,289	$2,081	$1,976
Operating Summary					
Revenues	$2,984	$2,525	$2,289	$2,081	$1,976
Personnel costs	1,215	1,004	887	805	726
Other costs	712	630	517	458	415
Income to Partners	$1,057	$ 891	$ 885	$ 818	$ 835
Statistical Data					
Average number of partners	9	9	9	8	8

Required

1. What percentages of total revenues did LPW earn by performing assurance services (similar to auditing), consulting services, and tax services during 2013? What were the percentages in 2017? Which type of service grew the most from 2013 to 2017?
2. Compute the average revenue per partner in 2017. Assume each partner works 1,900 hours per year. On average, how much does each partner charge a client for one hour of time?
3. How much net income did each LPW partner earn, on average, in 2017?

▷Try It! SOLUTIONS FOR CHAPTER 12

1. The partnership agreement is a contract, so transactions under the agreement are governed by contract law. If or when disputes arise, both partners are legally protected. A partnership agreement should contain the following items:
   - Name, location, and nature of the business
   - Name, capital investment, and duties of each partner
   - Procedures for admitting a new partner
   - Method of sharing profits and losses among the partners
   - Withdrawals of assets allowed to the partners
   - Procedures for settling disputes among the partners
   - Procedures for settling with a partner who withdraws from the firm
   - Procedures for removing a partner who will not withdraw or retire from the partnership voluntarily
   - Procedures for liquidating the partnership
2. Advantages as compared to proprietorships are that partnerships can raise more capital, partnerships bring together the abilities of more than one person, and partners working well together can achieve more than by working alone. Compared to corporations, partnerships are less expensive to organize and are subject to fewer governmental regulations and restrictions.

   The main disadvantage of partnerships is that partnership agreements may be difficult to formulate. Each time a new partner is admitted or a partner leaves the partnership, the business needs a new partnership agreement. Other disadvantages are that relationships among partners may be fragile, and mutual agency and unlimited liability create personal obligations for each partner.

3. This person would be a limited partner, so named because his or her personal obligation for the partnership's liabilities is limited to the amount he or she invested in the business.
4. a. The appraised value or current market value is the appropriate value to use because that is what the land is worth now, and the current market value was verified by independent professionals.

   b.

Land	50,000	
Marty Kaur, Capital		50,000

5. a. Burns: $50,000 × 60% = $30,000 net income
      White: $50,000 × 40% = $20,000 net income
   b. Betty: $200,000 × 3/10 = $60,000 net loss
      Luella: $200,000 × 4/10 = $80,000 net loss
      Pius: $200,000 × 3/10 = $60,000 net loss
   c. Losses are shared the same way as profits.
      Locke: $60,000 × 1/3 = $20,000 net loss
      Barnel: $60,000 × 2/3 = $40,000 net loss
   d. When there is no agreement, profits and losses are shared equally.
      Hampton: $90,000 × 1/2 = $45,000 net income
      Kirk: $90,000 × 1/2 = $45,000 net income

6. a.

Partnership capital before Phyllis is admitted ($25,000 + $75,000)	$100,000
Phyllis's investment in the partnership	20,000
Partnership capital after Phyllis is admitted	$120,000
Phyllis's capital in the partnership ($120,000 × 1/10)	$ 12,000
Bonus to the old partners ($20,000 − $12,000)	$ 8,000

   b.

Jun. 12	Cash	20,000	
	Phyllis, Capital		12,000
	Tina, Capital ($8,000 × 0.30)		2,400
	Jean, Capital ($8,000 × 0.70)		5,600
	To admit Phyllis with a 10% interest in the business.		

   c.

Jun. 12	Partners' capital balances:	
	Tina, capital ($25,000 + $2,400)	$ 27,400
	Jean, capital ($75,000 + $5,600)	80,600
	Phyllis, capital	12,000
	Total partnership capital	$120,000

7.

Partnership capital before Phyllis is admitted ($25,000 + $75,000)		$100,000
Phyllis's investment in the partnership		10,000
Partnership capital after Phyllis is admitted		$110,000
Phyllis's capital in the partnership ($110,000 × 1/10)		$ 11,000
Bonus to the new partner ($11,000 − $10,000)		$ 1,000

Jun. 12	Cash	10,000	
	Tina, Capital ($1,000 × 0.30)	300	
	Jean, Capital ($1,000 × 0.70)	700	
	Phyllis, Capital		11,000
	To admit Phyllis with a 10% interest in the business.		

8.

Aug. 31	Ruth, Capital	40,000	
	Nick, Capital	4,000	
	Adriana, Capital	6,000	
	Cash		50,000
	To record withdrawal of Ruth from the business. Nick's Capital is reduced by $4,000 [($50,000 − $40,000) × 2/5] and Adriana's Capital is reduced by $6,000 [($50,000 − $40,000) × 3/5].		

9.

Aug. 31	Ruth, Capital	40,000	
	Nick, Capital		4,000
	Adriana, Capital		6,000
	Cash		30,000
	To record withdrawal of Ruth from the business. Nick's Capital is increased by $4,000 [($40,000 − $30,000) × 2/5] and Adriana's Capital is increased by $6,000 [($54,000 − $30,000) × 3/5].		

10. a. The sale of the noncash assets for $20,000 creates a loss of $70,000 on the sale of noncash assets ($90,000 − $20,000 = $70,000).

b.

						Capital		
	Cash	+	Noncash Assets	=	Liabilities +	Lauren (60%) +	Andrews (20%) +	Benroudi (20%)
Balances before sale of assets	$10,000		$90,000		$30,000	$40,000	$20,000	$ 10,000
Sale of assets and sharing of loss	20,000		(90,000)			(42,000)	(14,000)	(14,000)
Balances	30,000		0		30,000	(2,000)	6,000	(4,000)
Payment of liabilities	(30,000)				(30,000)			
Balances	0		0		0	(2,000)	6,000	(4,000)
Disbursement of cash to partners	0					2,000	(6,000)	4,000
Balances	$ 0		$ 0		$ 0	$ 0	$ 0	$ 0

c. Lauren and Benroudi both have capital deficiencies. Both of these partners could contribute assets in the amount of their deficiencies to Andrews. However, if the deficient partners cannot contribute personal assets, then the deficits must be absorbed by Andrews. If Andrews absorbs the deficits, then she has a zero balance in her capital account. Since there is no remaining cash balance to distribute, she would be paid nothing more at liquidation.

13 CORPORATIONS: SHARE CAPITAL AND THE BALANCE SHEET

CONNECTING CHAPTER 13

LEARNING OBJECTIVE ① Identify the characteristics of a corporation

What is a corporation, and why is it an important form of business?

Corporations, page 730
   Characteristics of Corporations
   Organization of a Corporation
   Share Capital
Shareholders' Equity, page 733
   Contributed Capital
   Retained Earnings
   Dividends
   Shareholders' Rights

LEARNING OBJECTIVE ② Record the issuance of shares and prepare the shareholders' equity section of a corporation's balance sheet

How do we record and present share information?

Issuing Shares, page 736
   Common Shares
   Preferred Shares
   The Shareholders' Equity Section on a Balance Sheet
Ethical Considerations in Accounting for the Issuance of Shares, page 742
Organization Costs, page 742

LEARNING OBJECTIVE ③ Account for cash dividends

What are cash dividends and how do we account for them?

Accounting for Cash Dividends, page 743
   Dividend Dates
   Declaring and Paying Dividends
   Dividends on Cumulative and Noncumulative Preferred Shares

LEARNING OBJECTIVE ④ Use different share values in decision making

What is the difference between book value and market value of shares?

Different Values of Shares, page 746
   Market Value
   Book Value

LEARNING OBJECTIVE ⑤ Evaluate a company's ROA and ROE

What are the rate of return on total assets (ROA) and the rate of return on common shareholders' equity (ROE), and how do we calculate them?

Evaluating Operations, page 748
   Rate of Return on Total Assets
   Rate of Return on Common Shareholders' Equity

LEARNING OBJECTIVE ⑥ Identify the impact of IFRS on share capital

How does IFRS apply to share capital?
The Impact of IFRS on Share Capital, page 750

MyAccountingLab   The **Summary** for Chapter 13 appears on page 753. This lists all of the MyAccountingLab resources. **Accounting Vocabulary** with definitions for this chapter's material appears on page 754.

Have you ever wanted to be a DIRTTbag? That is what employees at DIRTT Environmental Solutions Ltd. proudly call themselves.[1] Their unique culture is one of the reasons that they have been recognized as one of Deloitte Canada's 50 Best Managed Companies more than once.

DIRTT stands for Doing It Right This Time. Their products are modular, adaptable, and environmentally friendly office systems. They manufacture, design, and sell systems for educational, industrial, corporate, retail, and residential use. These systems fit together like children's building blocks. Everything they create is completely customized for their clients—for them, "custom" is standard practice. Their ICE® 3D software makes a design work in such a way that each product can be reused and reconfigured as a client's needs change.

DIRTT started out in 2005 as a private corporation. At that time it did about $2.4 million in sales. In the company's 2013 annual report, it reported sales of $140 million. In order to expand further with more manufacturing facilities, the company needed more money. In November 2013 it "went public" (started selling shares on a stock exchange). DIRTT now lists its shares of stock on the Toronto Stock Exchange with the stock symbol DRT. Its *initial public offering* (IPO) raised almost $45 million for the company as 15,000,000 common shares were sold at $3.00 each before expenses.

So why does this matter to you? Well, in addition to possibly wanting to work there, you might want to invest in this business. Learning all about corporations in this chapter will help you make better decisions about corporations.

---

[1] Rosalynn Dodd and Houston Peschl, "DIRTT: A Story of DIRTTBags Revolutionizing the Building Industry," Management Innovation eXchange, May 11, 2012, accessed August 7, 2014, www.managementexchange.com/story/dirtt-story-dirttbags-revolutionizing-building-industry.

># Like

Indigo Books & Music Inc. and TELUS Corporation, DIRTT Environmental Solutions Ltd. is a corporation. From this point forward, we will focus on corporations, so this chapter marks a turning point. Fortunately, most of the accounting you have learned thus far also applies to corporations.

CORPORATIONS

LO 1

What is a corporation, and why is it an important form of business?

Corporations dominate business activity in Canada. Tim Hortons Inc. and Canadian Tire Corporation, Limited are two familiar examples. Although proprietorships and partnerships are more numerous, corporations transact more business and are larger in terms of total assets, sales revenue, and number of employees. Most well-known businesses, such as grocery store chain Loblaw Companies Limited, oil and gas producer EnCana Corporation, and drugstore chain The Jean Coutu Group (PJC) Inc., are corporations. Their full names include *Limited, Incorporated,* or *Corporation* (abbreviated *Ltd., Inc.,* or *Corp.*) to show they are corporations.

A corporation can be set up as a *public corporation*, such as the businesses just mentioned, or as a *private corporation*.

REAL WORLD EXAMPLE

Just because a company is a private corporation does not mean it is small. According to their website, the Jim Pattison Group is the second-largest private company in Canada, with sales over $8.4 billion and more than 39,000 employees in early 2015.

Public corporation   A **public corporation** is a company organized as a corporation that is listed and sells its shares on a stock exchange. Canadian generally accepted accounting principles (GAAP) require that these publicly accountable enterprises follow International Financial Reporting Standards (IFRS).

Private corporation   A **private corporation** is a company organized as a corporation that is not listed and does not sell its shares on a stock exchange. According to GAAP, private enterprises have the choice to follow either IFRS or Accounting Standards for Private Enterprises (ASPE). A company like DIRTT was a private corporation from 2005 until 2013 when it *went public*.

The majority of this chapter will focus on ASPE and what is common between IFRS and ASPE. At the end of the chapter, a few differences between the standards will be highlighted.

># Why It's Done This Way

Objective of Financial Reporting

As with partnerships, the principles and concepts in the accounting framework described in Chapter 1 (and repeated on the back inside cover of this book) apply equally to corporations.

Recall that the objective of financial reporting is to communicate useful information to users. With corporations, more information is presented because corporations can have more "owners" who may not have access to the financial details like a proprietor or a partner does.

The elements of financial statements (the accounts) do change a little. Accounting differences among types of organizations only relate to the equity section of the balance sheet, with corporations having contributed capital and retained earnings.

Characteristics of a Corporation

What makes the corporate form of organization so attractive? What are some of the reasons other forms of business organization are chosen?

KEY POINTS

Corporations can have one or more shareholders. For simplicity and ease of reading, this text will refer to "shareholders" rather than "shareholder(s)."

Separate Legal Entity   A corporation is a separate legal entity formed under federal or provincial law. The government approves the **articles of incorporation**, which is a document giving the owners permission to form a corporation. Neither a proprietorship nor a partnership requires federal or provincial approval to do business, because in the eyes of the law the business and the owner or owners are not separate entities. From a legal perspective, a corporation is a distinct entity—an artificial person that exists apart from its owners, who are called **shareholders**.

A corporation has many of the rights that a person has. For example, a corporation can buy, own, and sell property. Assets and liabilities in the business belong to the corporation rather than to the corporation's owners. The corporation can also enter into contracts, sue, and be sued, just like an individual.

Continuous Life and Transferability of Ownership   The owners' equity of a corporation is divided into **shares** of **stock**. The articles of incorporation specify how many shares the corporation can issue (sell) and lists the other details of its relationship with the federal or provincial government under whose laws it is incorporated. Most corporations have *continuous lives* regardless of changes in the ownership of their shares. In contrast, proprietorships and partnerships end when their ownership changes.

REAL WORLD EXAMPLE

The US term for common shares is *common stock*.

The shareholders of Tim Hortons, DIRTT Environmental Solutions, or any other corporation may sell or trade the shares to another person, give them away, bequeath them in a will, or dispose of them in any other way they desire. The transfer of the shares does not affect the continuity of the corporation.

No Mutual Agency   **Mutual agency** means that all the owners act as agents of the business. A contract signed by one owner is binding for the whole company. Mutual agency operates in partnerships and proprietorships, but *not* in corporations. A shareholder of Imperial Oil Limited cannot commit the corporation to a contract (unless the shareholder is also an officer of the corporation).

Limited Liability of Shareholders   Shareholders have **limited liability** for corporation debts. That means they have no personal obligation for corporation liabilities. The most that a shareholder can lose on an investment in a corporation's shares is the cost of the investment. In contrast, proprietors and partners are personally liable for all the debts of their businesses, unless the partnership is a limited liability partnership (LLP).

The combination of limited liability and no mutual agency means that investors can invest in a corporation without fear of losing all their personal wealth if the business fails. This feature enables a corporation to raise more money than proprietorships and partnerships can. Because of limited shareholder liability, many banks will lend money to a small corporation only if a third party (usually a corporate officer) guarantees payment of the loan personally in the event of default by the corporation.

Separation of Ownership and Management   Shareholders own a corporation, but a *board of directors*—elected by the shareholders—appoints corporate officers to manage the business. Shareholders may invest any amount of money without having to manage the company.

Corporate Taxation   Corporations are separate taxable entities. They pay a variety of taxes not required for proprietorships or partnerships, such as federal and provincial corporate income taxes. Corporate earnings are subject to some **double taxation:**

- First, corporations pay their own income taxes on corporate income.
- The shareholders then pay personal income tax on the dividends (distributions) that they receive from corporations, although the tax rate is usually lower than for regular income to minimize double taxation.

Proprietorships and partnerships pay no business income tax. Instead, owners are taxed on their share of the proprietorship or partnership income on their personal income tax return.

Government Regulation   Because of shareholders' limited liability for corporation debts, outsiders doing business with the corporation can look no further than the corporation for payment of its debts. To protect people who lend money to a corporation or who invest in its shares, the federal and provincial governments monitor the affairs of corporations. This government regulation consists mainly of ensuring that corporations disclose adequate business information for investors and creditors. This government regulation can be expensive for corporations.

REAL WORLD EXAMPLE

Public corporations are required to have an audit and file certain reports with the applicable provincial securities commission. These requirements add to a corporation's expenses without increasing its income, but they are necessary.

Unique Costs for Corporations   In Canada, legally, the directors of a corporation (defined below) have unlimited liability. However, insurance is available to cover any costs incurred by directors who may be sued by outsiders doing business with the corporation. If the corporation did not purchase this insurance for its directors, no one would agree to be a director of a corporation. In many small corporations there may only be one or a few shareholders, who would also be directors of the corporation. The cost for directors' insurance is unique to corporations—proprietorships or partnerships would not incur this cost.

Exhibit 13–1 summarizes the advantages and disadvantages of corporations.

EXHIBIT 13–1 | Advantages and Disadvantages of a Corporation

Corporation Advantages	Corporation Disadvantages
Can raise more money than a proprietorship or partnership.	Ownership and management are separated.
Has a continuous life.	Corporate earnings are subject to some double taxation.
Transferring ownership is easy.	Government regulation can be expensive.
No mutual agency exists among the shareholders.	Corporations may incur costs unique to corporations.
Shareholders have limited liability.	The board of directors often requires special insurance against lawsuits.

Organization of a Corporation

The process of creating a corporation begins when its organizers, called the *incorporators,* submit articles of incorporation to the federal or provincial government for approval. The articles of incorporation include the **authorization of shares** for the corporation to issue a certain number of shares of stock, which are shares of ownership in the corporation. The incorporators pay fees and file the required documents with the incorporating jurisdiction. Then the corporation comes into existence and becomes a legal entity. The incorporators agree to a set of **bylaws,** which act as the constitution for governing the corporation.

The ultimate control of the corporation rests with the shareholders, who usually receive one vote for each voting share they own. The shareholders elect the members of the **board of directors,** which has the following responsibilities:

- Sets policy for the corporation.
- Elects a **chairperson,** who is often the most powerful person in the corporation.
- Appoints the **president,** who is the chief executive officer (CEO) in charge of managing day-to-day operations.

Most corporations have a number of vice-presidents. Exhibit 13–2 shows a typical authority structure in a corporation.

EXHIBIT 13–2 | Typical Authority Structure in a Corporation

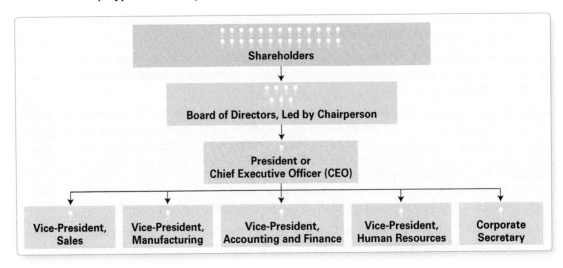

All corporations have an annual meeting at which the shareholders elect directors and make other shareholder decisions, such as appointing the external auditors. Shareholders unable to attend this annual meeting may vote on corporation matters by use of a **proxy**, which appoints another person to cast the vote on their behalf.

Share Capital

A corporation issues *share certificates* to its owners when they invest in the business. Shareholders rarely see or receive share certificates. Instead, their share purchase and sale transactions are listed on the monthly summary of activity in their brokerage or trading accounts. Because shares represent the corporation's capital, they are often called *share capital.* The basic unit of share capital is called a *share.* A corporation may issue a share certificate for any number of shares it wishes: 1 share, 100 shares, or any other number. Exhibit 13–3 depicts what an actual share certificate would look like and highlights key information found on a share certificate.

SHAREHOLDERS' EQUITY

A corporation reports assets and liabilities the same way as a proprietorship or a partnership. However, owners' equity of a corporation—called **shareholders' equity**—is reported differently. Business laws require corporations to report their sources of capital because some of the capital must be maintained by the company. The two most basic sources of capital are:

- **Contributed capital,** which represents investment amounts received from the shareholders of the corporation. Contributed surplus, which will be discussed later, is also a component of contributed capital.

- **Retained earnings,** which is capital earned from profitable operations.

While the Canada Business Corporations Act (CBCA) and several of the provincial incorporating acts use the term *stated capital* to describe share capital, this text

EXHIBIT 13–3 | Share Certificate

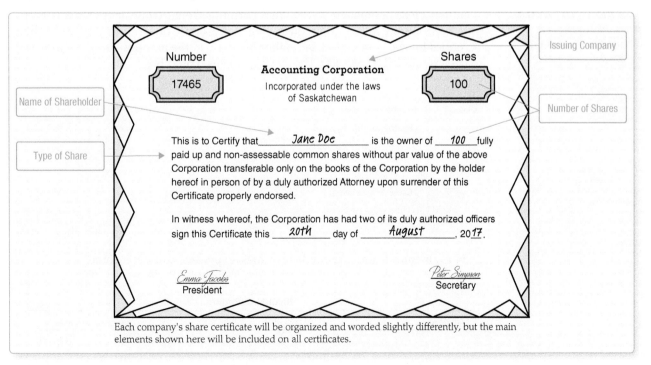

Each company's share certificate will be organized and worded slightly differently, but the main elements shown here will be included on all certificates.

will use the more common term *share capital*. Exhibit 13–4 is a summarized version of the shareholders' equity section of the balance sheet of Tim Hortons Inc., which is used to show how to report these categories of shareholders' equity.

EXHIBIT 13–4 | Summarized Shareholders' Equity at December 31, 2014, of Canadian Tire Corporation, Limited (adapted, amounts in millions)

Shareholders' Equity	
Contributed capital	$ 698.4
Retained earnings	4,157.1
Total shareholders' equity	$4,855.5

Contributed capital comes from shareholders.

Retained earnings come from profitable operations.

Contributed Capital

Common shares are regarded as the permanent capital of the business because the balance in the Common Shares account *cannot* be withdrawn by the shareholders. The entry to record the receipt of $200,000 cash and the issuance of common shares to shareholders is as follows:

Oct. 20	Cash	200,000	
	Common Shares		200,000
	Issued common shares.		

Issuing shares increases both the assets and the shareholders' equity of a corporation.

Retained Earnings

KEY POINTS

Sometimes students incorrectly view Retained Earnings as an asset, like Cash. Remember, Retained Earnings is a part of shareholders' equity and therefore should have a normal *credit* balance. A *debit* balance in Retained Earnings is called a *deficit*.

Profitable operations produce net income for the corporation, which increases shareholders' equity through a separate account called Retained Earnings.

Some people think of Retained Earnings as a fund of cash. It is not, because Retained Earnings is not an asset—it is an element of shareholders' equity. Retained earnings has no particular relationship to Cash or any other asset.

Corporations close their revenues and expenses into Income Summary, and then they close net income to Retained Earnings. To illustrate, let's consider a private corporation called Longbourn Golf & Resorts Corporation. Assume it had revenues for the year ended December 31, 2017, in the amount of $10,387,100 and expenses totalled $9,643,400. The closing entries would be:

Dec. 31	Revenues (detailed)	10,387,100	
	Income Summary		10,387,100
	To close revenue accounts.		
Dec. 31	Income Summary	9,643,400	
	Expenses (detailed)		9,643,400
	To close expenses.		

Now, Income Summary holds revenues, expenses, and net income:

Income Summary			
Expenses	9,643,400	Revenues	10,387,100
		Balance (net income)	743,700

Finally, the Income Summary's balance is closed to Retained Earnings:

Dec. 31	Income Summary	743,700	
	Retained Earnings		743,700
	To close net income to Retained Earnings.		

This closing entry completes the closing process. Income Summary is zeroed out, and Retained Earnings now holds net income.

If Longbourn Golf & Resorts had a net loss, Income Summary would have a debit balance. To close an assumed $100,000 loss, the closing entry credits Income Summary and debits Retained Earnings as follows:

Dec. 31	Retained Earnings	100,000	
	Income Summary		100,000
	To close Income Summary by transferring *net loss* to Retained Earnings.		

Negative Retained Earnings Is Called a Deficit   A loss or an accumulation of several years of losses may cause a debit balance in the negative Retained Earnings account. This condition—called a negative Retained Earnings or Accumulated **Deficit**—is reported as a negative amount in shareholders' equity. Great Canadian Gaming Corporation, which has its head office in Richmond, British Columbia, reported the following (adapted) in its 2013 annual report:

Shareholders' Equity (in millions of dollars)	December 31, 2013	December 31, 2012
Share capital and contributed surplus	$305.1	$313.5
Accumulated other comprehensive loss	0.4	(1.0)
Retained earnings (deficit)	2.0	(32.2)
	$307.5	$280.3

Dividends

A profitable corporation may distribute retained earnings to its shareholders. Such distributions are called **dividends**. Dividends are similar to the withdrawals of cash made by the owner of a proprietorship or by a partner of a partnership. Dividends are discussed in detail later in this chapter.

Shareholders' Rights

The owner of a share has certain rights that are set out in the corporation's articles of incorporation; these vary from company to company, and even between classes of shares within a company. In addition, the shareholder may have other rights granted by the legislation under which the corporation wrote its articles. An example of a right under the CBCA is that the shareholders may require the directors of the corporation to call a meeting of the shareholders.

Some of the rights generally attached to common shares[2] are:

- The right to sell the shares.
- The right to vote at shareholders' meetings.

---

[2] For a more complete listing, the interested reader is referred to the Canada Business Corporations Act in *The Revised Statutes of Canada.*

- The right to receive a **proportionate share** of any dividends declared by the directors for that class of shares.
- The right to receive a proportionate share of any assets on the winding-up of the company, after the creditors and any classes of shares that rank above that class have been paid. In reality, being last in line often means there is nothing left.
- A **preemptive right**—the right to maintain one's proportionate ownership in the corporation. If a shareholder owns 5 percent of the outstanding common shares and the corporation decides to issue 100,000 new shares, the shareholder would be entitled to purchase 5,000 of the new shares (0.05 × 100,000).

▷ Try It!

1. Compare and contrast the characteristics of proprietorships and corporations.

2. Describe the authority structure of a corporation, starting with the group or position that has the greatest authority.

Solutions appear at the end of this chapter and on MyAccountingLab

ISSUING SHARES

LO 2

How do we record and present share information?

Large corporations such as DIRTT Environmental Solutions, Tim Hortons Inc., and Kinross Gold Corp. need huge quantities of money to operate. They cannot expect to finance all their operations through borrowing. They can raise these funds by issuing shares. The articles of incorporation include an *authorization of shares*—that is, a provision for the business to issue (sell) a certain number of shares.

Underwriters   Corporations may sell their shares directly to the shareholders; however, they typically use the services of an **underwriter** to sell their shares, such as the brokerage firm RBC Dominion Securities or TD Securities Inc. The agreement between a corporation and its underwriter will vary, but typically the underwriter will commit to placing (selling) all of the share issue it can with its customers, and to buying any unsold shares for its own account. In another form of contract, the underwriter agrees to do its best to sell all of the share issue but makes no guarantees. The underwriter makes its money by selling the shares for a higher price than it pays to the corporation issuing the shares.

SEDAR   Companies often advertise the issuance of their shares to attract investors. A good source of such information is SEDAR (System for Electronic Document Analysis and Retrieval). SEDAR is a website developed under the authority of the Canadian Securities Administrators and administered by each of the provincial securities regulatory authorities.

IPO   Exhibit 13–5 is a reproduction of a portion of the *prospectus* dated November 21, 2013, of DIRTT Environmental Solutions's *initial public offering* of 15,000,000 common shares at $3.00 per share. A **prospectus** is a required legal document that describes the investment offering to potential purchasers. An **initial public offering** is the first time a corporation's shares are sold to investors or members of the public.

Number of Shares   Note the differences between the following terms:

- *Authorized shares.* The maximum number of shares the corporation can issue according to the articles of incorporation are the **authorized shares**. Most corporations are authorized to issue many more shares than they intend to issue originally. Management may hold some shares back and issue them later if the need for additional capital arises. If the corporation wants to issue more than the authorized shares, the articles of incorporation must be amended. Amendment

PROSPECTUS

Initial Public Offering   November 21, 2013

DIRTT

DIRTT ENVIRONMENTAL SOLUTIONS LTD.

$45,000,000

15,000,000 Common Shares

This Prospectus qualifies the distribution of 15,000,000 common shares ("**Common Shares**", with each Common Share being offered pursuant to this Prospectus, an "**Offered Share**") of DIRTT Environmental Solutions Ltd. (the "**Company**" or "**DIRTT**") at a price of $3.00 per Offered Share (the "**Offering Price**") for total gross proceeds of $45,000,000 (the "**Offering**").

The Common Shares sold pursuant to the Offering, including any additional Common Shares sold pursuant to the exercise of the Over-Allotment Option (as defined herein), are being offered by Raymond James Ltd. (the "**Lead Underwriter**"), Canaccord Genuity Corp., National Bank Financial Inc., TD Securities Inc. and Cormark Securities Inc. (together with the Lead Underwriter, the "**Underwriters**") pursuant to an underwriting agreement among DIRTT and the Underwriters dated November 21, 2013 (the "**Underwriting Agreement**"). The Offering Price was determined by negotiation between the Company and the Underwriters.

Price: $3.00 per Common Share

	Price to the Public	Underwriters' Fee[1]	Net Proceeds to the Company[2][3]
Per Common Share	$3.00	$0.18	$2.82
Total Offering	$45,000,000	$2,700,000	$42,300,000

---

of the articles of incorporation requires shareholder approval and may require government approval as well.

- *Issued shares.* The shares that the corporation does issue to shareholders are called **issued shares**. Only by issuing shares—not by receiving authorization—does the corporation increase the asset and shareholders' equity amounts on its balance sheet. The price that the shareholder pays to acquire shares from the corporation is called the **issue price**. A combination of underwriter opinion and market factors—including the company's comparative earnings record, financial position, prospects for success, and general business conditions—determines issue price.

- *Outstanding shares.* Shares that have been sold to and are held by shareholders are considered **outstanding shares**. The total number of a corporation's shares outstanding at any time represents 100 percent of its ownership.

Common Shares

Every corporation issues *common shares*, the most basic form of share capital. The common shareholders are the owners of the business. Companies may issue different classes of common shares. For example, Rogers Communications Inc. has issued Class A common shares, which carry the right to vote, and Class B common shares, which are nonvoting. (Classes of common shares may also be designated Series A, Series B, and so on, with each series having unique features.) There is a separate general ledger account for each class of common shares.

KEY POINTS

The following diagram shows the relationship among the authorized, issued, and outstanding shares:

REAL WORLD EXAMPLE

Some corporations issue several classes of common shares. One class may have the rights of common shares and the other may have some restrictions or enhancements. For example, Magna International Inc., a Canadian auto-parts supplier, has Class A shares with one vote each, while their Class B shares have 300 votes each.

Investors   Investors who buy common shares take a risk with a corporation. They are the owners of the business, but the corporation makes no promises to pay them. If the corporation succeeds, it may distribute dividends to its shareholders, but if Retained Earnings and Cash are too low, the shareholders may receive no dividends. The market value (selling price) of the shares of successful corporations increase, and investors enjoy the benefit of selling the shares at a gain. Thus, the holder of common shares can earn income both from dividends and from increases in the value of the shares.

But share prices can decrease, possibly leaving the investors with nothing of value. Because common shareholders take a risky investment position, they demand increases in share prices, high dividends, or both. If the corporation does not accomplish these goals and many shareholders sell their shares, the market price will fall. Short of bankruptcy, this is one of the worst things that can happen to a corporation because it means that the corporation cannot easily raise capital as needed. The period from the autumn of 2008 to the first part of 2009 highlighted this as most stock markets around the world saw share prices plummet. Exhibit 13–6 shows the performance of the Canadian stock market, represented by the performance of a group of corporate shares on the Toronto Stock Exchange. Notice the steep decline in values in 2008 and 2009. Imagine how difficult it must have been for shareholders and managers of corporations during that period.

No-Par-Value Shares   **No-par-value shares** are shares that do not have a value assigned to them by the articles of incorporation. The CBCA requires all newly issued shares in Canada to be no-par-value. **Par value** is an arbitrary value assigned to each share, and it might be seen in Canadian corporations that were established before the CBCA came into effect or when certain complex tax-planning arrangements are made.

Stated Value of Shares   The board of directors may assign a value to the shares when they are issued; this value is known as the **stated value**. For example, Dajol Inc. has authorization to issue 100,000 common shares, having no par value assigned to them by the articles of incorporation. Dajol Inc. needs $50,000 at incorporation, and might issue 10,000 shares for $5.00 per share, 2,000 shares at $25.00 per share, or 1,000 shares at $50.00 per share, and so on. The point is that Dajol Inc. can assign whatever value to the shares the board of directors wishes; however, the price the shares sell for on the market may be different from the stated value. To illustrate this, refer to the announcement of the share issue by DIRTT Environmental Solutions Ltd. in Exhibit 13–5. The initial price to the public at the bottom of the announcement of $3.00 per share is the stated value. Once the market opened, the price was $2.82 per share.

REAL WORLD EXAMPLE

If you looked at the balance sheet of a US corporation, you might see that its common shares had been issued at *par value*. This means the board of directors assigned a value to the common shares. If the shares were sold for more than par value, the difference was credited to Paid-in Capital in Excess of Par, or Additional Paid-in Capital. Most Canadian corporations credit the capital account for common shares for the full amount of the net proceeds from the sale of the shares.

EXHIBIT 13–6 | Canadian Stock Market Performance (TSX Composite)

Source: Globe and Mail, TSX Price Chart, www.theglobeandmail.com/globe-investor/markets/indexes/ chart/?q=TSX-I

The full amount of the proceeds from the sale of shares by a company must be allocated to the capital account for those shares, as shown in the next section.

Issuing Common Shares at a Stated Value Using the DIRTT information found in Exhibit 13–5, the share issuance entry (including fees and commissions) is:

Nov. 21	Cash	42,300,000	
	Discounts and Commissions Expense	2,700,000	
	Common Shares		45,000,000
	To issue 15,000,000 common shares at $3.00 per share, the stated value, less discounts and commissions expenses.		

The amount invested in the corporation, $45,000,000 in this case, is called share capital. The credit to Common Shares records an increase in the share capital of the corporation.

Issuing Common Shares for Assets Other Than Cash A corporation may issue shares in exchange for assets other than cash. It debits the assets received for their current market value and credits the Common Shares or Preferred Shares accounts accordingly. The assets' prior book value does not matter. Suppose the company we discussed earlier, Longbourn Golf & Resorts Corporation, issued 25,000 common shares (of the $100,000 authorized) for equipment worth $25,000 plus a building worth $125,000. The entry is:

Nov. 12	Equipment	25,000	
	Building	125,000	
	Common Shares		150,000
	To issue 25,000 common shares in exchange for equipment and a building.		

Common Shares increases by the amount of the assets' *current market value*, $150,000 in this case; the stated value or value assigned to the shares would be $6.00 ($150,000 ÷ 25,000) per share.

Preferred Shares

Preferred shares have special rights or preferences that give their owners certain advantages over common shareholders. Investors who buy preferred shares take less risk than do common shareholders:

- Preferred shareholders receive dividends before the common shareholders. The preferred dividend may be a set amount or a fixed percentage of some number, such as the prime interest rate at the date of declaration of the dividend.

- Preferred shareholders receive assets before the common shareholders if the corporation liquidates.

- Corporations often pay a fixed dividend on preferred shares. Investors usually buy preferred shares to earn those fixed dividends.

Because of the preferred shareholders' priorities, common shares represent the *residual ownership* in the corporation's assets after the liabilities and the claims of preferred shareholders have been subtracted.

Classes Often the right to vote is withheld from preferred shareholders. Companies may issue different classes of preferred shares (Class A and Class B or Series A and Series B, for example). Each class is recorded in a separate account.

KEY POINTS

Issuance of new shares increases the corporation's assets and shareholders' equity. Sales of shares by shareholders after this date are not reflected in the corporation's balance sheet because they are sales between shareholders and the company is not involved.

LEARNING TIPS

Whenever a corporation receives assets in exchange for share capital, assets and shareholders' equity will *increase*. Whenever a corporation distributes assets to shareholders (by paying dividends or retiring shares), assets and shareholders' equity will *decrease*.

For example, Bombardier Inc.'s December 31, 2013, annual report showed the company had the following classes of common and preferred shares:

	Number of Shares Authorized	Number of Shares Issued and Outstanding	Dividends
Class A Shares (Multiple Voting)	1,892,000,000	315,530,462	—
Class B Shares (Subordinate Voting)	1,892,000,000	1,424,759,510	—
Series 2 Cumulative Redeemable Preferred	12,000,000	9,692,521	50–100% of the Canadian prime rate per annum payable monthly
Series 3 Cumulative Redeemable Preferred	12,000,000	2,307,479	3.134% or $0.7835 per share per annum payable quarterly
Series 4 Cumulative Redeemable Preferred	9,400,000	9,400,000	6.25% per annum or $1.5625 per share per annum payable quarterly

Investors Investors usually buy preferred shares to earn these fixed dividends. Preferred shares' market values do not fluctuate much, so investor income from owning preferred shares is mostly from dividends rather than share-price increases. Individuals might also prefer to hold preferred shares because the income tax rate they pay on dividends they receive is lower than the income tax rate they pay on interest they receive. It's for this reason that the dividend rate on a company's preferred shares is usually lower than the interest rate on bonds the company issues (the bonds pay interest; the preferred shares pay dividends).

Debt versus Equity Corporations are faced with a number of choices when raising capital. Some of the things a corporation should consider when choosing to sell shares or issue long-term debt include the following:

REAL WORLD EXAMPLE

Another investment vehicle available to investors is called an *income trust* or *investment trust*. It is a portfolio of assets that is designed to provide safety of principal and a regular fixed income. An example of an income trust is Boston Pizza Royalties Income Fund. Unitholders receive monthly cash payments, but at the same time they maintain their equity position in the company. The monthly cash payments are roughly equivalent to dividends paid by corporations, but their tax treatment in the hands of unitholders is different.

	Common Shares	Preferred Shares	Long-term Debt
Annual Cost/Liability	None	Flexible. There may be dividends but only if declared by the board of directors	Required interest payment
Control	Vote	Usually no voting rights, so no change in control	Lenders have no voting rights, but may have influence through contracts
Repayment	No	No	Yes, fixed per terms of loan
Tax Implications for the Corporation	None	Dividends are not tax deductible because they are a distribution of earnings	Interest is a deductible expense for tax purposes

Not all corporations issue preferred shares. However, all corporations must issue at least one common share.

Issuing Preferred Shares Accounting for preferred shares follows the pattern illustrated for common shares.

Assume Longbourn Golf & Resorts Corporation's articles of incorporation authorize issuance of 10,000 preferred shares with an annual dividend of $5.00 per share. On July 31, the company issues 1,000 shares at a stated price of $100.00 per share and receives a cash payment of $100,000. The issuance entry is:

Jul. 31	Cash	100,000	
	Preferred Shares		100,000
	To issue 1,000 preferred shares for $100.00 per share (1,000 × $100).		

Convertible Preferred Shares   **Convertible preferred shares** are preferred shares that may be exchanged by the preferred shareholders, if they choose, for another specified class of shares in the corporation. For example, the preferred shares of Renewal Resources Inc. are convertible into the company's common shares. A note on Renewal's balance sheet describes the conversion terms as follows:

> **The . . . preferred shares are convertible at the rate of 7.00 common shares for each preferred share outstanding.**

If you owned 100 Renewal convertible preferred shares, you could convert them into 700 (100 × 7.00) common shares. Under what condition would you exercise the conversion privilege? You would do so if the market value of the common shares that you could receive from conversion was greater than the market value of the preferred shares that you presently hold. This way, you as an investor could increase your personal wealth.

Renewal Resources Inc.'s convertible preferred shares were issued at $100.00 per share, and the common shares were issued at $1.00. The company would record the conversion at the value of the 100 preferred shares on the Renewal Resources Inc. books, or $10,000 (100 × $100). The conversion of the 100 preferred shares into 700 common shares would be recorded as follows:

Mar. 7	Preferred Shares	10,000	
	Common Shares		10,000
	Conversion of preferred shares into common. (100 preferred shares converted into 700 common shares.)		

KEY POINTS
No gain or loss is reported on a conversion of shares.

At this point, the new common shares cannot be converted back to preferred shares.

The balance sheet would be updated to show the change in the equity section by reflecting the new numbers of each type of share.

The Shareholders' Equity Section of a Balance Sheet

The shareholders' equity section of Longbourn Golf & Resorts Corporation's balance sheet at December 31, 2017, appears in Exhibit 13–7.

EXHIBIT 13–7 | Shareholders' Equity Section of a Balance Sheet

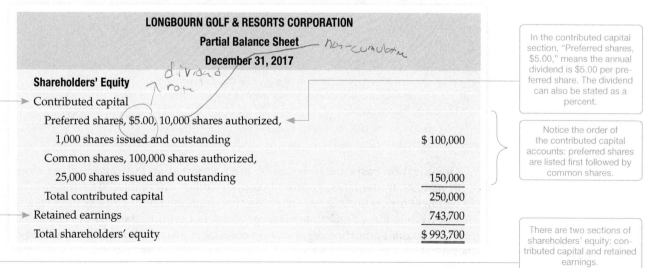

ETHICAL CONSIDERATIONS IN ACCOUNTING FOR THE ISSUANCE OF SHARES

Issuance of shares for *cash* poses no serious ethical challenge because the value of the asset received (cash) is clearly understood. The company simply receives cash and issues the shares to the shareholders. However, issuing shares for assets other than cash can pose an ethical challenge. The company issuing the shares wants to look successful, so it often wishes to record a large amount for the noncash asset received (such as land or a building) and for the shares being issued. Why? Because large asset and equity amounts make the business look prosperous, and financial ratios can be affected in a positive way.

REAL WORLD EXAMPLE

Sometimes, with publicly traded corporations, it is most objective to use the market value of the shares given in exchange for an asset as a measure of the asset's value.

A company is supposed to record an asset received at its current market value. However, one person may appraise land at a market value of $400,000, while another may honestly believe the land is worth only $300,000. A company receiving land in exchange for its shares must decide whether to record the land at $300,000, at $400,000, or at some amount in between based on external, independent evidence.

The ethical course of action is to record the asset at its current market value as determined by independent appraisers. Corporations are rarely found guilty of *understating* their assets, but companies have been sued for *overstating* asset values.

ORGANIZATION COSTS

The costs of organizing a corporation include legal fees for preparing documents and advising on procedures, fees paid to the incorporating jurisdiction, and charges by underwriters for selling the company's shares. These costs are grouped in an account titled Organization Costs, which is an asset because these costs contribute to a business's startup. Suppose BBV Holdings Inc. pays legal fees and incorporation fees of $5,000 to organize the corporation under the CBCA in Newfoundland. In addition, an investment dealer charges a fee of $15,000 for selling 30,000 common shares of BBV Holdings Inc. to investors for $225,000. Instead of being paid in cash, the broker receives 2,000 common shares as payment. BBV Holdings Inc.'s journal entries to record these organization costs are as follows:

Mar. 31	Organization Costs	5,000	
	Cash		5,000
	Legal fees and incorporation fees to organize the corporation.		
Apr. 3	Cash	225,000	
	Organization Costs	15,000	
	Common Shares		240,000
	To record receipt of funds from sale of 30,000 common shares and issue of 2,000 shares to investment dealer for selling shares in the corporation.		

REAL WORLD EXAMPLE

Notice that there is no rule for how long to amortize the organization costs. As you learn more accounting, you will find there are fewer rules and more room for professional judgment when recording transactions.

Organization costs are an *intangible asset,* reported on the balance sheet along with patents, trademarks, goodwill, and any other intangibles. The Income Tax Act allows corporations to expense a portion of organization costs against taxable income. While the *CPA Canada Handbook* does not require them to be amortized, most companies amortize organization costs over a short time period because of their relatively small size. As is true with other intangibles, amortization expense for the year should be disclosed in the financial statements.

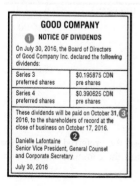

> Try It!

ACCOUNTING FOR CASH DIVIDENDS

Corporations share their wealth with the shareholders through dividends. Corporations declare dividends from *retained earnings* and usually pay the dividends with *cash*. A corporation must have enough retained earnings to declare the dividend and also have enough cash to pay the dividend. In addition, section 42 of the CBCA goes further to require that a "corporation shall not declare or pay a dividend if there are reasonable grounds for believing that (a) the corporation is or would after payment be unable to pay its liabilities as they become due; or (b) the realizable value of the corporation's assets would thereby be less than the aggregate of its liabilities and stated capital."

Companies also have the option to issue stock dividends, which are discussed in Chapter 14.

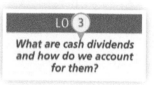

What are cash dividends and how do we account for them?

Dividend Dates

A corporation must declare a dividend before paying it. The corporation has no obligation to pay a dividend until the board of directors declares one. However, once the dividend is declared, it becomes a legal liability. Three dates for dividends are relevant and are illustrated in Exhibit 13-8.

Dividend announcements are published in the financial press and online to ensure that shareholders or potential shareholders are kept fully aware of the corporation's dividend policy.

KEY POINTS

Dividends are *not* an expense, but a distribution of earnings to owners. Cash dividends, like withdrawals, reduce assets and shareholders' equity.

EXHIBIT 13–8 | Dividend Notice

GOOD COMPANY
① NOTICE OF DIVIDENDS
On July 30, 2016, the Board of Directors of Good Company Inc. declared the following dividends:

Series 3 preferred shares	$0.195875 CDN pre shares
Series 4 preferred shares	$0.390625 CDN pre shares

These dividends will be paid on October 31, **③** 2016, to the shareholders of record at the close of business on October 17, 2016. **②**

Danielle Lafontaine
Senior Vice President, General Counsel and Corporate Secretary

July 30, 2016

① *Declaration date.* On the **declaration date**, the board of directors announces the intention to pay the dividend. The declaration creates a current liability called Dividends Payable for the corporation.

② *Date of record.* Those shareholders holding the shares on the **date of record**—a few weeks after declaration—will receive the dividend.

③ *Payment date.* Payment of the dividend usually follows the record date by two to four weeks.

Declaring and Paying Dividends

Declaration of a cash dividend is recorded by debiting Retained Earnings and crediting the current liability Dividends Payable as follows (amounts assumed):[3]

Oct. 3	Retained Earnings	20,000	
	Dividends Payable		20,000
	To declare a cash dividend for shareholders on the October 31 date of record. Payment date is November 15.		

There is no journal entry on October 31, the date of record. Shareholders who own shares on this date will receive the dividend on November 15.

To pay the dividend on the payment date, the transaction is recorded as follows:

Nov. 15	Dividends Payable	20,000	
	Cash		20,000
	To pay a cash dividend.		

When a company has issued both preferred and common shares, the preferred shareholders receive their dividends first. The common shareholders receive dividends only if the total declared dividend is large enough to satisfy the preferred requirements. Let's see how dividends are divided between preferred and common shares.

Guthrie Industries Inc. has 10,000 shares of $1.50 preferred shares outstanding plus common shares. Exhibit 13–9 shows the division of dividends between the preferred shares and common shares for two situations.

When a company has more than one class of preferred shares or common shares, the division of dividends among the various classes of shares depends on the order of priority created when each of the classes was issued.

EXHIBIT 13–9 | Dividing a Dividend between the Preferred Shares and Common Shares of Guthrie Industries Inc.

Case A:	Total dividend of $15,000	
	Preferred dividend (The full $15,000 goes to the preferred shares because the annual preferred dividend is $15,000 [$1.50 × 10,000].)	$15,000
	Common dividend (None, because the total dividend declared did not exceed the preferred dividend for the year.)	0
		$15,000
Case B:	Total dividend of $50,000*	
	Preferred dividend ($1.50 × $10,000)	$15,000
	Common dividend ($50,000 – $15,000)	35,000
		$50,000

*If Guthrie Industries Inc.'s annual dividend is large enough to exceed the preferred dividend for the year, the preferred shareholders receive their regular dividend and the common shareholders receive the remainder.

---

[3] Some accountants debit a Dividends account, a temporary account that is later closed to Retained Earnings, but most businesses debit Retained Earnings directly, as shown here.

Dividends on Cumulative and Noncumulative Preferred Shares

The allocation of dividends will involve additional calculations if the preferred shares are *cumulative*. If a corporation fails to pay the preferred dividend, the missed dividends are said to be in **arrears**. The owners of **cumulative preferred shares** must receive all dividends in arrears plus the current year's dividend before the corporation pays dividends to the common shareholders. "Cumulative" means that any dividends in arrears will accumulate, or carry over, to the future. The cumulative feature is not automatic to preferred shares but must be assigned to the preferred shares in the articles of incorporation. Common shares are never cumulative.

Let's assume the preferred shares of Guthrie Industries Inc. are cumulative and the company did not distribute the 2016 preferred dividend of $15,000. If Guthrie Industries now declares a $55,000 dividend in 2017, how much of this dividend goes to the preferred shareholders if the preferred shares are cumulative?

30,000 (the $15,000 in arrears + $15,000 for the current year)

How much goes to the common shareholders?

The remaining $25,000 ($55,000 – $30,000)

The entry to record the declaration of this dividend is:

2017			
Sep. 6	Retained Earnings	55,000	
	Dividends Payable, Preferred Shares		30,000
	Dividends Payable, Common Shares		25,000
	To declare a cash dividend. Preferred dividends are $30,000 ($15,000 × 2); common dividends are $25,000 ($55,000 – $30,000).		

If the preferred shares are not designated as cumulative, the corporation is not obligated to pay any dividends in arrears. Suppose that the Guthrie Industries Inc. preferred shares were noncumulative, and the company did not distribute a dividend in 2016. The preferred shareholders would lose the 2016 dividend forever. Before paying any common dividends in 2017, the company would have to pay only the 2017 preferred dividend of $15,000.

Having dividends in arrears on cumulative preferred shares is *not* a liability to the corporation. (A liability for dividends arises only after the board of directors declares the dividend.) Nevertheless, a corporation must report cumulative preferred dividends in arrears in the notes to the financial statements. This information alerts common shareholders to how much in cumulative preferred dividends must be paid before the common shareholders will receive any dividends.

Note disclosure of cumulative preferred dividends might take the following form on the balance sheet:

Preferred shares, $1.50, 50,000 shares authorized, 10,000 shares issued (Note 3)	$ 80,000
Common shares, 100,000 shares authorized, 40,000 shares issued	200,000
Retained earnings (Note 3)	414,000

> **Note 3: Cumulative preferred dividends in arrears. At December 31, 2017,** dividends on the company's $1.50 preferred shares were in arrears for 2016 and 2017 in the amount of $30,000 ($1.50 × 10,000 × 2 years).

> Try It!

4. CRS Robotics Inc. was organized on January 1, 2016, with 500,000 shares authorized; 200,000 shares were issued on January 5, 2016. CRS Robotics Inc. earned $250,000 during 2016 and declared a dividend of $0.25 per share on December 16, 2016, payable to shareholders on January 6, 2017.

   a. Journalize the declaration and payment of the dividend.

   b. Compute the balance of Retained Earnings on December 31, 2016.

5. Trivision Corp. has outstanding 20,000 common shares and 10,000 $2.00 cumulative preferred shares. The company has declared no dividends for the past two years but plans to pay $90,000 this year.

   a. Compute the dividends for the preferred and common shares.

   b. By how much will the dividends reduce Retained Earnings?

Solutions appear at the end of this chapter and on MyAccountingLab

DIFFERENT VALUES OF SHARES

What is the difference between book value and market value of shares?

The business community refers to several different *share values*. Both market value and book value are used for decision making.

Market Value

A share's **market value**, or *market price*, is the price for which a person can buy or sell a share. The issuing corporation's net income, financial position, future prospects, and the general economic conditions determine market value. Most companies' websites track their share prices, as do many business news sites and brokerage firms. *In almost all cases, shareholders are more concerned about the market value of a share than any other value.* At August 26, 2015, the common shares of DIRTT Environmental Solutions were *listed at* (an alternative term is *quoted at*) $5.35, which meant they sold for, or could be bought for, $5.35 per share. The purchase of 1,000 common shares of DIRTT would cost $5,350 ($5.35 × 1,000) plus a commission. If you were selling 1,000 common shares, you would receive cash of $5,350 less a commission. The commission is the fee an investor pays to a stockbroker for buying or selling the shares. If you buy shares in DIRTT from another investor, DIRTT gets no cash. The transaction is a sale between investors. DIRTT records only the change in shareholder name.

Book Value

LEARNING TIPS

Book value per share uses the number of shares *outstanding*, not the number of shares authorized.

The **book value** of a share is the amount of shareholders' equity on the company's books for each share. If the company has only common shares outstanding, divide total shareholders' equity by the number of shares *outstanding*. If a company has both common shares and preferred shares, the preferred shareholders have the first claim to shareholders' equity. Therefore, the preferred shareholders' equity must be subtracted from total shareholders' equity to calculate the shareholders' equity available for the common shareholders. This is shown by the following formula:

$$\text{Book value per common share} = \frac{\text{Total shareholders' equity} - \text{Preferred equity}}{\text{Number of common shares outstanding}}$$

For example, a company with shareholders' equity of $180,000, no preferred shares, and 5,000 common shares outstanding has a book value of $36.00 per common share, calculated as follows:

$$\text{Book value per common share} = \frac{\text{Total shareholders' equity} - \text{Preferred equity}}{\text{Number of common shares outstanding}}$$

$$= \frac{\$180,000 - \$0}{5,000}$$

$$= \$36.00$$

If the company has both preferred and common shares outstanding, the preferred shareholders' equity must be calculated before the common shareholders' equity can be calculated. Ordinarily, preferred shares have a specified **liquidation value**, or redemption value, or call value. This is shown by the following formula:

$$\text{Book value per preferred share} = \frac{\text{Preferred equity}}{\text{Number of preferred shares outstanding}}$$

$$= \frac{\text{Liquidation value} + \text{Dividends in arrears}}{\text{Number of preferred shares outstanding}}$$

To illustrate, Garner Corp. reports the following amounts:

Shareholders' Equity	
Contributed capital	
Preferred shares, $7.00, $90 liquidation value, 5,000 shares authorized, 1,000 shares issued and outstanding	$100,000
Common shares, 20,000 shares authorized, 5,000 shares issued and outstanding	150,000
Total contributed capital	250,000
Retained earnings	90,000
Total shareholders' equity	$340,000

Suppose that three years of cumulative preferred dividends are in arrears. The current year preferred dividend must also be paid.

The book value for the preferred shares must be calculated first:

$$\text{Book value per preferred share} = \frac{\text{Liquidation value} + \text{Dividends in arrears}}{\text{Number of preferred shares outstanding}}$$

$$= \frac{(\$90 \times 1,000) + (\$7.00 \times 1,000 \times 4^*)}{1,000}$$

$$= \frac{\$90,000 + \$28,000}{1,000}$$

$$= \frac{\$118,000}{1,000} \longleftarrow \text{Preferred equity}$$

$$= \$118.00$$

*4 years of dividends = 3 years in arrears + current year

The book value for the common shares can then be calculated, as follows:

$$\text{Book value per common share} = \frac{\text{Total shareholders' equity} - \text{Preferred equity}}{\text{Number of common shares outstanding}}$$

$$= \frac{\$340,000 - \$118,000}{5,000}$$

$$= \$44.40$$

Using Book Value in Decision Making Book value may be a factor in determining the price to pay for a *closely held* corporation. A corporation is **closely held** when it is a private corporation that has only a few shareholders. A company may buy out a shareholder by agreeing to pay the book value of the shareholder's shares.

Some investors compare the book value of a share with its market value. The idea is that shares selling below book value are *underpriced* and thus are a *good buy*. But the relationship between book value and market value is far from clear. Other investors believe that, if shares sell at a price below book value, the company must be experiencing difficulty. Exhibit 13–10 contrasts the book values and market prices for the common shares of three Canadian companies. In all cases, the share price, which is the market value, exceeds book value—a sign of success.

EXHIBIT 13–10 | Book Value and Market Value

	Stock	Book Value	Share Price*
Canadian Tire Corporation Limited	CTC.A	$67.35	$117.19
Barrick Gold Corporation	ABX	$14.51	$ 16.25
DIRTT Environmental Solutions	DRT	$ 1.02	$ 4.48

* Share price on January 30, 2015. Retrieved February 1, 2015, from Google Finance.

≫ Try It!

6. Castle Corporation's balance sheet at year end shows the following:

Shareholders' Equity	
Contributed capital	
Preferred shares, 7%, $13.00 liquidation value, 5,000 shares authorized, 3,500 shares issued	$ 45,500
Common shares, 140,000 shares authorized and issued	74,500
Total contributed capital	120,000
Retained earnings	260,000
Total shareholders' equity	$380,000

Compute the shareholders' equity allocated to the preferred shareholders. Five years of cumulative preferred dividends are in arrears, including the current year.

7. Refer to the Castle Corporation data in the previous question. Compute the shareholders' equity available for the common shareholders and the book value per common share.

Solutions appear at the end of this chapter and on MyAccountingLab

EVALUATING OPERATIONS

LO 5

What are the rate of return on total assets (ROA) and the rate of return on total common shareholders' equity (ROE), and how do we calculate them?

Investors and creditors are constantly comparing companies' profits. However, the DIRTT Environmental Solutions Ltd. net income may not be comparable to that of a company in the oil and gas industry, such as EnCana Corporation, or of a brewery, such as Sleeman Breweries Ltd. To compare companies, investors, creditors, and managers turn dollar amounts into ratios to look at the *relationship between* amounts rather than the exact dollar amounts. Two important ratios are the rate of return on total assets and the rate of return on shareholders' equity. We will calculate both ratios using the figures from the TELUS Corporation Inc. annual report found on MyAccountingLab.

Rate of Return on Total Assets

The **rate of return on total assets**, or simply **return on assets (ROA)**, measures a company's success in using its assets to earn income. Two groups invest money to finance a corporation:

- Shareholders—they invest in shares and expect the company to earn net income.
- Creditors—they lend money to the corporation to earn interest.

The sum of net income and interest expense is the return to the two groups that have financed the corporation's assets, and this is the numerator of the return on assets ratio. The denominator is average total assets ([Beginning + Ending total assets] ÷ 2). Return on assets is computed as follows (amounts in millions of dollars):

$$\text{Rate of return on total assets} = \frac{\text{Net income} + \text{Interest expense}}{\text{Average total assets}}$$

$$= \frac{\$1{,}294 + \$447}{(\$19{,}237 + \$18{,}235)\,/\,2} = \frac{\$1{,}741}{\$18{,}736}$$

$$= 0.0929, \text{ or } 9.3\%$$

Net income and interest expense are taken from the income statement (or in TELUS's case, from the consolidated statements of earnings and other comprehensive earnings). Average total assets are computed from the consolidated statements of financial position.

How is this profitability measure used in decision making? It is used to compare companies. By relating the sum of net income and interest expense to average total assets, we have a standard measure that describes the profitability of all types of companies.

What is a good rate of return on total assets? There is no single answer to this question because rates of return vary widely by industry. For example, consumer products companies earn much higher returns than do utilities or grocery store chains. In most industries, a return on assets of 10 percent is considered very good.

Rate of Return on Common Shareholders' Equity

Rate of return on common shareholders' equity, often called **return on equity (ROE)**, shows the relationship between net income and average common shareholders' equity. The numerator is net income minus preferred dividends. This information is taken from the income statement and statement of retained earnings. Preferred dividends are subtracted because the preferred shareholders have the first claim to dividends from the company's net income. The denominator is average *common shareholders' equity*—total shareholders' equity minus preferred equity. TELUS's rate of return on common shareholders' equity is computed as follows (amounts in millions of dollars):

$$\text{Rate of return on common shareholders' equity} = \frac{\text{Net income} - \text{Preferred dividends}}{\text{Average common shareholders' equity}}$$

$$= \frac{\$1{,}294 - \$0}{(\$8{,}015 + \$7{,}686)\,/\,2} = \frac{\$1{,}294}{\$7{,}850.5} = 0.165, \text{ or } 16.5\%$$

Investors and creditors use return on common shareholders' equity in much the same way as they use return on total assets—to compare companies. The higher the rate of return, the more successful the company. A 12 percent return on common shareholders' equity is considered quite good in many industries. Investors also compare a company's return on shareholders' equity to interest rates available in the market. If interest rates are almost as high as return on equity, many investors will lend their money to earn interest or deposit it in a bank rather than invest in common shares. They choose to forgo the extra risk of investing in shares when the rate of return on equity is too low.

Leverage   Observe that the return on equity (16.5 percent) is higher than the return on assets (9.3 percent). This difference results from the interest expense component of return on assets. Companies such as TELUS borrow at one rate, say 5.5 percent, and invest the funds to earn a higher rate, say 7.5 percent. Borrowing at a lower rate than the return on investments is called *using leverage*. During good times, **leverage** produces high returns for shareholders. However, too much borrowing can make it difficult to pay the interest on the debt. The company's creditors are guaranteed a fixed rate of return on their loans. The shareholders, conversely, have no guarantee that the corporation will earn net income, so their investments are riskier. Consequently, shareholders demand a higher rate of return than do creditors, and this explains why return on equity should exceed return on assets.

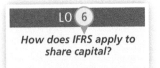

8. The financial statements of Riley Resources Corp. reported the following:

	2017	2016
Net income	$ 80,000	$ 90,000
Interest expense	20,000	24,000
$6.00 preferred shares (1,000 shares)	100,000	100,000
Common shares	200,000	200,000
Retained earnings	180,000	160,000
Total assets	840,000	760,000

Dividends were paid to preferred shareholders in 2016 and 2017. Dividends of $54,000 were declared and paid to common shareholders in 2017. Compute the return on assets for 2017.

9. Refer to the Riley Resources Corp. financial information in the previous question. Compute the return on common shareholders' equity for 2017.

10. Refer to the previous two questions. Compare the return on assets (ROA) and return on equity (ROE). Is there a favourable or unfavourable relationship between the two ratios?

Solutions appear at the end of this chapter and on MyAccountingLab

LO 6

How does IFRS apply to share capital?

THE IMPACT OF IFRS ON SHARE CAPITAL

ASPE	🌐	IFRS

The principles governing accounting for share capital are essentially the same under accounting standards for private enterprises (ASPE), as described in this chapter, and under IFRS.

ASPE	IFRS
The requirements under ASPE are less rigorous—they only require that disclosure be made for classes of shares that have actually been issued.	Under IFRS, companies must make certain disclosures about *all* classes of shares authorized by the corporation, whether those classes of shares have been issued or not.
When shares are issued for non-cash items, use fair value of either the item received or the item given up. Choose the information that is most reliable to record the transaction.	First consider the fair value of the non-cash item received in exchange for shares. If its value cannot be reliably determined, then use the fair value of the shares when recording the transaction.
Organization costs are capitalized under ASPE—recorded as an intangible asset—and then amortized.	Under IFRS, organization costs are expensed.

SUMMARY PROBLEM FOR YOUR REVIEW

Presented below are the accounts and related balances for ECOM Finance Ltd. at September 30, 2017:

Salary Payable	$ 3,000	Inventory	$ 85,000
Cash	15,000	Property, Plant, and Equipment, net	204,000
Accounts Payable	20,000	Accounts Receivable, net	25,000
Retained Earnings	80,000	Income Tax Payable	12,000
Organization Costs, net	1,000	Preferred Shares, $6.00, cumulative,	
Long-term Note Payable	70,000	20,000 shares authorized,	
Common Shares,		3,000 shares issued	50,000
60,000 shares authorized,			
25,000 shares issued	95,000		

Required

1. Prepare the classified balance sheet at September 30, 2017. Use the account format for the balance sheet.

2. Are the preferred shares cumulative or noncumulative? How can you tell?

3. What is the total amount of the annual preferred dividend?

4. Assume the common shares were all issued at the same time. What was the selling price per share?

5. Compute the book value per share of the preferred shares and the common shares. No prior-year preferred dividends are in arrears, and ECOM Finance Ltd. has not declared the current-year dividend.

SOLUTIONS

1.

ECOM FINANCE LTD.				
Balance Sheet				
September 30, 2017				
Assets			**Liabilities**	
Current assets:			Current liabilities:	
Cash	$ 15,000		Accounts payable	$ 20,000
Accounts receivable, net	25,000		Salary payable	3,000
Inventory	85,000		Income tax payable	12,000
Total current assets	125,000		Total current liabilities	35,000
Property, plant, and equipment, net	204,000		Long-term note payable	70,000
Intangible assets:			Total liabilities	105,000
Organization costs, net	1,000		**Shareholders' Equity**	
			Contributed capital:	
			Preferred shares, $6.00, cumulative, 20,000 shares authorized, 3,000 shares issued	$ 50,000
			Common shares, 60,000 shares authorized, 25,000 shares issued	95,000
			Total contributed capital	145,000
			Retained earnings	80,000
			Total shareholders' equity	225,000
			Total liabilities and	
Total assets	$330,000		shareholders' equity	$330,000

2. The preferred shares are cumulative, as is noted in their description.
3. Total annual preferred dividend: $18,000 (3,000 × $6.00)
4. Price per share: $3.80 ($95,000 ÷ 25,000 shares issued)
5. Book values per share of preferred and common shares:

Use the number of shares *issued*, not the number of shares authorized to calculate the share price.

Preferred	
Book value	$ 50,000
Cumulative dividend for current year (3,000 × $6.00)	18,000
Shareholders' equity allocated to preferred	$ 68,000
Book value per share ($68,000 ÷ 3,000 shares)	$ 22.67
Common	
Total shareholders' equity	$225,000
Less: Shareholders' equity allocated to preferred	68,000
Shareholders' equity available for common shareholders	$157,000
Book value per share ($157,000 ÷ 25,000 shares)	$ 6.28

Preferred: Remember to *add* any dividends in arrears, including the current year's dividends if they were not paid.

Common: Book value per common share must exclude any amounts pertaining to preferred shares.

SUMMARY

LEARNING OBJECTIVE **1** Identify the characteristics of a corporation

What is a corporation, and why is it an important form of business? Pg. 730

- A corporation is a separate legal and business entity. Shareholders are the owners of a corporation.
- Advantages of a corporation:
  - Continuous life
  - Ease of raising large amounts of capital
  - Ease of transferring ownership
  - Limited liability

  Disadvantages:
  - A degree of double taxation
  - Separation of ownership and management
  - Expensive government regulation
  - Additional costs

LEARNING OBJECTIVE **2** Record the issuance of shares and prepare the shareholders' equity section of a corporation's balance sheet

How do we record and present share information? Pg. 736

- Shares are classified as common or preferred, and there may be several classes or series. Preferred shares are further defined to include cumulative or noncumulative, and convertible
- The balance sheet carries the capital raised through share issuance under the heading Contributed Capital in the shareholders' equity section. Preferred shares are shown first and then common shares. Retained earnings is listed last.

LEARNING OBJECTIVE **3** Account for cash dividends

What are cash dividends and how do we account for them? Pg. 743

- There is a liability to pay dividends when the board of directors declares a dividend. Dividends are given to shareholders who own shares on the date of record and are paid after the date of record.
- Preferred shares have priority over common shares when dividends are paid. Preferred dividends are usually stated as a dollar amount per share.
- Preferred shares have a claim to dividends in arrears if the preferred shares are cumulative.

LEARNING OBJECTIVE **4** Use different share values in decision making

What is the difference between book value and market value of shares? Pg. 746

- A share's *market value* is the price for which a share may be bought or sold.
- *Book value* is the amount of shareholders' equity per share.

$$\text{Book value per common share} = \frac{\text{Total shareholder's equity} - \text{Preferred equity}}{\text{Number of common shares outstanding}}$$

$$\text{Preferred equity} = \text{Liquidation value} + \text{Dividends in arrears}$$

$$\text{Book value per preferred share} = \frac{\text{Liquidation value} + \text{Dividends in arrears}}{\text{Number of preferred shares outstanding}}$$

LEARNING OBJECTIVE **5** Evaluate a company's ROA and ROE

What are the rate of return on total assets (ROA) and the rate of return on common shareholders' equity (ROE), and how do we calculate them? Pg. 748

- These are two standard measures of profitability. A healthy company's return on equity will exceed its return on assets.

$$\text{ROA} = \frac{\text{Net income} + \text{Interest expense}}{\text{Average total assets}}$$

$$\text{ROE} = \frac{\text{Net income} - \text{Preferred dividends}}{\text{Average common shareholders' equity}}$$

MyAccountingLab **Video:** Real World Accounting

How does IFRS apply to share capital?   Pg. 750

- Accounting for shares under ASPE and IFRS is the same.
- IFRS requires that certain disclosures be made for classes of shares that have been authorized but not issued.
- IFRS requires fair market value of items received in exchange for shares to be considered first. If not reliable, then consider the fair market value of the shares as the transaction price.
- Organization costs are expensed under IFRS but capitalized as intangible assets and amortized under ASPE.

Check **Accounting Vocabulary** below for all key terms used in Chapter 13 and the **Glossary** at the back of the book for all key terms used in the textbook.

MORE CHAPTER REVIEW MATERIAL

MyAccountingLab

DemoDoc covering Common Shares

Student PowerPoint Slides

Audio Chapter Summary

Note: All MyAccountingLab resources can be found in the Chapter Resources section and the Multimedia Library.

ACCOUNTING VOCABULARY

Arrears To be behind or overdue in a debt payment (*p. 745*).

Articles of incorporation The document issued by the federal or provincial government giving the incorporators permission to form a corporation (*p. 730*).

Authorization of shares A provision in a corporation's articles of incorporation that permits a corporation to sell a certain number of shares of stock (*p. 732*).

Authorized shares The number of shares a corporation is allowed to sell according to the articles of incorporation (*p. 736*).

Board of directors A group elected by the shareholders to set policy for a corporation and to appoint its officers (*p. 732*).

Book value The amount of shareholders' equity on the company's books for each of its shares (*p. 746*).

Bylaws The constitution for governing a corporation (*p. 732*).

Chairperson (of board) An elected person on a corporation's board of directors; usually the most powerful person in the corporation (*p. 732*).

Closely held Describes a corporation with only a few shareholders (*p. 748*).

Common shares The most basic form of share capital. In describing a corporation, the common shareholders are the owners of the business (*p. 734*).

Contributed capital A corporation's capital from investments by the shareholders. Also called *share capital* or *capital stock* (*p. 733*).

Convertible preferred shares Preferred shares that may be exchanged by the preferred shareholders, if they choose, for another class of shares in the corporation (*p. 741*).

Cumulative preferred shares Preferred shares whose owners must receive all dividends in arrears before the

corporation pays dividends to the common shareholders (*p. 745*).

Date of record On this date, which is a few weeks after the declaration of the dividend, the list of shareholders who will receive the dividend is compiled (*p. 743*).

Declaration date The date on which the board of directors announces the dividend. There is a liability created on this date (*p. 743*).

Deficit A debit balance in the Retained Earnings account (*p. 735*).

Dividends Distributions by a corporation to its shareholders (*p. 735*).

Double taxation Corporations pay their own income taxes on corporate income. Then, the shareholders pay personal income tax on the cash dividends that they receive from corporations (*p. 731*).

Initial public offering (IPO) The first time a particular class of a corporation's shares are sold to investors (*p. 736*).

Issue price The price at which shareholders first purchase shares from the corporation (*p. 737*).

Issued shares Shares that are offered for sale to investors (*p. 737*).

Leverage The use of financial instruments to increase the potential return on investment by earning more income on borrowed money than the related expense, thereby increasing the earnings for the owners of the business. (*p. 750*).

Limited liability No personal obligation of a shareholder for corporation debts. The most that a shareholder can lose on an investment in a corporation's shares is the cost of the investment (*p. 731*).

Liquidation value (redemption value or call value) The amount of capital that a preferred shareholder would receive per preferred share upon liquidation of the corporation (p. 747).

Market value The price for which a person could buy or sell a share (p. 746).

Mutual agency Every owner can bind the business to a contract within the scope of the business's regular operations. This does not exist in a corporation (p. 731).

No-par-value shares Shares that do not have a value assigned to them by the articles of incorporation (p. 738).

Organization costs The costs of organizing a corporation, including legal fees and charges by promoters for selling the shares. Organization costs are an intangible asset under ASPE but are written off as an expense under IFRS (p. 742).

Outstanding shares Shares in the hands of shareholders (p. 737).

Par value An arbitrary value assigned when certain shares are initially offered to the public; these types of shares are not common in Canada (p. 738).

Preemptive right Existing shareholders are given the right to purchase additional shares of the company before the shares are offered to others. This would give existing shareholders the opportunity to maintain the same percentage of ownership as they would have had before the new shares were issued (p. 736).

Preferred shares Shares of stock that give their owners certain advantages over common shareholders, such as the priority to receive dividends before the common shareholders and the priority to receive assets before the common shareholders if the corporation liquidates (p. 739).

President The chief operating officer in charge of managing the day-to-day operations of a corporation (p. 732).

Private corporation A corporation that does not issue shares that are traded on a stock exchange (p. 730).

Proportionate share The same amount of shares in relation to others before and after an event such as a new issue of shares (p. 736).

Prospectus A mandatory legal document that describes an investment to potential purchasers (p. 736).

Proxy A formal appointment of one person to cast a vote for another person (p. 733).

Public corporation A corporation that issues shares that are traded on a stock exchange (p. 730).

Rate of return on common shareholders' equity Net income minus preferred dividends divided by average common shareholders' equity. A measure of profitability. Also called *return on equity (ROE)* or *return on common shareholders' equity* (p. 749).

Rate of return on total assets The sum of net income plus interest expense divided by average total assets. This ratio measures the success a company has in using its assets to earn income for the people who finance the business. Also called *return on assets (ROA)* (p. 748).

Retained earnings A corporation's capital that is earned through profitable operation of the business (p. 733).

Return on assets (ROA) Another name for *rate of return on total assets* (p. 748).

Return on equity (ROE) Another name for *rate of return on common shareholders' equity* (p. 749).

Shareholder A person or a company that owns shares in a corporation (p. 730).

Shareholders' equity Owners' equity of a corporation (p. 733).

Shares Units into which the owners' equity of a corporation is divided (p. 731).

Stated value An arbitrary amount assigned to a share of stock when it is issued (p. 738).

Stock Shares into which the owners' equity of a corporation is divided (p. 731).

Underwriter An independent firm that is hired to sell shares on a corporation's behalf (p. 736).

SIMILAR ACCOUNTING TERMS

Corp.	Corporation
Inc.	Incorporated
Initial public offering	IPO
Issue	Sell
Liquidation value	Redemption value; Call value; Call price
Ltd.	Limited
Market value	Market price
Rate of return on common shareholders' equity	Return on equity; ROE
Rate of return on total assets	Return on assets; ROA
Share capital	Capital stock; Stated capital
Shareholder	Stockholder (US terminology)
Stated capital	Share capital
Using leverage	Borrowing at a lower rate than the return on investments

SELF-STUDY QUESTIONS

Test your understanding of the chapter by marking the correct answer to each of the following questions:

1. Which characteristic of a corporation is most attractive to an owner (shareholder)? (*pp. 730–731*)
   a. Limited liability
   b. Double taxation
   c. Mutual agency
   d. All of the above

2. The person with the most power in a corporation is often the (*p. 732*)
   a. Accountant
   b. Chairperson of the board
   c. President
   d. Vice-president

3. The dollar amount of the shareholder investments in a corporation is called (*p. 733*)
   a. Outstanding shares
   b. Total shareholders' equity
   c. Contributed capital
   d. Retained earnings

4. The arbitrary value assigned to a share by the board of directors is called (*p. 738*)
   a. Market value
   b. Liquidation value
   c. Book value
   d. Stated value

5. Shares issued by a corporation incorporated under the Canada Business Corporations Act normally have (*p. 738*)
   a. No par value
   b. A par value set by management
   c. A par value set by the government
   d. A par value of $1.00

6. Magnum Corporation receives a building for 10,000 common shares. The building's book value is $275,000 and its current market value is $640,000. This transaction increases Magnum's share capital by (*p. 739*)
   a. $0 because the corporation received no cash
   b. $365,000
   c. $275,000
   d. $640,000

7. Organization costs are classified as a(n) (*p. 742*)
   a. Operating expense
   b. Current asset
   c. Contra item in shareholders' equity
   d. None of the above

8. The preferred shares of Glanville Inc. in the preceding question were issued at $55.00 per share. Each preferred share can be converted into 10 common shares. The entry to record the conversion of these preferred shares into common is (*p. 741*)

		Debit	Credit
a.	Cash	550,000	
	Preferred Shares		500,000
	Common Shares		50,000
b.	Preferred Shares	500,000	
	Cash		50,000
	Common Shares		550,000
c.	Preferred Shares	550,000	
	Common Shares		550,000
d.	Common Shares	550,000	
	Preferred Shares		550,000

9. Glanville Inc. has 10,000 $3.50 cumulative preferred shares and 100,000 common shares issued and outstanding. Two years' preferred dividends are in arrears.

   Glanville Inc. declares a cash dividend large enough to pay the preferred dividends in arrears, the preferred dividend for the current period, and a $1.50 dividend per common share. What is the total amount of the dividend? (*p. 745*)
   a. $255,000
   b. $220,000
   c. $150,000
   d. $105,000

10. When an investor is buying shares as an investment, the value of most direct concern is (*p. 746*)
   a. Par value
   b. Market value
   c. Liquidation value
   d. Book value

Answers to Self-Study Questions

1. a 2. b 3. c 4. d 5. a 6. d 7. d Intangible asset
8. c 9. a [(10,000 × $3.50 × 3 = $105,000) + (100,000 × $1.50 = $150,000) = $255,000] 10. b

ASSIGNMENT MATERIAL

QUESTIONS

1. Identify the characteristics of a corporation.

2. Explain how corporate earnings are subject to a degree of double taxation.

3. Briefly outline the steps in the organization of a corporation.

4. Compare the characteristics of a partnership and a corporation.

5. Name the five rights of a common shareholder. Are preferred shares automatically nonvoting?

6. Which event increases the assets of the corporation: authorization of shares or issuance of shares? Explain.

7. Suppose Bala Ltd. issued 1,400 shares of its $4.50 preferred shares for $110.00 per share. By how much would this transaction increase the company's contributed capital? By how much would it increase retained earnings? By how much would it increase annual cash dividend payments?

8. United Inc. issued 150 common shares for $9.00 per share and 250 shares for $8.50 per share. What would be the journal entry to record the combined issue?

9. How does issuance of 1,500 common shares for land and a building, together worth $200,000, affect contributed capital?

10. List the following accounts in the order in which they would appear on the balance sheet: Common Shares, Organization Costs, Preferred Shares, Retained Earnings, Dividends Payable. Also, give each account's balance sheet classification.

11. What type of account is Organization Costs? Briefly describe how to account for organization costs.

12. Briefly discuss the three important dates for a dividend.

13. Tapin Inc. has 2,500 shares of its $1.75 preferred shares outstanding. Dividends for 2015 and 2016 are in arrears. Assume that Tapin Inc. declares total dividends of $35,000 at the end of 2017. Show how to allocate the dividends to preferred and common shareholders (a) if preferred shares are cumulative, and (b) if preferred shares are noncumulative.

14. As a preferred shareholder, would you rather own cumulative or noncumulative preferred shares? If all other factors are the same, would the corporation rather issue cumulative or noncumulative preferred shares? Give your reasons.

15. How are cumulative preferred dividends in arrears reported in the financial statements? When do dividends become a liability of the corporation?

16. Distinguish between the market value of shares and the book value of shares. Which is more important to investors?

17. How is book value per common share computed when the company has both preferred shares and common shares outstanding?

18. Why should a healthy company's rate of return on shareholders' equity exceed its rate of return on total assets?

MyAccountingLab   Make the grade with MyAccountingLab: Most of the Starters, Exercises, and Problems marked in `red` can be found on MyAccountingLab. You can practise them as often as you want, and most feature step-by-step guided instructions to help you find the right answer.

STARTERS

Starter 13–1   Answer these questions about corporations.

Authority structure in a corporation

①

    1. Who is the most powerful person in the corporation?

    2. What group holds the ultimate power in a corporation?

    3. Who is in charge of day-to-day operations?

    4. Who is in charge of accounting?

Starter 13–2   How does a proprietorship's balance sheet differ from a corporation's balance sheet? How are the two balance sheets similar?

The balance sheets of a corporation and a proprietorship

①

Starter 13–3   Eagle Looking Incorporated has two classes of shares: common and preferred. Journalize Eagle Looking's June 11 issuance of

Issuing shares

②

    1. 1,000 common shares for $70.00 per share
    2. 1,000 preferred shares for a total of $32,000

Starter 13-4

Munsters Inc. issued all its shares during 2017 and reported the following on its balance sheet at December 31, 2017:

Common shares, Authorized: 5,000 shares	
Issued and outstanding: 3,000 shares	$ 2,900
Retained earnings	49,000

Journalize the company's issuance of the shares for cash on July 3.

Starter 13-5

At December 31, 2017, KD Corporation reported the following on its comparative balance sheet, which included 2016 amounts for comparison:

Allowed → to issue

	December 31,	
	2017	**2016**
Common shares		
Authorized: 10,000 shares		
Issued: 3,600 shares in 2017	$85,000	
3,490 shares in 2016		$79,000
Retained earnings	50,800 ←	46,800

1. How much did KD Corporation's total contributed capital increase during 2017? What caused total contributed capital to increase? How can you tell?

if no dividends
nothing deducted
r.e. earnings

2. Assuming no dividends were declared during 2017, did KD Corporation have a profit or a loss for 2017? How can you tell?

Starter 13-6

Hatteras Corporation reported the following accounts (a partial list):

Cost of Goods Sold	$29,400	Accounts Payable	$3,000
Common Shares,		Retained Earnings	8,000
40,000 shares issued		Unearned Revenue	2,600
and outstanding	29,500	Cash	12,000
Long-term Note Payable	3,800	Total assets	?

Prepare the shareholders' equity section of the Hatteras balance sheet.

Starter 13-7

Indicate whether each of the following favours the use of long-term debt to raise capital or the issuance of common shares:

a. Annual payment is optional.
b. Money must be repaid.
c. Issuance means dilution of existing control.
d. Annual cost is tax deductible.

Starter 13-8

Solve for the missing amounts in the partial balance sheet using the additional information provided below:

Shareholders' Equity	
Contributed Capital	
Preferred shares, $2.50, (A) issued, outstanding	$175,000
Common shares, 150,000 issued and outstanding	(B)
Total contributed capital	(C)
Deficit	(D)
Total Shareholders' Equity	$500,000

All of the shares were issued at one time. Common shares were sold for $3.00 per share and preferred shares were sold for $5.00 each. No dividends were paid for the year.

Starter 13–9 Gratto Corporation earned net income of $85,000 during the year ended December 31, 2016. On December 15, Gratto Corporation declared the annual cash dividend on its 5,000 $3.00 preferred shares and a $0.60 per share cash dividend on its 50,000 common shares. Gratto Corporation then paid the dividends on January 4, 2017.

Accounting for cash dividends
③

Cash, Jan. 4, 2017, $45,000

Journalize for Gratto Corporation:
1. Declaring the cash dividends on December 15, 2016
2. Paying the cash dividends on January 4, 2017

Starter 13–10 Xiong Inc. has the following shareholders' equity:

Dividing cash dividends between preferred and common shares
③

3. Preferred, $3,375; Common, $13,625

Preferred shares, $0.025, cumulative, liquidation value $0.50, 50,000 shares authorized, 45,000 shares issued and outstanding	$ 20,000
Common shares, 1,000,000 shares authorized and issued and outstanding	200,000
Retained earnings	130,000
Total shareholders' equity	$350,000

Answer these questions about Xiong's dividends:

1. Are Xiong Inc.'s preferred shares cumulative or noncumulative? How can you tell?
2. Suppose Xiong Inc. declares cash dividends of $17,000 for 2017. How much of the dividends goes to preferred shares? How much goes to common shares?
3. Suppose Xiong Inc. did not pay the preferred dividend in 2015 and 2016. In 2017, the company declares cash dividends of $17,000. How much of the dividends goes to preferred shares? How much goes to common shares?

Starter 13–11 Refer to the shareholders' equity information of Xiong Inc. in Starter 13–10. Xiong Inc. has not declared preferred dividends for five years (including the current year). Compute the book value per share of Xiong Inc.'s common shares. Round your answer to two decimal places.

Book value per common share
④

Book value per share, $0.32

Starter 13–12 Midnight Distribution Corporation's balance sheet reported the following information at December 31, 2016:

Calculating book value
④

Preferred shares, $3, cumulative, 11,000 shares issued, liquidation value $55 per share	$ 605,000
Common shares, 75,000 shares issued	2,000,000
Total contributed capital	2,605,000
Retained earnings	1,950,000
Total shareholders' equity	$4,555,000

Assuming there are two years' dividends in arrears (including 2016), determine the book value per share of both preferred and common shares.

Starter 13–13 Township Corp.'s 2017 financial statements reported the following items—with 2016 figures given for comparison:

Balance sheet	2017	2016
Total assets	$49,000	$44,800
Total liabilities	$25,400	$22,000
Total shareholders' equity (all common)	23,600	22,800
Total liabilities and equity	$49,000	$44,800

Income statement	
Net sales	$39,130
Cost of goods sold	14,210
Gross margin	24,920
Selling and administrative expenses	14,000
Interest expense	400
All other expenses, net	4,420
Net income	$ 6,100

Compute Township Corp.'s rate of return on total assets and rate of return on common shareholders' equity for 2017. Do these rates of return look high or low?

EXERCISES

MyAccountingLab

Exercise 13–1

Suppose you are forming a business and you need some outside money from other investors. Assume you have decided to organize the business as a corporation that will issue shares to raise the needed funds. Briefly discuss your most important reason for organizing as a corporation rather than as a partnership. If you had decided to organize as a partnership, what would be your most important reason for not organizing as a corporation?

Exercise 13–2

David Johnston and Lisa Jacobs are opening a decorating business to be named Student Decor Ltd. They need outside capital, so they plan to organize the business as a corporation. Because your accounting course is next to their design class, they come to you for advice. Write a memorandum informing them of the steps in forming a corporation. Identify specific documents used in this process, and name the different parties involved in the ownership and management of a corporation.

Exercise 13–3

Boogz Corp.'s new accounting intern prepared their adjusted trial balance in alphabetical order. All accounts have their normal balances.

Accounts Receivable	$ 56,000	Other Expenses	$ 35,400
Accumulated Amortization	14,000	Retained Earnings	68,400
Amortization Expense	40,800	Salaries Expense	170,000
Cash	112,000	Salaries Payable	3,400
Common Shares	50,000	Service Revenue	356,400
Computers & Equipment	74,800	Supplies	5,600
Interest Expense	8,800	Unearned Revenues	5,400
Interest Revenue	5,800		

Required

1. Prepare the appropriate closing entries for the January 31 year end.
2. What is the balance in the Retained Earnings account after the closing entries have been completed?

Exercise 13-4

Is each of the following statements true or false? For each false statement, explain why it is false.

Types of shares
(2)

   a. A shareholder may bind (obligate) the corporation to a contract.
   b. The policy-making body in a corporation is called the board of directors.
   c. The owner of 100 preferred shares has greater voting rights than the owner of 100 common shares.
   d. A company incorporated under the Canada Business Corporations Act must assign the proceeds of a share issue to the capital account for that type of share.
   e. All common shares issued and outstanding have equal voting rights.
   f. Issuance of 1,000 common shares at $12.00 per share increases shareholders' equity by $12,000.
   g. The stated value of a share is the value assigned to the shares by the company issuing them at the date issued.
   h. A corporation issues its preferred shares in exchange for land and a building with a combined market value of $200,000. This transaction increases the corporation's shareholders' equity by $200,000 regardless of the assets' prior book value.

Exercise 13-5

Atul Incorporated made the following share issuance transactions:

Issuing shares
(2)
2. Contributed capital,
$126,500

Jan.	19	Issued 4,500 common shares for cash of $11.00 per share.
Feb.	3	Sold 1,000 $1.50 Class A preferred shares for $14,000 cash.
	11	Received inventory valued at $20,000 and equipment with market value of $17,000 for 5,800 common shares.
	15	Issued 2,000 $1.00 Class B preferred shares for $13.00 per share.

Required

1. Journalize the transactions. Explanations are not required.
2. How much contributed capital did these transactions generate for Atul Incorporated?

Exercise 13-6

Shapalov Supplies Ltd. imports farm equipment. The corporation issues 10,000 common shares for $15.00 per share. Record issuance of the shares on March 4.

Recording issuance
of common shares
(2)

Exercise 13-7

Sutherland Equipment Ltd. has a choice about how it records the acquisition of property, plant, and equipment in return for shares. Make the journal entries on February 5 for each of the following cases:

Issuing shares to finance the
purchase of assets
(2)

Case A—Issue shares and buy the assets in separate transactions:
Sutherland Equipment Ltd. issued 7,000 common shares for cash of $1,460,000. In a separate transaction, Sutherland then used the cash to purchase an office building for $900,000 and equipment for $560,000. Journalize the two transactions.

Case B—Issue shares to acquire the assets:
Sutherland Equipment Ltd. issued 7,000 common shares to acquire an office building valued at $900,000 and equipment worth $560,000. Journalize this transaction.

Compare the balances in all accounts in Case A and Case B. Are the account balances similar or different?

Exercise 13-8

Issuing shares and preparing the shareholders' equity section of the balance sheet

(2)

2. Total shareholders' equity, $465,000

The articles of incorporation for Mid-way Consulting Inc. authorize the company to issue 500,000 $5 preferred shares and 1,000,000 common shares. During its first year of operations, Mid-way Consulting Inc. completed the following selected transactions:

2017

Jan.   4   Issued 5,000 common shares to the consultants who formed the corporation, receiving cash of $140,000.

       13   Issued 500 preferred shares for cash of $55,000.

       14   Issued 4,000 common shares in exchange for land valued at $120,000.

Dec. 31   Earned a profit for the fiscal year and closed the $150,000 net income into Retained Earnings.

Required

1. Record the transactions in the general journal.
2. Prepare the shareholders' equity section of the Mid-way Consulting Inc. balance sheet at December 31, 2017.

Exercise 13-9

Contributed capital for a corporation

(2)

Total contributed capital, $520,000

Yippee Corp. has recently incorporated. The company issued common shares to a lawyer who provided legal services worth $7,500 to help organize the corporation. It issued common shares to another person in exchange for his patent with a market value of $50,000. In addition, Yippee Corp. received cash both for 2,500 of its $1.50 preferred shares at $10.00 per share and for 35,000 of its common shares at $12.50 per share. Without making journal entries, determine the total contributed capital created by these transactions.

Exercise 13-10

Shareholders' equity section of a balance sheet

(2)

2. Total shareholders' equity, $271,500

The articles of incorporation for Novak Technology Inc. authorize the issuance of 100,000 preferred shares and 250,000 common shares. During a two-month period, Novak Technology Inc. completed these share-issuance transactions:

Mar. 23   Issued 12,000 common shares for cash of $10.00 per share.

Apr. 12   Received inventory valued at $60,000 and equipment with a market value of $10,000 for 5,000 common shares.

       17   Issued 1,500 $2.25 preferred shares. The issue price was cash of $11.00 per share.

Required

1. Journalize the transactions, with explanations.
2. Prepare the shareholders' equity section of the Novak Technology Inc. balance sheet for the transactions given in this exercise. Retained Earnings has a balance of $65,000.

Exercise 13-11

Excel Spreadsheet Template
Shareholders' equity section of a balance sheet

(2)

Total shareholders' equity, $284,500

Skeet Corporation has the following selected account balances at June 30, 2017. Prepare the shareholders' equity section of the company's balance sheet.

Common Shares,		Inventory	$70,000
500,000 shares authorized,		Machinery and Equipment	82,500
100,000 shares issued	$100,000	Preferred Shares, $1.25,	
Accumulated Amortization—		100,000 shares authorized,	
Machinery and Equipment	32,500	10,000 shares issued	87,500
Retained Earnings	97,000	Organization Costs, net	2,500
Cost of Goods Sold	42,500		

Exercise 13-12

The following is an alphabetical list of accounts of CHFI Services Inc. as at January 31, 2016. The balances are *prior* to the closing journal entries. All accounts have normal balances.

Balance sheet presentation

(2)

Total assets, $4,634,000

Accrued Liabilities	$ 50,400
Accounts Payable	90,000
Accounts Receivable, net	318,000
Cash	494,000
Common Shares, 500,000 shares authorized; 200,000 shares issued	2,500,000
Interest Expense	29,000
Inventory	420,000
Long-term Note Payable	600,000
Organization Costs	18,000
Prepaid Expenses	3,600
Preferred Shares, $2.50, cumulative, 24,000 authorized and issued	240,000
Property, Plant, and Equipment, net	3,360,000
Retained Earnings	623,600
Trademark, net	20,400

Additional information:

Net income for 2016 was $530,000.

No new shares were issued in 2016.

Required Prepare a classified balance sheet as at January 31, 2016.

Exercise 13-13

Melbourne Incorporated has 75,000 shares of $2 cumulative preferred shares outstanding as well as 110,000 common shares. There are no dividends in arrears on the preferred shares. The following transactions were reported during November 2016:

Accounting for cash dividends

(3)

Nov. 1 Declared the required dividend on the preferred shares and a $0.23 per share dividend on the common shares.

14 The date of record for the dividend declared on November 1.

28 Paid the dividend declared on November 1.

30 Closed out the Income Summary account. Net income for the year was $257,000.

Required

1. Prepare journal entries to record the above transactions. No explanations are required.
2. Assuming the balance of Retained Earnings on December 1, 2015, was $52,100, determine the balance of Retained Earnings on November 30, 2016.

Exercise 13-14

Refer to the shareholders' equity of Longbourn Golf & Resort Corporation (Longbourn) in Exhibit 13-7, page 741. Answer these questions about Longbourn's dividends:

Dividing cash dividends between preferred and common shares

(3)

4. Common, $35,000

1. How much in dividends must Longbourn declare each year before the common shareholders receive cash dividends for the year?
2. Suppose Longbourn declares cash dividends of $20,000 for 2017. How much of the dividends go to preferred shareholders? How much goes to common shareholders?
3. Are Longbourn's preferred shares cumulative or noncumulative? How can you tell?
4. Suppose Longbourn did not pay the preferred dividend in 2015 and 2016. In 2017, Longbourn declares cash dividends of $40,000. How much of the dividends go to preferred shareholders? How much goes to common shareholders?

Exercise 13–15

Computing dividends on
preferred and common shares

③

Common gets $35,000

The following elements of shareholders' equity are adapted from the balance sheet of Brzynski Marketing Ltd.:

Shareholders' Equity	
Preferred shares, $0.10, cumulative, 100,000 shares authorized, 60,000 shares issued and outstanding	$ 60,000
Common shares, 2,000,000 shares authorized, 900,000 shares issued and outstanding	1,500,000

The company has paid all dividends through 2015.

Required Compute the dividends paid to preferred shareholders and to common shareholders for 2016 and 2017 if total dividends are $0 in 2016, and $47,000 in 2017. Round your answers to the nearest dollar.

Exercise 13–16

Book value per share of
preferred and common shares

④

Common, $12.10 per share

The balance sheet of Nature's Design Technology Inc. reported the following:

Cumulative preferred shares, 300 shares issued and outstanding, liquidation value $15,000	$ 15,000
Common shares, 25,000 shares issued and outstanding	187,500

Assume that Nature's Design had paid preferred dividends for the current year and all prior years (no dividends in arrears). Retained Earnings was $115,000.

Required Compute the book value per share of the preferred shares and the common shares.

Exercise 13–17

Book value per share of
preferred and common shares;
preferred dividends in arrears

③ ④

Preferred, $78.00 per share;
common, $11.76 per share

Refer to Exercise 13–16. Compute the book value per share of the preferred shares and the common shares, assuming that four years of preferred dividends (including dividends for the current year) are in arrears. Assume the preferred shares are cumulative and their dividend rate is $7.00 per share.

Exercise 13–18

Evaluating profitability

⑤

ROA, 8.45%

Woldenga Equipment Inc. reported the figures shown below for 2017 and 2016:

	2017	2016
Income statement:		
Interest expense	$ 5,200	$ 3,700
Net income	3,250	5,200
Balance sheet:		
Total assets	105,000	95,000
Preferred shares, $1.15, 200 shares issued and outstanding	1,000	1,000
Common shareholders' equity	46,700	43,000
Total shareholders' equity	47,700	44,000

Compute the rate of return on total assets (ROA) and the rate of return on common shareholders' equity (ROE) for 2017. Do these rates of return suggest strength or weakness? Give your reasons.

Exercise 13-19

You have been asked to consider investing in ASAP Printing Services Inc.

ASAP Printing Services Inc.
Balance Sheet
December 31, 2016

Assets			Liabilities		
Current assets:			Current liabilities:		
Cash	$384,000		Accounts payable	$90,000	
Accounts receivable, net	318,000		Accrued liabilities	50,400	
Inventory	420,000		Total current liabilities		$140,400
Prepaid expenses	3,600		Long-term note payable		600,000
Total current assets		$1,125,600	Total liabilities		$740,400
Property, plant, and equipment, net		3,360,000			
Intangible assets:			**Shareholders' Equity**		
Trademark, net	$20,400		Preferred shares, $2.50, cumulative, 24,000, authorized and issued	$ 240,000	
Organization costs	18,000		Common shares, 300,000 shares authorized, 200,000 shares issued	2,500,000	
Total intangible assets		38,400	Retained earnings	1,043,600	
			Total shareholders' equity		3,783,600
Total assets		$4,524,000	Total liabilities and shareholders' equity		$4,524,000

Additional information:

Total assets at January 1, 2016, were $4,100,000.

Net income for 2016 was $420,000.

No new shares were issued in 2016.

Required Calculate the following for 2016:

1. Rate of return on total assets
2. Rate of return on common shareholders' equity
3. If the minimum rate of return for each of the above ratios is 12 percent, will you invest in this business?

SERIAL EXERCISE

This exercise continues the Lee Management Consulting situation from Exercise 12–17 of Chapter 12. If you did not complete any Serial Exercises in earlier chapters, you can still complete Exercise 13–20 as it is presented.

Exercise 13–20

Incorporation of a going concern and corporate transactions

① ②

Michael Lee has been operating Lee Management Consulting as a proprietorship but is planning to expand operations in the near future. In Chapter 12, Michael had considered taking on a partner, but decided not to form a partnership after all. To raise cash for future expansion, he has now decided to incorporate and create Lee Consulting Corporation. He has gone through all the legal steps to incorporate his business; as of August 1, 2016, Lee Consulting Corporation is authorized to issue an unlimited number of common shares and 50,000 $2.00 preferred shares.

The Lee Management Consulting July 31, 2016, balance sheet appears below, adjusted to reflect all amounts at current market value:

Lee Management Consulting Balance Sheet July 31, 2016	
Assets	
Cash	$21,650
Accounts receivable	5,900
Inventory	2,713
Supplies	100
Prepaid rent	6,000
Equipment	1,000
Accumulated amortization—equipment	(75)
Furniture	5,000
Accumulated amortization—furniture	(267)
Total assets	$42,021
Liabilities and Equity	
Accounts payable	$ 9,600
Salary payable	1,000
Unearned service revenue	1,200
Notes payable	0
Michael Lee, capital	30,221
Total liabilities and capital	$42,021

Required

1. Create the journal entry to record the incorporation of the business on August 1, 2016. To do this, you need to record each asset and liability account at its current market value. For equipment and furniture, this would be the net book value of each—there would not be any accumulated amortization accounts at the beginning of the new corporation's life. The Michael Lee, Capital balance would become the value of the 20,000 common shares Michael issues to himself.

2. To raise $50,000 in additional cash, Lee Consulting Corporation issued 1,000 of the preferred shares for $50.00 per share on August 2, 2016. Journalize this transaction.

3. Lee Consulting Corporation incurred $1,500 in legal fees and incorporation fees to organize the corporation under the Canada Business Corporations Act in Ontario. Prepare the journal entry for these organization costs paid on August 5.

CHALLENGE EXERCISE

Mussalem Motors Inc. reported these comparative shareholders' equity data:

Accounting for shareholders' equity transactions
② ③

	December 31,	
	2017	2016
Common shares	$1,530,000	$ 300,000
Retained earnings	2,318,000	1,538,000

During 2017, Mussalem Motors Inc. completed these transactions and events:

   a. Net income, $1,430,000.

   b. Cash dividends, $650,000.

   c. Issuance of common shares for cash, 3,000 shares at $60.00 per share.

   d. Issuance of common shares to purchase another company (Mussalem Motors debited the Investments account), 15,000 shares at $70.00 per share.

Required Without making journal entries, show how Mussalem Motors Inc.'s 2017 transactions and events accounted for the changes in the shareholders' equity accounts. For each shareholders' equity account, start with the December 31, 2016, balance and work toward the balance at December 31, 2017.

BEYOND THE NUMBERS

Beyond the Numbers 13–1

Answer the following questions to enhance your understanding of the shareholders' equity of corporations:

Characteristics of corporations' shareholders' equity
② ④

1. Why do you think contributed capital and retained earnings are shown separately in the shareholders' equity section?

2. Vivien Chan, major shareholder of Nah Inc., proposes to sell some land she owns to the company for common shares in Nah Inc. What problem does Nah Inc. face in recording the transaction?

3. Preferred shares generally have preference over common shares for dividends and on liquidation. Why would investors buy common shares when preferred shares are available?

4. If you owned 100 shares of Tim Hortons Inc. and someone offered to buy the shares for their book value, would you accept the offer? Why or why not?

5. What is a convertible preferred share? Why would an investor exercise the conversion privilege?

ETHICAL ISSUE

Note: This case is based on a real situation.

Jason Wertz paid $50,000 for a franchise that entitled him to market Success software programs in the countries of the European Union. Wertz intended to sell individual franchises for the major language groups of Western Europe—German, French, English, Spanish, and Italian. Naturally, investors considering buying a franchise from Wertz asked to see the financial statements of his business.

Believing the value of the franchise to be greater than $50,000, Wertz sought to capitalize his own franchise at $375,000. The law firm of St. Charles and LaDue helped Wertz form a corporation authorized to issue 500,000 common shares. Lawyers suggested the following chain of transactions:

1. A third party borrows $375,000 and purchases the franchise from Wertz.

2. Wertz pays the corporation $375,000 to acquire all its shares.

3. The corporation buys the franchise from the third party, who repays the loan.

In the final analysis, the third party is debt-free and out of the picture. Wertz owns all the corporation's shares, and the corporation owns the franchise. The corporation's balance sheet lists a franchise acquired at a cost of $375,000. This balance sheet is Wertz's most valuable marketing tool.

Required

1. What is unethical about this situation?
2. Who can be harmed? How can they be harmed? What role does accounting play?

PROBLEMS (GROUP A) MyAccountingLab

Problem 13–1A

Organizing a corporation

(1)

Mark Mathews and Karen Willamas are opening a software company. They have developed a new and effective software to manage small business operations. Their most fundamental decision is how to organize the business. Mathews thinks the partnership form is best. Willamas favours the corporate form of organization. They seek your advice.

Required Write a memo to Mathews and Willamas to make them aware of the advantages and the disadvantages of organizing the business as a corporation. Use the following format for your memo:

Date:	_____
To:	Mark Mathews and Karen Willamas
From:	[Student Name]
Subject:	Advantages and disadvantages of the corporate form of business organization

Problem 13–2A

Journalizing corporation transactions and preparing the shareholders' equity section of the balance sheet

(2)

2. Total shareholders' equity, $667,500

The partnership of Nuan Zhang and Jen Phuah needed additional capital to expand into new markets, so the business incorporated as A-1 Services Inc. The articles of incorporation under the Canada Business Corporations Act authorize A-1 Services Inc. to issue 500,000 $2.50 preferred shares and 2,000,000 common shares. In its first year, A-1 Services Inc. completed the following share-related transactions:

2017

Aug. 2 Paid incorporation fees of $6,000 and paid legal fees of $16,000 to organize as a corporation.

2 Issued 20,000 common shares to Zhang and 25,000 common shares to Phuah in return for cash. Zhang paid $150,000 cash, and Phuah paid $187,500 cash.

Dec. 10 Issued 1,000 preferred shares to acquire a computer system with a market value of $80,000.

16 Issued 15,000 common shares for cash of $120,000.

Required

1. Record the transactions in the general journal.
2. Prepare the shareholders' equity section of the A-1 Services Inc. balance sheet at December 31, 2017. The ending balance in Retained Earnings is $130,000.

Problem 13–3A

Issuing shares and preparing the shareholders' equity section of the balance sheet

(2)

5. Total shareholders' equity, $613,750

Riverbend Inc. was organized in 2016. At December 31, 2016, Riverbend Inc.'s balance sheet reported the following shareholders' equity:

Preferred shares, $4.00, 200,000 shares authorized, none issued	$ 0
Common shares, 1,000,000 shares authorized, 150,000 shares issued and outstanding	225,000
Retained earnings (Deficit)	(50,000)
Total shareholders' equity	$175,000

Required

Answer the following questions, making journal entries as needed:

1. What does the $4.00 mean for the preferred shares? If Riverbend Inc. issues 2,500 preferred shares, how much in cash dividends will it expect to pay?

2. At what average price per share did Riverbend Inc. issue the common shares during 2016?

3. Were first-year operations profitable? Give your reason.

4. During 2017, the company completed the following selected transactions:

   a. Issued for cash 1,500 preferred shares at $20.00 per share.

   b. Issued for cash 5,000 common shares at a price of $1.75 per share.

   c. Issued 100,000 common shares to acquire a building valued at $250,000.

   d. Net income for the year was $150,000, and the company declared no dividends. Make the closing entry for net income.

   Journalize each transaction. Explanations are not required.

5. Prepare the shareholders' equity section of the Riverbend Inc. balance sheet at December 31, 2017.

Problem 13–4A

The following summaries for Ruby Distributors Ltd. and Gem Wholesalers Inc. provide the information needed to prepare the shareholders' equity section of each company's balance sheet. The two companies are independent.

Ruby Distributors Ltd. This company is authorized to issue 150,000 common shares. All the shares were issued at $3.00 per share. The company incurred a net loss of $75,000 in 2014 (its first year of operations) and a net loss of $30,000 in 2015. It earned net incomes of $35,000 in 2016 and $60,000 in 2017. The company declared no dividends during the four-year period.

Gem Wholesalers Inc. Gem Wholesalers Inc.'s articles of incorporation authorize the company to issue 200,000 cumulative preferred shares and 1,000,000 common shares. Gem Wholesalers Inc. issued 2,000 preferred shares at $12.50 per share. It issued 100,000 common shares for $300,000. The company's Retained Earnings balance at the beginning of 2017 was $75,000. Net income for 2017 was $50,000, and the company declared the specified preferred share dividend for 2017. Preferred share dividends for 2016 were in arrears. The preferred dividend was $1.10 per share per year.

Required For each company, prepare the shareholders' equity section of its balance sheet at December 31, 2017. Show the computation of all amounts. Journal entries are not required.

Problem 13–5A

Redfern Limited reported the following information in its December 31, 2016, annual report:

Shareholders' Equity	
Preferred shares, $2.75, cumulative,	
600,000 shares authorized, 100,000 shares issued and outstanding	$ 400,000
Common shares, unlimited number of shares	
authorized, 1,300,000 shares issued and outstanding	1,850,000
Retained earnings	5,850,000
Total shareholders' equity	$8,100,000

Required

1. Identify the different issues of shares that Redfern Limited has outstanding.

2. What is the average issue price per preferred share?

3. Make two summary journal entries to record issuance of all the Redfern shares for cash on March 1, 2017. Explanations are not required.

4. Assume no preferred dividends are in arrears. Journalize the declaration of a $400,000 dividend at June 30, 2017. Use separate Dividends Payable accounts for preferred and common shares. An explanation is not required.

Excel Spreadsheet Template
 Shareholders' equity section of the balance sheet
② ③
Ruby Distributors Ltd.
Total shareholders' equity, $440,000

Analyzing the shareholders' equity of a corporation
② ③

Excel Spreadsheet
Template
Computing dividends on preferred and common shares
(3)
1. b. 2015: Common, $64,000

Problem 13–6A

Rainy Day Corporation has 50,000 $0.50 preferred shares and 600,000 common shares issued and outstanding. During a three-year period, Rainy Day Corporation declared and paid cash dividends as follows: 2014, $0; 2015, $114,000; and 2016, $260,000.

Required

1. Compute the total dividends to preferred shares and common shares for each of the three years if

    a. Preferred shares are noncumulative.

    b. Preferred shares are cumulative.

2. For requirement 1b, record the declaration of the 2016 dividends on December 22, 2016, and the payment of the dividends on January 12, 2017.

Problem 13–7A

Analyzing the shareholders'
equity of a corporation
(3) (4)
4. Book value per share:
Common, $14.36

The balance sheet of Tulameen Systems Inc. reported the following:

Shareholders' Equity	
Preferred shares, cumulative convertible, authorized 25,000 shares	$200,000
Common shares, authorized 50,000 shares, issued 44,000 shares	528,000
Retained earnings	168,000
Total shareholders' equity	$896,000

Notes to the financial statements indicate that 10,000 $1.20 preferred shares were issued and outstanding. The preferred shares have a liquidation value of $24.00 per share. Preferred dividends are in arrears for two years, including the current year. On the balance sheet date, the market value of the Tulameen Systems Inc. common shares was $28.00 per share.

Required

1. Are the preferred shares cumulative or noncumulative? How can you tell?
2. What is the total contributed capital of the company?
3. What is the total market value of the common shares?
4. Compute the book value per share of the preferred shares and of the common shares.

Problem 13–8A

Recording the issuance of
shares; allocating cash dividends;
calculating book value; preparing
the liability and shareholders'
equity sections of the balance
sheet
(2) (3) (4)
2. Total shareholders' equity,
$2,430,000

At January 1, 2015, Computer Metals Processing Ltd.'s balance sheet reported the following shareholders' equity:

Shareholders' Equity	
Contributed capital:	
Preferred shares, $1.25, cumulative (2 years in arrears), liquidation price of $20, 100,000 shares authorized, 30,000 shares issued and outstanding	$ 200,000
Common shares:	
Class A, 20,000 shares authorized and issued and outstanding	125,000
Class B, unlimited number of shares authorized, 150,000 shares issued and outstanding	1,500,000
Total contributed capital	1,825,000
Retained earnings	300,000
Total shareholders' equity	$2,125,000

The company had the following transactions on the dates indicated:

2015

Dec. 1 The company declared dividends of $180,000, payable on January 15, 2016, to the shareholders of record on December 31. Indicate the amount that would be payable to the preferred shareholders and to the common shareholders. The dividend rate for Class A and Class B shares is the same.

31 The company reported net income after taxes of $60,000 for the year and then closed the Income Summary account.

2016

Jan. 7 The company sold 10,000 preferred shares at $23.50 per share.

15 The company paid the dividend declared on December 1, 2015.

Feb. 14 The company sold 15,000 Class B common shares at $11.00 per share.

Dec. 2 The company declared dividends of $120,000, payable on January 15, 2017, to the shareholders of record on December 31, 2016. Indicate the amount that would be payable to the preferred shareholders and to the common shareholders.

31 The company reported net income after taxes of $145,000 and then closed the Income Summary account.

2017

Jan. 15 Paid the dividend declared on December 2, 2016.

Required

1. Record the transactions in the general journal.
2. Prepare the liability and shareholders' equity sections of the balance sheet as of the close of business on December 31, 2016.
3. Calculate the book value per share of the preferred shares and of the common shares (Class A and Class B combined) on December 31, 2016.
4. What was the average price at which the Class A common shares were issued?

Problem 13–9A

The following accounts and related balances of Etse Manufacturing Inc. are arranged in no particular order:

Preparing a corporation's balance sheet; measuring profitability
② ⑤

Accounts Payable	$ 36,000	Accrued Liabilities	$ 23,000
Retained Earnings	?	Long-term Note Payable	100,500
Common Shares,		Accounts Receivable, net	100,000
100,000 shares		Preferred Shares, $0.15	
authorized, 33,000 shares		25,000 shares authorized,	
issued and outstanding	165,000	6,000 shares issued	30,000
Dividends Payable	4,500	Cash	35,000
Total assets, Dec. 31, 2016	567,500	Inventory	190,500
Net income	140,750	Property, Plant, and	
Common Shareholders'		Equipment, net	381,000
Equity, Dec. 31, 2016	520,000	Prepaid Expenses	15,500
Interest Expense	10,850	Patent, net	37,000

Required

1. Prepare the company's classified balance sheet in the report format at December 31, 2017.
2. Compute the rate of return on total assets and the rate of return on common shareholders' equity for the year ended December 31, 2017.
3. Do these rates of return suggest strength or weakness? Give your reason.

PROBLEMS (GROUP B)

Problem 13–1B

Organizing a corporation

(1)

Jack Rudd and Pam Kines are opening an office supply store. The area where the store is located is growing, and no competitors are located in the immediate vicinity. Their most fundamental decision is how to organize the business. Rudd thinks the partnership form is best. Kines favours the corporate form of organization. They seek your advice.

Required Write a memo to Rudd and Kines to make them aware of the advantages and disadvantages of organizing the business as a corporation. Use the following format for your memo:

Date:	_____
To:	Jack Rudd and Pam Kines
From:	[Student Name]
Subject:	Advantages and disadvantages of the corporate form of business organization

Problem 13–2B

Journalizing corporation transactions and preparing the shareholders' equity section of the balance sheet

(2)

The articles of incorporation authorize Gingrich Solutions Ltd. to issue 100,000 $2.00 preferred shares and 250,000 common shares. In its first year, Gingrich Solutions Ltd. completed the following selected transactions:

2017

Jan. 2 Paid incorporation costs of $2,500 and legal fees of $6,000 to organize as a corporation.

6 Issued 20,000 common shares for equipment with a market value of $175,000.

12 Issued 100 preferred shares to acquire software with a market value of $19,500.

22 Issued 5,000 common shares for $7.00 cash per share.

Required

1. Record the transactions in the general journal.

2. Prepare the shareholders' equity section of the Gingrich Solutions Ltd. balance sheet at December 31, 2017. The ending Retained Earnings balance is $60,000.

Problem 13–3B

Issuing shares and preparing the shareholders' equity section of the balance sheet

(2)

Sloboda Corporation was organized in 2016. At December 31, 2016, Sloboda Corporation's balance sheet reported the following shareholders' equity:

Preferred shares, $0.20, 50,000 shares authorized, none issued	$ 0
Common shares, 100,000 shares authorized, 10,000 shares issued and outstanding	87,500
Retained earnings (Deficit)	(20,000)
Total shareholders' equity	$67,500

Required

1. What does the $0.20 mean for the preferred shares? If Sloboda Corporation issued 4,000 preferred shares, how much in cash dividends will Sloboda Corporation expect to pay per year?

2. At what average price per share did Sloboda Corporation issue the common shares?

3. Were first-year operations profitable? Give your reason.

4. During 2017, the company completed the following selected transactions. Journalize each transaction. Explanations are not required.

   a. Issued for cash 10,000 preferred shares at $2.50 per share.

   b. Issued for cash 1,000 common shares at a price of $9.00 per share.

c. Issued 25,000 common shares to acquire a building valued at $235,000.

d. Net income for the year was $62,500, and the company declared no dividends. Make the closing entry for net income.

5. Prepare the shareholders' equity section of the Sloboda Corporation balance sheet at December 31, 2017.

Problem 13–4B

Excel Spreadsheet Template
Shareholders' equity section of the balance sheet
② ③

Shareholders' equity information is given for Rexell Inc. and Raonic Corp. The two companies are independent.

Rexell Inc. Rexell Inc. is authorized to issue 100,000 common shares. All the shares were issued at $10.00 per share. The company incurred a net loss of $30,000 in 2015, its first year of business. It earned net income of $45,000 in 2016 and $50,000 in 2017. The company declared no dividends during the three-year period.

Raonic Corp. Raonic Corp.'s articles of incorporation authorize the company to issue 50,000 $1.25 cumulative preferred shares and 500,000 common shares. Raonic Corp. issued 4,000 preferred shares at $10.00 per share. It issued 60,000 common shares for a total of $150,000. The company's Retained Earnings balance at the beginning of 2017 was $55,000, and net income for the year was $62,500. During 2017, the company declared the specified dividend on preferred shares and a $0.50 per share dividend on common shares. Preferred dividends for 2016 were in arrears.

Required For each company, prepare the shareholders' equity section of its balance sheet at December 31, 2017. Show the computation of all amounts. Journal entries are not required.

Problem 13–5B

Analyzing the shareholders' equity of a corporation
② ③

Reckless Phones Ltd. included the following shareholders' equity on its year-end balance sheet at December 31, 2017:

Shareholders' Equity	
Preferred shares, $0.25, cumulative, unlimited authorization, 10,000 shares issued and outstanding	$ 32,500
Common shares, unlimited authorization, 230,000 shares issued and outstanding	100,000
Retained earnings	1,000,000
Total shareholders' equity	$1,132,500

Required

1. Identify the different issues of shares that Reckless has outstanding.

2. Are the preferred shares cumulative or noncumalative? How can you tell?

3. Give two summary journal entries to record issuance of all the Reckless shares on August 31, 2017. All the shares were issued for cash. Explanations are not required.

4. Assume that preferred dividends are in arrears for 2016. Record the declaration of a $15,000 dividend on December 31, 2017. Use separate Dividends Payable accounts for preferred shares and common shares.

Problem 13–6B

Excel Spreadsheet Template
Computing dividends on preferred and common shares
③

Tijiu Broadcasting Inc. has 15,000 $2.50 preferred shares and 75,000 common shares outstanding. Tijiu Broadcasting Inc. declared and paid the following dividends during a three-year period: 2015, $45,000; 2016, $0; and 2017, $120,000.

Required

1. Compute the total dividends on preferred shares and common shares for each of the three years if

   a. Preferred shares are noncumulative.

   b. Preferred shares are cumulative.

2. For Requirement 1(b), record the declaration of the 2017 dividends on December 28, 2017, and the payment of the dividends on January 17, 2018. Use separate Dividends Payable accounts for preferred shares and common shares.

Problem 13–7B

Analyzing the shareholders' equity of a corporation ③ ④

The balance sheet of Sonic Sales Limited reported the following at December 31, 2017:

Shareholders' Equity	
Preferred shares, redeemable, nonvoting, cumulative, authorized 16,000 shares, liquidation value $350,000	$350,000
Common shares, authorized 200,000 shares, issued 90,000 shares	340,000
Retained earnings	120,000
Total shareholders' equity	$810,000

Notes to the financial statements indicate that 16,000 of the cumulative preferred shares were issued and outstanding. The shares paid a dividend of $1.40. Preferred dividends have not been paid for three years, including the current year. On the balance sheet date, the market value of Sonic Sales Limited's common shares was $3.00 per share.

Required

1. Are the preferred shares cumulative or noncumulative? How can you tell?
2. Which class of shareholders controls the company? Give your reason.
3. What is the total contributed capital of the company?
4. What was the total market value of the common shares?
5. Compute the book value per share of the preferred shares and the common shares.

Problem 13–8B

Recording the issuance of shares; allocating cash dividends; calculating book value; preparing the shareholders' equity section of the balance sheet ② ③ ④

At January 1, 2015, Bohemia Nursery Ltd.'s balance sheet reported the following shareholders' equity:

Shareholders' Equity	
Contributed capital:	
Preferred shares, $0.75, cumulative (3 years in arrears), liquidation price of $25, 100,000 shares authorized, 40,000 shares issued and outstanding	$ 800,000
Common shares:	
Class A, 15,000 shares authorized, issued, and outstanding	120,000
Class B, unlimited number of shares authorized, 75,000 shares issued and outstanding	375,000
Total contributed capital	1,295,000
Retained earnings	300,000
Total shareholders' equity	$1,595,000

The company had the following transactions on the dates indicated:

2015

Dec.   1 The company declared dividends of $170,000, payable on January 14, 2016, to the shareholders of record on December 31, 2015. Indicate the amount that would be payable to the preferred shareholders and to the common shareholders. Class A and Class B shares receive the same per-share dividend.

      31 The company reported net income after taxes of $80,000 and closed the Income Summary account.

2016

Jan. 7 The company sold 10,000 preferred shares at $22.50 per share.

14 The company paid the dividend declared on December 1, 2015.

Feb. 14 The company sold 15,000 Class B common shares at $5.00 per share.

Dec. 2 The company declared dividends of $75,000, payable on January 13, 2017, to the shareholders of record on December 31, 2016. Indicate the amount that would be payable to the preferred shareholders and to the common shareholders.

31 The company reported net income after taxes of $63,000 and closed the Income Summary account.

2017

Jan. 13 Paid the dividend declared on December 2, 2016.

Required

1. Record the transactions in the general journal.

2. Prepare the shareholders' equity section of the balance sheet as of the close of business on December 31, 2016.

3. Calculate the book value per share of the preferred shares and of the common shares on December 31, 2016.

4. What was the average price at which the Class A common shares were issued?

Problem 13–9B

The accounts and related balances of Labelle Systems Ltd. are arranged in no particular order:

Preparing a corporation's balance sheet; measuring profitability
② ⑤

Trademark, net............................$19,000		Common Shareholders'	
Preferred Shares, $0.20,		Equity, June 30, 2016	$200,000
10,000 shares authorized,		Net income	25,000
issued and outstanding........ 29,500		Total assets, June 30, 2016...................	410,000
Cash... 15,000		Interest Expense	7,200
Accounts Receivable, net 52,500		Property, Plant, and	
Accrued Liabilities.................... 30,000		Equipment, net	300,000
Long-term Note Payable.......... 48,500		Common Shares, 500,000	
Inventory.................................... 93,500		shares authorized; 272,000	
Dividends Payable.................... 10,500		shares issued and outstanding......	300,000
Retained Earnings...................... ?		Prepaid Expenses	12,000
Accounts Payable...................... 36,000			

Required

1. Prepare the company's classified balance sheet in report format at June 30, 2017.

2. Compute the rate of return on total assets and the rate of return on common shareholders' equity for the year ended June 30, 2017.

3. Do these rates of return suggest strength or weakness? Give your reason.

CHALLENGE PROBLEMS

Problem 13–1C

Your friend Bryan McNair has come to you for advice. He has a very successful antiques store that had sales of more than $800,000 in the year just ended. He would like to expand and will need to borrow $350,000 to finance an enlarged inventory. He has learned that he can buy the store adjoining his for $250,000 and estimates that $60,000 of renovations would be needed to make the store compatible with his present store. Expansion would mean adding three or four employees to the current two employees.

The pros and cons of incorporation
①

Bryan's accountant has suggested that he incorporate his business and that Bryan hold all the shares. He has cited several reasons to Bryan, including the benefits of limited liability. Bryan has talked to his banker about the possibility of incorporating; the banker has pointed out that if Bryan does incorporate, the bank will need personal guarantees for any loans Bryan arranges with the bank.

Required Consider Bryan's situation and discuss the pros and cons of incorporation for Bryan. What would you suggest?

Problem 13–2C

Issuing shares; preparing and analyzing the shareholders' equity section

②

Franklin Technologies Inc., incorporated under the Canada Business Corporations Act, had three transactions during the year ended December 31, 2017, involving its common shares. On January 15, 2017, 50,000 Class A voting shares were issued at their stated value of $8.00 per share. On February 28, 2017, 10,000 Class B nonvoting shares were issued at their stated value of $10.00 per share. On August 8, 2017, 15,000 Class B shares were issued in exchange for land with a market value of $165,000. Franklin's articles of incorporation state that 100,000 Class A voting and 200,000 Class B nonvoting common shares are authorized.

Required

1. Prepare the journal entry to record the transaction of January 15, 2017.
2. Prepare the journal entry to record the transaction of February 28, 2017.
3. Prepare the journal entry to record the transaction of August 8, 2017.
4. Create the shareholders' equity section for Franklin Technologies Inc. after the three transactions have taken place. Assume Retained Earnings was $100,000 at this time.
5. What was the average issue price of each Class B common share?
6. How did Franklin Technologies Inc. withhold the voting privilege from its Class B common shareholders?

Problem 13–3C

Deciding on an investment in shares; evaluating different types of shares

④ ⑤

You have just received a bequest of $2,000 from an aunt and you have decided to invest the money in shares of Electronic Recycling Inc., a company that is listed on the Toronto Stock Exchange. Electronic Recycling Inc. (ERI) has common shares; cumulative preferred shares; noncumulative, convertible preferred shares; and noncumulative preferred shares. The common shares are trading at $40.00 and currently are paying a dividend of $2.40 per share. The cumulative preferred shares are selling at $50.00 and have a stated dividend of $3.50. The convertible preferred shares are selling for $78.50 and are convertible at the rate of 2 common for 1 preferred; the dividend rate is $5.30. The noncumulative preferred shares are trading at $25.00 and have a dividend rate of $1.55.

Required Evaluate each of the four different shares as an investment opportunity. After performing your analysis, select which shares you will buy and explain your choice.

EXTENDING YOUR KNOWLEDGE

DECISION PROBLEM

Evaluating alternative ways of raising capital

②

Kimberly Carlyle and Erron Friesen have written a spreadsheet program (Viacalc) to rival Excel. They need additional capital to market the product, and they plan to incorporate the business. They are considering the capital structure. Their primary goal is to raise as much capital as possible without giving up control of the business. Carlyle and Friesen plan to sell the Viacalc software to the corporation in exchange for 100,000 common shares. The partners have been offered $100,000 for the software.

The corporation's plans for the articles of incorporation include an authorization to issue 10,000 preferred shares and 1,000,000 common shares. Carlyle and Friesen are uncertain about the most desirable features for the preferred shares. Prior to incorporating, the partners have discussed their plans with two investment groups. The corporation can obtain capital from outside investors under either of the following plans:

Plan 1 Group 1 will invest $100,000 to acquire 1,000 shares of $7.50, cumulative preferred shares and $72,000 to acquire 60,000 common shares. Each preferred share will receive 50 votes if preferred dividends are more than two years in arrears.

Plan 2 Group 2 will invest $150,000 to acquire 1,200 shares of $8.50 nonvoting, noncumulative preferred shares.

Required Assume the corporation receives its articles of incorporation.

1. Journalize the issuance of common shares to Kimberly Carlyle and Erron Friesen.
2. Journalize the issuance of shares to the outsiders under both plans.
3. Assume that net income for the first year is $184,000, and total dividends of $34,800 are properly subtracted from retained earnings. Prepare the shareholders' equity section of the corporation's balance sheet under both plans.
4. Recommend one of the plans to Carlyle and Friesen. Give your reasons.

FINANCIAL STATEMENT CASES

Financial Statement Case 1

The Indigo Books & Music Inc. fiscal 2014 financial statements appear in Appendix A at the end of this book and on MyAccountingLab. Answer the following questions about the company's share capital:

Shareholders' equity
②

1. Where can you find information about Indigo's share capital? What classes of shares does Indigo have issued and outstanding? How many shares are authorized and how many are issued and outstanding?
2. Were any shares issued during the year? How do you know?

Financial Statement Case 2

The TELUS Communications Corp. 2013 financial statements appear on MyAccountinglab. Answer the following questions about the company's share capital:

Shareholders' equity
②
4. Basic EPS, $2.02

1. What classes of shares has TELUS issued? How many shares are authorized and how many are issued and outstanding?
2. What change was made to the common shares?
3. What is the book value per share at December 31, 2013? The market price of the shares closed at $36.49 on that date. Why is the market price different from the book value per share?
4. What did TELUS earn per common share in 2013? Where did you find that information?

IFRS MINI-CASE

Plaid Robots Inc. is a small, privately held corporation that had a great first year of operations. Management is considering taking the company public in the next three to five years. Since this is its first year of operations, its CEO, Pete Seckler, must now ask the accounting department to prepare its year-end financial statements. He still hasn't decided if the company will report using accounting standards for private enterprises (ASPE) or international financial reporting standards (IFRS). Pete has heard that there is "more" disclosure needed if the company follows IFRS but does not know what that means. Since he is not an accountant, he would like to see the shareholders' equity section of the balance sheet for this company prepared under both ASPE and IFRS to see for himself what all the fuss is about.

The following information is available to you to prepare the comparison:

- 250,000 Class A common shares were issued and outstanding at $5 each. There are 1,000,000 authorized Class A shares.
- 400,000 Class B common shares have been authorized but none have been issued.
- 10,000 preferred shares were issued and outstanding at $10 each, 50,000 authorized.
- Net income for the period May 1, 2016, to April 30, 2017, was $110,000.

Required

1. Prepare the shareholders' equity section of the balance sheet as it would be presented under ASPE. Use the minimum acceptable disclosure.
2. Prepare the shareholders' equity section of the balance sheet as it would be presented if Plaid Robots reported under IFRS.
3. Would IFRS allow another presentation than what you have shown in Requirement 2?

>Try It! SOLUTIONS FOR CHAPTER 13

1. *Proprietorship*
   - Legally, the owner and the business are one entity.
   - Limited to the life of the proprietor.
   - Unlimited liability of the owner.
   - Management by owner.
   - Business income is included in calculating the owner's taxable income.

   Corporation
   - Separate legal entity.
   - Continuous life.
   - Limited liability of shareholders.
   - Often has separation of ownership and management.
   - Pays corporate income tax.
   - May incur additional costs compared to proprietorships.

2. The authority structure in a corporation typically begins with the *shareholders*, who have the ultimate control in a corporation. The shareholders elect a *board of directors*, who elect a *chairperson of the board*. The board and its chairperson elect a *president* or *chief executive officer (CEO)*, who manages day-to-day operations; then *vice-presidents* are hired.

3. a. Jul. 31

Cash	200,000	
Preferred Shares		100,000
Common Shares		100,000
To issue 1,000 preferred shares with a stated value of $100 per share, and 2,000 common shares at $50 per share.		

   b. Contributed capital:

Preferred Shares	$ 100,000
Common Shares	100,000
Total contributed capital	200,000
Retained earnings	50,000
Total shareholders' equity	$250,000

c. Converting preferred shares into common shares occurs at the original value of the preferred shares, not at their current market value.

Preferred Shares	1,000	
Common Shares		1,000
To record conversion of 10 preferred shares into 20 common shares (10 preferred shares × 2 common shares/preferred share).		

4. a. December 16, 2016, declaration of the dividend:

Retained Earnings	50,000	
Dividends Payable		50,000
To declare a dividend on common shares to be paid on January 6, 2017 (200,000 shares × $0.25 per share).		

   January 6, 2017, payment of the dividend:

Dividends Payable	50,000	
Cash		50,000
To pay the dividend on common shares declared on December 16, 2016.		

   b. The balance in Retained Earnings is $200,000 ($250,000 − $50,000). The declaration on December 16, 2016—not the payment on January 6, 2017—reduces Retained Earnings.

5. a. Preferred Shares:

Dividends in arrears ($2.00 × 10,000 × 2 years)	$40,000
Current dividend	20,000
Total to Preferred Shareholder	$60,000
Common Shares:	
Remainder of dividend ($90,000 – $60,000)	30,000
Total dividend	$90,000

b. Dividends will reduce Retained Earnings by $90,000.

6. Shareholders' equity allocated to preferred shareholders:

Preferred shares ($13 × 3,500)	$ 45,500
Dividends in arrears ($45,500 × 7% × 5 years)	15,925
Shareholders' equity for preferred shares	$ 61,425

7. Shareholders' equity allocated to common shareholders:

Total shareholders' equity	$380,000
Less: Shareholders' equity allocated to preferred shareholders	61,425
Shareholders' equity available for common shareholders	$318,575
Book value per common share = ($318,575 ÷ 140,000 shares)	$ 2.28

8. Return on assets is 12.5 percent:

(Net income + Interest expense) ÷ Average total assets
= ($80,000 + $20,000) ÷ [($840,000 + $760,000) ÷ 2]
= $100,000 ÷ $800,000
= 0.125, or 12.5%

9. Return on equity is 20 percent:

(Net income – Preferred dividends) ÷ Average common shareholders' equity
= [$80,000 – ($6.00 × 1,000)] ÷ [($380,000 + $360,000) ÷ 2]
= $74,000 ÷ $370,000
= 0.20, or 20%

10. The return on equity (ROE) is higher than the return on assets (ROA), which indicates that the company is using leverage favourably.

14 CORPORATIONS: RETAINED EARNINGS AND THE INCOME STATEMENT

CONNECTING CHAPTER 14

LEARNING OBJECTIVE (1) Account for stock dividends and stock splits

How do we account for stock dividends and stock splits?

Stock Dividends, page 783
   Reasons for Stock Dividends
   Recording Stock Dividends
Stock Splits, page 785
   Consolidation
   Similarities and Differences between Stock Dividends and Stock Splits

LEARNING OBJECTIVE (2) Account for repurchased shares

Why are shares repurchased, and how do we account for them?

Repurchase of Its Shares by a Corporation, page 788
   Treasury Shares
   Share Repurchases
   Share Repurchase at Average Issue Price
   Share Repurchase below Average Issue Price
   Share Repurchase above Average Issue Price
   Recording the Sale of Repurchased Shares
Ethical and Legal Issues for Share Transactions, page 791

LEARNING OBJECTIVE (3) Prepare a detailed corporate income statement

How do we prepare a corporate income statement?

The Corporate Income Statement, page 792
   Continuing Operations
   Discontinued Operations
   Earnings per Share (EPS)

LEARNING OBJECTIVE (4) Prepare a statement of retained earnings and a statement of shareholders' equity

How do we prepare a statement of retained earnings and a statement of shareholders' equity?

Statement of Retained Earnings, page 798
Statement of Shareholders' Equity, page 799
   Variations in Reporting Shareholders' Equity
Accounting for Errors and Changes in Accounting Policy and Circumstances, page 800
   Errors
   Change in Accounting Policy
   Change in Circumstances
Restrictions on Retained Earnings, page 802
   Appropriations of Retained Earnings
   Limits on Dividends and Share Repurchases

LEARNING OBJECTIVE (5) Identify the impact of IFRS on the income statement and the statement of shareholders' equity

What is the impact of IFRS on the income statement and the statement of shareholders' equity?

The Impact of IFRS on the Income Statement and the Statement of Shareholders' Equity, page 803

MyAccountingLab   The **Summary** for Chapter 14 appears on page 808. This lists all of the MyAccountingLab resources. **Accounting Vocabulary** with definitions for this chapter's material appears on page 809.

Dollarama Inc., Canada's largest dollar store chain, is a retail success story in a market dominated by large, American retailers. In early 2015 it had over 900 locations across Canada. Dollarama carries seasonal and consumable products and general merchandise, all priced at $3 or less.

Dollarama Inc. (listed as DOL on the Toronto Stock Exchange) is a Canadian public corporation. It is unusual because it is still managed by members of the family that started it. The retail enterprise has its roots in a store started in 1910 by Salim Rossy. His chain of stores was expanded by his son George and again by George's son Larry, who founded Dollarama in its present form in 1992.

The corporation went public in 2009. Since then, it has continued to be successful. In fiscal 2015, revenues increased to over $2.3 billion and net income was just over $295 million. One way that companies share these profits is by issuing dividends. Dollarama's shareholders have received increasingly larger dividends each year. In April 2014, the dividend was increased 14 percent to $0.16 per share and remained at that level in 2015.

Senior managers in a corporation have lots of choices available to help them keep investors interested in purchasing their shares. Recently, Dollarama has done this by paying dividends. In 2014, Dollarama's management announced in its "normal course issuer bid" announcement that "The Board of Directors of Dollarama believes that the purchase by Dollarama of its common shares represents an appropriate and desirable use of its available cash to increase shareholder value."[1]

---

[1] Dollarama, "Dollarama Announces the Renewal of Its Normal Course Issuer Bid," press release, June 12, 2014. Retrieved from www.dollarama.com/wp-content/uploads/2014/06/Dollarama-Announces-the-Renewal-of-Normal-Course-Issuer-Bid.pdf.

>Chapter 13

introduced corporations and covered the basics of shareholders' equity. We saw that a corporation's balance sheet is the same as that for a proprietorship or a partnership except for the owner's equity section, which is called shareholders' equity for a corporation and has some different accounts. The topics covered in Chapter 13 apply to private corporations, whose shares tend to be held by a small number of shareholders and are not traded on a stock exchange, as well as public corporations, whose shares trade on stock exchanges.

All corporations' financial reporting is governed by Canadian generally accepted accounting principles (GAAP). Public corporations are governed by International Financial Reporting Standards (IFRS), which are discussed in Learning Objective 5 in this chapter. Private enterprises have a choice to follow either IFRS or Accounting Standards for Private Enterprises (ASPE). While ASPE forms the basis for this textbook, some examples in this chapter use public corporations to illustrate concepts more easily and to acknowledge that the accounting information students will see in the business press and in everyday dealings will be generated mainly by public corporations.

This chapter takes corporate equity a few steps further, as follows:

Chapter 13 covered	Chapter 14 covers
Contributed capital	Retained earnings
Issuing shares	Repurchasing shares
Cash dividends	Stock dividends and stock splits
Corporate balance sheet	Corporate income statement

RETAINED EARNINGS

We have seen that the contributed capital accounts and retained earnings make up the shareholders' equity section of a corporation's balance sheet. We studied contributed capital in Chapter 13. Now let's focus on retained earnings.

Retained Earnings carries the balance of the business's accumulated lifetime net income less all net losses from operations and less all dividends. *Retained* means "held onto" or "kept." The normal balance of Retained Earnings is a credit. A debit balance in Retained Earnings is called a *deficit*. Retained Earnings deficits are not common because they often indicate that the corporation may be facing corporate failure and bankruptcy.

When you read a balance sheet, remember these facts about retained earnings:

- In a proprietorship, investments, net income, and withdrawals are all recorded in the Capital account. In a corporation, *shareholders' equity is split into contributed capital and retained earnings.* The contributed capital section holds capital invested, or contributed. Retained earnings is used to record net income, net loss, and dividends.

- *Credits to the Retained Earnings account arise only from net income.* Retained Earnings shows how much net income a corporation has earned and retained in the business. Its balance is the cumulative, lifetime earnings of the company less all net losses and all dividends.

- *The Retained Earnings account is not a reservoir of cash.* Retained Earnings represents no particular asset. In fact, the corporation may have a large balance in Retained Earnings but too little cash to pay a dividend.

  - To *declare* a dividend, the company must have a credit balance in Retained Earnings both before and after the declaration of dividends.

  - To *pay* the dividend, it must have the cash.

LEARNING TIPS

Remember:

Beginning Retained Earnings

+ Net Income, or

− Net Loss

− Dividends

= Ending Retained Earnings

Retained Earnings

	Beginning
Net loss	balance
Dividends	Net income
	Ending
	balance

KEY POINTS

Retained Earnings is not a cash account. A $500,000 balance in Retained Earnings means that $500,000 of capital has been created by profits left in or reinvested in the business over its lifetime.

- *Retained Earnings' ending balance is computed as follows* (amounts assumed):

Beginning balance	$ 70,000
Add: Net income for the year	80,000
Less: Net loss (none this year)	
Dividends for the year	(50,000)
Ending balance	$100,000

> In a particular year, a corporation can have a net income or a net loss, but not both.

STOCK DIVIDENDS

A **stock dividend**, also called a **share dividend**, is a distribution of a corporation's own shares to its shareholders. Stock dividends are fundamentally different from cash dividends because stock dividends do not give any cash to the shareholders. Stock dividends increase Common Shares and decrease Retained Earnings. Both of these accounts are elements of shareholders' equity, so total shareholders' equity is unchanged. There is merely a transfer from Retained Earnings to Common Shares.

To illustrate the effects of a stock dividend, assume Sugar Bay Parts Inc. offered a 10 percent stock dividend to its shareholders. Since 75,000 shares were issued and outstanding before the stock dividend, then 7,500 new shares would be issued as a result of the stock dividend (75,000 × 10% = 7,500). This gives a total of 82,500 shares issued and outstanding after the stock dividend (75,000 + 7,500 = 82,500). Assume the market price of the shares was $1.50 per share on the date of the stock dividend, so the total value of the new 7,500 shares is $11,250.

The shareholders' equity section of Sugar Bay Parts Inc. before and after the stock dividend appears in Exhibit 14–1. Notice the change in the Retained Earnings and Common Shares balances after the stock dividend—each balance has changed by the $11,250 value of the 7,500 shares from the stock dividend. Total shareholders' equity is unchanged.

> **LO 1**
> *How do we account for stock dividends and stock splits?*

EXHIBIT 14–1 | Effects of a Stock Dividend

Before		After		
Shareholders' equity:		Shareholders' equity:		
Retained earnings	$150,000	Retained earnings	$138,750	↓ by $11,250
Common shares (75,000)	100,000	Common shares (82,500)	111,250	↑ by $11,250
Total shareholders' equity		Total shareholders'		
	$250,000	equity	$250,000	

Suppose you owned 20 percent of Sugar Bay Parts Inc.'s shares before the stock dividend, which is 15,000 shares (75,000 × 20% = 15,000). A 10 percent stock dividend gives you 1,500 new shares (15,000 × 10% = 1,500), for a total of 16,500 shares (15,000 + 1,500 = 16,500). After the stock dividend you still own 20 percent of the total shares (16,500 ÷ 82,500 = 20%). This proves that you are in the same relative ownership position (20 percent ownership) after the stock dividend as you were before the stock dividend.

Amount of Retained Earnings Transferred in a Stock Dividend Stock dividends are said to be **capitalized retained earnings** because they transfer an amount from retained earnings to contributed capital. The contributed capital accounts are more permanent than retained earnings because they cannot be paid out as dividends.

KEY POINTS

When a shareholder receives a stock dividend, the shareholder's percentage ownership in the company does not change.

Many shareholders view stock dividends as distributions that are little different from cash dividends.

Stock dividends, like cash dividends, are taxable in the hands of the recipient. The value of the stock dividend is equal to the amount of the increase in the capital of the company paying the dividend. The increase is usually the fair market value of the shares issued.

Reasons for Stock Dividends

Why do companies issue stock dividends?

- *To continue dividends but conserve cash.* A company may wish to continue dividends in some form but may need to keep its cash in the business.

- *To reduce the market price per share of its shares.* For companies whose shares trade on a stock exchange, a stock dividend may cause the market price of a company's shares to fall because of the increased supply of the shares. Fairfax Financial Holdings Limited's common shares traded at $687 in January 2015. If the company doubled the number of its shares outstanding by issuing a stock dividend, the market price of the shares would likely drop by approximately half. The objective of such a large stock dividend would be to make the shares less expensive and thus more affordable and attractive to investors.

Recording Stock Dividends

As with a cash dividend, there are three key dates for a stock dividend:

1 Declaration date. The board of directors announces stock dividends on the declaration date. The declaration of a stock dividend does *not* create a liability because the corporation is not obligated to pay out assets. (Recall that a liability is a claim on *assets*.) Instead, the corporation has declared its intention to distribute its shares.

2 Date of record.

3 Distribution date (payment date).

One concern about stock dividends is how to determine the amount to transfer from Retained Earnings to the Common Shares account. The Canada Business Corporations Act suggests that the market value of the shares issued is the appropriate amount to transfer, while other incorporating acts allow the directors to set a value on the shares. If market value were to be used, it would be the market value on the date the dividend is declared. This is the valuation used in this text.

Assume Tweeter Corporation has the following shareholders' equity prior to a stock dividend:

Shareholders' Equity	
Contributed capital	
Common shares, 100,000 shares authorized, 40,000 shares issued	$400,000
Retained earnings	100,000
Total shareholders' equity	$500,000

Assume Tweeter Corporation declares a 10 percent common stock dividend on November 17. The company will distribute 4,000 (40,000 × 0.10) shares in the dividend. On November 17, the market value of its common shares is $16.00 per share. Using the market value approach, Tweeter Corporation makes the following entry on the declaration date:

1 Nov. 17	Retained Earnings	64,000	
	Common Stock Dividend Distributable		64,000
	To declare a 10 percent common stock dividend. (40,000 × 0.10 × $16)		

The accounting equation for this transaction shows that a stock dividend does not affect assets, liabilities, or total shareholders' equity. It merely rearranges the information within the shareholders' equity accounts.

Assets	=	Liabilities	+	Shareholders' Equity	
				−64,000	Retained Earnings
0	=	0		+64,000	Common Stock Dividend Distributable

If the company prepares financial statements after the declaration of the stock dividend but before issuing it, Common Stock Dividend Distributable is reported in the shareholders' equity section of the balance sheet immediately after Common Shares. However, this account holds the value of the dividend shares only from the declaration date to the date of distribution.

On the distribution date, the company records issuance of the dividend shares as follows:

KEY POINTS

Never credit a payable account for a stock dividend. No liability is created when a stock dividend is declared, as compared to a cash dividend, which does create a liability.

❸ Dec. 12	Common Stock Dividend Distributable	64,000	
	Common Shares		64,000
	To issue common shares in a stock dividend.		

The following tabulation shows the changes in shareholders' equity caused by the stock dividend:

Shareholders' Equity	Before the Dividend	After the Dividend	Change
Contributed capital			
Common shares, 100,000 shares authorized			
40,000 shares issued	$400,000		
44,000 shares issued		$464,000	Up by $64,000
Total contributed capital	400,000	464,000	**Up by $64,000**
Retained earnings	100,000	36,000	**Down by $64,000**
Total shareholders' equity	$500,000	$500,000	Unchanged

STOCK SPLITS

A **stock split** is fundamentally different from a stock dividend. A stock split increases the number of authorized and outstanding shares with a proportionate reduction in the book value per share. For example, if the company splits its stock 2 for 1, the number of outstanding shares is doubled and each share's book value is halved. Many large companies in Canada—Lululemon Athletica Inc., Scotiabank, Loblaw Companies Limited, and others—have split their stock.

Assume that the market price of one common share of Marcato Corp. is $100 and that the company wishes to decrease the market price to approximately $50. Marcato decides to split the common shares 2 for 1 in the expectation that the share's market price would fall from $100 to $50. A 2-for-1 stock split means that the company would have two times as many shares outstanding after the split as it had before and that each share's book value would be halved. Assume Marcato had 400,000 common shares issued and outstanding before the split. Exhibit 14–2 shows how a 2-for-1 stock split affects Marcato Corp.'s shareholders' equity:

- It doubles the number of shares authorized and issued.
- It leaves all account balances and total shareholders' equity unchanged.

REAL WORLD EXAMPLE

Stock splits are more common than stock dividends. Bell Canada Enterprises has split its stock three times: 4 for 1 in 1948, 3 for 1 in 1979, and 2 for 1 in 1997.

EXHIBIT 14–2 | A 2-for-1 Stock Split

Shareholders' Equity before 2-for-1 Stock Split		Shareholders' Equity after 2-for-1 Stock Split	
Contributed capital		Contributed capital	
Common shares, unlimited number of shares authorized,		Common shares, unlimited number of shares authorized,	
400,000 shares issued and outstanding	$4,000,000	800,000 shares issued and outstanding	$4,000,000
Retained earnings	1,800,000	Retained earnings	1,800,000
Total shareholders' equity	$5,800,000	Total shareholders' equity	$5,800,000

Because the stock split affects no account balances, no formal journal entry is necessary. Instead, the split is often recorded in a **memorandum entry**—a note in the journal without debits or credits—such as the following:

Aug. 19	Distributed one new common share for each old share previously outstanding. This increased the number of common shares issued and outstanding from 400,000 to 800,000.

Consolidation

REAL WORLD EXAMPLE

Luna Gold Corporation, a Vancouver gold exploration company, consolidated its shares in early 2012 when it was selling at $0.64 per share. The 1-for-5 consolidation raised the share price to $3.20 on the day it happened.

A company may engage in a **consolidation** (or **reverse split**) to decrease the number of shares outstanding and increase the market price per share. If the number of shares outstanding is decreased, then existing shareholders may have a better chance of maintaining control over a corporation's shares. There are fewer shares available to be traded and purchased by new shareholders. For example, Marcato Corp. could consolidate its stock 1 for 4, which would reduce the number of shares issued from 400,000 to 100,000 and increase the share price from, for example, $25 per share to $100 per share. Consolidations are rare but are sometimes done to allow companies to continue trading their shares on stock exchanges that require a minimum share price if the company's share price falls below the minimum.

Similarities and Differences between Stock Dividends and Stock Splits

A 2-for-1 stock split and a 100 percent stock dividend appear remarkably similar on the surface, but there are a number of differences between the two choices.

Similarities

- Both increase the number of shares owned per shareholder.
- Neither a stock dividend nor a stock split changes the investor's total cost of the shares owned. For example, assume you paid $32,000 to acquire 1,000 common shares of LOM Ltd. In both cases, your 1,000 shares increase to 2,000, but your total cost is still $32,000.
- Both a stock dividend and a stock split increase the corporation's number of shares issued and outstanding. The number of authorized shares also increases unless they were unlimited to begin with.
- Both double the outstanding shares and are likely to initially cut the stock's market price per share in half.

Differences

- Stock splits and stock dividends differ in the way they are treated for tax purposes.
  - A stock *split* does not create taxable income to the investor.
  - A stock *dividend* creates taxable income because stock dividends are taxed in the same way as cash dividends. The stock dividend is valued at the market value of the shares on the date the stock dividend is declared, and this amount is included as taxable income. This is one reason why stock dividends are less popular than stock splits; investors must pay income tax on a stock dividend even though no cash is received.
- A stock *dividend* shifts an amount from retained earnings to contributed capital, leaving the total book value unchanged. However, the book value *per share* will decrease because of the increased number of shares outstanding. A stock *split* affects no account balances whatsoever but instead changes the book value of each share.

Exhibit 14–3 provides a summary of the effects of all dividends and stock splits.

EXHIBIT 14–3 | Effects of Dividends and Stock Splits

Effect on:	Cash Dividend	Stock Dividend	Stock Split
Common Shares account	None	Increase	None
Number of common shares issued and outstanding	None	Increase	Increase
Number of shares authorized	None	None	Increase (except when an unlimited number of shares are authorized)
Retained earnings	Decrease	Decrease	None
Total shareholders' equity	Decrease	None	None
Taxes to be paid by a shareholder	Yes	Yes	No
Book value per share	No	Yes	Yes

> Try It!

1. Beachcomber Pool Supply Inc. has 16,000 common shares outstanding for a total contributed capital value of $48,000. Beachcomber declares a 10 percent stock dividend on July 15 when the market value of its shares is $8 per share. The date of record is August 15 and the distribution date is August 31.

   a. Journalize the declaration of the stock dividend on July 15 and the distribution on August 31.

   b. What is the overall effect on Beachcomber's total assets?

   c. What is the overall effect on total shareholders' equity?

   d. If Beachcomber declared a 2-for-1 stock split instead of a stock dividend, what would be the journal entry on July 15? On August 31?

   e. What would be the effect of the stock split on shareholders' equity?

   Solutions appear at the end of this chapter and on MyAccountingLab

REPURCHASE OF ITS SHARES BY A CORPORATION

LO 2

Why are shares repurchased, and how do we account for them?

REAL WORLD EXAMPLE

It is normal for businesses to repurchase their own shares. There are announcements ahead of time for "normal course issuer bids" that tell the public a repurchase will take place. This is what Dollarama did in 2014.

Corporations may **repurchase shares** from their shareholders for several reasons:

- The corporation may have issued all its authorized shares and need to recover shares for distributions to officers and employees under bonus plans or share purchase plans.
- The purchase may help support the shares' current market price by decreasing the supply of shares available to the public.
- Management may want a more tax-efficient means of sharing earnings. An increased share price will not trigger an income tax expense, but a cash dividend will.
- The corporation may need to meet share-ownership requirements or limits, which may be a percentage of the total for foreign ownership or some other legislated requirement.

The Canada Business Corporations Act requires a corporation that purchases its own shares to cancel the shares bought. Those shares are then treated as authorized but unissued. Most incorporating acts do not permit a corporation to acquire its own shares if such reacquisition would result in the corporation putting itself into financial jeopardy and being unable to pay its liabilities as they become due.

Treasury Shares

Several of the provincial incorporating acts also require that the shares be cancelled, while other jurisdictions inside and outside of Canada permit the corporation to hold the shares as **treasury shares** (in effect, the corporation holds the shares in its treasury) and resell them. Because of the complex and varied treatment of treasury shares, they are covered more fully in intermediate and advanced accounting courses and will not be covered further in this text.

Share Repurchases

The first step in recording a share repurchase is to calculate the average cost per share. How a share repurchase is recorded depends on whether the shares are repurchased at a price equal to, less than, or greater than the average cost per share. We will examine each of these situations.

Share Repurchase at Average Issue Price

Assume the articles of incorporation for Dawson Resources Ltd., issued under the Canada Business Corporations Act, authorized it to issue 100,000 common shares. By February 28, 2017, Dawson Resources had issued 9,000 shares at an average issue price of $20.00 per share, and its shareholders' equity appeared as follows:

Shareholders' Equity	
Contributed capital	
Common shares, 100,000 shares authorized, 9,000 shares issued and outstanding	$180,000
Retained earnings	24,000
Total shareholders' equity	$204,000

On March 20, 2017, Dawson Resources Ltd. repurchases 1,000 shares at $20.00 per share, an amount equal to the average issue price. The company records the transaction as follows:

2017			
Mar. 20	Common Shares	20,000	
	Cash		20,000
	Purchased 1,000 shares at $20.00 per share.		

The repurchase of its own shares by a company decreases the company's assets (cash) and its shareholders' equity (common shares). The shareholders' equity section of Dawson Resources Ltd.'s balance sheet would appear as follows after the transaction:

Shareholders' Equity	
Contributed capital	
Common shares, 100,000 shares authorized, 8,000 shares issued and outstanding (Note 6)	$160,000
Retained earnings	24,000
Total shareholders' equity	$184,000

Note 6: During the year, the company acquired 1,000 common shares at a price of $20.00 per share; the shares had been issued at $20.00 per share.

Observe that the purchase of the shares decreased the number of shares issued and outstanding. Only *outstanding* shares have a vote, receive cash dividends, and share in assets if the corporation liquidates.

Share Repurchase below Average Issue Price

The *CPA Canada Handbook* requires a company that purchases its own shares at a price less than the *average issue price* to debit Common Shares (or Preferred Shares, as the case may be) for the average issue price. The excess of the average issue price over the purchase price should be credited to a new account: Contributed Surplus—Share Repurchase. (If the company has more than one class or series of shares, the Contributed Surplus—Share Repurchase account name would include the class or series.)

Let's continue the Dawson Resources Ltd. example. On April 30, 2017, Dawson repurchases 1,000 shares at $15.00 per share. The average issue price was $20.00 per share. The company records the transaction as follows:

2017			
Apr. 30	Common Shares	20,000	
	Contributed Surplus—Share Repurchase		5,000
	Cash		15,000
	Purchased 1,000 shares at $15.00 per share.		

- Issued at $20 × 1,000
- Excess of issue price over purchase price ($20,000 – $15,000)

The shareholders' equity section of Dawson Resources Ltd.'s balance sheet would appear as follows after the transaction:

Shareholders' Equity	
Contributed capital	
Common shares, 100,000 shares authorized, 7,000 shares issued and outstanding	$140,000
Contributed Surplus—Share Repurchase (Note 6)	5,000
Total contributed capital	145,000
Retained earnings	24,000
Total shareholders' equity	$169,000

Note 6: During the year, the company acquired 1,000 common shares at a price of $20.00 per share and 1,000 common shares at a price of $15.00 per share; the shares had been issued at $20.00 per share.

Dawson Resources Ltd. now has a balance in the Contributed Surplus—Share Repurchase account.

Share Repurchase above Average Issue Price

When a company purchases its own shares at a price greater than the average issue price, the excess should first be debited to Contributed Surplus—Share Repurchase to reduce the balance in this account to $0, and any remaining excess should then be debited to Retained Earnings.

Balance in the Contributed Surplus—Share Repurchase Account   Let's continue the Dawson Resources Ltd. example. Suppose Dawson repurchased another 1,000 shares at $30.00 per share on May 10, 2017, and the Contributed Surplus—Share Repurchase account had the balance of $5,000 shown above. The company would reduce the balance in Contributed Surplus—Share Repurchase to nil before reducing the Retained Earnings account, as follows:

2017				
May 10	Common Shares	20,000		Issued at $20 × 1,000
	Contributed Surplus—Share Repurchase	5,000		First, reduce any contributed surplus to nil
	Retained Earnings	5,000		Then debit Retained Earnings for the remainder ($30,000 – $20,000 – $5,000)
	Cash		30,000	
	Purchased 1,000 shares at $30.00 per share.			

The shareholders' equity section of Dawson Resources Ltd.'s balance sheet would appear as follows after the transaction:

Shareholders' Equity	
Contributed capital	
Common shares, 100,000 shares authorized, 6,000 shares issued and outstanding (Note 6)	$120,000
Retained earnings	19,000
Total shareholders' equity	$139,000

Note 6: During the year, the company acquired 1,000 common shares at a price of $20.00 per share, 1,000 common shares at a price of $15.00 per share, and 1,000 common shares at a price of $30.00 per share; the shares had been issued at $20.00 per share.

No Balance in the Contributed Surplus—Share Repurchase Account   Suppose Dawson Resources Ltd. had repurchased 1,000 of its shares at $30.00 per share on May 10, 2017, and did not have a balance in the Contributed Surplus—Share Repurchase account. Retained Earnings would be debited for the difference between the purchase price and the issue price, which in this case is $10,000 ($30,000 – $20,000). The journal entry would be as follows:

> The repurchase and sale of its own shares do not affect a corporation's net income. A share repurchase affects balance sheet accounts, not income statement accounts.

2017			
May 10	Common Shares	20,000	
	Retained Earnings	10,000	
	Cash		30,000
	Purchased 1,000 shares at $30.00 per share.		

Recording the Sale of Repurchased Shares

A company incorporated under the Canada Business Corporations Act may reissue the shares that it previously had repurchased. The sale would be treated like a normal sale of authorized but unissued shares. The Contributed Surplus—Share Repurchase account is *not* affected when a company sells its own repurchased shares.

Exhibit 14–4 summarizes the journal entries for share repurchases.

EXHIBIT 14–4 | Summary of Journal Entries for Share Repurchases

Repurchase at average issue price:

Common Shares	Number repurchased × Average cost per share	
Cash		Number repurchased × Price paid per share

Repurchase below average issue price:

Common Shares	Number repurchased × Average cost per share	
Contributed Surplus— Share Repurchase		Difference between Cash and Common Shares amounts
Cash		Number repurchased × Price paid per share

Repurchase above average issue price:

Common Shares	Number repurchased × Average cost per share	
Contributed Surplus—Share Repurchase	Use up the credit balance in this account first	
Retained Earnings	The amount of any remaining difference (the "plug" amount)	
Cash		Number repurchased × Price paid per share

ETHICAL AND LEGAL ISSUES FOR SHARE TRANSACTIONS

Share repurchase transactions have a serious ethical and legal dimension. A company buying its own shares must be extremely careful that its disclosures of information are complete and accurate. Otherwise, a shareholder who sold shares back to the company may claim that he or she was deceived into selling the shares at too low a price. For example, what would happen if a company repurchased its own shares at $17.00 per share and one day later announced a technological breakthrough that would generate millions of dollars in new business? The share price would likely increase in response to the new information. If it could be proved that management withheld the information, a shareholder selling shares back to the company might file a lawsuit to gain the difference per share. The shareholder would claim that, with the knowledge of the technological advance, he or she would have held the shares until after the price increase and been able to sell the shares at a higher price.

Insider Trading To keep the stock markets fair for everyone, people who work for public corporations are not allowed to buy or sell shares of the company when the information they have is not available to the public. They are also not allowed to share this information secretly with their friends. *Insiders* are allowed to buy and sell shares, but they must file reports with securities administrators. While jail terms for illegal **insider trading** action are rare, Barry Landen, the former vice-president of corporate affairs at Agnico Eagle Mines Ltd., was sentenced to 45 days in jail and assessed a $200,000 fine for insider trading under the Securities Act. He sold shares to avoid a loss of $115,000 based on "undisclosed material information."[2]

> Try It!

2. Whippet Industries Corporation has the following partial balance sheet information available at November 30, 2016:

Shareholders' Equity	
Contributed capital	
Common shares, 400,000 shares authorized,	
150,000 shares issued and outstanding	$ 900,000
Retained earnings	700,000
Total shareholders' equity	$1,600,000

If Whippet Industries repurchased 20,000 common shares on March 1, 2017, at a price of $4.50 per share, prepare the journal entry for the transaction.

3. Refer to the previous question. Suppose Whippet Industries repurchased 20,000 shares on March 1, 2017, at a price of $8.25 per share instead of $4.50. Prepare the journal entry for this transaction.

4. Prepare the shareholders' equity section of the balance sheet after the repurchase in the previous question.

Solutions appear at the end of this chapter and on MyAccountingLab

THE CORPORATE INCOME STATEMENT

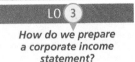

LO 3

How do we prepare a corporate income statement?

As we have seen, the shareholders' equity of a corporation is more complex than the capital of a proprietorship or a partnership. Also, a corporation's income statement includes some features that don't often apply to a proprietorship or a partnership. Most of the income statements you will see belong to corporations, so we turn now to the corporate income statement to explore these new features.

Net income is probably the most important piece of information about a company. Net income measures how successfully the company has operated. To shareholders, the larger the corporation's profit, the greater the likelihood of dividends or share-price increases. To creditors, the larger the corporation's profit, the better able it is to pay its debts. Net income builds up a company's assets and shareholders' equity. It also helps to attract capital from new investors who believe the company will be successful in the future.

Suppose you are considering investing in the shares of DIRTT Environmental Solutions Ltd., Dollarama Inc., or a private corporation. You would examine these companies' income statements. Of particular interest is the amount of net income they can expect to earn year after year. To understand net income, let's examine

---

[2] Megan Harman, "OSC Reveals New Sanctions against Landen," October 13, 2010. Retrieved from www.investmentexecutive.com/-/news-55298.

EXHIBIT 14–5 | Corporate Income Statement

KLR TECHNOLOGY INC.
Income Statement
For the Year Ended December 31, 2017

Sales revenue		$1,000,000	Continuing operations
Cost of goods sold		480,000	
Gross margin		520,000	
Operating expenses (listed individually)		362,000	
Operating income		158,000	
Other gains (losses)			
❶ Loss on restructuring operations	($20,000)		
❷ Gain on sale of machinery	42,000	22,000	
Income from continuing operations before income tax		180,000	
❸ Income tax expense		63,000	
Income from continuing operations		117,000	
❹ Discontinued operations			
Operating income, $60,000, less income tax of $21,000	39,000		
Gain on disposal, $10,000, less income tax of $3,500	6,500	45,500	Discontinued operations
Net income		$ 162,500	
❺ Earnings per common share (60,000 shares outstanding)			
Income from continuing operations		$ 1.95	
Income from discontinued operations		0.76	Earnings per share
Net income		$ 2.71	

Exhibit 14–5, which presents the multi-step income statement of KLR Technology Inc., a small manufacturer of electronic switching equipment that is owned by a few shareholders who run the company. Its shares do not trade on a stock exchange, so KLR Technology Inc. is a private corporation.

A single-step income statement is illustrated in the Summary Problem at the end of this chapter. It does not show the gross margin calculation nor does it break down other other gains/losses in the same amount of detail as shown here.

Continuing Operations

Income from a business's continuing operations helps financial statement users make predictions about the business's future earnings. In the income statement of Exhibit 14–5, the top section reports income from continuing operations. This part of the business is expected to continue from period to period. We may use this information to try to predict that KLR Technology Inc. will earn income of approximately $117,000 next year.

The continuing operations of KLR Technology Inc. include three items deserving explanation:

❶ During 2017, the company had a $20,000 loss on restructuring operations. Restructuring costs include severance pay to laid-off workers, moving expenses for employees transferred to other locations, and environmental cleanup expenses. The restructuring loss is part of continuing operations because KLR Technology Inc. is remaining in the same line of business. But the restructuring loss is highlighted as an "other" item (unusual item) on the income statement because its cause—restructuring—falls outside KLR's main business endeavour, which is selling electronics equipment.

❷ KLR Technology Inc. had a gain on the sale of machinery ($42,000), which is also outside the company's core business activity. It is shown in the continuing operations section because it is related to the machinery, which is used in operations.

The gains or losses from any unusual or infrequent transactions that are outside a company's core business activity would be disclosed separately on the income statement as part of income from continuing operations. Other examples in addition to those shown in Exhibit 14–5 could include:

- Losses due to lawsuits
- Losses due to employee labour strikes
- Losses due to floods, fire, or other forces of nature

These items are *not* shown net of tax effects.

③ Income tax expense ($63,000) has been deducted in arriving at income from continuing operations. The tax corporations pay on their income is a significant expense. The combined federal and provincial income tax rates for corporations varies by the type and size of company, and from province to province. We will use an income tax rate of 35 percent in our illustrations. The $63,000 income tax expense in Exhibit 14–5 equals the pretax income from continuing operations multiplied by the tax rate ($180,000 × 0.35 = $63,000).

After continuing operations, an income statement may include a section for gains and losses from discontinued operations.

Discontinued Operations

Many corporations engage in several lines of business. For example, The Jim Pattison Group of Vancouver is the second-largest private corporation in Canada and includes a diverse group of businesses. They include companies that sell illuminated signs, wholesale food, and retail automobiles, while others are involved in packaging, media, and periodical distribution, to name just a few. We call each significant part of a company a **segment of the business**.

A company may sell a segment of its business. Such a sale is not a regular source of income because a company cannot keep on selling its segments indefinitely. The sale of a business segment is viewed as a one-time transaction. Financial analysts and potential investors typically do not include income or loss on discontinued operations in their predictions about a company's future income. The discontinued segments will generate no income in the future.

④ The income statement presents information on the segment that has been disposed of under the heading Discontinued Operations. This section of the income statement is divided into two components:

- Operating income (or loss) from the segment that is disposed of
- Gain (or loss) on the disposal

Assume income and gains are taxed at the 35 percent rate. They would be reported as follows:

Discontinued operations	
Operating income $60,000, less income tax, $21,000	$39,000
Gain on disposal, $10,000 less income tax, $3,500	6,500
	$45,500

This presentation appears in Exhibit 14–5. An alternate presentation is shown in this chapter's Summary Problem on page 807.

It is necessary to separate discontinued operations into these two components because the company may operate the discontinued segment for part of the year. This is the operating income (or loss) component; it should include the results of

KEY POINTS
Businesses operate to generate profits; without profits a business will not exist for long. The main source of income for an ongoing business must be from regular, continuing operations, not from sources such as selling off a business segment.

KEY POINTS
The tax effect of the discontinued segment's operating income (or loss) is not included in income tax expense ($63,000 in Exhibit 14–5 ③); rather, it is added or deducted in the discontinued operations part of the income statement ④.

operations of the segment from the beginning of the period to the disposal date. There is usually also a gain (or loss) on disposal. Both the operating income (or loss) and the gain (or loss) on disposal are shown net of tax. This is because income tax is such a significant component of continuing operations and discontinued operations that investors and analysts need to know the tax effects. Operating losses and losses on disposal generate tax benefits because they reduce net income and thus reduce the amount of tax that needs to be paid.

If the transactions for discontinued operations have not been completed at the company's year end, the gain (or loss) may have to be estimated. To be conservative, the estimated net loss should be recorded in the accounts at year end while an estimated net gain would not be recognized until it was realized.

It is important that the assets, liabilities, and operations of the segment can be clearly identified as separate from those of other operations of the company. The notes to the financial statements should disclose fully the nature of the discontinued operations and other relevant information about the discontinued operations, such as revenue to the date of discontinuance.

Discontinued operations are common in business. General Motors decided to stop producing the Saturn line of vehicles, and Molson Coors Brewing Company sold part of its interest in Cervejarias Kaiser, a Brazilian brewing company.

Earnings per Share (EPS)

⑤ For many corporations, the final segment of a corporate income statement presents the company's earnings per share. **Earnings per share (EPS)** is the amount of a company's net income per outstanding common share. While ASPE does not require that corporations disclose EPS figures on the income statement or in a note to the financial statements, many corporations do provide this information because investors and financial analysts sometimes use it to assess a corporation's profitability. EPS is also widely reported in the financial press, so it is important to know how it is calculated and how it is used. Basic EPS is computed as follows:

REAL WORLD EXAMPLE

If showing a higher EPS is a good thing, what prevents companies from buying back shares just to make the EPS look better? Nothing really! This is why financial analysis is never done by looking at only one calculation. Prudent investors will look at many different factors when considering where to invest funds.

$$\text{Earnings per share} = \frac{\text{Net income} - \text{Preferred dividends}}{\text{Weighted average number of common shares outstanding*}}$$

* How to calculate the *weighted average number of common shares outstanding* is illustrated on the next page. If there is no change in the number of shares outstanding during the period, then use the total number of common shares outstanding.

Just as the corporation lists separately its different sources of income from continuing operations and discontinued operations, it should list separately the EPS figure for income before discontinued operations and net income for the period to emphasize the significance of discontinued operations to a company's overall results.

Consider the income statement of KLR Technology Inc. shown in Exhibit 14–5; in 2017 it had 60,000 common shares outstanding. Income from continuing operations was $117,000 and income from discontinued operations net of tax was $45,500. KLR Technology Inc. could present the following EPS information:

Earnings per common share		
Income from continuing operations	$1.95	$117,000 ÷ 60,000
Income from discontinued operations	0.76	$45,500 ÷ 60,000
Net income	$2.71	($117,000 + $45,500) ÷ 60,000

Weighted Average Number of Common Shares Outstanding Computing EPS is straightforward if the number of common shares outstanding does not change over the entire accounting period. For many corporations, however, this figure varies as the company issues new shares and repurchases its own shares over the course of the year. Consider a corporation that had 100,000 shares outstanding from January through November, then purchased 60,000 of its own shares. This company's EPS would be misleadingly high if computed using 40,000 (100,000 – 60,000) shares. To make EPS as meaningful as possible, corporations use the weighted average number of common shares outstanding during the period.

Let's assume the following figures for IMC Corporation. From January through May, 2017, the company had 240,000 common shares outstanding; from June through August, 200,000 shares; and from September through December, 210,000 shares. We compute the weighted average by considering the outstanding shares per month as a fraction of the year:

LEARNING TIPS

Remember that this is a *weighted* average and not a *simple* average. If you calculated the simple average [(240,000 + 200,000 + 210,000) ÷ 3], you would get an answer of 216,667, which is incorrect. The correct answer is 220,000, as shown to the right, because it reflects the fact that there are different amounts of shares held for different lengths of time.

Number of Common Shares Outstanding		Fraction of Year				Weighted Average Number of Common Shares Outstanding
240,000	×	$\frac{5}{12}$	(January through May)	=		100,000
200,000	×	$\frac{3}{12}$	(June through August)	=		50,000
210,000	×	$\frac{4}{12}$	(September through December)	=		70,000
Weighted average number of common shares outstanding during 2017				=		220,000

The 220,000 weighted average would be divided into net income to compute the corporation's EPS.

Stock Dividends and Stock Splits The calculation of weighted average number of common shares outstanding becomes complicated when there have been stock dividends or stock splits during the year. The number of shares outstanding during the year are restated to reflect the stock dividend or stock split *as if it had occurred at the beginning of the year*.

To illustrate, let's extend the IMC Corporation example above by assuming a stock dividend of 10 percent was effective on September 1. The effect of the 10 percent stock dividend is a multiplier of 1.10 for the period January to August to restate the number of outstanding shares as if the stock dividend had occurred at the beginning of the year. The number of outstanding shares for September to December already reflects the 10 percent stock dividend, so the effect is a multiplier of 1.00 for those months. We compute the weighted average by considering the outstanding shares per month as a fraction of the year:

Number of Common Shares Outstanding		Effect of Stock Dividend		Fraction of Year				Weighted Average Number of Common Shares Outstanding
240,000	×	1.10	×	$\frac{5}{12}$	(January through May)	=		110,000
200,000	×	1.10	×	$\frac{3}{12}$	(June through August)	=		55,000
231,000	×	1.00	×	$\frac{4}{12}$	(September through December)	=		77,000
Weighted average number of common shares outstanding during 2017						=		242,000

Amount includes the 10 percent stock dividend on 210,000 shares.

The 242,000 weighted average number of common shares outstanding would be divided into net income to compute the corporation's EPS.

To illustrate the results of a stock split, change the IMC Corporation example above by assuming a 2-for-1 stock split on September 1, 2017, instead of the 10 percent stock dividend shown above. The effect of the 2-for-1 stock split is 2.00, which doubles the number of shares for the period January to August to restate the number of outstanding shares as if the stock split had occurred at the beginning of the year. The number of outstanding shares for September to December already reflects the 2-for-1 stock split, so the effect is 1.00 for those months. Again, we compute the weighted average by considering the outstanding shares per month as a fraction of the year:

Number of Common Shares Outstanding		Effect of Stock Split		Fraction of Year				Weighted Average Number of Common Shares Outstanding
240,000	×	2.00	×	$\frac{5}{12}$	(January through May)	=		200,000
200,000	×	2.00	×	$\frac{3}{12}$	(June through August)	=		100,000
420,000	×	1.00	×	$\frac{4}{12}$	(September through December)	=		140,000
Weighted average number of common shares outstanding during 2017						=		440,000

Amount includes the 2-for-1 stock split of the 210,000 shares.

The 440,000 weighted average number of common shares outstanding would be divided into net income to compute the corporation's EPS.

Preferred Dividends Holders of preferred shares have no claim to the business's income beyond the stated preferred dividend. Even though preferred shares have no claims, preferred dividends do affect the EPS figure. Preferred dividends declared in the year are deducted from income to more accurately reflect what is left to be shared by the common shareholders. There is an exception to this rule if there are cumulative preferred shares. For cumulative preferred shares, the annual dividend is deducted in the formula even if it has not been declared.

If KLR Technology Ltd. (from Exhibit 14–5) had 10,000 cumulative preferred shares outstanding, each with a $1.50 dividend, the annual preferred dividend would be $15,000 (10,000 × $1.50). The $15,000 would be subtracted from income, resulting in the following EPS computations:

KEY POINTS

Dividends in arrears are not used in the EPS calculation. Only current dividends *declared* or the annual amount of cumulative preferred dividends (even if not declared) are deducted from net income.

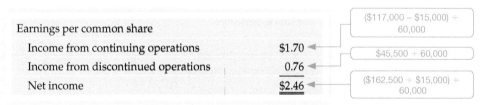

Earnings per common share		
Income from continuing operations	$1.70	($117,000 − $15,000) ÷ 60,000
Income from discontinued operations	0.76	$45,500 ÷ 60,000
Net income	$2.46	($162,500 − $15,000) ÷ 60,000

Dilution Some corporations make their bonds or preferred shares more attractive to investors by offering **conversion privileges**, which permit the holder to convert the bond or preferred shares into some specified number of common shares. If in fact the bonds or preferred shares are converted into common shares, then the EPS will be diluted (reduced) because more common shares are divided into net income. Because convertible bonds or convertible preferred shares can be traded for common shares, the common shareholders want to know the amount of the decrease in EPS that would occur if conversion took place. To provide this information, corporations with convertible bonds or preferred shares outstanding present two sets of EPS amounts:

- EPS based on actual outstanding common shares (**basic EPS**).
- EPS based on outstanding common shares plus the number of additional common shares that would arise from conversion of the convertible bonds and

convertible preferred shares into common shares (**fully diluted EPS**). Fully diluted EPS is always lower than basic EPS.

The topic of dilution can be very complex and is covered more fully in intermediate accounting texts.

Price–Earnings Ratio   EPS is one of the most widely used accounting figures. By dividing the market price of a company's share by its EPS, we compute a statistic called the **price–earnings ratio** or *price-to-earnings ratio*. Several websites as well as the business press, such as the *Globe and Mail Report on Business*, report the price–earnings ratios (listed as P/E) daily for companies listed on stock exchanges. The price–earnings ratio is explored more fully in Chapter 18.

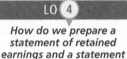

5. On September 1, 2017, Acme Equipment Corp. sells its division that manufactures mobile homes. The assets are sold at a taxable gain of $1,700,000. The loss from operations for the year up to the date of sale was $960,000. The tax rate is 30 percent. How would you present the loss for the year and the sale of the division on the income statement for the year ended December 31, 2017?

6. The net income of Hart Corp. amounted to $3,750,000 for the year ended December 31, 2017. Hart Corp. had 200,000 $9.00 cumulative preferred shares throughout the year, and 310,000 common shares at the end of the year. At January 1, 2017, Hart Corp. had 270,000 common shares outstanding and issued 40,000 common shares on April 1. Calculate Hart Corp.'s EPS.

Solutions appear at the end of this chapter and on MyAccountingLab

STATEMENT OF RETAINED EARNINGS

LO 4

How do we prepare a statement of retained earnings and a statement of shareholders' equity?

Retained earnings may be a significant portion of a corporation's shareholders' equity. It is so important that some corporations prepare a separate financial statement outlining the major changes in this equity account. The statement of retained earnings for KLR Technology Inc. appears in Exhibit 14–6.

EXHIBIT 14–6 | Statement of Retained Earnings

KLR TECHNOLOGY INC. Statement of Retained Earnings For the Year Ended December 31, 2017	
Retained earnings, January 1, 2017	$260,000
Net income for 2017	162,500
	422,500
Dividends for 2017	(42,000)
Retained earnings, December 31, 2017	$380,500

Some companies report income and retained earnings on a single statement. Exhibit 14–7 illustrates how KLR Technology Inc. would combine its income statement and its statement of retained earnings.

EXHIBIT 14–7 | Statement of Income and Retained Earnings

KLR TECHNOLOGY INC.
Statement of Income and Retained Earnings
For the Year Ended December 31, 2017

Income statement	Sales revenue	$1,000,000
	Cost of goods sold	480,000
	Gross margin	520,000
	Operating expenses (listed individually)	362,000
Statement of Retained Earnings	Net income for 2017	162,500
	Retained earnings, January 1, 2017	260,000
		422,500
	Dividends for 2017	(42,000)
	Retained earnings, December 31, 2017	$ 380,500

Earnings per common share (60,000 shares outstanding)	
Income from continuing operations	$1.95
Income from discontinued operations	0.76
Net income	$2.71

STATEMENT OF SHAREHOLDERS' EQUITY

In addition to the balance sheet and income statement, corporations that follow APSE *may* prepare a **statement of shareholders' equity**, or simply a **statement of equity**, to present changes in all components of equity, much as the statement of owner's equity presents information on changes in the equity of a proprietorship. The statement of shareholders' equity for KLR Technology Inc. appears in Exhibit 14–8, with some details added for illustration.

EXHIBIT 14–8 | Statement of Shareholders' Equity

Begins with the previous year's shareholders' equity balances and shows the changes that led to the current year's final balances.

Sales and repurchases of shares during the year may affect contributed capital.

The year's income increases the Retained Earnings balance.

Dividends decrease Retained Earnings.

This information is from the statement of retained earnings in Exhibit 14–6.

KLR TECHNOLOGY INC.
Statement of Shareholders' Equity
For the Year Ended December 31, 2017

	Common Shares	Contributed Surplus— Share Repurchases	Retained Earnings	Total Shareholders' Equity
Balance, December 31, 2016	$360,000	$ 0	$260,000	$620,000
Issuance of shares	100,000			100,000
Net income			162,500	162,500
Cash dividends			(42,000)	(42,000)
Repurchase of common shares	(40,000)	10,000		(30,000)
Balance, December 31, 2017	$420,000	$10,000	$380,500	$810,500

Variations in Reporting Shareholders' Equity

Accountants sometimes report shareholders' equity in ways that differ from our examples. We use a detailed format in this book to help you learn the components of shareholders' equity. Companies assume that investors and creditors understand the details.

An important skill you will learn in this book is how to be comfortable with the information presented in the financial statements of actual companies as it sometimes differs from the examples used for teaching. In Exhibit 14–9, we present a side-by-side comparison of our teaching format and a format adapted from the 2013 annual report of Canadian Tire Corporation, Limited.

EXHIBIT 14–9 | Formats for Reporting Shareholders' Equity*

Textbook Format		Real-World Format	
Shareholders' Equity ($ amounts in millions)		Equity ($ amounts in millions)	
Contributed capital			
Preferred shares, 100,000,000 authorized, 76,560,851 issued and outstanding ❹	$ 0.2	Share capital (Note 28) ❶ ❷	$ 587.0
Common shares, 3,423,366 authorized, issued, and outstanding	586.8		
Contributed surplus	6.2	Contributed surplus	6.2
		Accumulated other comprehensive income (loss)	47.4
Retained earnings	4,574.1	Retained earnings	4,526.7
Total shareholders' equity	$5,167.3	Equity attributable to owners of the Company ❸	$5,167.3

Note 28: Share Capital (adapted) Authorized
3,423,366 Common Shares
100,000,000 Class A Non-Voting Shares
Issued
3,423,366 Common Shares
76,560,851 Class A Non-Voting Shares

*ASPE and IFRS suggest the presentation of comparative data; in order to simplify the illustration, data are presented for 2013 only.

❶ Canadian Tire uses the heading Share Capital instead of Contributed Capital.

❷ Some companies combine all classes of contributed capital into a single line item and provide specifics in the notes to the financial statements.

❸ Often total shareholders' equity is not specifically labelled using that term.

❹ If this were a statement for a private enterprise following ASPE, the number of authorized shares would not need to be disclosed.

ACCOUNTING FOR ERRORS AND CHANGES IN ACCOUNTING POLICY AND CIRCUMSTANCES

The consistency principle is an important concept in accounting. But what if situations change and information on financial statements needs to be reported differently? Management might feel a different accounting method would provide better information to investors. Perhaps an error was made. Depending on the reason for the change, there are two ways this should be handled—with either *retrospective* (looking back) or *prospective* (looking forward) treatment.

Errors

What happens when a company makes an error in recording revenues or expenses? Detecting the error in the period in which it occurs allows the company to make a correction before preparing that period's financial statements. But failure to detect the error until a later period means that the business will have reported an incorrect amount of income on its income statement. After the revenue and expense accounts are closed, the Retained Earnings account will absorb the effect of the error, and its balance will be wrong until the error is corrected.

To correct an error, the correcting entry includes a debit or credit to Retained Earnings for the error amount and a debit or credit to the asset or liability account that was misstated.

Assume that Paquette Corporation recorded the closing inventory balance for 2016 as $30,000. When the inventory records were checked, it was discovered that the correct amount was $40,000. This error resulted in overstating 2016 expenses by $10,000 and understating net income by $10,000. The entry to record this error correction in 2017 is as follows:

Jun. 19	Inventory	10,000	
	Retained Earnings		10,000
	Correction of prior years' error in recording closing inventory in 2016.		

The credit to Retained Earnings adjusts its account balance to reflect the understated income in 2016. If Cost of Goods Sold were credited in 2017 when the correcting entry was recorded, income in 2017 would be overstated. The journal entry properly locates the adjustment in the period prior to 2017 (i.e., to 2016, when the error occurred). This is an example of **retrospective** treatment because numbers from the prior year are restated to reflect the correction of the error. However, instead of restating prior financial statements, the opening balance of Retained Earnings is adjusted for the error.

The error correction would appear on the statement of retained earnings as shown below, or on the statement of shareholders' equity in the Retained Earnings section (shown in the Summary Problem for Your Review on page 807):

PAQUETTE CORPORATION Statement of Retained Earnings For the Year Ended December 31, 2017	
Retained earnings, January 1, 2017 as originally reported	$390,000
Adjustment to correct error in recording closing inventory in 2016	10,000
Retained earnings, January 1, 2017, as adjusted	400,000
Net income for 2017	114,000
	514,000
Dividends for 2017	(41,000)
Retained earnings balance, December 31, 2017	$473,000

Change in Accounting Policy

A change in accounting policy should be applied *retrospectively*; in other words, prior periods should be restated to reflect the change. This would be done by restating any prior periods' comparative data provided in the current year's financial statements (not by reprinting the financial statements or annual reports from prior years). In addition, the facts of the restatement should be disclosed in the notes. An example would be a change in amortization method from straight line to units of production. The effect of the change on prior periods' results would appear as an item on the statement of retained earnings or on the statement of shareholders' equity in the Retained Earnings section, the same way an error would.

> The accounting framework characteristic of consistency (introduced in Chapter 6) reminds us that changes in policy should not happen too often.

Change in Circumstances

Companies must make estimates about many items on the financial statements, such as the amount of warranties or bad debts, inventory obsolescence, or the useful life of assets for amortization. If these estimates need to change to better reflect a change in circumstances, then the changes are made to the current year and all future financial statements. This **prospective** treatment is in response to new information and is done to make the information more useful. There is no change to past financial statements because the estimates at that time were correct based on what was known at that time.

RESTRICTIONS ON RETAINED EARNINGS

REAL WORLD EXAMPLE

How do restrictions protect creditors? By limiting how much managers can pay as dividends, they guarantee that some equity is left in the company in case it goes out of business. That way, managers who own a company can't sell all the assets and pay themselves a dividend, which leaves the lenders with nothing on which to collect the debts.

To ensure that corporations maintain a minimum level of shareholders' equity for the protection of creditors, incorporating acts restrict the amount of its own shares that a corporation may repurchase and the amount of dividends that can be declared. In addition, companies may voluntarily create reserves, or *appropriations*. Companies report their restrictions in notes to the financial statements.

Appropriations of Retained Earnings

Appropriations are restrictions of retained earnings that are recorded by formal journal entries. A corporation may appropriate—that is, segregate in a separate account—a portion of retained earnings for a specific use. For example, the board of directors may appropriate part of retained earnings for expanding a manufacturing plant. A debit to Retained Earnings and a credit to a separate account—Retained Earnings Restricted for Plant Expansion—records the appropriation. Appropriated Retained Earnings is normally reported directly above the regular Retained Earnings account, with a footnote where the appropriation is more fully described. *Retained earnings appropriations are rare.* Presentation of this information on the balance sheet may take this form:

Shareholders' Equity		
Total contributed capital		$325,000
Retained earnings:		
Appropriated for plant expansion	$125,000	
Unappropriated	50,000	
Total retained earnings		175,000
Total shareholders' equity		$500,000

Or the retained earnings could be shown with a notation that refers the reader to the notes for more details:

Shareholders' Equity	
Total contributed capital	$325,000
Retained earnings (Note X)	175,000
Total shareholders' equity	$500,000

Note X: The board of directors appropriated part of Retained Earnings to expand a manufacturing plant.

Limits on Dividends and Share Repurchases

Cash dividends and repurchases of shares require a cash payment. In fact, repurchases of shares are returns of their investment to the shareholders. These outlays decrease assets, so the corporation has fewer resources to pay liabilities. A bank may agree to lend $500,000 only if the borrowing corporation limits dividend payments and repurchases of its shares. A corporation might agree to restrict dividends as a condition for receiving a loan in order to get a lower interest rate.

This type of restriction on the payment of dividends is more often seen, as shown in the following note:

> **Restriction on Dividends:** Certain terms of the Company's preferred shares and debt instruments could restrict the Company's ability to declare dividends on preferred and common shares. At year end, such terms did not restrict or alter the company's ability to declare dividends.

> Try It!

7. Complete the following statement of shareholders' equity by calculating the missing amounts a, b, c, and d.

		CHECKPOINT INDUSTRIES INC.		
		Statement of Shareholders' Equity		
		For the Year Ended April 30, 2017		

	Common Shares	Contributed Surplus— Share Repurchases	Retained Earnings	Total Shareholders' Equity
Balance, April 30, 2016	$260,000	$ 0	(a)	$360,000
Issuance of shares	100,000			100,000
Net income			62,500	(c)
Cash dividends			(22,000)	(22,000)
Repurchase of common shares	(60,000)	(b)		(50,000)
Balance, April 30, 2017	$300,000	$10,000	$140,500	(d)

8. Identify whether each of the following independent cases is a correction of an error, a change in policy, or a change in estimate, *and* indicate whether there should be retrospective or prospective changes to the financial statements of CP Industries Inc. for three unrelated situations.

Situation	Change in estimate	Change in policy	Error	Retrospective Statement	Prospective Statement
A. Accountants felt it was better to use the units-of-production method of amortization for its vehicles rather than the straight-line method that had been used so far.					
B. Management decided that its equipment would last three years longer than it had originally anticipated.					
C. During 2017, the accountant discovered that a supplies invoice in the amount of $16,500 had not been recorded in 2016.					

Solutions appear at the end of this chapter and on MyAccountingLab

THE IMPACT OF IFRS ON THE INCOME STATEMENT AND THE STATEMENT OF SHAREHOLDERS' EQUITY

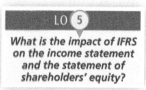

LO 5

What is the impact of IFRS on the income statement and the statement of shareholders' equity?

ASPE	IFRS
The statements are less complex and require fewer disclosures because it is assumed that private corporation shareholders and lenders can get access to the information they need directly from the corporation.	Typically, shareholders and lenders need more information (disclosure) because they do not have access to this information any other way. *(Continued)*

(Continued)

ASPE	IFRS
Does not require that an accounting policy change only be made under specific circumstances.	May only change an accounting policy if it meets the criteria of providing more *relevant* or *reliable* information.
Requires that the change be reported by restating any prior periods' comparative data in the current financial statements.	When there is a retrospective restatement of information, a statement of financial position must be prepared for the earliest period in which the accounting policy change resulted in a restated balance or a reclassified item.
Section 1506 of the *CPA Canada Handbook* for ASPE does not allow corporations to be exempt from restating financial information retroactively.	In International Accounting Standard (IAS) 8, a corporation may be exempt from restating financial information retroactively if it is *impractical* to do so.
EPS information is not required on the income statement. However, many private corporations do provide EPS information for current and potential investors.	IFRS requires companies to disclose EPS information on the income statement. When EPS information is included, it must be shown separately for both basic and diluted amounts, and results from continuing and discontinued operations must be shown separately, even if the results are negative.
Companies may prepare a statement of shareholders' equity.	Companies prepare a statement of changes in equity rather than a statement of retained earnings. The statement of changes in equity is similar to the statement of shareholders' equity described in this chapter.
Companies are not required to report **other comprehensive income**. Other comprehensive income arises from a number of sources, including unrealized gains and losses on certain classes of investment securities due in part to the use of fair value measurement.	Corporations are required to report *other comprehensive income*. May choose to prepare an income statement and a separate statement of comprehensive income, or combine this information into one statement. Exhibit 14–10 shows how the same information can be presented two different ways for the same company. Notice that the amount of income tax is shown separately for each component.

EXHIBIT 14–10 | **Examples of a Consolidated Statement of Earnings and Comprehensive Income, and a Statement of Comprehensive Income**

WEEKEE INDUSTRIES LIMITED
Consolidated Statement of Earnings and Comprehensive Income
For the Years Ended March 31, 2017 and 2016

	2017	2016
Profit before income tax	$799,500	$705,600
Income tax expense	239,850	211,680
Profit from continuing operations	559,650	493,920
Discontinued operations		
Profit (loss) from discontinued operation net of income tax	38,000	
Profit	597,650	493,920
Other comprehensive income		
Foreign currency translation differences for foreign operations, net of income tax	8,000	2,000
Net change in fair value of available-for-sale financial assets, net of income tax	9,250	7,500
Other comprehensive income for the period, net of income tax	17,250	9,500
Comprehensive income	$614,900	$503,420

(Continued)

WEEKEE INDUSTRIES LIMITED
Consolidated Statement of Earnings and Comprehensive Income
For the Years Ended March 31, 2017 and 2016

	2017	2016
Continuing operations		
Revenue	$1,650,000	$1,400,000
Cost of sales	750,000	600,000
Gross profit	900,000	800,000
Administrative expenses	50,000	45,000
Distribution expenses	30,000	27,000
Research and development expenses	15,000	13,000
Other expenses	5,000	9,000
Results from operating activities	800,000	706,000
Finance income	1,000	800
Finance costs	(1,500)	(1,200)
Net finance costs	(500)	(400)
Profit before income tax	799,500	705,600
Income tax expense	239,850	211,680
Profit from continuing operations	559,650	493,920
Discontinued operations		
Profit (loss) from discontinued operation, net of income tax	38,000	
Profit for the period	597,650	493,920
Other comprehensive income		
Foreign currency translation differences for foreign operations, net of income tax	8,000	2,000
Net change in fair value of available-for-sale financial assets, net of income tax	9,250	7,500
Other comprehensive income for the period, net of income tax	17,250	9,500
Total comprehensive income for the period	$ 614,900	$ 503,420
Earnings per share		
Basic earnings per share	$3.15	$2.58
Earnings per share from continuing operations	$2.87	$2.53

Note: Earnings per share is presented as part of the income statement if the income statement is separate from the statement of comprehensive income.

REAL WORLD EXAMPLE

Expense presentation by *nature* would include depreciation, transportation costs, and advertising, whereas by *function* these would be shown on the income statement as administrative costs, distribution costs, and selling costs.

> Why It's Done This Way

Objective of Financial Reporting

In this chapter you were introduced to new features presented on most corporate income statements, specifically the separation of income from continuing and discontinued operations, and earnings per share calculations. As we have seen in earlier chapters, the multi-step income statement is designed to communicate *useful* information to interested users to help them assess the success of the company—this is the objective of the accounting framework. The multi-step income statement approach is a useful tool for users for the *relevance* and *comparability* features of the information contained in the statement, as well as the format of the statement.

Users of the financial statements want to assess the future profitability of the company and will

(Continued)

(Continued)

use the income statement to achieve that objective. Users are also interested in assessing management's *stewardship* of the company. Stewardship is the concept of how well management uses the company's assets to meet company objectives such as earning a profit, serving specific markets, treating employees fairly, minimizing risks that face the company, and providing a good return to shareholders. Conveniently, the corporate multi-step income statement allows both objectives to be achieved. Future profitability can be estimated by studying the income from continuing operations, the ongoing operations that should continue into the future. Reporting unusual or infrequent activities separately on the income statement as part of ongoing operations helps users adjust their estimates of future profitability even more. Management stewardship may be assessed by examining the composition of the net income or, perhaps, comprehensive income for companies that report under IFRS.

SUMMARY PROBLEM FOR YOUR REVIEW

The following information was taken from the ledger of Kajal Exports Ltd. at December 31, 2017:

Loss on sale of discontinued operations...............................	$ 20,000	Selling expenses..................................	$ 78,000
Prior year error—credit to Retained Earnings..............	5,000	Common shares, 40,000 shares issued and outstanding................	125,000
		Sales revenue	620,000
Gain on sale of property............	61,000	Interest expense.................................	30,000
Income tax expense (saving)		Cost of goods sold............................	380,000
Continuing operations............	42,000	Operating income, discontinued operations...............	30,000
Discontinued operations			
Operating income...............	10,500	Loss due to lawsuit............................	11,000
Loss on sale	(7,000)	General expenses................................	62,000
Total dividends..........................	19,000	Preferred shares, $4.00, cumulative, 1,000 shares issued and outstanding................	50,000
Retained earnings, January 1, 2017, as originally reported	108,000		

Required

Prepare a single-step income statement first, then a statement of retained earnings, then a statement of shareholders' equity for Kajal Exports Ltd. for the year ended December 31, 2017. Include the EPS presentation and show computations. Assume no changes in the share accounts during the year, and assume a 35 percent tax rate.

SOLUTION

KAJAL EXPORTS LTD.
Income Statement
For the Year Ended December 31, 2017

Revenue and gains			
Sales revenue			$620,000
Gain on sale of property			61,000
Total revenues and gains			681,000
Expenses and losses			
Cost of goods sold		$380,000	
General expenses		62,000	
Income tax expense		42,000	
Interest expense		30,000	
Loss due to lawsuit		11,000	
Selling expenses		78,000	
Total expenses and losses			603,000
Income from continuing operations			78,000
Discontinued operations			
Operating income	$30,000		
Less income tax	(10,500)	19,500	
Loss on sale of discontinued operations	(20,000)		
Less income tax saving	7,000	(13,000)	6,500
Net income			$ 84,500
Earnings per share ←			
Income from continuing operations			$1.85
Income from discontinued operations			0.16
Net income			$2.01

Recall that a single-step income statement shows cost of goods sold as an expense and does not show the calculation for gross profit. In addition, gains and losses are shown as part of income from continuing operations and not as a separate section. A multi-step version is illustrated in Exhibit 14–5 on page 793.

Expenses include all normal operating costs related to the revenue reported. Income tax expense is included here.

Discontinued operations are reported net of income tax of 35 percent. Exhibit 14–5 on page 793 shows an alternative layout for this section.

[($78,000 – $4,000) ÷ 40,000 shares]
($6,500 ÷ 40,000 shares)
[($84,500 – $4,000) ÷ 40,000 shares]

$$\text{Earnings per share} = \frac{\text{Net income} - \text{Preferred dividends}}{\text{Weighted average number of common shares outstanding}}$$

Preferred dividends: $1,000 \times \$4.00 = \$4,000$

KAJAL EXPORTS LTD.
Statement of Retained Earnings
For the Year Ended December 31, 2017

Retained earnings, January 1, 2017, as originally reported	$108,000
Correction of prior year error—credit	5,000
Retained earnings, January 1, 2017, as adjusted	113,000
Net income for current year	84,500
	197,500
Dividends for 2017	(19,000)
Retained earnings, December 31, 2017	$178,500

Prior period adjustments must be disclosed in a separate line in the statement of retained earnings.

KAJAL EXPORTS LTD. Statement of Shareholders' Equity For the Year Ended December 31, 2017				
	Common Shares	Preferred Shares	Retained Earnings	Total Shareholders' Equity
Balance, December 31, 2016	$125,000	$50,000	$108,000	$283,000
Adjustment to correct error			5,000	5,000
Net income			84,500	84,500
Cash dividends			(19,000)	(19,000)
Balance, December 31, 2017	$125,000	$50,000	$178,500	$353,500

The Retained Earnings column of the statement of shareholders' equity contains the same information as the statement of retained earnings created earlier.

SUMMARY

LEARNING OBJECTIVE ① Account for stock dividends and stock splits

How do we account for stock dividends and stock splits?   Pg. 783

- *Stock dividends*, or *share dividends*, are distributions of the corporation's own shares to its shareholders. At the date of declaration, the following journal entry would be made:

Date	Retained Earnings	Market value	
	Common Stock Dividend Distributable		Market value

- *Stock dividends* have the following effects:

Retained Earnings ↓	↑ Common Shares	Total Shareholders' Equity is unchanged by a stock dividend.

- *Stock splits* do not change any account balances.
- Stock splits and stock dividends increase the number of shares outstanding and, thus, lower the market price per share.

LEARNING OBJECTIVE ② Account for repurchased shares

Why are shares repurchased, and how do we account for them?   Pg. 788

- *Repurchased shares* are the corporation's own shares that have been issued and reacquired by the corporation.

Repurchase at average issue price:

Common Shares	Number repurchased × Average cost per share	
Cash		Number repurchased × Price paid per share

Repurchase below average issue price:

Common Shares	Number repurchased × Average cost per share	
Contributed Surplus— Share Repurchase		Difference between Cash and Common Shares amounts
Cash		Number repurchased × Price paid per share

Repurchase above average issue price:

Common Shares	Number repurchased × Average cost per share	
Contributed Surplus— Share Repurchase	Use up the credit balance in this account first	
Retained Earnings	The amount of any remaining difference (the "plug" amount)	
Cash		Number repurchased × Price paid per share

How do we prepare a corporate income statement? Pg. 792

- The corporate *income statement* lists separately the various sources of income—*income from continuing operations* (which includes unusual gains and losses), and *discontinued operations*—as well as related *income tax expense*.
- The bottom line of the income statement reports *net income* or *net loss* for the period. *Earnings per share* figures may also appear on the income statement.
- Earnings per share is calculated as follows:

$$\text{Earnings per share} = \frac{\text{Net income} - \text{Preferred dividends}}{\text{Weighted average number of common shares outstanding}}$$

LEARNING OBJECTIVE ④ Prepare a statement of retained earnings and a statement of shareholders' equity

How do we prepare a statement of retained earnings and a statement of shareholders' equity? Pg. 798

- A corporation must prepare a statement of retained earnings, which reports the changes in the Retained Earnings account, including prior period adjustments, net income or net loss, and dividends paid. This statement may be combined with the income statement.
- Corporations may prepare a statement of shareholders' equity, which reports the changes in all the shareholders' equity accounts, including sales and repurchases of a corporation's own shares, cash and stock dividends paid, and net income or loss.

LEARNING OBJECTIVE ⑤ Identify the impact of IFRS on the income statement and the statement of shareholders' equity

What is the impact of IFRS on the income statement and statement of shareholders' equity? Pg. 803

- Companies that report under IFRS must present EPS information on their income statement and must report comprehensive income in a statement of comprehensive income.
- Under IFRS, the statement of shareholders' equity is called the statement of changes in equity. No statement of retained earnings is prepared.

Check **Accounting Vocabulary** below for all key terms used in Chapter 14 and the Glossary at the back of the book for all key terms used in the textbook.

MORE CHAPTER REVIEW MATERIAL

MyAccountingLab

DemoDoc covering Stock Splits and Stock Dividends

Student PowerPoint Slides

Audio Chapter Summary

Note: All MyAccountingLab resources can be found in the Chapter Resources section and the Multimedia Library.

ACCOUNTING VOCABULARY

Appropriations Restriction of retained earnings that is recorded by a formal journal entry *(p. 802)*.

Basic EPS Earnings per share calculated using the number of outstanding common shares *(p. 797)*.

Capitalized retained earnings Retained earnings that are not available for distribution. Stock dividends result in retained earnings being moved to contributed capital *(p. 783)*.

Consolidation A decrease in the number of shares outstanding by a fixed ratio. Also called a *reverse split* *(p. 786)*.

Conversion privileges Shareholders with this right may exchange specified bonds or shares into a stated number of common shares *(p. 797)*.

Earnings per share (EPS) The amount of a company's net income per outstanding common share *(p. 795)*.

Fully diluted EPS Earnings per share calculated using the number of outstanding common shares plus the number of additional common shares that would arise from conversion of convertible bonds and convertible preferred shares into common shares *(p. 798)*.

Insider trading According to the Canada Business Corporations Act, the purchase/sale of a security by someone who knows information not known by the general public that might affect the price of that security *(p. 792)*.

Memorandum entry   A journal entry without debits and credits   *(p. 786).*

Other comprehensive income   Income that arises from a number of sources, including unrealized gains and losses on certain classes of investment securities due in part to the use of fair value measurement   *(p. 804).*

Price–earnings ratio   (or price-to-earnings ratio, or P/E) The market price of a common share divided by the company's earnings per share. Measures the value that the stock market places on $1 of a company's earnings   *(p. 798).*

Prospective   In the future. For example, changes in accounting estimates are reflected in future financial statements, *not* in past financial statements   *(p. 802).*

Repurchase shares   When a corporation purchases its own shares that it issued previously   *(p. 788).*

Retrospective   In the past. For example, changes in accounting policies are reflected in past financial statement figures as if those policies had always been in place   *(p. 801).*

Reverse split   Another name for a share *consolidation* *(p. 786).*

Segment of the business   A significant part of a company   *(p. 794).*

Share dividend   Another name for a *stock dividend* *(p. 783).*

Statement of equity   Another name for *statement of shareholders' equity*   *(p. 799).*

Statement of shareholders' equity   Presents changes in all components of equity. Also called *statement of equity* *(p. 799).*

Stock dividend   A proportional distribution by a corporation of its own shares to its shareholders. Also called a *share dividend*   *(p. 783).*

Stock split   An increase in the number of authorized and outstanding shares coupled with a proportionate reduction in the book value of each share   *(p. 785).*

Treasury shares   When a corporation repurchases its own shares and holds the shares in its treasury for resale   *(p. 788).*

SIMILAR ACCOUNTING TERMS

Consolidation	Reverse split
Income Statement	Statement of Earnings
Price–earnings ratio	Price-to-earnings ratio; P/E ratio
Shareholders' equity	Stockholders' equity (US term)
Statement of shareholders' equity	Statement of equity; Statement of changes in equity
Stock dividend	Share dividend

SELF-STUDY QUESTIONS

Test your understanding of the chapter by marking the best answer for each of the following questions:

1. A corporation has total shareholders' equity of $100,000, including Retained Earnings of $38,000. The Cash balance is $40,000. The maximum cash dividend the company can declare and pay is *(pp. 782–783)*
    a. $38,000   c. $30,000
    b. $40,000   d. $100,000

2. A stock dividend, or share dividend, *(p. 783)*
    a. Decreases shareholders' equity
    b. Decreases assets
    c. Leaves total shareholders' equity unchanged
    d. Does none of the above

3. Acres Ltd. has 10,000 common shares outstanding. The shares were issued at $20.00 per share, and now their market value is $40.00 per share. Acres' board of directors declares and distributes a common stock dividend of one share for every 10 held. Which of the following

entries shows the full effect of declaring and distributing the dividend? *(pp. 784–785)*

a.	Retained Earnings	40,000	
	Common Stock Dividend		
	Distributable		40,000
b.	Retained Earnings	20,000	
	Common Shares		20,000
c.	Retained Earnings	20,000	
	Cash		20,000
d.	Retained Earnings	40,000	
	Common Shares		40,000

4. Lang Real Estate Investment Corporation declared and distributed a 50 percent stock dividend. Which of the following stock splits would have the same effect on the number of Lang shares outstanding? *(p. 785)*
    a. 2 for 1   c. 4 for 3
    b. 3 for 2   d. 5 for 4

5. Deer Lake Outfitters Ltd. purchased 10,000 of its common shares that had been issued at $1.50 per share, paying $7.00 per share. This transaction (p. 788)
   a. Has no effect on company assets
   b. Has no effect on shareholders' equity
   c. Decreases shareholders' equity by $15,000
   d. Decreases shareholders' equity by $70,000

6. A restriction of retained earnings (p. 802)
   a. Has no effect on total retained earnings
   b. Reduces retained earnings available for the declaration of dividends
   c. Is usually reported by a note
   d. Does all of the above

7. Which of the following items is not reported on the income statement? (p. 793)
   a. Issue price of shares
   b. Unusual gains and losses
   c. Income tax expense
   d. Earnings per share

8. The income statement item that is likely to be most useful for predicting income from year to year is (pp. 793–794)
   a. Unusual items
   b. Discontinued operations
   c. Income from continuing operations
   d. Net income

9. In computing earnings per share (EPS), dividends on cumulative preferred shares are (p. 795)
   a. Added because they represent earnings to the preferred shareholders
   b. Subtracted because they represent earnings to the preferred shareholders
   c. Ignored because they do not pertain to the common shares
   d. Reported separately on the income statement

10. Which of the following financial statements is not required under ASPE? (p. 804)
    a. Statement of retained earnings
    b. Statement of income
    c. Statement of shareholders' equity
    d. Statement of financial position

ASSIGNMENT MATERIAL

QUESTIONS

1. Identify the two main sections of shareholders' equity and explain how they differ.

2. Identify the account debited and the account credited from the last closing entry a corporation makes each year. What is the purpose of this entry?

3. Hoc Automotive Ltd. reported a Cash balance of $2 million and a Retained Earnings balance of $12 million. Explain how Hoc Automotive Ltd. can have so much more retained earnings than cash. In your answer, identify the nature of retained earnings and state how it ties to cash.

4. Give two reasons why a corporation might distribute a stock dividend.

5. A friend of yours receives a stock dividend on an investment. She believes stock dividends are the same as cash dividends. Explain why the two are not the same.

6. Poly Panels Inc. declares a stock dividend on June 21 and reports Stock Dividend Payable as a liability on the June 30 balance sheet. Is this correct? Give your reason.

7. What value is normally assigned to shares issued as a stock dividend?

8. Explain the similarity and difference between a 100 percent stock dividend and a 2-for-1 stock split to the corporation issuing the stock dividend and the stock split.

9. Give three reasons why a corporation may repurchase its own shares.

10. What effect does the repurchase and cancellation of common shares have on the (a) assets, (b) authorized shares, and (c) issued and outstanding shares of the corporation?

11. Are there any cases when a company does not cancel its repurchased shares? If so, what are they?

12. Incorporating legislation frequently has a prohibition on a corporation purchasing its own shares in certain circumstances. What are those circumstances? Why does the prohibition exist?

13. Why do creditors wish to restrict a corporation's payment of cash dividends and repurchases of the corporation's shares?

14. Why is it necessary to use the *weighted* average number of common shares in the earnings per share calculation rather than the average number of common shares?

15. What is the earnings per share of Phukett Realty Ltd., which had net income of $48,750 and a weighted average number of common shares of 15,000?

16. What are two ways to report a retained earnings restriction? Which way is more common?

17. Identify two items on the income statement that generate income tax expense. What is an income tax saving, and how does it arise?

18. Why is it important for a corporation to report income from continuing operations separately from discontinued operations?

19. Give four examples of gains and losses that are unusual and reported separately in the continuing operations section of the income statement.

20. For errors made in prior periods, what account do all corrections affect? On what financial statement are these corrections reported?

MyAccountingLab   Make the grade with MyAccountingLab: Most of the Starters, Exercises, and Problems marked in `red` can be found on MyAccountingLab. You can practise them as often as you want, and most feature step-by-step guided instructions to help you find the right answer.

STARTERS

Interpreting retained earnings
(1)

Starter 14–1 The Retained Earnings account has the following transactions in 2017 shown in a T-account format:

Retained Earnings

	180,000
20,000	X
	220,000

1. What does X represent?
2. How much is X?
3. What does the amount of $20,000 represent?

Recording a stock dividend
(1)

1. Dr Retained Earnings, $36,000

Starter 14–2 Rad Roadsters Ltd. has 10,000 common shares outstanding. Rad distributes a 20 percent stock dividend when the market value of its shares is $18.00 per share.

1. Journalize Rad's declaration of the stock dividend on September 30, 2017, and the distribution of the stock dividend on October 30, 2017. Explanations are not required.
2. What is the overall effect of the stock dividend on Rad's total assets? On total shareholders' equity?

Comparing and contrasting cash dividends and stock dividends
(1)

Starter 14–3 Compare and contrast the accounting for cash dividends and stock dividends. In the space provided, insert either "Cash dividends," "Stock dividends," or "Both cash dividends and stock dividends" to complete each of the following statements:

1. _____decrease Retained Earnings.
2. _____have no effect on a liability.
3. _____increase contributed capital by the same amount that they decrease retained earnings.
4. _____decrease both total assets and total shareholders' equity, resulting in a decrease in the size of the company.

Accounting for a stock split
(1)

1. Total shareholders' equity, $332,000

Starter 14–4 Jurgen's Farms Inc. recently reported the following shareholders' equity:

Common shares, 250,000 shares authorized, 55,000 shares issued and outstanding	$121,500
Retained earnings	210,500
Total shareholders' equity	$332,000

Suppose Jurgen's Farms split its common shares 2 for 1 to decrease the market price of its shares. The company's shares were trading at $83.00 immediately before the split.

1. Prepare the shareholders' equity section of Jurgen's Farms Inc.'s balance sheet after the stock split.
2. Which account balances changed after the stock split? Which account balances remain unchanged?

Starter 14–5

Anderson Products Inc. issued 100,000 common shares at $10.00 per share. Later, when the market price was $15.00 per share, the company distributed a 10 percent stock dividend. Then Anderson Products Inc. repurchased 500 shares at $20.00 per share. What is the final balance in the Common Shares account?

Stock dividend and repurchase
① ②

Starter 14–6

Boris' Dollar Store Inc. repurchased 1,000 common shares, paying cash of $12.00 per share on April 16, 2017. The shares were originally issued for $5.00 per share. Journalize the transaction. An explanation is not required.

Accounting for the repurchase of common shares
②

Starter 14–7

Justice Inc. began 2017 with the following account balances:

Common shares, 150,000 shares authorized, 75,000 issued	$2,175,000
Retained earnings	820,000

In early 2017, Justice Inc. reported the following transactions:

Jan. 10	Repurchased 7,500 of its own shares for $31 per share.
Feb. 20	Sold 4,000 of the repurchased shares for $32 per share.
Mar. 30	Sold the remaining repurchased shares for $25 per share.

Record journal entries for the above transactions.

Share repurchase entries
②

March 30, $87,500

Starter 14–8

List the major parts of a multi-step corporate income statement for Star Pilates Trainers Inc. for the year ended December 31, 2017. Include all the major parts of the income statement, starting with net sales revenue and ending with net income (net loss). Remember to separate continuing operations from discontinued operations. You may ignore dollar amounts and earnings per share.

Preparing a corporate income statement
③

Starter 14–9

Answer these questions about a corporate income statement:

1. How do you measure gross margin?
2. What is the title of those items that are unusual, infrequent, and over which management has no influence or control?
3. Which income number is the best predictor of future net income?
4. What does *EPS* abbreviate?

Explaining the items on a complex corporate income statement
③

Starter 14–10

Gala Fruit Corp's accounting records include the following items, listed in no particular order, at December 31, 2017:

Other gains (losses)............	$(12,500)	Net sales revenue............	$100,000
Cost of goods sold.............	35,000	Operating expenses..........	30,000
Gain on discontinued operations.......................	8,500	Accounts receivable.........	9,500

Income tax of 30 percent applies to all items.

Prepare Gala Fruit Corp.'s multi-step income statement for the year ended December 31, 2017. Omit earnings per share.

Preparing a corporate income statement
③

Net income, $21,700

Starter 14–11 Return to the Gala Fruit Corp. data in Starter 14–10. Gala Fruit had 10,000 common shares outstanding on January 1, 2017. Gala Fruit declared and paid preferred dividends of $1,500 during 2017. In addition, Gala Fruit paid a 20 percent common stock dividend on June 30.

Show how Gala Fruit Corp. reported EPS data on its 2017 income statement.

Starter 14–12 Figero Inc. has $350,000 of income in 2017. During that same time it declared preferred dividends in the amount of $13,000. The following activities affecting common shares occurred during the year:

Jan. 1	120,000 common shares were outstanding
Aug. 1	Sold 35,000 common shares
Sep. 1	Issued a 10 percent common stock dividend

1. Calculate the weighted average number of common shares outstanding during the year.
2. Calculate earnings per share. Round to the nearest cent.

Starter 14–13 The net income of Hart Corporation amounted to $3,750,000 for the year ended December 31, 2017. There were 200,000, $9.00 cumulative preferred shares throughout the year. At January 1, 2017, Hart Corporation had 270,000 common shares outstanding and issued 40,000 common shares on April 1. Then, on October 1, there was a 3-for-1 stock split of the common shares. Calculate Hart Corporation's EPS.

Starter 14–14 PR Investments Corp. ended its fiscal year on October 31, 2016, with Retained Earnings of $60,000. During 2017, the company earned net income of $155,000 and declared dividends of $17,000. The company ended 2016 with $75,000 in common shares and $15,000 in $2 preferred shares. Additional common shares were sold in 2017 for $25,000. Complete PR Investments Corp.'s statement of shareholders' equity for the year ended October 31, 2017.

PR INVESTMENTS CORP.
Statement of Shareholders' Equity
For the Year Ended October 31, 2017

	Common Shares	Preferred Shares	Retained Earnings	Total Shareholders' Equity
Balance, October 31, 2016				
Balance October 31, 2017				

Starter 14–15 Oak Research Inc. (ORI) ended 2016 with Retained Earnings of $37,500. During 2017 ORI earned net income of $40,000 and declared dividends of $15,000. Also during 2017 ORI got a $12,000 tax refund from the Canada Revenue Agency. A tax audit revealed that ORI paid too much income tax in 2015 in error.

Prepare ORI's statement of retained earnings for the year ended December 31, 2017, to report the correction of the prior period error.

Starter 14–16 Return to the Oak Research Inc. (ORI) data in Starter 14–15. ORI ended 2016 with $20,000 in common shares and $15,000 in $0.50 preferred shares. No shares were sold or repurchased during 2017. Create ORI's statement of shareholders' equity for the year ended December 31, 2017.

Starter 14-17 For each of the following situations, indicate whether there is a change in estimate, a change of policy, or an error by inserting a check mark in the correct box. Then indicate if the correction needs to be applied retrospectively (change past statement information) or prospectively (only future statements will be affected) by checking the correct box in the right two columns.

Describing accounting changes ④

	Change in Estimate	Change in Policy	Error	Retrospective Statement	Prospective Statement
A switch from the weighted-average method of inventory to the FIFO method.					
Management decided the welding equipment will last 12 years and not the original estimate of 10 years.					
Missing expense invoices were found after the financial statements were finalized.					

Starter 14-18 BLT Corporation's agreement with its bank lender restricts BLT's dividend payments. Why would a bank lender restrict a corporation's dividend payments and share repurchases?

Interpreting a restriction of retained earnings ④

Starter 14-19 Companies reporting under IFRS are required to report two types of information in their financial statements that are not required for companies reporting under ASPE. Describe each type of information and the financial statement on which it is reported.

Reporting under IFRS ⑤

Starter 14-20 Companies reporting under ASPE, as described in the chapter, sometimes create a statement of shareholders' equity. What is the name of a similar statement for companies reporting under IFRS?

Comparing IFRS and ASPE ⑤

Starter 14-21 Prepare a simple statement of comprehensive income for Yoshi Corporation using the following information:

- For the year ended June 30, 2017
- Loss for the year is $25,000
- Gain on equity investments is $60,000
- Tax rate is 25 percent

Preparing a statement of comprehensive income ⑤

Comprehensive income, $20,000

EXERCISES

MyAccountingLab

Exercise 14-1

The shareholders' equity for King Paving Inc. on June 30, 2017 (end of the company's fiscal year), follows:

Journalizing a stock dividend and reporting shareholders' equity ①

2. Total shareholders' equity, $680,000

Common shares, 800,000 shares authorized, 80,000 shares issued and outstanding	$300,000
Retained earnings	380,000
Total shareholders' equity	$680,000

On August 8, 2017, the market price of King Paving Inc.'s common shares was $12.00 per share and the company declared a 20 percent stock dividend. King Paving Inc. issued the dividend shares on August 31, 2017.

Required

1. Journalize the declaration and distribution of the stock dividend.
2. Prepare the shareholders' equity section of the balance sheet after the stock dividend distribution.

Exercise 14–2

Journalizing equity transactions

①

Stock dividend, $120,000

Nguyen Limited reports the following transactions for 2016:

Feb. 1   Sold 6,000 shares of $1.50, noncumulative, preferred shares for $70 per share.

Feb. 20   Sold 30,000 common shares for $9 per share.

Oct. 13   Declared a 10 percent stock dividend on the common shares. The current market price of the common shares is $12 per share. There are 100,000 common shares outstanding on October 13.

Nov. 16   Distributed the stock dividend declared on October 13.

Dec. 11   Declared the annual dividend required on the preferred shares and a $0.35 per share dividend on the common shares. There are 20,000 preferred shares outstanding at this time.

Required Prepare journal entries for the above transactions. Explanations are not required.

Exercise 14–3

Journalizing dividends and reporting shareholders' equity

①

3. Total shareholders' equity, $850,350

Poco Travel Ltd. is authorized to issue 500,000 common shares. The company issued 70,000 shares at $7.50 per share. On June 10, 2017, when the Retained Earnings balance was $360,000, Poco Travel Ltd. declared a 10 percent stock dividend using the market value of $4.00 per share. It distributed the stock dividend on July 20, 2017. On August 5, 2017, Poco Travel Ltd. declared a $0.45 per share cash dividend, which it paid on September 15, 2017.

Required

1. Journalize the declaration and distribution of the stock dividend.
2. Journalize the declaration and payment of the cash dividend.
3. Prepare the shareholders' equity section of the balance sheet after both dividends.

Exercise 14–4

Reporting shareholders' equity after a stock split

①

Total shareholders' equity, $600,000

Halifax Metal Products Ltd. had the following shareholders' equity at October 31, 2017:

Common shares, unlimited shares authorized, 60,000 shares issued and outstanding	$150,000
Retained earnings	450,000
Total shareholders' equity	$600,000

On November 14, 2017, Halifax Metal Products Ltd. split its common shares 2 for 1. Make the memorandum entry to record the stock split, and prepare the shareholders' equity section of the balance sheet immediately after the split.

Exercise 14–5

Accounting for a reverse stock split (consolidation)

①

Total shareholders' equity, $600,000

Examine Halifax Metal Products Ltd.'s shareholders' equity section for October 31, 2017, in Exercise 14–4. Suppose Halifax Metal Products Ltd. consolidated its common shares 1 for 2 (a reverse stock split) to increase the market price of its shares. The company's shares were trading at $6.00 immediately before the reverse split. Make the memorandum entry to record the share consolidation, and prepare the shareholders' equity section of Halifax Metal Products Ltd.'s balance sheet after the share consolidation. What would you expect the market price to be, approximately, after the reverse split?

Exercise 14–6

Using a stock split or a stock dividend to decrease the market price of a share

①

Usurp Corp., an Internet service provider, has prospered during the past seven years, and recently the company's share price has shot up to $244.00. Usurp's management wishes to decrease the share price to the range of $116.00 to $124.00, which will be attractive to more investors. Should the company issue a 100 percent stock dividend or split the stock? Why? If you propose a stock split, state the split ratio that will accomplish the company's objective. Show your computations.

Exercise 14–7

Identify the effects of these transactions on shareholders' equity. Has shareholders' equity increased, decreased, or remained the same? Each transaction is independent.

a. A 10 percent stock dividend. Before the dividend, 400,000 common shares were outstanding; market value was $7.50 at the time of the dividend.

b. A 2-for-1 stock split. Prior to the split, 50,000 common shares were outstanding.

c. Repurchase of 5,000 common shares at $7.00 per share. The average issue price of these shares was $5.00.

d. Sale of 2,000 repurchased common shares for $6.50 per share.

Effects of share issuance, dividends, and share repurchase transactions
① ②

Exercise 14–8

Journalize the following transactions that Fritter Technologies Ltd. conducted during 2017:

Feb.	19	Issued 10,000 common shares at $15.00 per share.
Apr.	24	Repurchased 2,000 common shares at $13.00 per share. The average issue price of the shares was $14.00.
Jun.	30	Repurchased 2,000 common shares at $18.00 per share. The average issue price of the shares was $14.00.

Journalizing share repurchase transactions
②
April 24 contributed surplus, $2,000

Exercise 14–9

Debon Ltd. had the following shareholders' equity on March 26, 2017:

Common shares, unlimited shares authorized, 140,000 shares issued and outstanding	$420,000
Retained earnings	475,000
Total shareholders' equity	$895,000

On May 3, 2017, the company repurchased and cancelled 5,000 common shares at $3.50 per share.

1. Journalize this transaction and prepare the shareholders' equity section of the balance sheet at June 30, 2017.

2. How many common shares are outstanding after the share repurchase?

Journalizing repurchase of company shares and reporting shareholders' equity
②
1. Total shareholders' equity, $877,500

Exercise 14–10

Shareholders' Equity ($ amounts in millions)	
Adapted from a corporation's annual report	
Contributed capital	
Preferred shares (Note 15)*	$ 4,384
Common shares (Note 16)**	8,432
Retained earnings	24,662
Accumulated other comprehensive income (loss)	(4,718)
	$32,760

*Note 15: Preferred Shares (adapted) Authorized

An unlimited number of Preferred Shares without nominal or par value.

Issued and fully paid

Preferred shares   175,345,767 shares

**Note 16: Common Shares (adapted) Authorized

An unlimited number of Common Shares without nominal or par value.

Issued and fully paid

Common shares   1,088,972,173

Accounting for the repurchase of preferred shares
②
(b) Reduced by $4,384 million

Suppose the corporation repurchased its preferred shares. What would be the amount of the reduction of the company's total shareholders' equity if the cost to repurchase the preferred shares was (a) $5,000 million? (b) $4,384 million? (c) $4,000 million?

Exercise 14–11

Preparing a single-step income statement

③

Net income, $61,230

The following accounts are from Mizuko Limited's general ledger. All data are shown before tax.

Sales revenue	$306,000	Cost of goods sold	$199,000
Interest revenue	13,000	Loss on discontinued operations	10,000
Interest expense	4,500	Operating expenses	46,000
Gain on sale of vehicle	19,000		

Required Prepare a single-step income statement for the year ended December 31, 2017. Omit earnings per share. The income tax rate is 22 percent. (Hint: This format is presented in the Summary Problem on page 807.)

Exercise 14–12

Excel Spreadsheet Template
Preparing a multi-step income statement

③

Net income, $32,500

The ledger of Pottery Supplies Inc. contains the following information for operations for the year ended September 30, 2017:

Sales revenue	$350,000	Income tax expense—gain on discontinued operations	$ 8,500
Operating expenses (excluding income tax)	67,500	Other loss	22,500
Cost of goods sold	230,000	Income tax expense— operating income	10,000
Gain on discontinued operations	21,000		

Required Prepare a multi-step income statement for the year ended September 30, 2017. Omit earnings per share. Was 2017 a good year or a bad year for Pottery Supplies Inc.? Explain your answer in terms of the outlook for 2018.

Exercise 14–13

Computing earnings per share

③

EPS = $1.16

Zelda Solutions Inc. earned net income of $122,000 in 2017. The ledger reveals the following figures:

Preferred shares, $1.50, 4,000 shares issued and outstanding	$ 50,000
Common shares, unlimited shares authorized, 100,000 shares issued	300,000

Required Compute Zelda Solutions Inc.'s EPS for 2017, assuming no changes in the share accounts during the year.

Exercise 14–14

Computing earnings per share

③

EPS for net income, $0.40

LeDuc Construction Ltd. had 60,000 common shares and 20,000, $0.75 cumulative preferred shares outstanding on December 31, 2016. On April 30, 2017, the company issued 6,000 additional common shares and split the common shares 2 for 1 on December 1, 2017. There were no other share issuances and no share repurchases during the year ended December 31, 2017. Income for the year from continuing operations was $70,000, and loss on discontinued operations (net of income tax) was $4,000.

Required Compute LeDuc Construction Ltd.'s EPS amounts for the year ended December 31, 2017.

Exercise 14–15

Reporting a retained earnings restriction

②

a. Total shareholders' equity, $587,500

The agreement under which Karset Transport Ltd. issued its long-term debt requires the restriction of $150,000 of the company's Retained Earnings balance. Total Retained Earnings is $337,500, and total contributed capital is $250,000.

Required Show how to report shareholders' equity (including retained earnings) on Karset Transport Ltd.'s balance sheet at December 31, 2017, assuming:

a. Karset Transport Ltd. discloses the restriction in a note. Write the note.

b. Karset Transport Ltd. appropriates retained earnings in the amount of the restriction and includes no note in its statements.

Exercise 14–16

Excel Spreadsheet Template
Preparing a statement of retained earnings
(4)
Retained earnings, Dec. 31, 2017, $275.0 million

Pacific Hotels Inc., a large hotel chain, had Retained Earnings of $250.0 million at the beginning of 2017. The company showed these figures at December 31, 2017:

	($ millions)
Net income	$75.0
Cash dividends—Preferred	1.5
Common	44.5
Debit to retained earnings due to repurchase of preferred shares	4.0

Required Prepare the statement of retained earnings for Pacific Hotels Inc. for the year ended December 31, 2017.

Exercise 14–17

Excel Spreadsheet Template
Preparing a statement of retained earnings with a correction of a prior period error
(4)
Retained earnings, Dec. 31, 2017, $2,745,000

Lankin Concrete Products Ltd. reported the correction of an error made in the year ended December 31, 2017. An inventory error caused net income of the prior year to be overstated by $50,000. Retained Earnings at January 1, 2017, as previously reported, stood at $2,408,000. Net income for the year ended December 31, 2017, was $448,000, and dividends were $61,000.

Required Prepare the company's statement of retained earnings for the year ended December 31, 2017.

Exercise 14–18

Preparing a statement of shareholders' equity
(3)
Total shareholders' equity, Dec. 31, 2017, $2,352,000

For the year ended December 31, 2016, Evans Inc. reported the following shareholders' equity:

Common shares, 400,000 shares authorized, 140,000 shares issued and outstanding	$1,400,000
Retained earnings	672,000
Total shareholders' equity	$2,072,000

During 2017, Evans Inc. completed these transactions and events (listed in chronological order):

a. Declared and issued a 10 percent stock dividend. At the time, Evans Inc.'s common shares were quoted at a market price of $11.50 per share.

b. Sold 1,000 common shares for $12.50 per share.

c. Sold 1,000 common shares to employees at $10.00 per share.

d. Net income for the year was $397,500.

e. Declared and paid cash dividends of $140,000.

Required Prepare Evans Inc.'s statement of shareholders' equity for 2017.

Exercise 14–19

Prepare the shareholders' equity section of a balance sheet
(4)

The shareholders' equity of Inspiration Management Corp. as of December 31, 2016, follows:

Preferred shares, $3, noncumulative 20,000 shares authorized, 4,000 shares issued	$ 200,000
Common shares, unlimited shares authorized, 200,000 shares issued	2,000,000
Total contributed capital	2,200,000
Retained earnings	626,900
Total shareholders' equity	$2,826,900

Inspiration Management Corp. completed the following transactions during 2017:

Feb. 6   Declared the required annual cash dividend on preferred shares and a $0.20 per share cash dividend on the common shares.

    26   Paid the cash dividend that was declared on February 6.

Jun. 4   Purchased 6,000 of its own common shares for $15.25 per share.

Jul. 5   Distributed a 2-for-1 stock split on the common shares.

The net loss for the year was 78,000.

Required Prepare the shareholders' equity section of the balance sheet of Inspiration Management Corp. as of December 31, 2017. Do not prepare journal entries for the above transactions.

SERIAL EXERCISE

This exercise continues the Lee Consulting Corporation situation from Exercise 13–20 of Chapter 13. If you did not complete any Serial Exercises in earlier chapters, you can still complete Exercise 14–20 as it is presented.

Exercise 14–20

Journalizing and reporting share sale and repurchase transactions
② ③
2. Common Shares ending balance, $41,529

To raise cash for future expansion, Michael Lee incorporated his proprietorship and created Lee Consulting Corporation. The corporation is authorized to issue an unlimited number of common shares and 50,000 $2.00 preferred shares. In July 2016, Michael Lee purchased 20,000 common shares for his proprietorship equity of $30,221 and issued 1,000 of the preferred shares for $50.00 per share to increase his investment in the business.

In August 2016, Lee Consulting Corporation has the following transactions related to its common shares:

Aug. 3   The company sold 1,000 of its common shares for $10.00 per share to a small number of people who believed in the company's potential for profit.

    20   The company repurchased 100 of its common shares for $12.00 per share from a shareholder who was having financial difficulties.

    30   The company sold 100 common shares for $15.00 per share.

Required

1. Journalize the entries related to the transactions.
2. Calculate the ending balance in the Common Shares account.
3. Prepare the statement of shareholders' equity for August 31, 2016. Assume that net income for the period was $67,500.

CHALLENGE EXERCISE

Exercise 14–21

Analyzing stock split and share repurchase transactions
②
6. b. Common Shares outstanding, 13,000

Scopis Ltd. reported its shareholders' equity as shown below:

Shareholders' Equity		
Preferred shares, $1.00		
Authorized: 10,000 shares		
Issued and outstanding: None	$	0
Common shares		
Authorized: 100,000 shares		
Issued and outstanding: 14,000 shares		70,000
Retained earnings		84,000
		$154,000

Required

1. What was the average issue price per common share?

2. Journalize the issuance of 1,200 common shares at $8.00 per share. Use Scopis Ltd.'s account titles.

3. After completing Requirement 2, how many Scopis Ltd. common shares are now outstanding?

4. How many common shares would be outstanding after Scopis Ltd. splits its common shares (computed in Requirement 3) 3 for 1?

5. Using Scopis Ltd.'s account titles, journalize the declaration of a 10 percent stock dividend when the market price of Scopis Ltd.'s common shares is $6.00 per share. Use the shares outstanding from Requirement 3.

6. Ignore the prior transactions and return to the Scopis Ltd. shareholders' equity information in Requirement 1, which shows 14,000 common shares issued.

   a. Journalize the following share repurchase transactions by Scopis Ltd., assuming they occur in the order given:

      i. Scopis Ltd. repurchases 500 of its own shares at $16.00 per share.

      ii. Scopis Ltd. repurchases 500 of its own shares at $4.00 per share.

   b. How many Scopis Ltd. common shares would be outstanding after the transactions in part (a) take place?

Exercise 14–22

Tillay Environmental Products Inc. (TEPI) began 2017 with 1.6 million common shares issued and outstanding for $4.0 million. Beginning Retained Earnings was $4.5 million. On February 26, 2017, TEPI issued 100,000 common shares at $3.50 per share. On November 16, 2017, when the market price was $5.00 per share, the board of directors declared a 10 percent stock dividend, which was paid on December 20, 2017. Net income for the year was $550,000.

Recording a stock dividend and preparing a statement of retained earnings

① ④

2. Retained Earnings, Dec. 31, 2017, $4,200,000

Required

1. Make the journal entries for the issuance of shares for cash and for the 10 percent stock dividend.

2. Prepare the company's statement of retained earnings for the year ended December 31, 2017.

BEYOND THE NUMBERS

Beyond the Numbers 14-1

The following accounting issues have arisen at Tri-City Computers Corp.:

Reporting special items

② ③

1. An investor noted that the market price of shares seemed to decline after the date of record for a cash dividend. Why do you think that would be the case?

2. Corporations sometimes repurchase their own shares. When asked why, Tri-City Computers Corp.'s management responded that the shares were undervalued. What advantage would Tri-City Computers Corp. gain by repurchasing its own shares under these circumstances?

3. Tri-City Computers Corp. earned a significant profit in the year ended June 30, 2017, because land that it held was expropriated for a low-rental housing project. The company proposes to treat the sale of land to the government as operating revenue. Why do you think Tri-City Computers Corp. is proposing such treatment? Is this treatment appropriate?

ETHICAL ISSUE

Sparkly Gold Mine Ltd. is a gold mine in Ontario. In February 2017, company geologists discovered a new vein of gold-bearing ore that tripled the company's reserves. After this discovery, but prior to disclosing the new vein to the public, top managers of the company quietly bought most of the outstanding Sparkly Gold Mine Ltd. shares for themselves personally. After the announcement of the discovery, Sparkly Gold Mine Ltd.'s share price increased from $4.00 to $30.00.

Required

1. Did Sparkly Gold Mine Ltd. managers behave ethically? Explain your answer.
2. Who was helped and who was harmed by management's action?

PROBLEMS (GROUP A)
MyAccountingLab

Problem 14–1A

Using a stock split to fight off a takeover of the corporation

①

Skiptrace Software Inc. is positioned ideally in the manufacturing and distribution sectors. It is the only company providing highly developed inventory tracking software. The company does a brisk business with companies such as Home Hardware and Roots. Skiptrace Software Inc.'s success has made the company a prime target for a takeover. Against the wishes of Skiptrace Software Inc.'s board of directors, an investment group is attempting to buy 55 percent of Skiptrace Software Inc.'s outstanding shares. Board members are convinced that the investment group would sell off the most desirable pieces of the business and leave little of value.

At the most recent board meeting, several suggestions were advanced to fight off the hostile takeover bid. One suggestion was to increase the shares outstanding by splitting the company's shares 2 for 1.

Required As a significant shareholder of Skiptrace Software Inc., write a short memo to the board advising how a stock split would affect the investor group's attempt to take over Skiptrace Software Inc. Include in your memo a discussion of the effect that the stock split would have on assets, liabilities, and total shareholders' equity; that is, the split's effect on the size of the corporation.

Problem 14–2A

Journalizing shareholders' equity transactions

① ②

Assume Frelix Construction Ltd. completed the following selected transactions during the year 2017:

Apr. 19 Declared a cash dividend on the $8.50 preferred shares (3,000 shares outstanding). Declared a $2.00 per share dividend on the 100,000 common shares outstanding. The date of record was May 2, and the payment date was May 25.

May 25 Paid the cash dividends.

Jun. 7 Split the company's 100,000 common shares 2 for 1; one new common share was issued for each old share held.

Jul. 29 Declared a 5 percent stock dividend on the common shares to holders of record on August 22, with distribution set for September 9. The market value was $36.00 per common share.

Sep. 9 Issued the stock dividend shares.

Nov. 26 Repurchased 5,000 of the company's own common shares at $40.00 per share. They had an average issue price of $28.00 per share.

Required Record the transactions in the general journal.

Problem 14–3A

Excel Spreadsheet Template
Journalizing dividend and share-repurchase transactions, reporting shareholders' equity

① ② ③

2. Total shareholders' equity, $435,000

The balance sheet of Gaitree Ltd. at December 31, 2016, reported 250,000 common shares authorized, with 75,000 shares issued and a Common Shares balance of $187,500. Retained Earnings had a credit balance of $150,000. During 2017, the company completed the following selected transactions:

Mar. 15 Repurchased 10,000 of the company's own common shares at $2.75 per share.

Apr. 29 Declared a 5 percent stock dividend on the 65,000 outstanding common shares to holders of record on May 2, with distribution set for May 16. The market value of Gaitree Ltd. common shares was $6.00 per share.

May 16 Issued the stock dividend shares.

Dec. 19 Split the common shares 2 for 1 by issuing one new share for each old share held on December 30, 2017.

31 Earned net income of $125,000 during the year.

Required

1. Record the transactions in the general journal. Explanations are not required.
2. Prepare the shareholders' equity section of the balance sheet at December 31, 2017.
3. Calculate the average issue price per share on December 31, 2017. Assume no shares were issued or repurchased after December 19, 2017.

Problem 14–4A

The information below was taken from the ledger and other records of Stahl Metalworks Corp. at September 30, 2017:

Preparing a single-step income statement

① ② ③

Net income, $21,450

Cost of goods sold	$157,500
Loss on sale of property	17,500
Sales returns	3,500
Income tax expense (saving)	
Continuing operations	13,500
Discontinued segment:	
Operating loss	(1,800)
Gain on sale	600
Gain on sale of discontinued segment	1,750
Interest expense	4,250
General expenses	42,000
Interest revenue	1,750
Preferred shares, $1.00, 15,000 shares authorized, 7,500 shares issued and outstanding	93,750
Retained earnings, October 1, 2016	30,500
Selling expenses	50,750
Common shares, 50,000 shares authorized, issued, and outstanding	165,000
Sales revenue	315,000
Dividends	11,000
Operating loss, discontinued segment	5,250
Loss on insurance settlement	4,000

Required Prepare a single-step income statement, including earnings per share, for Stahl Metalworks Corp. for the fiscal year ended September 30, 2017. Evaluate income for the year ended September 30, 2017, in terms of the outlook for 2018. Assume 2017 was a typical year and that Stahl Metalworks Corp.'s managers hoped to earn income from continuing operations equal to 10 percent of net sales.

Problem 14–5A

The capital structure of Renault Marketing Inc. at December 31, 2016, included 50,000, $0.50 preferred shares and 74,000 common shares. The 50,000 preferred shares were issued in 2009. Common shares outstanding during 2017 were 74,000 January through April and 80,000 May through September. A 20 percent stock dividend was paid on October 1. Income from continuing operations during 2017 was $122,000. The company discontinued a segment of the business at a gain (net of tax) of $9,250. The Renault Marketing Inc. board of directors restricts $125,000 of retained earnings for contingencies.

Computing earnings per share and reporting a retained earnings restriction

③

1. EPS for net income, $1.14

Required

1. Compute Renault Marketing Inc.'s earnings per share. Start with income from continuing operations. Income of $122,000 is net of income tax.
2. Show two ways of reporting Renault Marketing Inc.'s retained earnings restriction. Retained Earnings at December 31, 2016, was $145,500, and total contributed capital at December 31, 2017, is $375,000. The company declared dividends of $49,500 in 2017.

Problem 14–6A

Journalizing dividend and
stock repurchase transactions;
reporting shareholders' equity;
calculating earnings per share

① ② ③ ④

2. Total shareholders' equity,
$1,041,250

The balance sheet of Augen Vision Ltd. at December 31, 2016, reported the following share-holders' equity:

Common shares, 200,000 shares authorized, 50,000 shares issued and outstanding	$ 750,000
Retained earnings	250,000
Total shareholders' equity	$1,000,000

During 2017, Augen Vision Ltd. completed the following selected transactions:

Apr.	29	Declared a 10 percent stock dividend on the common shares. The market value of Augen Vision Ltd.'s common shares was $15.00 per share. The record date was May 20, with distribution set for June 3.
Jun.	3	Issued the stock dividend shares.
Jul.	29	Repurchased 5,000 of the company's own common shares at $13.50 per share; average issue price was $14.91.
Nov.	1	Sold 1,000 common shares for $16.50 per share.
	25	Declared a $0.25 per share dividend on the common shares outstanding. The date of record was December 16, and the payment date was January 6, 2018.
Dec.	31	Closed the $105,000 credit balance of Income Summary to Retained Earnings.

Required

1. Record the transactions in the general journal.
2. Prepare a statement of shareholders' equity at December 31, 2017.
3. Calculate earnings per share at December 31, 2017. (Hint: Use issue dates in your calculations.)

Problem 14–7A

Preparing a corrected
combined statement of income
and retained earnings

③ ④

Net income, $44,100

Muriel Thomas, accountant for Duchlorol Ltd., was injured in a hiking accident. Another employee prepared the income statement shown on the next page for the fiscal year ended December 31, 2017.

The individual amounts listed on the income statement are correct. However, some accounts are reported incorrectly, and others do not belong on the income statement at all. Also, income tax (30 percent) has not been applied to all appropriate figures. Duchlorol Ltd. issued 64,000 common shares in 2012 and has not issued or repurchased common shares since that time. The Retained Earnings balance, as originally reported at December 31, 2016, was $242,500. There were no preferred shares outstanding at December 31, 2017.

Required Prepare a corrected combined statement of income and retained earnings for the year ended December 31, 2017; include earnings per share. Prepare the income statement portion in single-step format.

DUCHLOROL LTD.
Income Statement
2017

Revenue and gains		
Sales		$295,000
Proceeds from sale of preferred shares		66,000
Gain on repurchase of preferred shares		
(issued for $76,000; repurchased for $66,500)		9,500
Total revenues and gains		370,500
Expenses and losses		
Cost of goods sold	$ 83,000	
Selling expenses	54,000	
General expenses	58,500	
Sales returns	7,500	
Dividends	5,500	
Sales discounts	4,500	
Income tax expense	29,200	
Total expenses and losses		242,200
Income from operations		128,300
Other gains and losses		
Loss on sale of discontinued operations	$ (2,500)	
Flood loss	(15,000)	
Operating loss on discontinued segment	(7,000)	
Correction for 2016 due to an inventory error	(2,000)	
Total other losses		(26,500)
Net income		$101,800
Earnings per share		$1.59

Problem 14–8A

Timpano Communication Inc. had the following shareholders' equity on January 1, 2017:

Preferred shares, $2.00, cumulative (1 year in arrears), liquidation price of $20, 100,000 shares authorized, 15,000 shares issued and outstanding	$240,000
Common shares, unlimited number of shares authorized, 25,000 shares issued and outstanding	200,000
Total contributed capital	440,000
Retained earnings	512,000
Total shareholders' equity	$952,000

Accounting for stock dividends, stock splits, share transactions, and preparing the statement of shareholders' equity

① ② ④

2. Total shareholders' equity, $1,169,750

The following transactions took place during 2017:

Jan. 14 Declared a $90,000 cash dividend, payable on March 1 to the shareholders of record on February 1. Indicate the amount payable to each class of shareholder.

Feb. 28 Issued 10,000 common shares for $6.00 per share.

Mar. 1 Paid the cash dividend declared on January 14.

Apr. 1 Declared a 10 percent stock dividend on the common shares, distributable on May 2 to the shareholders of record on April 15. The market value of the shares was $6.40 per share.

May 2 Distributed the stock dividend declared on April 1.

Jul. 4 Repurchased 3,000 of the company's own common shares at $7.00 per share.

Sep. 2 Issued 2,500 common shares for $7.50 per share.

Nov. 2 Split the common shares 2 for 1.

Dec. 31 Reported net income of $250,000. Closed the Income Summary account.

Required

1. Record the transactions in the general journal. Explanations are not required.
2. Prepare the statement of shareholders' equity for the year ended December 31, 2017.

Problem 14–9A

Accounting for stock dividends, stock splits, and errors from a prior period; preparing a combined statement of income and retained earnings; calculating earnings per share

① ③ ④

2. Net income, $730,600

ArtnMotion Inc. specializes in truck tires and had the following shareholders' equity on January 1, 2017:

Preferred shares, $2.50, convertible to common on a 2-for-1 basis, 100,000 shares authorized, 50,000 shares issued and outstanding	$1,500,000
Common shares, unlimited number of shares authorized, 150,000 shares issued and outstanding	1,500,000
Total contributed capital	3,000,000
Retained earnings	1,200,000
Total shareholders' equity	$4,200,000

The following information is available for the year ending December 31, 2017:

Feb.	1	Declared a cash dividend of $275,000, payable on March 1 to the shareholders of record on February 15. Indicate the amount payable to each class of shareholder.
Mar.	1	Paid the cash dividend declared on February 1.
May	2	Declared a 20 percent stock dividend on the common shares, distributable on July 4 to the shareholders of record on June 15. The market value of the shares was $11.00 per share.
Jul.	4	Distributed the common shares dividend declared on May 2.
Aug.	8	The company discovered that amortization expense recorded in 2015 was understated in error by $30,000. (Ignore any tax consequences.)
Dec.	31	ArtnMotion Inc.'s records show the following:

Sales for the year...	$3,150,000
Cost of goods sold...	1,290,000
Operating expenses...	792,000
Income from discontinued operations............................	132,000
Loss on sale of discontinued operations........................	76,000

Close only the Income Summary account, assuming the company pays taxes at the rate of 35 percent.

Required

1. Record the transactions in the general journal. Explanations are not required.
2. Prepare a combined statement of income and retained earnings for the year ended December 31, 2017. Include earnings per share information. For purposes of the earnings per share calculation, the weighted average number of common shares is 180,000.

PROBLEMS (GROUP B)   MyAccountingLab

Problem 14–1B

Repurchasing shares to fight off a takeover of the corporation

②

Fundybay Corporation is positioned ideally in its industry. Located in Nova Scotia, Fundybay Corporation is the only company with a reliable record for its locally managed transport company. The company does a brisk business with local corporations. Fundybay Corporation's recent success has made the company a prime target for a takeover. An investment group from Halifax is attempting to buy 51 percent of the company's outstanding shares against the wishes of Fundybay Corporation's board of directors. Board members are convinced that the Halifax investors would sell off the most desirable pieces of the business and leave little of value.

At the most recent board meeting, several suggestions were advanced to fight off the hostile takeover bid. The suggestion with the most promise is to repurchase and cancel a huge quantity of shares. Fundybay Corporation has the cash to carry out this plan.

Required

1. As a significant shareholder of Fundybay Corporation, write a memorandum to explain to the board how the repurchase and cancellation of shares might make it more difficult for the Halifax group to take over Fundybay Corporation. Include in your memo a discussion of the effect that repurchasing shares would have on shares outstanding and on the size of the corporation.

2. Suppose Fundybay Corporation management is successful in fighting off the takeover bid and later issues shares at prices greater than the purchase price. Explain what effect the sale of these shares will have on assets, shareholders' equity, and net income.

Problem 14–2B

CNZ Corporation Inc. completed the following selected transactions during 2017:

Feb.	4	Declared a cash dividend on the 30,000, $1.40 preferred shares. Declared a $0.20 per share cash dividend on the 40,000 common shares outstanding. The date of record was February 15, and the payment date was February 18.
	18	Paid the cash dividends.
Apr.	18	Declared a 15 percent stock dividend on the common shares to holders of record on April 29, with distribution set for May 31. The market value of the common shares was $14.00 per share.
May	31	Issued the stock dividend shares.
Jun.	17	Repurchased 3,000 shares of the company's own common shares at $11.00 per share; average issue price was $8.00 per share.
Nov.	14	Issued 1,000 common shares for $9.00 per share.

Required Record the transactions in the general journal.

Journalizing shareholders' equity transactions
① ②

Problem 14–3B

The balance sheet of Investtech Inc. at December 31, 2016, reported 2,000,000 common shares authorized with 250,000 shares issued at an average price of $4.00 each. Retained Earnings had a balance of $700,000. During 2017, the company completed the following selected transactions:

Feb.	15	Repurchased 20,000 of the company's own common shares at $4.00 per share.
Mar.	8	Sold 8,000 common shares for $4.25 per share.
Sep.	28	Declared a 5 percent stock dividend on the 238,000 outstanding common shares to holders of record on October 15, with distribution set for October 31. The market value of Investtech Inc. common shares was $4.50 per share.
Oct.	31	Issued the stock dividend shares.
Nov.	5	Consolidated the common shares 1 for 2 (reverse split); one new common share was issued for every two existing shares held. Prior to the split, the corporation had 249,900 shares issued and outstanding.
Dec.	31	Earned net income of $230,000 during the year.

Excel Spreadsheet Template
Journalizing dividend and share-repurchase transactions, reporting shareholders' equity

Required

1. Record the transactions in the general journal. Explanations are not required.
2. Prepare the shareholders' equity section of the balance sheet at December 31, 2017.
3. Calculate the average issue price per common share on December 31, 2017.

Problem 14–4B

Preparing a single-step income statement
(3)

The information below was taken from the ledger and other records of Make a Statement Inc. at September 30, 2017:

General expenses..	$ 220,000
Loss on sale of discontinued segment..	18,000
Cost of goods sold...	570,000
Income tax expense (saving)	
Continuing operations...	44,000
Discontinued segment:	
Operating income...	2,000
Loss on sale	(6,000)
Interest expense	27,000
Gain on settlement of lawsuit...	27,000
Sales returns	23,000
Contributed surplus from repurchase of preferred shares	18,000
Sales discounts..	7,000
Sales revenue	1,000,000
Operating income, discontinued segment...	8,000
Loss on sale of property, plant, and equipment	5,000
Dividends on preferred shares	12,500
Preferred shares, $0.50, cumulative, 50,000 shares authorized,	
25,000 shares issued and outstanding	350,000
Dividends on common shares	25,000
Retained earnings, October 1, 2016..	197,000
Selling expenses	33,000
Common shares, unlimited shares authorized, 40,000 shares	
issued and outstanding	433,000

Required Prepare a single-step income statement, including earnings per share, for Make a Statement Inc. for the fiscal year ended September 30, 2017. Evaluate income for the year ended September 30, 2017, in terms of the outlook for 2018. Assume 2017 was a typical year and that Make a Statement's managers hoped to earn income from continuing operations equal to 12 percent of net sales.

Problem 14–5B

Computing earnings per share and reporting a retained earnings restriction
(3) (4)

The capital structure of Redding Design Ltd. at December 31, 2016, included 15,000, $1 preferred shares and 420,000 common shares. Common shares outstanding during 2017 were 330,000 in January through March; 348,000 during April; 385,000 May through September; and 420,000 during October through December. Income from continuing operations during 2017 was $446,000. The company discontinued a segment of the business at a gain of $61,500. The board of directors of Redding Design Ltd. has restricted $82,500 of retained earnings for expansion of the company's office facilities.

Required

1. Compute Redding Design Ltd.'s earnings per share. Start with income from continuing operations. Income and loss amounts are net of income tax.

2. Show two ways of reporting Redding Design Ltd.'s retained earnings restriction. Retained Earnings at December 31, 2016, was $172,000, and total contributed capital at December 31, 2017, is $575,000. Redding Design Ltd. declared cash dividends of $250,000 during 2017.

Problem 14–6B

The balance sheet of Collingwood International Inc. at December 31, 2016, presented the following shareholders' equity:

Journalizing dividends and stock repurchase transactions; reporting shareholders' equity

① ② ③ ④

Contributed capital	
Common shares, 2,000,000 shares authorized, 500,000 shares issued and outstanding	$3,000,000
Retained earnings	820,000
Total shareholders' equity	$3,820,000

During 2017, Collingwood International Inc. completed the following selected transactions:

Mar. 29 Declared a 10 percent stock dividend on the common shares. The market value of Collingwood International Inc. common shares was $5.00 per share. The record date was April 29, with distribution set for May 29.

May 29 Issued the stock dividend shares.

Jul. 30 Repurchased 30,000 of the company's own common shares at $5.00 per share; average issue price was $5.91.

Oct. 4 Sold 20,000 common shares for $7.50 per share.

Dec. 27 Declared a $0.20 per share dividend on the common shares outstanding. The date of record was January 17, 2018, and the payment date was January 31, 2018.

31 Closed the $650,000 net income to Retained Earnings.

Required

1. Record the transactions in the general journal.
2. Prepare the statement of shareholders' equity for the year ended December 31, 2017.
3. Calculate earnings per share at December 31, 2017. (Hint: Use issue dates in your calculations.)

Problem 14–7B

Thomas Wong, accountant for APB Bikes Ltd., was injured in a biking accident. Another employee prepared the income statement shown on the next page for the fiscal year ended September 30, 2017.

Preparing a corrected combined statement of income and retained earnings

③ ④

The individual amounts listed on the income statement are correct. However, some accounts are reported incorrectly, and others do not belong on the income statement at all. Also, income tax (25 percent) has not been applied to all appropriate figures. APB Bikes Ltd. issued 30,000 common shares in 2012 and has not issued or repurchased common shares since that date. The Retained Earnings balance, as originally reported at September 30, 2016, was $660,000. There were no preferred shares outstanding at September 30, 2017.

Required Prepare a corrected combined statement of income and retained earnings for fiscal year 2017; include earnings per share. Prepare the income statement portion in single-step format.

APB BIKES LTD.
Income Statement
September 30, 2017

Revenues and gains		
Sales		$1,000,000
Gain on repurchase of preferred shares		
(issued for $60,000; repurchased for $48,000)		12,000
Total revenues and gains		1,012,000
Expenses and losses		
Cost of goods sold	$478,000	
Selling expenses	133,000	
General expenses	60,000	
Sales returns	13,000	
Correction of an error from a prior period—		
understated income tax for 2016 due to error	10,000	
Dividends	14,000	
Sales discounts	18,000	
Income tax expense	98,700	
Total expenses and losses		824,700
Income from operations		187,300
Other gains and losses		
Operating income on discontinued segment	16,000	
Loss on sale of discontinued operations	(32,000)	
Total other gains		(16,000)
Net income		$ 171,300
Earnings per share		$5.71

Problem 14–8B

Accounting for stock dividends, stock splits, share transactions, and preparing the statement of shareholders' equity

① ② ④

Orillia Outfitters Ltd. had the following shareholders' equity on January 1, 2017:

Preferred shares, $0.75, cumulative (1 year in arrears), liquidation price of $5.00, 50,000 shares authorized, 15,000 shares issued and outstanding	$150,000
Common shares, unlimited number of shares authorized, 25,000 shares issued and outstanding	125,000
Total contributed capital	275,000
Retained earnings	220,000
Total shareholders' equity	$495,000

The following transactions took place during 2017:

Jan.	28	Declared a $25,000 cash dividend, payable on March 1 to the shareholders of record on February 15. Indicate the amount payable to each class of shareholder.
Feb.	25	Issued 10,000 common shares for $7.00 per share.
Mar.	1	Paid the cash dividend declared on January 28.
Apr.	4	Declared a 10 percent stock dividend on the common shares, distributable on May 15 to the shareholders of record on April 15. The market value of the shares was $8.00 per share.
May	15	Distributed the stock dividend declared on April 4.
Jul.	6	Repurchased 10,000 of the company's own common shares at $8.50 per share.
Sep.	3	Issued 5,000 common shares for $8.50 per share.
Nov.	2	Split the common shares 2 for 1.
Dec.	31	Reported net income of $100,000. Closed the Income Summary account.

Required

1. Record the transactions in the general journal. Explanations are not required.
2. Prepare the statement of shareholders' equity for the year ended December 31, 2017.

Problem 14–9B

Red Deer Hardware Ltd. had the following shareholders' equity on January 1, 2017:

Accounting for stock dividends, stock splits, and prior period adjustments; preparing a combined statement of income and retained earnings; calculating earnings per share

① ③ ④

Preferred shares, $0.50 cumulative, convertible to common on a 2-for-1 basis, 50,000 shares authorized, 20,000 shares issued and outstanding	$ 55,000
Common shares, unlimited number of shares authorized, 50,000 shares issued and outstanding	62,500
Total contributed capital	117,500
Retained earnings	110,000
Total shareholders' equity	$227,500

The following information is available for the year ending December 31, 2017:

Mar. 7 Declared a cash dividend of $12,500, payable on April 1 to the shareholders of record on March 15. Indicate the amount payable to each class of shareholder.

Apr. 1 Paid the cash dividend declared on March 7.

Jun. 6 Declared a 5 percent stock dividend on the common shares, distributable on August 5 to the shareholders of record on July 4. The market value of the shares was $1.50 per share.

Aug. 5 Distributed the common shares dividend declared on June 6.

Sep. 15 Received notification from the Canada Revenue Agency that Red Deer Hardware Ltd. had made an error in filing its 2014 taxes. The reassessment showed that the company had reported and overpaid $4,000 in taxes.

Dec. 31 Red Deer Hardware Ltd.'s records show the following:

Sales for the year..	$212,500
Cost of goods sold..	95,000
Operating expenses...	65,000
Income from discontinued operations....................	4,000
Loss on sale of discontinued operations................	(2,500)

Close the Income Summary account, assuming the income tax on all types of income is 40 percent.

Required

1. Record the transactions in the general journal. Explanations are not required.
2. Prepare a combined multi-step statement of income and retained earnings for the year ended December 31, 2017. Include earnings per share information.

CHALLENGE PROBLEM

Problem 14–1C

Assume Watawa Inc., a private corporation with a small number of shareholders, had issued 20,000 common shares at incorporation at a price of $22.00 each. The book value per share was $34.00 at the most recent year end. The company has been paying an annual dividend of $1.56 per share. Recently, the company had offered to repurchase 3,000 shares at $28.00 per share.

Explaining the effects of a share repurchase

②

You and a friend bought 100 shares each when the shares were issued. Your friend wonders whether she should sell her shares back to Watawa Inc. since the company was offering 27 percent more than she had paid.

Required Analyze the information provided to help your friend decide whether or not she should sell her shares back to the company.

EXTENDING YOUR KNOWLEDGE

DECISION PROBLEM

Analyzing cash dividends and
stock dividends

(1)

2. 2015 dividends, $20,000;
2017 dividends, $16,500

Fraser Valley Technologies Inc. had the following shareholders' equity on December 31, 2017:

Common shares, 200,000 shares issued and outstanding	$2,000,000
Retained earnings	1,200,000
Total shareholders' equity	$3,200,000

In the past, Fraser Valley Technologies Inc. has paid an annual cash dividend of $2.00 per share. In 2016, despite a large Retained Earnings balance, the board of directors wanted to conserve cash for expansion and did not pay a cash dividend but distributed a 10 percent stock dividend. During 2017, the company's cash position improved, so the board declared and paid a cash dividend of $1.50 per share.

Suppose you own 10,000 Fraser Valley Technologies Inc. common shares, acquired January 2, 2015. The market price was $25.00 per share before any of the above dividends.

Required

1. How did the stock dividend affect your proportionate ownership in the company? Explain.

2. What amount of cash dividends did you receive in 2015? What amount of cash dividends did you receive in 2017? Would you expect the dividend per share to remain unchanged between 2015 and 2017?

3. Immediately after the stock dividend was distributed, the market value of Fraser Valley Technologies Inc. shares decreased from $25.00 per share to $22.72 per share. Does this represent a loss to you? Explain.

4. Suppose Fraser Valley Technologies Inc. announces at the time of the stock dividend that the company will continue to pay the annual $2.00 cash dividend per share, even after the stock dividend. Would you expect the market price of the shares to decrease in 2016 to $22.72 per share as in Requirement 3 above? Explain.

FINANCIAL STATEMENT CASES

Financial Statement Case 1

Corporate income statement and
earnings per share

(3) (4) (5)

Use the Indigo Books & Music Inc. financial statements in that appear in Appendix A at the end of this book and on MyAccountingLab to answer the following questions:

1. Which income statement format—single-step or multi-step—does Indigo's consolidated statement of income more closely resemble?

2. Does Indigo present a statement of comprehensive income that is separate from the income statement or combined with it?

3. Indigo's basic earnings per share at March 29, 2014, was ($1.21) per share. For purposes of this calculation, what was the weighted average number of shares outstanding?

Financial Statement Case 2

Understanding financial
statements and the effects of
reporting under IFRS

(2) (3) (4) (5)

Use the TELUS Corporation 2013 financial statements that appear on MyAccountingLab to answer the following questions:

1. Which income statement format—single-step or multi-step—does TELUS's consolidated statement of income more closely resemble?

2. What was TELUS's earnings per share in 2013? Did this increase or decrease from 2012?

3. Did the company pay dividends in 2011? If so, how much were they?

IFRS MINI-CASE

Golden Goods Ltd is a Canadian importer that does business around the world. To obtain credit to do business in other countries, it has to present its financial statements to suppliers, who assess the statements and decide whether to extend credit to Golden. Because of this, Golden prepares its financial statements using IFRS.

Preparing financial statements under IFRS

③ ④ ⑤

Your task as an employee of Golden Goods Ltd. is to complete two key financial statements.

Required

1. Calculate the missing amounts to complete the Golden Goods Ltd. income statement. Show your calculations.

GOLDEN GOODS LTD. Income Statement For the Year Ended December 31, 2017		
Sales revenue		$800,000
Cost of goods sold		380,000
Gross margin		a
Operating expenses (listed individually)		342,000
Operating income		b
Other gains (losses)		
Gain on sale of land	$80,000	
Loss due to labour dispute	(20,000)	c
Income from continuing operations before income tax		d
Income tax expense		51,000
Income from continuing operations		e
Discontinued operations		
Operating loss, $60,000, plus income tax saving of $21,000	f	
Gain on disposal, $21,000, less income tax of $7,000	14,000	g
Net income		$ h
Earnings per common share (20,000 shares outstanding):		
Income from continuing operations		$ i
Income from discontinued operations		j
Net income		$ k

2. Dividends paid during 2017 totalled $60,000. Calculate the missing amounts to complete the Golden Goods Ltd. statement of changes in equity. Show your calculations.

GOLDEN GOODS LTD.
Statement of Changes in Equity
For the Year Ended December 31, 2017

	Common Shares	Contributed Surplus— Share Repurchases	Retained Earnings	Total Shareholders' Equity
Balance, December 31, 2016	$160,000	$ 0	$ A	$400,000
Issuance of shares	E			E
Net income			B	B
Cash dividends			C	C
Repurchase of common shares	(20,000)	5,000		F
Balance, December 31, 2017	$240,000	$5,000	$ D	$ G

>Try It! SOLUTIONS FOR CHAPTER 14

1. a. July 15

Retained Earnings	12,800	
Common Stock Dividend Distributable		12,800
To declare a 10 percent common stock dividend. (16,000 × 0.10 × $8)		

August 31

Common Stock Dividend Distributable	12,800	
Common Shares		12,800
To issue common shares in a stock dividend.		

b. & c. The accounting equation for this transaction shows that a stock dividend does not affect assets, liabilities, or total shareholders' equity.

Assets	=	Liabilities	+	Shareholders' Equity
				−12,800 Retained earnings
0	=	0	+	12,800 Common shares

d. On July 15, Beachcomber would only issue an announcement or press release. On August 31, there would be a memorandum journal entry only, such as: Distributed one new common share for each old share previously outstanding. This increased the number of common shares issued from 16,000 to 32,000.

e. The only effect of the 2-for-1 stock split on shareholders' equity would be to change the number of outstanding shares, in this case from 16,000 to 32,000 common shares. It would also double the number of authorized shares, if the number is not unlimited.

2. Average price per share = 900,000 ÷ 150,000 = $6
20,000 shares × $6.00 = $120,000
20,000 shares × $4.50 = $90,000

Mar. 1	Common shares	120,000	
	Contributed Surplus— Share Repurchase		30,000
	Cash		90,000

3. 20,000 shares × $8.25 = $165,000

Mar. 1	Common Shares	120,000	
	Retained Earnings	45,000	
	Cash		165,000

4.

Shareholders' Equity	
Contributed capital	
Common shares,	
400,000 shares authorized, 150,000 shares issued and outstanding	$ 780,000
Retained earnings	$ 655,000
Total shareholders' equity	$1,435,000

5. In the Discontinued Operations section of the income statement, you would list two items:

Operating loss, $960,000, less income tax savings, $288,000	$ (672,000)
Gain on disposal, $1,700,000 less income tax, $510,000	1,190,000
	$ 518,000

6. To calculate Hart Corp.'s EPS, first calculate the weighted average number of common shares outstanding during the year:

Weighted average number of common shares:
For January to March $270,000 \times {}^{3}\!/_{12} =$ 67,500
For April to December $310,000 \times {}^{9}\!/_{12} =$ 232,500
                                              300,000 shares

EPS = [$3,750,000 − (200,000 × $9)] ÷ 300,000 shares
    = ($3,750,000 − $1,800,000) ÷ 300,000
    = $6.50

7.

CHECKPOINT INDUSTRIES INC.
Statement of Shareholders' Equity
For the Year Ended April 30, 2017

	Common Shares	Contributed Surplus— Share Repurchases	Retained Earnings	Total Shareholders' Equity
Balance, April 30, 2016	$260,000	$ 0	$100,000 (a)	$360,000
Issuance of shares	100,000			100,000
Net income			62,500	62,500 (b)
Cash dividends			(22,000)	(22,000)
Repurchase of common shares	(60,000)	10,000 (c)		(50,000)
Balance, April 30, 2017	$300,000	$10,000	$140,500	$450,500 (d)

8.

	Change in estimate	Change in policy	Error	Retrospective Statement	Prospective Statement
A.		✔		✔	
B.	✔				
C.			✔	✔	✔

15 LONG-TERM LIABILITIES

CONNECTING CHAPTER 15

LEARNING OBJECTIVE ① Define bonds payable and the types of bonds

What are bonds?

Bonds: An Introduction, page 838
Types of Bonds

LEARNING OBJECTIVE ② Determine the price of a bond, and account for basic bond transactions

How do we account for the sale of a bond?

Bond Prices, page 841
Present Value
Bond Interest Rates
Issuing Bonds to Borrow Money, page 843
Issuing Bonds at Par Value
Issuing Bonds and Notes between Interest Dates
Issuing Bonds at a Discount
Issuing Bonds at a Premium

LEARNING OBJECTIVE ③ Amortize a bond discount and premium by the straight-line amortization method and the effective-interest amortization method

How do we allocate a bond discount or premium over the life of a bond?

Amortization of a Bond Discount and a Bond Premium, page 849
Straight-Line Method
Effective-Interest Method
Reporting Liabilities and Bonds Payable, page 855
Adjusting Entries for Interest Expense, page 855
Adjusting Entries Using the Straight-Line Method
Adjusting Entries Using the Effective-Interest Method

LEARNING OBJECTIVE ④ Account for retirement and conversion of bonds

How do we account for changes in a bond issue?

Retirement of Bonds, page 858
Convertible Bonds and Notes, page 859

LEARNING OBJECTIVE ⑤ Show the advantages and disadvantages of borrowing

How do we decide whether to issue debt versus equity?

Advantages and Disadvantages of Issuing Bonds versus Shares, page 860

LEARNING OBJECTIVE ⑥ Account for other long-term liabilities

How do we account for other long-term liabilities?

Mortgages and Other Long-Term Liabilities, page 862
Mortgages: An Introduction
Balance Sheet Presentation
Other Long-Term Liabilities

LEARNING OBJECTIVE ⑦ Account for operating leases and for assets acquired through a capital lease

How do we account for leases?

Lease Liabilities, page 863
   Operating Leases
   Capital Leases

LEARNING OBJECTIVE ⑧ Identify the effects of IFRS on long-term liabilities

How does IFRS affect long-term liabilities?

The Effects on Long-Term Liabilities of IFRS, page 867

LEARNING OBJECTIVE A1 Compute the future value of an investment

How do we find the future value of an investment?

Future Value, page 897
   Future Value Tables
   Future Value of an Annuity

LEARNING OBJECTIVE A2 Compute the present value of a single future amount and the present value of an annuity

How do we find the present value of an investment?

Present Value, page 901
   Present Value Tables
   Present Value of an Annuity
   Present Value of Bonds Payable

MyAccountingLab   The **Summary** for Chapter 15 appears on page 870. This lists all of the MyAccountingLab resources. **Accounting Vocabulary** with definitions for this chapter's material appears on page 872.

Completing major projects requires an organization to take on risk as well as large investments of capital. These elements are often too much for one institution to bear, so bonds are a good way to raise funds from many lenders and thereby spread the risk of investing among these groups. For example Newfoundland and Labrador, in collaboration with the governments of Canada and Nova Scotia as well as Nalcor Energy and Emera Inc., have signed a deal to finance the Muskrat Falls energy project.

An undertaking of this size requires a huge investment of money. In 2013, Toronto-Dominion Bank and the Goldman Sachs Group became involved as underwriters in a $5 billion bond sale for the project. There was a lot of worry about the sale of these bonds, because the market was not very vibrant at the time. However, the deal ended up selling well, indicating that there was a high demand for fixed income among investors. The federal government also recognized the importance of this project to the region and became involved by committing to loan guarantees in December 2013.

The loan guarantees enabled Newfoundland and Labrador to negotiate a lower rate on the issue of the bond indenture, saving approximately $1 billion in interest costs over the 40-year term of the bonds. The issuer is a trust formed by Newfoundland and Labrador and Nalcor Energy, and the interest rate of the indenture is 3.8 percent.[1]

---

[1] Newfoundland and Labrador, "Investing in Muskrat Falls for an Energized Economy," press release, December 10, 2013. Retrieved from www.releases.gov.nl.ca/releases/2013/exec/1210n05.htm.

>This chapter

discusses the third way to finance a company—borrowing money on long-term liabilities. Recall from Chapter 4 that **long-term liabilities** are debts due to be paid in more than a year or more than one of the entity's operating cycles if an operating cycle is greater than one year. Examples include bonds and debentures payable, long-term notes payable, and lease liabilities. The chapter appendix provides background on the valuation of long-term liabilities.

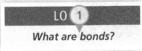

KEY POINTS

The three ways to finance a company are through contributed capital (investing or selling shares), profitable operations (retained earnings), and borrowing money (long-term liabilities).

LO 1

What are bonds?

BONDS: AN INTRODUCTION

Large companies, such as McDonald's Corporation, Canadian National Railway Company (CN), and WestJet Airlines Ltd., cannot borrow billions of dollars from a single lender because no lender will risk lending that much money to a single company. Even for smaller companies it may be impossible to borrow all they need from a bank.

How, then, do large corporations borrow a huge amount of money? They may issue bonds to the public. A **bond** is a formal arrangement between the issuer of the bond and the holder of the bond. The bondholder (the person or company that buys the bond) lends a fixed amount of money to the issuer. The issuer, such as Nalcor Energy, promises to pay the fixed amount at some future date and to pay regular payments of interest to the bondholder over the life of the bond. The details of the formal arrangement are contained in the **bond indenture** or offering circular. A bond is a debt of the company that issued the bond. **Bonds payable** are groups of notes payable issued to multiple lenders, called bondholders. TELUS Corporation, the parent company of TELUS Communications Inc., can borrow large amounts from thousands of individual investors, each investor buying a small amount of TELUS Corporation bonds. Most investments, including bonds, are made using a licensed dealer who receives a commission or fee on the purchase.

Purchasers of bonds may receive a bond certificate, which shows the name of the company that borrowed the money, exactly like a note payable. Today transactions are completed electronically, thereby reducing the need for paper

REAL WORLD
EXAMPLE

Banks and other lenders diversify their risk by lending relatively small amounts to numerous customers. That way, if one borrower cannot repay the lender is not devastated.

shares or certificates. The certificate also states the **principal value**, which is the amount that the company has borrowed from the bondholder. The bond's principal amount is also called the bond's **maturity value, par value,** or **face value**. The issuing company must pay each bondholder the principal amount at a specific future date, called the **maturity date**, which also appears on the certificate. In Chapter 11 we saw how to account for short-term notes payable. There is a lot of similarity between accounting for short-term notes payable and long-term notes payable.

Bondholders lend their money to earn interest. The bond certificate states the **coupon rate**, which is the interest rate that the issuer will pay the bondholder and the dates that the interest payments are due (generally twice a year). Some bond certificates name the bondholder (the investor). Exhibit 15–1 shows a bond certificate issued by XYZ Corporation (with legal details in the middle omitted).

EXHIBIT 15–1 | Bond Certificate

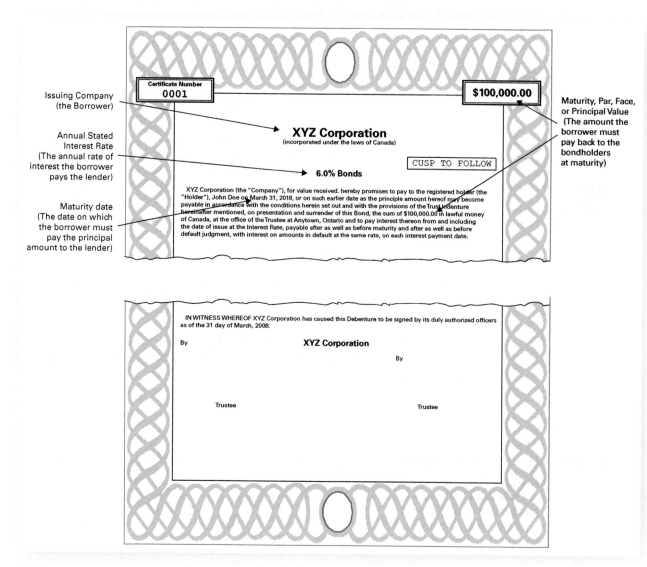

Let's compare bonds with shares, which were covered in Chapters 13 and 14:

Shares	Bonds
1. Shares represent *ownership* (equity) of the corporation. Each shareholder is an *owner*.	1. Bonds represent a *debt* (liability) of the corporation. Each bondholder is a *creditor* with no voting rights.
2. The corporation is *not* obligated to repay the amount invested by the shareholders.	2. The corporation *must* repay the bonds at maturity.
3. The corporation may or may not pay dividends on the shares.	3. The corporation *must* pay interest on the bonds.
4. Dividends are *not* an expense and are not tax deductible by the corporation.	4. Interest is a tax-deductible expense of the corporation.

Types of Bonds

There are various types of bonds, which are summarized in Exhibit 15–2.

EXHIBIT 15–2 | Types of Bonds

Type of Bond	Explanation
Term bonds	Bonds that all mature at the same time.
Serial bonds	Bonds that mature in instalments at regular intervals. For example, a $500,000, five-year serial bond may mature in $100,000 annual instalments over a five-year period.
Secured bonds	Bonds that give the bondholder the right to take specified assets of the issuer (called collateral) if the issuer *defaults*, that is, fails to pay principal or interest. A mortgage is an example of a secured bond. Details of the collateral must be provided in the notes to the financial statements. The Muskrat Falls bond in the opener is secured by the federal government.
Debentures	Unsecured bonds that are backed only by the good faith of the issuer. The bond shown in Exhibit 15–1 is a debenture because there are no rights to specific assets given in the first paragraph on the bond.
Bearer bonds	Bonds payable to the person that has possession of them. They are also called **unregistered bonds**.

KEY POINTS

A debenture is an unsecured bond and, therefore, is riskier than a bond, which is secured.

The discussion in this chapter will generally refer simply to *bonds*, since secured bonds and debentures (unsecured bonds) are treated essentially the same way for accounting purposes.

1. Refer to the bond certificate illustrated in Exhibit 15–1 and answer the following questions:
   a. What is the name of the corporation issuing the bond?
   b. What is the face value of the bond?
   c. What is the maturity date of the bond?
   d. What is the name of the bondholder?
   e. What is the stated interest rate the issuer will pay the bondholder?

   Solutions appear at the end of this chapter and on MyAccountingLab

BOND PRICES

A bond can be issued at any price agreed upon by the issuer and the bondholders. There are three basic categories of bond prices. A bond can be issued at;

- Par, maturity, face, or principal value. Example: A $1,000 bond issued for $1,000. A bond issued at par has no discount or premium.

- **Discount**, a price below (par) maturity value. Example: A $1,000 bond issued for $980. The discount is $20 ($1,000 – $980).

- **Premium**, a price above (par) maturity value. Example: A $1,000 bond issued for $1,015. The premium is $15 ($1,015 – $1,000).

The issue price of a bond does not affect the required payment at maturity. In all cases, the issuer must pay the maturity value of the bonds when they mature.

Bonds sell at a premium or a discount when the interest rate that will be paid on the bond is different from the interest rate available to investors elsewhere in the market at the time of the bond issuance. This will soon be explained more fully. As a bond nears maturity, its market price moves toward its maturity value. On the maturity date, the market value of a bond equals exactly its maturity value because the company that issued the bond pays that amount to retire the bond.

After a bond is issued, investors may buy and sell it through bond markets. The bond market in Canada is called the **over-the-counter (OTC) market**. It is a network of investment dealers who trade bonds issued by the Government of Canada and Crown corporations, the provinces, municipalities, regions, and corporations. You can find bond prices at canadianfixedincome.ca and globeinvestor.com, but you will likely need a representative to make the trade.

Bond prices are quoted at a percentage of their maturity value, using $100 as a base. For example:

- A $1,000 bond quoted at 100 is bought or sold for 100 percent of par value ($1,000).

- A $1,000 bond quoted at 101.5 has a price of $1,015 ($1,000 × 1.015).

- A $1,000 bond quoted at 98.5 has a price of $985 ($1,000 × 0.985).

Exhibit 15–3 contains actual price information for a TELUS Corporation bond, as quoted on the website canadianfixedincome.ca on September 9, 2014. On that date, TELUS Corporation's 3.650 percent par-value bond maturing May 25, 2016, was quoted at 103.09, which was a bid price of $1,030.90 for a $1,000.00 bond. This bid price provided a yield of 1.80 percent (the yield rate of a bond is influenced by the market interest rate and time to maturity).

LO 2

How do we account for the sale of a bond?

Bond issued at par:
Selling price = $1,000

$1,000 BOND

Bond issued at discount:
Selling price < $1,000

$1,000 BOND – Discount

Bond issued at premium:
Selling price > $1,000

$1,000 BOND + Premium

EXHIBIT 15–3 | **Bond Price Information**

Bonds	Coupon	Eff. Maturity	Price	Yield
TELUS Corporation	3.650	May 25/2016	103.09	1.80

In Exhibit 15–3, "Price" is the **bid price**, the highest price that a buyer is willing to pay for the bond. "Coupon" is the contractual rate of interest that TELUS must pay the bondholders, "Eff. Maturity" is the date that the bond term ends, and "**Yield**" is the interest rate that an investor will receive, based on a compounding period of one year.

Present Value[2]

A dollar received today is worth more than a dollar received in the future. Why? Because you can invest today's dollar and earn income from it. Likewise, deferring any payment until later gives your money a period of time to grow. Money earns income over time, a concept called the *time value of money*. Let's examine how the time value of money affects the pricing of bonds.

Assume a $1,000 bond reaches maturity three years from today and carries no interest. Would you pay $1,000 to purchase this bond? No, because paying $1,000 today to receive the same amount in the future provides you with no income on the investment. You would not be taking advantage of the time value of money. Just how much should you pay today to receive $1,000 at the end of three years? The answer is some amount less than $1,000. The diagram below shows the relationship between a bond's price (present value) and its maturity amount (future value).

KEY POINTS

Present value is always less than future value. You should be able to invest today's money (present value) so that its value will increase (future value). The difference between present value and future value is interest earned.

$$\frac{Present}{Value} + \frac{Interest}{Earned} = \frac{Future}{Value}$$

Suppose $850 is a fair market price.

By investing $850 now to receive $1,000 later, you earn $150 interest revenue over the three years.

2014

Present value is always less than future value

2017

Present value: Bond price $850

Future value: Maturity amount $1,000

The exact **present value** of any future amount depends on the following:

1. The amount of the future payment (or receipt)
2. The length of time from the date of the investment to the date when the future amount is to be received (or paid)
3. The interest rate during the period

We show how to compute present value in this chapter's appendix. You need to be aware of the present-value concept, however, in the discussion of bond prices that follows. If your instructor so directs you, please study the appendix now.

Bond Interest Rates

Bonds are sold at their market price, which is the amount that investors are willing to pay at any given time. Market price is the bond's present value, which equals the present value of the principal payment plus the present value of the cash interest payments. The cash interest payments can be made once every three months (quarterly), once every six months (semi-annually), or once per year (annually) over the term of the bond.

Two interest rates work to set the price of a bond:

KEY POINTS

When you buy a bond, you are really "buying" two future cash flows: principal and interest payments. The principal is a single sum received at maturity, and the interest payments are a series of receipts received each period until maturity.

- The **stated interest rate**, or **contract interest rate**, determines the amount of cash interest the borrower pays—and the investor receives—each year. The stated interest rate is printed on the bond and is set by the bond contract. It may

---

[2] The appendix for this chapter covers present value in more detail.

be fixed or adjustable. If the rate is fixed, it *does not change* during the life of the bond. For example, XYZ Corporation's 6 percent bonds have a stated interest rate of 6 percent (Exhibit 15–1). Thus, XYZ Corporation pays $6,000 of interest annually on each $100,000 bond. Each semi-annual interest payment is $3,000 ($100,000 × 0.06 × 1/2).

- The **market interest rate**, or **effective interest rate**, is the rate that investors demand for lending their money. The market interest rate changes constantly. A company may issue bonds with a stated interest rate that differs from the prevailing market interest rate. XYZ Corporation may issue its 6 percent bonds when the market rate for bonds issued by companies with a similar level of risk has risen to 7 percent. Will the XYZ Corporation bonds attract investors in this market? No, because investors can earn 7 percent on other bonds with a similar level of risk. In order to receive a 7 percent return on their investment, investors will purchase XYZ Corporation bonds only at a price less than the maturity value. The difference between the lower price and the bonds' maturity value is a *discount*. Conversely, if the market interest rate is 5 percent, XYZ Corporation's 6 percent bonds will be so attractive that investors will pay more than the maturity value for them. The difference between the higher price and the maturity value is a *premium*.

Exhibit 15–4 shows how the stated interest rate and the market interest rate interact to determine the issue price, or selling price, of a bond.

EXHIBIT 15–4 | How the Stated Interest Rate and the Market Interest Rate Interact to Determine the Issue Price of a Bond

Example: Bond with a Stated (Contract) Interest Rate of 9%			
Bond's Stated Interest Rate		Market Interest Rate	Issue Price of the Bond
9%	=	9%	⇒ Maturity value of the bond (face or par value)
9%	<	10%	⇒ Discount (price below maturity value)
9%	>	8%	⇒ Premium (price above maturity value)

ISSUING BONDS TO BORROW MONEY

The basic journal entry to record the issuance of bonds debits Cash and credits Bonds Payable. The company may issue bonds for three different bond prices:

- At *par* (maturity) value
- At a *discount*
- At a *premium*

Issuing Bonds at Par Value

We begin with the simplest case: issuing bonds at par value.

Suppose that UVW Corporation has $100 million in 6 percent bonds that mature in 10 years. Assume that UVW Corporation issued these bonds at par on January 2, 2017. The issuance entry is as follows:

2017			
Jan. 2	Cash	100,000,000	
	Bonds Payable		100,000,000
	To issue 6%, 10-year bonds at par.		

UVW Corporation, the borrower, makes this one-time entry to record the receipt of cash and issuance of bonds. Afterward, investors buy and sell the bonds through the bond markets, in a similar way to buying and selling shares through the stock market. Many of these transactions can be completed online. The buy-and-sell transactions between investors do not involve the company that issued the bonds. The company does not keep records of these transactions, except for the names and addresses of the bondholders. (This information is needed for mailing the interest and principal payments. The company may also have bondholder account information so that interest and principal payments can be directly deposited into bondholders' bank or investment accounts.)

Interest payments for these bonds occur each January 2 and July 2. UVW Corporation's entry to record the first semi-annual interest payment is:

KEY POINTS

Recall the formula for computing interest:
Amount of interest = Principal × Rate × Time

MyAccountingLab

Interactive Figure: Interact with Long-Term Notes Payable

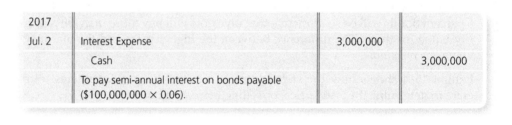

2017			
Jul. 2	Interest Expense	3,000,000	
	Cash		3,000,000
	To pay semi-annual interest on bonds payable ($100,000,000 × 0.06).		

Each semi-annual interest payment follows this same pattern.
At maturity, UVW Corporation will record payment of the bonds as follows:

2027			
Jan. 2	Bonds Payable	100,000,000	
	Cash		100,000,000
	To pay bonds payable at maturity.		

Issuing Bonds and Notes between Interest Dates

The foregoing entries to record UVW Corporation's bond transactions are straightforward because the company issued the bonds on an interest payment date (January 2). However, corporations often issue bonds between interest dates because they may not need the funds in one lump sum or the bonds may take longer to sell than originally planned.

Suppose Manitoba Hydro issues $200 million of 5 percent bonds due June 15, 2023. These bonds are dated June 15, 2017, and carry the price "100 plus accrued interest." An investor purchasing the bonds after the bond date must pay market value *plus accrued interest*. The issuing company will pay the full semi-annual interest amount to the bondholder at the next interest payment date. Companies do not split semi-annual interest payments among two or more investors who happen to hold the bonds during a six-month interest period since the recordkeeping for this would be difficult.

Assume that Manitoba Hydro sells $100,000 of its bonds on July 15, 2017, one month after the bond date of June 15. Also assume that the market price of the bonds on July 15 is the face value when issuing these bonds. Manitoba Hydro receives one month's accrued interest in addition to the bond's face value, as shown in the following timeline:

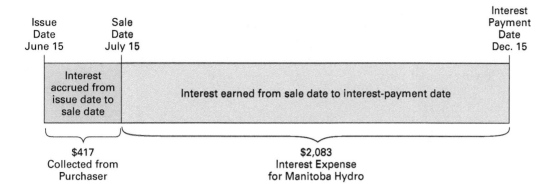

Manitoba Hydro's entry to record the issuance of the bonds payable is:

2017			
Jul. 15	Cash	100,417	
	Bonds Payable		100,000
	Interest Payable		417
	To issue 5%, 10-year bonds at par, one month after the original issue date. Interest payable is $417 ($100,000 × 0.05 × $\frac{1}{12}$).		

Manitoba Hydro has collected one month's interest in advance. On December 15, 2017, Manitoba Hydro's entry to record the first semi-annual interest payment on this $100,000 is:

2017			
Dec. 15	Interest Expense	2,083	
	Interest Payable	417	
	Cash		2,500
	To pay semi-annual interest on bonds payable. Interest expense is $2,083 ($100,000 × 0.05 × $\frac{5}{12}$); cash paid is $2,500 ($100,000 × 0.05 × $\frac{6}{12}$).		

The debit to Interest Payable eliminates the credit balance in that account from July 15. Manitoba Hydro has now paid that liability.

Note that Manitoba Hydro pays a full six months' interest on December 15. After subtracting the one month's accrued interest received at the time of issuing the bond, Manitoba Hydro has recorded interest expense for five months ($2,083). This interest expense is the correct amount for the five months that the bonds have been outstanding.

If Manitoba Hydro prepared financial statements immediately after December 15, 2017, it would report nothing on the balance sheet, because Interest Payable is $0, and would report Interest Expense of $2,083 on the income statement.

Issuing Bonds at a Discount

Unlike shares, bonds are often issued at a discount. We know that market conditions may force a company like UVW Corporation to accept a discount price for its bonds. Suppose UVW Corporation issues $1,000,000 of its 6 percent, 10-year bonds when the market interest rate is 6.27 percent. As a result, the market price of the bonds drops to a rounded factor of 98.00, which means 98 percent of face or

> **REAL WORLD EXAMPLE**
>
> When an investor sells bonds or debentures to another investor between interest dates, the price is always "plus accrued interest." Suppose you hold a bond for two months of a semi-annual interest period and sell the bonds to another investor before you receive your interest. The person who buys the bonds will receive your two months of interest on the next specified interest date. Thus, you must collect your share of the interest from the buyer when you sell your investment, which happens when the price is "plus accrued interest."

par value. To simplify the example we will use a factor; however, a more accurate calculation of the bond price is in the Learning Tip in the margin. The factor 98 can be calculated by dividing the PV/FV or ($980,163.82 ÷ 1,000,000 × 100). UVW Corporation receives $980,000 ($1,000,000 × 0.98) at issuance and makes the following journal entry:

2017			
Jan. 2	Cash	980,000	
	Discount on Bonds Payable	20,000	
	Bonds Payable		1,000,000
	To issue 6%, 10-year bonds at a discount. Cash received was $980,000 ($1,000,000 × 0.98).		

After posting, the bond accounts have the following balances:

Main Account: Bonds Payable	Contra Account: Discount on Bonds Payable
1,000,000	20,000

Bond carrying value = $980,000

Discount on Bonds Payable is a contra account to Bonds Payable. Bonds Payable *minus* the discount gives the book value, or carrying value, of the bonds. The relationship between Bonds Payable and the Discount account is similar to the relationships between Equipment and Accumulated Amortization, and between Accounts Receivable and Allowance for Doubtful Accounts. Thus, UVW Corporation's liability is $980,000, which is the amount the company borrowed. UVW Corporation's balance sheet immediately after issuance of the bonds reports the following:

Long-term liabilities		
Bonds payable, 6%, due 2027	$1,000,000	
Less: Discount on bonds payable	20,000	$980,000

If UVW Corporation were to pay off the bonds immediately (an unlikely occurrence), the company's required outlay would be $980,000 because the market price of the bonds is $980,000.

Interest Expense on Bonds Issued at a Discount We saw earlier that a bond's stated interest rate may differ from the market interest rate. Suppose the market rate is 6.27 percent when UVW Corporation issues its 6 percent bonds. The 0.27 percent interest rate difference creates the $20,000 discount on the bonds. UVW Corporation borrows $980,000 cash but must pay $1,000,000 cash when the bonds mature 10 years later. What happens to the $20,000 balance of the discount account over the life of the bond issue?

Borrows in 2017	Pays backs in 2027	Discount	
			How do we account for this?
$980,000	$1,000,000	$20,000	

The cash flow of the UVW bond, as payable to the bondholder, is shown below:

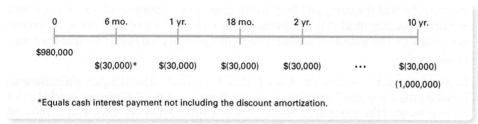

*Equals cash interest payment not including the discount amortization.

The $20,000 is in reality an additional interest expense to the issuing company. That amount is a cost—beyond the stated interest rate—that the business pays for borrowing the investors' money. The discount has the effect of raising the interest expense on the bonds to the market interest rate of 6.27 percent.

The discount amount is an interest expense not paid until the bond matures. However, the borrower—the bond issuer—benefits from the use of the investors' money each accounting period over the full term of the bond issue. The matching objective directs the business to match an expense against its revenues on a period-by-period basis, so the discount is allocated to Interest Expense through amortization for each accounting period over the life of the bonds. We will examine this in more detail shortly.

REAL WORLD EXAMPLE

Why are bonds issued at a premium less common than bonds issued at a discount? Because companies prefer to issue bonds that pay a lower stated interest rate than the market interest rate, so they price the bonds to sell at a discount.

Issuing Bonds at a Premium

To illustrate issuing bonds at a premium, let's change the UVW Corporation example. Assume that the market interest rate is 5.5 percent when the company issues its 6 percent, 10-year bonds. These 6 percent bonds are attractive in a 5.5 percent market, so investors will pay a premium price to acquire them. We can use a factor again for simplicity by dividing the present value as calculated accurately using a financial calculator by the future value, or $1,038,068.13 ÷ 1,000,000. If the bonds are priced at 103.81 (103.81 percent of par value), UVW Corporation receives $1,038,100 cash upon issuance. The entry is as follows:

2017			
Jan. 2	Cash	1,038,100	
	Bonds Payable		1,000,000
	Premium on Bonds Payable		38,100
	To issue 6%, 10-year bonds at a premium.		
	Cash received is $1,038,100 ($1,000,000 × 1.0381).		

After posting, the bond accounts have the following balances:

Main Account: Bonds Payable	Companion Account: Premium on Bonds Payable
1,000,000	38,100

Bond carrying value = $1,038,100

UVW Corporation's balance sheet immediately after issuance of the bonds reports the following:

Long-term liabilities		
Bonds payable, 6%, due 2027	$1,000,000	
Premium on bonds payable	38,100	$1,038,100

LEARNING TIPS

Using a financial calculator, the price would be $1,038,068.13, based on

$1,000,000 = **FV**

20 = **N**

2.75 = **I/Y**

$30,000 = **PMT**

CPT **PV**

The difference between $1,038,068.13 and $1,038,100 (which is $31.87) is due to rounding.

Premium on Bonds Payable is added to Bonds Payable to show the book value, or carrying value, of the bonds. UVW Corporation's liability is $1,038,100, which is the amount that the company borrowed. Immediate payment of the bonds would require an outlay of $1,038,100, because the market price of the bonds at issuance is $1,038,100. The investors would be unwilling to give up bonds for less than their market value.

Interest Expense on Bonds Issued at a Premium   The 0.5 percent difference between the 6 percent contract rate on the bonds and the 5.5 percent market interest rate creates the $38,100 premium. UVW Corporation borrows $1,038,100 cash but must pay only $1,000,000 cash at maturity:

Borrows in 2017	Pays back in 2027	Premium
		How do we
$1,038,100	$1,000,000	$38,100	account for this?

The cash flow of the UVW bond, payable to the bondholder, is shown below:

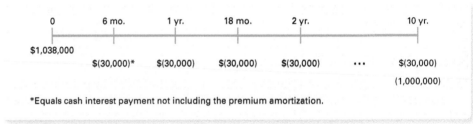

*Equals cash interest payment not including the premium amortization.

Rather than treat the premium as additional income to simplify the entry, we treat the premium as a reduction of interest expense to UVW Corporation. The premium reduces UVW Corporation's cost of borrowing the money and reduces the company's interest expense to an effective interest rate of 5.5 percent, the market rate. We account for the premium much as we handled the discount. We amortize the bond premium as a *decrease* in interest expense over the life of the bonds.

> **Try It!**

2. In each of the following situations, will the bonds sell at par, at a premium, or at a discount?
   a. 4 percent bonds sold when the market rate is 4.5 percent
   b. 4 percent bonds sold when the market rate is 3.8 percent
   c. 3.5 percent bonds sold when the market rate is 3.5 percent
3. Sunwood Insurance Corp. issued $1,000,000 of 3.75 percent, 10-year bonds at the market price of 99.00.
   a. Were the bonds issued at par, at a discount, or at a premium?
   b. Record the journal entry for the issuance of the bonds. Include an explanation.
   c. What is the carrying or present value of the bonds?
4. Parksville Insurance Corp. issued $1,000,000 of 3.75 percent, 10-year bonds at the market price of 101.50.
   a. Were the bonds issued at par, at a discount, or at a premium?
   b. Make the journal entry for the issuance of the bonds. Include an explanation.
   c. What is the carrying or present value of the bonds?

Solutions appear at the end of this chapter and on MyAccountingLab

AMORTIZATION OF A BOND DISCOUNT AND A BOND PREMIUM

There are two methods for amortizing a bond discount and a bond premium: the straight-line method and the effective-interest method. Each of these will be discussed in turn.

LO 3

How do we allocate a bond discount or premium over the life of a bond?

Straight-Line Method

We can amortize a bond discount or a bond premium by dividing the discount or premium into equal amounts for each interest period. This method is called **straight-line amortization**.

Straight-Line Amortization of a Bond Discount   In our UVW Corporation example on page 846, the beginning discount is $20,000 and there are 20 semi-annual interest periods during the bonds' 10-year life. Therefore, 1/20 of the $20,000 bond discount ($20,000 ÷ 20 = $1,000) is amortized each interest period. UVW Corporation's semi-annual interest entry on July 2, 2017, is as follows:

2017			
Jul. 2	Interest Expense	31,000	
	Cash		30,000
	Discount on Bonds Payable		1,000
	To pay semi-annual interest of $30,000 ($1,000,000 × 0.06 × $^{6}/_{12}$) and amortize discount on bonds payable, $1,000 ($20,000 ÷ 20).[3]		

Interest expense of $31,000 for each six-month period is the sum of:

- The stated interest ($30,000, which is paid in cash)
- *Plus* the amortization of the discount ($1,000)

Discount on Bonds Payable has a debit balance. Therefore, we credit the Discount account to amortize (reduce) its balance. Since Discount on Bonds Payable is a contra account, each reduction in its balance increases the book value or carrying value of Bonds Payable. Twenty amortization entries (semi-annual journal entries for 10 years) will decrease the discount balance to zero, which means that the Bonds Payable book or carrying value will have increased by

---

[3] Some accountants may record the payment of interest and the amortization of the discount in two separate entries, as follows (both approaches are equally correct):

2017			
Jul. 2	Interest Expense	30,000	
	Cash		30,000
	Paid semi-annual interest ($1,000,000 × 0.06 × $^{6}/_{12}$).		
2	Interest Expense	1,000	
	Discount on Bonds Payable		1,000
	Amortized discount on bonds payable ($20,000 ÷ 20).		

$20,000 up to its face value of $1,000,000 by the maturity date. The entry to pay the bonds at maturity is:

2027			
Jan. 2	Bonds Payable	1,000,000	
	Cash		1,000,000
	To pay the bonds payable at maturity.		

Straight-Line Amortization of a Bond Premium   In our UVW Corporation example on page 847, the beginning premium is $38,100 and there are 20 semi-annual interest periods during the bonds' 10-year life. Therefore, 1/20 of the $38,100 ($1,905) of bond premium is amortized each interest period. UVW Corporation's semi-annual interest entry on July 2, 2017, is as follows:

2017			
Jul. 2	Interest Expense	28,095	
	Premium on Bonds Payable	1,905	
	Cash		30,000
	To pay semi-annual interest ($1,000,000 × 0.06 × $\frac{6}{12}$) and amortize premium on bonds payable ($38,100 ÷ 20).[4]		

Interest expense of $28,095 is

- The stated interest ($30,000)
- *Minus* the amortization of the premium ($1,905)

The debit to Premium on Bonds Payable reduces its normal balance, which is a credit.

At July 2, 2017, immediately after amortizing the bond premium, the bonds have a carrying amount of:

$1,036,195 [calculated as $1,000,000 + ($38,100 − $1,905)]

Long-term liabilities		
Bonds payable, 6%, due 2027	$1,000,000	
Premium on bonds payable	36,195	$1,036,195

---

[4] The payment of interest and the amortization of the bond premium can be recorded in two separate entries as follows:

2017			
Jul. 2	Interest Expense	30,000	
	Cash		30,000
	Paid semi-annual interest ($1,000,000 × 0.06 × $\frac{6}{12}$).		
2	Premium on Bonds Payable	1,905	
	Interest Expense		1,905
	Amortized premium on bonds payable by reducing interest expense ($38,100 ÷ 20).		

At January 2, 2018, the bonds' carrying amount will be:

$1,034,290 [calculated as $1,000,000 + ($38,100 − $1,905 − $1,905)]

Long-term liabilities		
Bonds payable, 6%, due 2027	$1,000,000	
Premium on bonds payable	34,290	$1,034,290

At maturity on January 2, 2027, the bond premium will have been fully amortized and the bonds' carrying amount will be $1,000,000.

Effective-Interest Method

The straight-line amortization method has a theoretical weakness. Each period's amortization amount for a premium or discount is the same dollar amount over the life of the bonds. However, over that time the bonds' carrying value continues to increase (with a discount) or decrease (with a premium). Thus the fixed dollar amount of amortization changes as a percentage of the bonds' carrying value, making it appear that the bond issuer's interest rate changes over time. This appearance is misleading because in fact the issuer locked in a fixed interest rate when the bonds were issued. The stated interest *rate* on the bonds does not change.

Effective-interest amortization keeps each interest expense amount at the same percentage of the bonds' carrying value or book value for every interest payment over the bonds' life. The total amount of bond discount or bond premium amortized over the life of the bonds is the same under both methods. International Financial Reporting Standards (IFRS) specify that the effective-interest method should be used because it does a better job of matching the interest expense to the revenue earned. However, the straight-line method is popular because of its simplicity, and in practice, if there is no material difference, then the cost–benefit constraint results in companies using straight-line amortization. (Note: Accounting Standards for Private Enterprises (ASPE) allows both methods of amortization.)

Effective-Interest Method of Amortizing a Bond Discount Assume that on January 2, 2017, UVW Corporation issues $1,000,000 of 5 percent bonds at a time when the market rate of interest is 6 percent. Also assume that these bonds mature in five years and pay interest semi-annually, so there are 10 semi-annual interest payments. The issue price of the bonds is $957,349.[5] The discount on these bonds is $42,651 ($1,000,000 − $957,349). Exhibit 15–5 illustrates amortization of the discount by the effective-interest method.

Recall that we want to present interest expense amounts over the full life of the bonds at a fixed percentage of the bonds' carrying value. The 3 percent rate—the effective-interest rate (6 ÷ 2)—*is* that percentage. We have calculated the cost of the money borrowed by the bond issuer—the interest expense—as a constant percentage of the carrying value of the bonds. The *dollar amount* of interest expense varies from period to period, but the interest percentage applied to the carrying value remains the same.

The *accounts* debited and credited under the effective-interest amortization method and the straight-line method are the same. Only the *amounts* differ. We may take the amortization *amounts* directly from the table in Exhibit 15–5. We assume

🔑 KEY POINTS

The amount of *cash* paid each semi-annual interest period is calculated with the formula Interest paid = Face value × (Stated rate ÷ 2). This amount does not change over the term of the bond.

---

[5] We show how to compute this amount in the appendix for this chapter. The calculation shown here was made with a calculator. In the appendix, the amount is computed using the present-value tables that appear in the appendix.

EXHIBIT 15–5 | Effective-Interest Method of Amortizing a Bond Discount

Panel A: Bond Data

Maturity value—$1,000,000
Stated (contract) interest rate—5%
Interest paid—2.5% semi-annually—$25,000 ($1,000,000 × 0.025)
Market interest rate at time of issue—6% annually, 3% semi-annually

The amount of semi-annual interest expense can be manually calculated with the formula Interest expense = Bond carrying value (Col. E) × (Market interest rate ÷ 2). Note that both amounts will change each period.

KEY POINTS

$1,000,000 = **FV**
10 = **N**
6/2 = **I/Y**
$25,000 = **PMT**
CPT **PV** = Issue
price—$957,349

KEY POINTS

$1,000,000 = **FV**
10 = **N**
6/2 = **I/Y**
$25,000 = **PMT**
CPT **PV**
2nd **PV** (AMORT) (for
period 1 and first row of table)
Five amounts will show in the
screen using the up arrows: ⇑
P1 = 1, INT = $28,720, PRN =
$−3,720, BAL = $−961,069,
P2 = 1
Note: Each time you hit the up
arrow on the calculator a corresponding amount will appear on
the calculator screen.

Panel B: Amortization Table

	A	B	C	D	E
Semi-annual Interest Period	Interest Payment (2.5% of Maturity Value)	Interest *Expense* (3% of Preceding Bond Carrying Amount)	Discount Amortization (B – A)	Unamortized Discount Account Balance (Preceding D – Current C)	Bond Carrying Amount ($1,000,000 – D)
Issue Date				$42,651	$ 957,349*
1	$25,000	$28,720	$3,720	38,931	961,069
2	25,000	28,832	3,832	35,099	964,901
3	25,000	28,947	3,947	31,152	968,848
4	25,000	29,065	4,065	27,087	972,913
5	25,000	29,187	4,187	22,900	977,100
6	25,000	29,313	4,313	18,587	981,413
7	25,000	29,442	4,442	14,145	985,855
8	25,000	29,576	4,576	9,569	990,431
9	25,000	29,713	4,713	4,856	995,144
10	25,000	29,856	4,856	0	1,000,000

*Minor differences because of the effect of rounding.

Notes

Column A	The semi-annual interest payments are constant because they are fixed by the stated interest rate and the bonds' maturity value (the orange line in Exhibit 15–6, Panel A, on page 853; this number is manually calculated).
Column B	The interest expense each period is computed by multiplying the preceding bond carrying amount by the market interest rate. The effect of this *effective-interest rate* determines the interest expense each period. The amount of interest each period increases as the effective-interest rate, a constant, is applied to the increasing bond carrying amount (E) (the green line in Exhibit 15–6, Panel A).
Column C	The excess of each interest expense amount (B) over each interest payment amount (A) is the discount amortization for the period (the shaded amount in Exhibit 15–6, Panel A).
Column D	The unamortized discount balance decreases by the amount of amortization for the period (C), from $42,651 at the bonds' issue date to zero at their maturity (the shaded amount in Exhibit 15–6, Panel B). The balance of the discount plus the bonds' carrying amount equals the bonds' maturity value at all times; this is manually calculated.
Column E	The bonds' carrying amount increases from $957,349 at issuance to $1,000,000 at maturity (the blue line in Exhibit 15–6, Panel B).

that the first interest payment occurs on July 2 and use the appropriate amounts from Exhibit 15–5, reading across the line for the first interest payment date:

Jul. 2	Interest Expense	28,720	
	Discount on Bonds Payable		3,720
	Cash		25,000
	To pay semi-annual interest (Column A) and amortize discount (Column C) on bonds payable. Interest expense is calculated as the cash paid plus the discount amortization (Column B).		

Panel A of Exhibit 15–6 shows the interest expense over the life of bonds issued at a discount. Panel B shows how the carrying amount of the bonds rises to the maturity date. All amounts are taken from Exhibit 15–5. Focus on the highlighted items in Exhibit 15–6 and the references in Exhibit 15–5 to understand the main points of Exhibit 15–6.

EXHIBIT 15–6 | Interest Expense and Bond Carrying Amount Both Increase for Bonds Issued at a Discount

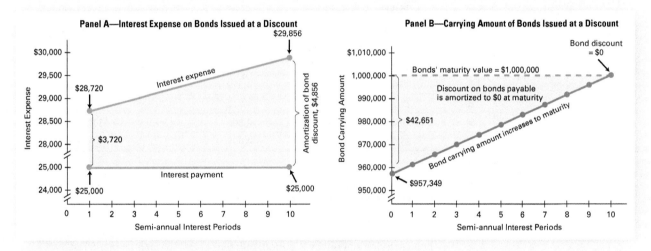

Effective-Interest Method of Amortizing a Bond Premium   Let's modify the UVW Corporation example to illustrate the effective-interest method of amortizing a bond premium. Assume that on April 30 UVW Corporation issues $1,000,000 of five-year, 5 percent bonds that pay interest semi-annually. If the bonds are issued when the market interest rate is 4 percent, their issue price is $1,044,913.[6] The premium on these bonds is $44,913, and Exhibit 15–7 illustrates amortization of the premium by the effective-interest method.

Assuming that the first interest payment occurs on October 31, we read across the line in Exhibit 15–7 for the first interest payment date and pick up the appropriate amounts.

Oct. 31	Interest Expense	20,898	
	Premium on Bonds Payable	4,102	
	Cash		25,000
	To pay semi-annual interest (column A) and amortize premium (column C) on bonds payable.		

---

[6] Again, we compute the present value of the bonds using a calculator. In the appendix for this chapter, the amount is computed using present-value tables.

EXHIBIT 15-7 | Effective-Interest Method of Amortizing a Bond Premium

KEY POINTS

$1,000,000 = **FV**

10 = **N**

4/2 = **I/Y**

$25,000 = **PMT**

CPT **PV** = Issue price—$1,044,913

2ⁿᵈ **PV** (AMORT) #1 (for period 1 and first row of table) Five amounts will show in the screen using the up arrows: ⇑ P1 = 1, INT = $20,898, PRN = $4,102, BAL = $-1,040,811, P2 = 1

Note: Each time you hit the up arrow on the calculator a corresponding amount will appear on the calculator screen.

Panel A: Bond Data

Maturity value—$1,000,000
Stated (contract) interest rate—5%
Interest paid—2.5% semi-annually, $25,000 ($1,000,000 × 0.025)
Market interest rate at time of issue—4% annually, 2% semi-annually

Panel B: Amortization Table

	A	B	C	D	E
	Interest Payment (2.5% of Maturity Value)	**Interest Expense** (2% of Preceding Bond Carrying Amount)	**Premium Amortization** (A – B)	**Unamortized Premium Account Balance** (Preceding D – Current C)	**Bond Carrying Amount** (1,000,000 + D)
Semi-annual Interest Period					
Issue Date				$44,913	$1,044,913
1	$25,000	$20,898	$4,102	40,811	1,040,811
2	25,000	20,816	4,184	36,627	1,036,627
3	25,000	20,733	4,267	32,360	1,032,360
4	25,000	20,647	4,353	28,007	1,028,007
5	25,000	20,560	4,440	23,567	1,023,567
6	25,000	20,471	4,529	19,038	1,019,038
7	25,000	20,381	4,619	14,419	1,014,419
8	25,000	20,288	4,712	9,707	1,009,707
9	25,000	20,194	4,806	4,901	1,004,901
10	25,000	20,099	4,901	0	1,000,000

Notes:

Column A   The semi-annual interest payments are a constant amount fixed by the stated interest rate and the bonds' maturity value (the orange line in Exhibit 15–8, Panel A).

Column B   The interest expense each period is computed by multiplying the preceding bond carrying amount by the effective-interest rate. The amount of interest decreases each period as the bond carrying amount decreases (the green line in Exhibit 15–8, Panel A).

Column C   The excess of each interest payment (A) over the period's interest expense (B) is the premium amortization for the period (the shaded area in Exhibit 15–8, Panel A).

Column D   The premium balance decreases by the amount of amortization for the period (C) from $44,913 at issuance to zero at maturity (the shaded area in Exhibit 15–9, Panel B). The bonds' carrying amount minus the premium balance equals the bonds' maturity value.

Column E   The bonds' carrying value decreases from $1,044,913 at issuance to $1,000,000 at maturity (the blue line in Exhibit 15–8, Panel B)

LEARNING TIPS

The interest and principal portion of the long-term debt should be separated and listed in the current liabilities section of the balance sheet. This was discussed in Chapter 11 on current liabilities.

Panel A of Exhibit 15–8 diagrams the interest expense over the life of the bonds issued at a premium. Panel B shows how the carrying amount of the bonds decreases to maturity. All amounts are taken from Exhibit 15–7. Focus on the highlighted items in Exhibit 15–8 and the references in Exhibit 15–7.

Does the method of amortizing a bond premium or discount affect the amount of cash interest paid on a bond? No. The amortization method for a bond premium or discount has *no effect* on the amount of cash interest paid on a bond. The amount of cash interest paid depends on the contract interest rate stated

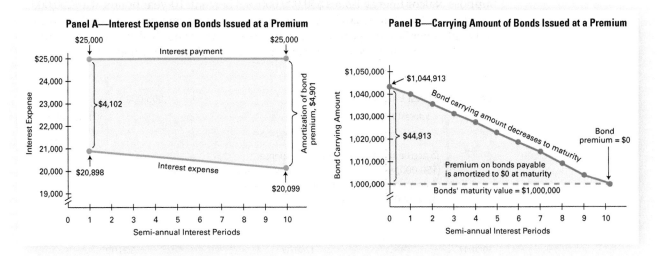

on the bond. That interest rate, and the amount of cash interest paid, are fixed and therefore remain constant over the life of the bond. To see this, examine Column A of Exhibits 15–5 and 15–7.

REPORTING LIABILITIES AND BONDS PAYABLE

The long-term liabilities are divided into their current and long-term portions for reporting on the balance sheet. For each long-term liability, the portion that is due to be paid within the next year is classified as a current liability and is shown on the balance sheet as the liability "Current portion of long-term debt." The long-term debt is reduced by the same amount so that only the portion of the debt due to be paid in more than a year is listed as a long-term liability on the balance sheet.

Bonds payable are reported on the balance sheet at their maturity amount plus any unamortized premium or minus any unamortized discount. For example, consider the UVW Corporation example on page 850. At December 31, 2018, UVW Corporation would have amortized the premium on bonds payable for three semi-annual periods ($1,905 × 3 = $5,715). The issue date is January 2, 2017, first payment is July 2, 2017, second payment is January 2, 2018, and third payment is July 2, 2018. The UVW Corporation balance sheet at December 31, 2018, would show the bonds payable as follows:

Long-term liabilities		
Bonds Payable, 6% due 2027	$1,000,000	
Premium on bonds payable [$38,100 – (3 × $1,905)]	32,385	$1,032,385

Over the life of the bonds, 20 amortization entries will decrease the premium balance to zero. The payment at maturity will debit Bonds Payable and credit Cash for $1,000,000.

ADJUSTING ENTRIES FOR INTEREST EXPENSE

Companies issue bonds when they need cash. The interest payments seldom occur on the end of the company's fiscal year. Nevertheless, interest expense must be accrued at the end of the period to measure net income accurately. The accrual entry may often be complicated by the need to amortize a discount or a premium for only a partial interest period.

LEARNING TIPS

You may recall that Chapter 3 introduced adjusting entries to accrue expenses. We are now adding a bond discount or premium amortization entry to the interest accrual entry.

Adjusting Entries Using the Straight-Line Method

Suppose Nalcor Energy issues $50,000,000 of 8 percent, 10-year bonds at a $200,000 discount on October 1, 2017. Assume that interest payments occur on March 31 and September 30 each year. If December 31 is its year end, Nalcor records interest for the three-month period (October, November, and December) as follows:

2017			
Dec. 31	Interest Expense	1,005,000	
	Interest Payable		1,000,000
	Discount on Bonds Payable		5,000
	To accrue three months' interest expense ($50,000,000 × 0.08 × $\frac{3}{12}$) and amortize the discount on bonds payable for three months ($200,000 ÷ 10 × $\frac{3}{12}$).		

10/01/17	12/31/17	3/31/18
Issue Bonds	Accrue 3 mo. bond int. at Y/E and amortize 3 mo. discount	Pay 6 mo. interest
$50,000,000 – $200,000*	$1,000,000 + $5,000	$2,000,000

*Interest Expense is split evenly between 2017 and 2018 ($1,000,000 each) after the $2,000,000 March 31 payment.

Interest Payable is credited for the three months of cash interest that have accrued since September 30. Discount on Bonds Payable is credited for three months of amortization.

The Nalcor Energy balance sheet at December 31, 2017, reports Interest Payable of $1,000,000 as a current liability. Bonds Payable appears as a long-term liability, presented as follows:

Long-term liabilities		
Bonds payable, 8%, due 2027	$50,000,000	
Less: Discount on bonds payable	195,000	$49,805,000

Observe that the balance of Discount on Bonds Payable decreases by $5,000. The bonds' carrying value increases by the same amount. The bonds' carrying value continues to increase over their 10-year life, reaching $50,000,000 at maturity when the discount will be fully amortized.

The next semi-annual interest payment occurs on March 31, 2018, as follows:

2018			
Mar. 31	Interest Expense	1,005,000	
	Interest Payable	1,000,000	
	Cash		2,000,000
	Discount on Bonds Payable		5,000
	To pay semi-annual interest ($50,000,000 × 0.08 × $\frac{6}{12}$), of which $1,000,000 was accrued, and amortize three months' discount on bonds payable ($200,000 ÷ 10 × $\frac{3}{12}$).		

Amortization of a premium over a partial interest period is similar except that the account Premium on Bonds Payable is debited.

Adjusting Entries Using the Effective-Interest Method

At year end, it is necessary to make an adjusting entry for accrued interest and amortization of the bond premium for a partial period. In our example on page 853, the last interest payment occurred on October 31. The adjustment for November and December must cover two months, or one-third of a semi-annual period.

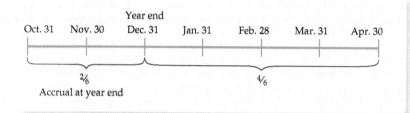

The entry, with amounts drawn from line 2 in Exhibit 15–7 on page 854, is:

Dec. 31	Interest Expense	6,939	
	Premium on Bonds Payable	1,395	
	Interest Payable		8,334
	To accrue two months' interest expense ($20,816 × $\frac{2}{6}$), amortize the premium on bonds payable for two months ($4,184 × $\frac{2}{6}$), and record interest payable ($25,000 × $\frac{2}{6}$).		

The second interest payment occurs on April 30 of the following year. The payment of $25,000 includes interest expense for four months (January through April), the reversal of the interest payable liability created at December 31, and premium amortization for four months. The payment entry is as follows:

Apr. 30	Interest Expense	13,877	
	Interest Payable	8,334	
	Premium on Bonds Payable	2,789	
	Cash		25,000
	To record semi-annual interest for four months ($13,877 = $20,816 × $\frac{4}{6}$), reverse interest payable accrual ($8,334), amortize the premium on bonds payable for four months ($4,184 × $\frac{4}{6}$), and make the cash interest payment of $25,000.		

This timeline shows the total effects of the December 31 accrual and the April 30 semi-annual interest payment:

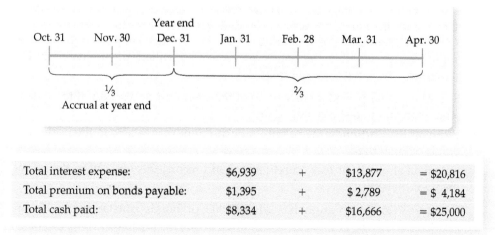

Total interest expense:	$6,939	+	$13,877	=	$20,816
Total premium on bonds payable:	$1,395	+	$2,789	=	$4,184
Total cash paid:	$8,334	+	$16,666	=	$25,000

If these bonds had been issued at a discount, procedures for these interest entries would be the same except that Discount on Bonds Payable would be credited.

▷ Try It!

5. Assume that Ontario Hydro has 6 percent, 10-year bonds that mature on May 1, 2027. Further, assume that $10,000,000 of the bonds are issued at 94.00 on May 1, 2017, and that Ontario Hydro pays interest each April 30 and October 31.

   a. Record issuance of the bonds on May 1, 2017.

   b. Record the interest payment and straight-line amortization of the premium or discount on October 31, 2017.

   c. Accrue interest and amortize the premium or discount on December 31, 2017.

   d. Show how the company would report the bonds on the balance sheet at December 31, 2017.

   e. Record the interest payment on April 30, 2018.

6. Refer to the example of the bonds issued at a premium illustrated in Exhibit 15–7. Use the data in Exhibit 15–7 to accrue interest and amortize the bond premium at the end of the second year, December 31, 2018 (line 4). Then record the April 30, 2019, payment of interest.

7. Refer to Exhibits 15–5 and 15–7 to answer the following questions:

   a. Will the periodic amount of interest expense increase or decrease over the life of a bond issued at a *discount* under the effective-interest amortization method?

   b. Will the periodic amount of interest expense increase or decrease for a bond issued at a *premium*? Assume the effective-interest method of amortizing the premium.

   c. Consider bonds issued at a discount. Which will be greater, the cash interest paid per period or the amount of interest expense? Answer the same question for bonds issued at a premium.

   Solutions appear at the end of this chapter and on MyAccountingLab

RETIREMENT OF BONDS

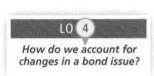

LO 4

How do we account for changes in a bond issue?

KEY POINTS

Callable bonds may be paid off at the corporation's option. The bondholder does not have the choice of refusing and must surrender the bond for retirement.

Normally companies wait until maturity to pay off, or retire, their bonds payable. All the bond discount or premium has been amortized, and the retirement entry debits Bonds Payable and credits Cash for the bonds' maturity value, as we saw earlier. But companies sometimes retire their bonds prior to maturity. The main reason for retiring bonds early is to relieve the pressure of making interest payments. Interest rates fluctuate. The company may be able to borrow at a lower interest rate and use the proceeds from new bonds to pay off the old bonds, which bear a higher rate.

Redeemable bonds are bonds that give the purchaser the option of retiring them at a stated dollar amount prior to maturity. Other bonds are **callable**, which means that the company may *call* or pay off those bonds at a specified price whenever it so chooses normally to take advantage of lower interest rates. The call price is usually a few percentage points above the face value or par, perhaps 104.00 or 105.00, to make the bonds attractive to lenders. An alternative to calling the bonds is to purchase them in the open market at their current market price. When bonds are retired early—whether the bonds are redeemed, called, or purchased in the open market—the same steps are followed:

1 Record a partial-period amortization of the premium or discount if the date is other than an interest payment date.

2 Write off the portion of the premium or discount that relates to the portion of bonds being retired.

3 Calculate any gain or loss on retirement and record this amount in the retirement journal entry.

Suppose XYZ Corporation has $10,000,000 of bonds outstanding with an unamortized discount of $40,000. Lower interest rates in the market may convince management to retire these bonds on June 30, immediately after an interest date. Assume that the bonds are callable at 103.00. If the market price of the bonds is 99.50, will XYZ Corporation call the bonds or purchase them in the open market? The market price is lower than the call price, so the market price is the better choice. Retiring the bonds at 99.50 results in a gain of $10,000, computed as follows:

Face value of bonds being retired	$10,000,000
Unamortized discount	40,000
[❶ (no partial-period amortization in this case) and ❷]	
Book value, or carrying value	9,960,000
Factor × the face value ($10,000,000 × 0.9950) or market price paid to retire the bonds	9,950,000
Gain on retirement of bonds ❸	$ 10,000

The following entry records retirement of these bonds, which happens to be immediately after an interest date:

Jun. 30	Bonds Payable	10,000,000	
	Discount on Bonds Payable		40,000
	Cash		9,950,000
	Gain on Retirement of Bonds Payable		10,000
	To retire bonds payable before maturity.		

After posting, the bond accounts have zero balances.

Bonds Payable		Discount on Bonds Payable	
Retirement 10,000,000	Prior bal. 10,000,000	Prior bal. 40,000	Retirement 40,000

The entry removes the bonds payable and the related discount from the accounts and records a gain on retirement. Of course, any existing premium would be removed with a debit to the Premium on Bonds Payable account.

If XYZ Corporation had retired only half of these bonds, the accountant would remove half of the discount or premium. Likewise, if the price paid to retire the bonds exceeded their carrying value, the retirement entry would record a loss with a debit to the account Loss on Retirement of Bonds. ASPE requires that gains and losses on early retirement of debt that are both abnormal in size and unusual be reported separately as a line item on the income statement before the line items for income tax and discontinued operations.

CONVERTIBLE BONDS AND NOTES

Corporations often add incentives or *sweeteners* to their bonds—features to make the bonds more attractive to potential investors. Many corporate bonds, debentures, and notes payable have the feature of being convertible into the common shares of the issuing company at the option of the investor. These bonds and notes, called **convertible bonds** (or **convertible notes**), combine the safety of assured receipts of principal and interest on the bonds with the opportunity for large gains on the shares. The conversion feature is so attractive that investors usually accept a lower stated interest rate than they would on nonconvertible bonds. The lower interest rate benefits the issuer. Convertible bonds are recorded like any other debt at issuance.

If the market price of the issuing company's shares gets high enough, the bond-holders will convert the bonds into shares. The corporation records conversion by debiting the bond accounts and crediting the shareholders' equity accounts.

REAL WORLD EXAMPLE

Canada Savings Bonds are different from the bonds described in this chapter, as can be seen by the terms described here. They are *debentures* issued by the Canadian government, available in regular and compounding interest, have a guaranteed minimum interest rate, are cashable at any time, and come in denominations of $100, $300, $500, $1,000, $5,000, and $10,000. The interest rate is guaranteed for one year and fluctuates with market conditions for the remaining nine years until the bonds mature.

Normally, the carrying value of the bonds becomes the book value of the newly issued shares, and *no gain or loss is recorded*.

Assume that XYZ Corporation bondholders converted $100,000 of XYZ Corporation bonds into 20,000 common shares on May 1, 2017. The bonds were issued at par. XYZ Corporation's entry to record the conversion would be:

2017			
May 1	Bonds Payable	100,000	
	Common Shares		100,000
	To record conversion of $100,000 bonds outstanding into 20,000 common shares.		

The entry brings the Bonds Payable account to zero, exactly the same as for a bond retirement. The carrying value of the bonds ($100,000) becomes the amount of increase in shareholders' equity.

> Try It!

8. Suppose Bunzell Corporation has $5,000,000 of bonds outstanding with an unamortized premium of $30,000. The call price is 105.00. To reduce interest payments, the company retires half of the bonds at the 100.50 market price. Calculate the gain or loss on retirement, and record the retirement immediately after an interest date.

9. Suppose Bunzell Corporation has $5,000,000 of bonds outstanding with an unamortized premium of $30,000. The bonds are convertible. Assume bondholders converted half of the bonds into 1,000,000 common shares on September 1, 2017. Record the conversion of these bonds into common shares.

10. Suppose Bunzell Corporation has $5,000,000 of bonds outstanding that were issued on different dates with a total unamortized premium of $30,000. Of these amounts, $1,500,000 of the bonds and $5,000 of the unamortized premium are due in one year. How would Bunzell Corporation report the debt on its year-end balance sheet?

Solutions appear at the end of this chapter and on MyAccountingLab

ADVANTAGES AND DISADVANTAGES OF ISSUING BONDS VERSUS SHARES

LO 5

How do we decide whether to issue debt versus equity?

Businesses acquire assets in different ways. Management may decide to purchase or to lease equipment. If management decides to purchase, the money to pay for the asset may be financed by the business's retained earnings, a note payable, a share issue, or a bond issue. Each financing strategy has its advantages and disadvantages, as follows:

Advantages of Financing Operations by	
Issuing Shares	**Issuing Notes or Bonds**
• Creates no liabilities or interest expense, which must be paid even during bad years; is less risky to the issuing corporation.	• Does not dilute share ownership or control of the corporation.
• Raises capital without increasing debt and adversely affecting some key ratios.	• May result in higher earnings per share because interest expense is tax deductible.
• Carries no obligation to pay dividends.	• Can create greater returns for shareholders if leveraged profitably.

Exhibit 15–9 illustrates the earnings-per-share advantage of borrowing. Recall from Chapter 14 that earnings per share (EPS) is a company's net income per common share outstanding. Suppose XYZ Corporation has net income of $600,000 and

	Plan 1: Borrow $1,000,000 at 10%	Plan 2: Issue $1,000,000 of Common Shares
Net income after interest and income tax, before expansion	$600,000	$600,000
Project income before interest and income tax	300,000	300,000
Less: Interest expense ($1,000,000 × 0.10)	100,000	0
Project income before income tax	200,000	300,000
Less: Income tax expense (40%)	80,000	120,000
Project net income	120,000	180,000
Total company net income	$720,000	$780,000
Earnings per share including expansion:		
Plan 1 ($720,000 ÷ 200,000 shares)	$3.60	
Plan 2 ($780,000 ÷ 300,000 shares)		$2.60

200,000 common shares outstanding before a new project. The company needs $1,000,000 for expansion, and management is considering two financing plans:

- Plan 1 is to issue $1,000,000 of 10 percent bonds.
- Plan 2 is to issue 100,000 common shares for $1,000,000.

XYZ Corporation management believes the new cash can be invested in operations to earn income of $300,000 before interest and taxes.

The EPS amount is higher if the company borrows (Plan 1). The business earns more on the investment ($120,000) than the interest it pays on the bonds ($100,000). Earning more income than the cost of borrowing increases the earnings for common shareholders and is called **trading on the equity**. It is widely used in business to increase earnings per common share.

Borrowing has its disadvantages. Debts must be paid during bad years as well as during good years. Interest expense may be high enough to eliminate net income and lead to a cash crisis and even bankruptcy. This happened to many Internet startups. In contrast, a company that issues shares can omit paying dividends during a bad year.

Spreadsheets are useful in evaluating financing alternatives such as issuing common shares, preferred shares, or bonds. This assessment is often called "what if" analysis—for instance, "what if we finance with common shares?" The answers to "what if" questions can be modelled on a spreadsheet to project the company's financial statements over the next few years.

 **Try It!**

11. If trading on the equity can improve EPS, how might it be to the corporation's *disadvantage* to finance with debt?

12. Suppose Zen Corporation has net income of $600,000 and 200,000 common shares outstanding before a new project. The company needs $1,000,000 for expansion, and management is considering two financing plans:

- Plan 1 is to issue $1,000,000 of 12 percent bonds.
- Plan 2 is to issue 50,000 common shares for $1,000,000.

Zen Corporation management believes the new cash can be invested in operations to earn income of $300,000 before interest and taxes. Which plan seems more favourable given the corporation's tax rate of 40 percent? Why?

Solutions appear at the end of this chapter and on MyAccountingLab

MORTGAGES AND OTHER LONG-TERM LIABILITIES

Mortgages: An Introduction

A **mortgage** is a *loan secured* by *real property* using a *mortgage note*. The mortgage is repaid in equal monthly instalments. A portion of each payment represents interest on the unpaid balance of the loan and the remainder reduces the principal, or the outstanding balance of the loan. Such payments are known as **blended payments**. Mortgage payments can be made at any point in the month, and to pay off a mortgage sooner payments can also be made weekly or biweekly. The principal and interest portions of each mortgage payment can be calculated and presented in a *mortgage instalment payment schedule*, also called a *mortgage amortization schedule*. The following is a partial mortgage instalment payment schedule for a 10-year, 5 percent, $200,000 mortgage obtained on October 1, 2017, with monthly blended payments of $2,121. All amounts are rounded to the nearest dollar.

	Partial Mortgage Instalment Payment Schedule			
	Blended Mortgage Payments			
	A	**B**	**C**	**D**
Period	**Blended Monthly Mortgage Payment**	**5% Interest for the Month (Preceding D × 0.05 ÷ 12)**	**Reduction in Principal (A − B)**	**Mortgage Balance (Preceding D − Current C)**
Oct. 1, 2017				$200,000
Nov. 1, 2017	$2,121	$833	$1,288	198,712
Dec. 1, 2017	2,121	828	1,293	197,419
Jan. 1, 2018	2,121	823	1,298	196,121

The blended mortgage payment ($2,121 in Column A) is a blend of both interest and principal. Notice how the reduction in principal (Column C) increases each month so that more of the principal is paid off as the mortgage note matures.

Journal Entry for Mortgage Payments On November 1, 2017, the journal entry to record the first monthly payment on this $200,000 mortgage is:

2017			
Nov. 1	Interest Expense	833	
	Mortgage Payable	1,288	
	Cash		2,121
	To pay monthly mortgage loan and record interest portion of the blended payment.		

Balance Sheet Presentation

The current and long-term portions of mortgage loans are reported on the balance sheet. In the mortgage instalment payment schedule above, the mortgage balance in column D represents the total mortgage debt, and this amount is divided into the current portion of the debt due in one year and the long-term portion due after one year. On December 31, 2017, the current portion of the mortgage is classified as a current liability, as well as the interest on the mortgage that has accrued since the December 1, 2017, payment. Using the amounts for the blended mortgage payments shown, the liabilities section of the balance sheet would appear as follows:

December 31, 2017	
Current liabilities	
Current portion of mortgage*	$ 25,452
Long-term debt	
Mortgage**	$170,669

*Calculated as 12 × $2,121, which should normally be split to show the interest and principal portions separately but is not done here for simplicity. If the mortgage instalment payment schedule were extended to show all the payments in 2018, you would add the 12 principal payments for the year from the schedule to calculate the current portion of the mortgage.

**Calculated as $196,121 – $25,452, which is the mortgage balance at December 31, 2017, (from column D) less the current portion of the mortgage shown as a current liability on the balance sheet.

Other Long-Term Liabilities

Other long-term liabilities shown on published balance sheets would include **shareholder loans**, pension obligations, deferred compensation plans, and future income taxes. These topics will be left for more advanced accounting courses.

> ## Try It!

13. Suppose Austin Metal purchases land and a building for $200,000 on October 1, 2017. Austin obtains a mortgage at an annual rate of 5 percent and will make monthly payments for 10 years. Using the instalment payment schedule in this section on page 862, journalize the entries for the receipt of the mortgage and for the purchase of the land and building, assuming the land is assessed at $40,000 and the building is assessed at $160,000.

14. Refer to the previous question. Journalize the entry for the second mortgage payment, which is made on December 1, 2017.

Solutions appear at the end of this chapter and on MyAccountingLab

LEASE LIABILITIES

A **lease** is an agreement in which the asset user (**lessee**) agrees to make regular, periodic payments to the property owner (**lessor**) in exchange for the exclusive use of the asset. Leasing is the way the lessee avoids having to make the large initial cash down payment that purchase agreements require. Accountants divide leases into two types when considering the lease from the lessee's perspective: operating and capital. From the lessor's perspective, there are again two categories of leases, operating and capital, with capital leases further divided into two kinds: *sales-type leases*, in which the lessor is usually a manufacturer or dealer, and *direct financing leases*, in which the lessor is usually not a manufacturer or dealer but provides financing. This text will consider the broader term, *capital lease*, and not the kinds of capital leases.

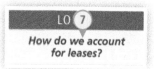

LO 7

How do we account for leases?

Operating Leases

Operating leases are usually short term or cancellable. Many apartment leases and most short-term car rental agreements extend for a year or less. These operating leases give the lessee the right to use the asset but provide the lessee with no continuing rights to the asset. The lessor retains the usual risks and rewards of owning the leased asset. To account for an operating lease, the lessee makes the following journal entry for a $2,000 lease payment:

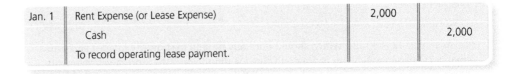

Jan. 1	Rent Expense (or Lease Expense)	2,000	
	Cash		2,000
	To record operating lease payment.		

The lessee's books report neither the leased asset nor any lease liability (except perhaps a prepaid rent amount or a rent accrual at the end of the period). However, the future lease payments for each of the next five years should be given in the notes to the financial statements. The nature of the **provisions**, or lease commitments, should also be stated in the notes.

Capital Leases

Many businesses use capital leasing to finance the acquisition of some assets. A capital lease is long-term, noncancellable financing that is a form of debt.

How do you distinguish a capital lease from an operating lease? Section 3065 of the *CPA Canada Handbook,* Part II, Accounting Standards for Private Enterprises, defines a **capital lease** as one that substantially transfers all the benefits and risks incident to ownership of the property to the lessee. The section goes on to suggest that a lease is a capital lease from the perspective of the lessee if one or more of the following conditions are present at the beginning of the lease:

1. There is reasonable assurance that the lessee will obtain ownership of the leased asset at the end of the lease term.

2. The lease term is of such a length that the lessee will obtain almost all (usually 75 percent or more) of the benefits from the use of the leased asset over its life.

3. The lessor will both recover the original investment and earn a return on that investment from the lease.

A lease that does not meet any of the above conditions is probably an operating lease and should be accounted for as such.

A lease is a capital lease from the perspective of the lessor if any one of the three conditions outlined above is present and *both* of the following are present:

1. The credit risk associated with the lease is normal.

2. The amounts of any unreimbursable costs to the lessor are estimable.

Accounting for a Capital Lease Accounting for a capital lease is much like accounting for a purchase. The lessee enters the asset into its accounts and records a lease liability at the beginning of the lease term. Thus, the lessee capitalizes the asset on its own financial statements even though the lessee may never take legal title to the property.

How does a lessee compute the cost of an asset acquired through a capital lease? Consider that the lessee gets the use of the asset but does *not* pay for the leased asset in full at the beginning of the lease. A capital lease is, therefore, similar to borrowing money to purchase the leased asset. The lessee must record the leased asset at the present value of the lease liability. The time value of money must also be taken into account.

The cost of the asset to the lessee is the sum of any payment made at the beginning of the lease period plus the present value of the future lease payments. The lease payments are equal amounts occurring at regular intervals—that is, they are annuity payments.

Consider a 20-year building lease signed by Sierra Wireless, Inc. The lease starts on January 2, 2017, and requires 20 annual payments of $20,000 each, with the first payment due immediately. If the interest rate in the lease is 10 percent, then the present value of the 19 future payments is $167,298 (see the Learning Tip for the calculation of this amount). Sierra's cost of the building is $187,298 (the sum of the initial payment, $20,000, plus the present value of the future payments, $167,298).

This lease meets the second condition for a capital lease given above: The arrangement is similar to purchasing the building on an instalment plan. In an instalment purchase, Sierra would debit Building and credit Cash and Instalment Note Payable. The company would then pay interest and principal on the note payable and record amortization on the building. Accounting for a capital lease follows this same pattern—debit an asset, credit Cash, and credit a payable for the future lease payments—as shown next.

Sierra records the building at cost, which is the sum of the $20,000 initial payment plus the present value of the 19 future lease payments of $20,000 each, or $187,298.[7] The company credits Cash for the initial payment and credits Lease Liability for the present value of the future lease payments. At the beginning of the lease term, Sierra Wireless makes the following entry:

LEARNING TIPS

To compute the present value of the lease asset using a financial calculator, ensure that the **BGN** key is on, then enter:

PMT = $20,000
I/Y = 10%
N = 20
FV = 0

This gives PV of $−187,298 (negative numbers indicate the direction of cash flow; in this case, cash is flowing *out*).
If using the tables, use ($20,000 × PV of annuity at 10 percent for 19 periods, or 8.365 from Exhibit 15A–7 = $187,300). The $2 difference is due to rounding in the tables.

2017			
Jan. 2	Building under Capital Lease	187,298	
	Cash		20,000
	Capital Lease Liability		167,298
	To lease a building ($20,000 + $167,298) and make the first annual lease payment on the capital lease ($20,000).		

Sierra's lease liability at January 2, 2017, is for 19 payments of $20,000 each on January 2, 2018, to January 2, 2036. However, included in those payments is interest calculated at 10 percent. The lease liability is as follows:

Cash payments January 2, 2018, to January 2, 2036 (19 × $20,000)	$380,000
Interest embedded in the lease payments	212,702
Present value of future lease payments	$167,298

If Sierra Wireless were to record the liability at $380,000, it would also have to record the interest included in that amount as a contra amount. Most companies net the interest against the cash payments and show the liability as the net amount (principal).

Because Sierra has capitalized the building, the company records amortization (using the straight-line method). Assume the building has an expected life of 25 years. It is amortized over the lease term of 20 years because the lessee has the use of the building only for that period. No residual value normally enters into the amortization computation because the lessee will have no residual asset when

---

[7] The appendix to this chapter explains present value.

the building is returned to the lessor at the expiration of the lease. Therefore, the annual amortization entry is:

2017			
Dec. 31	Amortization Expense	9,365	
	Accumulated Amortization— Building under Capital Lease		9,365
	To record amortization on leased building of $9,365 ($187,298 ÷ 20).		

KEY POINTS

For an operating lease, the lessor, not the lessee, records the amortization expense on the leased asset. For a capital lease, the lessee records the amortization expense.

Note that a lessee, such as Sierra, might obtain ownership of the leased asset at the end of the lease term. In such a situation, the lessee would amortize the leased asset over its useful life instead of over the term of the lease. At year end, Sierra must also accrue interest on the lease liability. Interest expense is computed by multiplying the lease liability by the interest rate on the lease. The following entry credits Capital Lease Liability (not Interest Payable) for this interest accrual:

2017			
Dec. 31	Interest Expense	16,730	
	Capital Lease Liability		16,730
	To accrue interest on the lease liability ($167,298 × 0.10, rounded).		

To distinguish between assets that an entity owns and assets it only has a right to use, information about assets acquired through capital leases must be disclosed separately from all other long-term assets. This information includes leased assets' costs, amortization, and interest expense. For the previous example, the balance sheet at December 31, 2017, reports the following:

Assets		
Capital assets:		
Building under capital lease	$187,298	
Less: Accumulated amortization	9,365	$177,933
Liabilities		
Current liabilities:		
Lease liability (next payment due on Jan. 2, 2018)*		$ 20,000
Long-term liabilities:		
Lease liability		164,028**

*The information in brackets is for student reference only. It would not appear on the balance sheet.

**$164,028 = [Beginning balance ($167,298) + Interest accrual ($16,730) – Current portion ($20,000)]

In addition, the lessee must report the minimum capital lease payments for the next five years in the notes to the financial statements.

The lease liability is split into current and long-term portions because the next payment ($20,000) is a current liability and the remainder is long term. The January 2, 2018, lease payment is recorded as follows:

2018			
Jan. 2	Lease Liability	20,000	
	Cash		20,000
	To make second annual lease payment on building.		

15. Bedrock Construction Inc. acquired equipment under a capital lease that requires six annual lease payments of $30,000. The first payment is due when the lease begins on January 2, 2017. Future payments are due on January 2 of each year of the lease term. The interest rate in the lease is 12 percent and the present value of the five future lease payments is $108,143. Journalize (a) the acquisition of the equipment, (b) the amortization for 2017, (c) the accrued interest at December 31, 2017, and (d) the second lease payment on January 2, 2018.

Solutions appear at the end of this chapter and on MyAccountingLab

THE EFFECTS ON LONG-TERM LIABILITIES OF IFRS

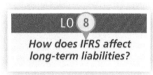

LO 8

How does IFRS affect long-term liabilities?

ASPE	IFRS
In Canada, both IFRS and ASPE are prepared under the authority of the Accounting Standards Board and are published as part of the *CPA Canada Handbook*.	
ASPE allows either straight-line amortization or the effective-interest method.	IFRS requires the use of the effective-interest method

> Why It's Done This Way

Objective of Financial Reporting

Issuing bonds is one common way of raising capital to fund existing or new operations and projects. Corporations may prefer to raise capital with debt—by issuing bonds—because interest payments are tax deductible and the rate of interest paid is, in most cases, fixed. The market, in this case defined as the creditors who purchase the bonds, assess the risk of the company issuing the bonds and compare the bond interest rate with other investments available in the market to determine the interest rate they must earn when they purchase the bonds. This is the market rate of interest we discussed in this chapter.

The action of the market in determining the market rate of interest for bonds leads to either the creation of a discount or a premium, the accounting for which you have studied in this chapter. Since bondholders are always reassessing the risk of their investments, the market rate of interest can change daily. How is this constantly changing market rate of interest reflected in a company's financial statements? Under IFRS, companies can fairly value their bonds at the end of each fiscal period, which means they recalculate the present

value of the bonds each year. This annual update to fair value is consistent with the characteristics of *relevance* and *reliability* in the accounting framework described in Chapter 1. Using the current rate of interest to calculate the fair value of bond debt is relevant information to the users of the financial statements. Since the rate of interest is determined by market forces, it is also reliable. Under ASPE, companies are not required to recalculate the fair value of their bond debt every year. This is because, typically, there are not as many bondholders in a private corporation and those bondholders have access to information directly from the owners and managers of the company.

Under both ASPE and IFRS, details of the corporation's various bond issues must be disclosed in the notes to the financial statements, as described by the *recognition* and *measurement criteria* in the framework. Thus, the valuation of bonds and disclosure of bond information in the financial statements *communicate useful information to interested users* to help them assess the success of the company—this is the objective of the accounting framework.

SUMMARY PROBLEM FOR YOUR REVIEW

Name: Astoria Inc.
Accounting Period:
The years 2017, 2018, 2019

Astoria Inc. has outstanding an issue of 8 percent convertible bonds that mature in 2027. Suppose the bonds were issued October 1, 2017, and pay interest each April 1 and October 1.

Required

1. Complete the following effective-interest amortization table through October 1, 2019.

   Bond data: Maturity value—$2,000,000
   Contract interest rate—8%
   Interest paid—4% semi-annually, $80,000 ($2,000,000 × 0.04)
   Market interest rate at time of issue—9% annually, 4.5% semi-annually
   Issue proceeds—$1,869,921

Amortization table:

	A	B	C	D	E
				Unamortized	
Semi-annual Interest Period	**Interest Payment (4% of Maturity Value)**	**Interest Expense (4.5% of Preceding Bond Carrying Amount)**	**Discount Amortization (B – A)**	**Discount Account Balance (Preceding D – Current C)**	**Bond Carrying Amount ($2,000,000 – D)**
Oct. 1, 2017					
Apr. 1, 2018					
Oct. 1, 2018					
Apr. 1, 2019					
Oct. 1, 2019					

2. Using the amortization table, record the following transactions:

   a. Issuance of the bonds on October 1, 2017.

   b. Accrual of interest and amortization of discount on December 31, 2017.

   c. Payment of interest and amortization of discount on April 1, 2018.

   d. Conversion of one-third of the bonds payable into common shares on October 2, 2019.

   e. Retirement of two-thirds of the bonds payable on October 2, 2019. Purchase price of the bonds was 102.00.

SOLUTION

Requirement 1

Amortization table:

Money received on issue

	A	B	C	D	E
Semi-annual Interest Period	Interest Payment (4% of Maturity Value)	Interest Expense (4.5% of Preceding Bond Carrying Amount)	Discount Amortization (B – A)	Unamortized Discount Account Balance (Preceding D – Current C)	Bond Carrying Amount ($2,000,000 – D)
Oct. 1, 2017				$130,079	$1,869,921
Apr. 1, 2018	$80,000	$84,146	$4,146	125,933	1,874,067
Oct. 1, 2018	80,000	84,333	4,333	121,600	1,878,400
Apr. 1, 2019	80,000	84,528	4,528	117,072	1,882,928
Oct. 1, 2019	80,000	84,732	4,732	112,340	1,887,660

Column A: The semi-annual interest payment is the same each period ($80,000).
Column B: The interest expense is calculated as 4.5 percent of the previous period's carrying value ($1,869,921 × 0.045 = $84,146).

Requirement 2

	2017			
a.	Oct. 1	Cash	1,869,921	
		Discount on Bonds Payable	130,079	
		Bonds Payable		2,000,000
		To issue 8%, 10-year bonds at a discount.		

a. The bonds were issued for less than $2,000,000, reflecting a discount. Use the amounts from columns D and E for Oct. 1, 2017, from the amortization table.

b.	Dec. 31	Interest Expense	42,073	
		Discount on Bonds Payable		2,073
		Interest Payable		40,000
		To accrue interest expense for three months ($84,146 × ³⁄₆) and amortize bond discount for three months ($4,146 × ³⁄₆), and record payable for three months ($80,000 × ³⁄₆).		

b. The accrued interest is calculated, and the bond discount is amortized. Use $\frac{3}{6}$ of the amounts from columns A, B, and C for Apr. 1, 2018.

	2018			
c.	Apr. 1	Interest Expense	42,073	
		Interest Payable	40,000	
		Discount on Bonds Payable		2,073
		Cash		80,000
		To pay semi-annual interest, part of which was accrued on December 31, 2017, and amortize three months' discount on bonds payable ($4,146 × ³⁄₆).		

c. The semi-annual interest payment is made ($80,000 from Column A). Only the January–March 2018 interest expense is recorded, since the October–December interest expense was already recorded in Requirement 2b. The same is true for the discount on bonds payable. Reverse Interest Payable from Requirement 2b, since cash is paid now.

	2019			
d. When converting bonds to common shares, retire the full amount of the bonds ($\frac{1}{3} \times$ $2,000,000) and the discount account balance ($\frac{1}{3} \times$ $112,240 from column D for Oct. 1, 2019).	d. Oct. 2	Bonds Payable	666,667	
		Discount on Bonds Payable		37,447
		Common Shares		629,220
		To record conversion of $\frac{1}{3}$ of the bonds payable ($2,000,000 $\times$ $\frac{1}{3}$). Remove $\frac{1}{3}$ of the discount ($112,340 $\times$ $\frac{1}{3}$).		
e. The cash paid on retirement was $102 for every $100 of bonds. Use $\frac{2}{3}$ of the amount from column D for Oct. 1, 2019, to calculate Discount on Bonds Payable. The loss on retirement reflects the excess of the book value over the cash received and is the "plug" figure in the journal entry calculated as $1,333,333 − $74,893 − $1,360,000 = $101,560 debit.	e. Oct. 2	Bonds Payable	1,333,333	
		Loss on Retirement of Bonds	101,560	
		Discount on Bonds Payable		74,893
		Cash		1,360,000
		To retire remaining bonds payable ($2,000,000 $\times$ $\frac{2}{3}$) and discount ($112,340 $\times$ $\frac{2}{3}$) before maturity. Cash paid ($2,000,000 $\times$ $\frac{2}{3}$ $\times$ 1.02).		

SUMMARY

LEARNING OBJECTIVE ① Define bonds payable and the types of bonds

What are bonds?

Pg. 838

- A corporation may borrow money by issuing long-term notes and bonds.
- Bondholders are the people or companies that lend the money to the bond or note issuer.
- A bond indenture or contract specifies the maturity value of the bonds, the stated interest rate, and the dates for paying interest and principal.
- Bonds may be secured (e.g., a mortgage) or unsecured (e.g., a debenture). Bonds and debentures are accounted for similarly.

LEARNING OBJECTIVE ② Determine the price of a bond, and account for basic bond transactions

How do we account for the sale of a bond?

Pg. 841

- Bonds are traded through organized markets, such as the over-the-counter market.
- Bonds are typically divided into $1,000 units. Their prices are quoted at the price per $100.00 bond.
- Market interest rates fluctuate and may differ from the stated rate on a bond.
- If a bond's stated rate exceeds the market rate, the bond sells at a premium.
- A bond with a stated rate below the market rate sells at a discount.
- Money earns income over time, a fact that gives rise to the present value concept.
- An investor will pay a price for a bond equal to the present value of the bond principal plus the present value of the stream of bond interest receipts.
- Accrued interest may be factored into the purchase if the bond is sold between interest dates.

MyAccountingLab **Interactive Figure:** Interact with Long-Term Notes Payable

LEARNING OBJECTIVE ③ Amortize a bond discount and premium by the straight-line amortization method and the effective-interest amortization method

How do we allocate a bond discount or premium over the life of a bond? Pg. 849

- Straight-line amortization allocates an *equal dollar amount* of premium or discount to each interest period.
- The effective-interest method of amortization allocates a different dollar amount of premium or discount to each interest period because it allocates a *constant percentage* of premium or discount to each interest period. The market rate at the time of issuance is multiplied by the bonds' carrying amount to determine the interest expense for each period and to compute the amount of discount or premium amortization.

LEARNING OBJECTIVE ④ Account for retirement and conversion of bonds

How do we account for changes in a bond issue? Pg. 858

- Companies may retire their bonds payable before maturity.
- Redeemable bonds are bonds that give the purchaser the option of retiring the bonds at a stated dollar amount prior to maturity.
- Callable bonds give the borrower the right to pay off the bonds at a specified call price; otherwise, the company may purchase the bonds in the open market.
- Convertible bonds and notes give the investor the privilege of trading the bonds in for shares of the issuing corporation. The carrying amount of the bonds becomes the book value of the newly issued shares.

LEARNING OBJECTIVE ⑤ Show the advantages and disadvantages of borrowing

How do we decide whether to issue debt versus equity? Pg. 860

- A key advantage of raising money by borrowing versus issuing shares is that interest expense on debt is tax deductible. Thus, borrowing is less costly than issuing shares.
- If the company can earn more income than the cost of borrowing, EPS will increase.
- Borrowing's disadvantages result from the fact that the company must repay the loan and its interest, unlike issuing shares, where dividends do not have to be declared and paid.

LEARNING OBJECTIVE ⑥ Account for other long-term liabilities

How do we account for other long-term liabilities? Pg. 862

- A mortgage is a loan secured by real property using a mortgage note. The mortgage is repaid in equal monthly instalments.
- A portion of each payment represents interest on the unpaid balance of the loan and the remainder reduces the principal, or the outstanding balance of the loan.
- Other liabilities such as shareholder loans may appear in this section of the balance sheet.

    MyAccountingLab **Interactive Figure:** Interact with Mortgages Payable

LEARNING OBJECTIVE ⑦ Account for operating leases and for assets acquired through a capital lease

How do we account for leases? Pg. 863

- A lease is an agreement between the lessor who owns an item and rents it to the lessee who has the use of the item.
- In an operating lease, the lessor retains the usual risks and rights of owning the asset. The lessee debits Rent Expense and credits Cash when making lease payments.
- A capital lease is long term, non-cancellable, and similar to an instalment purchase of the leased asset. In a capital lease, the lessee capitalizes and amortizes the leased asset and reports a lease liability on its balance sheet.

LEARNING OBJECTIVE ⑧ Identify the effects of IFRS on long-term liabilities

How does IFRS affect long-term liabilities? Pg. 867

- Under ASPE, liabilities for bond indebtedness are reported at amortized cost. Under IFRS, the liability may be reported at amortized cost or fair value.
- Under IFRS, companies are required to disclose more lease information than under ASPE.

Check **Accounting Vocabulary** on page 872 for all key terms used in Chapter 15 and the **Glossary** at the back of the book for all key terms used in the textbook.

MORE CHAPTER REVIEW MATERIAL

MyAccountingLab

DemoDoc covering Bond Transactions

Student PowerPoint Slides

Audio Chapter Summary

Note: All MyAccountingLab resources can be found in the Chapter Resources section and the Multimedia Library.

ACCOUNTING VOCABULARY

Bearer bonds Bonds payable to the person that has possession of them. Also called *unregistered bonds* (p. 840).

Bid price The highest price that a buyer is willing to pay for a bond (p. 841).

Blended payments Payments that are a constant amount, and the amount of interest and principal that are applied to the loan change with each payment (p. 862).

Bond A formal agreement in which a lender loans money to a borrower who agrees to repay the money loaned at a future date and agrees to pay interest regularly over the life of the bond (p. 838).

Bond indenture The contract that specifies the maturity value of the bonds, the stated (contract) interest rate, and the dates for paying interest and principal (p. 838).

Bonds payable Groups of notes payable (bonds) issued to multiple lenders called bondholders (p. 838).

Callable bond Bonds that the issuer may call or pay off at a specified price whenever the issuer wants (p. 858).

Capital lease A lease agreement that substantially transfers all the benefits and risks of ownership from the lessor to the lessee (p. 864).

Contract interest rate The interest rate that determines the amount of cash interest the borrower pays and the investor receives each year. Also called the *stated interest rate* (p. 842).

Convertible bond Bonds that may be converted into the common shares of the issuing company at the option of the investor (p. 859).

Convertible note Notes that may be converted into the common shares of the issuing company at the option of the investor (p. 859).

Coupon rate The contractual rate of interest that the issuer must pay the bondholders (p. 839).

Debenture An unsecured bond, backed only by the good faith of the issuer (p. 840).

Discount The amount of a bond's issue price under its maturity (par) value; also called bond discount (p. 841).

Effective-interest amortization An amortization method in which a different amount of bond discount or premium is written off through interest expense each year (or period) of the bond's life. The amount of amortization expense is the same percentage of a bond's carrying value for every period over a bond's life (p. 851).

Effective interest rate The interest rate that investors demand in order to loan their money. Also called the *market interest rate* (p. 843).

Face value Another name for the principal or maturity value of a bond (p. 839).

Lease An agreement in which the tenant (lessee) agrees to make rent payments to the property owner (lessor) in exchange for the exclusive use of the asset (p. 863).

Lessee The tenant, or user of the asset, in a lease agreement (p. 863).

Lessor The property owner in a lease agreement (p. 863).

Long-term liabilities Debts due to be paid in more than a year or more than one of the entity's operating cycles if an operating cycle is greater than one year (p. 838).

Market interest rate The interest rate that investors demand in order to loan their money. Also called the *effective interest rate* (p. 843).

Maturity date The date on which the borrower must pay the principal amount to the lender (p. 839).

Maturity value A bond issued at par that has no discount or premium. Also another name for a bond's principal value (p. 839).

Mortgage The borrower's promise to transfer the legal title to certain assets to the lender if the debt is not paid on schedule. A mortgage is a special type of *secured bond* (p. 862).

Operating lease Usually a short-term or cancellable rental agreement (p. 864).

Over-the-counter (OTC) market The decentralized market where bonds are traded between dealers. Unlike the stock market, there isn't a central bond exchange where transaction prices are posted for all to see (p. 841).

Par value Another name for the principal or maturity value of a bond (p. 839).

Premium The excess of a bond's issue price over its maturity (par) value; also called bond premium (p. 841).

Present value The amount a person would invest now to receive a greater amount at a future date (p. 842).

Principal value The amount a company borrows from a bondholder. Also called the bond's *maturity value, par value,* or *face value* (p. 839).

Provision An account that represents a liability of one entity to another entity (p. 864).

Redeemable bonds Bonds that give the purchaser the option of retiring them at a stated dollar amount prior to maturity *(p. 858)*.

Secured bond A bond that gives the bondholder the right to take specified assets of the issuer if the issuer fails to pay principal or interest *(p. 840)*.

Serial bond A bond that matures in instalments over a period of time *(p. 840)*.

Shareholder loan A loan that is obtained from the owner either in the form of cash or in kind. This amount can be shown as a liability or as a receivable on the balance sheet, depending on whether the balance is a debit or credit *(p. 863)*.

Stated interest rate The interest rate that determines the amount of cash interest the borrower pays and the investor receives each year. Also called the *contract interest rate* *(p. 842)*.

Straight-line amortization Allocating a bond discount or a bond premium to expense by dividing the discount or premium into equal amounts for each interest period *(p. 849)*.

Term bond Bonds that all mature at the same time for a particular issue *(p. 840)*.

Trading on the equity Earning more income on borrowed money than the related expense, thereby increasing the earnings for the owners of the business *(p. 861)*.

Unregistered bonds Another name for *bearer bonds* *(p. 840)*.

Yield The interest rate that an investor will receive based on a compounding period of one year *(p. 841)*.

SIMILAR ACCOUNTING TERMS

Bond	Secured bond; Mortgage bond
Bond principal	Maturity value; Face value; Par value; Principal value
Capital lease liability	Obligation under capital lease
Debenture	Unsecured bond
Mortgage instalment payment schedule	Mortgage amortization schedule
Market interest rate	Effective interest rate
Operating lease	Short-term lease; Short-term rental
Stated interest rate	Contract interest rate; Indenture rate

SELF-STUDY QUESTIONS

Test your understanding of the chapter by marking the best answer for each of the following questions:

1. Which type of bond is unsecured? *(p. 840)*
   a. Serial bond
   b. Common bond
   c. Debenture bond
   d. Mortgage bond

2. How much will an investor pay for a $200,000 bond priced at 102.5? *(p. 841)*
   a. $200,000
   b. $204,000
   c. $205,000
   d. $202,500

3. A bond with a stated interest rate of 6.5 percent is issued when the market interest rate is 6.75 percent. This bond will sell at *(p. 843)*
   a. Par value
   b. A discount
   c. A premium
   d. A price minus accrued interest

4. Imported Cars Inc. has $1,000,000 of 10-year bonds payable outstanding. These bonds had a discount of $80,000 at issuance, which was five years ago. The company uses the straight-line amortization method. The carrying amount or balance of the Imported Cars Inc. bonds payable is *(pp. 849–850)*
   a. $920,000
   b. $960,000
   c. $1,000,000
   d. $1,040,000

5. Imported Cars issued its 8 percent bonds payable at a price of $880,000 (maturity value is $1,000,000). The market interest rate was 10 percent when Imported Cars issued its bonds. The company uses the effective-interest method for the bonds. Interest expense for the first year is *(pp. 851–853)*
   a. $70,400
   b. $80,000
   c. $88,000
   d. $100,000

6. Bonds payable with a face value of $1,800,000 and a balance or carrying value of $1,728,000 are retired before their scheduled maturity with a cash outlay of $1,752,000. Which of the following entries correctly records this bond retirement? (*pp. 858–859*)

a.

Bonds Payable	1,800,000	
Discount on Bonds Payable	72,000	
Cash		1,752,000
Gain on Retirement of Bonds Payable		120,000

b.

Bonds Payable	1,800,000	
Loss on Retirement of Bonds Payable	24,000	
Discount on Bonds Payable		72,000
Cash		1,752,000

c.

Bonds Payable	1,800,000	
Discount on Bonds Payable		36,000
Cash		1,752,000
Gain on Retirement of Bonds Payable		12,000

d.

Bonds Payable	1,728,000	
Discount on Bonds Payable	72,000	
Gain on Retirement of Bonds Payable		48,000
Cash		1,752,000

7. YYZ Corporation has $3,450,000 of debt outstanding at year end, of which $990,000 is due in one year. What will this company report on its year-end balance sheet? (*pp. 862–863*)
a. Long-term debt of $3,450,000
b. Current liability of $990,000 and long-term debt of $3,450,000

c. Current liability of $990,000 and long-term debt of $2,460,000
d. None of the above

8. An advantage of financing operations with debt versus shares is (*pp. 860–861*)
a. The tax deductibility of interest expense on debt
b. The legal requirement to pay interest and principal
c. Lower interest payments compared to dividend payments
d. All of the above

9. Which of the following statements is true for mortgage notes payable requiring blended payments? (*p. 862*)
a. Payments include an increasing amount of interest and a decreasing amount of principal over the life of the mortgage.
b. Payments include an increasing amount of principal and a decreasing amount of interest over the life of the mortgage.
c. Payments include an equal amount of principal and interest for every period over the life of the mortgage.
d. The total cost of the asset secured by a mortgage is equal to the present value of the mortgage.

10. In a capital lease, the lessee records (*pp. 864–866*)
a. A leased asset and a lease liability
b. Amortization on the leased asset
c. Interest on the lease liability
d. All of the above

11. Which of the following would *note* qualify as a capital lease? (*p. 864*)
a. There is reasonable assurance that the lessee will obtain ownership of the leased asset at the end of the lease term.
b. The lease term is of such a length that the lessee will obtain almost all of the benefits (75 percent or more) from the use of the leased asset over its life.
c. The lessor retains the usual risks and rewards of owning the leased asset.
d. The lessor would both recover the original investment and earn a return on that investment from the lease.

Answers to Self-Study Questions

1. c 2. c [$200,000 × 1.025 = $205,000] 3. b 4. b 5. c 6. b 7. c 8. a 9. b
10. d 11. c

ASSIGNMENT MATERIAL

QUESTIONS

1. How do bonds payable differ from a note payable?
2. How does an underwriter assist with the issuance of bonds?

3. Compute the price to the nearest dollar for the following bonds with a face value of $10,000:
a. 93.00 b. 101.375 c. 100.00

4. In which of the following situations will bonds sell at par? At a premium? At a discount?
   a. 9 percent bonds sold when the market rate is 9 percent
   b. 9 percent bonds sold when the market rate is 10 percent
   c. 9 percent bonds sold when the market rate is 8 percent

5. Identify the accounts using journal entries to debit and credit for transactions (a) to issue bonds at *par*, (b) to pay interest, (c) to accrue interest at year end, and (d) to pay off bonds at maturity.

6. Identify the accounts using journal entries to debit and credit for transactions (a) to issue bonds at a *discount*, (b) to pay interest, (c) to accrue interest at year end, and (d) to pay off bonds at maturity.

7. Identify the accounts using journal entries to debit and credit for transactions (a) to issue bonds at a *premium*, (b) to pay interest, (c) to accrue interest at year end, and (d) to pay off bonds at maturity.

8. Why are bonds sold for a price "plus accrued interest"? What happens to accrued interest when bonds are sold by an individual?

9. How does the straight-line method of amortizing a bond discount (or premium) differ from the effective-interest method?

10. A company retires 10-year bonds payable of $100,000 after five years. The business issued the bonds at 104.00 and called them at 103.00. Compute the amount of gain or loss on retirement. How is this gain or loss reported on the income statement? Assume the straight-line method of amortization is used.

11. Bonds payable with a maturity value of $200,000 are callable at 102.50. Their market price is 101.25. If you are the issuer of these bonds, how much will you pay to retire them before maturity?

12. Why are convertible bonds attractive to investors? Why are they popular with borrowers?

13. Silver Corp. has $156 million of bonds outstanding at December 31, 2017. Of the total, $26 million are due in 2018 and the balance in 2019 and beyond. How would Silver Corp. report its bonds payable on its 2017 balance sheet?

14. Contrast the effects of a company of issuing bonds versus issuing shares.

15. Identify the accounts a lessee debits and credits when making operating lease payments.

16. What characteristics distinguish a capital lease from an operating lease?

17. A business signs a capital lease for the use of a building. What accounts are debited and credited (a) to begin the lease term and make the first lease payment, (b) to record amortization, (c) to accrue interest on the lease liability, and (d) to make the second lease payment? The lease payments are made on the first day of the fiscal year.

18. What are blended mortgage payments?

19. Describe how each portion of a blended mortgage payment changes over the life of the mortgage.

20. Show how a lessee reports on the balance sheet any leased equipment and the related lease liability under a capital lease.

MyAccountingLab

Make the grade with MyAccountingLab: Most of the Starters, Exercises, and Problems marked in red can be found on MyAccountingLab. You can practise them as often as you want, and most feature step-by-step guided instructions to help you find the right answer.

STARTERS

Starter 15–1 Match the following terms by entering in the blank space the letter of the phrase that best describes each term.

Bond terms and definitions
①

Bond terms and definitions

_____ Bond indenture

_____ Secured bonds

_____ Debentures

_____ Convertible bonds

_____ Over-the-counter market

_____ Bond discount

_____ Contract interest rate

_____ Unregistered bonds

_____ Bearer bonds

_____ Serial bonds

_____ Redeemable bonds

_____ Market interest rate

_____ Bond premium

a. Interest rate that investors demand in order to loan their money
b. May be converted into the company's common shares
c. Matures in instalments over a period of time
d. Unsecured bond backed only by the good faith of the issuer
e. Contract agreed to between the issuer of the bonds and the purchaser
f. Excess of a bond's maturity value over its issue price
g. Assets of the issuer are provided as collateral
h. Another name for bearer bonds
i. Interest rate that determines the amount of cash interest the borrower pays and the investor receives each year
j. Principal is payable to the person that has possession of the bonds
k. Bonds that give the buyer an option of retiring the bonds before maturity
l. A place where bonds are bought and sold by investors
m. Excess of a bond's issue price over its par value

Determining bond price
②

Starter 15–2

Determine the present value of a $1,000 bond payable issued at maturity value, at a premium, or at a discount (interest is payable annually on this 10-year bond) in each of the situations below.

a. The market interest rate is 7 percent. Jersey Corp. issues bonds payable with a stated rate of 6.5 percent.
b. Frobisher Bay Inc. issued 7 percent bonds payable when the market rate was 6.75 percent.
c. Carola Corporation issued 8 percent bonds when the market interest rate was 8 percent.
d. Black Hawk Corp. issued bonds payable that pay stated interest of 7 percent. At issuance, the market interest rate was 8.25 percent.

Pricing bonds
②
2. 104,500

Starter 15–3

Compute the price of the following 4 percent bonds of Quebec Telecom:
1. $100,000 issued at 98.5
2. $100,000 issued at 104.5
3. $100,000 issued at 92.6

Maturity value of a bond
②

Starter 15–4

For which bond in Starter 15–3 will Quebec Telecom have to pay the most at maturity? Explain your answer.

Journalizing basic bond payable transactions
②
2. Interest expense, $8,125

Starter 15–5

Hunter Corp. issued a $500,000, 3.25 percent, 10-year bond payable on January 1, 2017. Journalize the following transactions for Hunter Corp. Include a calculation for each entry.
1. Issuance of the bond payable at par on January 1, 2017.
2. Payment of semi-annual cash interest on July 1, 2017. (Round to the nearest dollar.)
3. Payment of the bonds payable at maturity. (Give the date.)

Determining bonds payable amounts
②
3. Interest $30,000

Starter 15–6

C&W Drive-Ins Ltd. borrowed money by issuing $1,000,000 of 6 percent bonds payable at 98.
1. How much cash did C&W receive when it issued the bonds payable?
2. How much must C&W pay back at maturity?
3. How much cash interest will C&W pay every six months?

Bond interest rates
②

Starter 15–7

A 7 percent, 10-year bond was issued at a price of 93. Was the market interest rate per annum at the date of issuance closer to 6 percent, 7 percent, or 8 percent? Explain.

Issuing bonds payable and accruing interest
②
2. Interest expense, $12,000

Starter 15–8

Reliable Limited issued $800,000 of 6 percent, 10-year bonds payable on October 1, 2017, at par value. Reliable's accounting year ends on December 31. Journalize the following transactions. Include an explanation for each entry.
1. Issuance of the bonds on October 1, 2017.
2. Accrual of interest expense on December 31, 2017.
3. Payment of the first semi-annual interest amount on April 1, 2018.

Issuing bonds payable between interest dates and then paying the interest
②
2. Interest expense, $7,500

Starter 15–9

Veltman Corp. issued $750,000 of 6 percent, 10-year bonds at par value on May 1, 2017, four months after the bond's original issue date of January 1, 2017. Journalize the following transactions. Include an explanation for each entry.
1. Issuance of the bonds payable on May 1, 2017.
2. Payment of the first semi-annual interest amount on July 1, 2017.

Starter 15–10 Jobs Inc. issued a $500,000, 4 percent, 10-year bond payable at a price of 95 on January 1, 2017. Journalize the following transactions for Jobs Inc. Include an explanation for each entry.
1. Issuance of the bond payable on January 1, 2017.
2. Payment of semi-annual interest and amortization of bond discount on July 1, 2017. Jobs uses the straight-line method to amortize the bond discount.

Issuing bonds payable at a discount, paying interest, and amortizing a discount by the straight-line method
② ③
2. Interest expense, $11,250

Starter 15–11 Surf Sisters Corp. issued a $400,000, 7 percent, 10-year bond payable at a price of 105 on January 1, 2017. Journalize the following transactions for Surf Sisters Corp. Include an explanation for each entry.
1. Issuance of the bond payable on January 1, 2017.
2. Payment of semi-annual interest and amortization of bond premium on July 1, 2017. Surf Sisters uses the straight-line method to amortize the premium.

Issuing bonds payable at a premium, paying interest, and amortizing a premium by the straight-line method
② ③
2. Interest expense, $13,000

Starter 15–12 Live Nation Inc. issued $1,500,000 of 6 percent, 10-year bonds payable and received cash proceeds of $1,393,407 on March 31, 2017. The market interest rate at the date of issuance was 7 percent, and the bonds pay interest semi-annually.
1. Did the bonds sell at a premium or a discount?
2. Prepare an effective-interest amortization table for the bond discount through the first two interest payments. Use Exhibit 15–5 as a guide, and round amounts to the nearest dollar. Students can use a financial calculator if so instructed.
3. Record Live Nation Inc.'s issuance of the bonds on March 31, 2017, and payment of the first semi-annual interest amount and amortization of the bond discount on September 30, 2017. Explanations are not required.
4. If we were to amortize the bond discount using the straight-line method instead of the effective-interest method, record the first interest amortization entry.

Issuing bonds payable and amortizing a discount by the effective-interest method
③
3. Interest expense, $48,769

Starter 15–13 Moe Jones Inc. issued $400,000 of 8 percent, 10-year bonds payable at a price of 114.88 on May 31, 2017. The market interest rate at the date of issuance was 6 percent, and the Moe Jones Inc. bonds pay interest semi-annually.

The effective-interest amortization table for the bond premium is presented here for the first two interest periods:

Issuing bonds payable and amortizing a premium by the effective-interest method
③
3. Interest expense, $13,651

Amortization Table

	A	B	C	D	E
End of Semi-annual Interest Period	Interest Payment (4% of Maturity Value)	Interest Expense (3% of Preceding Bond Carrying Amount)	Premium Amortization (A – B)	Unamortized Premium Account Balance (Previous D – Current C)	Bond Carrying Amount ($400,000 – D)
May 31, 2017				$59,520	$459,520
Nov. 30, 2017	$16,000	$13,786	$2,214	57,306	457,306
May 31, 2018	16,000	13,719	2,281	55,025	455,025

1. How much cash did Moe Jones Inc. receive upon issuance of the bonds payable?
2. Continue the effective-interest amortization table for the bond premium for the next two interest payments. Round amounts to the nearest dollar.
3. Record issuance of the bonds on May 31, 2017, and payment of the third semi-annual interest amount and amortization of the bond premium on November 30, 2018. Explanations are not required.

Accounting for the retirement of bonds payable
④
3. Gain, $31,000

Starter 15–14 On January 1, 2017, Nanke Inc. issued $500,000 of 9 percent, five-year bonds payable at 104. Nanke has extra cash and wishes to retire all the bonds payable on January 1, 2018, immediately after making the second semi-annual interest payment. Nanke uses the straight-line method of amortization. To retire the bonds, Nanke pays the market price of 97.
1. What is Nanke's carrying amount of the bonds payable on the retirement date?
2. How much cash must Nanke pay to retire the bonds payable?
3. Compute Nanke's gain or loss on the retirement of the bonds payable.

Accounting for the conversion of bonds payable
④
1. Carrying amount, $3,030,000

Starter 15–15 Freshfood Corp. has $3,000,000 of convertible bonds payable outstanding, with a bond premium of $30,000 also on the books. The bondholders have notified Freshfood that they wish to convert the bonds into shares. Specifically, the bonds may be converted into 400,000 of Freshfood's common shares.
1. What is Freshfood's carrying amount of its convertible bonds payable prior to the conversion?
2. Journalize Freshfood's conversion of the bonds payable into common shares. No explanation is required.

Earnings-per-share effects of financing with bonds versus shares
⑤
EPS: Plan A, $3.78

Starter 15–16 T&T Marina needs to raise $2 million to expand. T&T's president is considering two plans:
- Plan A: Issue $2,000,000 of 8 percent bonds payable to borrow the money
- Plan B: Issue 100,000 common shares at $20.00 per share

Before any new financing, T&T expects to earn net income of $600,000, and the company already has 200,000 common shares outstanding. T&T believes the expansion will increase income before interest and income tax by $400,000. The income tax rate is 35 percent.

Prepare an analysis similar to Exhibit 15–9 to determine which plan is likely to result in higher earnings per share. Which financing plan would you recommend?

Reporting liabilities
③ ⑥
Total current liabilities, $38,500

Starter 15–17 Talon Inc. includes the following selected accounts in its general ledger at December 31, 2017:

Notes Payable, Long-term	$ 60,000	Accounts Payable	$ 26,000
Bonds Payable.............................	100,000	Discount on Bonds Payable.........	3,000
Interest Payable (due next year).............................	500	Mortgage Payable (payments are $1,000 per month)	100,000

Prepare the liabilities section of Talon Inc.'s balance sheet at December 31, 2017, to show how the company would report these items. Report a total for current liabilities.

Applying mortgage concepts to a loan
⑥

Starter 15–18 You qualified for a student loan in the amount of $10,000. Once you graduate, you are required to repay this loan over 10 years at a rate of interest of 4 percent. The monthly interest and principal repayments are calculated like a mortgage. The following table illustrates the first four payments beginning November 1, 2017:

Student Loan Payments				
Period	Loan Payment	Interest	Reduction in Loan	Loan Balance
Nov. 1, 2017				$10,000.00
Dec. 1, 2017	$101.25	$33.33	$67.92	9,932.08
Jan. 1, 2018	101.25	33.11	68.14	9,863.94
Feb. 1, 2018	101.25	32.88	68.37	9,795.57
Mar. 1, 2018	101.25	32.65	68.60	9,726.97

Using the information from the table, record the journal entry for the January 1, 2018, loan payment.

Starter 15–19 On January 1, 2017, Thames Company purchases a vehicle and signs a six-year loan for $60,000 at 4 percent. Complete the partial amortization schedule below assuming they will make a monthly payment of $980:

Account for long-term notes payable
④
Current portion, $11,760

Payment Number	Date	Equal Payment	Interest Expense	Principal Portion	Balance
	Jan. 1, 2017				60,000.00
1	Jan. 31, 2017				
2	Feb. 28, 2017				
3	Mar. 31, 2017				
4	Apr. 30, 2017				
5	May 31, 2017				
6	Jun. 30, 2017				

At the end of 2017, what amount would be shown on the balance sheet for the current portion of the loan?

Starter 15–20 Best Corp. agrees to lease a store in a mall and open a coffee shop. On January 2, 2017, the company pays a non-refundable $20,000 deposit to secure the store and agrees to a lease amount of $10,000 per month for two years. Journalize the initial lease deposit, the first monthly lease payment, and the December 31 year-end adjustment of the $20,000 deposit. Explanations are not required. Would Best Corp. report the lease information in the notes to the financial statements? Why or why not?

Reporting lease liabilities
⑦

Starter 15–21 Briefly answer the following questions:
a. When accounting for bonds, what is the primary difference between ASPE and IFRS?
b. When accounting for leases, what is the primary difference between ASPE and IFRS?

Difference between ASPE and IFRS
⑧

EXERCISES

MyAccountingLab

Exercise 15–1

Air Canada needs to raise some funds to finance the purchase of a fleet of energy-efficient aircraft to replace the current fleet of aging planes. Air Canada is planning on issuing bonds to finance this proposal. You are the CFO of Air Canada. What would be the best type of bond to issue? As an investor, what would be the best type of bond to purchase in this case?

Bond types
①

Exercise 15–2

Tyler Corp. is planning to issue long-term bonds payable to borrow for a major expansion. The chief executive, Robert Tyler, asks your advice on some related matters:

a. At what type of bond price will Tyler have total interest expense equal to the cash interest payments?

b. Under which type of bond price will Tyler's total interest expense be greater than the cash interest payments?

c. The stated interest rate on the bonds is 3 percent, and the market interest rate is 4 percent. What type of price can Tyler expect for the bonds?

d. Tyler could raise the stated interest rate on the bonds to 5 percent (market rate is 4 percent). In that case, what type of price can Tyler expect for the bonds?

Determining whether the bond price will be at par, at a discount, or at a premium
②

Exercise 15–3

Issuing bonds and
paying interest
②
b. Interest expense, $60,000

Sea-Link Distributors Inc. issues $2,000,000 of 6 percent, semi-annual, 20-year bonds dated April 30. Record (a) the issuance of bonds at par on April 30 and (b) the next semi-annual interest payment on October 31.

Exercise 15–4

Issuing bonds; paying and
accruing interest
② ③
b. Interest expense, $150,000

On February 1, Lasquiti Logistics Inc. issues 20-year, 3 percent bonds payable with a maturity value of $10,000,000. The bonds sell at par and pay interest on January 31 and July 31. Record (a) the issuance of the bonds on February 1, (b) the semi-annual interest payment on July 31, and (c) the interest accrual on December 31.

Exercise 15–5

Issuing bonds; paying
and accruing interest
② ③
b. Interest expense, $125,000

Saturna Corp. issues 20-year, 6 percent bonds with a maturity value of $5,000,000 on April 30. The bonds sell at par and pay interest on March 31 and September 30. Record (a) the issuance of the bonds on April 30, (b) the payment of interest on September 30, and (c) the accrual of interest on December 31.

Exercise 15–6

Issuing bonds between
interest dates
②

Refer to the data for Saturna Corp. in Exercise 15–5. If Saturna Corp. issued the bonds on June 30, how much cash would Saturna Corp. receive upon issuance of the bonds?

Exercise 15–7

Issuing bonds, paying and
accruing interest, and
amortizing a discount by the
straight-line method
② ③
b. Interest expense, $90,000

On April 1, Avalon Inc. issued 20-year, 3.5 percent bonds with a maturity value of $5,000,000. The bonds sell at 98.00 and pay interest on September 30 and March 31. Avalon Inc. amortizes bond discounts by the straight-line method. Record (a) the issuance of the bonds on April 1, (b) the semi-annual interest payment on September 30, and (c) the interest accrual on December 31.

Exercise 15–8

Issuing bonds, paying and
earning interest, and amortizing
a premium by the straight-line
method
② ③
b. Interest expense, $59,250

Lafayette Corp. issues $1,500,000 of 20-year, 8 percent bonds on February 1, 2017. The bonds sell at 102.00 and pay interest on January 31 and July 31. Assume Lafayette Corp. amortizes the premium by the straight-line method. Record (a) the issuance of the bonds on February 1, (b) the payment of interest on July 31, (c) the accrual of interest on December 31, and (d) the payment of interest on January 31, 2018.

Exercise 15–9

Excel Spreadsheet
Template
Preparing an effective-interest
amortization table;
recording interest payments
and the related discount
amortization
③
2. Interest expense on June 30,
$133,288

Life Fitness Ltd. is authorized to issue $6,000,000 of 5 percent, 10-year bonds. On January 2, 2017, the contract date, when the market interest rate is 6 percent, the company issues $4,800,000 of the bonds and receives cash of $4,442,941. Interest is paid on June 30 and December 31 each year. Life Fitness Ltd. amortizes bond discounts by the effective-interest method.

Required

1. Prepare an amortization table for the first four semi-annual interest periods. Follow the format of Panel B in Exhibit 15–5 on page 852.

2. Record the issue of the bonds on January 2, the first semi-annual interest payment on June 30, and the second payment on December 31.

3. Show the balance sheet presentation of the bond on the date of issue and on December 31, 2018.

Exercise 15–10

Excel Spreadsheet
Template
Preparing an effective-interest
amortization table; recording
interest accrual and payment
and the related premium
amortization
③
2. Interest expense on Dec. 31,
$147,738

On September 30, 2017, when the market interest rate is 6 percent, LeHigh Ltd. issues $8,000,000 of 8 percent, 20-year bonds for $9,849,182. The bonds pay interest on March 31 and September 30. Lehigh Ltd. amortizes a bond premium by the effective-interest method.

Required

1. Prepare an amortization table for the first four semi-annual interest periods. Follow the format of Panel B in Exhibit 15–7 on page 854.
2. Record the issuance of the bonds on September 30, 2017, the accrual of interest at December 31, 2017, and the semi-annual interest payment on March 31, 2018.

Exercise 15–11

On January 2, 2017, Omni Industries Inc. issued $4,000,000 of 8.5 percent, 5-year bonds when the market interest rate was 10 percent. Omni Industries pays interest annually on December 31. The issue price of the bonds was $3,772,553.

Required Create a spreadsheet model to prepare a schedule to amortize the discount on these bonds. Use the **effective-interest** method of amortization. Round to the nearest dollar, and format your answer as follows:

Excel Spreadsheet Template
Debt payment and preparing a discount amortization schedule using a spreadsheet
③
Interest expense, $377,255

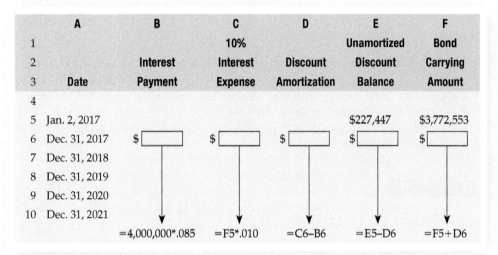

	A	B	C	D	E	F
1			10%		Unamortized	Bond
2		Interest	Interest	Discount	Discount	Carrying
3	Date	Payment	Expense	Amortization	Balance	Amount
4						
5	Jan. 2, 2017				$227,447	$3,772,553
6	Dec. 31, 2017	$ ☐	$ ☐	$ ☐	$ ☐	$ ☐
7	Dec. 31, 2018					
8	Dec. 31, 2019					
9	Dec. 31, 2020					
10	Dec. 31, 2021					
		=4,000,000*.085	=F5*.010	=C6–B6	=E5–D6	=F5+D6

Exercise 15–12

Saint Martin Inc. issued $300,000, 12 percent, 10-year bonds on July 1, 2016. Interest payments dates are January 2 and July 1. The issue price was $293,400. The bonds are convertible into common shares at the rate of 15 common shares for each $1,000 bond. The market price of Saint Martin Inc. common shares has risen steadily over the last two years, and on July 1, 2018, half of the bonds are converted into common shares.

Account for retirement and conversion of bonds
④

Required

1. Compute the balance in the premium or discount account on the date of conversion. Saint Martin Inc. uses the straight-line method of amortization.
2. Prepare the entry to convert half of the bonds into common shares.

Exercise 15–13

Y&R Corporation issued $10,000,000 of 7 percent, 20-year bonds at a premium. The bonds are retired prior to maturity at 102. The book value of the bonds is $10,453,000 at this time. Y&R Corporation amortizes bond premiums using the effective-interest method.

Account for the retirement of bonds
④

Required

1. Was the contract rate on the bonds at the time of issuance greater or less than the market rate of interest? Explain.
2. Prepare the journal entry to record the retirement of the bonds.
3. Assume that the bonds were redeemed at maturity. Would the total cash interest paid be different if the company used the straight-line method of amortization of premiums? Explain.

Exercise 15-14

Recording retirement of
bonds payable
(4)
Interest expense Oct. 1, 2018,
$255,502

Weisbrod Management Inc. issued 8 percent bonds with a maturity value of $6,000,000 for $5,662,980 on October 1, 2017, when the market rate of interest was 9 percent. These bonds mature on October 1, 2025, and are callable at 102.00. Weisbrod Management Inc. pays interest each April 1 and October 1. On October 1, 2018, when the bonds' market price is 103.00, Weisbrod Management Inc. retires the bonds in the most economical way available.

Required Record the payment of interest and the amortization of the bond discount at October 1, 2018; also record the retirement of the bonds on that date. Weisbrod Management Inc. uses the effective-interest method to amortize the bond discount.

Exercise 15-15

Recording conversion of
bonds payable
(4)
2. Carrying amount at Dec. 31,
2018, $7,252,500

Kellogg Imaging Ltd. issued $7,500,000 of 8.5 percent, 15-year convertible bonds payable on July 1, 2017, at a price of 97.0. Each $1,000 face amount of bonds is convertible into 80 common shares. On December 31, 2018, bondholders exercised their right to convert the bonds into common shares.

Required

1. What would cause the bondholders to convert their bonds into common shares?
2. Without making journal entries, compute the carrying amount of the bonds payable at December 31, 2018. Kellogg Imaging Ltd. uses the straight-line method to amortize a bond premium or discount on an annual basis.
3. All amortization has been recorded properly. Journalize the conversion transaction at December 31, 2018.

Exercise 15-16

Recording early retirement and
conversion of bonds payable
(4)
1. Cr Cash, $824,000

Seville Products Ltd. reported the following at September 30, 2017:

Long-term liabilities		
Convertible bonds payable, 9%, due September 30, 2023	$1,600,000	
Discount on bonds payable	60,000	$1,540,000

Required

1. Record the retirement of one-half of the bonds on October 1, 2017, at the call price of 103.00.
2. Record the conversion of one-fourth (of the original $1,600,000) of the bonds into 20,000 common shares of Seville Products Ltd. on October 1, 2017.

Exercise 15-17

Analyzing alternative plans
for raising money
(5)
EPS: Plan A, $5.78

Pudong Transport Ltd. is considering two plans for raising $4,000,000 to expand operations. Plan A is to borrow at 9 percent, and Plan B is to issue 400,000 common shares. Before any new financing, Pudong Transport Ltd. has net income after interest and income tax of $2,000,000 and 400,000 common shares outstanding. Management believes the company can use the new funds to earn income of $840,000 per year before interest and taxes. The income tax rate is 35 percent.

Required Analyze Pudong Transport Ltd.'s situation to determine which plan will result in higher earnings per share. Use Exhibit 15-9 on page 861 as a guide.

Exercise 15-18

Earnings-per-share effects
of financing with bonds
versus shares
(5)
EPS: Plan A, $4.12

Knutsen Financial Services Ltd. needs to raise $3,000,000 to expand company operations. Knutsen's president is considering two options:

- Plan A: $3,000,000 of 4 percent bonds payable to borrow the money
- Plan B: 300,000 common shares at $10.00 per share

Before any new financing, Knutsen Financial Services Ltd. expects to earn net income of $900,000, and the company already has 300,000 common shares outstanding. The president believes the expansion will increase income before interest and income tax by $600,000. The company's income tax rate is 30 percent.

Required Prepare an analysis similar to Exhibit 15–9 on page 861, to determine which plan is likely to result in the higher earnings per share. Which financing plan would you recommend for Knutsen Financial Services Ltd.? Give your reasons.

Exercise 15–19

The chief accounting officer of Giffen Productions Ltd. is considering how to report long-term notes. The company's financial accountant has assembled the following for long-term notes payable:

Reporting long-term debt on the balance sheet
③ ⑥

Note 5: Long-Term Debt	
Total	$2,400,000
Less: Current portion	300,000
Less: Unamortized discount	16,000
Long-term debt	$2,084,000

None of the unamortized discount relates to the current portion of long-term debt. Show how Giffen Productions Ltd.'s balance sheet would report these liabilities.

Exercise 15–20

Spirit World Corp. borrowed $500,000 in the form of a mortgage on January 1, 2017, to finance the purchase of a small warehouse. The mortgage rate is 5 percent, the term is 20 years, and semi-annual payments of $19,918 are made on January 1 and July 1. The following chart shows the first five mortgage payments:

Recording and reporting mortgage liabilities
⑥

Semi-annual Interest Period	A Cash Payment	B Interest Expense 2.5%	C Reduction of Principal	D Principal Balance
Jan. 1, 2017				$500,000
July 1, 2017	$19,918	$12,500	$7,418	492,582
Jan. 1, 2018	19,918	12,315	7,603	484,979
July 1, 2018	19,918	12,124	7,794	477,185
Jan. 1, 2019	19,918	11,930	7,988	469,197
July 1, 2019	19,918	11,730	8,188	461,009

Required

1. Journalize the establishment of the mortgage and the first mortgage payment made on July 1, 2017.

2. Show the balance sheet presentation of this mortgage on December 31, 2018, separating the current and long-term portions.

Exercise 15–21

Reporting liabilities, including
capital lease obligations
(7)

Total liabilities $1,600,000

HMR Associates Inc. includes the following selected accounts in its general ledger at December 31, 2017:

Bonds Payable................................	$1,020,000	Current Obligation under Capital Lease..................................	$ 12,000
Equipment under Capital Lease..............................	350,000	Accounts Payable..............................	57,000
Interest Payable (due March 1, 2018)..................	31,000	Long-term Capital Lease Liability...	136,000
Current Portion of Bonds Payable..........................	162,000	Discount on Bonds Payable (all long term)	18,000
Notes Payable, Long-term	200,000		

Required Prepare the liabilities section of HMR Associates Inc.'s balance sheet at December 31, 2017, to show how the company would report these items. Report a total for both current and long-term liabilities.

Exercise 15–22

Journalizing capital lease and
operating lease transactions
(7)

2. Dec. 31, 2017, amortization
expense, $27,036

A capital lease agreement for equipment requires Granger Transport Ltd. to make 10 annual payments of $40,000, with the first payment due on January 2, 2017, the date of the inception of the lease. The present value of the nine future lease payments at 10 percent is $230,360.

Required

1. Calculate the present value of the lease at 5 percent if your instructor has taught present value.
2. Journalize the following lessee transactions:

2017
Jan.   2   Beginning of lease term and first annual payment.
Dec. 31   Amortization of equipment (10 percent).
      31   Interest expense on lease liability.
2018
Jan.   2   Second annual lease payment.

3. Assume now that this is an operating lease. Journalize the January 2, 2017, lease payment.

SERIAL EXERCISE

This exercise continues the Lee Consulting Corporation situation from Exercise 14–20 of Chapter 14. If you did not complete any Serial Exercises in earlier chapters, you can still complete Exercise 15–23 as it is presented.

Exercise 15–23

Bonds transactions
(2)

3. Oct. 1, 2017, interest expense,
$17,274

Lee Consulting Corporation is considering raising capital for a planned business expansion to a new market. Lee believes the company will need $500,000 and plans to raise the capital by issuing 6 percent, 10-year bonds on April 1, 2017. The bonds pay interest semi-annually on April 1 and October 1. On April 1, 2017, the market rate of interest required by similar bonds by investors is 8 percent, causing the bonds to sell for $431,850.

Required

1. Were the Lee Consulting Corporation bonds issued at par, a premium, or a discount?
2. Record the cash received on the bond issue date.
3. Journalize the first interest payment on October 1, 2017, and amortize the premium or discount using the effective-interest method.
4. Journalize the entry required, if any, on December 31, 2017, related to the bonds.

CHALLENGE EXERCISE

Exercise 15–24

The (partial) advertisement below appeared in the *Financial Post*:

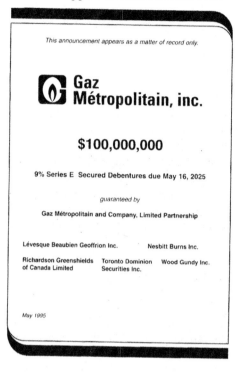

This announcement appears as a matter of record only.

Gaz Métropolitain, inc.

$100,000,000

9% Series E Secured Debentures due May 16, 2025

guaranteed by

Gaz Métropolitain and Company, Limited Partnership

Lévesque Beaubien Geoffrion Inc.   Nesbitt Burns Inc.

Richardson Greenshields   Toronto Dominion   Wood Gundy Inc.
of Canada Limited   Securities Inc.

May 1995

Interest is payable on November 16 and May 16.

Required   Answer these questions about Gaz Métropolitain's secured debentures (bonds):

1. Suppose investors purchased these securities at 98.50 on May 16, 2017. Describe the transaction in detail, indicating who received cash, who paid cash, and how much.
2. Compute the annual cash interest payment on the Gaz Métropolitain bonds.
3. Prepare an effective-interest amortization table for Gaz Métropolitain's first two payments, on November 16, 2017, and May 16, 2018. Assume the market rate at the date of issuance was 9.2 percent.
4. Compute Gaz Métropolitain's interest expense for the first full year ended May 16, 2018, under the effective-interest amortization method.
5. Another company's issue of unsecured bonds for $20,000,000 was issued the same day; it bore an interest rate of 12 percent. Why was the rate so much higher for this issue than for the Gaz Métropolitain issue?

Exercise 15–25

Refer to the bond situation of Gaz Métropolitain in Exercise 15–24. Assume Gaz Métropolitain issued the bonds at a price of 98.50 and that the company uses the effective-interest amortization method. The company's year end is December 31.

Required

1. Journalize the following bond transactions of Gaz Métropolitain:

2017

May 16   Issuance of the bonds.

Nov. 16   Payment of interest expense and amortization of the discount on the bonds payable. The market rate on the date of issuance was 9.2 percent.

Dec. 31   Accrual of interest expense and amortization of the discount on the bonds payable.

2. What is Gaz Métropolitain's carrying amount of the bonds payable at
   a. November 16, 2017?
   b. December 31, 2017?
   c. May 16, 2018?

BEYOND THE NUMBERS

Beyond the Numbers 15–1

Questions about long-term debt
② ⑥

The following questions are not related.

1. IMAX Corporation obtains the use of most of its theatre properties through leases. IMAX Corporation prefers operating leases over capital leases. Why is this a good idea? Consider IMAX Corporation's debt ratio.

2. IMAX Corporation likes to borrow for longer periods when interest rates are low and for shorter periods when interest rates are high. Why is this a good business strategy?

3. Suppose IMAX Corporation needs to borrow $2,000,000 to open new theatres. The company can borrow $2,000,000 by issuing 8 percent, 20-year bonds at a price of 96. How much will IMAX Corporation actually be borrowing under this arrangement? How much must the company repay at maturity?

ETHICAL ISSUE

Cavell Products Inc., a manufacturer of electronic devices, borrowed heavily during the early 2000s to exploit the advantage of financing operations with debt. At first, Cavell Products was able to earn operating income much higher than its interest expense and was therefore quite profitable. However, when the business cycle turned down, Cavell Products' debt burden pushed the company to the brink of bankruptcy. Operating income was less than interest expense.

Required Is it unethical for managers to commit a company to a high level of debt? Or is it just risky? Who could be hurt by a company's taking on too much debt? Discuss.

PROBLEMS (GROUP A)   MyAccountingLab

Problem 15–1A

Journalizing bond transactions (at par) and reporting bonds payable on the balance sheet
②
1. b. Interest expense, $200,000

The board of directors of Jeter Production Co. Ltd. authorizes the issuance of 4 percent, 10-year bonds with a maturity value of $12,000,000. The semi-annual interest dates are May 31 and November 30. The bonds are issued through an underwriter on June 30, 2017, at par plus accrued interest from June 1, 2017. Jeter's year end is December 31.

Required

1. Journalize the following transactions:
   a. Issuance of the bonds on June 30, 2017.
   b. Payment of interest on November 30, 2017.
   c. Accrual of interest on December 31, 2017.
   d. Payment of interest on May 31, 2018.

2. Report interest payable and bonds payable as they would appear on the Jeter Production Co. Ltd. balance sheet at December 31, 2017.

3. Why do we need to accrue interest on June 30 and again on December 31, twice in 2017?

Problem 15–2A

On March 1, 2017, Shaw Systems Ltd. issues 8.5 percent, 20-year bonds payable with a maturity value of $5,000,000. The bonds pay interest on February 28 and August 31. Shaw Systems Ltd. amortizes premiums and discounts by the straight-line method.

Issuing bonds at a discount, amortizing by the straight-line method, and reporting bonds payable on the balance sheet
(2) (3)
3. b. Interest expense, $216,250

Required

1. If the market interest rate is 7.5 percent when Shaw Systems issues its bonds, will the bonds be priced at par, at a premium, or at a discount? Explain.

2. If the market interest rate is 9 percent when Shaw Systems issues its bonds, will the bonds be priced at par, at a premium, or at a discount? Explain.

3. Assume the issue price of the bonds is 97.00. Journalize the following bond transactions:

   a. Issuance of the bonds on March 1, 2017.

   b. Payment of interest and amortization of the discount on August 31, 2017.

   c. Accrual of interest and amortization of the discount on December 31, 2017, Shaw Systems' year end.

   d. Payment of interest and amortization of the discount on February 28, 2018.

4. Report interest payable and bonds payable as they would appear on the Shaw Systems Ltd. balance sheet at December 31, 2017.

Problem 15–3A

The notes to Shaolin Biotech Inc.'s financial statements recently reported the following data on June 30, 2017, the company's year end:

Excel Spreadsheet Template
Analyzing a company's long-term debt, journalizing its transactions, and reporting the long-term debt on the balance sheet
(2) (3)
4. Interest expense, $40,000

NOTE 4: INDEBTEDNESS

Long-term debt at June 30, 2017, included the following:

6.00 percent debentures due June 30, 2036, with an effective interest rate of 7.00 percent, net of unamortized discount of $206,712 .... $1,793,288

Other indebtedness with an interest rate of 5.00 percent, due $408,000 in 2021 and $392,000 in 2022.. 800,000

Assume Shaolin Biotech Inc. amortizes a discount by the effective-interest method.

Required

1. Answer the following questions about Shaolin Biotech's long-term liabilities:

   a. What is the maturity value of the 6 percent debentures?

   b. What are Shaolin Biotech's annual cash interest payments on the 6 percent debentures?

   c. What is the carrying amount of the 6 percent debentures at June 30, 2017? 2018?

   d. How many years remain in the life of the 6 percent debentures?

2. Prepare an amortization table through June 30, 2020, for the 6 percent debentures. Round all amounts to the nearest dollar, and assume Shaolin Biotech pays interest annually on June 30.

3. Record the June 30, 2019 and 2020, interest payments on the 6 percent debentures.

4. There is no premium or discount on the other indebtedness. Assuming annual interest is paid on June 30 each year, record Shaolin Biotech Inc.'s June 30, 2018, interest payment on the other indebtedness.

Problem 15–4A

On December 31, 2017, Belagio Holdings Ltd. issues 6 percent, 10-year convertible bonds with a maturity value of $6,000,000. The semi-annual interest dates are June 30 and December 31. The market interest rate is 5 percent and the issue price of the bonds is 107.79458. Belagio Holdings Ltd. amortizes any bond premium and discount by the effective-interest method.

Excel Spreadsheet Template
Issuing convertible bonds at a premium, amortizing by the effective-interest method, retiring bonds early, converting bonds, and reporting the bonds payable on the balance sheet
(2) (3) (4)
2. b. Interest expense, $161,692

Required

1. Prepare an effective-interest-method amortization table for the first four semi-annual interest periods.
2. Journalize the following transactions:
   a. Issuance of the bonds on December 31, 2017. Credit Convertible Bonds Payable.
   b. Payment of interest on June 30, 2018.
   c. Payment of interest on December 31, 2018.
   d. Retirement of bonds with maturity value of $3,000,000 on July 2, 2019. Belagio Holdings pays the call price of 104.00.
   e. Conversion by the bondholders on July 2, 2019, of bonds with maturity value of $2,000,000 into 40,000 of Belagio Holdings Ltd. common shares.
3. Prepare the balance sheet presentation of the bonds payable that are outstanding at December 31, 2019.

Problem 15–5A

Amortizing a bond discount and premium by the effective-interest method; retirement of bonds; conversion of bonds
② ③ ④
1. June 30, 2017, interest expense, $221,209

Shield Transport Ltd. is authorized to issue 10-year, 6 percent convertible bonds with a maturity value of $16,000,000. Interest is payable on June 30 and December 31. The bonds are convertible on the basis of 50 common shares for each $1,000 bond. The following bond transactions took place:

2017

Jan. 2	Issued bonds with $6,400,000 maturity value. Since the market rate of interest on this date was 8 percent, the bonds sold for $5,530,219.
Jun. 30	Paid semi-annual interest and amortized the discount using the effective-interest amortization method.
Dec. 31	Paid semi-annual interest and amortized the discount using the effective-interest amortization method.

2018

Jun. 30	Paid semi-annual interest and amortized the discount using the effective-interest amortization method.
Jul. 2	Retired bonds with a $3,200,000 maturity value at a rate of 94.00.
2	Bondholders converted bonds with a $1,600,000 maturity value into common shares.

Required

1. Create an amortization schedule for the first three interest periods for the bonds sold on January 2, 2017. Round all amounts to the nearest whole dollar. Use the values from the schedule and any other information to journalize all the transactions above.
2. Show the balance sheet presentation of the bonds payable on July 2, 2018.

Problem 15–6A

Financing operations with debt or with shares
⑤

Two businesses must consider how to raise $10,000,000.

Blackburn Inc. is in the midst of its most successful period since it began operations 48 years ago. For each of the past 10 years, net income and earnings per share have increased by 15 percent. The outlook for the future is equally bright, with new markets opening up and competitors unable to manufacture products of Blackburn Inc.'s quality. Blackburn Inc. is planning a large-scale expansion and would like to purchase equipment. The bank is reluctant to lend any more funds to this company as the lending rules have become stricter.

Sage Consulting Limited has fallen on hard times. Net income has remained flat for five of the last six years, even falling by 10 percent from last year's level of profits. Top management has experienced unusual turnover, and the company lacks strong leadership. To become competitive again, Sage Consulting Limited desperately needs $10,000,000 for expansion.

Required

1. Propose a plan for each company to raise the needed cash. Which company should borrow? Which company should issue shares? Consider the advantages and disadvantages of raising money by borrowing and by issuing shares, and discuss them in your answer.

2. How will what you have learned in this chapter help you manage a business?

Problem 15–7A

Domaine Wines Ltd. issued an $800,000, 5-year, 6 percent mortgage note payable on December 31, 2017, to help finance a new warehouse. The terms of the mortgage provide for semi-annual blended payments of $93,784 on June 30 and December 31 of each year.

1. Prepare a mortgage instalment payment schedule for the first two years of this mortgage. Round all amounts to the nearest whole dollar.

2. Record the issuance of the mortgage note payable on December 31, 2017.

3. Report interest payable and the mortgage note payable on the December 31, 2017, balance sheet.

4. Journalize the first two instalment payments on June 30, 2018, and December 31, 2018.

Accounting for a mortgage
⑥
1. Dec. 31, 2019, principal balance, $508,049

Problem 15–8A

Journalize the following transactions of Mecina Technologies Inc.:

Journalizing bonds payable and capital lease transactions
② ⑦
July 2, 2017, interest expense, $182,500

2017

Jan.	2	Issued 7 percent, 10-year bonds with a maturity value of $5,000,000 at 97.00.
Jan.	2	Signed a five-year capital lease on equipment. The agreement requires annual lease payments of $400,000, with the first payment due immediately (BGN). The present value of the five lease payments is $1,724,851 (8 percent is the interest rate).
Jul.	2	Paid semi-annual interest and amortized the discount by the straight-line method on the 7 percent bonds.
Dec.	31	Accrued semi-annual interest expense and amortized the discount by the straight-line method on the 7 percent bonds.
	31	Recorded amortization on the leased equipment using the straight-line method (five years).
	31	Accrued interest expense at 8 percent on the lease liability.

2027

Jan.	2	Paid the 7 percent bonds at maturity. (Ignore the final interest payment.)

Problem 15–9A

Castlegar Systems Inc. had the following information available on bonds payable outstanding at December 31, 2017, its year end:

Amortizing a bond premium by the effective-interest method; accounting for lease transactions
③ ⑦
1. Apr. 2, 2018, interest expense, $204,452

- $5,000,000—Bonds Payable, 9 percent, interest paid on April 2 and October 2. The bonds had been issued on April 2, 2017, for $5,131,053 when the market rate of interest was 8 percent, and are due April 2, 2020.

The following transactions took place after December 31, 2017:

2018

Jan.	2	Castelgar Systems Inc. signed a lease to rent a warehouse for expansion of its operations. The lease is five years with an option to renew and calls for annual payments of $50,000 per year payable on January 2. Castelgar Systems gave a cheque for the first year upon signing the contract.
	2	Castelgar Systems Inc. signed a lease for equipment. The lease is for 10 years with payments of $40,000 per year payable on January 2 (the first year's payment was made at the signing). At the end of the lease the equipment will become the property of Castelgar Systems. The future payments on the lease have a present value (at 10 percent) of $270,361. The equipment has a 10-year useful life and 10 percent residual value.

Apr.	2	Paid the interest on the bonds payable and amortized the premium using the effective-interest method. Assume half of the interest expense, amortization of the bond premium, and interest payable had been accrued properly on December 31, 2017.
Oct.	2	Paid the interest on the bonds payable and amortized the premium using the effective-interest method.
Dec.	31	Recorded any adjustments required at the end of the year for the bonds payable and the lease(s).

2019

Jan.	2	Made the annual payments on the leases.
Apr.	2	Paid the interest on the bonds payable and amortized the premium using the effective-interest method.

Required

1. For the bonds issued on April 2, 2017, prepare an amortization schedule for the three-year life of the bonds. Round all amounts to the nearest whole dollar.

2. Record the general journal entries for the 2018 and 2019 transactions.

3. Show the liabilities section of the balance sheet on December 31, 2019.

Problem 15–10A

The accounting records of Sleeman Resources Inc. include the following items:

Reporting liabilities on the balance sheet

⑥ ⑦

Current portion of bond payable, $103,091

Capital Lease Liability, Long-term..	$538,000	Mortgage Note Payable, Long-term.............................	$ 501,000
Bonds Payable, Long-term................	960,000	Building Acquired under Capital Lease.........................	800,000
Premium on Bonds Payable..............	78,000		
Interest Expense	300,000	Bonds Payable, Current Portion	96,000
Interest Payable	98,820	Accumulated Amortization,	
Interest Revenue...............................	61,800	Building...............................	448,000
Capital Lease Liability, Current...	74,000	Mortgage Note Payable, Short-term	201,000

Required
Show how these items would be reported on the Sleeman Resources Inc. balance sheet, including headings for property, plant, and equipment; current liabilities; long-term liabilities; and so on. Note disclosures are not required. Remember that the premium on bonds payable must be split between the current and long-term portions of the bonds payable.

PROBLEMS (GROUP B) MyAccountingLab

Problem 15–1B

Journalizing bond transactions (at par) and reporting bonds payable on the balance sheet

②

The board of directors of Farrell Communications Ltd. authorizes the issuance of 6 percent, 20-year bonds with a maturity value of $10,000,000. The semi-annual interest dates are March 31 and September 30. The bonds are issued through an underwriter on April 30, 2017, at par plus accrued interest. Farrell's year end is December 31.

Required

1. Journalize the following transactions:

   a. Issuance of the bonds on April 30, 2017.

   b. Payment of interest on September 30, 2017.

   c. Accrual of interest on December 31, 2017.

   d. Payment of interest on March 31, 2018.

2. Report interest payable and bonds payable as they would appear on the Farrell Communications Ltd. balance sheet at December 31, 2017.

3. Why do we need to accrue interest on April 30 and again on December 31, twice in 2017?

Problem 15–2B

On April 1, 2017, Pettington Corp. issues 7 percent, 10-year bonds payable with a maturity value of $3,000,000. The bonds pay interest on March 31 and September 30, and Pettington Corp. amortizes premiums and discounts by the straight-line method.

Issuing bonds at a premium, amortizing by the straight-line method, and reporting bonds payable on the balance sheet
② ③

Required

1. If the market interest rate is 9 percent when Pettington Corp. issues its bonds, will the bonds be priced at par, at a premium, or at a discount? Explain.

2. If the market interest rate is 5 percent when Pettington Corp. issues its bonds, will the bonds be priced at par, at a premium, or at a discount? Explain.

3. Assume the issue price of the bonds is 103.00. Journalize the following bonds payable transactions:

   a. Issuance of the bonds on April 1, 2017.

   b. Payment of interest and amortization of the premium on September 30, 2017.

   c. Accrual of interest and amortization of the premium on December 31, 2017, the year end.

   d. Payment of interest and amortization of the premium on March 31, 2018.

4. Report interest payable and bonds payable as they would appear on the Pettington Corp. balance sheet at December 31, 2017.

Problem 15–3B

Assume that the notes to Echo Valley Ltd.'s financial statements reported the following data on September 30, 2017:

NOTE E: LONG-TERM DEBT

5 percent debentures due 2033, net of unamortized discount of $223,162
(effective interest rate of 6.0 percent) $1,776,838

Echo Valley Ltd. amortizes the discount by the effective-interest method.

Excel Spreadsheet Template
Analyzing a company's long-term debt, journalizing its transactions, and reporting the long-term debt on the balance sheet
② ③

Required

1. Answer the following questions about Echo Valley's long-term liabilities:

   a. What is the maturity value of the 5 percent debentures?

   b. What is the carrying amount of the 5 percent debentures at September 30, 2017? 2018?

   c. What are Echo Valley's annual cash interest payments on these debentures?

2. Prepare an amortization table through September 30, 2019, for the 5 percent debentures. Echo Valley pays interest annually on September 30.

3. Record the September 30, 2019, interest payments on the 5 percent debentures.

4. What is Echo Valley's carrying amount of the 5 percent debentures at September 30, 2019, immediately after the interest payment?

Problem 15–4B

On December 31, 2017, Sierra Corp. issues 4 percent, 10-year convertible bonds with a maturity value of $4,500,000. The semi-annual interest dates are June 30 and December 31. The market interest rate is 5 percent, and the issue price of the bonds is 92.2054. Sierra Corp. amortizes bond premium and discount by the effective-interest method.

Excel Spreadsheet Template
Issuing convertible bonds at a discount, amortizing by the effective-interest method, retiring bonds early, converting bonds, and reporting bonds payable on the balance sheet
② ③ ④

Required

1. Prepare an effective-interest method amortization table for the first four semi-annual interest periods.

2. Journalize the following transactions:

   a. Issuance of the bonds on December 31, 2017. Credit Convertible Bonds Payable.

   b. Payment of interest on June 30, 2018.

   c. Payment of interest on December 31, 2018.

d. Retirement of the bonds with a maturity value of $200,000 on July 2, 2019. Sierra Corp. purchases the bonds at 96.00 in the open market.

e. Conversion by the bondholders on July 2, 2019, of bonds with a maturity value of $400,000 into 5,000 Sierra Corp. common shares.

3. Prepare the balance sheet presentation of the bonds payable that are outstanding at December 31, 2019.

Problem 15–5B

Amortizing a bond discount and premium by the effective-interest method; retirement of bonds; conversion of bonds

② ③ ④

Tasis Ventures Inc. is authorized to issue 10-year, 5 percent convertible bonds with a maturity value of $9,000,000. Interest is payable on June 30 and December 31. The bonds are convertible on the basis of 40 common shares for each $1,000 bond. The following bond transactions took place:

2017

Jan.	2	Issued bonds with $5,400,000 maturity value. Since the market rate of interest on this date was 4 percent, the bonds sold for $5,841,488.
Jun.	30	Paid semi-annual interest and amortized the premium using the effective-interest method.
Dec.	31	Paid semi-annual interest and amortized the premium using the effective-interest method.

2018

Jun.	30	Paid semi-annual interest and amortized the premium using the effective-interest method.
Jul.	2	Retired bonds with a $600,000 maturity value at a rate of 101.
	2	Bondholders converted bonds with a $600,000 maturity value into common shares.

Required

1. Create an amortization schedule for the first three interest periods for the bonds sold on January 2, 2017. Round all amounts to the nearest whole dollar. Use the values from the schedule and any other information to journalize all the transactions above.

2. Show the balance sheet presentation of the bonds payable on July 2, 2018.

Problem 15–6B

Financing operations with debt or with shares

⑤

Marketing studies have shown that consumers prefer upscale restaurants, and recent trends in industry sales have supported the research. To capitalize on this trend, Orca Ltd. is embarking on a massive expansion. Plans call for opening five new restaurants within the next 18 months. Each restaurant is scheduled to be 30 percent larger than the company's existing restaurants, furnished more elaborately, with more extensive menus. Management estimates that company operations will provide $15 million of the cash needed for the expansion, and Orca also owns the existing waterfront property that the head office is located on. Orca Ltd. must raise the remaining $15 million from outsiders since the bank has tightened up lending. The board of directors is considering obtaining the $15 million either through borrowing or by issuing common shares.

Required Write a memo to company management. Discuss the advantages and disadvantages of borrowing and of issuing common shares to raise the needed cash. Use the following format for your memo:

Date:	
To:	Management of Orca Ltd.
From:	Student Name
Subject:	Advantages and disadvantages of borrowing and issuing shares to raise $15 million for expansion
Advantages and disadvantages of borrowing:	
Advantages and disadvantages of issuing shares:	

Problem 15–7B

Werstirener Brewing Ltd. issued a $600,000, 5-year, 6 percent mortgage note payable on December 31, 2017, to help finance a new distribution centre. The terms of the mortgage provide for semi-annual blended payments of $70,338 due June 30 and December 31 of each year.

Accounting for a mortgage ⑥

Required

1. Prepare a mortgage instalment payment schedule for the first two years of this mortgage. Round all amounts to the nearest whole dollar.
2. Record the issuance of the mortgage note payable on December 31, 2017.
3. Report interest payable and the mortgage note payable on the December 31, 2017, balance sheet.
4. Journalize the first two instalment payments on June 30, 2018, and December 31, 2018.

Problem 15–8B

Journalize the following transactions of Fayuz Communications Inc.:

Journalizing bonds payable and capital lease transactions ② ⑦

2017

Jan.	2	Issued $8,000,000 of 7 percent, 10-year bonds payable at 97.00.
	2	Signed a five-year capital lease on machinery. The agreement requires annual lease payments of $80,000, with the first payment due immediately. The present value of the five lease payments is $333,589, using a market rate of 10 percent.
Jul.	2	Paid semi-annual interest and amortized the discount by the straight-line method on the 7 percent bonds payable.
Dec.	31	Accrued semi-annual interest expense and amortized the discount by the straight-line method on the 7 percent bonds.
	31	Recorded amortization on the leased machinery using the straight-line method.
	31	Accrued interest expense at 10 percent on the lease liability.

2027

Jan.	2	Paid the 7 percent bonds at maturity. (Ignore the final interest payment.)

Problem 15–9B

Moncton Manufacturing Ltd. had the following information available on bonds payable outstanding at December 31, 2016, its year end:

Amortizing bond discount by the effective-interest method; accounting for lease transactions ③ ⑦

- $7,500,000—Bonds Payable, 6 percent, interest paid on April 2 and October 2. The bonds had been sold on October 2, 2016, for $7,330,686 when the market rate of interest was 7 percent. The bonds mature on April 2, 2019.

The following transactions took place after December 31, 2016:

2017

Jan.	2	Moncton Manufacturing Ltd. signed a lease to rent a building for expansion of its operations. The lease is for six years, with an option to renew, and calls for annual payments of $37,500 per year payable on January 2. Moncton Manufacturing Ltd. gave a cheque for the first year upon signing the lease.
	2	Moncton Manufacturing Ltd. signed a lease for equipment. The lease is for 10 years with payments of $22,500 per year payable on January 2 (the first year's payment was made at the signing). At the end of the lease, the equipment will become the property of Moncton Manufacturing Ltd. The future payments on the lease have a present value (at 10 percent) of $129,578. The equipment has a 10-year useful life and zero residual value.
Apr.	2	Paid the interest on the bonds payable and amortized the discount using the effective-interest method. Assume interest payable of $112,500 had been accrued on December 31, 2016.
Oct.	2	Paid the interest on the bonds payable and amortized the discount using the effective-interest method.

Dec. 31 Recorded any adjustments required at the end of the year for the bonds payable and the lease(s).

2018

Jan. 2 Made the annual payments on the leases.

Apr. 2 Paid the interest on the bonds payable and amortized the discount using the effective-interest method.

Oct. 2 Paid the interest on the bonds payable and amortized the discount using the effective-interest method.

Dec. 31 Recorded any adjustments required at the end of the year for the bonds payable and the lease(s).

Required

1. For the bonds issued on October 2, 2016, prepare an amortization schedule for the life of the bonds. Round all amounts to the nearest whole dollar.

2. Record the general journal entries for the 2017 and 2018 transactions.

3. Show the liabilities section of the balance sheet on December 31, 2018.

Problem 15–10B

Reporting liabilities on the balance sheet
(7)

The accounting records of Carter Technologies Inc. include the following items:

Equipment Acquired under Capital Lease	$591,000	Interest Expense	$171,000
Bonds Payable—Current Portion	225,000	Mortgage Note Payable—Long-term	238,000
Capital Lease Liability—Long-term	162,000	Accumulated Amortization—Equipment	123,000
Discount on Bonds Payable—Long-term	21,000	Capital Lease Liability—Current	64,000
Interest Revenue	15,000	Mortgage Note Payable—Current	69,000
Interest Payable	84,000	Bonds Payable—Long-term...	900,000

Required Show how these items would be reported on the Carter Technologies Inc. balance sheet, including headings for property, plant, and equipment; current liabilities; long-term liabilities; and so on. Note disclosures are not required. Remember that the premium on bonds payable must be split between the current and long-term portions of the bonds payable.

CHALLENGE PROBLEMS

Problem 15–1C

Understanding present value
(3)

A friend tells you that she always buys bonds that are at a discount because "You always get more than you paid when the bond matures."

Required Discuss your friend's understanding of present value.

Problem 15–2C

Evaluating alternative methods of financing growth
(5)

You have just inherited $50,000 and have decided to buy shares. You have narrowed your choice down to QT Logistics Inc. and Next Systems Ltd. You carefully read each company's annual report to determine which company's shares you should buy. Your research indicates that the two companies are very similar. QT Logistics Inc.'s annual report states "The Company has financed its growth through long- and short-term borrowing," while the Next report contains the statement "The Company has financed its growth out of earnings retained in the business."

QT's shares are trading at $25.00 while Next's shares are trading at $13.00. You wonder if that is because QT has been paying an annual dividend of $2.00 per share while Next has been paying a dividend of $1.10.

You recall that the morning newspaper had an article about the economy that predicted that interest rates were expected to rise and stay at a much higher rate than at present for the next two to three years.

Required   Explain which shares you would buy and indicate why you have selected them.

EXTENDING YOUR KNOWLEDGE

DECISION PROBLEMS

Decision Problem 1

Business is going well for Valley Forest Products Inc. The board of directors of this family-owned company believes that the company could earn an additional $9,000,000 in income after interest and taxes by expanding into new markets. However, the $30,000,000 that the business needs for growth cannot be raised within the family. The directors, who strongly wish to retain family control of Valley Forest Products Inc., must consider issuing securities to outsiders. They are considering three financing plans:

Analyzing alternative ways of raising $10,000,000
⑤
1. EPS: Plan A, $10.66

- Plan A is to borrow at 8 percent.
- Plan B is to issue 300,000 common shares.
- Plan C is to issue 300,000 nonvoting, $7.50 cumulative preferred shares.

The company presently has net income before tax of $18,000,000 and has 1,500,000 common shares outstanding. The income tax rate is 35 percent.

Required

1. Prepare an analysis similar to Exhibit 15–9 to determine which plan will result in the highest earnings per common share.
2. Recommend one plan to the board of directors. Give your reasons.

Decision Problem 2

The following questions are not related.

Questions about long-term debt
⑦ Ⓐ2

1. Why do you think corporations prefer operating leases over capital leases? How do you think a shareholder would view an operating lease?
2. If you were to win $3,000,000 from Lotto 6/49, you would receive the $3,000,000 today, whereas if you were to win $3,000,000 in one of the US lotteries, you would receive 20 annual payments of $150,000. Are the prizes equivalent? If not, why not?

FINANCIAL STATEMENT CASES

Financial Statement Case 1

The Indigo Books and Music Inc. financial statements that appear in Appendix A at the end of this book and on MyAccountingLab provide details about the company's long-term debt. Use the data to answer the following questions:

Long-term debt
⑥ ⑦

1. How much did Indigo report in bank and long-term debt during the fiscal year ended March 29, 2014? How much long-term debt did Indigo repay during fiscal 2014? During fiscal 2013?

2. What type of long-term debt is listed on the balance sheet at March 29, 2014? See Note 18.

3. What is the interest rate charged on the long-term line of credit?

4. What types of shares are outstanding? What was the amount of the dividends paid during 2014?

5. Did Indigo have any operating or capital/finance leases outstanding during fiscal 2014?

Financial Statement Case 2

Long-term debt
⑥ ⑦

TELUS Corporation's income statement and balance sheet on MyAccountingLab provide details about the company's long-term debt and equity. Use the data to answer the following questions:

1. What did TELUS have listed as long-term debt obligations?

2. List the long-term liability amounts at December 31, 2013 and 2012.

3. What lease payments are due in the year ended December 31, 2013? How much is due in the years beyond 2013?

4. How much financing cost did TELUS record on the income statement for 2013 and 2012? What was the main reason for the increase?

5. What types of shares is TELUS authorized to issue? Which types of shares were outstanding at December 31, 2013? What was their dollar amount? Were dividends paid during the year ended December 31, 2013? If so, how much were they?

IFRS MINI-CASE

Sun-Rype Products Limited is a manufacturer and marketer of juice-based beverages and fruit-based snacks based in the fruit-growing district of British Columbia but with sales across Canada. Appearing below is an excerpt from the Sun-Rype notes to the consolidated financial statements for the years ended December 31, 2011 and 2010. Sun-Rype reports under IFRS. This chapter discussed disclosure requirements under ASPE. Compare Sun-Rype's reporting below with a company reporting similar information under ASPE.

Note 11 (c) Bank term loans (all amounts in thousands of Canadian dollars)

	Currency	Annual principal payments required	Interest rate	Dec. 31, 2011	Dec. 31, 2010	January 1, 2010
Term loan	US dollar	US$1,480	Bank prime lending rate plus 0.5% (3.75% at December 31, 2011)	$14,035 $ —	$5,470	$ —
Term loan	Canadian dollar	$ 486	Bank prime lending rate plus 0.5% (3.5% at December 31, 2011)	2,308 —	—	—
Term loan	Canadian dollar	$1,500	Bank prime lending rate plus 0.5%	—	—	4,750
Balance outstanding				16,343	5,470	4,750
Current portion				1,961	547	1,500
Non-current portion				$14,382	$4,923	$3,250

During 2011, the Company received secured bank loan advances of US$9.0 million to fund business acquisition payments and $2.4 million to fund capital expenditures.

CHAPTER 15 APPENDIX

TIME VALUE OF MONEY: FUTURE VALUE AND PRESENT VALUE

The following discussion of future value lays the foundation for present value but is not essential. For the valuation of long-term liabilities, some instructors may wish to begin on page 901.

The phrase *time value of money* refers to the fact that money earns interest over time. Interest is the cost of using money. To borrowers, interest is the expense of renting money. To lenders, interest is the revenue earned from lending. When funds are used for a period of time, we must recognize the interest. Otherwise we overlook an important part of the transaction. Suppose you invest $4,545 in corporate bonds that pay interest of 10 percent each year. After one year the value of your investment has grown to $5,000. The difference between your original investment ($4,545) and the future value of the investment ($5,000) is the amount of interest revenue you will earn during the year ($455). If you ignored the interest, you would fail to account for the interest revenue you have earned. Interest becomes more important as the time period lengthens because the amount of interest depends on the span of time the money is invested.

Let's consider a second example, but from the borrower's perspective. Suppose you purchase a machine for your business. The cash price of the machine is $8,000, but you cannot pay cash now. To finance the purchase, you sign an $8,000 note payable. The note requires you to pay the $8,000 plus 10 percent interest one year from the date of purchase. Is your cost of the machine $8,000, or is it $8,800 [$8,000 plus interest of $800 ($8,000 $\times$ 0.10)]? The cost is $8,000. The additional $800 is interest expense and not part of the cost of the machine, although interest expense is certainly a part of the decision of whether or not to purchase the machine.

FUTURE VALUE

The main application of future value *in this book* is to calculate the accumulated balance of an investment at a future date. In our first example, the investment earned 10 percent per year. After one year, $4,545 grew to $5,000, as shown in the timeline in Exhibit 15A–1.

> **LO A1**
> *How do we find the future value of an investment?*

EXHIBIT 15A–1 | Future Value

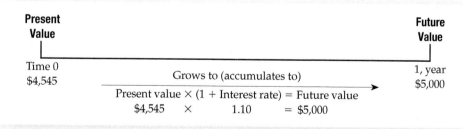

If the money were invested for five years, you would have to perform five such calculations. You would also have to consider the compound interest that your investment is earning. *Compound interest* is the interest you earn not only on your principal amount but also the interest you receive on the interest you have already earned. Most business applications include compound interest. The table below shows the interest revenue earned each year at 10 percent:

End of Year	Interest	Future Value
0	—	$4,545
1	$4,545 × 0.10 = $455	5,000
2	5,000 × 0.10 = 500	5,500
3	5,500 × 0.10 = 550	6,050
4	6,050 × 0.10 = 605	6,655
5	6,655 × 0.10 = 666	7,321

Earning 10 percent, a $4,545 investment grows to $5,000 at the end of one year, to $5,500 at the end of two years, and so on. Throughout this discussion we round off to the nearest dollar to keep the numbers simple, although calculations like these are usually rounded to the nearest cent.

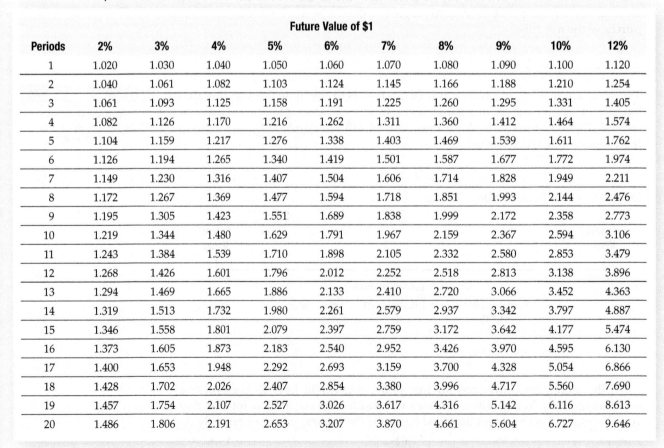

KEY POINTS

The formula for future value is
$FV = PV(1 + i)^n$
where
FV = future value
PV = present value
i = interest rate per period
n = number of compounding periods

Future Value Tables

The process of computing a future value is called *accumulating* or *compounding* because the future value is *more* than the present value. Mathematical tables ease the computational burden. You can also use financial calculators and functions in spreadsheet programs to calculate future value. (In the real world, calculators are used rather than tables—we use tables here to demonstrate the concepts.) Exhibit 15A–2, Future Value of $1, gives the future value for a single sum (a present value), $1, invested to earn a particular interest rate for a specific number of periods. Future value depends on three factors: (1) the amount of the investment, (2) the length of time between investment and future accumulation, and (3) the interest rate.

EXHIBIT 15A–2 | Future Value of $1

Future Value of $1

Periods	2%	3%	4%	5%	6%	7%	8%	9%	10%	12%
1	1.020	1.030	1.040	1.050	1.060	1.070	1.080	1.090	1.100	1.120
2	1.040	1.061	1.082	1.103	1.124	1.145	1.166	1.188	1.210	1.254
3	1.061	1.093	1.125	1.158	1.191	1.225	1.260	1.295	1.331	1.405
4	1.082	1.126	1.170	1.216	1.262	1.311	1.360	1.412	1.464	1.574
5	1.104	1.159	1.217	1.276	1.338	1.403	1.469	1.539	1.611	1.762
6	1.126	1.194	1.265	1.340	1.419	1.501	1.587	1.677	1.772	1.974
7	1.149	1.230	1.316	1.407	1.504	1.606	1.714	1.828	1.949	2.211
8	1.172	1.267	1.369	1.477	1.594	1.718	1.851	1.993	2.144	2.476
9	1.195	1.305	1.423	1.551	1.689	1.838	1.999	2.172	2.358	2.773
10	1.219	1.344	1.480	1.629	1.791	1.967	2.159	2.367	2.594	3.106
11	1.243	1.384	1.539	1.710	1.898	2.105	2.332	2.580	2.853	3.479
12	1.268	1.426	1.601	1.796	2.012	2.252	2.518	2.813	3.138	3.896
13	1.294	1.469	1.665	1.886	2.133	2.410	2.720	3.066	3.452	4.363
14	1.319	1.513	1.732	1.980	2.261	2.579	2.937	3.342	3.797	4.887
15	1.346	1.558	1.801	2.079	2.397	2.759	3.172	3.642	4.177	5.474
16	1.373	1.605	1.873	2.183	2.540	2.952	3.426	3.970	4.595	6.130
17	1.400	1.653	1.948	2.292	2.693	3.159	3.700	4.328	5.054	6.866
18	1.428	1.702	2.026	2.407	2.854	3.380	3.996	4.717	5.560	7.690
19	1.457	1.754	2.107	2.527	3.026	3.617	4.316	5.142	6.116	8.613
20	1.486	1.806	2.191	2.653	3.207	3.870	4.661	5.604	6.727	9.646

The heading in Exhibit 15A–2 states $1. Future value tables and present value tables are based on $1 because unity (the value 1) is so easy to work with. Observe the Periods column and the Interest Rate columns 2% through 12%. In business applications, interest rates are usually assumed to be for the annual period of one year unless specified otherwise. In fact, an interest rate can be stated for any period, such as 3 percent per quarter or 5 percent for a six-month period. The length of the period is arbitrary. For example, an investment may promise a return (income) of 3 percent per quarter for two quarters (six months). In that case you would be working with 3 percent interest for two periods. It would be incorrect to use 6 percent for one period because the interest is 3 percent compounded quarterly, and that amount differs somewhat from 6 percent compounded semi-annually. Take care in studying future value and present value problems to align the interest rate with the appropriate number of periods.

Let's use Exhibit 15A–2. The future value of $1.00 invested at 4 percent for one year is $1.04 ($1.00 × 1.040, which appears at the junction under the 4% column and across from 1 in the Periods column). The figure 1.040 includes both the principal (1.000) and the compound interest for one period (0.040).

Suppose you deposit $5,000 in a savings account that pays annual interest of 4 percent. The account balance at the end of the year will be $5,200. To compute the future value of $5,000 at 4 percent for one year, multiply $5,000 by 1.040 to get $5,200. Now suppose you invest in a 10-year, 6 percent certificate of deposit (CD). What will be the future value of the CD at maturity? To compute the future value of $5,000 at 6 percent for 10 periods, multiply $5,000 by 1.791 (from Exhibit 15A–2) to get $8,955. This future value of $8,955 indicates that $5,000 earning 6 percent interest compounded annually grows to $8,955 at the end of 10 years. In this way, you can find any present amount's future value at a particular future date. Future value is especially helpful for computing the amount of cash you will have on hand for some purpose in the future.

Future Value of an Annuity

In the preceding example, we made an investment of a single amount. Other investments, called annuities, include multiple payments of an equal periodic amount at fixed intervals over the duration of the investment. Consider a family investing for a child's education. The Dietrichs can invest $4,000 annually to accumulate a college fund for 15-year-old Helen. The investment can earn 7 percent annually until Helen turns 18—a three-year investment. How much will be available for Helen on the date of the last investment? Exhibit 15A–3 shows the accumulation—a total future value of $12,860.

EXHIBIT 15A–3 | Future Value of an Annuity

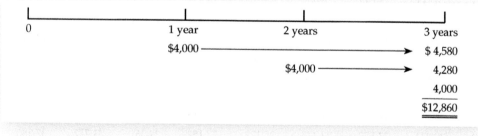

The first $4,000 invested by the Dietrichs grows to $4,580 over the investment period. The second $4,000 invested grows to $4,280, and the third $4,000 invested stays at $4,000 because it has no time to earn interest. The sum of the three future values ($4,580 + $4,280 + $4,000) is the future value of the annuity ($12,860), which can be computed as follows:

End of Year	Annual Investment	Interest	Increase for the Year	Future Value of Annuity
0	—	—	—	$ 0
1	$4,000	—	$ 4,000	4,000
2	4,000 + ($4,000 × 0.07 = $280) = 4,280		8,280	
3	4,000 + ($8,280 × 0.07 = $580) = 4,580		12,860	

These computations are laborious. As with the future value of $1 (a lump sum), mathematical tables ease the strain of calculating annuities. Exhibit 15A–4, Future Value of Annuity of $1, gives the future value of a series of investments, each of equal amount, at regular intervals.

What is the future value of an annuity of three investments of $1 each that earn 7 percent? The answer, 3.21,5 can be found in the 7% column and across from 3 in the Periods column of Exhibit 15A–4. This amount can be used to compute the future value of the investment for Helen's education, as follows:

Amount of each periodic investment	×	Future value of annuity of $1 (Exhibit 15A–4)	=	Future value of investment
$4,000	×	3.215	=	$12,860

EXHIBIT 15A–4 | Future Value of Annuity of $1

Future Value of Annuity of $1

Periods	2%	3%	4%	5%	6%	7%	8%	9%	10%	12%
1	1.000	1.000	1.000	1.000	1.000	1.000	1.000	1.000	1.000	1.000
2	2.020	2.030	2.040	2.050	2.060	2.070	2.080	2.090	2.100	2.120
3	3.060	3.091	3.122	3.153	3.184	3.215	3.246	3.278	3.310	3.374
4	4.122	4.184	4.246	4.310	4.375	4.440	4.506	4.573	4.641	4.779
5	5.204	5.309	5.416	5.526	5.637	5.751	5.867	5.985	6.105	6.353
6	6.308	6.468	6.633	6.802	6.975	7.153	7.336	7.523	7.716	8.115
7	7.434	7.663	7.898	8.142	8.394	8.654	8.923	9.200	9.487	10.089
8	8.583	8.892	9.214	9.549	9.897	10.260	10.637	11.028	11.436	12.300
9	9.755	10.159	10.583	11.027	11.491	11.978	12.488	13.021	13.579	14.776
10	10.950	11.464	12.006	12.578	13.181	13.816	14.487	15.193	15.937	17.549
11	12.169	12.808	13.486	14.207	14.972	15.784	16.645	17.560	18.531	20.655
12	13.412	14.192	15.026	15.917	16.870	17.888	18.977	20.141	21.384	24.133
13	14.680	15.618	16.627	17.713	18.882	20.141	21.495	22.953	24.523	28.029
14	15.974	17.086	18.292	19.599	21.015	22.550	24.215	26.019	27.975	32.393
15	17.293	18.599	20.024	21.579	23.276	25.129	27.152	29.361	31.772	37.280
16	18.639	20.157	21.825	23.657	25.673	27.888	30.324	33.003	35.950	42.753
17	20.012	21.762	23.698	25.840	28.213	30.840	33.750	36.974	40.545	48.884
18	21.412	23.414	25.645	28.132	30.906	33.999	37.450	41.301	45.599	55.750
19	22.841	25.117	27.671	30.539	33.760	37.379	41.446	46.018	51.159	63.440
20	24.297	26.870	29.778	33.066	36.786	40.995	45.762	51.160	57.275	72.053

This one-step calculation is much easier than computing the future value of each annual investment and then summing the individual future values. In this way, you can compute the future value of any investment consisting of equal periodic amounts at regular intervals. Businesses make periodic investments to accumulate funds for equipment replacement and other uses—an application of the future value of an annuity.

PRESENT VALUE

LO A2

How do we find the present value of an investment?

Often a person knows a future amount and needs to know the related present value. Recall Exhibit 15A–1, in which present value and future value are on opposite ends of the same timeline. Suppose an investment promises to pay you $5,000 at the *end* of one year. How much would you pay *now* to acquire this investment? You would be willing to pay the present value of the $5,000, which is a future amount.

Present value also depends on three factors: (1) the amount of payment (or receipt), (2) the length of time between investment and future receipt (or payment), and (3) the interest rate. The process of computing a present value is called *discounting* because the present value is *less* than the future value.

In our investment example, the future receipt is $5,000. The investment period is one year. Assume that you demand an annual interest rate of 10 percent on your investment. With all three factors specified, you can compute the present value of $5,000 at 10 percent for one year:

$$\text{Present value of \$5,000 at 10 percent for one year}$$
$$= \frac{\text{Future value}}{1 + \text{Interest rate}} = \frac{\$5,000}{1.10} = \$4,545$$

By turning the problem around, we verify the present value computation:

Amount invested (present value)	$4,545
Expected earnings ($4,545 × 0.10)	455
Amount to be received one year from now (future value)	$5,000

This example illustrates that present value and future value are based on the same equation:

$$\text{Present value} \times (1 + \text{Interest rate}) = \text{Future value}$$
$$\text{Present value} = \frac{\text{Future value}}{1 + \text{Interest rate}}$$

KEY POINTS

The formula for present value is
$PV = FV \times (1 + i)^n$
where
PV = present value
FV = future value
i = interest rate per period
n = number of compounding periods

If the $5,000 is to be received two years from now, you will pay only $4,132 for the investment, as shown in Exhibit 15A–5.

EXHIBIT 15A–5 | Two-Year Investment

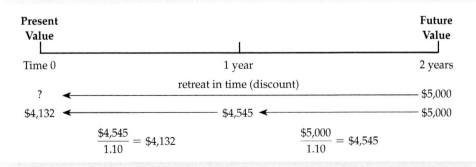

By turning the data around, we verify that $4,132 accumulates to $5,000 at 10 percent for two years:

Amount invested (present value)	$4,132
Expected earnings for first year ($4,132 × 0.10)	413
Amount invested after one year	4,545
Expected earnings for second year ($4,545 × 0.10)	455
Amount to be received two years from now (future value)	$5,000

You would pay $4,132—the present value of $5,000—to receive the $5,000 future amount at the end of two years at 10 percent per year. The $868 difference between the amount invested ($4,132) and the amount to be received ($5,000) is the return on the investment, the sum of the two interest receipts: $413 + $455 = $868.

Present Value Tables

We have shown the simple formula for computing present value. However, calculating present value "by hand" for investments spanning many years presents too many opportunities for arithmetical errors and it is too much work. Present value tables ease our work and allow us to see at a glance the relationship between time (in the Periods column) and each interest rate. (In the real world, calculators and computers are used rather than tables—we use tables here to demonstrate the concepts.) Let's re-examine our examples of present value by using Exhibit 15A–6: Present Value of $1.

EXHIBIT 15A–6 | Present Value of $1

				Present Value of $1					
Periods	2%	3%	4%	5%	6%	7%	8%	10%	12%
1	0.980	0.971	0.962	0.952	0.943	0.935	0.926	0.909	0.893
2	0.961	0.943	0.925	0.907	0.890	0.873	0.857	0.826	0.797
3	0.942	0.915	0.889	0.864	0.840	0.816	0.794	0.751	0.712
4	0.924	0.889	0.855	0.823	0.792	0.763	0.735	0.683	0.636
5	0.906	0.863	0.822	0.784	0.747	0.713	0.681	0.621	0.567
6	0.888	0.838	0.790	0.746	0.705	0.666	0.630	0.564	0.507
7	0.871	0.813	0.760	0.711	0.665	0.623	0.583	0.513	0.452
8	0.854	0.789	0.731	0.677	0.627	0.582	0.540	0.467	0.404
9	0.837	0.766	0.703	0.645	0.592	0.544	0.500	0.424	0.361
10	0.820	0.744	0.676	0.614	0.558	0.508	0.463	0.386	0.322
11	0.804	0.722	0.650	0.585	0.527	0.475	0.429	0.350	0.287
12	0.789	0.701	0.625	0.557	0.497	0.444	0.397	0.319	0.257
13	0.773	0.681	0.601	0.530	0.469	0.415	0.368	0.290	0.229
14	0.758	0.661	0.577	0.505	0.442	0.388	0.340	0.263	0.205
15	0.743	0.642	0.555	0.481	0.417	0.362	0.315	0.239	0.183
16	0.728	0.623	0.534	0.458	0.394	0.339	0.292	0.218	0.163
17	0.714	0.605	0.513	0.436	0.371	0.317	0.270	0.198	0.146
18	0.700	0.587	0.494	0.416	0.350	0.296	0.250	0.180	0.130
19	0.686	0.570	0.475	0.396	0.331	0.277	0.232	0.164	0.116
20	0.673	0.554	0.456	0.377	0.312	0.258	0.215	0.149	0.104

For the 10 percent investment for one year, we find the junction under 10% and across from 1 in the Period column. The table figure of 0.909 is computed as follows: 1 ÷ 1.10 = 0.909. This work has been done for us, and only the present values are given in the table. The heading in Exhibit 15A–6 states present value for $1. To calculate present value for $5,000, we multiply 0.909 by $5,000. The result is $4,545, which matches the result we obtained by hand.

For the two-year investment, we read down the 10% column and across the Period 2 row. We multiply 0.826 (computed as 0.909 ÷ 1.10 = 0.826) by $5,000 and get $4,130, which confirms our earlier computation of $4,132 (the difference is due to rounding in the present value table). Using the table we can compute the present value of any single future amount.

While we focus on tables in this text, you can also use financial calculators and functions in spreadsheet programs to calculate present value.

Present Value of an Annuity

Return to the investment example beginning on the previous page. That investment provided the investor with only a single future receipt ($5,000 at the end of two years). Annuity investments provide multiple receipts of an equal amount at fixed intervals over the investment's duration.

Consider an investment that promises *annual* cash receipts of $10,000 to be received at the end of each of three years. Assume that you demand a 12 percent return on your investment. What is the investment's present value? What would you pay today to acquire the investment? The investment spans three periods, and you would pay the sum of three present values. The computation is as follows:

Year	Annual Cash Receipt		Present Value of $1 at 12% (Exhibit 15A–6)	Present Value of Annual Cash Receipt
1	$10,000	×	0.893	$ 8,930
2	10,000	×	0.797	7,970
3	10,000	×	0.712	7,120
Total present value of investment				$24,020

The present value of this annuity is $24,020. By paying this amount today, you will receive $10,000 at the end of each of three years while earning 12 percent on your investment.

The example illustrates repetitive computations of the three future amounts, a time-consuming process. One way to ease the computational burden is to add the three present values of $1 (0.893 + 0.797 + 0.712) and multiply their sum (2.402) by the annual cash receipt ($10,000) to obtain the present value of the annuity ($10,000 × 2.402 = $24,020).

An easier approach is to use a present value of an annuity table. Exhibit 15A–7 shows the present value of $1 to be received periodically for a given number of periods. The present value of a three-period annuity at 12 percent is 2.402 (the junction of the Period 3 row and the 12% column). Thus, $10,000 received annually at the end of each of three years, discounted at 12 percent, is $24,020 ($10,000 × 2.402), which is the present value.

Present Value of Annuity of $1

Periods	2%	3%	4%	5%	6%	7%	8%	10%	12%
1	0.980	0.971	0.962	0.952	0.943	0.935	0.926	0.909	0.893
2	1.942	1.914	1.886	1.859	1.833	1.808	1.783	1.736	1.690
3	2.884	2.829	2.775	2.723	2.673	2.624	2.577	2.487	2.402
4	3.808	3.717	3.630	3.546	3.465	3.387	3.312	3.170	3.037
5	4.714	4.580	4.452	4.329	4.212	4.100	3.993	3.791	3.605
6	5.601	5.417	5.242	5.076	4.917	4.767	4.623	4.355	4.111
7	6.472	6.230	6.002	5.786	5.582	5.389	5.206	4.868	4.564
8	7.326	7.020	6.733	6.463	6.210	5.971	5.747	5.335	4.968
9	8.162	7.786	7.435	7.108	6.802	6.515	6.247	5.759	5.328
10	8.983	8.530	8.111	7.722	7.360	7.024	6.710	6.145	5.650
11	9.787	9.253	8.760	8.306	7.887	7.499	7.139	6.495	5.938
12	10.575	9.954	9.385	8.863	8.384	7.943	7.536	6.814	6.194
13	11.348	10.635	9.986	9.394	8.853	8.358	7.904	7.103	6.424
14	12.106	11.296	10.563	9.899	9.295	8.745	8.244	7.367	6.628
15	12.849	11.938	11.118	10.380	9.712	9.108	8.559	7.606	6.811
16	13.578	12.561	11.652	10.838	10.106	9.447	8.851	7.824	6.974
17	14.292	13.166	12.166	11.274	10.477	9.763	9.122	8.022	7.120
18	14.992	13.754	12.659	11.690	10.828	10.059	9.372	8.201	7.250
19	15.679	14.324	13.134	12.085	11.158	10.336	9.604	8.365	7.366
20	16.351	14.878	13.590	12.462	11.470	10.594	9.818	8.514	7.469

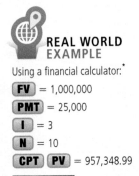

REAL WORLD EXAMPLE

Using a financial calculator:*

FV = 1,000,000

PMT = 25,000

I = 3

N = 10

CPT PV = 957,348.99

* Financial calculator keys and results may differ from those shown. Financial calculator results will also differ from those obtained with tables because of the rounding in present value and future value tables.

Present Value of Bonds Payable

The present value of a bond—its market price—is the present value of the future principal amount at maturity plus the present value of the future contract interest payments. The principal is a single amount to be paid at maturity. The interest is an annuity because it occurs periodically.

Let's compute the present value of 5 percent, five-year bonds of UVW Corporation. The face value of the bonds is $1,000,000, and they pay 2.5 percent contract (cash) interest semi-annually. At issuance the market interest rate is 6 percent, but it is computed at 3 percent semi-annually. Therefore, the effective-interest rate for each of the 10 semi-annual periods is 3 percent. We use 3 percent in computing the present value of the maturity and of the interest. The market price of these bonds is $957,250, as follows:

	Effective annual interest rate ÷ 2	Number of semi-annual interest payments	
PV of principal:			
$1,000,000 × **PV of single amount** at ($1,000,000 × 0.744—Exhibit 15A–6)	3%	for 10 periods	$744,000
PV of interest:			
($1,000,000 × 0.025) × **PV of annuity** at ($25,000 × 8.530—Exhibit 15A–7)	3%	for 10 periods	213,250
PV (market price) of bonds			$957,250

The market price of the UVW Corporation bonds shows a discount because the contract interest rate on the bonds (5 percent) is less than the market interest rate (6 percent). We discuss these bonds in more detail on page 845.

Let's consider a premium price for the UVW Corporation bonds. Assume that UVW Corporation issues $1,000,000 of 5 percent bonds when the market interest rate is 4 percent at issuance. The effective-interest rate is 2 percent for each of the 10 semi-annual periods.

	Effective annual interest rate ÷ 2	Number of semi-annual interest payments	
PV of principal:			
$1,000,000 × **PV of single amount** at ($1,000,000 × 0.820—Exhibit 15A–6)	2%	for 10 periods	$ 820,000
PV of interest:			
($1,000,000 × 0.025) × **PV of annuity** at ($25,000 × 8.983—Exhibit 15A–7)	2%	for 10 periods	224,575
PV (market price) of bonds			$1,044,575

We discuss accounting for these bonds on page 847.

Many calculators and spreadsheet software packages can quickly and accurately perform present value calculations for bonds and leases.

APPENDIX PROBLEMS

Problem 15A–1

For each situation, compute the required amount using the tables in this appendix.

1. Summit Enterprises Ltd. is budgeting for the acquisition of land over the next several years. The company can invest $800,000 at 9 percent. How much cash will Summit Enterprises Ltd. have for land acquisitions at the end of five years? At the end of six years?

2. Alton Associates Inc. is planning to invest $10,000 each year for five years. The company's investment advisor believes that Alton Associates Inc. can earn 6 percent interest without taking on too much risk. What will be the value of Alton's investment on the date of the last deposit if Alton can earn 6 percent? If Alton can earn 8 percent?

Computing the future value of an investment
(A1)
2. At 6%, $56,370

Problem 15A–2

For each situation, compute the required amount using the tables in this appendix.

1. XS Technologies Inc.'s operations are generating excess cash that will be invested in a special fund. During 2017, XS Technologies invests $12,000,000 in the fund for a planned advertising campaign for a new product to be released six years later, in 2023. If XS Technologies's investments can earn 5 percent each year, how much cash will the company have for the advertising campaign in 2023?

2. XS Technologies Inc. will need $20 million to advertise a new product in 2019. How much must XS Technologies invest in 2017 to have the cash available for the advertising campaign? XS Technologies's investments can earn 5 percent annually.

3. Explain the relationship between your answers to (1) and (2).

Relating the future and present values of an investment
(A1) (A2)
1. $16,080,000

Problem 15A–3

Computing the present values of various notes and bonds

(A2)

3. $254,280

4. $200,040

Determine the present value of the following notes and bonds using the tables in this appendix (notes are accounted for in the same way as bonds):

1. $100,000, five-year note payable with a contract interest rate of 9 percent, paid annually. The market interest rate at issuance is 10 percent.

2. Ten-year bonds payable with a maturity value of $200,000 and a contract interest rate of 12 percent, paid semi-annually. The market rate of interest is 10 percent at issuance.

3. Same bonds payable as in Requirement 2, but the market interest rate is 8 percent.

4. Same bonds payable as in Requirement 2, but the market interest rate is 12 percent.

Problem 15A–4

Computing a bond's present value; recording its issuance at a discount and interest payments

(A2)

1. $569,183

On December 31, 2017, when the market interest rate is 8 percent, Churchill Land Corporation issues $600,000 of 10-year, 7.25 percent bonds payable. The bonds pay interest semi-annually.

Required

1. Determine the present value of the bonds at issuance using the tables in this appendix.

2. Assume that the bonds are issued at the price computed in Requirement 1. Prepare an effective-interest method amortization table for the first two semi-annual interest periods.

3. Using the amortization table prepared in Requirement 2, journalize the issuance of the bonds and the first two interest payments.

Problem 15A–5

Deciding between two payment plans

(A2)

Ontario Children's Choir needs a fleet of vans to transport the children to singing engagements throughout Ontario. Ford offers the vehicles for a single payment of $120,000 due at the end of four years. Toyota prices a similar fleet of vans for four annual payments of $28,000 each. Ontario Children's Choir could borrow the funds at 6 percent, so this is the appropriate interest rate. Which company should get the business, Ford or Toyota? Base your decision on present value and give your reason.

>Try It! SOLUTIONS FOR CHAPTER 15

1. a. XYZ Corporation
   b. $100,000.00
   c. March 31, 2018
   d. John Doe
   e. 6% per year; the frequency of interest payments is not shown in Exhibit 15–1, but interest is typically paid twice a year (3 percent every 6 months).

2. a. At a discount
   b. At a premium
   c. At par

3. a. The bonds were issued at a discount.

   b.

Cash	990,000	
Discount on Bonds Payable	10,000	
Bonds Payable		1,000,000
To issue 3.75%, 10-year bonds at a discount. Cash received was $990,000 ($1,000,000 × 0.99).		

   c. The carrying value of these bonds is $990,000 ($1,000,000 − $10,000 discount).

4. a. The bonds were issued at a premium.

   b.

Cash	1,015,000	
Bonds Payable		1,000,000
Premium on Bonds Payable		15,000
To issue 3.75%, 10-year bonds at a premium. Cash received was $1,015,000 ($1,000,000 × 101.50).		

   c. The carrying value of these bonds is $1,015,000 ($1,000,000 + $15,000 premium).

5. a. Compare the bond issue date (May 1, 2017) to the bonds' interest payment dates (April 30 and October 31). If time has passed between the interest payment date and the issue date, then include

interest for this time in the amount paid for the bonds. In this case, no time has passed from April 30 to May 1, so no interest needs to be calculated. Also, determine whether there is a premium or a discount. Since bonds were issued at 94.00, which is less than 100.00, there is a discount.

2017			
May 1	Cash	9,400,000	
	Discount on Bonds Payable	600,000	
	Bonds Payable		10,000,000
	Issued 6 percent, 10-year bonds at a discount ($10,000,000 × 0.94).		

b. Check for any interest accruals or partial amortization of a bond premium or discount. Since the six-month period of May 1 to October 31, 2017, occurs before year end, no accruals or partial amortization are necessary on October 31.

Oct. 31	Interest Expense	330,000	
	Cash		300,000
	Discount on Bonds Payable		30,000
	Paid semi-annual interest ($10,000,000 × 0.06 × $\frac{6}{12}$) and amortized discount ($600,000 ÷ 20).		

c. Calculate the time period from the last interest payment (October 31, 2017) to the year end (December 31, 2017). Accrue interest and amortize the premium or discount for this time period (2 months).

Dec. 31	Interest Expense	110,000	
	Discount on Bonds Payable		10,000
	Interest Payable		100,000
	Accrued interest ($10,000,000 × 0.06 × $\frac{2}{12}$) and amortized bond discount for two months ($600,000 ÷ 20 × $\frac{2}{6}$).		

d. Make sure all amortization of the bond discount is reflected in Discount on Bonds Payable, including the accrual calculated in part (c). Then subtract the discount from Bonds Payable to show the net liability for bonds payable.

Long-term liabilities

Bonds payable, 6%, due 2027	$10,000,000		
Discount on bonds payable			
($600,000 – $30,000 – $10,000)*		560,000	$9,440,000

*The calculation is for your reference only. It would not appear on the balance sheet.

e. The cash payment of interest is always the same: Bonds payable × Stated rate × Time. Reverse the year-end accrual (Interest Payable amount), then calculate interest and amortization of the discount or premium for the period January 1 to April 30, 2018.

2018			
Apr. 30	Interest Expense	220,000	
	Interest Payable	100,000	
	Cash		300,000
	Discount on Bonds Payable		20,000
	Paid semi-annual interest ($10,000,000 × 0.06 × $\frac{6}{12}$), part of which was accrued ($100,000), and amortized four months' discount on bonds payable ($600,000 ÷ 20 × $\frac{4}{6}$).		

Here are some suggestions for checking your solutions. While you don't have to follow these procedures for every problem, you can use them to check your solutions for reasonableness as well as accuracy.

On April 30, 2018, the bonds have been outstanding for one year. After the entries have been recorded, the account balances should show the results of one year's cash interest payments and one year's bond premium amortization.

Fact 1   Cash interest payments should be $600,000 ($10,000,000 × 0.06).

Accuracy check   Two credits to Cash of $300,000 each = $600,000. Cash payments are correct.

Fact 2   Discount amortization should be $60,000 ($600,000 ÷ 20 semi-annual periods × 2 semi-annual periods in 1 year).

Accuracy check   Three debits to Discount on Bonds Payable ($30,000 + $10,000 + $20,000 = $60,000). Discount amortization is correct.

Fact 3   Also, we can check the accuracy of interest expense recorded during the year ended December 31, 2017.

The bonds in this problem will be outstanding for a total of 10 years, or 120 (that is, 10 × 12) months. During 2017, the bonds are outstanding for 8 months (May through December).

(Continued)

(Continued)

Interest expense for 8 months *equals* payment of cash interest for 8 months plus discount amortization for 8 months.

Interest expense should therefore be ($10,000,000 × 0.06 × 8/12 = $400,000) plus [($600,000/120) × 8 = $40,000] or ($400,000 + $40,000 = $440,000).

Accuracy check: Two debits to Interest Expense ($330,000 + $110,000) = $440,000. Interest expense for 2017 is correct.

6.

2018			
Dec. 31	Interest Expense	6,882	
	Premium on Bonds Payable	1,451	
	Interest Payable		8,333
	To accrue two months' interest expense ($20,647 × $\frac{2}{6}$), amortize premium on bonds payable for two months ($4,353 × $\frac{2}{6}$), and record interest payable ($25,000 × $\frac{2}{6}$).		

2019			
Apr. 30	Interest Expense	13,765	
	Interest Payable	8,333	
	Premium on Bonds Payable	2,902	
	Cash		25,000
	To pay semi-annual interest ($20,647 × $\frac{4}{6}$), some of which was accrued, and amortize premium on bonds payable for four months ($4,353 × $\frac{4}{6}$).		

7. a. The periodic amount of interest expense *increases* because the carrying amount of the bond *increases* toward maturity value. To see this, refer to columns B and E of Exhibit 15–5. The upward-sloping line in Exhibit 15–6, Panel A, illustrates the increasing amount of interest expense.

b. The periodic amount of interest expense *decreases* because the carrying amount of the bond *decreases* toward maturity value. To see this, study columns B and E of Exhibit 15–7. The downward-sloping line in Exhibit 15–8, Panel A, illustrates the decreasing amount of interest expense.

c. For bonds issued at a discount, interest expense will be greater than cash interest paid by the amount of the discount amortized for the period. Remember that the company received less than face value when it issued the bonds. But at maturity, the company must pay the full value back to the bondholders. Thus, a discount increases the company's interest expense above the amount of cash interest paid each period.

For bonds issued at a *premium*, cash interest paid will be greater than interest expense by the amount of the premium amortized for the period. This is because the premium amount received at issuance decreases the interest expense below the amount of cash interest paid each period.

8. Calculation of the gain or loss on retirement:

Face value of bonds being retired ($5,000,000 × $\frac{1}{2}$)	$2,500,000
Unamortized premium ($30,000 × $\frac{1}{2}$)	15,000
Book value, or carrying value	2,515,000
Market price paid to retire the bonds ($2,500,000 × 1.0050)	2,512,500
Gain on retirement of bonds	$ 2,500

The journal entry to record the retirement:

Bonds Payable	2,500,000	
Premium on Bonds Payable	15,000	
Cash		2,512,500
Gain on retirement of bonds		2,500
To retire bonds payable before maturity.		

9.

2017			
Sep. 1	Bonds Payable	2,500,000	
	Premium on Bonds Payable	15,000	
	Common Shares		2,515,000
	To record conversion of $2,515,000 of bonds outstanding into 1,000,000 common shares.		

10.

Current liabilities		
Current portion of long-term debt	$1,500,000	
Premium on bonds payable	5,000	$1,505,000
Long-term debt, excluding current portion	3,500,000	
Premium on bonds payable	25,000	3,525,000

11. While trading on the equity can improve EPS, it might be to the corporation's *disadvantage* to finance with debt. This is because the corporation would suffer (1) if the interest rate on its debt is greater than the rate of earnings from that money, and (2) if the company borrows so much that it cannot meet interest and principal payments.

12.

	Plan 1 Borrow $1,000,000 at 10%	Plan 2 Issue $1,000,000 of Common Shares
Net income after interest and income tax, before expansion	$600,000	$600,000
Project income before interest and income tax	$300,000	$300,000
Less: Interest expense ($1,000,000 × 0.12)	120,000	0
Project income before income tax	180,000	300,000
Less: Income tax expense (40%)	72,000	120,000
Project net income	$108,000	$180,000
Total company net income	$708,000	$780,000
Earnings per share including expansion:		
Plan 1 ($708,000 ÷ 200,000 shares)	$3.54	
Plan 2 ($780,000 ÷ 250,000 shares)		$3.12

Plan 1 seems more favourable because the EPS is higher. However, the EPS is only 13 percent higher than Plan 2. The company's ability to pay the interest on the bonds must also be considered—at 12 percent, the interest payments may limit the company from making other future expenditures as they are needed, so both plans should be considered carefully.

13.

2017			
Oct. 1	Cash	200,000	
	Mortgage Payable		200,000
	To record the receipt of proceeds from a 10-year, 5 percent mortgage loan.		
Oct. 1	Building	140,000	
	Land	60,000	
	Cash		200,000
	To record the purchase of land and a building for $200,000.		

14.

2017			
Dec. 1	Interest Expense	828	
	Mortgage Payable	1,293	
	Cash		2,121
	To pay monthly mortgage loan and record interest portion.		

15.

a.

2017			
Jan. 2	Equipment	138,143	
	Cash		30,000
	Capital Lease Liability		108,143
	To lease equipment and make the first annual lease payment on a capital lease. (Equipment = $30,000 + $108,143 = $138,143).		

(If using a financial calculator:

PMT = $30,000, N = 6,
I = 12%, FV = 0,
CPT PV = $−138,143.29).

b.

Dec. 31	Amortization Expense	23,024	
	Accumulated Amortization—Leased Equipment		23,024
	To record amortization on leased equipment ($138,143 ÷ 6)		

c.

Dec. 31	Interest Expense	12,977	
	Capital Lease Liability		12,977
	To accrue interest expense on the capital lease liability ($108,143 × 0.12).		

d.

2018			
Jan. 2	Capital Lease Liability	30,000	
	Cash		30,000
	To make second annual lease payment on equipment.		

16 INVESTMENTS AND INTERNATIONAL OPERATIONS

CONNECTING CHAPTER 16

LEARNING OBJECTIVE ① Account for short-term investments

How do we account for short-term investments?

Share Investments, page 912
  Share Prices
  Investors and Investees
  Classifying Investments
Accounting for Short-Term Investments, page 914
  Share (Equity) Investments
  Reporting Short-Term Bond (Debt) Investments

LEARNING OBJECTIVE ② Account for long-term share investments

How do we account for long-term share investments?

Accounting for Long-Term Share Investments, page 917
  Long-Term Equity Investments without Significant Influence

LEARNING OBJECTIVE ③ Use the equity method to account for investments

What is the equity method, and how do we use it?

Long-Term Share Investments Accounted for by the Equity Method, page 920
  Joint Ventures
Long-Term Share Investments Accounted for by the Consolidation Method, page 923
  Long-Term Equity Investments

LEARNING OBJECTIVE ④ Describe and create consolidated financial statements

What is consolidation, and how do we perform a simple consolidation?

Consolidated Financial Statements, page 925
  Consolidated Balance Sheet—Parent Owns All Subsidiary's Shares
  Parent Buys Subsidiary's Shares and Pays for Goodwill
  Consolidated Balance Sheet—Parent Owns Less than 100 Percent of Subsidiary's Shares
  Income of a Consolidated Entity

LEARNING OBJECTIVE ⑤ Account for investments in bonds

How do we record investments in bonds?

Investments in Bonds, page 931
  Short-Term Investments in Bonds
  Long-Term Investments in Bonds

LEARNING OBJECTIVE ⑥ Account for foreign-currency transactions

How do we record transactions in foreign currencies?

Foreign-Currency Transactions, page 935
  Foreign Currencies and Foreign-Currency Exchange Rates
  Foreign-Currency Transactions
  Paying Cash in a Foreign Currency

Collecting Cash in a Foreign Currency
Minimizing Risk

LEARNING OBJECTIVE (7) Identify the impact of IFRS on accounting for investments and international transactions

How does IFRS apply to investments and international transactions?
The Impact of IFRS on Accounting for Investments and International Transactions, page 940

MyAccountingLab   The **Summary** for Chapter 16 appears on page 944. This lists all of the MyAccountingLab resources. **Accounting Vocabulary** with definitions for this chapter's material appears on page 945.

K inross Gold Corporation is a Canadian-based gold mining company with both Canadian and international operations. Kinross states that its "core purpose is to lead the world in generating value through responsible mining." Their 10 Guiding Principles for Corporate Responsibility for ethics and the environment helped them get named to the Dow Jones Sustainability Index from 2010 to 2013.[1]

Kinross has more than a dozen subsidiary companies whose results are combined into the corporation's consolidated financial statements. In addition, it has a number of companies in which it has a small ownership interest whose results are also reported within the Kinross annual report. The accounting treatment for investments in other companies varies depending on the percentage of ownership acquired (based on the number of shares purchased) and *management's intention* for the acquired company. The first part of this chapter will explore investments in other companies.

Kinross's investments are mostly in companies located outside of Canada, in places including Russia, Brazil, Chile, Mauritania, Ghana, and the United States. Kinross is ahead of many companies in investing in businesses in countries with developing economies. It is the largest Canadian investor in Russia and has spent over $3 billion there, making it the largest foreign mining investor in that country. Working in different countries means transacting in different currencies. This chapter will also address how foreign-currency transactions are recorded.

---

[1] Kinross Gold Corporation website, www.kinross.com.

this course, you have become increasingly familiar with the financial statements of companies such as Tim Hortons Inc., Dollarama Inc., Indigo Books & Music Inc., and TELUS Corporation. This chapter continues to examine the real world of accounting by discussing investments and international operations.

SHARE INVESTMENTS

Share Prices

LO 1

How do we account for short-term investments?

Investors can purchase shares directly from the issuing company or from other investors who wish to sell their shares. Investors buy more shares in transactions with other investors than in purchases directly from the issuing company. Each share is issued only once, but it may be traded among investors multiple times thereafter. People and businesses buy shares from and sell shares to each other in markets, such as the Toronto Stock Exchange (TSX) and the TSX Venture Exchange. Recall that share ownership is transferable. Investors trade (buy and sell) millions of shares each day. Brokers like RBC Dominion Securities and CIBC Investor Services Inc. handle share transactions for a commission. Individuals may also choose to do the trading themselves using discount trading/brokerage accounts to reduce transaction costs. Exhibit 16–1 presents information for the common shares of several Canadian companies listed on the TSX.

EXHIBIT 16–1 | Share Price Information for Three Canadian Companies

52 Weeks		Stock	Daily High	Daily Low	Cls or Latest	% Chge	Volume	P/E Ratio
High	Low							
62.11	40.05	Dollarama Inc	60.53	59.55	59.80	−.99%	335,373	30.10
44.63	36.97	TELUS Corporation	43.98	42.85	43.16	−1.3%	838,496	19.30
5.99	2.27	Kinross Gold Corp.	4.23	4.04	4.04	−5.61%	2,347,095	n/a

Source: Toronto Stock Exchange, Closing information for February 6, 2015.

REAL WORLD EXAMPLE

Companies listed on stock exchanges have their name and type of shares shown in short form on many reports. WestJet Airlines Ltd.'s shares are shown under WJA or WJA.A depending on the class of shares.

A broker (or website) may "quote a share price," which refers to the current market price per share. Exhibit 16–1 shows Kinross Gold Corp. common shares traded at $4.04 on February 6, 2015. This information is available from a variety of websites, including the website for the Toronto Stock Exchange—www.tsx.com. At some point during the previous 52 weeks, Kinross common shares reached a high of $5.99 and, at some other point, a low of $2.27. The TSX website continually updates this information while the stock market is open and then provides a summary at the end of each trading day. The closing price was 5.61 percent lower than the closing price one trading day earlier. From this information, we also learn that 2,347,095 shares of Kinross stock were traded. The P/E ratio (ratio of the share price to earnings per share) is not applicable because the business does not currently have positive earnings.

Investors and Investees

A person or a company that owns shares in a corporation is an *investor*. The corporation that issued the shares is the *investee*. If you own common shares of Kinross, you are an investor and Kinross is the investee.

Why do individuals and corporations invest in shares? You would probably make an investment to earn dividend revenue and to sell the shares at a higher price than you paid for them. Corporations and investment companies such as pension funds, mutual funds, insurance companies, bank trust departments, and other investment-related corporations buy shares for this reason.

Many companies invest in shares for a second reason: to influence or to control another company that is in a related line of business. Kinross Gold Corporation holds 100 percent of the shares of a Canadian company called Underworld

Resources Inc., which means Kinross can exert complete control over the affairs of that company. It owns 25 percent, or one-fourth, of Compania Minera Casale (Chile). While Kinross doesn't own all the shares of the Chilean company, it owns "enough" to influence the decisions of its management and, therefore, it reports in the notes to the financial statements that it has influence over the affairs of that company.

The term **significant influence** is used when a company participates in the decision making of another company without having full control over it. Somewhere in the range of 20 to 50 percent of the ownership of the company is usually sufficient for this to be the case. An investor holding more than 50 percent of the outstanding common shares has controlling interest in the investee. Determining the amount of influence requires the use of professional judgment. This is necessary because different accounting methods apply to different types of investments.

Classifying Investments

Investments are assets to the investor. Equity investments are reported as current or long term based on the length of time management *intends* to own them. Investments in the shares of other businesses are called equity investments because some share of the ownership is purchased.

KEY POINTS

Management *intent* is the key determinant about whether an investment is categorized as long term or short term.

Short-Term Investments

- **Short-term investments** may also be described as marketable securities or temporary investments.
- They may include **treasury bills, certificates of deposit, money market funds**, as well as shares and bonds of other companies.
- Short-term investments are **actively traded**, with the primary objective being to make a profit from changes in short-term market values.
- They must be liquid (readily convertible to cash).

Long-Term Investments

- An investment in the equity of a company that is *not* a short-term investment is categorized as a *long-term investment.*
- **Long-term investments** are those investments the investor intends to convert to cash in more than one year.

Investments in debt instruments of other companies, such as notes and bonds, can be either short-term or long-term investments. These will be discussed separately in this chapter.

Exhibit 16–2 provides an example of the presentation of the investment accounts on the balance sheet.

EXHIBIT 16–2 | Reporting Investments on the Balance Sheet

Current assets		
Cash	$x	
Short-term investments	x	
Accounts receivable	x	
Inventories	x	
Prepaid expenses	x	
Total current assets		$x
Long-term investments (or simply **Investments**)—Note X		x
Property, plant, and equipment		x

Note X—Long-Term Investments
Details of the long-term investments in shares where there is no significant influence, long-term investments in shares where there is significant influence, and long-term investments in bonds would be given in this note.

We report assets in order of their liquidity, starting with cash. Short-term investments are shown as current assets, while long-term investments and investments subject to significant influence are reported as long-term assets. Notice that these long-term investments are reported before property, plant, and equipment, and that there is no subtitle for long-term assets like there is for current assets.

"Long-term" is not often used in the account title. It is assumed that unless it is specifically labelled as short-term, it is long-term.

ACCOUNTING FOR SHORT-TERM INVESTMENTS

Unless otherwise stated, we assume all short-term investments in this chapter have an available market price.

The **fair value method**, or **market value method**, is used to account for short-term investments in shares. If there is an available market price for the investment, the historic cost is used only as the initial amount for recording investments and as the basis for measuring gains and losses on their sale. These investments are reported on the balance sheet at their fair values. (If there is not an available market price for the investment, it is recorded and reported on the balance sheet at historic cost.)

Share (Equity) Investments

Let's work through an example to show how share transactions are recorded and the share information is reported on the financial statements.

Investment   All investments are recorded initially at cost. Cost is the price paid for the shares. Section 3856 of Part II of the *CPA Canada Handbook* states that brokerage commissions and other transaction costs are expensed.

Suppose that Elk Valley Ltd. purchases 1,000 common shares of the 687,000 outstanding shares from Finning International Inc. at the market price of $16.00 per share and pays a $500 commission. Elk Valley Ltd. intends to sell this investment within one year or less and, therefore, classifies it as a short-term investment. Elk Valley Ltd.'s entry to record the investment is as follows:

1,000 × $16.00 = $16,000

Aug. 22	Short-Term Investments	16,000	
	Brokerage Commissions Expense	500	
	Cash		16,500
	Purchased 1,000 common shares of Finning International Inc. at $16.00 per share plus commission of $500.		

Cash Dividend   Assume Elk Valley Ltd. receives a $0.25 per share cash dividend on the Finning shares. Elk Valley Ltd.'s entry to record receipt of the dividends is:

Oct. 14	Cash	250	
	Dividend Revenue		250
	Received $0.25 per share cash dividend (1,000 × $0.25) on Finning International Inc. common shares.		

Dividends do not accrue with the passage of time (as interest does). An investor makes no accrual entry for dividend revenue at year end in anticipation of a dividend declaration. However, if a dividend declaration does occur before year end, say, on December 28, the investor *may* debit Dividend Receivable and credit Dividend Revenue on that date. The investor would then report this receivable and the revenue in the December 31 financial statements. Receipt of the cash dividend in January would be recorded by a debit to Cash and a credit to Dividend Receivable. The more common practice, however, is to record the dividend as income when it is received.

Stock Dividend   Receipt of a stock dividend does not require a formal journal entry. As we have seen, a stock dividend increases the number of shares held by the investor but does not affect the total cost of the investment. The *cost per share* of the share investment therefore decreases. The investor usually makes a memorandum entry of the number of stock dividend shares received and the new cost per share.

Assume that Elk Valley Ltd. receives a 10 percent stock dividend on its 1,000 share investment in Finning International Inc. that cost $16,000. Elk Valley Ltd. would make a memorandum entry like this:

Nov. 22	Received 100 Finning International Inc. common shares in a 10 percent stock dividend. New cost per share is $14.55 ($16,000 ÷ 1,100 shares).

Gain or Loss on Sale Prior to Adjustments to Fair Value   Any gain or loss on the sale of the investment is the difference between the sale proceeds and the **carrying value** of the investment.

Assume that Elk Valley Ltd. sells 400 shares of Finning International Inc. for $20.00 per share, less a $300 commission. The entry to record the sale is:

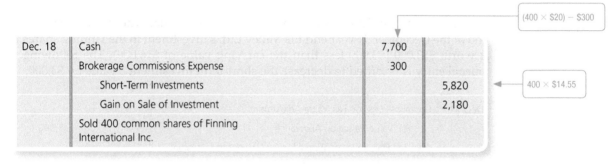

Dec. 18	Cash	7,700	
	Brokerage Commissions Expense	300	
	Short-Term Investments		5,820
	Gain on Sale of Investment		2,180
	Sold 400 common shares of Finning International Inc.		

(Annotations: $(400 \times \$20) - \$300$ pointing to 7,700; $400 \times \$14.55$ pointing to 5,820)

The carrying value per share of the investment ($14.55) is based on the total number of shares held, including those received as a stock dividend.

Reporting Short-Term Investments   ASPE requires that equity investments where there is no significant influence be reported at their fair value, or current market value, at year end. There is no significant influence in this case because Elk Valley owns only a small percentage of the total outstanding shares of Finning International Inc. (Elk Valley owns only 700 of Finning's total of 755,700 common shares after the stock dividend, which is less than $\frac{1}{10}$ of 1 percent of Finning's shares.) Any gain or loss is recorded as an unrealized gain or loss in the non-operating section of the company's income statement under "Other gains and losses."

In our previous example, Elk Valley Ltd. had purchased 1,000 shares of Finning International Inc. for $16.00 per share. Ignoring the stock dividend and the December 18 sale, assume that the fair value of the shares at the December 31 year end had increased to $18.00 per share. Elk Valley Ltd. must adjust the value of the short-term investment to $18,000 (1,000 shares × $18.00) from its carrying value of $16,000, which is an increase of $2,000.

To record this adjustment, a Fair Value Valuation Allowance account is created, which is a **companion account** to the Short-Term Investments or Long-Term Investments account:

Dec. 31	Fair Value Valuation Allowance	2,000	
	Unrealized Gain on Fair Value Adjustment		2,000
	Adjusted Finning International Inc. investment to fair value.		

Unrealized means that the gain or loss resulted from a change in fair value, not from a sale of the investment. A gain or loss on the sale of an investment is said to be *realized* when the company receives cash.

Elk Valley Ltd.'s balance sheet would report short-term investments, and its income statement would report the increase in the short-term investment as follows:

Balance Sheet (partial)	
Current Assets	
Cash	$ xxx
Short-term investments, at fair value	18,000
Accounts receivable,	
net of allowance of $xxx	xxx

Income Statement (partial)	
Other gains and losses:	
Unrealized gain on short-term investments	$2,000
Income before income taxes	xxx
Income tax expense	xxx
Net income (or net loss)	$ xxx

The amount presented here includes $16,000 for the Short-Term Investments account balance plus $2,000 for the companion Fair Value Valuation Allowance account balance.

Now assume instead that the Finning International Inc. shares decreased, in value, and at the December 31 year end Elk Valley Ltd.'s investment in the Finning shares is worth $13,000 ($3,000 less than the carrying value of $16,000). The following journal entry is recorded to decrease the short-term investment's value by $3,000:

Dec. 31	Unrealized Loss on Fair Value Adjustment	3,000	
	Fair Value Valuation Allowance		3,000
	Adjusted Finning International Inc. investment to fair value.		

Elk Valley Ltd.'s balance sheet would report short-term investments, and its income statement would report the decrease in the short-term investments, as follows:

Balance Sheet (partial)	
Current Assets	
Cash	$ xxx
Short-term investments, at fair value	13,000
Accounts receivable,	
net of allowance of $xxx	xxx

Income Statement (partial)	
Other gains and losses:	
Unrealized loss on short-term investments	$3,000
Income before income taxes	xxx
Income tax expense	xxx
Net income (or net loss)	$ xxx

The amount presented here includes $16,000 for the Short-Term Investments account balance less $3,000 for the companion Fair Value Valuation Allowance account balance.

Selling a Short-Term Equity Investment   When a company sells an equity investment, the gain or loss on the sale is the difference between the sale proceeds and the last carrying amount.

We now continue the previous loss example. If Elk Valley Ltd. sells the Finning International Inc. shares after year end for $12,000, Elk Valley Ltd. would record the sale and the $1,000 loss ($12,000 selling price − $13,000 carrying value) as follows:

Change in fair value since the investment was purchased.

Original cost of the investment, adjusted for any stock dividends or stock splits.

Jan. 19	Cash	12,000	
	Loss on Sale of Short-Term Investments	1,000	
	Fair Value Valuation Allowance	3,000	
	Short-Term Investments		16,000
	Sold Finning International Inc. shares at a loss.		

These entries remove the fair value of the investment from the books.

Companies would normally account for each investment separately, which can be done quite easily with computerized record keeping. Elk Valley Ltd.'s income statement would report the *realized* loss on the sale of the short-term investment in the "Other gains and losses" section.

Reporting Short-Term Bond (Debt) Investments

The fair value method is used to account for short-term investments in bonds. Like shares, short-term bond investments are valued at fair value, or market value. Premiums or discounts are not amortized as the intent is to hold the bonds for only a short period.

1. Calculate the price per share immediately after each of the following actions. This is a short-term investment and the investor does not have a significant influence on the investee.

   a. 1,000 shares were purchased for $18,700 plus commission of $300.
   b. The shares were split 2 for 1 one month later.
   c. The shares' total market value at year end was $16,000.
   d. All the shares were sold after year end for $20,000 plus commission of $250.

2. Levon Ltd. completed the following investment transactions during 2016 and 2017. Journalize the transactions, providing explanations.

   2016

Sep. 30	Purchased 1,200 of the 50,000 outstanding common shares of Betam Ltd. at a price of $36.00 per share, intending to sell the investment within the next year. Commissions were $125.
Dec. 21	Received a cash dividend of $0.09 per share on the Betam Ltd. shares.
31	At Levon Ltd.'s year end, adjusted the investment to its fair value of $33.50 per share.

   2017

   | Apr. 13 | Sold the Betam Ltd. shares for $31.00 per share. Commissions were $120. |

3. At what amount should the following investment portfolio be reported on the December 31 year-end balance sheet? All the investments are less than 5 percent of the investee's shares. Prepare one adjusting journal entry for the portfolio rather than making separate journal entries.

Shares	Carrying Value	Current Fair Value
All Seasons Hotels	$ 88,000	$ 97,000
Tangerine Manufacturing Corp.	140,000	124,000
Prairie Grocers Inc.	74,000	76,000

Solutions appear at the end of this chapter and on MyAccountingLab

ACCOUNTING FOR LONG-TERM SHARE INVESTMENTS

Long-term investments vary in how they are reported, depending on the purpose of the investment and thus the percentage of voting interest acquired. Each of the types and their related accounting method is introduced on the following pages and summarized in Exhibit 16–3.

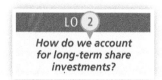

LO 2

How do we account for long-term share investments?

EXHIBIT 16–3 | Types of Investments and Accounting Methods under ASPE

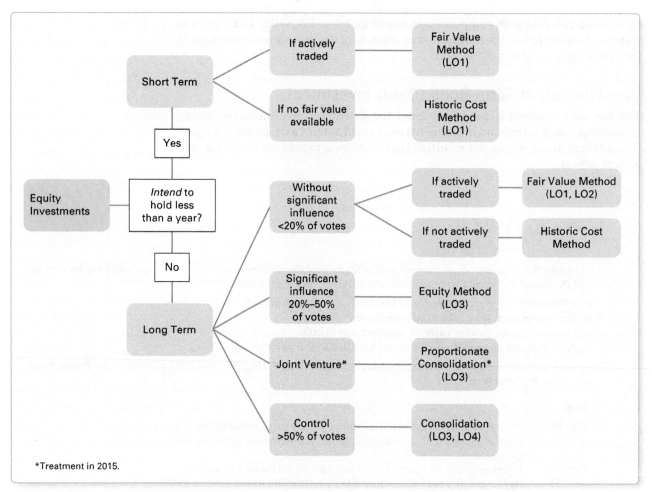

*Treatment in 2015.

Long-Term Equity Investments without Significant Influence

An investor may make a long-term investment in the shares of another corporation where the purpose is similar to that of short-term investing—the investor will hold the investment to earn dividend revenue or make a profit from selling the investment at a higher price than its purchase price. In such a situation, the investor will generally hold less than 20 percent of the voting interest of the investee and would normally play no important role in the investee's operations. They would normally account for the investment using the *fair value method* (*market value method*), if the market value for the shares of the investee is readily available, and at cost if there is no market price available. ***This is the same treatment as for short-term equity investments.***

Investment   Suppose Elm Corporation purchases 1,000 common shares of Molson Coors Brewing Company at the market price of $48.00 per share plus a brokerage commission of $1,000. Elm plans to hold these shares for longer than a year and classifies them as a long-term investment. Elm's entry to record the investment is:

Feb. 23	Long-Term Investments	48,000	
	Brokerage Commission Expense	1,000	
	Cash		49,000
	Purchased 1,000 common shares of Molson Coors Brewing Company at $48 per share.		

Cash Dividend   Assume that Elm receives a $1.00 per share cash dividend on the Molson Coors Brewing Company shares. Elm's entry for receipt of the dividend is:

Jul. 14	Cash	1,000	
	Dividend Revenue		1,000
	Received dividend on the Molson Coors Brewing Company shares (1,000 × $1.00).		

Reporting Long-Term Investments at Fair Value   Reporting at fair value requires an adjustment to current market value on the balance sheet date. Assume that the fair value of Elm's investment in Molson Coors Brewing Company shares has increased to $50,000 on December 31, its year end. In this case, Elm makes the following adjustment:

Dec. 31	Fair Value Valuation Allowance	2,000	
	Unrealized Gain on Fair Value Adjustment		2,000
	Adjusted long-term investment to $50,000 fair value ($50,000 − $48,000).		

The balance sheet would report the investment at the fair (market) value of $50,000.

Long-Term Investments	**Fair Value Valuation Allowance**
48,000	2,000

Investment carrying amount = Market value of $50,000

Here the Fair Value Valuation Allowance account has a debit balance because the investment has increased in value. If the investment's value declines, the allowance is credited. In that case, the investment carrying amount is cost *minus* the allowance. Fair Value Valuation Allowance with a credit balance becomes a contra account.

The other side of the December 31 adjusting journal entry credits Unrealized Gain on Fair Value Adjustment. If the investment declines, the company debits Unrealized Loss on Fair Value Adjustment.

Selling a Long-Term Investment Where There Is No Significant Influence   The sale of a long-term investment where there is no significant influence usually results in a *realized* gain or loss. Suppose Elm Corporation sells its investment in the Molson Coors Brewing Company shares for $52,000 during the next year, with brokerage commissions of $1,050. Elm would record the sale as follows:

Apr. 16	Cash	50,950		
	Brokerage Commissions Expense	1,050		$52,000 − $1,050 = $50,950 cash received
	Gain on Sale of Long-Term Investment		2,000	
	Long-Term Investments		48,000	These two accounts are closed since the asset is no longer owned.
	Fair Value Valuation Allowance		2,000	
	Sold Molson Coors Brewing Company shares at a gain.			

Elm Corporation would report the Gain on Sale of Long-Term Investment as an "Other gain or loss" in the non-operating section of the income statement.

> Try It!

4. Focus Ltd. completed the following investment transactions. Journalize the transactions, providing explanations.

2016

Oct. 16   Purchased 10,000 of the 60,000 outstanding common shares of Levell Inc. at a price of $45.00 per share; Levell Inc. is known for its generous dividends, so Focus Ltd. plans to hold the investment for more than one year. Commissions were $425.

Dec. 1   Received a cash dividend of $2.00 per share on the Levell Inc. shares.

    31   At Focus Ltd.'s year end, adjusted the investment to its fair value of $46.00 per share.

2017

Feb. 15   Suddenly needing cash, Focus Ltd. sold half the Levell Inc. shares for $49.00 per share. Commissions were $260.

Solutions appear at the end of this chapter and on MyAccountingLab

LONG-TERM SHARE INVESTMENTS ACCOUNTED FOR BY THE EQUITY METHOD

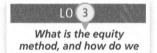

What is the equity method, and how do we use it?

KEY POINTS

An investor who holds 20 percent of a company's shares can *usually influence* some decisions of the board of directors and gain influence in company decisions. With more than 50 percent ownership (majority ownership), the investor can *usually control* the affairs of the company.

An investor may make an investment in the investee by purchasing from 20 to 50 percent of the investee's voting shares. In this case, the investor will likely be able to exert a *significant influence* over the investee and how the investee operates the business. Such an investor can likely affect the investee's decisions on dividend policy, product lines, sources of supply, and other important matters. We often use the **equity method for investments** to account for investments in which the investor can significantly influence the decisions of the investee.

The ability to influence matters more than the actual percentage of ownership. In certain circumstances, an investor with less than a 20 percent holding may still exert significant influence if there are many other shareholders who all own a small number of shares. In another case, a shareholder with a larger holding, such as a 30 percent holding, may exert no significant influence if another shareholder owns 51 percent of the shares and thus has control of the corporation.

Investment   Investments accounted for by the equity method are recorded initially at cost. Suppose Saturna Corp. pays $4,000,000 for 30 percent of the common shares of Galiano Corporation. Brokerage commissions are $5,000. Saturna Corp.'s entry to record the purchase of this investment is as follows:

2017			
Jan. 6	Investment in Galiano Corporation Common Shares	4,000,000	
	Brokerage Commissions Expense	5,000	
	Cash		4,005,000
	To purchase a 30% investment in Galiano Corporation common shares.		

Recording a Share of Income/Loss   Under the equity method, Saturna Corp., as the investor, records its share of the investee's net income and dividends as revenue. If Galiano Corporation reports net income of $1,000,000 for the year, Saturna

Corp. records 30 percent of this amount as an increase in the investment account and as equity method investment revenue, as follows:

Equity Method Investment in Galiano Corp.

Original cost	Share of losses
Share of income	Share of dividends
Balance	

Dec. 31	Investment in Galiano Corporation Common Shares	300,000	
	Equity Method Investment Revenue		300,000
	To record 30% of Galiano Corporation net income, $300,000 ($1,000,000 × 0.30).		

Equity Method Investment Revenue is specifically identified separately from other revenue. It is put into its own account for the same reason that we distinguish Sales Revenue from Service Revenue—to get better management information from the financial statements.

The investor increases the Investment (asset) account and records Investment Revenue when the investee reports income because of the close relationship between the two companies. As the investee's shareholders' equity increases, so does the value of the investment on the books of the investor.

Recording a Share of Dividends Saturna Corp. records its cash dividends received from Galiano Corporation. Assuming Galiano Corporation declares and pays a cash dividend of $600,000, Saturna Corp. receives 30 percent of this dividend, recording it as follows:

Dec. 31	Cash	180,000	
	Investment in Galiano Corporation Common Shares		180,000
	To record receipt of 30% of Galiano Corporation cash dividend, $180,000 ($600,000 × 0.30).		

Observe that the Investment account is credited for the receipt of a dividend on an equity method investment. Why? It is because the dividend decreases the investee's shareholders' equity, so it also reduces the investor's investment. In effect, the investor received cash for this portion of the investment.

After the above entries are posted, Saturna Corp.'s Investment account reflects its equity in the net assets of Galiano Corporation (also known as its *carrying value*):

Investment in Galiano Corporation Common Shares

2017					
Jan. 6	Purchase	4,000,000	Dec. 31	Dividends	180,000
Dec. 31	Net income	300,000			
2017					
Dec. 31	Balance	4,120,000			

Gain or Loss on the Sale of an Equity Method Investment The gain or loss on sale is measured as the difference between the sale proceeds and the carrying value of the investment.

If next year Saturna Corp. sold $\frac{1}{10}$ of the Galiano Corporation common shares for $400,000 with brokerage fees of $500, the transaction would be recorded as follows:

2018			
Feb. 13	Cash	399,500	
	Brokerage Commissions Expense	500	
	Loss on Sale of Investment	12,000	
	Investment in Galiano Corporation Common Shares		412,000
	Sold $\frac{1}{10}$ of investment in Galiano Corporation common shares at a loss of $12,000 [$400,000 − ($4,120,000 × $\frac{1}{10}$)].		

This account is reported in the non-operating section of the income statement.

Companies with investments accounted for by the equity method often refer to the investee as an **affiliated company**. The account titles Investments in Affiliated Companies or Investments Subject to Significant Influence also refer to investments that are accounted for by the equity method.

Write-downs Sometimes a company must write down an investment accounted for by the equity method because of what is expected to be a permanent decline in the value of the asset. These **write-downs** are rare. The following was reported in the 2013 Kinross Gold Corporation annual report about its 100 percent investment in the Fruita del Norte (FDN) project in Ecuador:

> Kinross' decision to cease the development of FDN resulted in a charge of $720.0 million in the second quarter of 2013, which was included in expenses and reflected a write-down of the Company's carrying value of the FDN project of $714.7 million, and $5.3 million of severance and other closure costs.

LEARNING TIPS

A write-down means there was a credit (decrease) to the asset account and a debit to an expense account, which reduces profit on the income statement.

Joint Ventures

A **joint venture** is a separate entity or project owned and operated by a small group of businesses. Joint ventures are common in risky endeavours such as the petroleum, mining, and construction industries. Moreover, they are widely used in developing countries such as Brazil, Russia, India, and China (the BRIC countries), where the political and economic systems are not the same as in North America. Many Canadian and US companies that do business abroad enter into joint ventures.

Section 3055 of Part II of the *CPA Canada Handbook* requires the use of **proportionate consolidation** when accounting for a joint venture. Proportionate consolidation means the venturer combines its proportionate interest in the assets, liabilities, revenues, and expenses of a joint venture with its own assets, liabilities, revenues, and expenses.[2] For example, assume V Ltd. has inventory of $500,000 and a 40 percent interest in a joint venture. The joint venture has inventory of $200,000. V Ltd. would report inventory on its consolidated financial statements of $580,000 ($500,000 + 40% of $200,000).

Private enterprises can choose to use the equity method or the cost method to account for joint ventures if the costs of using proportionate consolidation outweighed the benefits.

---

[2] This standard was in effect at the time this book was written in 2015. As of January 2016, section 3056 replaces section 3055 of the *CPA Canada Handbook*. Some examples of changes include the term *joint venture* is replaced with *joint arrangement* and *venturer* is replaced by *investor in a joint arrangement*. Specific details of the joint arrangement determine the method of recognizing the investment.

LONG-TERM SHARE INVESTMENTS ACCOUNTED FOR BY THE CONSOLIDATION METHOD

A **controlling interest** (or **majority interest**) is normally the ownership of more than 50 percent of the investee's voting shares. Such an investment enables the investor to elect a majority of the investee's board of directors and so control the investee. In such a situation, the investor is called the **parent company** and the investee company is called the **subsidiary**. The financial statements of subsidiaries are normally *consolidated* with those of the parent. For example, Galen Weston and other shareholders own George Weston Limited. In turn, that company owns 63 percent of Loblaw Companies Limited and 100 percent of Weston Foods, as shown in Exhibit 16–4. It can be said that George Weston Limited has control over both Loblaw Companies Limited and Weston Foods.

EXHIBIT 16–4 | **Partial Ownership Structure of George Weston Limited**

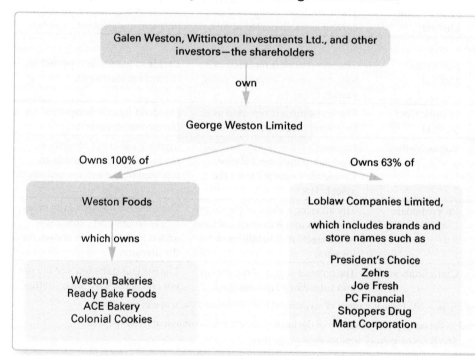

Why have subsidiaries? Why not have the corporation take the form of a single legal entity? Subsidiaries may limit the parent's liabilities in a risky venture; may make mergers, acquisitions, and sales easier; and may ease expansion into foreign countries. For example, George Weston Limited sold off Neilson Dairy to Saputo Inc. for $465 million and purchased ACE Bakery for $110 million. These deals would have been much more complex if they were all part of one big company.

Consolidation accounting is a method of combining the financial statements of two or more companies that are controlled by the same owners. This method implements the entity concept by reporting a single set of financial statements for the consolidated entity, which carries the name of the parent company.

ASPE allows parent companies to account for their subsidiaries using the equity method or the cost method if the cost of providing **consolidated financial statements** is greater than the benefits for users who are able to gain access to financial information directly from the parent company. However, the *CPA Canada Handbook* emphasizes consolidation for companies with controlling interest, so we focus on consolidation accounting in such situations. The next section in this chapter will focus on how to do this.

REAL WORLD EXAMPLE

The *CPA Canada Handbook* provides guidance about how to record transactions and present financial information. It is not exclusively a book of rules. There are often alternatives from which companies need to choose based on what provides the best information to readers of financial statements at the most reasonable cost. In this case, there is an emphasis (or recommendation) to consolidate when there is controlling interest, but it is not the only choice.

Long-Term Equity Investments

So far we have introduced several types of ownership and several methods for recording and reporting information. Exhibit 16–5 summarizes the accounting method and financial statement presentation used generally for share investments according to the percentage of the investor's ownership in the investee company.

EXHIBIT 16–5 | Summary of Accounting for Investments under ASPE

Type of Investment (% of votes)	Primary* Accounting Method	Financial Statement Effects	
		Balance Sheet	Income Statement**
Short Term			
No significant influence (<20%, actively traded)	Fair Value Method	The investment is reported as a current asset. Reported using market value.	Dividend income is reported on the income statement.
No significant influence (<20%, not actively traded)	Historic Cost Method	The investment is reported as a current asset. Reported at cost.	Dividend income is reported on the income statement.
Long Term			
Without significant influence (<20%, actively traded)	Fair Value Method	The investment is reported as a long-term asset. Reported using market value.	Dividend income is reported on the income statement.
Without significant influence (<20%, not actively traded)	Historic Cost Method	The investment is reported as a long-term asset. Reported at cost.	Dividend income is reported on the income statement
Significant influence (20–50%)	Equity Method	Investor's share of income/loss is added to the asset balance. Dividends deducted from the asset balance.	Investor's share of investee's net income and dividends are reported on the income statement.
Joint venture***	Proportionate Consolidation	The investor's share of the investee's assets and liabilities is added to the assets and liabilities of the investor.	The investor's share of the investee's revenues and expenses is added to the amounts shown for the investor.
Control (>50%)	Consolidation	The balance sheets of the parent and subsidiary are combined.	The income statements of the parent and subsidiary are combined.

* Choices in the accounting method are possible for many types of investment and are beyond the scope of this chapter.

** Realized gains/losses are reported in the non-operating section of the income statement. Commission fees expensed.

*** Effective in 2015. See the *CPA Canada Handbook* Section 3056 for changes in 2016.

 Try It!

5. Identify the appropriate accounting method for each of the following independent situations involving investments in common shares:

   a. Purchase of 25 percent and investor plans to hold as a long-term investment
   b. Investor intends to sell three months after year end
   c. Purchase of more than 50 percent of investee's shares

6. Investor Ltd. paid $140,000 to acquire 40 percent of the common shares of Investee Ltd. The investment is subject to significant influence. At the end of the first year, Investee Ltd.'s net income was $180,000, and Investee Ltd. declared and paid cash dividends of $140,000. Journalize Investor Ltd.'s (a) purchase of the investment, (b) share of Investee Ltd.'s net income, (c) receipt of dividends from Investee Ltd., and (d) sale of all the Investee Ltd. shares for $160,000.

Solutions appear at the end of this chapter and on MyAccountingLab

CONSOLIDATED FINANCIAL STATEMENTS

Many published financial reports include consolidated statements. To understand the statements you are likely to encounter, you need to know the basic concepts underlying consolidation accounting.

Consolidated statements combine the balance sheets, income statements, and other financial statements of the parent company with those of the subsidiaries into an overall set as if the parent and its subsidiaries were a single entity. The goal is to provide a better perspective on operations than could be obtained by examining the separate reports of each of the individual companies. The assets, liabilities, revenues, and expenses of each subsidiary are added to the parent's accounts. The consolidated financial statements present the combined account balances. For example, the balance in the Cash account of Loblaw Companies Limited is added to the balance in the George Weston Limited Cash account, and the sum of the two amounts is presented as a single amount in the consolidated balance sheet of George Weston Limited. Loblaw Companies Limited and the names of all other George Weston Limited subsidiaries do not appear in the statement titles. But the names of the subsidiary companies are listed in the notes that accompany the parent company's annual report.

Exhibit 16–6 shows a corporate structure where the parent corporation owns controlling interests in five subsidiary companies and equity method investments in two other investee companies.

LO 4

What is consolidation, and how do we perform a simple consolidation?

EXHIBIT 16–6 | **Parent Company with Five Consolidated Subsidiaries and Two Equity Method Investments**

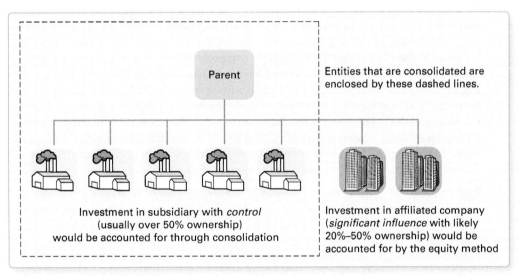

Consolidated Balance Sheet—Parent Owns All Subsidiary's Shares

Suppose that Parent Corporation purchased all the outstanding common shares of Subsidiary Corporation at its book value of $1,200,000 on June 14. In addition, Parent Corporation loaned Subsidiary Corporation $640,000 on June 30. The $1,200,000 is paid to the *former* owners (the shareholders) of Subsidiary Corporation as private investors. The $1,200,000 *is not* an addition to the existing assets and shareholders' equity of Subsidiary Corporation. That is, the books of Subsidiary Corporation are completely unaffected by Parent Corporation's initial investment and Parent's subsequent accounting for that investment. Subsidiary Corporation is not dissolved. It lives on as a separate legal entity but with a new owner, Parent Corporation.

REAL WORLD EXAMPLE

Buying shares is not the only way to purchase a company. It is also possible to buy the assets, but this alternative is covered in finance courses.

Parent Corporation Books					Subsidiary Corporation Books			
June 14	Investment in Subsidiary Corporation	1,200,000			June 14	No entry		
	Cash		1,200,000					
June 30	Notes Receivable from Subsidiary Corp.	640,000			June 30	Cash	640,000	
	Cash		640,000			Notes Payable to Parent Corp.		640,000

KEY POINTS

Each subsidiary company keeps its own set of books and pays its own taxes, just as the parent company does; however, for reporting purposes, the parent and subsidiary companies are treated as one economic unit when they are consolidated. Intercompany transactions must be eliminated.

Each legal entity has its individual set of books. The consolidated entity does not keep a separate set of books. Instead, a worksheet is used to prepare the consolidated statements. A major concern in consolidation accounting is this: *Do not double count—that is, do not include the same item twice.*

Companies may prepare a consolidated balance sheet immediately after acquisition. The consolidated balance sheet shows all the assets and liabilities of the parent and the subsidiary. The Investment in Subsidiary account on the parent's books represents all the assets and liabilities of Subsidiary Corporation. The consolidated statements cannot show both the investment account and the amounts for the subsidiary's assets and liabilities. Doing so would count the same net resources twice. To avoid this double counting, we eliminate ❶ the $1,200,000 Investment in Subsidiary Corporation on the parent's books, and the $1,200,000 shareholders' equity on the subsidiary's books ($800,000 Common Shares and $400,000 Retained Earnings), and ❷ the intercompany $640,000 note.

Explanation of Elimination-Entry ❶ (Ownership) Exhibit 16–7 shows the *worksheet* for consolidating the balance sheet. (Notice this is a much different sort of worksheet than what was shown in Chapter 4!) Consider the elimination entry for the parent–subsidiary ownership accounts, which are intercompany accounts. Entry ❶ credits the parent's Investment account to eliminate its debit balance. It also eliminates the subsidiary's shareholders' equity accounts by debiting Common Shares for $800,000 and Retained Earnings for $400,000. The resulting consolidated balance sheet reports no Investment in Subsidiary Corporation account, and the Common Shares and Retained Earnings are those of Parent Corporation only. The consolidated amounts are in the final column of the consolidation worksheet. Another way of stating this is to say that the subsidiary's equity is the parent company's investment balance—which represents the same resource. Therefore, including them both would amount to double counting.

REAL WORLD EXAMPLE

Notice that in the consolidation worksheet there are no dollar signs. That is because this is an internal working document and not a formal financial statement, and because all amounts are stated in dollars.

Explanation of Elimination-Entry ❷ (Intercompany Transactions) Parent Corporation loaned $640,000 to Subsidiary Corporation. Therefore, Parent Corporation's balance sheet includes a $640,000 note receivable, and Subsidiary Corporation's balance sheet reports a note payable for this amount. This loan was entirely within the consolidated entity and so must be eliminated. Entry ❷ in Exhibit 16–7 accomplishes this. The $640,000 credit in the elimination column of the worksheet offsets Parent Corporation's debit balance in Notes Receivable from Subsidiary Corporation. After this worksheet entry, the consolidated amount for notes receivable is zero and the resulting consolidated amount for notes payable is the amount owed to those outside the consolidated entity.

Parent Buys Subsidiary's Shares and Pays for Goodwill

A company may acquire a controlling interest in a subsidiary by paying a price above the fair value of the subsidiary's net assets (assets minus liabilities), which we assume is equal to the book value of the subsidiary's shareholders' equity. This excess is called goodwill. Accounting for goodwill was introduced in Chapter 10 on page 580.

The subsidiary does not record goodwill; only the purchaser does. The goodwill is shown as a separate line of the worksheet in the process of consolidating the parent and subsidiary financial statements.

EXHIBIT 16–7 | Worksheet for Consolidated Balance Sheet—Parent Corporation Owns All Subsidiary Corporation's Shares

	Parent Corporation	Subsidiary Corporation	Eliminations Debit	Eliminations Credit	Consolidated Amounts
Assets					
Cash	$ 96,000	$ 144,000			$ 240,000
Notes receivable from Subsidiary Corp.	640,000	—		❷$ 640,000	—
Inventory	832,000	728,000			1,560,000
Investment in Subsidiary Corp.	1,200,000	—		❶ 1,200,000	—
Other assets	1,744,000	1,104,000			2,848,000
Total	$4,512,000	$1,976,000			$4,648,000
Liabilities and Shareholders' Equity					
Accounts payable	$ 344,000	$ 136,000			$ 480,000
Notes payable	1,520,000	640,000	❷$ 640,000		1,520,000
Common shares	1,408,000	800,000	❶ 800,000		1,408,000
Retained earnings	1,240,000	400,000	❶ 400,000		1,240,000
Total	$4,512,000	$1,976,000	$1,840,000	$1,840,000	$4,648,000

Let's look at a new example in Exhibit 16–8. Suppose Par Corporation paid $2,700,000 to acquire 100 percent of the common shares of Sub Corporation, which had Common Shares of $1,200,000 and Retained Earnings of $1,080,000. Par's payment included $420,000 for goodwill ($2,700,000 − $1,200,000 − $1,080,000 = $420,000).[3]

EXHIBIT 16–8 | Worksheet for Consolidated Balance Sheet—Par Corporation Owns All Sub Corporation's Shares and Paid for Goodwill

	Parent Corporation	Subsidiary Corporation	Eliminations Debit	Eliminations Credit	Consolidated Amounts
Assets					
Cash	$ 880,000	$ 100,000			$ 980,000
Inventory	500,000	1,500,000			2,000,000
Investment in Sub Corp.	2,700,000	—		$2,700,000	—
Goodwill	—	—	$ 420,000		420,000
Other assets	816,000	785,000			1,601,000
Total	$4,896,000	$2,385,000			$5,001,000
Liabilities and Shareholders' Equity					
Accounts payable	$ 426,000	$ 25,000			$ 451,000
Notes payable	1,000,000	80,000			1,080,000
Common shares	1,280,000	1,200,000	1,200,000		1,280,000
Retained earnings	2,190,000	1,080,000	1,080,000		2,190,000
Total	$4,896,000	$2,385,000	$2,700,000	$2,700,000	$5,001,000

---

[3] For simplicity, we are assuming the fair market value of the subsidiary's net assets (Assets–Liabilities) equals the book value of the company's shareholders' equity. Advanced courses consider other situations.

Assume that Par Corporation recorded the purchase on December 31 as follows:

Dec. 31	Investment in Sub Corporation	2,700,000	
	Cash		2,700,000

The entry to eliminate Par Corporation's Investment account against Sub Corporation's equity accounts is:

In *actual* practice, this entry would be made only on the consolidation worksheet. Here we show it in general journal form for instructional purposes.

Dec. 31	Common Shares, Sub Corporation	1,200,000	
	Retained Earnings, Sub Corporation	1,080,000	
	Goodwill	420,000	
	Investment in Sub Corporation		2,700,000
	To eliminate cost of investment in Sub Corporation against Sub Corporation's equity balances and goodwill.		

The asset goodwill is reported as a separate line item on the consolidated balance sheet. For example, Kinross Gold Corporation's December 31, 2014, consolidated balance sheet includes goodwill of $162.7 million as a separate line item in the non-current assets section of the balance sheet.

Consolidated Balance Sheet—Parent Owns Less than 100 Percent of Subsidiary's Shares

When a parent company owns more than 50 percent (a majority) of the subsidiary's shares but less than 100 percent of them, a new category of balance sheet account, called *non-controlling interest*, must appear on the consolidated balance sheet. Suppose P Ltd. buys 75 percent of S Ltd.'s common shares. The non-controlling interest is the remaining 25 percent of S Ltd.'s equity. Thus, **non-controlling interest** (sometimes called **minority interest**) is the subsidiary's equity that is held by shareholders other than the parent company. While the *CPA Canada Handbook* is silent on where non-controlling interest should be disclosed on the balance sheet, accepted practice is to list it as a liability between liabilities and shareholders' equity. This is illustrated in Exhibit 16–10.

Assume P Ltd. buys 75 percent of S Ltd.'s common shares for $1,440,000 and there is no goodwill. Also, P Ltd. owes $600,000 on a note payable to S Ltd. P Ltd. would record this purchase on December 31 as follows:

Dec. 31	Investment in S. Ltd	1,440,000	
	Cash		1,440,000

KEY POINTS

The balance sheet elimination entry requires, at most, five steps:

- Eliminate intercompany receivables and payables.

- Eliminate the shareholders' equity accounts of the subsidiary.

- Eliminate the Investment in Subsidiary account.

- Record goodwill.

- Record non-controlling interest.

Exhibit 16–9 is the consolidation worksheet for this example.

- Entry ❶ eliminates P Ltd.'s Investment balance of $1,440,000 against the $1,920,000 shareholders' equity of S Ltd. Observe that all of S Ltd.'s equity is eliminated even though P Ltd. holds only 75 percent of S Ltd.'s shares. The remaining 25 percent interest in S Ltd.'s equity is credited to Non-controlling Interest ($1,920,000 × 0.25 = $480,000). Thus, entry ❶ *reclassifies* 25 percent of S Ltd.'s equity as non-controlling interest.

- Entry ❷ eliminates S Ltd.'s $600,000 note receivable against P Ltd.'s note payable of the same amount. The consolidated amount of notes payable ($504,000) is the amount that S Ltd. owes to outsiders.

The consolidated balance sheet of P Ltd., shown in Exhibit 16–10, is based on the worksheet of Exhibit 16–9.

	P Ltd.	S Ltd.	Eliminations Debit	Eliminations Credit	Consolidated Amounts
Assets					
Cash	$ 396,000	$ 216,000			$ 612,000
Notes receivable from P Ltd.	—	600,000		② $ 600,000	—
Accounts receivable, net	648,000	468,000			1,116,000
Inventory	1,104,000	792,000			1,896,000
Investment in S Ltd.	1,440,000	—		① 1,440,000	—
Property, plant, and equipment, net	2,760,000	1,476,000			4,236,000
Total	$6,348,000	$3,552,000			$7,860,000
Liabilities and Shareholders' Equity					
Accounts payable	$1,692,000	$1,128,000			$2,820,000
Notes payable	600,000	504,000	② $ 600,000		504,000
Non-controlling interest	—	—		① 480,000	480,000
Common shares	2,040,000	1,200,000	① 1,200,000		2,040,000
Retained earnings	2,016,000	720,000	① 720,000		2,016,000
Total	$6,348,000	$3,552,000	$2,520,000	$2,520,000	$7,860,000

EXHIBIT 16–10 | Consolidated Balance Sheet of P Ltd.

P LTD. Consolidated Balance Sheet December 31, 2017		
Assets		
Current assets		
Cash	$ 612,000	
Accounts receivable, net	1,116,000	
Inventory	1,896,000	
Total current assets		$3,624,000
Property, plant, and equipment, net		4,236,000
Total assets		$7,860,000
Liabilities		
Current liabilities		
Accounts payable		$2,820,000
Long-term liabilities		
Notes payable		504,000
Total liabilities		3,324,000
Non-controlling interest		480,000
Shareholders' equity		
Common shares	$2,040,000	
Retained earnings	2,016,000	
Total shareholders' equity		4,056,000
Total liabilities and shareholders' equity		$7,860,000

Even though the *CPA Canada Handbook* does not stipulate where to include non-controlling interest, common practice is to list is as a liability between liabilities and shareholders' equity, as shown here.

Income of a Consolidated Entity

The income of a consolidated entity is the net income of the parent plus the parent's proportion of the subsidiaries' net income. Suppose Mega-Parent Inc. owns all the shares of Subsidiary S-1 Inc. and 60 percent of the shares of Subsidiary S-2 Inc. During the year just ended, Mega-Parent Inc. earned net income of $1,980,000, Subsidiary S-1 Inc. earned $900,000, and Subsidiary S-2 Inc. had a net loss of $600,000. Mega-Parent Inc. would report net income of $2,520,000, computed as follows:

	Net Income (Net Loss)	Mega-Parent Inc. Shareholders' Ownership	Mega-Parent Inc. Net Income (Net Loss)
Mega-Parent Inc.	$1,980,000	100%	$1,980,000
Subsidiary S-1 Inc.	900,000	100	900,000
Subsidiary S-2 Inc.	(600,000)	60	(360,000)
Consolidated net income			$2,520,000

The parent's net income is the same amount that would be recorded under the equity method. However, the equity method stops short of reporting the investee's assets and liabilities on the parent balance sheet because, with an investment in the range of 20 to 50 percent, the investor owns less than a controlling interest in the investee company.

The procedures for preparation of a consolidated income statement are similar to those outlined for the balance sheet, but it is discussed in an advanced accounting course.

> Why It's Done This Way

Objective of Financial Reporting

Why is it important to consolidate the financial results of companies under common control? The consolidated financial statements *communicate useful information* to interested users to help them assess the success of the company—this is the primary objective of the accounting framework. If the parent company provided financial information on each of its subsidiaries on a company-by-company basis only, users would find it difficult to pull all the pieces together on their own. Intercompany transactions would be difficult to identify unless a user had direct access to the same information as internal managers.

In the accounting framework, the *economic entity assumption* directs us to eliminate intercompany transactions because these occur *within* the larger economic entity (which is the consolidated group of companies)

and would cause double-counting errors if they were not eliminated.

The framework's characteristic of *understandability* promotes disclosure in the notes to the financial statements. The parent company's notes to the financial statements must list the subsidiary companies and the parent's percentage of ownership of each. GAAP also require that companies provide **segmented information** in their financial statement notes. This segmented information is either by industry or by geography, and it is reported by companies that operate in different industries or regions of the world, including parent and subsidiary companies.

By presenting details about a parent company's subsidiaries and segmented information in the notes, consolidated financial statements communicate even more *useful information* to users to help them assess the success of the company.

> Try It!

7. Answer these questions about consolidated financial statements:

   a. Whose name appears on the consolidated statements—the parent company's, the subsidiary company's, or both?

   b. Why does consolidated shareholders' equity (contributed capital + retained earnings) exclude the equity of a subsidiary corporation?

   c. Suppose A Ltd. owns 90 percent of B Ltd. What are the remaining 10 percent of B Ltd.'s shares called, and where do they appear, if at all, in A Ltd.'s consolidated financial statements?

   d. Suppose C Ltd. paid $2,000,000 to acquire D Ltd., whose shareholders' equity (which has the same fair value as net assets) totalled $1,400,000. What is the $600,000 excess called? Which company reports the excess? Where in the consolidated financial statements is the excess reported?

8. Parent Inc. paid $400,000 for all the common shares of Subsidiary Inc., and Parent Inc. owes Subsidiary Inc. $70,000 on a note payable. Assume the fair value of Subsidiary Inc.'s net assets is equal to book value. Complete the following consolidation worksheet:

	Parent Inc.	Subsidiary Inc.	Eliminations Debit	Eliminations Credit	Consolidated Amounts
Assets					
Cash	$ 38,000	$ 36,000			
Note receivable from Parent Inc.	—	70,000			
Investment in Subsidiary Inc.	400,000	—			
Goodwill	—	—			
Other assets	432,000	396,000			
Total	$870,000	$502,000			
Liabilities and Shareholders' Equity					
Accounts payable	$ 60,000	$ 42,000			
Notes payable	70,000	120,000			
Common shares	560,000	240,000			
Retained earnings	180,000	100,000			
Total	$870,000	$502,000			

Solutions appear at the end of this chapter and on MyAccountingLab

INVESTMENTS IN BONDS[4]

Industrial and commercial companies invest far more in shares than they do in bonds. The major investors in bonds are financial institutions, such as pension plans, trust companies, and insurance companies.

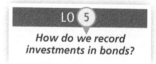

How do we record investments in bonds?

We looked at bonds in Chapter 15, but at that time it was from the perspective if the *issuer*. In this chapter we will look at how the *investor* records and reports the same transactions. The dollar amount of a bond transaction is the same for both, but the accounts debited and credited differ.

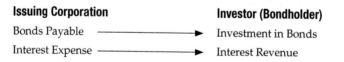

Issuing Corporation		Investor (Bondholder)
Bonds Payable	→	Investment in Bonds
Interest Expense	→	Interest Revenue

---

[4] Section 3856 of Part II of the *CPA Canada Handbook* addresses financial instruments. Much of the discussion is beyond the scope of this text and is covered in advanced accounting courses.

Short-Term Investments in Bonds

Short-term investments in bonds are rare, since the purpose of investing in bonds is to provide a stream of investment income over the life of the bonds, and bonds typically have a life that is longer than one year. We covered accounting for short-term bonds using the fair value method on page 915. Therefore, we focus here on long-term investments in bonds.

Long-Term Investments in Bonds

The accounting treatment of long-term bond investments is typically referred to as the **amortized cost method**, which involves the following journal entries:

1 Long-term bond investments are recorded at cost, which includes the purchase price and brokerage fees.

2 The accountant records interest and amortization on the cash interest dates.

3 At year end, interest receivable and the related amortization is accrued.

The discount or premium is amortized to account more precisely for interest revenue over the period the bonds will be held. The journal entries would be:

Discount:	Investment in Bonds	$X	
	Interest Revenue		$X
Premium:	Interest Revenue	$X	
	Investment in Bonds		$X

4 Long-term investments in bonds are reported at their *amortized cost*, which determines the carrying amount.

5 At maturity, the investor will receive the face value of the bonds.

Consider the following scenario to illustrate accounting for a bond investment:

- $100,000 of 6 percent Xpress Trucking Ltd. bonds were purchased on April 1, 2017, at a price of 98 (98 percent of par value)
- Interest dates are April 1 and October 1
- Bonds mature on April 1, 2021 (outstanding for 48 months)
- Brokerage charges are $800 and are added to the cost
- Purchaser's year end is December 31
- Use the straight-line method of amortization for the premium or discount. It is calculated the same way as it is calculated for bonds payable in Chapter 15 on pages 849–851.

The transactions for the bond investment are recorded as follows:

1 **Purchase at Cost** The $100,000, 6 percent bond was purchased at a price of 98. Brokerage costs are not expensed; they are added to the cost of the bond.

2017			
Apr. 1	Investment in Bonds	98,800	
	Cash		98,800
	To purchase long-term bond investment ($100,000 × 0.98) + $800 brokerage fee.		

2 **Amortization of Discount/Premium** The amortization of the discount or the premium on a bond investment affects Interest Revenue and the carrying amount of the bonds in the same way as for the company that issued the bonds.

The entries bring the investment balance to the bond's face value on the maturity date and record the correct amount of interest revenue each period. Recall that in Exhibit 15–6 on page 853 we looked at bond discounts from the perspective of the seller. Exhibit 16–11 shows a similar amortization of the discount except from the perspective of the purchaser in this Xpress Trucking Ltd. example.

At the first interest date, the interest revenue and bond discount amortization must be recorded:[5]

Oct. 1	Cash	3,000	
	Interest Revenue		3,000
	To receive semi-annual interest ($100,000 × 0.06 × $^6/_{12}$).		
1	Investment in Bonds	150	
	Interest Revenue		150
	To amortize discount on bond investment for six months ([($100,000 − $98,800) ÷ 48] × 6).		

EXHIBIT 16–11 | **Amortization of a Bond Discount by a Purchaser**

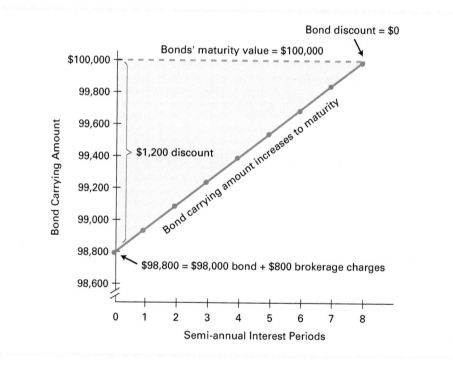

[5] Companies sometimes record the investment at par value and the premium or discount in a separate account. If so, the journal entries would be

Apr. 1	Investment in Bonds	100,000	
	Discount on Investment in Bonds		1,200
	Cash		98,800
Oct. 1	Discount on Investment in Bonds	150	
	Interest Revenue		150
	Cash	3,000	
	Interest Revenue		3,000

3 Year-end Accrual At year end, interest revenue must be accrued. The amortization of the bond discount is also recorded at this time.

Dec. 31	Interest Receivable	1,500	
	Interest Revenue		1,500
	To accrue interest revenue for three months ($100,000 × 0.06 × ³/₁₂).		
31	Investment in Bonds	75	
	Interest Revenue		75
	To amortize discount on bond investment for three months ([($100,000 − $98,800) ÷ 48] × 3).		

4 Reporting Long-Term Investments in Bonds If we assume that the bond's market price is 102 at December 31, 2017, the year-end financial statements report the following effects of this long-term investment in bonds, where $99,025 = $98,800 + $150 + $75:

Partial balance sheet at December 31, 2017:

Current assets:

Interest receivable	$ 1,500
Total current assets	x,xxx
Investments in bonds—Note 6	99,025

Note 6: Investments in Bonds
Investments in bonds are reported at their amortized cost. At December 31, 2017, the current market value of the investments in bonds was $102,000.

Partial income statement (multi-step) for the year ended December 31, 2017:

Other revenues:

Interest revenue	$4,725

$3,000 + $150 + $1,500 + $75

5 Maturity At maturity, the following journal entry would record the return of the face value of the bond. Interest revenue would be reported separately as shown in **2**.

2021			
Apr. 1	Cash	98,000	
	Investment in Bonds		98,000
	To collect face value of the bond at maturity.		

Write-down If the market value of a long-term bond investment declines below cost and the decline is considered to be other than temporary (thus it is an impairment), the investment should be *written down to market*. Suppose the market price for the bonds at December 31, 2017, was 97 (instead of the 102 noted in **4**). The journal entry to write down the investment would be:

2017			
Dec. 31	Impairment Loss	2,025	
	Investment in Bonds		2,025
	To record reduction in bond value not considered to be temporary ($99,025 book value − $97,000).		

If there is a subsequent improvement in the value, it is possible to reverse the adjustment and increase the book value of the investment to its amortized cost.

9. On April 30, 2017, Cana Corp. paid 97.50 for 4 percent bonds of Starr Limited as an investment. Maturity value of the bonds is $100,000 at October 31, 2022; they pay interest on April 30 and October 31. At December 31, 2017, the bonds' market value is 98.25. Cana Corp. plans to hold the bonds until they mature.

   a. What accounting treatment should Cana Corp. use to account for the bonds?
   b. Using the straight-line method of amortizing the discount, journalize all transactions on the bonds for 2017.
   c. Show how the investment in Starr Limited bonds would be reported on the Cana Corp. balance sheet at December 31, 2017.

10. Cana Corp. purchased $50,000 of 4 percent bonds from Xylomax Inc. on June 1, 2017. It paid $46,490 and intends to hold the bonds for three years or more. There were no brokerage fees. Interest is paid semi-annually on December 1 and June 1. Using the partial amortization schedule below, prepare the journal entries for June 1, 2017, and December 1, 2017. (Refer to Chapter 15 for information on the effective-interest method.)

Annual Interest Period	Interest Revenue 4.00%	Period Interest Revenue	Discount Amort.	Discount Balance	Bond Carrying Value
Jun. 1, 2017				$3,510	$46,490
Dec. 1, 2017	$1,000	$1,395	$395	3,115	46,885
Jun. 1, 2018	1,000	1,407	407	2,708	47,292

Solutions appear at the end of this chapter and on MyAccountingLab

FOREIGN-CURRENCY TRANSACTIONS

Accounting for business activities across national boundaries makes up the field of *international accounting*. Did you know that Bombardier earned more than 95 percent of revenues outside of Canada in 2012? And Kinross Gold Corporation earned 100 percent of its revenues in US dollars in 2013? It is common for Canadian companies to do a large part of their business abroad.

The economic environment varies from country to country. Canada may be booming while other countries may be depressed economically. International accounting must deal with such differences.

LO 6

How do we record transactions in foreign currencies?

Foreign Currencies and Foreign-Currency Exchange Rates

When companies engage in business transactions across national borders, there are no rules about which currency should be used. The choice of currency is just one of many business management decisions to be made. Assume BlackBerry sells 1,000 of its BlackBerry wireless devices to a US retailer. Will BlackBerry receive Canadian dollars or US dollars? If the transaction takes place in Canadian dollars, the US retailer must buy Canadian dollars to pay BlackBerry in Canadian currency. If the transaction takes place in US dollars, BlackBerry will receive US dollars and then exchange them for the Canadian dollars they need to pay their Canadian employees. In either case, a step has been added to the transaction: One company must convert domestic currency into foreign currency, or the other company must convert foreign currency into domestic currency.

The price of one nation's currency can be stated in terms of another country's monetary unit. The price of a foreign currency is called the **foreign-currency exchange rate**. In Exhibit 16–12, the Canadian dollar value of a Japanese yen is

$0.01051. This means that one Japanese yen could be bought for approximately one cent. Other currencies, such as the pound and the euro, are also listed in Exhibit 16–12.

LEARNING TIPS

Notice that the exchange rates are quoted to at least 5 decimal places in Exhibit 16–12. When using exchange rates in calculations, do not round calculations until the last step.

EXHIBIT 16–12 | Currency Exchange Rates

Country	Monetary Unit	Cost in Canadian Dollars	Country	Monetary Unit	Cost in Canadian Dollars
United States	Dollar	$1.25167	Britain	Pound	$ 1.90697
European Union	Euro	1.41591	n/a	Bitcoin	279.606
Japan	Yen	0.01051	Denmark	Krone	0.19039

Source: OANDA.com, Currency Converter. © 2015 OANDA Corporation.

We use the exchange rate to convert the price of an item stated in one currency to its price in a second currency. We call this conversion a **translation**. Suppose an item costs 200 euros. To compute its cost in dollars, we multiply the amount in euros by the conversion rate: 200 euros × $1.41591 = $283.18.

To aid the flow of international business, a market exists for foreign currencies. Traders buy and sell Canadian dollars, US dollars, euros, and other currencies in the same way that they buy and sell other commodities such as beef, corn, cotton, and automobiles. And just as supply and demand cause the prices of these other commodities to shift, so supply and demand for a particular currency cause exchange rates to fluctuate daily—even minute by minute. When the demand for a nation's currency exceeds the supply of that currency, its exchange rate rises. When supply exceeds demand, the currency's exchange rate falls.

Currencies are often described in the financial press as "strong" or "weak." What do these terms mean? The exchange rate of a **strong currency** is rising relative to other nations' currencies. The exchange rate of a **weak currency** is falling relative to other currencies.

The relationship between the Canadian and US dollar over the long term looks like this:

March 1, 2001   exchange rate was $1 US = $1.5480 Canadian
February 2, 2015   exchange rate was $1 US = $1.2578 Canadian

REAL WORLD EXAMPLE

A Canadian dollar at 1.2578 in February 2015 made travel to the US less attractive to Canadians than when the US dollar was at $0.9681 in May 2012.

Based on this limited information, we would come to the conclusion that it has taken *fewer* Canadian dollars to buy a US dollar over time. In other words, during this particular period the Canadian dollar appreciated or gained strength over the US dollar.

Exchange rates can rise and fall dramatically within a short period. Exhibit 16–13 shows how the US dollar has had periods in which it is falling and then rising. Buying goods in US dollars in April 2014 and paying for them in July 2014 makes money for the Canadian company because the exchange rate has decreased, which means each US dollar costs less. Buying goods in July 2014 and paying for them at any time later costs money for the Canadian company because the exchange rate has increased—each US dollar costs more.

Foreign-Currency Transactions

When a Canadian company transacts business with a foreign company, the transaction price can be stated either in Canadian dollars or in the national currency of the other company or in any other currency that is stipulated by contract. This

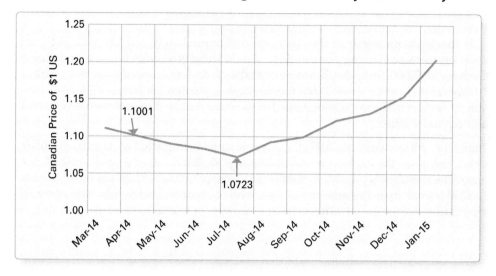

adds risk to the transactions because, as we just saw, exchange rates fluctuate over time.

Bombardier Inc. wrote in the Management Discussion and Analysis section of its 2013 annual report that for the Bombardier Aerospace (BA) division,

> A U.S. one-cent change in the value of the Canadian dollar compared to the U.S. dollar would impact BA's expected costs for the 12-month period ending December 31, 2014 by approximately $29 million . . .

First we will look at how to record transactions when foreign currencies are exchanged, and then we will look briefly at ways to minimize foreign-exchange risk.

Paying Cash in a Foreign Currency

If the transaction price is stated in units of the foreign currency, the Canadian company encounters two accounting steps. First, the transaction price must be translated into Canadian dollars for recording in the accounting records. Second, these transactions usually cause the Canadian company to experience a **foreign-currency transaction gain** or **foreign-currency transaction loss**. This type of gain or loss occurs when the exchange rate changes between the date of the purchase or sale on account and the date of the subsequent payment or receipt of cash.

If a company purchases products from a supplier in another country, Accounts Payable is created. It is recorded at the exchange rate in effect at the time of the transaction. Later, when the company pays the invoice, the exchange rate has almost certainly changed. Accounts Payable is debited for the amount recorded earlier, and Cash is credited for the amount paid at the current exchange rate. A debit difference is a loss, and a credit difference is a gain.

Purchase Date   Suppose on December 13, 2016, The Petit Parfum Boutique in Barrie imports Shalimar perfume from a French supplier at a price of 75,000 euros (which can also be shown as €75,000). If the exchange rate is $1.56 per euro, the Boutique records this credit purchase as follows:

KEY POINTS

For an accounts payable transaction, there is a *loss* if the exchange rate has moved *higher* in the period between the purchase and the payment. There is a *gain* if the exchange rate has moved *lower*.

2016			
Dec. 13	Inventory	117,000	
	Accounts Payable		117,000
	To record a purchase on credit (€75,000 × $1.56 per euro).		

The Boutique translates the euro price of the merchandise (€75,000) into Canadian dollars ($117,000) for recording the purchase and the related account payable.

If the Boutique were to pay this account immediately (which is unlikely in most business scenarios), the Boutique would debit Accounts Payable and credit Cash for $117,000. Suppose, however, that the credit terms specify payment within 60 days and suppose as well that the Boutique's year end is January 31, 2017. It is almost certain that the exchange rate for the euro will be different on the year-end and payment dates.

Year End On January 31, 2017, the payable must be reported at its current dollar value. Suppose the exchange rate at January 31, 2017, has changed to $1.57 per euro. The Boutique's payable would be $117,750 (€75,000 × $1.57 per euro), which is $750 higher than the amount of the payable recorded originally. The entry to record this change in the euro exchange rate at year end is:

2017			
Jan. 31	Foreign-Currency Transaction Loss	750	
	Accounts Payable		750
	To record the change in the exchange rate of the euro at year end [€75,000 × ($1.57 − $1.56)].		

Payment Date On February 2, 2017, when the Boutique pays this debt, suppose the exchange rate has changed to $1.58 per euro. The Boutique's payment entry is:

$117,000 purchase + $750 year-end exchange

Feb. 2	Accounts Payable	117,750	
	Foreign-Currency Transaction Loss	750	
	Cash		118,500
	To record payment of the account for a credit purchase (€75,000 × $1.58).		

The Boutique has a loss because the company has settled the debt with more dollars than the adjusted accounts payable balance. If on the payment date the exchange rate of the euro was less than $1.56, the Boutique would have paid fewer dollars than the $117,750 year-end valuation of the payable. The company would have recorded a gain on the transaction as a credit to Foreign-Currency Transaction Gain.

Collecting Cash in a Foreign Currency

International sales on account may also be measured in foreign currency.

Sale Date Suppose Bombardier sells some products to an American customer on January 30, 2017. The price of the products is US$140,000, and the exchange rate is $1.04. Bombardier's sale entry is:

Jan. 30	Accounts Receivable	145,600	
	Sales Revenue		145,600
	To record a sale on account (US$140,000 × $1.04).		

Collection Date Assume Bombardier collects from the American customer on March 2, 2017, when the exchange rate has fallen to $1.02. Bombardier receives fewer Canadian dollars than the recorded amount of the receivable and so experiences a foreign-currency transaction loss. The collection entry is:

Mar. 2	Cash	142,800	
	Foreign-Currency Transaction Loss	2,800	
	Accounts Receivable		145,600
	To record collection of a receivable (US$140,000 × $1.02).		

Foreign-currency transaction gains and losses are combined for each accounting period. The net amount of gain or loss can be reported as Other Revenue and Expense on the income statement.

Year-End Adjustment In addition, the year-end balance for accounts receivable must be updated to show any foreign currency amounts at the exchange rate in effect on the date of the financial statements. The gain or loss would be recorded to the same accounts as shown above.

REAL WORLD EXAMPLE

When a subsidiary prepares financial statements in a currency other than Canadian dollars, the subsidiary must translate the financial statements into Canadian dollars for the consolidated financial statements at the exchange rate in effect on the date of the financial statements.

Minimizing Risk

One way for Canadian companies to avoid foreign-currency transaction losses is to insist that international transactions be settled in Canadian dollars. This requirement puts the burden of currency translation on the foreign party. However, such a strategy may alienate customers and decrease sales, or it may cause customers to demand unreasonable credit terms to compensate for the risk they would need to take in the transaction.

Hedging Another way for a company to protect itself from the effects of fluctuating foreign-currency exchange rates is by hedging. **Hedging** means protecting oneself from losing money in one transaction by engaging in a **counterbalancing transaction**—a second, related transaction to offset the risk of the first one. Such an arrangement can be set up using one of several tactics—this example assumes that the company has a roughly equal amount of receivables and payables in different currencies.

Let's go back to the Boutique example for a moment. If the company sold goods online to be paid for in Mexican pesos, it would expect to receive a fixed number of pesos in the future. If the peso is losing value, the Canadian company would expect the pesos to be worth fewer dollars than the amount of the receivable—an expected loss situation. However, since the Boutique will accumulate payables stated in a different foreign currency—the euro, in this case—losses on the receipt of pesos may be approximately offset by gains on the payment of euros to the French supplier.

There are other strategies available for managing risk—**futures contracts, forward contracts**, and **currency options** to name a few—but they are outside the scope of this text and will be covered in more advanced accounting and finance courses.

11. In each of the following situations, determine whether the Canadian company will experience a foreign-currency transaction gain or loss, and explain why:

   a. A Canadian company purchased car parts from a German supplier at a price of 200,000 euros. On the date of the credit purchase, the exchange rate of the euro was $1.0891. On the payment date, the exchange rate of the euro is $1.0723. The payment is in euros.

   b. A Canadian company sold merchandise to a Danish company at a price of 500,000 kroner. On the date of the credit sale, the exchange rate of the krone was $0.20962. On the day the payment is received in kroner, the exchange rate of the krone is $0.21325.

(Continued)

(Continued)

    c. A Canadian company purchased electronics from a Japanese supplier at a price of 1,200,000 yen. On the date of the credit purchase, the exchange rate of the yen was $0.01172. On the payment date, the exchange rate of the yen is $0.01221. The payment is in yen.

    d. A Canadian company sold merchandise to a US company at a price of US$15,000. On the date of the credit sale, the exchange rate of the US dollar was $1.0891. On the day the payment is received in US dollars, the exchange rate of the US dollar is $1.0624.

12. Suppose Zippy Ltd. sells maple syrup to a British company on May 16. Zippy agrees to accept 80,000 British pounds sterling. On the date of sale, the pound is quoted at $1.7831. Zippy collects half the receivable on June 19, when the pound is worth $1.7614. Then, on July 16, when the price of the pound is $1.7792, Zippy collects the final amount. Journalize these three transactions for Zippy; include an explanation. Overall, did Zippy have a net foreign-currency gain or loss?

Solutions appear at the end of this chapter and on MyAccountingLab

LO 7

How does IFRS apply to investments and international transactions?

THE IMPACT OF IFRS ON ACCOUNTING FOR INVESTMENTS AND INTERNATIONAL TRANSACTIONS

ASPE		IFRS

Equity Investments

No Significant Influence (non-strategic investments)

ASPE	IFRS
Report using fair value or cost (if fair value is too difficult or costly to obtain).	Most **financial instruments** must be measured at fair value (market value). In many cases, determining the fair value can be difficult and costly. There is no option to measure at cost.
Gains and losses are reported under Net Income.	Gains and losses are reported under Other Comprehensive Income.

Where there is significant influence (strategic investments)

ASPE	IFRS
Use the cost or equity method.	Only the equity method may be used.
Significant influence depends on the situation rather than a specific percentage.	Significant influence is a **rebuttable presumption**. It is *presumed* that if an investor holds, directly or indirectly, 20 percent or more of the voting power of the investee it has significant influence, unless it can be clearly demonstrated that this is not the case.
Reversal of impairment losses is not permitted over the original cost.	Reversals of impairment losses are permitted and it is possible to increase the asset above its cost.

Joint Ventures

ASPE	IFRS
Reported using proportionate consolidation, equity, or cost method.* * Effective 2016, this is replaced by section 3056 of the *CPA Canada Handbook*.	Differentiates between *joint operations* and *joint ventures*. *Joint ventures* are accounted for using the equity method. *Joint operations* are accounted for by recording the owners' share of each of the accounts of the business according to the IFRS treatment for each account.

Where there is control (majority interest)

ASPE	IFRS
The parent company must consolidate its subsidiaries' financial results.	The parent company must consolidate its subsidiaries' financial results.

There is no guidance about where to report minority interest on the balance sheet.	Minority interest must be presented within the equity section, but separate from the parent's shareholders' equity.
Investments in Debt Instruments	
Short-term investments in bonds	
The standards are converged. Both suggest that these investments are measured and reported at fair value. (Use the cost method if no market price is available.)	
Long-term investments in bonds	
Amortized cost method uses either straight-line amortization or the effective-interest-rate method.	Must use the effective-interest-rate method.
Foreign-currency transactions	
Translation gains and losses are usually reported as Other Revenue and Expense.	Translation gains or losses are included in Other Comprehensive Income.
Hedging	
There are fewer categories of transactions that qualify as hedging relationships.	General cash flow hedges and fair value hedges are reported.

SUMMARY PROBLEMS FOR YOUR REVIEW

1. The January 31, 2017, year-end balance sheet of Shijie Corp. included an Investment in Bran Ltd. account in the amount of $10,000,000. The balance in the Short-Term Investments account was $86,000. Suppose the company completed the following investment transactions:

2017

Apr. 8	Purchased 3,000 common shares as a short-term investment, paying $25.00 per share plus brokerage commission of $400.
19	Purchased additional common shares in Bran Ltd. at a cost of $1,750,000. Commissions on the purchase were $30,000. Shijie Corp now owns 31 percent of Bran Ltd.'s equity. Shijie does not have control over Bran Ltd.
Sep. 15	Received the semi-annual cash dividend of $0.15 per share on the short-term investment purchased April 8.
Oct. 16	Sold 750 shares of the short-term investment purchased on April 8 for $28.00 per share, less brokerage commission of $300.
Dec. 1	Received a cash dividend of $150,000 from Bran Ltd.

2018

Jan. 31	Bran Ltd. reported total net income for the year of $2,100,000. Assume that the short-term investment's book value is the same as their market value at this date.

Required

a. Record the transactions in the general journal of Shijie Corp.

b. What are the balances in the Investments accounts at January 31, 2018?

2. Journalize the following transactions of Canada Corp.:

2016

Nov. 16   Purchased equipment on account for US$40,000 when the exchange rate was $1.07 per US dollar.

27   Sold merchandise on account to a Swiss company for 700,000 Swiss francs. Each Swiss franc is worth $0.81.

Dec. 22   Paid the US company when the US dollar's exchange rate was $1.05.

31   Adjusted for the change in the exchange rate of the Swiss franc. Its current exchange rate is $0.80.

2017

Jan. 4   Collected from the Swiss company. The exchange rate is $0.82.

SOLUTION

Requirement 1 a.

2017			
Apr. 8	Short-Term Investments	75,000	
	Brokerage Commissions Expense	400	
	Cash		75,400
	Purchased 3,000 shares at $25.00 plus commission of $400.		
19	Investment in Bran Ltd. Common Shares	1,750,000	
	Brokerage Commissions Expense	30,000	
	Cash		1,780,000
	Purchased additional shares of Bran Ltd.		
Sep.15	Cash	450	
	Dividend Revenue		450
	Received $0.15 per share cash dividend on short-term investment (3,000 × $0.15).		
Oct. 16	Cash	20,700	
	Brokerage Commissions Expense	300	
	Gain on Sale of Short-Term Investment		2,250
	Short-Term Investments		18,750
	Sold 750 shares of a short-term investment purchased Apr. 8. ($75,000 × 750/3,000 shares). Received cash of (750 × $28) − $300		
Dec. 1	Cash	150,000	
	Investment in Bran Ltd. Common Shares		150,000
	Received cash dividends from Bran Ltd.		
2018			
Jan. 31	Investment in Bran Ltd. Common Shares	651,000	
	Equity Method Investment Revenue		651,000
	To record proportion of Bran Ltd.'s net income ($2,100,000 × 0.31).		

Brokerage commissions are expensed and not capitalized.

Dividend and interest income on short-term investments are reported as revenue.

This is a gain because the shares were sold for $21,000 (750 × $28) less $300 commission yet they were valued at $18,750 ($25 × 750).

Requirement 1 b.

Investment in Bran Ltd.

2017						
Feb. 1	Balance	10,000,000	Dec. 1	Dividends	150,000
Apr. 19	Purchase	1,750,000			
2018					
Jan. 31	Net income	651,000			
Jan. 31	Balance	12,251,000			

Short-Term Investments

2017						
Feb. 1	Balance	86,000	Oct. 16	Sale	18,750
Apr. 8	Purchase	75,000			
2018					
Jan. 31	Balance	142,250			

Problem 2

Entries for transactions stated in foreign currencies:

2016			
Nov. 16	Equipment	42,800	
	Accounts Payable		42,800
	To record a purchase on credit (40,000 × $1.07).		
27	Accounts Receivable	567,000	
	Sales Revenue		567,000
	To record a sale on account (700,000 × $0.81).		
Dec. 22	Accounts Payable	42,800	
	Cash		42,000
	Foreign-Currency Transaction Gain		800
	To record payment of a credit purchase (40,000 × $1.05).		
31	Foreign-Currency Transaction Loss	7,000	
	Accounts Receivable		7,000
	Year-end exchange rate adjustment [700,000 × ($0.81 − $0.80)].		
2017			
Jan. 4	Cash	574,000	
	Accounts Receivable		560,000
	Foreign-Currency Transaction Gain		14,000
	Collection of account receivable = (700,000 × $0.82) Accounts Receivable ($567,000 − $7,000) Gain = [700,000 × ($0.92 − $0.90)]		

Always use the exchange rates in effect on the date of a transaction. When journalizing the payment or receipt for a foreign-currency transaction, calculate the cash payment or receipt amount first.
Then,
Cash payment > Payable
→ F-C transaction loss
Cash payment < Payable
→ F-C transaction gain
Cash receipt > Receivable
→ F-C transaction gain
Cash receipt < Receivable
→ F-C transaction loss

SUMMARY

LEARNING OBJECTIVE 1 Account for short-term investments

How do we account for short-term investments?   Pg. 912

- Use the fair value (or market value) method:
  - Change in value at year end is an unrealized gain or loss in the non-operating section of the income statement under "Other gains and losses."
  - Dividends and interest are recorded as income.
  - Brokerage commission fees are expensed.

LEARNING OBJECTIVE 2 Account for long-term share investments

How do we account for long-term share investments?   Pg. 917

Percentage investment in shares	Accounting method
< 20%	Fair value or market value
20% to 50%	Equity
> 50%	Consolidation
Joint venture	Proportionate consolidation*

*current to 2015

LEARNING OBJECTIVE 3 Use the equity method to account for investments

What is the equity method, and how do we use it?   Pg. 920

- Use when there is "significant influence" or ownership of about 20 to 50 percent of the shares.
- Investee income is recorded by the investor by debiting the Investment account and crediting the Equity Method Investment Revenue account.
- The investor records the receipt of dividends from the investee by crediting the Investment account.

LEARNING OBJECTIVE 4 Describe and create consolidated financial statements

What is consolidation, and how do we perform a simple consolidation?   Pg. 925

- Ownership of more than 50 percent of the voting shares—*consolidation* method must be used.
- Parent has "control" over the subsidiary.
- The subsidiary's financial statements are included in the consolidated statements of the parent company.
- Two features of consolidation accounting are:
  1. Addition of the parent and subsidiary accounts to prepare the parent's consolidated statements, and.
  2. Elimination of intercompany items.
- When a parent owns less than 100 percent of the subsidiary's shares, the portion owned by outside investors is called a *non-controlling interest.*

LEARNING OBJECTIVE 5 Account for investments in bonds

How do we record investments in bonds?   Pg. 931

- Long-term investments in bonds are *recorded at cost.* Fees are capitalized.
- Bonds are reported at their *amortized cost,* which means the discount or premium is amortized to account more precisely for interest revenue over the period the bonds will be held.
- At maturity the investor will receive the face value of the bonds.

LEARNING OBJECTIVE 6 Account for foreign-currency transactions

How do we record transactions in foreign currencies?   Pg. 935

- Foreign-currency transaction gains:
  - When a company receives foreign currency worth *more* in Canadian dollars than the amount of the receivable recorded earlier.

- When a company pays foreign currency that costs *less* in Canadian dollars than the amount of the payable recorded earlier.
- Foreign-currency transaction losses:
  - When a company receives foreign currency worth *less* in Canadian dollars than the amount of the receivable recorded earlier.
  - When a company pays foreign currency that costs *more* in Canadian dollars than the amount of the payable recorded earlier.

LEARNING OBJECTIVE 7 Identify the impact of IFRS on accounting for investments and international transactions

How does IFRS apply to investments and international transactions?　　　　　　　　**Pg. 940**

- In general, IFRS and ASPE require the same or similar treatment of investments and foreign-currency transactions.
- In many cases, ASPE allows companies more options for accounting for their investments.

Check **Accounting Vocabulary** below for all key terms used in Chapter 16 and the Glossary at the back of the book for all key terms used in the textbook.

MORE CHAPTER REVIEW MATERIAL

MyAccountingLab

Student PowerPoint Slides

Audio Chapter Summary

Note: All MyAccountingLab resources can be found in the Chapter Resources section and the Multimedia Library.

ACCOUNTING VOCABULARY

Actively traded　Financial instruments that are easily bought or sold because there are a lot of them in the market and it is easy to find someone who is willing to engage in a transaction (*p. 913*).

Affiliated company　An investment in a company in which there is significant influence and 20 to 50 percent ownership. These investments are accounted for using the equity method (*p. 922*).

Amortized cost method　To account for long-term bond investments, the discount or premium is amortized to more accurately reflect the interest revenue. These bonds are reported at their amortized cost (*p. 932*).

Carrying value　The amount at which an asset is reported on the balance sheet (*p. 915*).

Certificate of deposit　A secure form of investment with a fixed interest rate and term. Unlike a bank account, they must be held to maturity (*p. 913*).

Companion account　An account that is typically paired up with another account (*p. 915*).

Consolidated financial statements　Financial statements of the parent company plus those of majority-owned subsidiaries as if the combination were a single legal entity (*p. 923*).

Controlling interest　Ownership of more than 50 percent of an investee company's voting shares. Also called *majority interest* (*p. 923*).

Counterbalancing transaction　Engaging in a second transaction to offset the risk of the first transaction (*p. 939*).

Currency options　A contract that can be purchased to guarantee the right to a future exchange rate (*p. 939*).

Equity method for investments　The method used to account for investments in which the investor generally has 20 to 50 percent of the investee's voting shares and can significantly influence the decisions of the investee. The investment account is debited for ownership in the investee's net income and credited for ownership in the investee's dividends (*p. 920*).

Fair value method　The method of accounting for shares held as short-term investments that values them at their fair, or market, value on the year-end balance sheet date. Any gain or loss resulting from the change in fair value is recognized in net income for the period in which it arises, and fair value becomes the new carrying value of the shares. Also called the *market value method* (*p. 914*).

Financial instrument　A contract that creates an asset for one party and a liability or equity for another (*p. 940*).

Foreign-currency exchange rate　The measure of one currency against another currency (*p. 935*).

Foreign-currency transaction gain　The gain that occurs when a cash payment is less than the related account payable or a cash receipt is greater than the related account receivable due to a change in exchange rate between the transaction date and the payment date (*p. 937*).

Foreign-currency transaction loss The loss that occurs when a cash payment is greater than the related account payable or a cash receipt is less than the related account receivable due to a change in exchange rate between the transaction date and the payment date (*p. 937*).

Forward contract An agreement to purchase at a specified future date and price (*p. 939*).

Futures contract A contract that can be purchased to guarantee the right to a product at a specified price in the future (*p. 939*).

Hedging A way to protect oneself from losing money in a foreign-currency transaction by engaging in a counterbalancing foreign-currency transaction (*p. 939*).

Joint venture When two or more businesses enter into a contractual arrangement to own a separate entity or project. In 2016 this term will change to *joint arrangement* (*p. 922*).

Long-term investments Investments that a company intends to hold for more than one year (*p. 913*).

Majority interest Another name for *controlling interest* (*p. 923*).

Market value method Another name for the *fair value method* of accounting for short-term investments in shares (*p. 914*).

Minority interest Another name for *non-controlling interest* (*p. 928*).

Money market fund An investment product generally considered safe because it invests in short-term debt securities, such as certificates of deposit (*p. 913*).

Non-controlling interest A subsidiary company's equity that is held by shareholders other than the parent company. Also called *minority interest* (*p. 928*).

Parent company An investor company that generally owns more than 50 percent of the voting shares of a subsidiary company (*p. 923*).

Proportionate consolidation The venturer combines its share of the interest in the assets, liabilities, revenues, and expenses of a joint venture with its own assets, liabilities, revenues, and expenses in its consolidated financial statements (*p. 922*).

Rebuttable assumption A conclusion that something is true unless proven that it isn't (*p. 940*).

Segmented information Financial information presented in the notes to the financial statements either by industry or by geography (*p. 930*).

Short-term investments Investments that management intends to hold for less than one year (*p. 913*).

Significant influence When a company participates in the decision making of another company without having full control over it (*p. 913*).

Strong currency A currency that is rising relative to other nations' currencies (*p. 936*).

Subsidiary An investee company in which a parent company owns more than 50 percent of the voting shares (*p. 923*).

Translation Another term for a currency conversion or foreign-currency exchange (*p. 936*).

Treasury bills A short-term debt obligation issued by a government (*p. 913*).

Weak currency A currency that is falling relative to other nations' currencies (*p. 936*).

Write-down An accounting entry to recognize the decrease in the value of an asset by debiting an expense account and crediting the asset account (*p. 922*).

SIMILAR ACCOUNTING TERMS

CD	Certificates of deposit
Controlling interest	Majority interest
Fair value method	Market value method
Minority interest	Non-controlling interest
Short-term investments	Marketable securities; Temporary investments
Translation	Foreign-currency conversion
Trade shares	Buy/sell shares

SELF-STUDY QUESTIONS

Test your understanding of the chapter by marking the best answer for each of the following questions:

1. Short-term investments are reported on the balance sheet (*p. 913*)
   a. Immediately after inventory
   b. Immediately after accounts receivable
   c. Immediately after cash
   d. Immediately after current assets

2. Byforth Inc. distributes a stock dividend. An investor who owns Byforth Inc. shares as a short-term investment should (*pp. 914–915*)
   a. Debit Short-Term Investments and credit Dividend Revenue for the book value of the shares received in the dividend distribution
   b. Debit Short-Term Investments and credit Dividend Revenue for the market value of the shares received in the dividend distribution

c. Debit Cash and credit Short-Term Investments for the market value of the shares received in the dividend distribution

d. Make a memorandum entry to record the new cost per share of Byforth Inc. shares held

3. Short-term investments are reported at the (*pp. 915–916*)
   a. Total cost of the portfolio
   b. Total fair value of the portfolio
   c. Lower of total cost or total fair value of the portfolio, or lower of cost or fair value on an investment-by-investment basis
   d. Total equity value of the portfolio

4. Mulgarvey Corporation owns 30 percent of the voting shares of Turner Inc. Turner Inc. reports net income of $200,000 and declares and pays cash dividends of $80,000. Which method should Mulgarvey Corporation use to account for this investment? (*p. 920*)
   a. Cost
   b. Equity
   c. Fair value
   d. Consolidation

5. Refer to the facts of the preceding question. What effect do Turner Inc.'s income and dividends have on Mulgarvey Corporation's net income? (*pp. 920–922*)
   a. Increase of $24,000
   b. Increase of $36,000
   c. Increase of $60,000
   d. Increase of $84,000

6. In applying the consolidation method, elimination entries are (*p. 923*)
   a. Necessary
   b. Required only when the parent has a receivable from or a payable to the subsidiary
   c. Required only when there is a minority interest
   d. Required only for the preparation of the consolidated balance sheet

7. Parent Corp. reports net income of $200,000. Sub A Ltd., of which Parent Corp. owns 90 percent, reports net income of $80,000, and Sub B Ltd., of which Parent Corp. owns 60 percent, reports net income of $100,000. What is Parent Corp.'s consolidated net income? (*p. 930*)
   a. $200,000
   b. $332,000
   c. $335,000
   d. $380,000

8. On May 16, the exchange rate of the euro was $1.50. On May 20, the exchange rate was $1.52. Which of the following statements is true? (*p. 936*)
   a. The Canadian dollar has risen against the euro.
   b. The Canadian dollar has fallen against the euro.
   c. The Canadian dollar is stronger than the euro.
   d. The Canadian dollar and the euro are equally strong.

9. A strong Canadian dollar encourages (*p. 936*)
   a. Travel to Canada by foreigners
   b. Purchase of Canadian goods by foreigners
   c. Canadians to save dollars
   d. Canadians to travel abroad

10. Canadian Furniture Inc. purchased dining room suites from an English supplier at a price of 400,000 British pounds sterling. On the date of the credit purchase, the exchange rate of the British pound was $1.75. On the payment date, the exchange rate of the pound is $1.77. If payment is in pounds, Canadian Furniture experiences (*pp. 937–938*)
    a. A foreign-currency transaction gain of $8,000
    b. A foreign-currency transaction loss of $8,000
    c. Neither a transaction gain nor loss because the debt is paid in Canadian dollars
    d. None of the above

Answers to Self-Study Questions

1. c 2. d 3. b 4. b 5. c ($200,000 × 0.30 = $60,000; dividends have no effect on investor net income under the equity method) 6. a 7. b [$200,000 + ($80,000 × 0.90) + ($100,000 × 0.60) = $332,000] 8. b 9. d 10. b [400,000 × ($1.77 − $1.75) = $8,000; a loss since cash payment > payable]

ASSIGNMENT MATERIAL

QUESTIONS

1. If a company buys the shares of another company as an investment, what is the investor's cost of 1,000 Royal Bank of Canada non-cumulative preferred shares at $20.50 with a brokerage commission of $300?
2. What distinguishes a short-term investment in shares from a long-term investment in shares?
3. Show the positions of short-term investments and long-term investments on the balance sheet.
4. At the end of a fiscal period, all equity investments that are traded on public stock exchanges must be revalued on the balance sheet to their market value. Does this policy provide better information for the investor? Explain.
5. How does an investor record the receipt of a cash dividend on an investment accounted for by the fair value method? How does this investor record receipt of a stock dividend?

6. An investor paid $30,000 for 1,000 common shares and later that same year received a 10 percent stock dividend. Compute the gain or loss on sale of 500 common shares for $15,000 before year end.

7. Are the short-term and long-term equity investment portfolios mixed on the balance sheet, or are they kept separate?

8. When is an investment accounted for by the equity method? Outline how to apply the equity method. Include in your answer how to record the purchase of the investment, the investor's proportion of the investee's net income, and receipt of a cash dividend from the investee. Indicate how a gain or loss on the sale of the investment would be measured.

9. Identify three transactions that cause debits or credits to an equity method investment account.

10. What are two special features of the consolidation method for investments?

11. Why are intercompany items eliminated from consolidated financial statements? Name two intercompany items that are eliminated.

12. Name the account that expresses the excess of cost of an investment over the fair market value of the subsidiary's net assets. What type of account is this, and where in the financial statements is it reported?

13. When a parent company buys more than 50 percent but less than 100 percent of a subsidiary's shares, a certain type of equity is created. What is it called, and how do most companies report it?

14. How would you measure the net income of a parent company with three subsidiaries? Assume that two subsidiaries are wholly owned (100 percent) and that the parent owns 60 percent of the third subsidiary.

15. Weel Soo purchases Canadian Utilities Inc. bonds as a long-term investment. Suppose the face amount of the

bonds is $300,000 and the purchase price is 101.30. The bonds pay interest at the stated annual rate of 8 percent. How much did Soo pay for the bonds? How much principal will Soo collect at maturity?

16. The purchase date of the bond investment in the preceding question was August 1, 2017. The bonds pay semiannual interest on January 31 and July 31. How much interest will Soo earn during the year ended December 31, 2017?

17. Mentacos Inc. purchased inventory from a French company, agreeing to pay 150,000 euros. On the purchase date, the euro was quoted at $1.55. When Mentacos Inc. paid the debt, the price of a euro was $1.57. What account does Mentacos Inc. debit for the $3,000 difference between the cost of the inventory and the amount of cash paid?

18. Which of the following situations results in a foreign-currency transaction gain for a Canadian business? Which situation results in a loss?

   a. Credit purchase denominated in pesos, followed by weakness in the peso

   b. Credit purchase denominated in pesos, followed by weakness in the dollar

   c. Credit sale denominated in pesos, followed by weakness in the peso

   d. Credit sale denominated in pesos, followed by weakness in the dollar

19. What is the main difference between IFRS and ASPE for short-term investments?

20. What is the main difference between IFRS and ASPE for investments in subsidiaries?

MyAccountingLab

Make the grade with MyAccountingLab: Most of the Starters, Exercises, and Problems marked in red can be found on MyAccountingLab. You can practise them as often as you want, and most feature step-by-step guided instructions to help you find the right answer.

STARTERS

Computing the cost of an investment in shares

①

a. $9,075
b. $44,400

Starter 16–1 Compute the cost of each of the following short-term investments. Round to the nearest dollar.

a. 550 shares of Grey Ltd. at $16.50 per share. Brokerage fees were $175.

b. 600 shares of Red Corp. at $74 per share. Red Corp. pays a cash dividend of $0.66 per year. Brokerage fees were $550.

c. 1,000 shares of White Inc. at $55.10 per share. Brokerage fees were $560.

d. 70 shares of Tangerine Ltd. at $35.50 per share. Brokerage fees were $250.

Starter 16-2

Journalize Cold Publishing Ltd.'s investment transactions. Explanations are not required.

2016

Dec. 6   Purchased 1,000 shares of Georgian Graphics Inc. at a price of $41.00 per share, intending to sell the investment within three months. Brokerage fees were $350.

    23   Received a cash dividend of $1.10 per share on the Georgian Graphics Inc. shares.

    31   Adjusted the investment to its fair value of $45.00 per share.

2017

Jan. 27   Sold the Georgian Graphics Inc. shares for $46.00 per share, less brokerage fees of $370.

Accounting for a short-term investment

①

Jan. 27, 2017, gain on sale, $1,000

Starter 16-3

McBain Electronics completed the following investment transactions during 2016 and 2017:

2016

Dec. 12   Purchased 1,500 shares of Blackmore Ltd. at a price of $62.00 per share, intending to sell the investment within the next year. Commissions were $510.

    21   Received a cash dividend of $0.48 per share on the Blackmore Ltd. shares.

    31   Adjusted the investment to its fair value of $61.50 per share.

2017

Jan. 16   Sold the Blackmore Ltd. shares for $59.00 per share, less commissions of $490.

1. Classify McBain's investment as short term or long term.

2. Journalize McBain's investment transactions. Explanations are not required.

Accounting for a short-term investment

①

2. Jan. 16, 2017, loss on sale, $3,750

Starter 16-4

Baines Corp. purchased 1,000 common shares in each of three companies:

a. Investment in Cullen Corp. to be sold within the next 9 to 12 months.

b. Investment in Gerson Canada Ltd. to be sold within the next 90 days.

c. Investment in Arnold Ltd. to be sold within the next two years.

Classify each investment as a current asset or a long-term asset. None of these investments is subject to significant influence.

Classifying investments as short term or long term

① ②

Starter 16-5

Gerber Ltd. buys 2,000 of the 100,000 shares of Efron Inc., paying $35.00 per share. Suppose Efron distributes a 10 percent stock dividend. Later the same year, Gerber Ltd. sells the Efron shares for $29.00 per share. Disregard commissions on the purchase and sale.

1. Compute Gerber Ltd.'s new cost per share after receiving the stock dividend.

2. Compute Gerber Ltd.'s gain or loss on the sale of this long-term investment.

Measuring gain or loss on the sale of a share investment after receiving a stock dividend

②

2. Loss on sale, $6,200

Starter 16-6

Marsland Inc. completed these long-term investment transactions during 2017. Disregard commissions.

Jan. 14   Purchased 1,000 shares of Crew Ltd., paying $41.00 per share. Marsland intends to hold the investment for the indefinite future.

Aug. 22   Received a cash dividend of $3.28 per share on the Crew Ltd. shares.

Dec. 31   Adjusted the Crew Ltd. investment to its current fair value of $50,750.

Accounting for a long-term investment's unrealized gain or loss

②

1. Dec. 31, 2017, unrealized gain, $9,750

1. Journalize Marsland's investment transactions. Explanations are not required. Marsland Inc. exerts no significant influence on Crew Ltd.

2. Show how to report the investment and any unrealized gain or loss on Marsland's balance sheet at December 31, 2017.

Accounting for the sale of a
long-term investment
(2)

1. Gain on sale, $2,250

Starter 16–7 Use the data given in Starter 16-6. On August 4, 2018, Marsland Inc. sold its investment in Crew Ltd. for $53.00 per share. Disregard commissions.

1. Journalize the sale. No explanation is required.

2. How does the gain or loss that you recorded differ from the gain or loss that was recorded at December 31, 2017 (in Starter 16–6)?

Accounting for a 40 percent
investment in another company
(3)

3. Bal. $5,400,000

Starter 16–8 Suppose on January 6, 2017, Ling Corp. paid $5,000,000 for its 40 percent investment in True World Inc. Assume True World earned net income of $1,800,000 and paid cash dividends of $800,000 during 2017. Disregard commissions.

1. What method should Ling Corp. use to account for the investment in True World Inc.? Give your reason.

2. Journalize these three transactions on the books of Ling Corp. Include an explanation for each entry.

3. Post to the Investment in True World Inc. Common Shares T-account. What is its balance after all the transactions are posted?

Understanding consolidated
financial statements
(4)

Starter 16–9 Answer these questions about consolidation accounting:

1. Define "parent company." Define "subsidiary."

2. Which company's name appears on the consolidated financial statements? How much of the subsidiary's shares must the parent own before reporting consolidated statements?

3. How do consolidated financial statements differ from the financial statements of a single company?

Matching reporting methods
(1)(2)(3)(4)(5)

Starter 16–10 Match the following situations with the appropriate measurement method (letters may be used more than once):

1. Bonds held to maturity	A. Equity method
2. More than 50 percent ownership	B. Consolidation
3. Bonds held for less than one year	C. Fair value method
4. Between 20 and 50 percent ownership	D. Proportionate consolidation
5. Less than 20 percent ownership	E. Amortized cost
6. Joint venture	

Working with a bond investment
(5)

3. Annual interest revenue,
$66,000

Starter 16–11 Heinz Ltd. owns vast amounts of corporate bonds. Suppose the company buys $1,000,000 of Kuzawa Corporation bonds on January 2, 2017, at a price of 97. The Kuzawa bonds pay cash interest at the annual rate of 6 percent and mature on December 31, 2021.

1. How much did Heinz Ltd. pay to purchase the bond investment? How much will Heinz Ltd. collect when the bond investment matures?

2. How much cash interest will Heinz Ltd. receive each year from Kuzawa Corporation?

3. Compute Heinz Ltd.'s annual interest revenue on this bond investment. Use the straight-line method to amortize the discount on the investment.

Recording bond investment
transactions
(5)

b. Cash interest received,
$60,000

Starter 16–12 Return to Starter 16–11, the Heinz Ltd. investment in Kuzawa Corporation bonds. Journalize the following transactions on Heinz Ltd.'s books, along with an explanation:

a. Purchase of the bond investment on January 2, 2017. As Heinz Ltd. expects to hold the investment to maturity, it is classified as a long-term investment.

b. Receipt of the annual cash interest on December 31, 2017.

c. Amortization of the discount on December 31, 2017.

d. Collection of the investment's face value at its maturity date on December 31, 2021. (Assume that the interest and amortization of discount for 2021 have already been recorded, so you may ignore these entries.)

Starter 16–13 Suppose Fleetstar Ltd. sells athletic shoes to a German company on March 14. Fleetstar agrees to accept 2,000,000 euros. On the date of sale, the euro is quoted at $1.56. Fleetstar collects half the receivable on April 19, when the euro is worth $1.55. Then, on May 10, when the price of the euro is $1.58, Fleetstar collects the final amount.

Journalize these three transactions for Fleetstar; include an explanation. Overall, did Fleetstar have a net foreign-currency gain or loss?

Accounting for transactions stated in a foreign currency

⑥

Net foreign-currency gain, $10,000

Starter 16–14 Fill in the blanks to indicate how investments are reported under IFRS:

a. Financial instruments are measured at _____.

b. Gains or losses on equity investments with no significant influence are recorded under _____.

c. Significant influence is a rebuttable assumption. It is presumed if an investor holds (directly or indirectly) _____ or more of the votes.

d. Joint ventures are accounted for using the _____ method.

e. Minority interest is shown on the balance sheet _____ but separate from the parent's _____.

f. Short-term investments in bonds are measured and reported at _____.

g. Long-term investments in bonds are amortized using the _____.

IFRS reporting of investments

⑦

EXERCISES

MyAccountingLab

Exercise 16–1

Journalize the following investment transactions of Russell Corp.:

2017

Nov. 6	Purchased 1,200 common shares of Aveda Corporation at $78.00 per share, with brokerage commission of $500. The shares will be sold early in 2018.
30	Received a cash dividend of $3.85 per share on the Aveda Corporation investment.
Dec. 31	The share price for Aveda Corporation's common shares was $76.25 on December 31, 2017, which is Russell Corp.'s year end.

2018

Jun. 14	Sold the Aveda Corporation shares for $79.50 per share. Brokerage fees were $400.

Accounting for a short-term investment

①

June 14, 2018, gain on sale, $3,900

Exercise 16–2

BlackBerry Limited reported the following (adapted) information in the notes accompanying its 2014 financial statements:

Reporting investments at fair value

①

Current Assets	(in millions of US dollars)
Cash and cash equivalents	$1,579
Short-term investments (fair value)	950

Assume that the carrying value of BlackBerry's short-term investments is $945 million prior to the year-end adjustment to fair value.

Required Write a note to identify the method used to report short-term investments and to disclose cost and fair value. Show the journal entry that would have been made by BlackBerry if you determine that a journal entry was needed at year end.

Exercise 16–3

Accounting for a short-term investment

①

Jan. 20, 2018, gain on sale, $1,000

Suppose Carlton Ltd. completed the following investment transactions in 2017 and 2018:

2017

Nov. 6   Purchased 2,000 McGill Corporation common shares for $60,000. Carlton plans to sell the shares in the near future to meet its operating cash flow requirements. Commissions on the purchase were $800.

30   Received a quarterly cash dividend of $1.50 per share on the McGill Corporation shares.

Dec. 31   Current fair value of the McGill common shares is $62,000.

2018

Jan. 20   Sold the McGill Corporation shares for $63,000, less commissions on the sale of $900.

Required

1. Make the entries to record Carlton Ltd.'s investment transactions. Explanations are not required. Carlton Ltd.'s year end is December 31.

2. Show how Carlton Ltd. would report its investment in the McGill Corporation shares on the balance sheet at December 31, 2017.

Exercise 16–4

Classifying equity investments

① ②

Cummins Corp. reports its annual financial results on June 30 each year. Cummins Corp. purchased 1,000 shares in each of three companies. Classify each investment as a short-term or long-term investment.

a. Investment to be sold within the next 9 to 12 months.
b. Investment to be sold within the next 90 days.
c. Investment to be sold within the next two years.

Exercise 16–5

Journalizing transactions for a long-term investment

②

Dec. 4, gain on sale, $6,120

Journalize the following investment transactions of Vantage Inc.:

Aug. 6   Purchased 900 Rhodes Corporation common shares as a long-term investment, paying $90.00 per share. Vantage Inc. exerts no significant influence on Rhodes Corporation. Commissions on the purchase were $900.

Sep. 12   Received cash dividends of $1.60 per share on the Rhodes Corporation investment.

Nov. 23   Received 90 Rhodes Corporation common shares in a 10 percent stock dividend.

Dec. 4   Unexpectedly sold all the Rhodes Corporation shares for $88.00 per share, less commissions on the sale of $750.

Exercise 16–6

Journalizing transactions under the equity method

③

Kinross Gold Corp., introduced in the chapter-opening story, owns equity method investments in several companies. Suppose Kinross paid $12,000,000 to acquire a 40 percent investment in Minecraft Ltd. Further, assume Minecraft Ltd. reported net income of $1,780,000 for the first year and declared and paid cash dividends of $650,000. Record the following entries in Kinross's general journal: (a) purchase of the investment, (b) Kinross's proportion of Minecraft Ltd.'s net income, and (c) receipt of the cash dividends. Disregard commissions on the purchase.

Exercise 16–7

Using the information from Exercise 16–6, calculate the balance in the Investment in Minecraft Ltd. Common Shares account. Assume that after all the above transactions took place, Kinross sold its entire investment in Minecraft Ltd. common shares for $13,100,000 cash. Journalize the sale of the investment. Disregard commissions on sale.

Recording equity method transactions in the accounts
③
Gain on sale, $648,000

Exercise 16–8

⟍ ⟍ > equity method ←

Windsor Corporation paid $760,000 for a 35 percent investment in the common shares of Semmi Systems Inc. For the first year, Semmi Systems Inc. reported net income of $360,000 and at year end declared and paid cash dividends of $105,000. On the balance sheet date, the fair value of Windsor Corporation's investment in Semmi Systems Inc. shares was $780,000.

Applying the appropriate accounting method for investments
② ③

Required

1. Which method is appropriate for Windsor Corporation to use in accounting for its investment in Semmi Systems Inc.? Why?
2. Show everything that Windsor Corporation would report for the investment and any investment revenue in its year-end financial statements.
3. What role does the fair value of the investment play in this situation?

Exercise 16–9

Penfold Ltd. owns all the common shares of Simmons Ltd. Prepare a consolidation worksheet using the following information. Assume that the fair value of the assets and liabilities of Simmons Ltd. are equal to their book values.

Excel Spreadsheet Template
Completing a consolidation worksheet with 100 percent ownership
④
Total consolidated assets, $7,932,000

	Penfold Ltd.	Simmons Ltd.
Assets		
Cash	$ 225,000	$ 55,000
Accounts receivable, net	360,000	264,000
Note receivable from Simmons Ltd	76,000	—
Inventory	258,000	159,000
Investment in Simmons Ltd	2,350,000	—
Property, plant, and equipment, net	3,590,000	2,900,000
Total	$6,859,000	$3,378,000
Liabilities and Shareholders' Equity		
Accounts payable	$ 357,000	$ 180,000
Notes payable	462,000	759,000
Other liabilities	78,000	210,000
Common shares	1,980,000	670,000
Retained earnings	3,982,000	1,559,000
Total	$6,859,000	$3,378,000

Completing a consolidation worksheet with non-controlling interest
④
Total consolidated assets, $2,086,800

Exercise 16–10

Pettigrew Holdings Ltd. owns an 80 percent interest in Shortland Inc. Prepare a consolidation worksheet using the information below. Assume that the fair values of Shortland Inc.'s assets and liabilities are equal to their book values.

	Pettigrew Holdings Ltd.	Shortland Inc.
Assets		
Cash	$ 96,000	$ 36,000
Accounts receivable, net	210,000	144,000
Note receivable from Shortland Inc.	60,000	—
Inventory	246,000	216,000
Investment in Shortland Inc.	228,000	—
Property, plant, and equipment, net	720,000	312,000
Other assets	48,000	42,000
Total	$1,608,000	$750,000
Liabilities and Shareholders' Equity		
Accounts payable	$ 108,000	$ 66,000
Notes payable	120,000	96,000
Other liabilities	204,000	324,000
Non-controlling interest	—	—
Common shares	780,000	204,000
Retained earnings	396,000	60,000
Total	$1,608,000	$750,000

Exercise 16–11

Working with a bond investment

(5)

4. Annual interest revenue, $192,000

Credit Crunchers Ltd. has a large investment in corporate bonds. Suppose Credit Crunchers Ltd. buys $6,000,000 of Government of Alberta bonds at a price of 98. The Government of Alberta bonds pay cash interest at the annual rate of 3.0 percent and mature in 10 years. Credit Crunchers Ltd. plans to hold the bonds until maturity.

Required

1. How much did Credit Crunchers Ltd. pay to purchase the bond investment? How much will Credit Crunchers Ltd. collect when the bond investment matures?

2. How much cash interest will Credit Crunchers Ltd. receive each year from the Government of Alberta?

3. Will Credit Crunchers Ltd.'s annual interest revenue on the bond investment be more or less than the amount of cash interest received each year? Give your reason.

4. Compute Credit Crunchers Ltd.'s annual interest on this bond investment. Use the straight-line method to amortize the discount on the investment.

Exercise 16–12

Recording bond investment transactions using the straight-line method

(5)

3. Balance, $98,541

On March 31, 2017, Kingpin Corp. paid 98.25 for 4 percent bonds of Claim Limited as an investment. The maturity value of the bonds is $100,000 at September 30, 2021; they pay interest on March 31 and September 30. At December 31, 2017, the bonds' market value is 99.25. The company plans to hold the bonds until they mature.

Required

1. How should Kingpin Corp. account for the bonds?

2. Using the straight-line method of amortizing the discount, journalize all transactions on the bonds for 2017.

3. Show how the investment would be reported by Kingpin Corp. on the balance sheet at December 31, 2017.

Recording bond investment transactions using the effective-interest method

(5)

Exercise 16–13

Ace Properties Ltd. purchased a five-year, 4.5 percent Scotia bond on May 1, 2017, and intends to hold it until it matures. The market rate at the time was 5.2 percent. Interest is paid annually each April 30. Information about the bond appears in the table below. Journalize the purchase and the April 30, 2018, entries. Use Exhibit 15–5 on page 852 as a guide. Assume there were no brokerage fees.

Annual Interest Period	Interest Revenue 4.50%	Period Interest Revenue	Discount Amort.	Discount Balance	Bond Carrying Value
May 1, 2017				$30,100	$ 969,900
April 30, 2018	$ 45,000	$ 50,435	$ 5,435	24,665	975,335
April 30, 2019	45,000	50,717	5,717	18,948	981,052
April 30, 2020	45,000	51,015	6,015	12,933	987,067
April 30, 2021	45,000	51,327	6,327	6,606	993,394
April 30, 2022	45,000	51,606	6,606	0	1,000,000
Total	$225,000	$255,100	$30,100		

Exercise 16–14

Journalize the following foreign-currency transactions for Kingsway Import Inc.:

Journalizing foreign-currency transactions
⑥
Dec. 31, 2017, foreign-currency transaction loss, $2,400

2017

Nov. 17   Purchased goods on account from a Japanese company. The price was 500,000 yen, and the exchange rate of the yen was $0.0117.

Dec. 16   Paid the Japanese supplier when the exchange rate was $0.0120.

19   Sold merchandise on account to a French company at a price of 80,000 euros. The exchange rate was $1.57.

31   Adjusted for the decrease in the value of the euro, which had an exchange rate of $1.54. Kingsway Import Inc.'s year end is December 31.

2018

Jan. 14   Collected from the French company. The exchange rate was $1.58.

Exercise 16–15

Indicate the appropriate financial reporting standard by completing each sentence with either "ASPE" or "IFRS" in the blank.

Differences between ASPE and IFRS
① ② ③ ⑤ ⑦

a. Gains and losses are recorded under "other comprehensive income" under _____.
b. Equity investments with no significant influence can only be recorded at cost under _____.
c. Equity investments with over 20 percent ownership must be treated as having significant influence unless proven otherwise under _____.
d. When there is significant influence, impairment losses must be reversed under _____.
e. Joint ventures are accounted for using the proportionate consolidation method under _____.
f. For long-term investments in bonds, the straight-line amortization method is not allowed under _____.

SERIAL EXERCISE

This exercise continues the Lee Consulting Corporation situation from Exercise 15–23 of Chapter 15. If you did not complete Exercise 15–23, you can still complete Exercise 16–16 as it is presented.

Exercise 16–16

After issuing bonds in Chapter 15, Lee Consulting Corporation has some excess cash on hand. Michael Lee, the corporation's major shareholder, intends to invest some of the cash for different time periods to get better returns than from the bank and to have cash available when needed to expand the business into a new market. Assume Lee Consulting Corporation completed the following investment transactions:

Investment transactions
① ② ③ ⑤
2. Dec. 10, 2018, balance, $59,000

2017

Apr. 15	The business purchased 300 common shares of Canadian Tire Corporation, Limited for $114.00 per share. Michael Lee intends to hold this investment for less than a year. He thinks the share value will increase and knows Lee Consulting will need the cash for operations in less than a year. Assume there were no brokerage fees.
Jun. 2	Purchased 2,000 of the 6,000 common shares of Landers Consulting Ltd. at a cost of $40,000. Landers Consulting is a company formed by a colleague of Lee, so Lee hopes the investment will lead to future business opportunities for Lee Consulting.
15	Purchased $10,000 of 6 percent, four-year bonds of Consulting Suppliers Inc. at 115. Lee intends to hold these to maturity since the effective interest rate is still better than other investments he assessed.
Jul. 1	Received the quarterly cash dividend of $0.55 per share on the Canadian Tire investment.
Dec. 10	Received an annual dividend of $0.50 per share from Landers Consulting Ltd. Also received word that at November 30, Landers' year end, net income was $60,000.
15	Received semi-annual interest of $300 on the Consulting Suppliers Inc. bonds. Amortized the premium using the straight-line method.

Required

1. Record the transactions in the general journal of Lee Consulting Corporation. Disregard any commissions on purchases and sales of investments.

2. Post entries to the Investment in Landers Consulting Ltd. Common Shares T-account. Determine its balance at December 10, 2017, after the transaction shown on that date.

CHALLENGE EXERCISE

Exercise 16–17

Analyzing long-term investments

③

2017 dividends, $840

Canfor Corporation is a major integrated forest products company based in Vancouver. Suppose Canfor's financial statements reported the following items for affiliated companies whose shares Canfor owns in various percentages between 20 and 50 percent:

	(In thousands of dollars)	
	2017	**2016**
Balance Sheet (adapted)		
Equity method investments	$6,950	$6,800
Cash Flow Statement		
Increase in equity method investments	350	325
Income Statement		
Equity earnings in affiliates	640	400

Assume no sales of equity method investments during 2016 or 2017.

Required Prepare a T-Account for Equity Method Investments to determine the amount of dividends Canfor Corporation received from investee companies during 2017. The company's year end is December 31. Show your calculations.

BEYOND THE NUMBERS

Beyond the Numbers 16–1

Sophie Bu inherited some investments, and she has received the annual reports of the companies in which the funds are invested. The financial statements of the companies are puzzling to Sophie, and she asks you the following questions:

Analyzing long-term investments
④

a. The companies label their financial statements as *consolidated* balance sheet, *consolidated* income statement, and so on. What are consolidated financial statements?

b. Notes to the statements indicate that "certain intercompany transactions, loans, and other accounts have been eliminated in preparing the consolidated financial statements." Why does a company eliminate transactions, loans, and accounts? Sophie states that she thought a transaction was a transaction and that a loan obligated a company to pay real money. She wonders if the company is juggling the books to defraud the Canada Revenue Agency.

c. The balance sheet lists the asset Goodwill. What is goodwill? Does this mean that the company's shares have increased in value?

Required   Respond to each of Sophie Bu's questions.

ETHICAL ISSUE

Sherman Inc. owns 18 percent of the voting shares of Arbor Corporation. The remainder of the Arbor Corporation shares are held by numerous investors with small holdings. Ken Tung, president of Sherman Inc. and a member of Arbor Corporation's board of directors, heavily influences Arbor Corporation's policies.

Under the fair value method of accounting for investments, Sherman Inc.'s net income increases if or when it receives dividends from Arbor Corporation. Sherman Inc. pays Mr. Tung, as president, a bonus computed as a percentage of Sherman Inc.'s net income. Therefore, Tung can control his personal bonus to a certain extent by influencing Arbor Corporation's dividends.

Sherman Inc. has a bad year in 2017, and corporate income is low. Tung uses his power to have Arbor Corporation pay a large cash dividend. This action requires Arbor Corporation to borrow a substantial sum one month later to pay operating costs.

Required

1. In getting Arbor Corporation to pay the large cash dividend, is Tung acting within his authority as a member of the Arbor Corporation board of directors? Are Tung's actions ethical? Whom can his actions harm?

2. Discuss how using the equity method of accounting for investments would decrease Tung's potential for manipulating his bonus.

PROBLEMS (GROUP A)   MyAccountingLab

Problem 16–1A

Oliver Corp. owns numerous investments in the shares of other companies. Assume Oliver Corp. completed the following investment transactions:

Journalizing transactions under the fair value and equity methods
① ② ③
Feb. 6, 2018, loss on sale, $15,957

2017

May 1	Purchased 12,000 common shares (total issued and outstanding common shares, 50,000) of Larson Corp. at a cost of $950,000. Commissions on the purchase were $20,000.
Jul. 2	Purchased 2,000 Larson Corp. common shares at a cost of $162,000. Commissions on the purchase were $1,500.
Sep. 15	Received semi-annual cash dividend of $3.20 per share on the Larson Corp. investment.
Oct. 12	Purchased 1,000 Sharma Ltd. common shares as a short-term investment, paying $33.00 per share plus brokerage commission of $1,000.

Dec. 14	Received semi-annual cash dividend of $1.50 per share on the Sharma Ltd. investment.	
31	Received annual report from Larson Corp. Net income for the year was $800,000. Of this amount, Oliver Corp.'s proportion is 28 percent. The current market value for 1,000 Sharma Ltd. shares is $31,000.	

2018

Feb. 6	Sold 2,000 Larson Corp. shares for cash of $168,500, less commissions of $1,550.	

Required   Record the transactions in the general journal of Oliver Corp.; the company's year end is December 31.

Problem 16–2A

Applying the fair value method and the equity method

① ② ③

3. Dec. 31, 2017, balance, $525,000

The balance sheet of Spottified Corp. recently included:

Investments in significantly influenced and other companies	$2,500,000

Spottified Corp. included its short-term investments among the current assets; the investments described above were long-term. Assume the company completed the following investment transactions during 2017:

Mar. 3	Purchased 8,000 common shares as a short-term investment, paying $25.00 per share plus brokerage commission of $500.	
4	Purchased additional shares in a company that is significantly influenced by Spottified Corp. at a cost of $600,000 plus brokerage commission of $4,500.	
May 14	Received semi-annual cash dividend of $1.70 per share on the short-term investment purchased March 3.	
Jun. 15	Received cash dividend of $55,000 from a significantly influenced company.	
Aug. 28	Sold the short-term investment (purchased on March 3) for $24.00 per share, less brokerage commission of $500.	
Oct. 24	Purchased other short-term investments for $275,000, plus brokerage commission of $400.	
Dec. 15	Received cash dividend of $30,000 from a significantly influenced company.	
31	Received annual reports from significantly influenced companies. Their total net income for the year was $1,300,000. Of this amount, Spottified Corp.'s proportion is 30 percent.	

Required

1. Record the transactions in the general journal of Spottified Corp.

2. Post entries to the Investments in Significantly Influenced and Other Companies T-account, and determine its balance at December 31, 2017.

3. Assume the beginning balance of Short-Term Investments was at a cost of $250,000. Post entries to the Short-Term Investments T-account and determine its balance at December 31, 2017.

4. Assuming the market value of the short-term investment portfolio is $510,000 at December 31, 2017, show how Spottified Corp. would report short-term investments and investments in significantly influenced and other companies on the December 31, 2017, balance sheet. Use the following format:

Cash	$XXX
Short-term investments, at fair value	☐
Accounts receivable (net)	XXX
⌇	⌇
Total current assets	XXX
Investments in significantly influenced and other companies	☐

Problem 16–3A

The accounting for equity investments changes with the amount of shares held. BF Ltd. has a total of 30,000 shares outstanding. Complete the chart below to show the accounting differences between two different scenarios and how Niall Holdings Ltd. should record the transaction and balances if it owns different amounts of BF Ltd. shares as a long-term investment.

Compare accounting methods as share ownership percentage varies

① ② ③

Case B year-end balance in the investments account, $317,300

	Case A: 3,600 Shares	Case B: 11,400 Shares
Which accounting method should be used for this long-term investment?		
Journal entry to record purchase of shares at $27 each. No commissions.		
Journal entry to recognize share of $25,000 in dividends declared and paid.		
Journal entry to recognize $50,000 in net income declared by BF Ltd.		
Journal entry to recognize the year-end market value of $30 per share.		
What is the balance in the investments account at year end?		

Problem 16–4A

Pluto Corp. paid $750,000 to acquire all the common shares of Saturn Inc., and Saturn Inc. owes Pluto Corp. $170,000 on a note payable. The fair market value of Saturn Inc.'s net assets equalled the book value. Immediately after the purchase on May 31, 2017, the two companies' balance sheets were as follows:

Excel Spreadsheet Template
Preparing a consolidated balance sheet; goodwill; no non-controlling interest

④

Total consolidated assets, $2,420,000

	Pluto Corp.	Saturn Inc.
Assets		
Cash	$ 60,000	$ 100,000
Accounts receivable, net	210,000	150,000
Note receivable from Saturn Inc.	170,000	—
Inventory	300,000	440,000
Investment in Saturn Inc.	750,000	—
Property, plant, and equipment, net	600,000	500,000
Total	$2,090,000	$1,190,000
Liabilities and Shareholders' Equity		
Accounts payable	$ 250,000	$ 40,000
Notes payable	400,000	210,000
Note payable to Pluto Corp.	—	170,000
Other liabilities	156,000	80,000
Common shares	800,000	500,000
Retained earnings	484,000	190,000
Total	$2,090,000	$1,190,000

Required Prepare a consolidation worksheet.

Excel Spreadsheet
Template
Preparing a consolidated balance sheet with goodwill and
non-controlling interest

④

Total consolidated
assets, $8,299,600

Problem 16–5A

On July 18, 2017, Patrone Holdings Ltd. paid $1,920,000 to purchase 90 percent of the com-
mon shares of Smirnoff Inc., and Smirnoff Inc. owes Patrone Holdings Ltd. $240,000 on a
note payable. All historical cost amounts are equal to their fair market value on July 18,
2017. Immediately after the purchase, the two companies' balance sheets were as follows:

	Patrone Holdings Ltd.	Smirnoff Inc.
Assets		
Cash	$ 200,000	$ 340,000
Accounts receivable, net	720,000	480,000
Note receivable from Smirnoff Inc.	240,000	—
Inventory	1,480,000	920,000
Investment in Smirnoff Inc.	1,920,000	—
Property, plant, and equipment, net	2,190,000	1,540,000
Goodwill	—	—
Total	$6,750,000	$3,280,000
Liabilities and Shareholders' Equity		
Accounts payable	$1,060,000	$ 680,000
Notes payable	1,680,000	320,000
Note payable to Patrone Holdings Ltd.	—	240,000
Other liabilities	260,000	384,000
Common shares	1,540,000	1,060,000
Retained earnings	2,210,000	596,000
Total	$6,750,000	$3,280,000

Required Prepare a consolidation worksheet.

Problem 16–6A

Accounting for a long-term
bond investment purchased at a
discount

⑤

2. Carrying value,
$1,019,500

Financial institutions such as insurance companies and pension plans hold large quantities of bond investments. Suppose Sun Life Insurance Company purchases $1,000,000 of
3.00 percent bonds of Hydro-Québec at 102.00 on July 1, 2017. These bonds pay interest on
January 1 and July 1 each year. They mature on July 1, 2037. At December 31, 2017, the market price of the bonds is 101.00. Sun Life plans to hold these bonds to maturity. Disregard
commissions.

Required

1. Journalize Sun Life's purchase of the bonds as a long-term investment in bonds on July
   1, 2017, and accrual of interest revenue and amortization of the discount for six months
   at December 31, 2017. Assume the straight-line method is appropriate for amortizing the
   discount.

2. Calculate the carrying value of the Hydro-Québec bonds at December 31, 2017.

Computing the cost of a bond
investment and journalizing its
transactions using the effective-
interest method of amortizing a
discount

⑤

Carrying amount at Dec.
31, 2018, $651,863

Problem 16–7A

On December 31, 2017, when the market interest rate is 6 percent, an investor purchases
$700,000 of Solar Ltd. 10-year, 5 percent bonds at issuance for $647,929. Interest is paid
semi-annually. Assume that the investor plans to hold the investment to maturity. Disregard
commissions.

Required Prepare a schedule for amortizing the discount on the bond investment through December 31, 2018. The investor uses the effective-interest amortization method. Use Exhibit 15–5 on page 852 as a guide. Journalize the purchase on December 31, 2017, the first semi-annual interest receipt on June 30, 2018, and the year-end interest receipt on December 31, 2018.

Problem 16–8A

Sparta Investments Ltd. had the following short-term investments in marketable securities at fair value at December 31, 2016:

Accounting for short-term investments using the fair value method and long-term investments in bonds

① ⑤

Dec. 31, 2017, fair value valuation allowance, $107,727

Alberta Energy Co.	$310,000
Finning Ltd.	180,000
Canadian National Railway	285,000
Total short-term investments	$775,000

Sparta Investments Ltd. had the following investment transactions during 2017:

Jan.	5	Purchased 5,000 shares (2 percent) of HHN Ltd. as a short-term investment. The shares were purchased at $51.00 and the commission was $500.
	31	HHN Ltd. reported net income of $7,000,000 and declared a cash dividend of $2,100,000.
Feb.	15	Received $42,000 from HHN Ltd. as a cash dividend.
Apr.	1	Purchased $400,000 (face value) of bonds at 99 as a long-term investment. The bonds pay 5 percent interest (2.5 percent semi-annually) on October 1 and April 1. Sparta Investments Ltd. plans to hold the bonds until maturity in two years. The company chooses to use the straight-line method to amortize the discount.
Aug.	31	Received a 10 percent stock dividend from HHN Ltd.
Oct.	1	Received the interest on the bonds.
Nov.	1	HHN Ltd. declared and distributed a 2-for-1 stock split.
Dec.	15	Sold 4,000 shares of HHN Ltd. for $28.00 per share. The commission was $1,500.
	31	Recorded the adjustment for accrued interest on the bonds.
	31	The fair values of the investments were as follows:

Alberta Energy Co.	$ 280,000
Finning Ltd.	187,000
Canadian National Railway	290,000
HHN Ltd	288,000
Total short-term investments	$1,045,000

Required Prepare the general journal entries required to record the transactions of 2017.

Journalizing foreign-currency
transactions and reporting the
transaction gain or loss

⑥

1. Foreign-currency transaction
loss at Dec. 31, 2017, $9,400

Global Networking Corporation completed the following transactions:

2017

Dec. 1   Sold machinery on account to a Japanese company for $45,000. The exchange rate of the Japanese yen is $0.0113, and the Japanese company agrees to pay in Canadian dollars.

10   Purchased supplies on account from a US company at a price of US$125,000. The exchange rate of the US dollar is $1.06, and payment will be in US dollars.

17   Sold machinery on account to an English firm for 220,000 British pounds. Payment will be in pounds, and the exchange rate of the pound is $1.61.

22   Collected from the Japanese company. The exchange rate of the yen has not changed since December 1.

31   Adjusted the accounts for changes in foreign-currency exchange rates. Current rates: US dollar, $1.10; British pound, $1.59.

2018

Jan. 18   Paid the US company. The exchange rate of the US dollar is $1.08.

24   Collected from the English firm. The exchange rate of the British pound is $1.63.

Required

1. Record these transactions in Global Networking Corporation's general journal, and show how to report the transaction gain or loss on the income statement for the fiscal year ended December 31, 2017. For simplicity, use Sales Revenue as the credit.

2. How will what you have learned in this problem help you structure international transactions?

PROBLEMS (GROUP B)   MyAccountingLab

Big Seven Insurance Ltd. owns numerous investments in the shares of other companies. Assume Big Seven Insurance Ltd. completed the following investment transactions:

2017

Feb. 12   Purchased 30,000 (total issued and outstanding common shares, 120,000) common shares of Earl Mfg. Ltd. at a cost of $2,550,000. Commissions on the purchase were $15,000.

Jul. 2   Purchased 6,000 additional Earl Mfg. Ltd. common shares at a cost of $88.00 per share. Commissions on the purchase were $400.

Aug. 9   Received the annual cash dividend of $2.00 per share on the Earl Mfg. Ltd. investment.

Oct. 16   Purchased 2,000 Excellence Ltd. common shares as a short-term investment, paying $63.00 per share plus brokerage commission of $500.

Nov. 30   Received the semi-annual cash dividend of $2.50 per share on the Excellence Ltd. investment.

Dec. 31   Received the annual report from Earl Mfg. Ltd. Net income for the year was $1,160,000. Of this amount, Big Seven Insurance Ltd.'s proportion is 30 percent.

31   The current market value of the Excellence shares is $140,000.

2018

Jan. 14   Sold 5,000 Earl Mfg. Ltd. shares for $460,000, less commissions of $800.

Required   Record the transactions in the general journal of Big Seven Insurance Ltd. The company's year end is December 31.

Problem 16–2B

The December 31, 2016, balance sheet of FT Corporation included the following:

Applying the fair value method and the equity method
① ② ③

Investments—Associated Companies at Equity	$15,000,000

Suppose the company completed the following investment transactions during 2017:

Mar. 2   Purchased 2,000 common shares as a short-term investment, paying $38.00 per share plus brokerage commission of $900.

5   Purchased additional shares in an associated company at a cost of $1,600,000. Commissions on the purchase were $30,000.

Jul. 21   Received the semi-annual cash dividend of $1.50 per share on the short-term investment purchased March 2.

Aug. 17   Received a cash dividend of $160,000 from an associated company.

Oct. 16   Sold 1,100 shares of the short-term investment (purchased on March 2) for $36.00 per share, less brokerage commission of $600.

Nov. 8   Purchased short-term investments for $310,000, plus brokerage commission of $5,000.

17   Received a cash dividend of $280,000 from an associated company.

Dec. 31   Received annual reports from associated companies. Their total net income for the year was $6,900,000. Of this amount, FT's proportion is 24 percent.

Required

1. Record the transactions in the general journal of FT Corporation.

2. Post entries to the Equity Investments T-account and determine its balance at December 31, 2017.

3. Assume the beginning balance of Short-Term Investments was $104,000. Post entries to the Short-Term Investments T-account and determine its balance at December 31, 2017.

4. Assuming the market value of the short-term investment portfolio is $425,000 at December 31, 2017, show how FT Corporation would report short-term investments and investments in associated companies on the ending balance sheet. (No journal entry is required.) Use the following format:

Cash	$XXX
Short-term investments, at fair value	[ ]
Accounts receivable (net)	XXX
~	~
Total current assets	XXX
Investments—Associated companies at equity	[ ]

Problem 16–3B

The accounting for equity investments changes with the amount of shares held. Hughes Ltd. has a total of 35,000 shares outstanding. Complete the chart on the next page to show the accounting differences between two different scenarios and how Soochow Corp. should record the transaction and balances if it owns different amounts of Hughes Ltd. shares as a long-term investment:

Compare accounting methods as share ownership percentage varies
① ② ③

	Case A: 3,800 Shares	Case B: 11,900 Shares
Which accounting method should be used for this long-term investment?		
Journal entry to record purchase of shares at $35 each. No commissions.		
Journal entry to recognize share of $40,000 in dividends declared and paid.		
Journal entry to recognize $75,000 in net income declared by Hughes Ltd.		
Journal entry to recognize the year-end market value of $34 per share.		
What is the balance in the investments account at year end?		

Excel Spreadsheet Template
Preparing a consolidated balance sheet; goodwill, no non-controlling interest
4

Problem 16–4B

Pisa Inc. paid $1,040,000 to acquire all the common shares of Sienna Ltd., and Sienna Ltd. owes Pisa Inc. $120,000 on a note payable. The fair market value of Sienna's net assets equalled the book value. Immediately after the purchase on June 30, 2017, the two companies' balance sheets were as shown below:

	Pisa Inc.	Sienna Ltd.
Assets		
Cash	$ 80,000	$ 72,000
Accounts receivable, net	288,000	144,000
Note receivable from Sienna Ltd.	120,000	—
Inventory	480,000	388,000
Investment in Sienna Ltd.	1,040,000	—
Property, plant, and equipment, net	608,000	720,000
Total	$2,616,000	$1,324,000
Liabilities and Shareholders' Equity		
Accounts payable	$ 192,000	$ 128,000
Notes payable	588,000	224,000
Note payable to Pisa Inc.	—	120,000
Other liabilities	204,000	12,000
Common shares	880,000	440,000
Retained earnings	752,000	400,000
Total	$2,616,000	$1,324,000

Required Prepare a consolidation worksheet.

Excel Spreadsheet Template
Preparing a consolidated balance sheet; goodwill with non-controlling interest
4

Problem 16–5B

On March 22, 2017, Primary Investments Corp. paid $1,575,000 to purchase 70 percent of the common shares of Secondary Products Inc., and Primary Investments Corp. owes Secondary Products Inc. $400,000 on a note payable. The fair market value of Secondary Products Inc.'s net assets equalled the book value. Immediately after the purchase, the two companies' balance sheets were as follows:

	Primary Investments Corp.	Secondary Products Inc.
Assets		
Cash	$ 570,000	$ 150,000
Accounts receivable, net	540,000	440,000
Note receivable from Primary		
Investments Corp.	—	400,000
Inventory	750,000	540,000
Investment in Secondary Products Inc.	1,575,000	—
Property, plant, and equipment, net	1,797,000	1,520,000
Total	$5,232,000	$3,050,000
Liabilities and Shareholders' Equity		
Accounts payable	$ 480,000	$ 420,000
Notes payable	1,077,000	270,000
Note payable to Secondary Products Inc.	400,000	—
Other liabilities	155,000	230,000
Non-controlling interest	—	—
Common shares	1,170,000	540,000
Retained earnings	1,950,000	1,590,000
Total	$5,232,000	$3,050,000

Required Prepare a consolidation worksheet.

Problem 16–6B

Financial institutions such as insurance companies and pension plans hold large quantities of bond investments. Suppose Meridian Credit Union purchases $2,000,000 of 3.0 percent bonds of the Province of Manitoba at 105 on January 1, 2017. These bonds pay interest on January 1 and July 1 each year. They mature on January 1, 2027. Meridian plans to hold the bonds to maturity. Disregard commissions.

Accounting for a bond investment purchased at a premium
⑤

Required

1. Journalize Meridian's purchase of the bonds as a long-term investment on January 1, 2017, receipt of cash interest and amortization of premium on July 1, 2017, and accrual of interest revenue and amortization of premium at October 31, 2017, the fiscal year end. Assume the straight-line method is appropriate for amortizing the premium as there is no material difference from the effective-interest method.
2. Calculate the book value of the investment in the Province of Manitoba bonds at October 31, 2017.

Problem 16–7B

Suppose, on December 31, 2017, when the market interest rate is 6 percent, an investor purchases $5,000,000 of Belmont Products Inc.'s six-year, 5.5 percent bonds at issuance for $4,873,675. Interest is payable semi-annually. The investor plans to hold these bonds to maturity. Disregard commissions.

Computing the cost of a long-term bond investment and journalizing its transactions using the effective-interest method of amortizing a discount
⑤

Required Prepare a schedule for amortizing the discount on the bond investment through December 31, 2018. The investor uses the effective-interest amortization method. Use Exhibit 15–5 on page 852 as a guide. Journalize the purchase on December 31, 2017, the first semi-annual interest receipt on June 30, 2018, and the year-end interest receipt on December 31, 2018.

Problem 16–8B

Accounting for short-term
investments using the fair value
method; investments in bonds
① ⑤

Portal Holdings Ltd. had the following short-term investments in marketable securities on December 31, 2016, at fair value and book value:

Canadian Utilities Limited	$310,000
TELUS Corporation	425,000
Talisman Energy Ltd.	160,000
Total short-term investments	$895,000

Portal Holdings Ltd. had the following investment transactions during 2017:

Jan.	5	Purchased 5,000 shares (2 percent) of Salmon Ltd. as a short-term investment. The shares were purchased at $50.00 and the commission was $300.
	31	Salmon Ltd. reported net income of $1,500,000 and declared a cash dividend of $900,000.
Feb.	15	Received $18,000 from Salmon Ltd. as a cash dividend.
Apr.	1	Purchased $300,000 (face value) of bonds at 100 as a long-term investment. The bonds pay 6 percent interest (3 percent semi-annually) on October 1 and April 1 and mature in two years.
Aug.	31	Received a 10 percent stock dividend from Salmon Ltd.
Oct.	1	Received the interest on the bonds.
Nov.	1	Salmon Ltd. declared and distributed a 2-for-1 stock split.
Dec.	15	Sold 3,300 shares of Salmon Ltd. at $48.00 and the commission was $200.
	31	Recorded the adjustment for accrued interest on the bonds.
	31	The fair values of the investments were as follows:

Canadian Utilities Limited	$ 290,000
TELUS Corporation	420,000
Salmon Ltd.	270,000
Talisman Energy Ltd.	175,000
Total short-term investments	$1,155,000

Required Prepare the general journal entries required to record the transactions of 2017.

Problem 16–9B

Journalizing foreign-currency
transactions and reporting the
transaction gain or loss
⑥

Suppose Pickel Corp. completed the following transactions:

2017

Dec.	4	Sold product on account to a Mexican company for $110,000. The exchange rate of the Mexican peso was $0.078, and the customer agreed to pay in Canadian dollars.
	13	Purchased inventory on account from a US. company at a price of US$240,000. The exchange rate of the US dollar was $1.05, and payment will be in US dollars.

20	Sold goods on account to an English firm for 180,000 British pounds. Payment will be in pounds, and the exchange rate of the pound was $1.66.
27	Collected from the Mexican company. The exchange rate of the Mexican peso was $0.075.
31	Adjusted the accounts for changes in foreign-currency exchange rates. Current rates: US dollar, $1.07; British pound, $1.65.

2018

Jan. 21	Paid the American company. The exchange rate of the US dollar was $1.06.
Feb. 17	Collected from the English firm. The exchange rate of the British pound was $1.69.

Required

1. Record these transactions in Pickel Corp.'s general journal, and show how to report the transaction gain or loss on the income statement for the year ended December 31, 2017.

2. How will what you have learned in this problem help you structure international transactions?

CHALLENGE PROBLEMS

Problem 16–1C

The text lists general rules for accounting for long-term investments in the voting shares of another corporation. However, the management of the investing company may decide that, in their judgment, the rules do not apply in a particular situation.

Accounting for ownership of shares in another company
① ② ③ ④

Required

1. Identify a situation where an investing company that owns less than 20 percent might believe that the equity method was appropriate.

2. Identify a situation where an investing company that owns between 20 and 50 percent might believe that the fair value method was appropriate.

3. Identify a situation where an investing company that owns more than 50 percent might believe that the fair value method was appropriate.

Problem 16–2C

Canadian exporters are pleased when the Canadian dollar weakens against the US dollar, while the federal and provincial ministers of finance are likely not happy when this happens.

Accounting for foreign operations
⑥

Required   Explain why a weakening Canadian dollar makes Canadian exporters happy. Why would a weaker Canadian dollar make the finance ministers unhappy?

EXTENDING YOUR KNOWLEDGE

DECISION PROBLEM

Understanding the fair value and equity methods of accounting for investments

① ② ③

Margaret Joyce is the owner of Trickle Music Holdings Ltd., a newly formed company whose year end is December 31. The company made two investments during the first week of January 2017. Both investments are to be held for at least the next five years as investments. Information about each of the investments follows:

a. Trickle Music Holdings Ltd. purchased 30 percent of the common shares of Old Times Ltd. for its book value of $600,000. During the year ended December 31, 2017, Old Times Ltd. earned $240,000 and paid a total dividend of $150,000.

b. Trickle Music Holdings Ltd. purchased 10 percent of the common shares of Mountain Music Inc. for its book value of $150,000. During the year ended December 31, 2017, Mountain Music Inc. paid Trickle Music Holdings Ltd. a dividend of $10,000. Mountain Music Inc. earned a profit of $225,000 for that period. The market value of Trickle Music Holdings Ltd.'s investment in Mountain Music Inc. was $204,000 at December 31, 2017.

Joyce has come to you as her auditor to ask you how to account for the investments. Trickle Music Holdings Ltd. has never had such investments before. You attempt to explain the proper accounting to her by indicating that different accounting methods apply to different situations.

Required   Help Joyce understand by:

1. Describing the methods of accounting applicable to investments such as these.
2. Identifying which method should be used to account for the investments in Old Times Ltd. and Mountain Music Inc.

FINANCIAL STATEMENT CASES

Financial Statement Case 1

Investments and foreign-currency transactions

① ② ③ ④ ⑥

Indigo Books & Music Inc.'s (Indigo's) financial statements appear in Appendix A at the end of this book and on MyAccountingLab.

Required

1. The financial statements are labelled "consolidated." What evidence can you find in the financial statements that reveals how Indigo accounts for its subsidiaries?
2. What business(es) is(are) included in the consolidated statements?
3. Does Indigo have any foreign-currency transactions? How do you know?

Financial Statement Case 2

Investments and foreign-currency transactions

① ② ③ ④ ⑥

The TELUS Corporation December 31, 2013, financial statements appear on MyAccountingLab. Access them to answer the following questions.

Required

1. What information can you find about TELUS Corporation's policy on foreign-currency transactions?
2. Does TELUS Corporation have any subsidiaries or long-term investments in other businesses as of December 31, 2013? How can you tell?
3. Does the company have any other business investments?

1. a. $18.70 per share ($18,700 ÷ 1,000 shares; the commission is expensed, not included in the price per share)
    b. $9.35 per share ($18,700 ÷ 2,000 shares)
    c. $8.00 per share ($16,000 ÷ 2,000 shares)
    d. $10.00 per share ($20,000 ÷ 2,000 shares; the commission is expensed, not included in the price per share)

2.

2016			
Sep. 30	Short-Term Investments	43,200	
	Commission Expense	125	
	Cash		43,325
	Purchased 1,200 common shares of Betam Ltd. at $36.00 per share (1,200 × $36.00 = $43,200) plus commission of $125.		

Dec. 21	Cash	108	
	Dividend Revenue		108
	Received $0.09 per share cash dividend (1,200 × $0.09) on Betam Ltd. common shares.		

Dec. 31	Unrealized Loss on Fair Value Adjustment	3,000	
	Fair Value Valuation Allowance		3,000
	Adjusted Betam Ltd. investment to fair value [1,200 × ($36.00 − $33.50)].		

2017			
Apr. 13	Cash	37,080	
	Loss on Sale of Investment	3,000	
	Fair Value Valuation Allowance	3,000	
	Commission Expense	120	
	Short-Term Investments		43,200
	Sold all the Betam Ltd. common shares held for $31.00 per share. Carrying value of the common shares sold was $40,200 ($43,200 − $3,000). Loss on sale was $3,000 (1,200 × $31.00 − $40,200). Commission expense was $120.		

3.

Shares	Carrying Value	Current Fair Value
All Seasons Hotels	$ 88,000	$ 97,000
Tangerine Manufacturing Corp.	140,000	124,000
Prairie Grocers Inc.	74,000	76,000
Totals	$302,000	$297,000

Report the investments at fair value, $297,000, and report an unrealized loss of $5,000 ($297,000 − $302,000) in the non-operating section of the income statement. The adjusting journal entry would be:

Unrealized Loss on Fair Value Adjustment	5,000	
Fair Value Valuation Allowance		5,000*
Adjusted short-term investments to fair value.		

*Since most companies account for each investment separately, the $5,000 total gain is calculated as:

All Seasons Hotels: unrealized gain	$ 9,000
Tangerine Manufacturing Corp.: unrealized loss	(16,000)
Prairie Grocers Inc.: unrealized gain	2,000
Total (unrealized loss)	$ (5,000)

4.

2016			
Oct. 16	Long-Term Investments	450,000	
	Commission Expense	425	
	Cash		450,425
	Purchased 10,000 common shares of Levell Inc. at $45.00 per share (10,000 × $45.00 = $450,000) plus commission of $425.		

Dec. 1	Cash	20,000	
	Dividend Revenue		20,000
	Received $2.00 per share cash dividend (10,000 × $2.00) on Levell Inc. common shares.		

Dec. 31	Fair Value Valuation Allowance	10,000	
	Unrealized Gain on Fair Value Adjustment		10,000
	Adjusted Levell Inc. investment to fair value [10,000 × ($46.00 − $45.00)].		

2017			
Feb. 15	Cash	244,740	
	Commission Expense	260	
	Short-Term Investments		225,000
	Fair Value Valuation Allowance		5,000
	Gain on Sale of Investment		15,000
	Sold 5,000 of the Levell Inc. common shares held for $49.00 per share. Carrying value of the common shares sold was $230,000 [50% × ($450,000 + $10,000)]. Gain on sale was $15,000 (5,000 × $49.00 − $230,000). Commission expense was $260.		

5. Recall that for equity investments, the general rules are:
Less than 20% —> Fair value
20% to 50% —> Equity
Greater than 50% —> Consolidation

  a. An investment subject to significant influence is usually accounted for by the equity method.
  b. Fair value method
  c. Consolidation

6. For a 40 percent equity method investment, the Investment in Investee Ltd. Common Shares account includes the cost of the investment + 40% of the investee's net income − 40% of the investee's cash dividends.
Remember that cash dividends received from an equity method investment are credited to Investment in Investee Ltd. Common Shares, *not to Dividend Revenue.*

  a.
Investment in Investee Ltd. Common Shares	140,000	
Cash		140,000
To purchase 40 percent investment in Investee Ltd. common shares.		

  b.
Investment in Investee Ltd. Common Shares	72,000	
Equity Method Investment Revenue		72,000
To record 40 percent of Investee Ltd. net income ($180,000 × 0.40).		

  c.
Cash	56,000	
Investment in Investee Ltd. Common Shares		56,000
To record receipt of 40 percent of Investee Ltd. cash dividend ($140,000 × 0.40).		

  d.
Cash	160,000	
Investment in Investee Ltd. Common Shares		156,000
Gain on Sale of Investment		4,000
Sold investment in Investee Ltd. common shares ($140,000 + $72,000 − $56,000).		

7. a. Parent company only.
  b. The shareholders' equity of the consolidated entity excludes the shareholders' equity of a subsidiary because the shareholders' equity of the consolidated entity is that of the parent only, and because the subsidiary's equity and the parent company's investment balance represent the same resources. Therefore, including them both would amount to double counting.
  c. Non-controlling or minority interest—reported on A Ltd.'s (parent) consolidated balance sheet between the liabilities and shareholders' equity sections.
  d. Goodwill—reported on C Ltd.'s (parent) consolidated balance sheet as an asset.

8. ❶ Eliminate all parent-and-subsidiary intercompany transactions to avoid double counting items when consolidating.
❷ Check for goodwill by comparing the net assets purchased (represented by the subsidiary's shareholders' equity balance) with the amount paid. The completed worksheet appears below.

	Parent Inc.	Subsidiary Inc.	Eliminations Debit	Eliminations Credit	Consolidated Amounts
Assets					
Cash	$ 38,000	$ 36,000			$ 74,000
Note receivable from Parent Inc.	—	70,000		❶ $ 70,000	—
Investment in Subsidiary Inc.	400,000	—		❷ 400,000	—
Goodwill	—	—	❷ $ 60,000*		60,000
Other assets	432,000	396,000			828,000
Total	$870,000	$502,000			$962,000
Liabilities and Shareholders' Equity					
Accounts payable	$ 60,000	$ 42,000			$102,000
Notes payable	70,000	120,000	❶ 70,000		120,000
Common shares	560,000	240,000	❷ 240,000		560,000
Retained earnings	180,000	100,000	❷ 100,000		180,000
Total	$870,000	$502,000	$470,000	$470,000	$962,000

*$60,000 = $400,000 − ($240,000 + $100,000)

9. a. Cana Corp. should account for the bonds at amortized cost.

b.
2017			
Apr. 30	Investment in Bonds	97,500	
	Cash		97,500
	Purchased long-term Starr Limited bond investment ($100,000 × 0.975).		
Oct. 31	Cash	2,000	
	Interest Revenue		2,000
	Received semi-annual interest ($100,000 × 0.04 × $^6/_{12}$).		

Oct. 31	Investment in Bonds	227	
	Interest Revenue		227
	To amortize discount on bond investment for six months [($100,000 − $97,500) × $^6/_{66}$].		

Dec. 31	Interest Receivable	667	
	Interest Revenue		667
	To accrue interest revenue for two months ($100,000 × 0.04 × $^2/_{12}$).		

Dec. 31	Investment in Bonds	76	
	Interest Revenue		76
	To amortize discount on bond investment for two months [($100,000 − $97,500) × $^2/_{66}$].		

c.

Balance Sheet at December 31, 2017

Current assets:	
Interest receivable	$667
Total current assets	x,xxx
Investment in bonds—Note 3	97,803

Note 3: Investment in Bonds

Long-term bond investments are reported at amortized cost. At December 31, 2017, the current market value of long-term investments in bonds was $98,250.

10.
Jun. 1	Investment in Bonds	46,490	
	Cash		46,490
	To record purchase of bond held as a long-term investment.		

Dec. 1	Investment in Bonds	1,000	
	Interest Revenue		1,000
	To accrue interest revenue for six months ($50,000 × 0.04 × $^6/_{12}$).		

Dec. 1	Investment in Bonds	395	
	Interest Revenue		395
	To amortize bond discount using the effective-interest method according to the table provided.		

11. a. Foreign-currency translation gain—the payment is made in fewer Canadian dollars than when the purchase was recorded.
   b. Foreign-currency translation gain—the payment is received in more Canadian dollars than when the sale was recorded.
   c. Foreign-currency translation loss—the payment is made in more Canadian dollars than when the purchase was recorded.
   d. Foreign-currency translation loss—the payment is received in fewer Canadian dollars than when the sale was recorded.

12.
May 16	Accounts Receivable	142,648	
	Sales Revenue		142,648
	To record a sale on account (80,000 × $1.7831).		

Jun. 19	Cash	70,456	
	Foreign-Currency Transaction Loss	868	
	Accounts Receivable		71,324
	To record receipt of half the amount receivable (40,000 × $1.7614).		

Jul. 16	Cash	71,168	
	Foreign-Currency Transaction Loss	156	
	Accounts Receivable		71,324
	To record receipt of the remaining amount receivable (40,000 × $1.7792).		

Overall, Zippy had a net foreign-currency loss of $1,024 ($868 + $156).

COMPREHENSIVE PROBLEM FOR PART 3

ACCOUNTING FOR CORPORATE TRANSACTIONS

Greyhawk Investments Inc.'s articles of incorporation authorize the company to issue 1,000,000 common shares and 400,000 $9.00 preferred shares. During the first quarter of operations, Greyhawk Investments Inc. completed the following selected transactions:

2017

Oct.	1	Issued 50,000 common shares for cash of $30.00 per share.
	4	Signed a capital lease for equipment. The lease requires a down payment of $600,000, plus 20 quarterly lease payments of $60,000. The present value of the future lease payments is $981,086 at an annual interest rate of 8 percent.
Oct.	6	Issued 2,000 preferred shares, receiving cash of $300,000.
	22	Purchased land from the Province of Manitoba for $300,000 cash.
	30	Purchased 5,000 (25 percent) of the outstanding common shares of Big Sky Ltd. as a long-term investment, $270,000.
Nov.	1	Issued $1,000,000 of 6 percent, 10-year bonds payable at 98.
	16	Purchased short-term investments in the common shares of TELUS Corporation, $85,000, and ATCO Ltd., $87,000.
	19	Purchased $1,000,000 of inventory on account. Greyhawk Investments Inc. uses a perpetual inventory system.
	20	Repurchased 2,000 of the company's common shares at $15.00 per share for cancellation.
Dec.	1	Received cash dividends of $1,800 on the TELUS investment.
	16	Sold 1,000 of the company's common shares for cash of $24.00 per share.
	29	Received a report from Big Sky Ltd. indicating the combined net income for November and December was $25,000.
	30	Sold merchandise on account, $2,148,000. Cost of the goods was $945,000. Operating expenses totalled $557,000, with $498,000 of this amount paid in cash. Greyhawk Investments Inc. uses a perpetual inventory system.
	31	Accrued interest and amortized discount (straight-line method) on the bonds payable.
	31	Accrued interest on the capital lease liability.
	31	Amortized the equipment acquired by the capital lease. The company uses the double-declining-balance method.
	31	Market values of short-term investments: TELUS Corporation shares, $84,000, and ATCO Ltd. shares, $93,000.
	31	Accrued income tax expense of $240,000. Credit the Income Tax Payable account.
	31	Closed all revenues, expenses, and losses to Retained Earnings in a single closing entry.
	31	Declared a quarterly cash dividend of $2.25 per share on the preferred shares. Record date is January 11, 2018, with payment scheduled for January 19.

Required

1. Record these transactions in the general journal. Explanations are not required. Disregard commissions.

2. Prepare a single-step income statement for the quarter ended December 31, 2017, including earnings per share. (Hint: Use T-accounts to calculate account balances.)

3. Report the liabilities and the shareholders' equity as they would appear on the balance sheet at December 31, 2017.

17 THE CASH FLOW STATEMENT

CONNECTING CHAPTER 17

LEARNING OBJECTIVE ① Identify the purposes of the cash flow statement

What is a cash flow statement?

The Cash Flow Statement: Basic Concepts, page 978
Purpose of the Cash Flow Statement, page 979
  Cash and Cash Equivalents

LEARNING OBJECTIVE ② Identify cash flows from operating, investing, and financing activities

What are the main cash flows in a business?

Operating, Investing, and Financing Activities, page 981
  Discontinued Operations
  Interest and Dividends as Operating Activities
  Non-cash Investing and Financing Activities
Measuring Cash Adequacy: Free Cash Flow, page 984
Format of the Cash Flow Statement, page 985

LEARNING OBJECTIVE ③ Prepare a cash flow statement by the direct method

What is the direct method, and how is it used to prepare a cash flow statement?

The Cash Flow Statement: The Direct Method, page 986
  Cash Flows from Operating Activities
  Cash Flows from Investing Activities
  Cash Flows from Financing Activities

LEARNING OBJECTIVE ④ Compute the cash effects of a wide variety of business transactions

What are the cash effects of different business transactions?

Computing Individual Amounts for the Cash Flow Statement, page 991
  Computing the Cash Amounts of Operating Activities
  Computing the Cash Amounts of Investing Activities
  Computing the Cash Amounts of Financing Activities

LEARNING OBJECTIVE ⑤ Prepare a cash flow statement by the indirect method

What is the indirect method, and how is it used to prepare a cash flow statement?

The Cash Flow Statement: The Indirect Method, page 1000
  Theory behind the Indirect Method

LEARNING OBJECTIVE ⑥ Identify the impact of IFRS on the cash flow statement

How does IFRS affect the cash flow statement?

The Impact of IFRS on the Cash Flow Statement, page 1005

MyAccountingLab   The **Summary** for Chapter 17 appears on page 1012. This lists all of the MyAccountingLab resources. **Accounting Vocabulary** with definitions for this chapter's material appears on page 1013.

Many companies have needed to seek protection from their creditors due to mismanagement of the cash needed to sustain a business. This chapter focuses on the management or summarized changes in a company's cash account. An example of a company that has faced tough competition in the Canadian home and garden sector as well as stagnant economic conditions is RONA Inc.

RONA Inc. is a major Canadian retailer and distributor of hardware, building materials, and home renovation products. Major US retailers have been interested in RONA in recent years, but the company remains solid. RONA has over 530 franchises and affiliate stores under several different names or banners and in a number of strategically aligned formats. It has 13 distribution centres, and its specialized TruServ Canada wholesaler serves RONA's network as well as many other independent dealers operating under other names. Roughly 25,000 employees work at RONA, and the company has annual consolidated sales of $4.2 billion.

Fiscal 2013 was a rough year for Rona. Store closures and lower housing starts across the country led to a decline in consolidated revenue of 5.7 percent. However, strong capital management and the sale of one of its divisions for $214 million enabled RONA to generate cash flows of about $31 million. These funds were used to purchase shares as well as reduce corporate debt. Changes in RONA's cash position can be seen in the 2013 annual report.[1]

---

[1] RONA Inc., 2013 Annual Report. Retrieved from www.rona.ca/corporate/financial-documents.

> **The cash flow** statement, a required financial statement, reports where cash came from and how the company spent it. Like the income statement and the balance sheet, the cash flow statement provides important information about an organization. For RONA Inc., the results seem positive overall because RONA has made decisions that will improve operations, despite generating a negative overall change in cash flow of −$12,345,000 in 2013. However, RONA still managed to maintain a positive cash balance in the amount of $8,245,000 in 2013, largely due to the disposal of a division. This allowed RONA to pay down debt, buy back shares, and pay dividends (see the shaded items in Exhibit 17–1). Positive cash flow from operations is a positive signal about any

EXHIBIT 17–1 | RONA Inc.'s 2013 and 2012 Cash Flow Statements (Indirect Method for Operating Activities)

RONA Inc.
Consolidated Statement of Cash Flows
Years Ended December 29, 2013 and December 30, 2012
(in thousands of Canadian dollars)

	2013	2012
Operating activities		
(Loss) income before income taxes	$(198,071)	$24,700
Loss before income taxes from discontinued operations (Note 10)	(149,430)	(6,970)
(Loss) income before income taxes from continuing operations	(48,641)	31,670
Adjustments:		
Depreciation, amortization and impairment of nonfinancial assets (Note 5.2)	113,850	107,261
Change in provision for restructuring costs	52,130	23,135
Change in fair value of derivative financial instruments	3,062	(628)
Net gains on disposal of assets	(4,640)	(3,973)
Share of income of equity-accounted investees	(1,599)	(1,570)
Share-based payment (Note 24)	6,688	3,676
Difference between amounts paid for post-employment benefits and current year expenses	(851)	(1,939)
Reversal of straight-line lease provisions (Note 5.4)	(3,468)	(1,329)
Other	(760)	1,122
	115,771	157,425
Net change in working capital (Note 8)	(33,497)	(13,745)
	82,274	143,680
Interest received	3,945	3,822
Income taxes paid	(11,107)	(25,124)
Cash flows from continuing operating activities	75,112	122,378
Investing activities		
Business combinations (Note 9)	(22,812)	(11,808)
Proceeds on disposal of a business (Note 10)	213,667	—
Acquisition of property, plant and equipment (Note 13)	(35,825)	(30,047)
Acquisition of intangible assets (Note 16)	(25,925)	(45,676)
Acquisition of other financial assets	(2,433)	(2,947)
Proceeds on disposal of property, plant and equipment and non-current assets held for sale	29,106	16,462
Proceeds on disposal of intangible assets	784	—
Proceeds on disposal of other financial assets	2,975	1,751
Dividends received from equity-accounted investees	2,004	1,198
Interest received	868	790
Cash flows from (used for) continuing investing activities	162,409	(70,277)

RONA Inc.
Consolidated Statement of Cash Flows
Years Ended December 29, 2013 and December 30, 2012
(in thousands of Canadian dollars)

	2013	2012
Financing activities		
Bank loans	(7,533)	3,605
Net change in credit facilities	(176,068)	63,274
Other long-term debt	—	16
Financing costs	—	(80)
Repayment of other long-term debt	(15,328)	(18,173)
Proceeds from issuance of common shares	4,713	5,714
Repurchase of common shares (Note 23)	(15,375)	(66,767)
Dividends on common shares	(17,043)	(17,191)
Dividends on preferred shares	(9,263)	(9,062)
Cash dividends paid by a subsidiary to non-controlling interests	(3,430)	—
Interest paid	(10,546)	(9,429)
Cash flows used for continuing financing activities	(249,873)	(48,093)
Net (decrease) increase in cash from continuing operations	(12,352)	4,008
Net increase in cash from discontinued operations (Note 10)	7	303
Net change in cash during the year	(12,345)	4,311
Cash, beginning of year	20,590	16,279
Cash, end of year	$8,245	$20,590

company because operations should be the main source of cash. RONA had a positive cash flow from operations in both years in the amount of $75,112,000 in 2013 and $122,378,000 in 2012.

We begin this chapter by explaining the cash flow statement format preferred by the accounting standards for private enterprises (ASPE) described in the *CPA Canada Handbook*. These standards are very clear, and the preferred format is called the *direct method*. We end the chapter with the more common format of the cash flow statement, the *indirect method*. The method used by RONA Inc. in the chapter-opening vignette is the indirect method. By the time you have worked through this chapter, you will be better able to analyze the cash flows of any company you might encounter.

The cash flow statement reports where cash came from and how it was spent. We learned in Chapter 1 (page 23) that the cash flow statement is a required financial statement. Like the other two major financial reports—the income statement and the balance sheet—the cash flow statement enables investors and creditors to make informed decisions about a company. The income statement might present one picture of the company (e.g., relatively high income), while the cash flow statement might present a different picture (e.g., not enough cash). This example underscores the challenge of financial analysis: A company's signals may point in different directions. For instance, fraudulent pyramid or ponzi schemes could hide a cash shortage if the cash flow statement was missing from the annual report. Astute investors and creditors know what to look for, and increasingly they are focusing on cash flows.

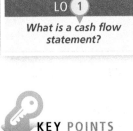

THE CASH FLOW STATEMENT: BASIC CONCEPTS

The balance sheet reports a company's cash balance at the end of the period. By comparing the beginning and ending balance sheets, you can tell whether cash increased or decreased during the period. However, the balance sheet does not indicate *why* the cash balance changed. The income statement reports revenues, expenses, and net income (or net loss)—clues about the sources and uses of cash—but it does not tell *why* cash increased or decreased.

The **cash flow statement** reports the entity's **cash flows**—cash receipts and cash payments—during the period.

KEY POINTS

A helpful feature of the cash flow statement is that you can calculate a check figure by placing the change in cash during the year at the bottom of the statement and ensuring that you balance to that number.

- It shows where cash came from (receipts) and how cash was spent (payments).
- It reports why cash increased or decreased during the period.
- It covers a period of time and is dated "For the Month Ended xxxx" or "For the Year Ended xxxx," the same as the income statement.

The cash flow statement is a summary of all the transactions that affected the Cash account for a period of time. Exhibit 17–2 shows the Cash T-account and some of the types of transactions that affect its balance during a period.

EXHIBIT 17–2 | **Some Transactions that Affect the Cash Account**

Cash (and cash equivalents)

Increases		Decreases
Beginning cash balance	Payments to suppliers	
Collections from customers	Payments to employees	
Interest received on notes	Payments for income tax	
Issuance of shares	Payments for assets	
Issuance of bonds	Loan to another company	
Receipt of dividends	Payment of dividends	
	Repayment of a bank loan	
	Repayment of long-term loans	
Ending cash balance		

Exhibit 17–3 illustrates the relationships among the balance sheet, the income statement, and the cash flow statement, and the time periods covered by each.

EXHIBIT 17–3 | **Timing of the Financial Statements**

KEY POINTS

The end of the day on December 31 of this year is considered to be the same as the beginning of the day on January 1 of next year.

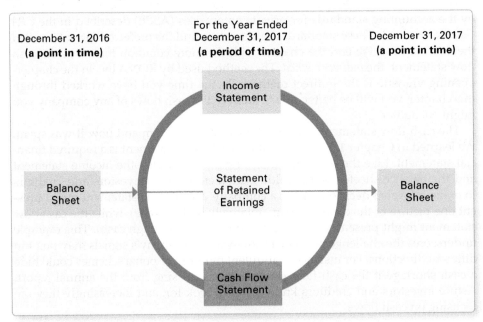

PURPOSE OF THE CASH FLOW STATEMENT

How do people use cash flow information?

- *Predict future cash flows.* It takes cash to pay the bills or take advantage of opportunities. In many cases, past cash receipts and cash payments help predict future cash flows.

- *Evaluate management decisions.* Wise decisions lead to profits and strong cash flows. Unwise decisions often bring bankruptcy. One of the areas that the cash flow statement reports on is the investments a company is making in itself and in outside companies so shareholders and other interested financial statement users can assess management's investment decisions.

- *Determine the company's ability to pay dividends and debts.* Shareholders are interested in receiving dividends on their investments in the company's shares. Creditors want to receive their principal and interest amounts on time. The cash flow statement helps investors and creditors predict whether the business can make dividend and debt payments.

- *Show the relationship between net income and cash flow.* Usually, cash and net income move together. High profits tend to lead to increases in cash and vice versa. However, a company's cash balance can decrease when net income is high, and cash can increase when net income is low. The failures of companies that were earning net income but had insufficient cash have pointed to the need for cash flow information.

It is clear that cash flows are important to a company's survival. A cash shortage is usually the most pressing problem of a struggling organization. Abundant cash allows a company to expand, invest in research and development, and hire the best employees. How, then, do investors (and their representatives, financial analysts) and creditors use cash flow information for decision making?

Neither cash flow data, net income information, balance sheet figures, nor the financial statement notes tell investors all they need to know about a company. Decision making is much more complex than inserting a few numbers into a simple formula. To decide whether to invest in a company's shares, investors analyze:

- A company's financial statements
- Articles in the financial press
- Data about the company's industry
- Predictions about the world and local economy

To evaluate a loan request, a bank loan officer may interview a company's top managers to decide whether they are trustworthy and whether their projections for the future of the company are reasonable. Both investors and creditors are interested mainly in a company's future. They want to make predictions about a company's future net income and future cash flows.

It has been said that cash flow data help to spot losers better than winners. This is often true. When a company's business is booming, profits are high and cash flows are usually improving. In almost all cases, a negative cash flow from operations warrants investigation. A cash downturn in a *single* year is not necessarily a danger signal. But negative cash flows for two or more *consecutive* years may lead to bankruptcy. Without cash flow from operations, a business simply cannot survive.

You may ask, "Can't the business raise money by issuing shares or by borrowing?" The answer is often no, because if operations cannot generate enough cash, then investors will not buy the company's shares, and bankers will not lend it money. *Over the long run, if a company cannot generate cash from operations it is doomed.*

Cash and Cash Equivalents

On the financial statements, *Cash* has a broader meaning than just cash on hand and cash in the bank. It includes **cash equivalents** (introduced in Chapter 8), which are highly liquid short-term investments convertible into cash with little delay. Because their liquidity is one reason for holding these investments, they are treated as cash. Examples of cash equivalents are investments in money market funds and investments in Government of Canada Treasury bills. Note 6 from the Indigo Books & Music 2014 annual report shows an example of cash and cash equivalents (see Exhibit 17–4). Businesses invest their extra cash in these types of liquid assets to earn interest income or to satisfy credit obligations. Throughout this chapter, the term *cash* refers to cash and cash equivalents.

EXHIBIT 17–4 | **Indigo's Note about Its Cash and Cash Equivalents (2014)**

6. CASH AND CASH EQUIVALENTS
Cash and cash equivalents consist of the following:

(thousands of Canadian dollars)	March 29, 2014	March 30, 2013
Cash	57,098	88,268
Restricted cash	3,369	470
Cash equivalents	97,111	121,824
Cash and cash equivalents	157,578	210,562

Restricted cash represents cash pledged as collateral for letter of credit obligations issued to support the Company's purchases of offshore merchandise.

> Try It!

1. Refer to the RONA Inc. cash flow statements illustrated in Exhibit 17–1 and answer the following questions:
   a. What is the period of time covered by RONA Inc.'s cash flow statements?
   b. What was RONA Inc.'s net income during the periods covered by the cash flow statement?
   c. In the "investing activities" section, where did RONA Inc. receive most of its cash from? How much cash did RONA receive on this category of investment? (Note that cash outflows, or cash payments, are indicated by dollar amounts in parentheses.)
   d. In the "financing activities" section, what did RONA Inc. spend most of its cash on? How much cash did the company spend on this category? (Note that net change in credit facilities is a reduction in debt.)
   e. What amount of cash and cash equivalents did RONA Inc. report on its balance sheet in 2013 and 2012?

2. Indicate whether each of the following items would increase (I) or decrease (D) the balance of cash and cash equivalents.
   _____ Payment of dividends
   _____ Issuance of shares
   _____ Payment to employees
   _____ Collections from customers
   _____ Payments for assets
   _____ Repayment of a bank loan
   _____ Issuance of bonds

Solutions appear at the end of this chapter and on MyAccountingLab

OPERATING, INVESTING, AND FINANCING ACTIVITIES

A business engages in three basic categories of business activities:

- **Operating activities**
- **Investing activities**
- **Financing activities**

The cash flow statement has a section for each category of cash flows. Exhibit 17–5 outlines what each section reports.

LO 2

What are the main cash flows in a business?

🔑 **KEY** POINTS

Once the business is up and running, *operations* are the most important activity, followed by *investing activities* and *financing activities.* Investing activities are generally more important than financing activities because *what* a company invests in is usually more important than *how* the company finances the investment.

EXHIBIT 17–5 | Sections of the Cash Flow Statement

Operating Activities . . .	• Create revenues, expenses, gains, and losses • Affect net income on the income statement • Affect current assets and current liabilities on the balance sheet • Are the most important category of cash flows because they reflect the day-to-day operations that determine the future of an organization
Investing Activities . . .	• Increase and decrease long-term assets, such as computers, software, land, buildings, and equipment, and purchases and sales of these long-term assets • Include purchases and sales of long-term share investments • Include long-term notes receivable in the form of loans to others as well as the collection of long-term loans • Are the next most important category of cash flows after operating activities
Financing Activities . . .	• Increase and decrease long-term liabilities and owners' equity • Include issuing shares, paying dividends, and repurchasing a company's own shares • Include borrowing money and paying off loans • Are the least important of all the activities because what a company invests in is usually more important than how the company finances the investment

Exhibit 17–6 shows the relationships among operating, investing, and financing cash flows and the various parts of the balance sheet.

EXHIBIT 17–6 | Operating, Investing, and Financing Cash Flows and the Balance Sheet Accounts

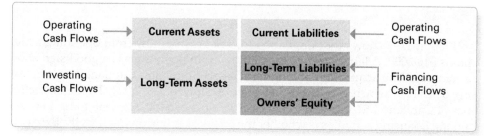

As you can see, operating cash flows affect the current accounts. Investing cash flows affect the long-term assets. Financing cash flows affect long-term liabilities and owners' equity.

The cash flow statement in Exhibit 17–7 shows how cash receipts and payments are divided into operating activities, investing activities, and financing activities for Capilano Ltd., a small manufacturer of glass products and the company we will refer to throughout this chapter.

EXHIBIT 17–7 | **Cash Flow Statement (Direct Method for Operating Activities)**

CAPILANO LTD. Cash Flow Statement For the Year Ended December 31, 2017		
Cash flows from operating activities		(in thousands)
Receipts:		
Collections from customers	$650	
Interest received on notes receivable	24	
Dividends received on investments in shares	22	
Total cash receipts		$696
Payments:		
To employees	(140)	
To suppliers for merchandise for resale	(270)	
To suppliers for operating expenses	(44)	
For interest	(38)	
For income tax	(36)	
Total cash payments		(528)
Net cash inflow from operating activities		168
Cash flows from investing activities		
Acquisition of property, plant, and equipment and intangible assets	(735)	
Loan to another company	(26)	
Cash received from selling property, plant, and equipment and intangible assets	149	
Net cash outflow from investing activities		(612)
Cash flows from financing activities		
Cash received from issuing common shares	242	
Cash received from issuing long-term notes payable	226	
Payment of long-term debt*	(27)	
Payment of dividends	(41)	
Net cash inflow from financing activities		400
Net increase (decrease) in cash and cash equivalents		(44)
Cash and cash equivalents at beginning of 2017		101
Cash and cash equivalents at end of 2017		$ 57

Brackets indicate an outflow of funds

Cash received from operations

Net cash used by business

Overall decrease in cash

Compare with Cash account balance

* This would also include the current portion of long-term debt payable, which is NIL in this case.

Exhibit 17–7 shows that Capilano Ltd.'s net cash inflow from operating activities is $168,000. A large positive cash inflow from operations is a good sign about a company. The acquisition of long-term assets dominates Capilano Ltd.'s investing activities, which produce a net cash outflow of $612,000. Financing activities of Capilano Ltd. brought in net cash receipts of $400,000. One thing to watch among financing activities is whether the business is borrowing heavily. Excessive

EXHIBIT 17–8 | Cash Receipts and Payments on the Cash Flow Statement

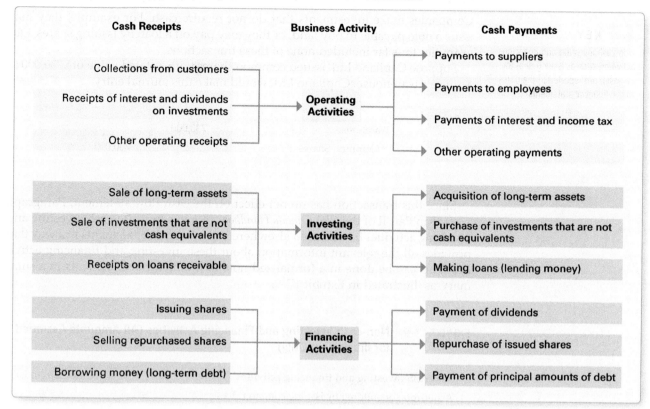

borrowing has been the downfall of many companies. Each of these categories of activities—operating, investing, and financing—includes both cash receipts and cash payments, as shown in Exhibit 17–8. The exhibit lists the more common cash receipts and cash payments that appear on the cash flow statement. (All amounts in the exhibit are in thousands of dollars.)

Discontinued Operations

Just as discontinued operations are shown separately on the income statement, they are also shown separately on the cash flow statement. The cash inflow or out-flow resulting from discontinued operations should be shown as part of operating, investing, or financing activities, as appropriate.

Interest and Dividends as Operating Activities

You may be puzzled by the inclusion of cash receipts of interest and dividends as operating activities. After all, these cash receipts result from investing activities. Interest comes from investments in loans, and dividends come from investments in shares. Equally puzzling is listing the payment of interest as part of operations. Interest expense results from borrowing money—a financing activity. *However, interest and dividends are included as operating activities because they affect the computation of net income and are received on a regular basis.* Interest revenue and dividend revenue increase net income, and interest expense decreases income. Therefore, cash receipts of interest and dividends and cash payments of interest are reported as operating activities on the cash flow statement.

In contrast, note that dividend payments are reported as a financing activity. This is because they do not enter into the computation of net income but rather are payments to the entity's shareholders, who finance the business by purchasing its shares.

KEY POINTS

Non-cash investing and financing activities, such as issuing debt for an asset, are reported in the notes to the financial statements.

Non-cash Investing and Financing Activities

Companies make investments that do not require cash. For example, they may issue a note payable to buy land, or they may pay off a loan by issuing shares. Our examples thus far included none of these transactions.

Suppose Capilano Ltd. issued common shares with a stated value of $730,000 to acquire a warehouse. Capilano Ltd. would make this journal entry:

Warehouse	730,000	
Common Shares		730,000

Since this transaction has no net effect on the cash flow statement, Paragraph 1540.48 in Part II of the *CPA Canada Handbook* requires that non-cash investing and financing activities be disclosed elsewhere in the financial statements in a way that provides all the relevant information about these investing and financing activities. This can be done in a formalized note to the financial statements in a summary, as illustrated in Exhibit 17–9.

EXHIBIT 17–9 | **Non-cash Investing and Financing Activities (All Amounts Assumed for Illustration Only)**

Non-cash investing and financing activities	(in thousands)
Acquisition of building by issuing common shares	$ 730
Acquisition of land by issuing note payable	172
Payment of long-term debt by transferring investments to the creditor	250
Acquisition of equipment by issuing short-term note payable	89
Total non-cash investing and financing activities	$1,241

When there is a cash component to a transaction, it is appropriate to show only the net effect of the transaction on the cash flow statement. For example, if the purchase of the building had been for common shares of $700,000 and for cash of $30,000, it would be appropriate to show only the net effect on cash of $30,000 and the other components of the transaction in the notes to the financial statements.

MEASURING CASH ADEQUACY: FREE CASH FLOW

So far we have focused on cash flows from operating, investing, and financing activities. Some investors want to know how much cash a company can "free up" for new opportunities. **Free cash flow** is the amount of cash available from operations after paying for planned investments in long-term assets. Free cash flow can be computed as follows:

	Net cash provided		Cash payments planned for
Free cash flow =	by operating	−	investments in property, plant,
	activities		equipment, and other long-term assets

PepsiCo Inc. uses free cash flow as part of a financial management strategy to manage its operations. Suppose PepsiCo expects net cash provided by operations of $2.9 billion. Assume PepsiCo plans to spend $2.3 billion to modernize its bottling factories. In this case, PepsiCo's free cash flow would be $0.6 billion ($2.9 billion − $2.3 billion). If a good investment opportunity comes along, PepsiCo should have $0.6 billion to invest in the opportunity. A large amount of free cash flow is preferable because it means a lot of cash is available for new investments.

FORMAT OF THE CASH FLOW STATEMENT

There are two ways to format operating activities on the cash flow statement:

- The **direct method**, which reports all the cash receipts and all the cash payments from operating activities
- The **indirect method** (sometimes called the **reconciliation method**), which reconciles net income to net cash provided by operating activities

The direct method, illustrated in Exhibit 17–7 on page 982, is the method preferred by the *CPA Canada Handbook* because it reports where cash came from and how it was spent on operating activities, for example, cash collected directly from customers.

In keeping with ASPE, companies' accounting systems are designed for accrual-basis rather than cash-basis accounting. To use the direct method, a company must be able to access information on cash inflows and cash outflows. However, accrual-based accounting systems make it easy for companies to compute cash flows from operating activities using the indirect method, which starts with net income and reconciles to cash flows from operating activities. Exhibit 17–10 gives an overview of the process of converting from accrual-basis income to the cash basis for the cash flow statement.

EXHIBIT 17–10 | **Converting from the Accrual Basis to the Cash Basis for the Cash Flow Statement**

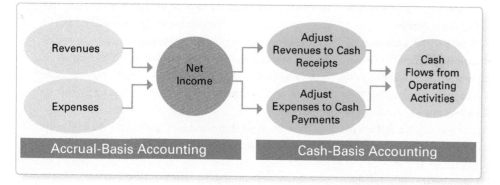

The direct method is easier to understand, and it provides better information for decision making, which is why the Accounting Standards Board and most financial analysts prefer it. However, accounting systems often don't produce the cash flow data easily. By learning how to compute the cash flow amounts for the direct method, you will be learning something far more important: how to determine the cash effects of business transactions. This is a critical skill for analyzing financial statements because accrual-basis accounting often hides cash effects. Then, after you have a firm foundation in cash flow analysis, it is easier to learn the indirect method. If your instructor chooses to focus solely on the indirect method, you can study that method, which begins on page 1000, with a minimum of references to earlier sections of this chapter.

The indirect and direct methods:

- Use different computations but produce the same amount of cash flow from operations
- Have no effect on investing activities or financing activities—they show the same net change in cash for the period.

3. Identify each of the following transactions as either an operating activity (O), an investing activity (I), a financing activity (F), or an activity that is not reported on a cash flow statement (N). Assume the direct method is used to report cash flows from operating activities.

_____ Payment of income taxes

_____ Issuance of preferred shares

_____ Payment of employee salaries

_____ Collections of accounts receivable

_____ Payment for a delivery truck

_____ Repayment of a long-term bank loan (principal only)

_____ Receipt of loan interest

_____ Payment of accounts payable

4. For the items listed in the previous question, indicate whether the transaction would increase (+), decrease (−), or have no effect (N) on cash.

Solutions appear at the end of this chapter and on MyAccountingLab

> Why it's Done this Way

Objective of Financial Reporting

Having seen the contents of the cash flow statement, we can turn to the accounting framework described in Chapter 1 to understand why the cash flow statement is one of the required financial statements for all companies.

The accounting framework states the objective of financial reporting is to communicate financial information that is *useful* in evaluating investment decisions and in assessing the success of a company. Supporting this objective, the framework describes the characteristics that financial statements must have to be useful. Two of those characteristics are *relevance* and *reliability*.

In previous chapters we discussed the role of the income statement in providing relevant and reliable information. Many investors feel that the cash flow statement provides the most relevant information of all of the financial statements. Why? While the income statement provides information about how much income was earned during the period, it does not state clearly how much cash was generated by the company. The income statement uses accruals to match revenues and expenses and reports them in the proper time period in which they were earned or incurred. However, the cash generated by a company and the use of that cash in the business is a significant predictor of future financial performance. We make the cash flow statement even more relevant and informative by classifying the cash flows as coming from operating, investing, or financing activities.

The cash flow statement is reliable since it deals only with cash transactions and, typically, cash transactions are easy to verify. There are no accrual assumptions to assess when dealing with cash transactions.

Thus, by being both relevant and reliable, the cash flow statement is critical to achieving the accounting framework's objective of providing information that helps users make investment decisions and assess company success.

THE CASH FLOW STATEMENT: THE DIRECT METHOD

LO 3

What is the direct method, and how is it used to prepare a cash flow statement?

There are two methods used in this text to illustrate the preparation of the cash flow statement. The first is to start with two years of financial statements and find the cash transactions by explaining the changes in the balances from the first year to the next. The other way is to start with the results of such a comparison. Let's see how to prepare the cash flow statement by the direct method illustrated in Exhibit 17–7 on page 982 using the second method. Suppose Capilano Ltd. has assembled the summary of 2017 transactions in Exhibit 17–11. These transactions give data for both the income statement and the cash flow statement. Some

EXHIBIT 17–11 | **Summary of Capilano Ltd.'s 2017 Transactions**

Operating Activities:

1. Sales on account, $682,000

2. Collections of accounts receivable and cash sales, $650,000

3. Interest revenue on notes receivable, $29,000

4. Collection of interest receivable, $24,000

5. Cash receipt of dividend revenue on investments in shares, $22,000

6. Cost of goods sold, $360,000

7. Purchases of inventory on credit, $353,000

8. Payments to suppliers for merchandise, $270,000, and operating expenses, $44,000

9. Salaries expense, $134,000

10. Payments of salaries, $140,000

11. Amortization expense, $43,000

12. Other operating expense, $41,000

13. Interest expense and payments, $38,000

14. Income tax expense and payments, $36,000

Investing Activities:

15. Cash payments to acquire property, plant, and equipment and intangible assets, $735,000

16. Loan to another company, $26,000

17. Cash receipts from sale of property, plant, and equipment and intangible assets, $149,000, including a $19,000 gain

Financing Activities:

18. Cash receipts from issuing common shares, $242,000

19. Cash receipts from issuing a long-term note payable, $226,000

20. Payment of long-term debt, $27,000

21. Declaration and payment of cash dividends, $41,000

Activities in blue indicate a cash flow transaction that is to be reported on the cash flow statement.

KEY POINTS

Note that cash collections from customers are not the same as sales. Cash collections from customers could include collections from sales that were made last year (beginning accounts receivable) but not credit sales from the current year that have not yet been collected (ending accounts receivable).

transactions affect one statement, some the other. Sales, for example, are reported on the income statement, but cash collections appear on the cash flow statement. Other transactions, such as the cash receipt of dividend revenue, affect both. *The cash flow statement reports only those transactions with cash effects* (those in blue in Exhibit 17–11).

To prepare the cash flow statement, follow these three steps:

1. Identify the activities that increased cash or decreased cash—those items in blue in Exhibit 17–11.

2. Classify each cash increase and each cash decrease as an operating activity, an investing activity, or a financing activity.

3. Identify the cash effect of each transaction.

Cash Flows from Operating Activities

Operating cash flows are listed first because they are the most important source of cash for most businesses. The failure of operations to generate the bulk of cash inflows for an extended period may signal trouble for a company. Exhibit 17–7 shows that Capilano Ltd. is sound; its operating activities generated the greatest amount of cash, $696,000 in operating receipts. Capilano's cash flows from operating activities section from Exhibit 17–7 is repeated here for reference. Refer to it as we organize the operating activities into receipts and payments based on the operating transactions shown in Exhibit 17–11. We will go through it line by line.

Cash flows from operating activities	(in thousands)	
Receipts:		
Collections from customers	$650	
Interest received on notes receivable	24	
Dividends received on investments in shares	22	
Total cash receipts		$696
Payments:		
To employees	(140)	
To suppliers for merchandise for resale	(270)	
To suppliers for operating expenses	(44)	
For interest	(38)	
For income tax	(36)	
Total cash payments		(528)
Net cash inflow from operating activities		$168

Cash Collections from Customers   Cash sales bring in cash immediately. Credit sales bring in cash later, when cash is collected. "Collections from customers" include both cash sales and collections of accounts receivable from credit sales—$650,000.

Cash Receipts of Interest   Interest revenue is earned on notes receivable. The income statement reports interest revenue. As time passes, interest revenue accrues, but *cash* interest is received only on specific dates. Only the cash receipts of interest appear on the cash flow statement—$24,000.

Cash Receipts of Dividends   Dividends are earned on share investments. Dividend revenue is ordinarily recorded on the income statement when cash is received. This cash receipt is reported on the cash flow statement—$22,000. (Dividends *received* are part of operating activities, but dividends *paid* are a financing activity.)

These cash receipts add to the total cash receipts of $696,000.

Cash Payments to Employees   Salaries, wages, commissions, and other forms of employee compensation require payments to employees. Accrued amounts are excluded because they have not yet been paid. The income statement reports the expense, including accrued amounts. The cash flow statement reports only the cash payments—$140,000.

Cash Payments to Suppliers   Payments to suppliers include all cash payments for inventory and most operating expenses, but not for interest, income taxes, and employee compensation expenses. *Suppliers* are entities that provide the business with its inventory and essential services. For example, a clothing store's payments to Levi Strauss & Co., Nygård International, and Stanfield's Ltd. are payments to suppliers. Other suppliers provide advertising, utilities, and other services. Payments to suppliers *exclude* payments to employees, payments for interest, and payments for income taxes because these are separate categories of operating cash payments. Capilano Ltd.'s payments to suppliers are $270,000 for merchandise for resale and $44,000 for operating expenses.

Cash Payments for Interest Expense and Income Tax Expense   These cash payments are reported separately from the other expenses. In the Capilano Ltd. example, interest and income tax expenses equal the cash payments. The cash flow statement reports the cash payments for interest of $38,000 and income tax of $36,000.

KEY POINTS

Using the direct method, cash receipts from issuing shares are *a financing activity.* Payment of dividends is also considered *a financing activity.* Cash receipts from and payments of short- or long-term borrowing are *financing activities.* But interest expense on these borrowings is considered an *operating* activity.

Therefore, the same amount appears on the income statement and the cash flow statement. In practice, this is rarely the case. Year-end accruals and other transactions usually cause the expense and cash payment amounts to differ.

Amortization Expense This expense is not listed on the cash flow statement because it does not affect cash. Amortization is recorded by debiting the expense and crediting Accumulated Amortization (there is no debit or credit to the Cash account).

Cash Flows from Investing Activities

Investing activities are important because a company's investments determine its future. Purchases of tangible assets such as property, plant, and equipment, as well as intangible assets such as patents, indicate the company is expanding, which is usually a good sign about the company. Low levels of investing activity over a lengthy period mean the business is not replenishing its property, plant, and equipment or intangible assets. Knowing the cash flows from investing activities helps investors and creditors evaluate the direction that managers are charting for the business.

Capilano's cash flows from investing activities listed in Exhibit 17–11 and shown in Exhibit 17–7 is repeated here for reference. Refer to it as we go through this section line by line.

Cash flows from investing activities		
Acquisition of property, plant, and equipment and intangible assets	$(735)	
Loan to another company	(26)	
Cash received from selling property, plant, and equipment and intangible assets	149	
Net cash outflow from investing activities		$(612)

Cash Payments for Property, Plant, and Equipment and Intangible Assets, Investments, and Loans to Other Companies All these cash payments acquire a long-term asset. The first investing activity reported by Capilano Ltd. on its cash flow statement is the purchase of property, plant, and equipment and intangible assets, such as land, buildings, equipment, and patents, for $735,000. The second transaction is a $26,000 loan; Capilano Ltd. obtained a long-term note receivable. These are investing activities because the company is mainly investing in assets for business use rather than for resale. The other typical transaction in this category, which is not shown for Capilano Ltd., is a purchase of long-term investments. Long-term notes or investments are assets with future economic value and serve to support the strategic initiatives of the business.

Cash Received from the Sale of Property, Plant, and Equipment and Intangible Assets, Investments, and the Collection of Loans These transactions are the opposite of making acquisitions of property, plant, and equipment or intangible assets, investments, and loans. They are cash receipts from investment transactions.

The sale of the property, plant, and equipment and intangible assets needs explanation. The cash flow statement reports that Capilano Ltd. received $149,000 cash on the sale of these assets. The income statement shows a $19,000 gain on this transaction. What is the appropriate amount to show on the cash flow statement? It is $149,000, the cash received from the sale. If we assume Capilano Ltd. sold equipment that cost $155,000 and had accumulated amortization of $25,000, the following journal entry would record the sale:

Cash	149,000	
Accumulated Amortization	25,000	
Equipment		155,000
Gain on Sale of Equipment (from income statement)		19,000

LEARNING TIPS

Notice the entry to record the sale of equipment. Any time Cash is debited in a journal entry, it must appear on the cash flow statement as a cash inflow. Likewise, a credit signals an outflow. To think this through, make journal entries but do not post them as they are merely a way to help you understand the cash effect of the transaction.

The analysis indicates the equipment cost $155,000 and its accumulated amortization was $25,000. Thus, the book value of the equipment was $130,000 ($155,000 − $25,000). However, the book value of the asset sold is not reported on the cash flow statement. Only the cash proceeds of $149,000 are reported on the cash flow statement. For the income statement, only the gain is reported.

Because a gain occurred, you may wonder why this cash receipt is not reported as part of operations. Operations consist of buying and selling merchandise or rendering services to earn revenue. Investing activities are the acquisition and disposition of assets used in operations. Therefore, the cash received from the sale of property, plant, and equipment and intangible assets, and the sale of investments should be viewed as cash inflows from investing activities. Any gain or loss on the sale is not cash, but rather an accounting amount based on the asset's book value in the accounting records.

Investors and creditors are often critical of a company that sells large amounts of its property, plant, and equipment and intangible assets. Such sales may signal an emergency need for cash and negative news. But selling property, plant, and equipment or intangible assets may be positive news if the company is selling an unprofitable division or a useless property, plant, and equipment asset. Whether sales of property, plant, and equipment or intangible assets are positive news or negative news, they should be evaluated in light of a company's overall picture.

Cash Flows from Financing Activities

Readers of the financial statements want to know how the entity obtains its financing. Cash flows from financing activities include several specific items. The majority are related to obtaining money from investors and lenders and paying them back.

Capilano's cash flows from financing activities listed in Exhibit 17–11 and shown in Exhibit 17–7 is repeated here for reference. Refer to it as we go through this section line by line.

MyAccountingLab

Video: Creating Cash Flow Statements by the Direct Method

Cash flows from financing activities	
Cash received from issuing common shares	$242
Cash received from issuing long-term notes payable	226
Payment of long-term debt	(27)
Payment of dividends	(41)
Net cash inflow from financing activities	$400

Cash Received from Issuing Shares and Debt Issuing shares (preferred and common) and debt are two common ways to finance operations. Capilano Ltd. issued common shares for cash of $242,000 and long-term notes payable for cash of $226,000.

Payment of Debt and Repurchases of the Company's Own Shares The payment of debt decreases Cash, which is the opposite of borrowing money. Capilano Ltd. reports debt payments of $27,000. Other transactions in this category are repurchases of the company's shares.

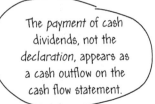

The payment of cash dividends, not the declaration, appears as a cash outflow on the cash flow statement.

Payment of Cash Dividends The payment of cash dividends decreases Cash and is therefore reported as a cash payment. Capilano Ltd.'s $41,000 payment is an example. A dividend in another form—such as a stock dividend—has no effect on Cash and is either *not* reported on the cash flow statement or is reported in the non-cash financing and investing footnote section described earlier in this chapter.

▷ Try It!

5. Suppose Markham Corp. sold land at a $3 million gain. The land cost Markham Corp. $2 million when it was purchased in 1995. What amount will Markham Corp. report as an investing activity on the cash flow statement?

Solutions appear at the end of this chapter and on MyAccountingLab

COMPUTING INDIVIDUAL AMOUNTS FOR THE CASH FLOW STATEMENT

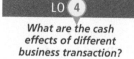

LO 4

What are the cash effects of different business transaction?

How do we compute the amounts for the cash flow statement? We use the income statement and *changes* in the related balance sheet accounts. For the *operating* cash flow amounts, the adjustment process follows this basic approach:

> Revenue or expense from the income statement ± Adjustment for the change in the related balance sheet account(s) = Amount for the cash flow statement

This is called the T-account approach and it will be illustrated in the next section, "Computing the Cash Amounts of Operating Activities." Learning to analyze T-accounts is one of the most useful accounting skills you will acquire. It will enable you to measure the cash effects of a wide variety of transactions.

The following discussions use Capilano Ltd.'s income statement in Exhibit 17–12, comparative balance sheet in Exhibit 17–13, and cash flow statement in Exhibit 17–14 (which is a repeat of Exhibit 17–7 for your convenience). Now let's compute the cash flows from operating activities.

LEARNING TIPS

The cash flow statement reports the changes in all non-cash accounts. To make sure that all changes have been accounted for, place a check mark by each account on the balance sheet after you have used it in preparing the statement. If a check mark is missing, further investigation may be required.

EXHIBIT 17–12 | Income Statement

CAPILANO LTD. Income Statement For the Year Ended December 31, 2017 (amounts in thousands)		
Revenues and gains:		
Sales revenue	$682	
Interest revenue	29	
Dividend revenue	22	
Gain on sale of property, plant, and equipment and intangible assets	19	
Total revenues and gains		$752
Expenses:		
Cost of goods sold	360	
Salaries expense	134	
Amortization expense	43	
Other operating expenses	41	
Interest expense	38	
Total expenses		616
Net income before income taxes		136
Income tax expense		36
Net income		$100

CAPILANO LTD. **Balance Sheet** **December 31, 2017 and 2016** **(amounts in thousands)**				

Assets	2017	2016	Increase (Decrease)	Changes in the following:
Current				
Cash	$ 57	$ 101	$ (44)	
Accounts receivable	224	192	32	
Interest receivable	8	3	5	Current assets—Operating
Inventory	323	330	(7)	
Prepaid expenses	18	17	1	
Long-term receivable from another company	26	—	26	Noncurrent
Property, plant, and equipment, net of amortization	1,087	525	562	assets—Investing
Total	$1,743	$1,168	$ 575	
Liabilities				
Current				Current liabilities—
Accounts payable	$ 220	$ 137	$ 83	**Operating** and change in current
Salaries payable	6	12	(6)	portion of long-term
Accrued liabilities	5	7	(2)	debt—**Financing**
Long-term debt	384	185	199	Most long-term liabilities and contributed capital—**Financing**
Shareholders' Equity				
Common shares	861	619	242	Change due to net
Retained earnings	267	208	59	income—**Operating** and change due
Total	$1,743	$1,168	$ 575	to dividends—**Financing**

Computing the Cash Amounts of Operating Activities

LEARNING TIPS

A *decrease* in Accounts Receivable indicates that cash collections were greater than sales. The decrease is *added* to Sales. An *increase* in Accounts Receivable indicates that cash collections were less than sales. The increase is *deducted* from Sales.

Cash Collections from Customers Collections can be computed by converting sales revenue (an accrual-basis amount) to the cash basis. Capilano Ltd.'s income statement (Exhibit 17–12) reports sales of $682,000. Exhibit 17–13 shows that Accounts Receivable increased from $192,000 at the beginning of the year to $224,000 at year end, a $32,000 increase. Based on those amounts, cash collections equals $650,000, as shown in the Accounts Receivable T-account:

Accounts Receivable				Cash	
Beginning balance	192,000			650,000	
Sales	682,000	Collections	650,000		
Ending balance	224,000				

Another explanation: Accounts Receivable increased by $32,000, so Capilano Ltd. must have received $32,000 less cash than sales revenue for the period.

EXHIBIT 17–14 | Cash Flow Statement (Direct Method for Operating Activities)

CAPILANO LTD. Cash Flow Statement For the Year Ended December 31, 2017		
Cash flows from operating activities		(in thousands)
Receipts:		
Collections from customers	$650	
Interest received on notes receivable	24	
Dividends received on investments in shares	22	
Total cash receipts		$696
Payments:		
To employees	(140)	
To suppliers for merchandise for resale	(270)	
To suppliers for operating expenses	(44)	
For interest	(38)	
For income tax	(36)	
Total cash payments		(528)
Net cash inflow from operating activities		168
Cash flows from investing activities		
Acquisition of property, plant, and equipment and intangible assets	(735)	
Loan to another company	(26)	
Cash received from selling property, plant, and equipment and intangible assets	149	
Net cash outflow from investing activities		(612)
Cash flows from financing activities		
Cash received from issuing common shares	242	
Cash received from issuing long-term debt	226	
Payment of long-term debt*	(27)	
Payment of dividends	(41)	
Net cash inflow from financing activities		400
Net increase (decrease) in cash and cash equivalents		(44)
Cash and cash equivalents at beginning of 2017		101
Cash and cash equivalents at end of 2017		$ 57

> Both the indirect and direct methods will balance to the same net cash inflow from operating activities—$168,000—and will reconcile to the same total cash change of $(44,000).

*This would also include the current portion of long-term debt payable, which is NIL in this case.

The following equation shows another way to compute cash collections from customers:

Accounts Receivable				
Beginning balance	**+ Sales**	**− Collections**	**= Ending balance**	
$192,000	+ $682,000	− X	= $224,000	
		−X	= $224,000 − $192,000 − $682,000	
		X	= $650,000	

A decrease in Accounts Receivable would mean that the company received more cash than the amount of sales revenue. *This computation is summarized as the first item in Exhibit 17–15 on page 996.*

LEARNING TIPS

Remember that each account contains four basic elements:

Beginning Balance
+ Increases
− Decreases
= Ending Balance

Apply this relationship to Accounts Receivable for Capilano Ltd.

Compute collections:

Beg. A/R	$192,000
+ Sales	682,000
− Collections*	?
= Ending Balance	$224,000

*Collections = $650,000

All collections of receivables are computed in the same way. In our example, Capilano Ltd.'s income statement, Exhibit 17–12, reports interest revenue of $29,000. Interest Receivable's balance in Exhibit 17–13 increased $5,000. Cash receipts of interest must be $24,000 (Interest Revenue of $29,000 minus the $5,000 increase in Interest Receivable). *Exhibit 17–15 on page 996 summarizes this computation.*

Payments to Suppliers This computation includes two parts, payments for inventory related to cost of goods sold and payments for operating expenses.

Payments for inventory are computed by converting cost of goods sold to the cash basis. We must analyze the Inventory and Accounts Payable accounts. To "analyze" an account means to explain each amount in the account. The computation of Capilano Ltd.'s cash payments for inventory is given by this analysis of the T-accounts (again, we are using Exhibit 17–12 and Exhibit 17–13 for our numbers):

Inventory					Accounts Payable			
Beg. Inventory 330,000	Cost of goods				Payments for		Beg. bal.	137,000
Purchases 353,000	sold	360,000			inventory 270,000		Purchases	353,000
End. Inventory 323,000							End. bal.	220,000

The first equation details the activity in the Inventory account to compute purchases, as follows:

Inventory							
Beginning inventory	+	Purchases	−	Cost of goods sold	=	Ending inventory	
$330,000	+	X	−	$360,000	=	$323,000	
		X			=	$323,000 − $330,000 + $360,000	
		X			=	$353,000	

Now we can insert the purchases figure into accounts payable to compute the amount of cash paid for inventory, as follows:

Accounts Payable							
Beginning balance	+	Purchases	−	Payments for inventory	=	Ending balance	
$137,000	+	$353,000	−	X	=	$220,000	
				−X	=	$220,000 − $137,000 − $353,000	
				X	=	$270,000	

LEARNING TIPS

The COGS calculation requires two adjustments. The adjustment for inventory gives the amount of purchases; the adjustment for accounts payable gives the payments for inventory.

Beginning and ending inventory amounts come from the balance sheet, and cost of goods sold comes from the income statement. *Exhibit 17–15 on page 996 shows the general approach to compute the payments to suppliers of inventory (fourth item).*

Payments for inventory appear in the Accounts Payable account, but we must first work through the Inventory account to calculate payments to suppliers of inventory.

Payments to Employees Companies keep separate accounts for salaries, wages, and other forms of employee compensation. It is convenient to combine all compensation amounts into one account for presentation purposes. Capilano Ltd.'s calculation adjusts Salaries Expense for the change in Salaries Payable, as shown in the following T-account:

Salaries and Wages Payable

		Beginning balance	12,000
Payments to employees	140,000	Salaries expense	134,000
		Ending balance	6,000

Salaries and Wages Payable

Beginning balance	+	Salaries expense	−	Payments	=	Ending balance
$12,000	+	$134,000	−	X	=	$6,000
				−X	=	$6,000 − $12,000 − $134,000
				X	=	$140,000

Exhibit 17–15 summarizes this computation under Payments to Employees.

Payments for Operating Expenses Payments for operating expenses is similar to payments to employees, but in this case there are two items affecting operating expenses that makes the calculation of the cash paid more difficult. Payments for operating expenses other than interest and income tax can be computed as "plug figures," or differences, by analyzing Prepaid Expenses and Accrued Liabilities, as follows for Capilano Ltd. (again, all numbers are taken from Exhibit 17–12 and Exhibit 17–13). The assumption here is that all prepaid items, such as rent, insurance, and advertising, or all accrued liabilities, such as entertainment, telephone, and utilities, flow through the one Operating Expenses account.

The question is how much cash did Capilano pay for operating expenses? An assumption is made regarding operating expenses in the following example. It assumes that all the prepaid expenses at the beginning of the year ($17,000) expired during the year and were adjusted in the current year by crediting the Prepaid Expenses account ❶ and debiting the applicable expense ❷. We know that accrued expenses during the year were $5,000, so we have enough data to determine how much cash was paid out for these operating expenses combined ($44,000).

Prepaid Expenses

Beg. bal. 17,000	❶ Expiration of prepaid expense 17,000
Payments 18,000	
End. bal. 18,000	

Accrued Liabilities

Payments 7,000	Beg. bal.	7,000	
	❷ Accrual of expense at year end	5,000	
	End. bal.	5,000	

Operating Expenses (other than Salaries, Wages, and Amortization)

❷ Accrual of expense at year end	5,000
❶ Expiration of prepaid expense	17,000
Payments	19,000
End. bal.	41,000

Total payments for operating expenses	=	$44,000
$18,000 + $7,000 + $19,000	=	$44,000

The following equations show another way to calculate payments for operating expenses:

Prepaid Expenses

Beginning balance	+	Payments	−	Expiration of prepaid expense	=	Ending balance
$17,000	+	X	−	$17,000	=	$18,000
		X			=	$18,000 − $17,000 + $17,000
		X			=	$18,000

LEARNING TIPS

Increases and decreases in other payables (Salary Payable, Interest Payable, and Income Tax Payable) are treated in the same way as increases and decreases in Accounts Payable and Accrued Liabilities. A *decrease* in the payable indicates that payments for salaries/interest/income taxes were greater than the expense. The decrease is *added* to the expense. An *increase* in the payable indicates that payments for salaries/interest/income taxes were less than the expense. The increase is *deducted* from the expense.

Accrued Liabilities

Beginning balance	+	Accrual of expense at year end	−	Payments	=	Ending balance
$7,000	+	$5,000	−	X	=	$5,000
				−X	=	$5,000 − $7,000 − $5,000
				X	=	$7,000

Operating Expenses

Accrual of expense at year end	+	Expiration of prepaid expense	+	Payments	=	Ending balance
$5,000	+	$17,000	+	X	=	$41,000
				X	=	$41,000 − $5,000 − $17,000
				X	=	$19,000

The expense total for operating expenses is $41,000. Once we remove the prepaid expirations and the expense accruals, the remaining balance must be the cash payments for expenses.

Payments of Interest and Income Tax   In our example, the expense and payment amount is the same for interest and income tax. Therefore, no analysis is required to determine the payment amount—we can use the expense amounts on the income statement for the cash flow statement. However, if the expense and the payment differ, the payment can be computed by analyzing the related liability or prepayment account. The payment computation follows the pattern illustrated for payments to employees.

Exhibit 17–15 shows how to compute operating cash flows under the direct method.

EXHIBIT 17-15 | Direct Method of Determining Cash Flows from Operating Activities

Cash Receipts and Payments	From the Income Statement (Exhibit 17–12)	From the Balance Sheet (Exhibit 17–13)
CASH RECEIPTS		
From customers	Sales Revenue	+ Decrease in Accounts Receivable − Increase in Accounts Receivable
Of interest	Interest Revenue	+ Decrease in Interest Receivable − Increase in Interest Receivable
Of dividends	Dividend Revenue	+ Decrease in Dividends Receivable − Increase in Dividends Receivable
CASH PAYMENTS		
To suppliers of inventory	Cost of Goods Sold	+ Increase in Inventory + Decrease in Accounts Payable − Decrease in Inventory − Increase in Accounts Payable
To suppliers of other items	Operating Expense	+ Increase in Prepaids + Decrease in Accrued Liabilities − Decrease in Prepaids − Increase in Accrued Liabilities
To employees	Salaries (Wages) Expense	+ Decrease in Salaries (Wages) Payable − Increase in Salaries (Wages) Payable
For interest	Interest Expense	+ Decrease in Interest Payable − Increase in Interest Payable
For income tax	Income Tax Expense	+ Decrease in Income Tax Payable − Increase in Income Tax Payable

This exhibit was created from a suggestion made by Barbara Gerrity.

Computing the Cash Amounts of Investing Activities

Investing activities affect long-term asset accounts, such as Property, Plant, and Equipment, intangible assets, Investments, and Notes Receivable. Cash flows from investing activities can be computed by analyzing these accounts. The income statement and beginning and ending balance sheets provide the data.

Acquisitions and Sales of Tangible and Intangible Assets Companies keep separate accounts for Land, Buildings, Equipment, and other tangible and intangible assets. It is helpful to combine these accounts into a single summary for computing the cash flows from acquisitions and sales of these assets. Also, we often subtract accumulated amortization from the assets' cost and work with a net figure for property, plant, and equipment and amortizable intangible assets, which is the book value. This approach allows us to work with a single total for tangible and intangible assets.

To illustrate, observe that Capilano Ltd.'s balance sheet (Exhibit 17–13) reports beginning property, plant, and equipment, net of amortization, of $525,000 and an ending net amount of $1,087,000. The income statement in Exhibit 17–12 shows amortization of $43,000 and a $19,000 gain on the sale of property, plant, and equipment. Further, the acquisitions are $735,000, an amount provided by the accounting records. How much are the proceeds from the sale of property, plant, and equipment? First, we must compute the book value of property, plant, and equipment sold as follows:

Property, Plant, and Equipment (net*)

Beginning balance (net)	525,000	Accumulated Amortization	43,000
Acquisitions	735,000	Book value of assets sold	130,000
Ending balance (net)	1,087,000		

*Accumulated amortization is subtracted

Property, Plant, and Equipment, Net

Beginning balance	+	Acquisitions	−	Accumulated Amortization	−	Book value of assets sold	=	Ending balance
$525,000	+	$735,000	−	$43,000	−	X	=	$1,087,000
						−X	=	$1,087,000 − $525,000 − $735,000 + $43,000
						X	=	$130,000

Now we can compute the proceeds from the sale of property, plant, and equipment as follows:

Sale proceeds	=	Book value of assets sold	+	Gain	−	Loss
	=	$130,000	+	$19,000	−	$0
	=	$149,000				

The journal entry for the sale would look like this:

Cash	$149,000	
Accumulated Amortization Old Asset	?	
Old Asset original cost		?
Gain on the sale of old asset		$19,000

$130,000 book value

Trace the sale proceeds of $149,000 to the cash flow statement in Exhibit 17–14. If the sale had resulted in a loss of $6,000, the sale proceeds would be $124,000 ($130,000 − $6,000), and the cash flow statement would report $124,000 as a cash receipt from this investing activity.

Acquisitions and Sales of Long-Term Investments and Long-Term Loans and Loan Collections The cash amounts of long-term investment and loan transactions can be computed in the manner illustrated for property, plant, and equipment and intangible assets. Investments are easier to analyze because there is no amortization to account for, as shown by the following T-account:

Investments			
Beginning balance*	xxx		
Purchases**	xxx	Cost of investments sold	xxx
Ending balance*	xxx		

*From the balance sheet
**From the accounting records, used to create the cash flow statement

Long-Term Investments (amounts assumed for illustration only)

Beginning balance	+	Purchases	−	Cost of investments sold	=	Ending balance
$200,000	+	$100,000		X	=	$280,000
				$-X$	=	$280,000 − $200,000 − $100,000
				X	=	$20,000

Sale proceeds	=	Cost of investments sold	+	Gain	−	Loss
	=	$20,000	+	$6,000	−	$0
	=	$26,000				

Loan transactions follow the pattern described on pages 992–994 for collections from customers. New loans made increase the receivable and decrease the amount of cash. Collections decrease the receivable and increase the amount of cash, as follows:

Loans and Notes Receivable (Long-Term)			
Beginning balance*	xxx		
New loans made**	xxx	Collections	xxx
Ending balance*	xxx		

*From the balance sheet
**From the accounting records, used to create the cash flow statement

Loans and Notes Receivable (amounts assumed for illustration only)

Beginning balance	+	New loans made	−	Collections	=	Ending balance
$180,000	+	$20,000	−	X	=	$60,000
				$-X$	=	$60,000 − $180,000 − $20,000
				X	=	$140,000

Computing the Cash Amounts of Financing Activities

Financing activities affect the long-term liability and shareholders' equity accounts, such as Notes Payable, Bonds Payable, Long-Term Debt, Common Shares, and Retained Earnings. To compute the cash flow amounts, analyze these accounts.

Issuances and Payments of Long-Term Debt Notes Payable, Bonds Payable, and Long-Term Debt accounts are related to borrowing, a financing activity. Their balances come from the balance sheet. If either the amount of new issuances or the amount of the payments is known, the other amount can be computed. New debt issuances totalled $226,000 for Capilano Ltd., as provided by the accounting records. Debt payments are computed from the

Long-Term Debt T-account, using amounts from Capilano Ltd.'s balance sheet, Exhibit 17–13:

Long-Term Debt

		Beginning balance	185,000
Payments	27,000	Issuance of new debt	226,000
		Ending balance	384,000

Long-Term Debt

Beginning balance	+	Issuance of new debt	−	Payments of debt	=	Ending balance
$185,000	+	$226,000	−	X	=	$384,000
				−X	=	$384,000 − $185,000 − $226,000
				X	=	$27,000

Issuances and Repurchases of Shares These financing activities are computed from the various share accounts. It is convenient to work with a single summary account for shares. Using data from Exhibit 17–13 and Exhibit 17–14, we have the following:

Common Shares

		Beginning balance	619,000
Retirements of shares	0	Issuance of new shares	242,000
		Ending balance	861,000

Common Shares

Beginning balance	+	Issuance of new share	−	Retirements of shares	=	Ending balance
$619,000	+	$242,000	−	X	=	$861,000
				−X	=	$861,000 − $619,000 − $242,000
				X	=	$0

Dividend Payments If the amount of the dividends is not given elsewhere (e.g., in a statement of retained earnings), it can be computed as follows:

Retained Earnings

		Beginning balance	208,000
Dividend declaration	41,000	Net income	100,000
		Ending balance	267,000

Dividends Payable

		Beginning balance	0
Dividend payments	41,000	Dividend declaration	41,000
		Ending balance	0

First, we must compute dividend declarations by analyzing Retained Earnings. Then we can solve for dividend payments with the Dividends Payable account. Capilano Ltd. has no Dividends Payable account, so dividend payments are the same as declarations. The following computations show how to compute Capilano Ltd.'s dividend payments:

Retained Earnings

Beginning balance	+	Net income	−	Dividend declarations	=	Ending balance
$208,000	+	$100,000	−	X	=	$267,000
				−X	=	$267,000 − $208,000 − $100,000
				X	=	$41,000

> Try It!

6. Pardellies Limited reported the following current asset and current liability amounts at year end:

	December 31,	
	2017	**2016**
Current assets		
Cash and cash equivalents	$38,000	$ 6,000
Accounts receivable	44,000	46,000
Inventories	68,000	62,000
Prepaid expenses	2,000	6,000
Current liabilities		
Notes payable (for inventory purchases)	$22,000	$14,000
Accounts payable	48,000	38,000
Accrued liabilities	14,000	18,000
Income and other taxes payable	22,000	20,000

Use this information to answer the following questions about the company:

a. Compute collections from customers during 2017. Sales totalled $240,000 and all sales were on credit.

b. Compute payments for inventory during 2017, assuming the change in Accounts Payable is due to inventory. Cost of goods sold was $140,000.

c. Compute payments for income taxes during 2017. Income tax expense for 2017 was $20,000.

d. Compute payments for prepaid expenses during 2017. Prepaid expenses of $8,000 expired during 2017.

7. Bolin Corp. reported the following (amounts in thousands):

Retirement of Bolin Corp. preferred shares	$ 90
Sale of bonds issued by Blue Ltd.	224
Payment of interest on mortgage note to bank	22
Purchase of land	316
Payment of income taxes	76
Sale of Bolin Corp. common shares	210
Collection of long-term note receivable	126
Payment of dividends	300

a. What is Bolin Corp.'s net change in cash from investing activities?

b. Categorize the other items.

8. Refer to the Bolin Corp. data in the previous question. What is Bolin Corp.'s net change in cash from financing activities?

Solutions appear at the end of this chapter and on MyAccountingLab

THE CASH FLOW STATEMENT: THE INDIRECT METHOD

LO 5

What is the indirect method, and how is it used to prepare a cash flow statement?

The indirect method of reporting cash flows from operating activities is a conversion or a reconciliation from net income to net cash inflow (or outflow) from operating activities. It is a conversion of accrual-based net income to the cash-based net income, which shows how the company's net income is related to net cash flows from operating activities. The indirect method starts with net income from the income statement and reconciles to operating cash flows.

This method shows the link between net income and cash flows from operations better than the direct method. Many companies use the indirect method for that reason. The main drawback of the indirect method is that it does not report the detailed operating cash flows—collections from customers and other cash receipts, payments to suppliers, payments to employees, and payments for interest and taxes. Although the Accounting Standards Board prefers the direct method, the vast majority of Canadian companies (and US companies) use the indirect method.

Exhibit 17–16 is Capilano Ltd.'s cash flow statement prepared by the indirect method. Only the operating section of the statement differs from the direct method format in Exhibit 17–14. The new items ➊, ➋, and ➌ are keyed to their explanations, which are discussed below. For ease of reference, we repeat Capilano Ltd.'s income statement and balance sheet here as Exhibits 17–17 and 17–18.

🔑 **KEY** POINTS

These two methods (direct and indirect) of preparing the cash flow statement affect only the operating activities section of the statement. No difference exists for investing activities or financing activities.

EXHIBIT 17–16 | **Cash Flow Statement (Indirect Method for Operating Activities)**

CAPILANO LTD. Cash Flow Statement For the Year Ended December 31, 2017		
Cash flows from operating activities		(in thousands)
Net income		$100
Add (subtract) items that affect net income and cash flow differently:		
➊ Amortization	$ 43	
➋ Gain on sale of property, plant, and equipment and intangible assets	(19)	
Increase in accounts receivable	(32)	
Increase in interest receivable	(5)	
Decrease in inventory	7	
➌ Increase in prepaid expenses	(1)	
Increase in accounts payable	83	
Decrease in salaries payable	(6)	
Decrease in accrued liabilities	(2)	
		68
Net cash inflow from operating activities		168
Cash flows from investing activities		
Acquisition of property, plant, and equipment and intangible assets	(735)	
Loan to another company	(26)	
Cash received from selling property, plant, and equipment and intangible assets	149	
Net cash outflow from investing activities		(612)
Cash flows from financing activities		
Cash received from issuing common shares	242	
Cash received from issuing long-term debt	226	
Payment of long-term debt	(27)	
Payment of dividends	(41)	
Net cash inflow from financing activities		400
Net increase (decrease) in cash and cash equivalents		(44)
Cash and cash equivalents at beginning of 2017		101
Cash and cash equivalents at end of 2017		$ 57

EXHIBIT 17–17 | Income Statement

CAPILANO LTD. Income Statement For the Year Ended December 31, 2017 (amounts in thousands)		
Revenues and gains:		
Sales revenue	$682	
Interest revenue	29	
Dividend revenue	22	
❷ Gain on sale of property, plant, and equipment and intangible assets	19	
Total revenues and gains		$752
Expenses:		
Cost of goods sold	360	
Salaries expense	134	
❶ Amortization expense	43	
Other operating expenses	41	
Interest expense	38	
Total expenses		616
Net income before income taxes		136
Income tax expense		36
Net income		$100

Theory behind the Indirect Method

The indirect method cash flow statement begins with accrual-basis net income from the income statement. Additions and subtractions follow. These are labelled "Add (subtract) items that affect net income and cash flow differently." We discuss these items in the following sections. Refer to Exhibit 17–16.

Amortization Expenses ❶ These expenses are added back to net income to compute cash flow from operations. Let's see why.

Amortization was originally recorded as follows:

Amortization Expense	43,000	
Accumulated Amortization		43,000

REAL WORLD EXAMPLE

Other adjustments commonly made to net income are for amortization of bond premium/discount and equity method revenue.

This entry neither debits nor credits Cash because amortization has no cash effect. However, amortization expense is deducted from revenues to compute income. Therefore, in going from net income to cash flows from operations, we add amortization back to net income. The add back cancels the earlier deduction.

The following example should help clarify this practice. Suppose a company had only two transactions during the period: a $5,000 cash sale and amortization expense of $1,000. Net income is $4,000 ($5,000 − $1,000). But cash flow from operations is $5,000. To go from net income ($4,000) to cash flow ($5,000), we must add back the amortization amount of $1,000.

Gains and Losses on the Sale of Assets ❷ Sales of property, plant, and equipment and of intangible assets are investing activities on the cash flow statement.

CAPILANO LTD. **Balance Sheet** **December 31, 2017 and 2016** **(amounts in thousands)**				
Assets	2017	2016	Increase (Decrease)	Changes in the following:
Current				
Cash	$ 57	$ 101	$ (44)	
❸ Accounts receivable	224	192	32	
❸ Interest receivable	8	3	5	
❸ Inventory	323	330	(7)	Current assets—**Operating**
❸ Prepaid expenses	18	17	1	
Long-term receivable from another company	26	—	26	
Property, plant, and equipment, net of amortization	1,087	525	562	Noncurrent assets—**Investing**
Total	$1,743	$1,168	$575	
Liabilities				
Current				
❸ Accounts payable	$ 220	$ 137	$ 83	Current liabilities—**Operating**
❸ Salaries payable	6	12	(6)	and current portion of
❸ Accrued liabilities	5	7	(2)	long-term debt—**Financing**
Long-term debt	384	185	199	Most long-term liabilities
Shareholders' Equity				and contributed
Common shares	861	619	242	capital—**Financing**
				Change due to net income—
Retained earnings	267	208	59	**Operating** and change due to
Total	$1,743	$1,168	$575	dividends—**Financing**

Refer to the calculations on page 997 regarding the sale of the Capilano Ltd. equipment with a book value of $130,000 for $149,000, producing a gain of $19,000. The $19,000 gain is reported on the income statement and is therefore included in net income. The cash receipt, or proceeds from the sale, is $149,000, and that is what we report on the cash flow statement. The $149,000 of cash received also includes the $19,000 gain on the sale. Gains and losses are bookkeeping amounts that we track on the income statement, but they do not represent the cash received of $149,000 from the sale, which is what we want to show in the investing section. Starting with net income, we subtract the gain, which removes the gain's earlier effect on income. The sale of property, plant, and equipment and of intangible assets is reported as a $149,000 cash receipt from an investing activity, as shown in Exhibit 17–16.

A loss on the sale of property, plant, and equipment and of intangible assets is also an adjustment to net income on the cash flow statement. A loss is *added back* to income to compute cash flow from operations. The cash received from selling the property, plant, and equipment and intangible assets is reported under investing activities on the cash flow statement.

To convert net income from accrual basis to cash basis:

- Expenses with no cash effects, such as accruals, are added back to net income on the cash flow statement.
- Revenues that do not provide cash, such as accrued income, are subtracted from net income.
- Items are either added or subtracted by calculating differences in current assets and current liabilities between the opening and closing amounts.

Changes in the Current Asset and Current Liability Accounts ③ Most current assets and current liabilities result from operating activities. Changes in the current accounts are reported as adjustments to net income on the cash flow statement. The following rules apply and are summarized in Exhibit 17–19:

- **An increase in a current asset other than cash is subtracted from net income to compute cash flow from operations.** Suppose a company makes a sale. Income is increased by the sale amount. However, collection of less than the full amount increases Accounts Receivable. For example, Exhibit 17–18 reports that Capilano Ltd.'s Accounts Receivable increased by $32,000 during 2017. To compute the impact of revenue on Capilano Ltd.'s cash flows, we must subtract the $32,000 increase in Accounts Receivable from net income in Exhibit 17–16. The reason is this: We have *not* collected this $32,000 in cash. The same logic applies to the other current assets. If they increase during the period, subtract the increase from net income.
- **A decrease in a current asset other than cash is added to net income.** Suppose Capilano Ltd.'s Accounts Receivable balance decreased by $8,000 during the period. Cash receipts cause Accounts Receivable to decrease and Cash to increase, so decreases in Accounts Receivable and the other current assets are *added* to net income.

- **A decrease in a current liability is subtracted from net income.** The payment of a current liability decreases both Cash and the current liability, so decreases in current liabilities are subtracted from net income. For example, in Exhibit 17–16, the $2,000 decrease in Accrued Liabilities is *subtracted* from net income to compute net cash inflow from operating activities.
- **An increase in a current liability is added to net income.** Capilano Ltd.'s Accounts Payable increased during the year. This increase can occur only if cash is not spent to pay this liability, which means that cash payments are less than the related expense. As a result, we have more cash on hand. Thus, increases in current liabilities are *added* to net income.

Computing net cash inflow or net cash outflow from *operating* activities by the indirect method takes a path that is very different from the direct method computation. However, both methods arrive at the same amount of net cash flow from operating activities, as shown in Exhibits 17–14 and 17–16: Both report a net cash inflow of $168,000.

Exhibit 17–19 summarizes the adjustments needed to convert net income to net cash inflow (or net cash outflow) from operating activities by the indirect method.

Item	Adjustment on Statement of Cash Flows	
Depreciation, Depletion, and Amortization Expense	+	
Gains on Disposal of Long-term Assets	–	
Losses on Disposal of Long-term Assets	+	
Increases in Current Assets	–	← Decrease in cash
Decreases in Current Assets	+	
Increases in Current Liabilities	+	← Increase in cash
Decreases in Current Liabilities	–	

> Try It!

9. The information listed below is taken from the financial statements of Vista Corp. for the year ended December 31, 2017, when net income is $150. All amounts are in thousands of dollars:

	Dec. 31, 2017	Jan. 1, 2017
Cash	$45	$15
Accounts Receivable	12	18
Inventory	66	48
Accounts Payable	20	9
Wages Payable	24	39

Compute cash flow from operating activities using the indirect method.

10. Examine Capilano Ltd.'s cash flow statement, Exhibit 17–16, and answer these questions:

a. Does Capilano Ltd. appear to be growing or shrinking? How can you tell?

b. Where did most of Capilano Ltd.'s cash for expansion come from?

c. Suppose Accounts Receivable decreased by $80,000 (instead of increasing by $32,000) during the current year. What would Capilano Ltd.'s cash flow from operating activities be?

Solutions appear at the end of this chapter and on MyAccountingLab

THE IMPACT OF IFRS ON THE CASH FLOW STATEMENT

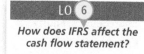

LO 6

How does IFRS affect the cash flow statement?

ASPE	IFRS
In Canada, both IFRS and ASPE are prepared under the authority of the Accounting Standards Board and are published as part of the *CPA Canada Handbook*.	
Interest and dividends that go through net income are considered operating activities, otherwise they are considered to be financing activities.	Interest and dividends need to be reported consistently from period to period as operating, investing, or financing activities.

While both ASPE and IFRS permit both the direct and indirect method, ASPE encourages the use of the direct method. Once a company chooses a method for its accounting policy, it must apply the policy consistently to all similar transactions.

SUMMARY PROBLEMS FOR YOUR REVIEW

Problem 1

The Adams Corporation reported the following income statement for 2017 and comparative balance sheet for 2017 and 2016, along with transaction data for 2017:

ADAMS CORPORATION Comparative Balance Sheet December 31, 2017 and 2016			
	2017	**2016**	**Increase (Decrease)**
Assets			
Current assets:			
Cash	$ 22,000	$ 3,000	$19,000
Accounts receivable	22,000	23,000	(1,000)
Merchandise inventory	35,000	34,000	1,000
Long-term assets:			
Plants assets	153,200	97,200	56,000
Accumulated amortization—Plant assets	(27,200)	(25,200)	(2,000)
Total assets	$205,000	$132,000	$73,000
Liabilities			
Current liabilities:			
Accounts payable	$ 35,000	$ 26,000	$ 9,000
Accrued liabilities	7,000	9,000	(2,000)
Income tax payable	10,000	10,000	0
Long-term liabilities:			
Bonds payable	84,000	53,000	31,000
Total liabilities	136,000	98,000	38,000
Shareholders' Equity			
Common shares	52,000	20,000	32,000
Retained earnings	27,000	19,000	8,000
Preferred shares	(10,000)	(5,000)	(5,000)
Total Shareholders' Equity	69,000	34,000	35,000
Total Liabilities and Shareholders' Equity	$205,000	$132,000	$73,000

ADAMS CORPORATION
Income Statement
Year Ended December 31, 2017

Sales revenue		$662,000
Cost of goods sold		560,000
Gross profit		102,000
Operating expenses:		
Salaries and wages expense	$46,000	
Amortization expense—Plant assets	10,000	
Rent expense	2,000	
Total operating expenses		58,000
Operating income		44,000
Other revenue and (expenses):		
Loss on disposal of plant assets	(2,000)	
Total other revenues and (expenses)		(2,000)
Net income before income taxes		42,000
Income tax expense		16,000
Net income		$ 26,000

Transaction data for 2017

Cash paid for purchase of equipment	$140,000
Cash payment of dividends	18,000
Issuance of common shares to retire bonds payable	13,000
Issuance of bonds payable to borrow cash	44,000
Cash receipt from issuance of common shares	19,000
Cash receipt from sale of equipment (cost, $84,000; accumulated amortization, $8,000)	74,000
Cash paid for purchase of preferred shares	5,000

Prepare Adams Corporation's cash flow statement for the year ended December 31, 2017. Format cash flows from operating activities by the indirect method.

Problem 2

Matheson Corporation's accounting records include the information shown below for the year ended December 31, 2017. Prepare Matheson Corporation's income statement and cash flow statement for the year ended December 31, 2017. Follow the cash flow statement format of Exhibit 17–7, using the direct method for operating cash flows, and follow the single-step format for the income statement (grouping all revenues together and all expenses together, as shown in Exhibit 17–12 on page 991). Net income is $61,000.

a. Salary expense, $290,000

b. Amortization expense on property, plant, and equipment, $104,000

c. Cash received from issuing common shares, $87,000

d. Declaration and payment of cash dividends, $62,000

e. Collection of interest on notes receivable, $20,000

f. Payments of salaries, $308,000

g. Collections from credit customers, $1,030,000

h. Loan to another company, $118,000

i. Cash received from selling property, plant, and equipment, $50,000, including a $3,000 loss

j. Payments to suppliers, $893,000

k. Income tax expense and payments, $45,000

l. Credit sales, $1,005,000

m. Cash sales, $258,000

n. Interest revenue, $22,000

o. Cash received from issuing short-term debt, $106,000

p. Payments of long-term debt, $160,000

q. Interest expense and payments, $31,000

r. Loan collections, $143,000

s. Cash received from selling investments, $61,000, including a $36,000 gain

t. Purchase of inventory on credit, $832,000

u. Dividends received in cash on investments in shares, $8,000

v. Cash payments to acquire property, plant, and equipment, $232,000

w. Cost of goods sold, $795,000

x. Cash balance:

December 31, 2016—$230,000

December 31, 2017—$144,000

Note that, for simplicity, uncollectible accounts have been ignored.

SOLUTION

Problem 1

ADAMS CORPORATION Statement of Cash Flows Year Ended December 31, 2017		
Cash flows from operating activities:		
Net Income		$26,000
Adjustments to reconcile net income to net cash Provided by operating activities:		
Amortization expense—plant assets	$ 10,000	
Loss on disposal of plant asset	2,000	
Decrease in accounts receivable	1,000	
Increase in merchandise inventory	(1,000)	
Increase in accounts payable	9,000	
Decrease in accrued liabilities	(2,000)	19,000
Net cash provided by operating activities		45,000
Cash flows from investing activities:		
Cash payment for acquisition of plant assets	(140,000)	
Cash receipt from disposal of plant assets	74,000	
Net cash used for investing activities		(66,000)
Cash flows from financing activities:		
Cash receipt from issuance of bonds payable	44,000	
Cash receipt from issuance of common shares	19,000	
Cash payment for purchase of preferred shares	(5,000)	
Cash payment of dividends	(18,000)	
Net cash provided by financing activities		40,000
Net increase (decrease) in cash		19,000
Cash balance, december 31, 2016		3,000
Cash balance, december 31, 2017		$22,000
Non-cash investing and financing activities:		
Issuance of common shares to retire bonds payable		$13,000
Total non-cash investing and financing activities		$13,000

The title must include the name of the company, "Cash Flow Statement," and the specific period of time covered. There are three sections: Cash flows from operating, investing, and financing activities.

For the indirect method, always begin with accrual-basis net income from the income statement (or from the data given, in this case).

Add back non-cash items: amortization and losses; deduct gains

Reflect changes in current assets and liabilities as follows:
Current asset increases—deduct
Current asset decreases—add
Current liability increases—add
Current liability decreases—deduct

For cash flows from investing activities, look for activities that have a cash impact on long-term asset accounts. Brackets indicate cash outflows (purchases).

For cash flows from financing activities, look for activities that have a cash impact on short-term debt (or note) accounts, long-term liability accounts, and equity accounts. Brackets indicate cash outflows.

The end result should equal the December 31, 2017, balance sheet amount of cash and cash equivalents, given as part of current assets. If it does not, there is an error in the cash flow statement.

Relevant T-accounts:

Plant Assets

Dec. 31, 2016	97,200		
Acquisitions	140,000	Disposals	84,000
Dec. 31, 2017	153,200		

Accumulated Amortization—Plant Assets

		Dec. 31, 2016	25,200
Disposals	8,000	Amort. exp.	10,000
		Dec. 31, 2017	27,200

Bonds Payable

		Dec. 31, 2016	53,000
Retirement	13,000	Issuance	44,000
		Dec. 31, 2017	84,000

Common Shares

		Dec. 31, 2016	20,000
Retirement	0	Issuance	13,000
		Issuance	19,000
		Dec. 31, 2017	52,000

Preferred Shares

Dec. 31, 2016	5,000		
Purchase	5,000	Disposal	0
Dec. 31, 2017	10,000		

Retained Earnings

		Dec. 31, 2016	19,000
		Net Income	26,000
Dividends	18,000		
		Dec. 31, 2017	27,000

Problem 2

To create the income statement, select revenues, expenses, gains, and losses from the list of items (a) to (x). Items can be listed in order of declining balances or in alphabetical order. Income tax expense is almost always shown separately, as the last item before net income.

Item (reference letter)	Matheson Corporation Income Statement For the Year Ended December 31, 2017		
			(amounts in thousands)
	Revenue and gains:		
l, m	Sales revenue ($1,005 + $258)	$1,263	
s	Gain on sale of investments	36	
n	Interest revenue	22	
u	Dividend revenue	8	
	Total revenues and gains		$1,329
	Expenses and losses:		
w	Cost of goods sold	795	
a	Salary expense	290	
b	Amortization expense	104	
q	Interest expense	31	
i	Loss on sale of property, plant, and equipment	3	
	Total expenses		1,223
	Net income before income tax		106
k	Income tax expense		45
	Net income		$ 61

Matheson Corporation
Cash Flow Statement
For the Year Ended December 31, 2017

		(amounts in thousands)	
	Cash flows from operating activities		
	Receipts:		
g, m	Collections from customers ($1,030 + $258)	$1,288	
e	Interest received on notes receivable	20	
u	Dividends received on investments in shares	8	
	Total cash receipts		$ 1,316
	Payments:		
j	To suppliers	(893)	
f	To employees	(308)	
q	For interest	(31)	
k	For income tax	(45)	
	Total cash payments		(1,277)
	Net cash inflow from operating activities		39
	Cash flows from investing activities		
v	Acquisition of property, plant, and equipment	$(232)	
h	Loan to another company	(118)	
s	Cash received from sale of investments	61	
i	Cash received from sale of property, plant, and equipment	50	
r	Collection of loans	143	
	Net cash outflow from investing activities		(96)
	Cash flows from financing activities		
o	Cash received from issuing short-term debt	106	
c	Cash received from issuing common shares	87	
p	Payments of long-term debt	(160)	
d	Dividends declared and paid	(62)	
	Net cash outflow from financing activities		(29)
	Net decrease in cash		(86)
x	Cash balance at beginning of 2017		230
x	Cash balance at end of 2017		$ 144

← Compare to Cash account

Cash flow (direct method) statement:
- Operating activities: Look for activities that have a cash impact on revenues (cash receipts) and expenses (cash payments).
- Financing activities: Look for activities that have a cash impact on short-term debt accounts, long-term liability accounts, and equity accounts.
- Investing activities: Look for activities that have a cash impact on long-term asset accounts.

SUMMARY

LEARNING OBJECTIVE 1   Identify the purposes of the cash flow statement

What is a cash flow statement?   Pg. 978

- The *cash flow statement* reports a business's cash receipts, cash payments, and change in cash for the accounting period.
- It shows *why* cash increased or decreased during the period.
- It is a required financial statement and it gives a different view of the business from that given by accrual-basis statements.
- The cash flow statement aids in the prediction of future cash flows and evaluation of management decisions.
- Cash includes cash on hand, cash in the bank, and *cash equivalents*, such as liquid short-term investments.

LEARNING OBJECTIVE 2   Identify cash flows from operating, investing, and financing activities

What are the main cash flows in a business?   Pg. 981

- The cash flow statement reports *operating activities, investing activities,* and *financing activities.*
- Operating activities create revenues and expenses in the entity's major line of business.
- Investing activities affect the long-term assets.
- Financing activities include the cash obtained from investors and creditors to launch and sustain the business.
- Each of these sections of the cash flow statement includes cash receipts and cash payments.
- The statement must agree with the change in cash reported on the comparative balance sheet.
- In addition, *non-cash investing* and *financing activities* are reported either in the notes to the financial statements or in a separate section.
- *Free cash flow* is the amount of cash available for new opportunities, calculated as cash available from operations after paying for planned investments in long-term assets.

LEARNING OBJECTIVE 3   Prepare a cash flow statement by the direct method

What is the direct method, and how is it used to prepare a cash flow statement?   Pg. 986

- Two formats can be used to report *operating* activities: the direct method and the indirect method.
- Examples of items that the *direct method* reports include collections from customers and receipts of interest and dividends minus cash payments to suppliers, payments to employees, and payments for interest and income taxes.
- Investing cash flows and financing cash flows are unaffected by the method used to report operating activities.

     MyAccountingLab **Video:** Creating Cash Flow Statements by the Direct Method

LEARNING OBJECTIVE 4   Compute the cash effects of a wide variety of business transactions

What are the cash effects of different business transactions?   Pg. 991

- The analysis of T-accounts aids in the computation of the cash effects of business transactions.
- The information needed comes from the balance sheet, the income statement, the statement of earnings, and the related accounts.

LEARNING OBJECTIVE 5   Prepare a cash flow statement by the indirect method

What is the indirect method, and how is it used to prepare a cash flow statement?   Pg. 1000

- The *indirect method* starts with net income and reconciles net income to cash flow from operations.

LEARNING OBJECTIVE 6   Identify the impact of IFRS on the cash flow statement

How does IFRS affect the cash flow statement?   Pg. 1005

- IFRS provides companies with some alternatives for classifying both the receipt and payment of interest and dividends on the cash flow statement.
- Specifically, the receipt of interest and dividends may be recorded as either operating or investing activities, while the payment of interest and dividends may be recorded as either operating or financing activities.
- Once the company chooses an accounting policy, however, it must apply the policy consistently to all transactions of a similar nature.

     MyAccountingLab **Video:** Creating Cash Flow Statements by the Indirect Method
                 Video: Real World Accounting

Check **Accounting Vocabulary** on page 1013 for all key terms used in Chapter 17 and the Glossary at the back of the book for all key terms used in the textbook.

MORE CHAPTER REVIEW MATERIAL

MyAccountingLab

DemoDoc covering **Operating, Investing,**
and Financing Activities
Student PowerPoint Slides
Audio Chapter Summary

Note: All MyAccountingLab resources can be found in
the Chapter Resources section and the Multimedia Library.

ACCOUNTING VOCABULARY

Cash equivalents Highly liquid short-term investments that can be converted into cash with little delay *(p. 980)*.

Cash flow statement Reports cash receipts and cash payments classified according to the entity's major activities: operating, investing, and financing *(p. 978)*.

Cash flows Cash receipts and cash payments (disbursements) *(p. 978)*.

Direct method The format of the operating activities section of the cash flow statement that shows cash receipts from and cash payments for operating activities *(p. 985)*.

Financing activity An activity that obtains the funds from investors and creditors needed to launch and sustain the business; a section of the cash flow statement *(p. 981)*.

Free cash flow The amount of cash available from operations after paying for planned investments in plant, equipment, and other long-term assets *(p. 984)*.

Indirect method The format of the operating activities section of the cash flow statement that starts with net income and shows the reconciliation from net income to operating cash flows. Also called the *reconciliation method* *(p. 985)*.

Investing activity An activity that increases and decreases the long-term assets available to the business; a section of the cash flow statement *(p. 981)*.

Operating activity An activity that creates revenue or expense in the entity's major line of business; a section of the cash flow statement. Operating activities affect the income statement *(p. 981)*.

Reconciliation method Another name for the *indirect method* of formatting the operating activities section of the cash flow statement *(p. 985)*.

SIMILAR ACCOUNTING TERMS

Cash flows	Cash receipts and cash payments
Cash flow statement	Statement of cash flows; Statement of changes in financial position
Cash payments	Disbursements
Cash receipts	Proceeds
Indirect method	Reconciliation method

SELF-STUDY QUESTIONS

Test your understanding of the chapter by marking the correct answer for each of the following questions:

1. The income statement and the balance sheet *(p. 978)*
   a. Report the cash effects of transactions
   b. Fail to report why cash changed during the period
   c. Report the sources and uses of cash during the period
   d. Are divided into operating, investing, and financing activities

2. The purpose of the cash flow statement is to *(p. 979)*
   a. Predict future cash flows
   b. Evaluate management decisions
   c. Determine the ability to pay liabilities and dividends
   d. Do all of the above

3. A successful company's major source of cash should be *(p. 981)*
   a. Operating activities
   b. Investing activities

c. Financing activities

d. A combination of the above

4. Dividends paid to shareholders are usually reported on the cash flow statement as a(n) *(p. 983)*

   a. Operating activity

   b. Investing activity

   c. Financing activity

   d. Combination of the above

5. Which of the following appears as a line on a cash flow statement prepared by the direct method? *(p. 988)*

   a. Amortization expense

   b. Decrease in accounts receivable

   c. Loss on sale of property, plant, and equipment and intangible assets

   d. Cash payments to suppliers

6. Falcon Lake Copy Centre had accounts receivable of $40,000 at the beginning of the year and $50,000 at year end. Revenue for the year totalled $150,000. How much cash did Falcon Lake Copy Centre collect from customers? *(pp. 992–993)*

   a. $160,000

   b. $190,000

   c. $200,000

   d. $140,000

7. Tancredi Ltd. sold a long-term investment for $50,000; the selling price included a loss of $2,500. The cash flow from investing activities will show *(p. 998)*

   a. An increase of $50,000

   b. An increase of $47,500

c. A decrease of $52,500

d. None of the above

8. Herdsman Corp. borrowed $100,000, issued common shares for $40,000, and paid dividends of $30,000. What was Herdsman Corp.'s net cash provided (used) by financing activities? *(pp. 998–999)*

   a. $0

   b. $110,000

   c. $(30,000)

   d. $140,000

9. In preparing a cash flow statement by the indirect method, the accountant will treat an increase in inventory as a(n) *(p. 1004)*

   a. Increase in investment cash flows

   b. Decrease in investment cash flows

   c. Decrease in operating cash flows

   d. Increase in operating cash flows

10. Net income is $40,000, and amortization is $12,000. In addition, the sale of property, plant, and equipment generated an $8,000 gain. Current assets other than cash increased by $12,000, and current liabilities increased by $16,000. What was the amount of cash flow from operations using the indirect method? *(pp. 1002–1004)*

    a. $64,000

    b. $48,000

    c. $40,000

    d. $72,000

Answers to Self-Study Questions

1. b 2. d 3. a 4. c 5. d 6. d 7. a 8. b 9. c

10. b ($40,000 + $12,000 − $8,000 − $12,000 + $16,000 = $48,000)

ASSIGNMENT MATERIAL

QUESTIONS

1. What information does the cash flow statement report that is not shown on the balance sheet, the income statement, or the statement of retained earnings?

2. Identify four purposes of the cash flow statement.

3. Identify and briefly describe the three types of activities that are reported on the cash flow statement.

4. How is the cash flow statement dated and why?

5. What is the check figure for the cash flow statement? In other words, which figure do you check to make sure you've done your work correctly? Where is it obtained, and how is it used?

6. What is the most important source of cash flow category on the cash flow statement for most successful companies?

7. How can cash decrease during a year when income is high? How can cash increase when income is low? How can investors and creditors learn these facts about the company?

8. How should issuance of a note payable to purchase land be reported in the financial statements? Identify three other transactions that fall into this same category.

9. What is free cash flow, and how is it calculated?

10. Fort Inc. prepares its cash flow statement using the *direct* method for operating activities. Identify the section of Fort Inc.'s cash flow statement where the results of each of the following transactions will appear. If the transaction does not appear on the cash flow statement, give the reason.

a. Cash	14,000	
Note Payable, Long-Term		14,000
b. Salary Payable	7,300	
Cash		7,300
c. Cash	28,400	
Sales Revenue		28,400
d. Amortization Expense	6,500	
Patent		6,500
e. Accounts Payable	1,400	
Cash		1,400

11. Why is amortization expense *not* reported on a cash flow statement that reports operating activities by the direct method? Why and how are these expenses reported on a statement prepared by the indirect method?

12. Winford Distributing Corp. collected cash of $102,000 from customers and $8,000 interest on notes receivable. Cash payments included $28,000 to employees, $18,000 to suppliers, $11,000 as dividends to shareholders, and $10,000 as a long-term loan to another company. How much was Winford Distributing Corp.'s net cash inflow from operating activities?

13. Summarize the major cash receipts and cash payments in the three categories of activities that appear on the cash flow statement prepared by the direct method.

14. Nelson Inc. recorded salary expense of $54,000 during a year when the balance of Salary Payable decreased from $8,000 to $2,000. How much cash did Nelson Inc. pay to employees during the year? Where on the cash flow statement should Nelson Inc. report this item?

15. Trail Corporation's beginning property, plant, and equipment balance, net of accumulated amortization, was $200,000, and the ending amount was $180,000. Trail Corporation recorded amortization of $35,000 and sold property, plant, and equipment with a book value of $10,000. How much cash did Trail Corporation pay to purchase property, plant, and equipment during the period? Where on the cash flow statement should Trail Corporation report this item?

16. Which format of the cash flow statement gives a clearer description of the individual cash flows from operating activities? Which format better shows the relationship between net income and operating cash flow?

17. An investment that cost $150,000 was sold for $160,000, resulting in a $10,000 gain. Show how to report this transaction on a cash flow statement prepared by the indirect method.

18. Using the indirect method, identify the cash effects of net increases and net decreases in current assets other than cash. What are the cash effects of net increases and net decreases in current liabilities?

19. Aggasiz Corporation earned net income of $90,000 and had amortization expense of $24,000. Also, non-cash current assets decreased by $18,000, and current liabilities decreased by $12,000. Using the indirect method, what was Aggasiz Corporation's net cash flow from operating activities?

20. What is the difference between the direct method and the indirect method of reporting investing activities and financing activities?

21. Degrout Corp. reports operating activities by the direct method. Does this method show the relationship between net income and cash flow from operations? If so, state how. If not, how can Greenwood Corp. satisfy this purpose of the cash flow statement?

MyAccountingLab   Make the grade with MyAccountingLab: Most of the Starters, Exercises, and Problems marked in red can be found on MyAccountingLab. You can practise them as often as you want, and most feature step-by-step guided instructions to help you find the right answer.

STARTERS

Starter 17–1   Describe how the cash flow statement helps investors and creditors perform each of the following functions:
1. Predict future cash flows.
2. Evaluate management decisions.
3. Predict the ability to make debt payments to lenders and pay dividends to shareholders.
4. Show the relationship of net income to cash flow.

Purposes of the cash flow statement
①

Starter 17–2   Answer these questions about the cash flow statement:
a. List the categories of cash flows in order of importance.
b. What is the "check figure" for the cash flow statement? Where do you get this check figure?
c. What is the first dollar amount to report for the direct method?
d. What is the first dollar amount to report for the indirect method?

Classifying cash flow items
①

Using a cash flow statement

①

Starter 17–3 Which company shown below is likely a startup company rather than an established company? Give reasons for your answer.

	Company X	Company Y
Cash inflow (outflow)—operating activities	$ (10,000)	$50,000
Cash inflow (outflow)—investing activities	(100,000)	30,000
Cash inflow (outflow)—financing activities	80,000	(20,000)
Income (loss) for the year	20,000	20,000

Free cash flow

②

Free cash flow, $56,000

Starter 17–4 Latham Company expects the following for 2017:
* Net cash provided by operating activities of $120,000
* Net cash provided by financing activities of $48,000
* Net cash used for investing activities of $64,000 (no sales of long-term assets)

How much free cash flow does Latham Company expect for 2017?

Preparing a cash flow statement—direct method

③

Net increase in cash, $10,000

Starter 17–5 Memmot Health Labs Inc. began 2017 with cash of $65,000. During the year, Memmot earned service revenue of $650,000 and collected $660,000 from customers. Expenses for the year totalled $470,000, of which Memmot paid $460,000 in cash to suppliers and employees. Memmot also paid $150,000 to purchase equipment and paid a cash dividend of $40,000 to its shareholders during 2017.

Prepare the company's cash flow statement for the year ended December 31, 2017. Format operating activities by the direct method.

Computing operating cash flows—direct method

③

Net cash provided, $40,000

Starter 17–6 Napanee Resources Inc. has assembled the following data for the year ended June 30, 2017:

Payment of dividends	$ 12,000
Cash received from issuing shares	40,000
Collections from customers	400,000
Cash received from sale of land	120,000
Payments to suppliers	220,000
Purchase of equipment	80,000
Payments to employees	140,000
Payment of note payable	60,000

Prepare only the *operating* activities section of Napanee's cash flow statement for the year ended June 30, 2017. Napanee uses the direct method for operating cash flows.

Preparing a cash flow statement—direct method

③

Net increase in cash, $48,000

Starter 17–7 Use the data in Starter 17–6 to prepare Napanee Resources Inc.'s complete cash flow statement for the year ended June 30, 2017. Napanee uses the *direct* method for operating activities. Use Exhibit 17–14 on page 993 as a guide, but you may stop after determining the net increase (or decrease) in cash.

Preparing a cash flow statement—investing

④

Starter 17–8 Refer to the Equipment T-account below. For the items to be reported on the cash flow statement, indicate the section where they are reported.

Equipment

Beginning Balance	$100,000		
Jul. 1	200,000		
		Jul. 15	$50,000
Aug. 1	57,000		
Ending balance	$307,000		

July 1 and July 15 were cash transactions.
August 1 was a purchase with a long-term note.

Techno Toys Ltd. had the following comparative balance sheet:

Computing operating cash
flows—direct method
③ ④
a. Collections from customers,
$402,000

TECHNO TOYS LTD.
Balance Sheet
December 31, 2017 and 2016

Assets	2017	2016	Liabilities	2017	2016
Current			Current		
Cash	$ 57,000	$ 48,000	Accounts payable	$ 141,000	$ 126,000
Accounts receivable	162,000	144,000	Salary payable	69,000	63,000
Inventory	240,000	232,000	Accrued liabilities	24,000	33,000
Prepaid expenses	9,000	6,000	Long-term notes payable	198,000	204,000
Long-term investments	225,000	270,000	**Shareholders' Equity**		
Property and equipment, net	675,000	575,000	Common shares	120,000	111,000
			Retained earnings	816,000	738,000
Total	$1,368,000	$1,275,000	Total	$1,368,000	$1,275,000

Compute the following for Techno Toys Ltd.:
a. Collections from customers during 2017. Sales totalled $420,000.
b. Payments for inventory during 2017, assuming the change in Accounts Payable is due to inventory. Cost of goods sold was $240,000.

Starter 17–10 Use the Techno Toys Ltd. data in Starter 17–9 to compute the following:
a. New borrowing or payment of long-term note payable, with Techno having only one long-term note payable transaction during the year.
b. Issuance of common shares, with Techno having only one common share transaction during the year.
c. Payment of cash dividends. Net income for the year ended December 31, 2017, was $120,000.
d. Net cash provided by operating activities using the direct method. Ignore Prepaid Expenses, Salary Payable, and Accrued Liabilities.

Computing financing cash flows
④
c. Dividends, $42,000

KS Media Corporation had the following income statement and balance sheet for 2017:

Computing investing and
financing cash flows
④
a. Acquisitions $16,500

KS MEDIA CORPORATION
Income Statement
For the Year Ended December 31, 2017

Service revenue	$120,000
Amortization expense	9,000
Other expenses	81,000
Net income	$ 30,000

KS MEDIA CORPORATION
Balance Sheet
December 31, 2017 and 2016

Assets	2017	2016	Liabilities	2017	2016
Current:			Current:		
Cash	$ 7,500	$ 6,000	Accounts payable	$ 12,000	$ 9,000
Accounts receivable	15,000	9,000	Long-term notes payable	15,000	18,000
Equipment, net	112,500	105,000			
			Shareholders' equity		
			Common shares	33,000	30,000
			Retained earnings	75,000	63,000
	$135,000	$120,000		$135,000	$120,000

Compute the following for KS during 2017:

a. Acquisition of equipment. KS sold no equipment during the year.

b. Payment of a long-term note payable. During the year, KS issued a $7,500 note payable.

Identifying items for reporting
cash flows from operations—
indirect method

(5)

a. O+
j. O−

Starter 17–12 Werstiner Corporation is preparing its cash flow statement by the *indirect* method. The company has the following items for you to consider in preparing the statement. Identify each item as a(n)

- Operating activity—addition to net income (O+) or subtraction from net income (O−)
- Investing activity (I)
- Financing activity (F)
- Activity that is not used to prepare the cash flow statement (N)

Answer by placing the appropriate symbol in the blank space.

_____ a. Loss on sale of land	_____ f. Increase in accounts payable
_____ b. Amortization expense	_____ g. Payment of dividends
_____ c. Increase in inventory	_____ h. Decrease in accrued liabilities
_____ d. Decrease in accounts receivable	_____ i. Issuance of common shares
_____ e. Purchase of equipment	_____ j. Gain on sale of building

Computing cash flows from
operating activities—indirect
method

(5)

Net cash provided, $61,000

Starter 17–13 Urgent Printers reported the following data for 2017:

Income Statement	
Net income	$63,000
Amortization expense	10,000
Balance sheet	
Increase in Accounts Receivable	7,000
Decrease in Accounts Payable	5,000

Compute Urgent Printers' net cash provided by operating activities using the indirect method.

Starter 17–14 Donna's Gourmet Shops earned net income of $88,000, which included amortization of $16,500. Donna's paid $132,000 for a building and borrowed $66,000 on a long-term note payable. How much did Donna's cash balance increase or decrease during the year?

Starter 17–15 Carbone Resources Inc. accountants have assembled the following data for the year ended June 30, 2017:

Payment of dividends	$12,000	Net income	$100,000
Cash receipt from issuance of common shares	40,000	Purchase of equipment	80,000
		Decrease in current liabilities	10,000
Increase in current assets other than cash	60,000	Payment of note payable	60,000
		Cash receipt from sale of land	120,000
Repurchase of Carbone shares	10,000	Amortization expense	40,000

Prepare the *operating* activities section of Carbone Resources Inc.'s cash flow statement for the year ended June 30, 2017. Carbone uses the *indirect* method for operating cash flows.

Starter 17–16 Use the data in Starter 17–15 to prepare Carbone Resources Inc.'s cash flow statement for the year ended June 30, 2017. Carbone uses the *indirect* method for operating activities. Use Exhibit 17–16 as a guide, but you may stop after determining the net increase (or decrease) in cash.

Starter 17–17

1. Under IFRS, what options does an entity have for classifying cash inflows from interest and dividends on the statement of cash flows? How does this differ from ASPE?

2. Under IFRS, what options does an entity have for classifying cash payments of interest and dividends on the statement of cash flows? How does this differ from ASPE?

EXERCISES

Exercise 17–1

Hazelton Properties Ltd., a real estate developer, has experienced 10 years of growth in net income. Nevertheless, the business is facing bankruptcy. Creditors are calling all Hazelton Properties Ltd.'s outstanding loans for immediate payment, and the cash is simply not available. Where did Hazelton Properties Ltd. go wrong? Managers placed too much emphasis on net income and gave too little attention to cash flows.

Identifying the purposes of the cash flow statement
①

Required

Write a brief memo, in your own words, to explain for Hazelton Properties Ltd. managers the purposes of the cash flow statement.

Exercise 17–2

Suppose Whiteshell Inc.'s cash flow statement showed a net cash outflow from operations of $6,000,000.

Using a cash flow statement
①

Required

1. Suggest possible reasons for the cash outflow from operations.
2. What is the main danger signal this situation reveals?
3. Suppose Whiteshell Inc. has two more years with the cash flows mentioned above. What is likely to happen to the company?

Exercise 17–3

Identify each of the following transactions as an operating activity (O), an investing activity (I), a financing activity (F), a non-cash investing and financing activity (NIF), or a transaction that is not reported on the cash flow statement (N). For each cash flow, indicate whether the item increases (+) or decreases (–) cash. Assume the *indirect* method is used to report cash flows from operating activities.

Identifying activities for the cash flow statement
②
a. O+
e. F+
g. O+

Activity	(+)/(−)	Transactions
a.	_____	Amortization of equipment
b.	_____	Sale of long-term investment at a loss
c.	_____	Payment of cash dividend
d.	_____	Increase in inventory
e.	_____	Issuance of preferred shares for cash
f.	_____	Prepaid expenses decreased during the year
g.	_____	Accrual of salaries expense
h.	_____	Issuance of long-term note payable to borrow cash
i.	_____	Cash sale of land
j.	_____	Payment of long-term debt

Exercise 17–4

Consider three independent cases for the cash flow data of Rennie Recreation Products Inc.:

Interpreting a cash flow statement—indirect method
②

	Case A	Case B	Case C
Cash flows from operating activities:			
Net income	$120,000	$ 12,000	$120,000
Amortization	44,000	44,000	44,000
Increase in current assets	(4,000)	(28,000)	(76,000)
Decrease in current liabilities	0	(32,000)	(24,000)
	160,000	(4,000)	64,000

Cash flows from investing activities:			
Acquisition of property, plant, and equipment	$(364,000)	$(364,000)	$(364,000)
Sales of property, plant, and equipment	16,000	16,000	388,000
	(348,000)	(348,000)	24,000
Cash flows from financing activities:			
New borrowing	200,000	516,000	64,000
Payment of debt	(36,000)	(116,000)	(84,000)
	164,000	400,000	(20,000)
Net increase (decrease) in cash	$ (24,000)	$ 48,000	$ 68,000

Required For each case, identify from the cash flow statement the primary method that Rennie Recreation Products Inc. used to generate the cash to acquire new property, plant, and equipment.

Exercise 17–5

Interpreting cash flow statements—indirect method
(2)

Refer to the data in Exercise 17–4 for Rennie Recreation Products Inc. Which case indicates the best financial position? Give the reasons for your answer by analyzing each case.

Exercise 17–6

Distinguishing among operating, investing, and financing activities
(2)

Describe operating activities, investing activities, and financing activities. For each category, give an example of (a) a cash receipt and (b) a cash payment.

Exercise 17–7

Identifying activities for the cash flow statement
(2)
a. NIF
e. I–
g. O+

Identify each of the following transactions as an operating activity (O), an investing activity (I), a financing activity (F), a non-cash investing and financing activity (NIF), or a transaction that is not reported on the cash flow statement (N). For each cash flow, indicate whether the item increases (+) or decreases (–) cash. Assume the direct method is used to report cash flows from operating activities.

Activity	(+)/(−)	Transactions
a.	_____	Acquisition of a building by issuance of common shares
b.	_____	Issuance of common shares for cash
c.	_____	Payment of accounts payable
d.	_____	Acquisition of equipment by issuance of note payable
e.	_____	Purchase of long-term investment
f.	_____	Payment of wages to employees
g.	_____	Collection of cash interest
h.	_____	Distribution of stock dividend
i.	_____	Repurchase of common shares
j.	_____	Amortization of bond discount
k.	_____	Collection of accounts receivable

Exercise 17–8

Preparing a cash flow statement—direct method
(2) (3)
a. Cash balance end of the year,
$73,000

Use the information provided to prepare a cash flow statement for Starr Karaoke using the direct method for December 31, 2017. Assume that the beginning balance of cash is $55,000. Identify by letter which entry matched the line item on the cash flow statement.

a.	Land	185,000	
	Cash		185,000
b.	Dividends Payable	40,000	
	Cash		40,000

(Continued)

c.	Furniture and Fixtures	43,000	
	Note Payable, Short-Term		43,000
d.	Salaries Expense	19,000	
	Cash		19,000
e.	Equipment	137,000	
	Cash		137,000
f.	Cash	125,000	
	Long-Term Investment in Bonds		125,000
g.	Cash	80,000	
	Bonds Payable		80,000
h.	Building	210,000	
	Note Payable, Long-Term		210,000
i.	Cash	85,000	
	Accounts Receivable		85,000
j.	Accounts Payable	39,000	
	Cash		39,000
k.	Cash	140,000	
	Common Shares		140,000
l.	Cash	8,000	
	Interest Revenue		8,000

Exercise 17–9

The accounting records of Koltire Auto Parts Ltd. reveal the following:

Computing cash flows from operating activities—direct method

③

Net cash inflow from operating activities, $60,000

Acquisition of land	$ 89,000	Loss on sale of land	$ 6,000
Amortization	50,000	Net income	78,000
Cash sales	78,000	Payment of accounts payable	110,000
Collection of accounts receivable	186,000	Payment of dividends	25,000
Collection of dividend revenue	4,000	Payment of income tax	8,000
Decrease in current liabilities	52,000	Payment of interest	14,000
Increase in current assets other than cash	48,000	Payment of salaries and wages	76,000

Required Compute cash flows from operating activities by the direct method. Use the format of the operating activities section of Exhibit 17–14.

Exercise 17–10

Tech Arts Ltd. began 2017 with cash of $112,000. During the year, the company earned service revenue of $2,400,000 and collected $2,360,000 from clients. Expenses for the year totalled $1,760,000, of which the company paid $1,640,000 in cash to employees and $60,000 in cash for supplies. Tech Arts Ltd. also paid $480,000 to purchase computer equipment and paid a cash dividend of $80,000 to its shareholders during 2017.

Preparing a cash flow statement—direct method

② ③

3. Net increase in cash, $100,000

Required

1. Compute net income for the year.
2. Determine the cash balance at the end of the year.
3. Prepare the company's cash flow statement for the year. Format operating activities by the direct method.

Exercise 17-11

Preparing a cash flow statement—direct method

② ③

Net cash from operating, $288,000; investing, $(182,000); financing, $(86,000)

The income statement and additional data of Flashpoint Consulting Ltd. follow:

FLASHPOINT CONSULTING LTD. Income Statement For the Year Ended September 30, 2017		
Revenues		
Consulting revenue		$548,000
Expenses		
Salaries expense	$296,000	
Amortization expense	58,000	
Rent expense	14,000	
Office supplies expense	16,000	
Insurance expense	4,000	
Interest expense	4,000	
Income tax expense	36,000	428,000
Net income		$120,000

Additional data:
a. Collections from clients were $114,000 more than revenues.
b. Increase in cash balance, $20,000.
c. Payments to employees are $8,000 less than salaries expense.
d. Interest expense and income tax expense equal their cash amounts.
e. Acquisition of computer equipment is $232,000. Of this amount, $202,000 was paid in cash and $30,000 by signing a long-term note payable.
f. Cash received from sale of land, $20,000.
g. Cash received from issuance of common shares, $84,000.
h. Payment of long-term note payable, $40,000.
i. Payment of cash dividends, $130,000.
j. Payments for rent and insurance were equal to expense.
k. Payment for office supplies was $12,000 more than expense.

Prepare Flashpoint Consulting Ltd.'s cash flow statement by the direct method and the note to the financial statements giving the summary of non-cash investing and financing activities. Evaluate Flashpoint's cash flow for the year. Mention all three categories of cash flows and the reason for your evaluation.

Exercise 17-12

Computing amounts for the cash flow statement—direct method

④

a. $104,000

Compute the following items for the cash flow statement:

a.	Beginning Accounts Receivable	$ 25,000
	Ending Accounts Receivable	21,000
	Credit sales for the period	100,000
	Cash collections	?
b.	Cost of goods sold	$ 80,000
	Beginning Inventory balance	20,000
	Ending Inventory balance	16,000
	Beginning Accounts Payable	12,000
	Ending Accounts Payable	8,000
	Cash payments for inventory	?

Exercise 17–13

Selected accounts of Acorn Storage Centres show the following:

Identifying items for the cash flow statement—direct method
④

Accounts Receivable

Beginning balance	27,000	Cash receipts from customers	354,000
Service revenue	360,000		
Ending balance	33,000		

Land

Beginning balance	640,000	
Acquisitions paid with cash	81,000	
Ending balance	721,000	

Long-Term Debt

Payments	207,000	Beginning balance	819,000
		Issuance of debt for cash	249,000
		Ending balance	861,000

Required For each account, identify the item or items that should appear on a cash flow statement prepared by the direct method. Also, state each item's amount and where to report the item.

Exercise 17–14

Compute the following items for the cash flow statement:

Computing investing and financing amounts for the cash flow statement
② ④
a. $45,000

a.		
	Beginning Retained Earnings	$120,000
	Ending Retained Earnings	160,000
	Net income for the period	150,000
	Stock dividends	65,000
	Cash dividend payments	?

b.		
	Beginning Property, Plant, and Equipment	$320,000 net
	Ending Property, Plant, and Equipment	365,000 net
	Amortization for the period	36,000
	Acquisitions of new property, plant, and equipment	104,000

Property, plant, and equipment was sold at an $8,000 loss. What was the amount of the cash receipt from the sale?

Exercise 17–15

Indicate whether or not each of the items below would be shown on a cash flow statement with operating activities reported using the *indirect* method. Indicate whether the adjustment is added to, deducted from, or has no effect on the cash flow statement. If the transaction affects the cash flow statement, state whether it relates to operating activities, investing activities, or financing activities. Provide the reason for your answer.

Classifying transactions for the cash flow statement
② ④

a. The payment of interest on long-term debt.

b. The declaration and distribution of a common stock dividend.

c. A decrease in accounts payable.

d. The sale of office equipment for its book value.

e. The borrowing of funds for future expansion through the sale of bonds.

f. A gain on the sale of property, plant, and equipment.

g. The purchase of equipment in exchange for common shares.

h. Amortization expense—buildings.

i. A decrease in merchandise inventory.

j. An increase in prepaid expenses.

k. Amortization of the premium on bonds payable.

l. An investment in a money market fund.

m. The receipt of interest on long-term investments.

n. The purchase of office equipment.

o. Receiving funds for future expansion through the sale of common shares.

p. Amortization of intangible assets.

Exercise 17–16

Classifying transactions for the cash flow statement

② ④

Two transactions of LRT Logistics Inc. are recorded as follows:

a.	Cash	80,000	
	Accumulated Amortization—Computer Equipment	830,000	
	Computer Equipment		870,000
	Gain on Sale of Computer Equipment		40,000

b.	Land	2,900,000	
	Cash		1,300,000
	Note Payable		1,600,000

Required

1. Indicate where, how, and in what amount to report these transactions on the cash flow statement and accompanying schedule of non-cash investing and financing activities. Are they cash receipts or payments? LRT Logistics Inc. reports cash flows from operating activities by the *direct* method.

2. Repeat Requirement 1, assuming that LRT Logistics Inc. reports cash flows from operating activities by the *indirect* method.

Exercise 17–17

Computing net income using cash flows from operating activities—indirect method

⑤

Repage Inc. reported a net cash flow from operating activities of $40,625 on its cash flow statement for the year ended December 31, 2017. The following information was reported in the Cash Flows from Operating Activities section of the cash flow statement, which uses the *indirect* method:

∠ L	Decrease in legal fees payable	$1,000
ℒ A	Increase in prepaid expenses	400
✓ CA	Amortization	3,350
✓ CA	Loss on sale of equipment	1,500
✓A	Increase in accounts payable	600
ℒA	Decrease in inventories	2,175
ℒA	Increase in trade accounts receivable	2,000

Required Determine the net income reported by Repage Inc. for the year ended December 31, 2017.

Exercise 17–18

Computing cash flows from operating activities—indirect method

⑤

Cash outflows from operating activities, $(24,000)

The accounting records of Iberia Corporation reveal the following:

Acquisition of land............................	$ 444,000	Increase in current assets other than cash	$252,000
Amortization.......................................	156,000	Loss on sale of land.........................	60,000
Cash sales	108,000	Net income	288,000
Collection of accounts receivable....	1,116,000	Payment of accounts payable.......	576,000

Collection of dividend revenue.......	108,000	Payment of dividends	84,000
Decrease in current liabilities	276,000	Payment of income tax.................	96,000
		Payment of interest........................	192,000
		Payment of salaries and wages....	432,000

Compute cash flows from operating activities by the indirect method. Use the format of the operating activities section of Exhibit 17–16. Then evaluate Iberia Corporation's operating cash flows as strong or weak (omit the date from the statement heading).

Exercise 17–19

Use the income statement of Flashpoint Consulting Ltd. in Exercise 17–11 plus these additional data during fiscal year 2017:

a. Acquisition of computer equipment was $232,000. Of this amount, $202,000 was paid in cash and $30,000 by signing a long-term note payable. Flashpoint Consulting Ltd. sold no computer equipment during fiscal year 2017.

b. Cash received from sale of land, $20,000.

c. Cash received from issuance of common shares, $84,000.

d. Payment of long-term note payable, $40,000.

e. Payment of dividends, $130,000.

f. Change in cash balance, $?

g. From the comparative balance sheet:

Preparing the cash flow statement by the indirect method
② ⑤
Net cash flow from operating, $288,000; investing, $(182,000); financing, $(86,000)

FLASHPOINT CONSULTING LTD. Balance Sheet (partial) September 30, 2017 and 2016		
	2017	2016
Current assets:		
Cash	$56,000	$ 36,000
Accounts receivable	30,000	144,000
Office supplies	18,000	6,000
Prepaid expenses	10,000	10,000
Current liabilities:		
Accounts payable	$68,000	$ 56,000
Accrued liabilities	38,000	42,000

Required

1. Prepare Flashpoint Consulting Ltd.'s cash flow statement for the year ended September 30, 2017, using the indirect method.

2. Evaluate Flashpoint Consulting Ltd.'s cash flows for the year. In your evaluation, mention all three categories of cash flows and give the reason for your evaluation.

Exercise 17–20

White's Printing Ltd.'s year end is February 28. The accounting records of White's Printing Ltd. at March 31, 2017, include the selected accounts shown below.

Computing cash flows from operating activities—indirect method
⑤
Net cash outflow from operating activities, $21,000

Cash			
Mar. 1	75,000	Dividend	24,000
Collections	126,000	Payments	138,000
Mar. 31	39,000		

Accounts Receivable			
Mar. 1	54,000		
Sales	228,000	Collections	126,000
Mar. 31	156,000		

Inventory			
Mar. 1	57,000		
Purchases	111,000	Cost of sales	108,000
Mar. 31	60,000		

Equipment		
Mar. 1	279,000	
Mar. 31	279,000	

Accumulated Amortization—Equipment				Accounts Payable		
	Mar. 1	78,000			Mar. 1	42,000
	Amortization	9,000	Payments	96,000	Purchases	111,000
	Mar. 31	87,000			Mar. 31	57,000

Accrued Liabilities				Retained Earnings		
	Mar. 1	27,000	Quarterly		Mar. 1	192,000
Payments	42,000	Expenses	33,000	dividend	24,000	Net income	69,000
	Mar. 31	18,000			Mar. 31	237,000

Required Compute White's Printing Ltd.'s net cash inflow or outflow from operating activities during March 2017. Use the *indirect* method. Does White's Printing Ltd. have trouble collecting receivables or selling inventory? How can you tell?

Exercise 17–21

Preparing the cash flow statement by the indirect method

② ⑤

Net cash flow from operating, $180,000; investing, $(128,000); financing, $12,000

Prepare the 2017 cash flow statement for Valemont Corporation using the indirect method to report cash flows from operating activities.

Transaction data for 2017

Amortization expense	$ 40,000		Payment of cash dividends	$ 72,000
Issuance of long-term note payable to borrow cash	28,000		Net income	104,000
			Purchase of long-term investment	32,000
Issuance of common shares for cash	76,000		Issuance of long-term note payable to purchase patent	148,000
Cash received from sale of building	296,000		Issuance of common shares to retire $52,000 of bonds	52,000
Repurchase of own shares	20,000			
Loss on sale of building	8,000			
Purchase of equipment	392,000			

	December 31,	
	2017	2016
Current assets		
Cash and cash equivalents	$ 76,000	$ 12,000
Accounts receivable	88,000	92,000
Inventories	136,000	124,000
Prepaid expenses	4,000	12,000
Current liabilities		
Notes payable (for inventory purchases)	$ 44,000	$ 28,000
Accounts payable	96,000	76,000
Accrued liabilities	28,000	36,000
Income and other taxes payable	40,000	40,000

The income statement and additional data of Wandell Consulting Ltd. follow:

Preparing the cash flow statement under IFRS—direct method
② ⑤ ⑥
Net cash flow from operating, $47,000; investing, $(45,500); financing, $3,500

Wandell CONSULTING LTD. Income Statement For the Year Ended December 31, 2017		
Revenues:		
Consulting revenue		$137,000
Expenses:		
Salaries expense	$74,000	
Amortization expense	14,500	
Rent expense	6,000	
Office supplies expense	1,500	
Insurance expense	1,000	
Interest expense	1,000	
Income tax expense	9,000	107,000
Net income		$ 30,000

Additional data:

a. Collections from clients are $3,500 more than revenues.

b. Increase in cash balance, $5,000.

c. Payments to employees are $2,000 less than salaries expense.

d. Interest expense and income tax expense equal their cash amounts.

e. Acquisition of property, plant, and equipment is $58,000. Of this amount, $50,500 is paid in cash, $7,500 by signing a long-term note payable.

f. Cash received from sale of land, $5,000.

g. Cash received from issuance of common shares, $21,000.

h. Payment of long-term note payable, $10,000.

i. Payment of cash dividends, $7,500.

j. Payments for rent and insurance are equal to expense.

k. Payment for office supplies is $3,000 more than expense.

l. Opening cash balance, $8,000.

Required

1. Prepare Wandell Consulting Ltd.'s cash flow statement by the direct method for operating activities and a note to the financial statements providing a summary of non-cash investing and financing activities.

2. Assume Wandell Consulting Ltd. has adopted IFRS. What would be the difference in the cash flow statement using this framework?

SERIAL EXERCISE

This exercise continues the Lee Consulting Corporation situation from Exercise 16–16 of Chapter 16. If you did not complete any Serial Exercises in earlier chapters, you can still complete Exercise 17–23 as it is presented.

Exercise 17–23

Preparing the cash flow statement—indirect method
② ⑤
Net cash flow from operating, $39,900; investing, $(83,000); financing, $40,000

Suppose, at December 31, 2017, Lee Consulting Corporation has the following comparative balance sheet:

LEE CONSULTING CORPORATION Balance Sheet December 31, 2017 and 2016		
	2017	2016
Current assets		
Cash	$ 5,000	$ 8,100
Accounts receivable	2,200	1,700
Supplies	420	300
Equipment	10,000	2,000
Furniture	3,600	3,600
Building	55,000	—
Less: accumulated amortization	(2,753)	(93)
Land	20,000	—
Total assets	$93,467	$15,607
Current liabilities		
Accounts payable	$ 350	$ 3,900
Salary payable	2,500	—
Long-term liabilities		
Notes payable	40,000	—
Shareholders' equity		
Common shares	20,000	10,000
Retained earnings	30,617	1,707
Total liabilities and shareholders' equity	$93,467	$15,607

Additional information: Lee Consulting Corporation declared and paid $10,000 in dividends during 2017. Net income for the year ended December 31, 2017, was $38,910.

Required Using this information, prepare the cash flow statement for Lee Consulting Corporation using the indirect method for operating activities.

CHALLENGE EXERCISE

Exercise 17–24

Canadian Tire Corporation, Limited's cash flow statement for the years ended December 28, 2013, and December 29, 2012, is reproduced below:

Analyzing an actual company's cash flow statement
① ②

CANADIAN TIRE CORPORATION, LIMITED Consolidated Cash Flow Statement (adapted)		
For the Years Ended (Dollars in millions)	December 28, 2013	December 29, 2012
Operating activities		
Net income	$ 564.4	$ 498.9
Adjustments for:		
Gross impairment loss on loans receivable	326.1	323.7
Depreciation on property and equipment	253.8	248.9
Income tax expense	220.2	177.9
Net finance costs	105.8	126.2
Amortization of intangible assets	91.5	86.2
Changes in fair value of derivative instruments	(37.9)	(7.7)
Gain on disposal of property and equipment	(10.3)	(7.9)
Other	15.1	21.3
Cash generated from operations	1,528.7	1,467.5
Change in operating working capital and other	270.2	(29.8)
Change in loans receivable	(600.2)	(521.7)
Change in deposits	(96.2)	134.7
Interest paid	(126.5)	(155.3)
Interest received	12.0	8.9
Income taxes paid	(191.2)	(161.3)
Cash generated from operating activities	796.8	743.0
Investing activities		
Acquisition of Pro Hockey Life Sporting Goods Inc.	(58.0)	—
Acquisition of short-term investments	(339.2)	(264.0)
Proceeds from the maturity and disposition of short-term investments	(193.8)	360.7
Acquisition of long-term investments	(55.1)	(130.0)
Proceeds from the disposition of long-term investments	0.4	4.7
Additions to property and equipment	(404.3)	(222.3)
Proceeds on disposition of property and equipment	20.6	45.0
Additions to intangible assets	(105.9)	(64.3)
Long-term receivables and other assets	(21.5)	17.6
Other	(17.2)	(8.9)
Cash used for investing activities	(786.4)	(261.5)
Financing activities		
Net repayment of short-term borrowings	(20.4)	(233.7)
Issuance of loans payable	235.9	235.3
Repayment of loans payable	(248.5)	(240.3)
Issuance of share capital	5.8	12.4
Repurchase of share capital	(105.9)	(33.1)
Issuance of long-term debt	265.8	637.4
Repayment of long-term debt and finance lease liabilities	(659.2)	(30.1)
Dividends paid	(113.0)	(97.7)
Other	274.0	(3.2)
Cash (used for) generated from financing activities	(365.5)	247.0
Cash (used) generated in the year	(355.1)	728.5
Cash and cash equivalents, beginning of year	929.5	201.0
Effect of exchange rate fluctuations on cash held	(0.2)	—
Cash and cash equivalents, end of year	$ 574.2	$ 929.5

Adapted from the Canadian Tire Annual Report 2013. Reprinted with permission.

Required

1. Which format did Canadian Tire Corporation, Limited use for reporting cash flows from operating activities?
2. What was Canadian Tire's largest source of cash during the year ended December 28, 2013? During the previous year December 29, 2012?
3. What was Canadian Tire's largest use of cash during the year ended December 28, 2013? During the year ended December 29, 2012?
4. Which section—operating, investing, or financing—did Canadian Tire have the largest source of cash shown for 2013 and 2012? Comment on your findings.
5. During the year ended December 28, 2013, Canadian Tire has a large negative cash flow from investing activities. Does this mean Canadian Tire is expanding, downsizing, or remaining stable?
6. Why are Canadian Tire's year ends shown as December 28, 2013, and December 29, 2012?

BEYOND THE NUMBERS

Using cash flow data to evaluate an investment
① ②

Beyond the Numbers 17–1

Gillam Ltd. and Genoway Inc. are asking you to recommend their shares to your clients. Gillam Ltd. and Genoway Inc. earn about the same net income and have similar financial positions, so your decision depends on their cash flow statements, summarized as follows:

	Gillam Ltd.		Genoway Inc.	
Net cash inflows from operating activities		$ 90,000		$ 50,000
Net cash inflows (outflows) from investing activities:				
Purchase of property, plant, and equipment	$(100,000)		$ (20,000)	
Sale of property, plant, and equipment	10,000	(90,000)	40,000	20,000
Net cash inflows (outflows) from financing activities:				
Issuance of common shares	30,000		—	
Issuance of long-term debt	—		80,000	
Repayment of long-term debt	—	30,000	(120,000)	(40,000)
Net increase in cash		$ 30,000		$ 30,000

Based on their cash flows, which company looks better? Give your reasons.

ETHICAL ISSUE

Eurocheapo Travel Ltd. is experiencing a bad year. Net income is only $60,000. Also, two important clients are falling behind in their payments to Eurocheapo Travel Ltd., and the agency's accounts receivable are increasing dramatically. The company desperately needs a loan. The company's board of directors is considering ways to put the best face on the company's financial statements. The company's bank closely examines cash flow from operations. Trent Belland, a director, suggests reclassifying as long term the receivables from the slow-paying clients. He explains to the other members of the board that removing the $40,000 rise in accounts receivable will increase net cash inflow from operations. This approach will increase the company's cash balance and may help Eurocheapo Travel Ltd. get the loan.

Required

1. Using only the amounts given, compute net cash inflow from operations both without and with the reclassification of the receivables. Which reporting makes Eurocheapo Travel Ltd. look better?

2. Where else in Eurocheapo's cash flow statement will the reclassification of the receivable be reported? What cash flow effect will this item report? What effect would the reclassification have on overall cash flow from all activities?

3. Under what condition would the reclassification of the receivables be ethical? Unethical?

PROBLEMS (GROUP A)   MyAccountingLab

Problem 17–1A

Top managers of Upland Communications Corp. are reviewing company performance for 2017. The income statement reports an 18 percent increase in net income, which is excellent. The balance sheet shows modest increases in assets, liabilities, and shareholders' equity. The assets with the largest increases are plant and equipment because the company is halfway through an expansion program. No other assets and no liabilities are increasing dramatically. A summarized version of the cash flow statement reports the following:

Using cash flow information to evaluate performance
①

Net cash inflow from operating activities	$ 1,240,000
Net cash outflow from investing activities	(1,140,000)
Net cash inflow from financing activities	280,000
Increase in cash during 2017	$ 380,000

Required Write a memo to give top managers of Upland Communications Corp. your assessment of 2017 and your outlook for the future. Focus on the information content of the cash flow data.

Problem 17–2A

Sawyer Products Ltd.'s accountants have developed the following data from the company's accounting records for the year ended July 31, 2017:

Preparing the cash flow statement—direct method
② ③

1. Net cash flow from operating, $(240,000); investing, $307,800; financing $401,200

a. Salaries expense, $631,800.

b. Cash payments to purchase property, plant, and equipment, $1,035,000.

c. Proceeds from issuance of long-term debt, $264,600.

d. Payments of long-term debt, $142,800.

e. Proceeds from sale of property, plant, and equipment, $318,200.

f. Interest revenue, $72,600.

g. Cash receipt of dividend revenue on investments in shares, $56,200.

h. Payments to suppliers, $4,129,800.

i. Interest expense and payments, $226,800.

j. Cost of goods sold, $2,886,600.

k. Collection of interest revenue, $30,200.

l. Acquisition of equipment by issuing short-term note payable, $213,000.

m. Payment of salaries, $804,000.

n. Credit sales, $3,648,600.

o. Income tax expense and payments, $338,400.

p. Amortization expense, $309,600.

q. Collections on accounts receivable, $4,038,600.

r. Collection of long-term notes receivable, $486,400.

s. Proceeds from sale of investments, $538,200.

t. Payment of long-term debt by issuing common shares, $900,000.

u. Cash sales, $1,134,000.

v. Proceeds from issuance of common shares, $589,400.

w. Payment of cash dividends, $310,000.

x. Cash balance:

July 31, 2016—$654,800

July 31, 2017—$?

Required

1. Prepare Sawyer Products Ltd.'s cash flow statement for the year ended July 31, 2017, using the direct method for the operating activities section. Follow the format of Exhibit 17–14, but do *not* show amounts in thousands. Include a note to the financial statements giving a summary of non-cash investing and financing activities.

2. Evaluate 2017 in terms of cash flow. Give your reasons.

Excel Spreadsheet
Template
Preparing the cash flow
statement—direct method
② ③ ④
1. Net cash flow from
operating, $666,000;
investing, $(526,000);
financing, $(249,000)

Problem 17–3A

The 2017 comparative balance sheet and income statement of Whitbey Group Inc. follow:

WHITBEY GROUP INC. Balance Sheet August 31, 2017 and 2016		
	2017	**2016**
Current assets		
Cash and cash equivalents	$ 47,000	$ 156,000
Accounts receivable	415,000	431,000
Interest receivable	6,000	9,000
Inventories	993,000	899,000
Prepaid expenses	17,000	22,000
Plant and equipment, net	1,009,000	937,000
Land	401,000	200,000
Total assets	$2,888,000	$2,654,000
Current liabilities		
Accounts payable	$ 114,000	$ 179,000
Interest payable	63,000	67,000
Wages payable	71,000	14,000
Lease liabilities	181,000	187,000
Income tax payable	73,000	38,000
Long-term liabilities		
Notes payable	450,000	650,000
Shareholders' equity		
Common shares	1,411,000	1,223,000
Retained earnings	525,000	296,000
Total liabilities and shareholders' equity	$2,888,000	$2,654,000

WHITBEY GROUP INC.		
Income Statement		
For the Year Ended August 31, 2017		
Revenues:		
Sales revenue		$4,380,000
Interest revenue		17,000
Total revenues		4,397,000
Expenses:		
Cost of goods sold	$1,952,000	
Salaries expense	814,000	
Amortization expense	253,000	
Other operating expenses*	497,000	
Interest expense	246,000	
Income tax expense	169,000	
Total expenses		3,931,000
Net income		$ 466,000

*Includes lease liability and prepaid expense.

Whitbey Group had no non-cash investing and financing transactions during 2017. During the year, there were no sales of land or plant and equipment, no issuances of notes payable, and no repurchase of common shares.

Required

1. Prepare the 2017 cash flow statement, formatting operating activities by the direct method.
2. Evaluate the 2017 cash flow for this company.

Problem 17–4A

Use the Whitbey Group Inc. data from Problem 17–3A.

Required

1. Prepare the 2017 cash flow statement by the indirect method. If your instructor also assigned Problem 17–3A, prepare only the operating activities section.
2. Evaluate the 2017 cash flow for this company.

Problem 17–5A

Accountants for Natures Design Ltd. have assembled the following data for the year ended December 31, 2017:

	December 31,	
	2017	2016
Current accounts (all result from operations)		
Current assets		
Cash and cash equivalents	$ 9,050	$ 8,700
Accounts receivable	17,025	18,425
Inventories	29,625	24,125
Prepaid expenses	800	525
Current liabilities		
Notes payable (for inventory purchases)	7,575	9,200
Accounts payable	18,025	16,875
Income tax payable	1,475	1,950
Accrued liabilities	12,075	5,800

Transaction data for 2017:

Acquisition of building by issuing long-term note payable.............................	$33,000	Issuance of common shares, class B, for cash......................	$14,050
		Net income	12,625
Acquisition of farm equipment............	18,500	Payment of cash dividends......	10,700
Acquisition of long-term investment..	11,200	Payment of long-term debt......	16,950
Amortization expense	5,075	Retirement of bonds payable by issuing preferred shares.....................	
Collection of loan	2,575		22,350
Gain on sale of investment	875	Sale of long-term investment for cash..	5,550
Issuance of long-term debt to borrow cash	17,750	Share dividends..........................	10,150

Required

1. Prepare Natures Design Ltd.'s cash flow statement using the *indirect* method to report operating activities. Include a note regarding non-cash investing and financing activities.

2. Evaluate Natures Design Ltd.'s cash flows for the year. Mention all three categories of cash flows, and give the reason for your evaluation.

Problem 17–6A

Preparing the cash flow statement—direct and indirect methods

② ③ ④ ⑤

1. Net cash flow from operating, $84,100; investing, $(51,500); financing, $(44,500)

To prepare the cash flow statement, accountants for Fothingham Sales Ltd. have summarized 2017 activity in two T-accounts as follows:

Cash

Beginning balance	87,100	Payments of operating expenses	46,100
Sale of common shares	80,800	Payment of long-term debt	78,900
Receipts of dividends	17,900	Repurchase of common shares	30,400
Sale of investments	28,400	Payment of income tax	6,000
Receipts of interest	22,200	Payments on accounts payable	101,600
Collections from customers	307,000	Payments of dividends	16,000
		Payments of salaries and wages	67,500
		Payments of interest	41,800
		Purchase of equipment	79,900
Ending balance	75,200		

Common Shares

Repurchase of common shares	30,400	Beginning balance	103,500
		Issuance for cash	80,800
		Issuance to acquire land	64,500
		Issuance to retire long-term debt	31,600
		Ending balance	250,000

Fothingham Sales Ltd.'s 2017 income statement and selected balance sheet data follow:

FOTHINGHAM SALES LTD. Income Statement For the Year Ended October 31, 2017		
Revenues and gains:		
Sales revenue		$317,000
Interest revenue		22,200
Dividend revenue		17,900
Gain on sale of investments		700
Total revenues and gains		357,800
Expenses:		
Cost of goods sold	$103,600	
Salaries and wages expense	66,800	
Amortization expense	10,900	
Other operating expenses	44,700	
Interest expense	44,100	
Income tax expense	9,200	
Total expenses		279,300
Net income		$ 78,500

FOTHINGHAM SALES LTD. Balance Sheet Data For the Year Ended October 31, 2017	
	Increase (Decrease)
Current assets	
Cash and cash equivalents	$?
Accounts receivable	10,000
Inventories	5,700
Prepaid expenses	(1,900)
Investments	(27,700)
Plant and equipment, net	69,000
Land	75,000
Current liabilities	
Accounts payable	7,700
Interest payable	2,300
Salaries payable	(700)
Other accrued liabilities	(3,300)
Income tax payable	3,200
Long-term debt	(100,000)
Common shares	146,500
Retained earnings	62,500

Required

1. Prepare Fothingham Sales Ltd.'s cash flow statement for the year ended October 31, 2017, using the *direct* method to report operating activities. Also prepare a note to the financial statements summarizing the non-cash investing and financing activities.

2. Prepare a schedule showing cash flows from operating activities using the *indirect* method. All activity in the current accounts results from operations.

Brentwood Bay Inc.'s comparative balance sheet at September 30, 2017, and its 2017 income
statement are shown below:

BRENTWOOD BAY INC.
Balance Sheet
September 30, 2017 and 2016

	2017	2016
Current assets		
Cash	$ 194,800	$ 96,400
Accounts receivable	167,600	164,000
Interest receivable	16,400	11,200
Inventories	486,800	467,600
Prepaid expenses	34,400	37,200
Long-term investments	204,400	55,200
Plant and equipment, net	527,600	416,400
Land	188,400	297,200
	$1,820,400	$1,545,200
Current liabilities		
Notes payable, short-term	$ 40,000	$ 0
Accounts payable	247,200	281,200
Income tax payable	47,200	46,400
Accrued liabilities	71,600	116,400
Interest payable	18,000	12,800
Salaries payable	6,000	4,400
Long-term note payable	492,000	525,600
Common shares	543,600	336,000
Retained earnings	354,800	222,400
	$1,820,400	$1,545,200

BRENTWOOD BAY INC.
Income Statement
For the Year Ended September 30, 2017

Sales revenue		$1,468,400
Cost of goods sold		646,000
Gross margin		822,400
Operating expenses:		
Amortization	$ 34,000	
Salaries	253,600	
Other	118,400	406,000
Operating income		416,400
Other revenues and expenses:		
Revenues and gains:		
Interest	39,200	
Gain on sale of land	43,600	82,800
		499,200
Interest expense		64,000
Income before income taxes		435,200
Income tax expense		85,600
Net income		$ 349,600

Other information for the year ended September 30, 2017:

a. Acquired equipment by issuing long-term note payable, $89,200, and paying $16,000 cash.

b. Paid long-term note payable, $122,800.

c. Received $207,600 cash for issuance of common shares.

d. Paid cash dividends, $217,200.

e. Acquired equipment by issuing short-term note payable, $40,000.

Required

1. Prepare Brentwood Bay Inc.'s cash flow statement for the year ended September 30, 2017, using the *direct* method to report operating activities. Also prepare a note to the financial statements giving a summary of non-cash investing and financing activities. All current accounts, except short-term notes payable, result from operating transactions.

2. Prepare a supplementary schedule showing the cash flows from operating activities using the *indirect* method.

Problem 17–8A

The financial statements for Facetime Corp. for the year ended December 31, 2017, are as follows:

Distinguishing among operating, investing, and financing activities; using the financial statements to compute the cash effects of a wide variety of business transactions; preparing a cash flow statement by the indirect method

② ④ ⑤

1. Net cash flow from operating, $586,000; investing, $(204,000); financing, $(430,000)

FACETIME CORP. Balance Sheet December 31, 2017 and 2016		
	2017	2016
Assets		
Cash	$ 10,000	$ 18,000
Investment in money market fund	0	40,000
Accounts receivable	189,000	175,000
Merchandise inventory	280,000	610,000
Prepaid expenses	30,000	23,000
Plant and equipment	1,798,000	1,654,000
Less accumulated amortization	(160,000)	(120,000)
Investment	200,000	0
Goodwill	90,000	100,000
Total assets	$2,437,000	$2,500,000
Liabilities		
Accounts payable	$ 176,000	$ 120,000
Salaries payable	110,000	100,000
Loan payable	350,000	400,000
Total liabilities	636,000	620,000
Shareholders' equity		
Preferred shares	800,000	500,000
Common shares	500,000	500,000
Retained earnings	501,000	880,000
Total shareholders' equity	1,801,000	1,880,000
Total liabilities and shareholders' equity	$2,437,000	$2,500,000

FACETIME CORP.
Income Statement
For the Year Ended December 31, 2017

Net sales		$1,600,000
Cost of goods sold		840,000
Gross margin		760,000
Operating expenses:		
Selling expenses	350,000	
Administrative expenses	230,000	
Interest expense	40,000	
Total operating expenses		620,000
Operating income		140,000
Income taxes		39,000
Net income		$ 101,000

Additional information:

a. The administrative expenses included the following:

Amortization expense on plant and equipment, $100,000.

Write-down of goodwill, $10,000.

b. Sold equipment for its book value. The equipment cost $430,000 and had been amortized for $60,000.

c. Purchased additional equipment in December for $574,000.

d. Issued preferred shares for an investment purchase of $200,000.

e. Declared and paid cash dividends: preferred, $230,000; common, $250,000.

f. Sold 20,000 preferred shares for $5.00 per share.

g. Paid $90,000 (of which $40,000 was interest) on the loans.

Required

1. Prepare a cash flow statement for Facetime Corp. for the year ended December 31, 2017, using the *indirect* method. The investment in the money market fund is a cash equivalent.

2. Did the company improve its cash position in 2017? Give your reasons.

Problem 17–9A

Preparing the cash flow statement under IFRS—direct method

② ③ ⑥

1. Net cash flow from operating, $(170,000); investing, $92,600; financing, $260,400

Sahanji Products Ltd.'s accountants have developed the following data from the company's accounting records for the year ended December 31, 2017:

a. Salaries expense, $210,600.

b. Cash payments to purchase property, plant, and equipment, $345,000.

c. Proceeds from issuance of long-term debt, $88,200.

d. Payments of long-term debt, $37,600.

e. Proceeds from sale of property, plant, and equipment, $119,400.

f. Interest revenue, $24,200.

g. Cash receipt of dividend revenue on investments in shares, $5,400.

h. Payments to suppliers, $1,376,600.

i. Interest expense and payments, $75,600.

j. Cost of goods sold, $962,200.

k. Collection of interest revenue, $33,400.

l. Acquisition of equipment by issuing short-term note payable, $91,000.

m. Payment of salaries, $468,000.

n. Credit sales, $1,216,200.

o. Income tax expense and payments, $112,800.

p. Depreciation expense, $103,200.

q. Collections on accounts receivable, $1,346,200.

r. Collection of long-term notes receivable, $138,800.

s. Proceeds from sale of investments, $179,400.

t. Payment of long-term debt by issuing preferred shares, $400,000.

u. Cash sales, $578,000.

v. Proceeds from issuance of common shares, $209,800.

w. Payment of cash dividends, $100,000.

x. Cash balance:

   December 31, 2016—$151,600

   December 31, 2017—$?

Required

1. Prepare Sahanji's cash flow statement for the year ended December 31, 2017, reporting operating activities by the direct method. Include a note to the financial statements providing a summary of non-cash investing and financing activities.

2. Assume that Sahanji Products Ltd. has adopted IFRS and has elected to classify cash inflows from interest and dividends as investing activities and cash outflows for the payment of interest and dividends as financing activities. How would this reclassification change the balances in the three sections of the cash flow statement? Note the balances of each section and comment.

PROBLEMS (GROUP B)
MyAccountingLab

Problem 17–1B

Top managers of Burley Guys Delivery Ltd. are reviewing company performance for 2017. The income statement reports a 20 percent increase in net income over 2016. However, most of the net income increase resulted from an unusual gain of $60,000 on the sale of equipment. The cash proceeds were $180,000. The balance sheet shows a large increase in receivables. The cash flow statement, in summarized form, reports the following:

Using cash flow information to evaluate performance
①

Net cash outflow from operating activities	$(330,000)
Net cash inflow from investing activities	300,000
Net cash inflow from financing activities	150,000
Increase in cash during 2017	$ 120,000

Required Write a memo to give the managers of Burley Guys Delivery Ltd. your assessment of 2017 operations and your outlook for the future. Focus on the information content of the cash flow data.

Problem 17–2B

Accountants for Direct Builders' Supply Ltd. have developed the following data from the company's accounting records for the year ended April 30, 2017:

Preparing the cash flow statement—direct method
② ③

a. Credit sales, $728,125.

b. Income tax expense and payments, $47,375.

c. Cash payments to acquire property, plant, and equipment, $49,250.

d. Cost of goods sold, $478,250.

e. Cash received from issuance of long-term debt, $85,000.

f. Payment of cash dividends, $80,500.

g. Collection of interest, $34,250.

h. Acquisition of equipment by issuing short-term note payable, $40,500.

i. Payment of salaries, $129,500.

j. Cash received from sale of property, plant, and equipment, $28,000, including an $8,500 loss.

k. Collections on accounts receivable, $578,250.

l. Interest revenue, $4,750.

m. Cash receipt of dividend revenue on investment in shares, $25,125.

n. Payments to suppliers, $460,625.

o. Cash sales, $214,875.

p. Amortization expense, $78,500.

q. Cash received from issuance of short-term debt, $69,500.

r. Payments of long-term debt, $62,500.

s. Interest expense and payments, $16,625.

t. Salaries expense, $119,125.

u. Collections of notes receivable, $35,000.

v. Cash received from sale of investments, $11,375, including $2,500 gain.

w. Payment of short-term note payable by issuing long-term note payable, $78,750.

x. Cash balance:

    May 1, 2016—$99,125

    April 30, 2017—$?

Required

1. Prepare Direct Builders' Supply Ltd.'s cash flow statement for the year ended April 30, 2017, using the direct method for the operating activities section. Follow the format of Exhibit 17–14, but do not show amounts in thousands. Include a note regarding the non-cash investing and financing activities.

2. Evaluate 2017 from a cash flow standpoint. Give your reasons.

Excel Spreadsheet Template
Preparing the cash flow statement—direct method
② ③ ④

Problem 17–3B

The 2017 comparative income statement and balance sheet of Flowell Design Ltd. follow:

FLOWELL DESIGN LTD. Income Statement For the Year Ended June 30, 2017		
Revenues:		
Sales revenue		$257,000
Interest revenue		13,600
Total revenues		270,600
Expenses:		
Cost of goods sold	$76,600	
Salaries expense	27,800	
Amortization expense	4,000	
Other operating expenses	10,500	
Interest expense	16,600	
Income tax expense	27,800	
Total expenses		163,300
Net income		$107,300

FLOWELL DESIGN LTD.
Balance Sheet
June 30, 2017 and 2016

	2017	2016
Current assets		
Cash and cash equivalents	$ 7,200	$ 6,300
Accounts receivable	31,600	26,900
Interest receivable	1,900	700
Inventories	33,600	57,200
Prepaid expenses	2,500	1,900
Plant and equipment, net	66,500	49,400
Land	103,000	54,000
Total assets	$246,300	$196,400
Current liabilities		
Accounts payable	$ 31,400	$ 28,800
Interest payable	4,400	4,900
Salaries payable	3,100	6,600
Other accrued liabilities	13,700	16,000
Income tax payable	8,900	7,700
Long-term liabilities		
Notes payable	75,000	95,000
Shareholders' equity		
Common shares	68,300	34,700
Retained earnings	41,500	2,700
Total liabilities and shareholders' equity	$246,300	$196,400

Flowell Design Ltd. had no non-cash financing and investing transactions during 2017. During the year, there were no sales of land or plant and equipment, and no issuances of notes payable.

Required

1. Prepare the 2017 cash flow statement, formatting operating activities by the direct method.
2. Evaluate the 2017 cash flow for this company.

Problem 17–4B

Use the Flowell Design Ltd. data from Problem 17–3B.

Required

1. Prepare the 2017 cash flow statement by the indirect method. If your instructor also assigned Problem 17–3B, prepare only the operating activities section of the statement.
2. Evaluate the 2017 cash flow for this company.

Excel Spreadsheet
Template
Preparing the cash flow
statement—indirect method
② ⑤

Problem 17–5B

Roanoke Ltd.'s accountants have assembled the following data for the year ended December 31, 2017:

	December 31,	
	2017	2016
Current accounts (all result from operations)		
Current assets		
Cash and cash equivalents	$ 75,500	$ 56,750
Accounts receivable	174,250	155,500
Inventories	271,500	212,500
Prepaid expenses	13,250	10,250
Current liabilities		
Notes payable (for inventory purchases)	56,500	45,750
Accounts payable	132,250	139,500
Income tax payable	96,500	41,750
Accrued liabilities	38,750	68,000

Transaction data for 2017:

Acquisition of building	$325,750	Issuance of long-term note	
Acquisition of land by issuing long-term note payable..........................	237,500	payable to borrow cash	$ 36,000
		Loss on sale of equipment.............	16,750
Acquisition of long-term investment...	79,000	Net income	199,000
		Payment of cash dividends...........	90,750
Amortization expense	60,250	Repurchase and retirement	
Collection of loan	71,750	of common shares	85,750
Issuance of common shares for cash...	123,000	Retirement of bonds payable by issuing common shares........	157,500
Stock dividends..................................	79,500	Sale of equipment for cash............	145,000

Required

1. Prepare Roanoke Ltd.'s cash flow statement using the *indirect* method to report operating activities. Note any additional disclosures that are required.

2. Evaluate Roanoke Ltd.'s cash flows for the year. Mention all three categories of cash flows, and give the reason for your evaluation.

Problem 17–6B

Preparing the cash flow
statement—direct and indirect
methods
② ③ ⑤

To prepare the cash flow statement, accountants for Tofino Inc. have summarized activity for the year 2017 in two accounts as follows:

Cash

Beginning balance	64,320	Payments on accounts payable	447,720
Collection of loan	39,600	Payments of dividends	52,640
Sale of investment	31,440	Payments of salaries and wages	172,560
Receipts of interest	39,120	Payments of interest	56,280
Collections from customers	814,440	Purchase of equipment	37,680
Issuance of common shares	33,360	Payments of operating expenses	41,160
Receipts of dividends	25,400	Payment of long-term debt	73,560
		Repurchase of common shares	20,280
		Payment of income tax	22,680
Ending balance	123,120		

Repurchase of shares	20,280	Beginning balance	101,280
		Issuance for cash	33,360
		Issuance to acquire land	77,320
		Issuance to retire long-term debt	42,800
		Ending balance	234,480

Tofino Inc.'s income statement and selected balance sheet data follow:

TOFINO INC.
Income Statement
For the Year Ended December 31, 2017

Revenues:		
Sales revenue		$847,560
Interest revenue		39,120
Dividend revenue		25,400
Total revenues		912,080
Expenses and losses:		
Cost of goods sold	$420,720	
Salaries and wages expense	180,960	
Amortization expense	29,160	
Other operating expenses	52,920	
Interest expense	58,560	
Income tax expense	19,440	
Loss on sale of investments	3,720	
Total expenses		765,480
Net income		$146,600

TOFINO INC.
Balance Sheet Data
For the Year Ended December 31, 2017

	Increase (Decrease)
Current assets	
Cash and cash equivalents	$?
Accounts receivable	33,120
Inventories	(14,160)
Prepaid expenses	720
Loan receivable	(39,600)
Long-term investments	(35,160)
Plant and equipment, net	8,520
Land	97,320
Current liabilities	
Accounts payable	(41,160)
Interest payable	2,280
Salaries payable	8,400
Other accrued liabilities	12,480
Income tax payable	(3,240)
Long-term debt	(96,360)
Common shares	133,200
Retained earnings	93,960

Required

1. Prepare the cash flow statement of Tofino Inc. for the year ended December 31, 2017, using the *direct* method to report operating activities. Also prepare a summary of non-cash investing and financing activities that will be part of a note to the financial statements.

2. Use the data from Tofino Inc.'s 2017 income statement and the selected balance sheet data to prepare a supplementary schedule showing cash flows from operating activities by the *indirect* method. All activity in the current accounts results from operations.

Problem 17–7B

Preparing the cash flow statement—direct and indirect methods

Main Street Antiques Ltd.'s comparative balance sheet at December 31, 2017, and its 2017 income statement are as follows:

MAIN STREET ANTIQUES LTD. Balance Sheet December 31, 2017 and 2016		
	2017	**2016**
Current assets		
Cash	$ 188,000	$ 43,000
Accounts receivable	370,000	241,500
Interest receivable	14,500	18,000
Inventories	343,000	301,000
Prepaid expenses	18,500	14,000
Long-term investment	50,500	26,000
Plant and equipment, net	422,500	368,000
Land	212,000	480,000
	$1,619,000	$1,491,500
Current liabilities		
Notes payable, short-term	$ 67,000	$ 90,500
Accounts payable	234,500	201,500
Income tax payable	69,000	72,500
Accrued liabilities	41,000	48,500
Interest payable	18,500	14,500
Salaries payable	4,500	13,000
Long-term note payable	237,000	470,500
Common shares	319,500	256,000
Retained earnings	628,000	324,500
	$1,619,000	$1,491,500

MAIN STREET ANTIQUES LTD. Income Statement For the Year Ended December 31, 2017		
Net sales		$1,327,000
Cost of goods sold		402,000
Gross margin		925,000
Operating expenses:		
Salaries expense	$194,000	
Amortization expense	27,000	
Other expenses	210,000	431,000
Operating income		494,000

MAIN STREET ANTIQUES LTD.
Income Statement
For the Year Ended December 31, 2017

Other revenues and expenses:		
Revenues and gains:		
Interest revenue		53,000
Expenses and losses:		
Interest expense	(30,500)	
Loss on sale of land	(33,500)	(64,000)
Income before income taxes		483,000
Income tax expense		49,500
Net income		$ 433,500

Other information for the year ended December 31, 2017:

a. Acquired equipment by issuing a long-term note payable, $76,500, and paying $5,000 cash.

b. Purchased a long-term investment for cash.

c. Received cash for issuance of common shares, $40,000.

d. Only cash dividends were issued during the year.

e. Paid short-term note payable by issuing common shares.

Required

1. Prepare the cash flow statement of Main Street Antiques Ltd. for the year ended December 31, 2017, using the *direct* method to report operating activities. Also prepare a note to the financial statements providing a summary of non-cash investing and financing activities. All current accounts, except short-term notes payable, result from operating transactions.

2. Prepare a supplementary schedule showing cash flows from operations by the *indirect* method.

Problem 17–8B

Cloverdale Sales Corp. had the financial statements for the year ended December 31 shown below:

Distinguishing among operating, investing, and financing activities; using the financial statements to compute the cash effects of a wide variety of business transactions; preparing a cash flow statement by the indirect method

② ④ ⑤

CLOVERDALE SALES CORP.
Income Statement
For the Year Ended December 31, 2017

Net sales		$267,000
Cost of goods sold		120,000
Gross margin		147,000
Operating expenses		
Selling expenses	73,800	
Administrative expenses	43,500	
Interest expense	8,700	
Total operating expenses		126,000
Operating income		21,000
Income taxes		8,400
Net income		$ 12,600

CLOVERDALE SALES CORP.
Balance Sheet
December 31, 2017 and 2016

	2017	2016
Assets		
Cash	$ 6,000	$ 27,600
Investments in money market funds	1,500	4,500
Accounts receivable	12,700	34,200
Merchandise inventory	45,900	107,815
Prepaid expenses	3,600	2,850
Plant and equipment	285,600	235,535
Less accumulated amortization	(24,000)	(15,000)
Land	90,000	0
Goodwill	18,000	22,500
Total assets	$439,300	$420,000
Liabilities		
Accounts payable	$ 21,300	$ 22,500
Salaries payable	34,000	21,000
Loans payable	84,000	99,000
Total liabilities	139,300	142,500
Shareholders' equity		
Common shares	165,000	150,000
Retained earnings	135,000	127,500
Total shareholders' equity	300,000	277,500
Total liabilities and shareholders' equity	$439,300	$420,000

Additional information:

a. The administrative expenses included the following:

Amortization expense on plant and equipment = $24,000

Write-down of goodwill = $4,500

b. Sold equipment for its net book value. The equipment cost $44,685 and had been amortized for $15,000.

c. Purchased additional equipment for $94,750.

d. Exchanged common shares for land valued at $90,000.

e. Declared and paid cash dividends on common shares, $5,100.

f. Repurchased common shares for $75,000.

g. Paid $23,700 (of which $8,700 was interest) on the loans.

Required

1. Prepare a cash flow statement for Cloverdale Sales Corp. for the year ended December 31, 2017, using the *indirect* method. Consider the investments in money market funds to be a cash equivalent.

2. Comment on the results indicated by the cash flow statement.

Problem 17–9B

Preparing the cash flow statement under IFRS—direct method
② ③ ⑥

Accountants for Giovanni's Builders' Supply Ltd. have developed the following data from the company's accounting records for the year ended December 31, 2017:

a. Credit sales, $291,950.

b. Income tax expense and payments, $18,950.

c. Cash payments to acquire property, plant, and equipment, $29,700.

d. Cost of goods sold, $191,300.

e. Cash received from issuance of long-term debt, $34,000.

f. Payment of cash dividends, $24,200.

g. Collection of interest, $13,700.

h. Acquisition of equipment by issuing short-term note payable, $18,200.

i. Payment of salaries, $43,800.

j. Cash received from sale of property, plant, and equipment, $11,200, including a $3,400 loss.

k. Collections on accounts receivable, $231,300.

l. Interest revenue, $1,900.

m. Cash receipt of dividend revenue on investment in shares, $2,050.

n. Payments to suppliers, $184,250.

o. Cash sales, $85,950.

p. Depreciation expense, $31,400.

q. Cash received from issuance of short-term debt, $29,800.

r. Payments of long-term debt, $25,000.

s. Interest expense and payments, $16,650.

t. Salaries expense, $47,650.

u. Collections of notes receivable, $24,000.

v. Cash received from sale of investments, $4,550, including $1,000 gain.

w. Payment of short-term note payable by issuing long-term note payable, $31,500.

x. Cash balance:

December 31, 2016—$39,650

December 31, 2017—$?

Required

1. Prepare Giovanni's cash flow statement for the year ended December 31, 2017, reporting operating activities by the direct method. Include a note to the financial statements providing a summary of non-cash investing and financing activities.

2. Assume that Giovanni's Builders' Supply Ltd. has adopted IFRS and has elected to classify cash inflows from interest and dividends as investing activities and cash outflows for the payment of interest and dividends as financing activities. How would this reclassification change the balances in the three sections of the cash flow statement? Note the balances in each section and comment.

CHALLENGE PROBLEMS

Problem 17–1C

Both the Accounting Standards Board (AcSB) in Canada and the Financial Accounting Standards Board (FASB) in the United States prefer the direct method of preparing the operating activities section of the cash flow statement. Yet most companies use the indirect method when preparing their cash flow statement.

Distinguishing between the direct method and indirect method
③ ⑤

Required Discuss why you think companies use the indirect method when the direct method is preferred by the standard-setting bodies.

Problem 17–2C

Initially, the *CPA Canada Handbook* did not require financial statements to include information about non-cash investing and financing activities. The financial statements reported only changes in working capital (defined as current assets less current liabilities), so transactions such as the use of long-term debt to purchase property, plant, and equipment or conversion of debt into equity were excluded.

Accounting for non-cash financing and investing activities
④

Required Discuss the present *CPA Canada Handbook*'s requirements with respect to disclosure of non-cash financing and investing decisions, and explain why you think the required disclosure does or does not benefit users.

EXTENDING YOUR KNOWLEDGE

DECISION PROBLEMS

Decision Problem 1

Preparing and using the cash
flow statement to evaluate
operations
④ ⑤

1. Net cash flow from
operating, $60,000;
investing, $(66,500);
financing, $(18,500)

The 2017 comparative income statement and the 2017 comparative balance sheet of Eclipse Golf Inc. (shown below) have just been distributed at a meeting of the company's board of directors.

In discussing the company's results of operations and year-end financial position, the members of the board raise a fundamental question: Why is the cash balance so low? This question is especially puzzling to the board members because 2017 showed record profits. As the controller of the company, you must answer the question.

ECLIPSE GOLF INC.
Income Statement
For the Years Ended December 31, 2017 and 2016
(amounts in thousands)

	2017	2016
Revenues and gains:		
Sales revenue	$222.0	$155.0
Gain on sale of equipment (sale price, $17.5)	—	9.0
Total revenues and gains	222.0	164.0
Expenses and losses:		
Cost of goods sold	110.5	81.0
Salaries expense	24.0	14.0
Amortization expense	28.5	16.5
Interest expense	6.5	10.0
Loss on sale of land (sale price, $30.5)	—	17.5
Total expenses and losses	169.5	139.0
Net income	$ 52.5	$ 25.0

ECLIPSE GOLF INC.
Balance Sheet
December 31, 2017 and 2016
(amounts in thousands)

Assets	2017	2016
Cash	$ 6.5	$ 31.5
Accounts receivable, net	46.0	30.5
Inventories	97.0	90.5
Property, plant, and equipment, net	74.0	30.5
Patents, net	88.5	94.0
Total assets	$312.0	$277.0
Liabilities and Shareholders' Equity		
Notes payable, short-term (for general borrowing)	$ 16.0	$ 50.5
Accounts payable	31.5	28.0
Accrued liabilities	6.0	8.5
Notes payable, long-term	73.5	81.5
Common shares	74.5	30.5
Retained earnings	110.5	78.0
Total liabilities and shareholders' equity	$312.0	$277.0

Required

1. Prepare a cash flow statement for 2017 in the format that best shows the relationship between net income and operating cash flow. The company sold no capital assets or long-term investments and issued no notes payable during 2017. The changes in all current accounts except short-term notes payable arose from operations. There were no non-cash financing and investing transactions during the year. Show all amounts in thousands. Amortization expense on the patent was $5,500.

2. Answer the board members' question: Why is the cash balance so low? In explaining the business's cash flows, identify two significant cash receipts that occurred during 2016 but not in 2017. Also point out the two largest cash payments during 2017.

3. Considering net income and the company's cash flows during 2017, was it a good year or a bad year for Eclipse Golf Inc.? Give your reasons.

Decision Problem 2

In the not-too-distant past, the cash flow statement included information in only two categories: sources of funds and uses of funds. Funds were usually defined as working capital (current assets minus current liabilities). The present-day statement provides information about cash flows from operating activities, investing activities, and financing activities. The earlier statement permitted the information to be about changes in working capital or in cash, while today's cash flow statement deals specifically with information about flows in cash and cash equivalents.

Using the cash flow statement to evaluate a company's operations ①

Required

1. Explain why you think the present-day cash flow statement, with its disclosure of the three different kinds of activities, is or is not an improvement over the earlier model that showed only sources and uses of funds.

2. Is information about cash flows more informative to users than information about working capital flows?

3. Briefly explain why comparative balance sheets and a cash flow statement are more informative than just comparative balance sheets.

FINANCIAL STATEMENT CASES

Financial Statement Case 1

Indigo Books & Music Inc.'s Consolidated Statements of Cash Flow appear in Appendix A at the end of this book and on MyAccountingLab. Use these statements along with the other material in the annual report to answer the following questions:

Using the cash flow statement ② ④

1. Which method does Indigo use to report net cash flows from operations? How can you tell?
2. Did Indigo improve its cash position in the year ended March 29, 2014? If so, by how much? If not, by how much did it decline?
3. By how much did Indigo's cash from operations increase or decrease in the year ended March 29, 2014? Why is it important for cash from operating activities to be a positive number?
4. What were the major investing activities during fiscal 2014? Financing activities?
5. Was Indigo expanding or contracting in fiscal 2014? Support your answer with specific references to the financial statements.

Financial Statement Case 2

TELUS Corporation's Statements of Cash Flows appear on MyAccountingLab. Use these statements along with the other material in the annual report to answer the following questions:

Using the cash flow statement ② ④

1. Which method does TELUS use to report net cash flows from operations? How can you tell?
2. Did TELUS improve its cash position in 2013? If so, by how much?
3. TELUS, and many other companies, report items differently in the operating section than the method illustrated or described in the chapter. Explain why this is the case.

4. Explain the cause for the large outflow in the investing section and discuss.
5. Was TELUS expanding, contracting, or holding steady in 2013? Support your answer with specific references to the financial statements.

IFRS MINI-CASE

The income statement and additional data of ENVIRO Consulting Ltd. follow:

ENVIRO CONSULTING LTD. Income Statement For the Year Ended December 31, 2017		
Revenues:		
Consulting revenue		$274,000
Expenses:		
Salaries expense	$148,000	
Depreciation expense	29,000	
Rent expense	12,000	
Office supplies expense	3,000	
Insurance expense	2,000	
Interest expense	2,000	
Income tax expense	18,000	214,000
Net income		$ 60,000

Additional data:

a. Collections from clients are $7,000 more than revenues.

b. Increase in cash balance, $10,000.

c. Payments to employees are $4,000 less than salaries expense.

d. Interest expense and income tax expense equal their cash amounts.

e. Acquisition of property, plant, and equipment is $116,000. Of this amount, $101,000 is paid in cash, $15,000 by signing a long-term note payable.

f. Cash received from sale of land, $10,000.

g. Cash received from issuance of common shares, $42,000.

h. Payment of long-term note payable, $20,000.

i. Payment of cash dividends, $15,000.

j. Payments for rent and insurance are equal to expense.

k. Payment for office supplies is $6,000 more than expense.

l. Opening cash balance, $16,000.

Required

1. Assume ENVIRO Consulting Ltd. has adopted IFRS and elects to classify as operating activities all cash inflows and outflows for interest and dividends. Prepare ENVIRO Consulting Ltd.'s cash flow statement by the direct method for operating activities, and write a note to the financial statements providing a summary of non-cash investing and financing activities.
2. Assume ENVIRO Consulting Ltd. has adopted IFRS and elects to classify as investing or financing activities all cash inflows and outflows for interest and dividends. Prepare ENVIRO Consulting Ltd.'s cash flow statement by the direct method for operating activities, and write a note to the financial statements providing a summary of non-cash investing and financing activities.
3. Compare and summarize the effects of the accounting choice in Requirement 1 with that of Requirement 2. Can ENVIRO change the method used and classifications from one year to the next?

>Try It! SOLUTIONS FOR CHAPTER 17

1. a. Two years: 2013 and 2012.
   b. Net loss of $48,641,000 in 2013 and net income of $31,670,000 in 2012.
   c. Disposal of a business operation in the amount of $213,667,000 in 2013.
   d. Payment of debt owing: $176,068,000 million in 2013.
   e. $8,245,000 million in 2013 and $20,590,000 million in 2012.

2. __D__ Payment of dividends
   __I__ Issuance of shares
   __D__ Payment to employees
   __I__ Collections from customers
   __D__ Payments for assets
   __D__ Repayment of a bank loan
   __I__ Issuance of bonds

3. __O__ Payment of income taxes
   __F__ Issuance of preferred shares
   __O__ Payment of employee salaries

   __O__ Collections of accounts receivable
   __I__ Payment for a delivery truck
   __F__ Repayment of a long-term bank loan (principal only)
   __O__ Receipt of loan interest
   __O__ Payment of accounts payable

4. __−__ Payment of income taxes
   __+__ Issuance of preferred shares
   __−__ Payment of employee salaries
   __+__ Collections of accounts receivable
   __−__ Payment for a delivery truck
   __−__ Repayment of a long-term bank loan (principal only)
   __+__ Receipt of loan interest
   __−__ Payment of accounts payable

5. Markham Corp. will report a cash receipt of $5 million (cost of $2 million plus the gain of $3 million).

6. a. Cash collections from customers:

Accounts Receivable

Beginning balance	+ Sales	− Collections	= Ending balance
$46,000	+ $240,000	− X	= $44,000
		−X	= $44,000 − $46,000 − $240,000
		X	= $242,000

b. Payments for inventory:

Inventory

Beginning balance	+ Purchases	− Cost of goods sold	= Ending balance
$62,000	+ X	− $140,000	= $68,000
		X	= $68,000 − $62,000 + $140,000
		X	= $146,000

Accounts and Notes Payable

Beginning balance	+ Purchases	− Payments for inventory	= Ending balance
$52,000	+ $146,000	− X	= $70,000
		−X	= $70,000 − $52,000 − $146,000
		X	= $128,000

c. Payments for income taxes:

Income and Other Taxes Payable

Beginning balance	+	Income tax expense	–	Payments	=	Ending balance
$20,000	+	$20,000	–	X	=	$22,000
				–X	=	$22,000 – $20,000 – $20,000
				X	=	$18,000

d. Payments for prepaid expenses:

Prepaid Expenses

Beginning balance	+	Payments	–	Expiration of prepaid expenses	=	Ending balance
$6,000	+	X	–	$8,000	=	$2,000
				X	=	$2,000 – $6,000 + $8,000
				X	=	$4,000

7. a. Net change in cash from investing activities (amounts in thousands):

Sale of bonds issued by Blue Ltd.	$ 224
Purchase of land	(316)
Collection of long-term note receivable	126
	$ 34 a net increase

b. *Operating activities:* Payment of interest, payment of income taxes
Financing activities: Retirement of preferred shares, sale of common shares, payment of dividends

8. Net change in cash from financing activities (amounts in thousands):

Retirement of Bolin Corp. preferred shares	$ (90)
Sale of Bolin Corp. common shares	210
Payment of dividends	(300)
	$(180) a net decrease

9. Computation of cash flow from operating activities using the indirect method:

Net income	$150
Add (subtract):	
Decrease in accounts receivable	6
Increase in inventory	(18)
Increase in accounts payable	11
Decrease in wages payable	(15)
Cash flow from operating activities	$134

10. a. Capilano Ltd. appears to be growing. The company acquired more property, plant, and equipment and intangible assets ($735,000) than it sold during the year ($149,000), and current assets changed very little.

b. Most of the cash for expansion came from issuing common shares ($242,000) and from borrowing ($226,000). However, cash from the balance on January 1, 2017, and cash from operating activities could have been used for expansion too.

c. Accounts Receivable ↓, Cash ↑

Therefore, net cash inflow from operating activities would be $280,000 ($168,000 + $80,000 + $32,000).

18 FINANCIAL STATEMENT ANALYSIS

CONNECTING CHAPTER 18

**LEARNING OBJECTIVE ① ** Perform a horizontal analysis of financial statements

How do we compare several years of financial information?

Horizontal Analysis, page 1057
  Trend Percentages

**LEARNING OBJECTIVE ② ** Perform a vertical analysis of financial statements

What is vertical analysis, and how do we perform one?

Vertical Analysis, page 1061

**LEARNING OBJECTIVE ③ ** Prepare and use common-size financial statements

What are common-size financial statements, and how do we use them?

Common-Size Statements, page 1063
  Benchmarking

**LEARNING OBJECTIVE ④ ** Compute the standard financial ratios

How do we compute standard financial ratios, and what do they mean?

Using Ratios to Make Decisions, page 1066
  Measuring the Ability to Pay Current Liabilities
  Measuring the Ability to Sell Inventory and Collect Receivables
  Measuring the Ability to Pay Long-Term Debt (Solvency)
  Measuring Profitability
  Analyzing Shares as an Investment
Limitations of Financial Analysis, page 1076
Investor Decisions, page 1077
  Annual Reports
  Look for Red Flags When Analyzing Financial Statements

**LEARNING OBJECTIVE ⑤ ** Describe the impact of IFRS on financial statement analysis

What is the impact of IFRS on financial statement analysis?

The Impact of IFRS on Financial Statement Analysis, page 1081

MyAccountingLab The **Summary** for Chapter 18 appears on page 1083. This lists all of the MyAccountingLab resources. Accounting Vocabulary with definitions for this chapter's material appears on page 1085.

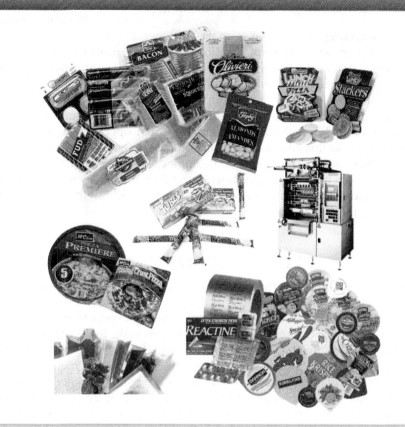

Winpak manufactures and sells high-quality packaging materials and packaging machines. Customers use Winpak packaging for perishable foods, beverages, pharmaceuticals, and medical applications. Customers include Proctor & Gamble, McCain Foods Limited, High Liner Foods Inc., and Maple Leaf Foods Inc.

Everyone wants to know "how is the company doing?" There are a number of different ways to answer that question because there are a number of different tools to use.

- Investors and management of Winpak compare the performance of the most recent period against prior periods. Financial results for two or more years are presented in annual reports for this reason.
- Investors can compare Winpak's earnings to its number of shareholders to measure success against other companies which you might invest in. By comparing different amounts of earnings against different numbers of shareholders, *relative* performance is considered rather than just the total dollar amounts, which is another form of analysis.
- Investors and creditors compare Winpak against its competitors in the same field of business and the industry in general.
- Managers might analyze inventory levels to see if they are too high so that operations managers can adjust production, marketing managers can see whether changes to advertising results in increased sales, and human resources managers can see if labour costs are in line with other companies in the industry.

So how is Winpak doing? See for yourself. In this chapter, we will explore ratios and other forms of financial statement analysis for Winpak and other companies.

>As the opening vignette illustrates, managers rely on accounting information to make business decisions. Investors and creditors also rely on accounting information. Often they want to compare two or more similar companies. The way to compare companies of different sizes is to use *standard* measures. In earlier chapters, we have discussed financial ratios, such as the current ratio, inventory turnover, and return on shareholders' equity. These ratios are standard measures that enable investors to compare companies of similar sizes or different sizes, or companies that operate in the same or different industries. In this chapter, we discuss many of the basic ratios and related measures that managers use to run a company. Investors and lenders use the same tools to search for good investments and loan prospects. It is important to know how ratios are calculated to better understand and interpret the results of financial statement analysis.

OBJECTIVES OF FINANCIAL STATEMENT ANALYSIS

Financial statement analysis focuses on techniques used by internal managers and by analysts external to the organization.

Investors who purchase a company's shares expect to receive dividends and hope the shares' value will increase. Creditors make loans with the expectation of receiving cash for the interest and principal. Both groups bear the risk they will not receive their expected returns. They use financial statement analysis to predict the amount of expected returns and assess the risks associated with those returns.

Creditors generally expect to receive specific fixed amounts and have the first claim on a company's assets if the company goes bankrupt, so creditors are most concerned with assessing short-term liquidity and long-term solvency. **Short-term liquidity** is an organization's ability to meet current payments as they become due. **Long-term solvency** is the ability to generate enough cash to pay long-term debts as they mature.

In contrast, *investors* are more concerned with profitability, dividends, and future share prices. Why? Because dividends and future share prices depend on profitable operations. Creditors also assess profitability because profitable operations are the company's prime source of cash to repay loans.

However, investors and creditors cannot evaluate a company by looking at only one year's data. This is one reason why most financial statements present results for at least two periods. This chapter illustrates some of the analytical tools for charting a company's progress over time.

Exhibit 18–1 shows graphical data taken from the 2014 annual report of Winpak Ltd. Management presents information this way to show how the company performed over a ten year period.

KEY POINTS

When performing financial analysis, it is important to not look at only one period or one ratio. Think of analysis as solving a mystery, where one clue leads to another until a conclusion can be reached based on all the clues fitting together.

EXHIBIT 18–1 | **Financial Data from Winpak Ltd.'s 2014 Annual Report**

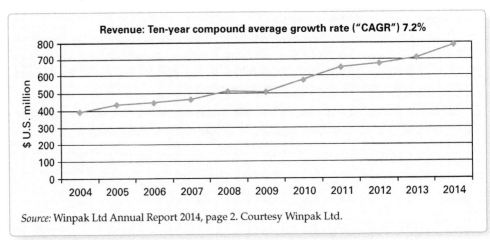

Source: Winpak Ltd Annual Report 2014, page 2. Courtesy Winpak Ltd.

How can we decide what we really think about Winpak's performance? We can analyze a company's performance in different ways:

- From year to year
- Compared with a competing company
- Compared with the company's industry

Then we can better judge the company's current situation and try to predict what might happen in the near future.

METHODS OF ANALYSIS

There are three main ways to analyze financial statements:

- Perform horizontal analysis to provide a year-to-year comparison of performance in different periods.
- Perform vertical analysis to compare different companies.
- Calculate and interpret financial ratios.

HORIZONTAL ANALYSIS

Many managerial decisions hinge on whether the numbers—revenues, expenses, and net income—are increasing or decreasing. Have revenues risen from last year? By how much? The fact that revenues may have risen by $20,000 may be interesting, but considered alone it is not very useful for decision making. Did $2,000,000 or $200,000 in revenues increase by $20,000? The *percentage change* in the net revenues over time is more useful because it shows the changes over time in *relative* terms. It is more useful to know that revenues increased by 20 percent than to know that revenues increased by $20,000.

The study of percentage changes in comparative statements is called **horizontal analysis**. Computing a percentage change in comparative statements requires three steps:

① Lay out at least two periods of financial statement information side by side.

② Compute the dollar amount of the change from the earlier period to the later period.

③ Divide the dollar amount of the change by the earlier-period amount and multiply by 100. We call the earlier period the *base period*.

Let's look at how horizontal analysis, which is illustrated for Winpak Ltd. in Exhibit 18–2 and Exhibit 18–3, is done.

① Organize financial information into a chart format, as shown here:

LO ❶

How do we compare several years of financial information?

🔑 **KEY** POINTS

Horizontal analysis often involves a percentage change, calculated as follows:

$$\frac{\$ \text{ change}}{\text{Base year } \$} \times 100 = \% \text{ change}$$

It is important to consider both dollar changes and percentage changes in horizontal analysis. The dollar increase may be growing, but the percentage change may be growing less because the base is greater each year.

	(US dollar amounts in millions)		Increase (Decrease)	
	2014	2013	Amount	Percent
Sales	$786.8	$714.9		
Net income*	78.4	71.4		

*Net income attributable to equity holders

② Compute the dollar amount of change in each account during the most recent year:

	(US dollar amounts in millions)		Increase (Decrease)	
	2014	2013	Amount	Percent
Sales	$786.8	$714.9	$71.9	
Net earnings	78.4	71.4	7.0	

③ Divide the dollar amount of change by the base-period amount and multiply by 100 to compute the percentage change during the later period. For sales, the calculation is as follows:

$$\text{Percentage change} = \frac{\text{Dollar amount of change}}{\text{Base-year amount}} = \frac{\$71.9}{\$714.9} \times 100 = 10.1 \text{ percent}$$

	(US dollar amounts in millions)		Increase (Decrease)	
	2014	2013	Amount	Percent
Sales	$786.8	$714.9	$71.9	10.1
Net earnings	78.4	71.4	7.0	9.8

REAL WORLD EXAMPLE

Spreadsheet programs like Excel are ideal for performing horizontal analysis.

The comparative income statement for Winpak Ltd. shown in Exhibit 18–2 shows that sales increased by $71.9 million, or 10.1 percent. The gross margin increased only 7.8 percent because the cost of goods sold (cost of sales) increased by 11 percent, which is more than the increase in sales.

EXHIBIT 18–2 | Comparative Income Statement—Horizontal Analysis

WINPAK LTD.				
Consolidated Statements of Income (adapted)				
For the Years Ended December 28, 2014, and December 29, 2013				
(US dollar amounts in millions except per-share amounts)*				
			Increase (Decrease)	
	2014	2013	Amount	Percent
Sales	$786.8	$714.9	$ 71.9	10.1%
Cost of sales	562.4	506.8	55.6	11.0
Gross margin	224.4	208.1	16.3	7.8
Expenses				
Selling, general, & administrative	99.4	88.7	10.7	13.6
Research and technical	14.3	13.1	1.2	9.2
Pre-production	1.4	3.0	(1.6)	(53.3)
Earnings from operations	115.1	104.8	10.3	9.8
Interest expense	(0.1)	0.4	(0.5)	(125.0)
Earnings before income taxes	115.2	104.4	10.8	10.3
Income tax expense	35.5	32.3	3.2	9.9
Net earnings	$ 79.7	$ 72.1	$ 7.6	10.5
Earnings per share (basic and fully diluted)	$ 1.21	$ 1.10	$ 0.1	9.1

* Numbers may not add up due to rounding.
Note: Net earnings shown here are not the same as net income attributable to equity holders shown earlier. This company has a "non-controlling interest" that has a right to a share of the earnings.

The comparative balance sheet in Exhibit 18–3 shows the changes between 2013 and 2014. Total assets increased by $21.1 million, or 3 percent, and total liabilities increased by $12.4 million, or 10.2 percent. The increase in retained earnings was $7.9 million, or 1.4 percent. These numbers are highlighted in Exhibit 18-3 for easy reference.

EXHIBIT 18–3 | Comparative Balance Sheet—Horizontal Analysis

WINPAK LTD.
Consolidated Balance Sheet (adapted)*
December 28, 2014, and December 29, 2013
(US dollar amounts in millions)

	2014	2013	Increase (Decrease) Amount	Increase (Decrease) Percent
Assets				
Current assets:				
Cash and equivalents	$143.8	$161.1	$(17.3)	(10.7%)
Accounts receivable	112.5	98.4	14.1	14.3
Income taxes receivable	2.9	3.6	(0.7)	(19.4)
Inventory	100.6	92.3	8.3	9.0
Prepaid expenses	4.3	3.1	1.2	38.7
Total current assets	364.0	358.5	5.5	1.5
Property, plant, and equipment	348.0	329.7	18.3	5.6
Other assets, intangible assets, and goodwill	22.3	25.0	(2.7)	(10.8)
Total assets	$734.3	$713.2	$ 21.1	3.0
Liabilities and Shareholders' Equity				
Current liabilities:				
Accounts payable and accrued liabilities	70.4	64.6	5.8	9.0
Income taxes payable	0.7	2.0	(1.3)	(43.3)
Total current liabilities	71.1	66.6	4.5	6.8
Non-current liabilities:				
Employee benefit plan liabilities	7.7	3.4	4.3	126.5
Deferrals	47.6	44.1	3.5	7.9
Provisions	6.6	6.5	0.1	1.5
Total non-current liabilities	61.9	54.0	7.9	14.6
Total liabilities	132.9	120.6	12.3	10.2
Shareholders' equity:				
Common shares	29.2	29.2	0.0	0.0
Retained earnings	555.1	547.2	7.9	1.4
Non-controlling interests**	17.1	16.2	0.9	5.6
Total shareholders' equity	601.4	592.6	8.8	1.5
Total liabilities and shareholders' equity	$734.3	$713.2	$21.1	3.0

Note: Percentage changes are typically not computed for shifts from a negative amount to a positive amount, and vice versa. In addition, a decrease from any number to zero is a decrease of 100 percent. We will treat an increase from zero to any positive number as an increase of 100 percent.

* Slight differences are due to rounding throughout the statement.

** Winpak reports using IFRS.

KEY POINTS

There are no equal sign lines for the total in the Percent column. This column will never add up because a separate percentage has been calculated for each item, as is always done in horizontal analysis.

Trend Percentages

Trend percentages are a form of horizontal analysis. Trends are important indicators of the direction a business is taking. To gain a realistic view of the company, it is often necessary to examine more than just a two- or three-year period. How have sales changed over a five-year period? What trend does gross margin show? These questions can be answered by analyzing trend percentages over a recent period, such as the most recent five years or ten years.

Trend percentages are computed by selecting a base year. The base-year amounts are set to 100 percent. The amounts for each following year are expressed as a percent of the base amount. To compute trend percentages, divide each item for following years by the base-year amount and multiply by 100 percent.

$$\text{Trend \%} = \frac{\text{Any year \$}}{\text{Base-year \$}} \times 100\%$$

Using financial statements from more than one year, we can create a summary chart to show Winpak's sales and income from operations for the past five years:

	(Amounts in millions)				
	2014	**2013**	**2012**	**2011**	**2010**
Sales	$786.8	$714.9	$670.1	$652.1	$579.4
Income from operations	115.1	104.8	103.2	95.0	79.0
Net income*	78.4	71.4	71.3	63.8	55.3

*Selected data from page 2 of the Winpak Ltd. 2014 Annual Report.

We want trend percentages for a four-year period, 2010 through 2014, so we use 2010 as the base year. Trend percentages for sales are computed by dividing each sales amount by the 2010 amount of $579.4 million. The same steps are done for the other accounts. The resulting trend percentages follow:

$115.1 \div 79.0 \times 100 = 145.7\%$

	2014	**2013**	**2012**	**2011**	**2010**
Sales	135.8%	123.4%	115.7%	112.6%	100%
Income from operations	145.7	132.7	130.6	120.3	100
Net income	141.8	129.1	128.9	115.4	100

Winpak's sales have trended upward from 2010; 2014 sales are 135.8 percent of 2010 sales. Income from operations has also trended upward from 2010, and net income followed the same upwards trend, from $55.3 million in 2010 to $78.4 million in 2014; 2014's net income was 141.8 percent of 2010's net income. Further analysis would need to be completed to confirm whether the upward trends are expected to continue.

> Try It!

1. Perform a horizontal analysis of the comparative income statement of Umoja Inc. State whether 2017 was a good year or a bad year and give your reasons.

UMOJA INC. Income Statement For the Years Ended December 31, 2017 and 2016	2017	2016
Net sales	$275,000	$225,000
Expenses:		
Cost of goods sold	194,000	165,000
Engineering, selling, and administrative expenses	54,000	48,000
Interest expense	5,000	5,000
Income tax expense	9,000	3,000
Other expense (income)	1,000	(1,000)
Total expenses	263,000	220,000
Net income	$ 12,000	$ 5,000

2. Suppose Umoja Inc. reported the following net sales and net income amounts:

	(in thousands)			
	2017	2016	2015	2014
Net sales	$275,000	$225,000	$210,000	$200,000
Net income	12,000	5,000	6,000	3,000

a. Show Umoja Inc.'s trend percentages for net sales and net income. Use 2014 as the base year.
b. Which measure increased faster between 2014 and 2017?

Solutions appear at the end of this chapter and on MyAccountingLab

VERTICAL ANALYSIS

As we have seen, horizontal analysis and trend percentages highlight changes in an item over time. However, no single technique provides a complete picture of a business. Another way to analyze a company is called vertical analysis.

Vertical analysis of a financial statement reveals the relationship of each statement item to a base, which is shown as 100 percent.

$$\text{Vertical analysis \%} = \frac{\text{Each account}}{\text{Base amount*}} \times 100\%$$

* Base amount for an income statement is sales. Base amount for a balance sheet is total assets.

For example, when an income statement for a merchandising company is subjected to vertical analysis, net sales is usually the base. Every other item on the income statement is then reported as a percentage of that base.

Suppose under normal conditions a company's gross margin is 40 percent of net sales. A drop in gross margin to 30 percent of net sales may cause the company to report a net loss on the income statement. Management, investors, and creditors view a large decline in gross margin with alarm. If analysis were performed using just dollar amounts, it is possible that this decline would be missed because an increase in sales and gross margin might not show the *relative* decline in the gross margin.

LO 2

What is a vertical analysis, and how do we perform one?

KEY POINTS

While horizontal analysis shows the relationship among numbers over several years, vertical analysis shows the relationship among numbers on the financial statements for the same year.

EXHIBIT 18–4 | Comparative Income Statement—Vertical Analysis

WINPAK LTD.
Consolidated Statements of Income (adapted)
For the Years Ended December 28, 2014, and December 29, 2013
(US dollar amounts in millions)

	2014		2013	
	Amount	Percent*	Amount	Percent*
Sales	$786.8	100.0%	$714.9	100.0%
Cost of sales	562.4	71.5	506.8	70.9
Gross margin	224.4	28.5	208.1	29.1
Expenses:				
Selling, general, & administrative	99.4	12.6	88.7	12.4
Research and technical	14.3	1.8	13.1	1.8
Pre-production	1.4	0.2	3.0	0.4
Earnings from operations	115.1	14.6	104.8	14.7
Interest	(0.1)	(0.01)	0.4	0.1
Earnings before income taxes	115.2	14.6	104.4	14.6
Income tax expense	35.5	4.5	32.3	4.5
Net earnings	$ 79.7	10.1	$ 72.1	10.1
Earnings per share (basic and fully diluted)	$ 1.21		$ 1.10	

* Percentages may not add up due to rounding.

Exhibit 18–4 shows the vertical analysis of Winpak Ltd.'s income statement as a percentage of sales. Notice that the total sale dollars, cost of sales, and gross margin dollars *increased*, but the gross margin *decreased* from 29.1 percent of sales in 2013 to 28.5 percent of sales in 2014. This tells us the same sort of information as horizontal analysis—that cost of sales rose and the gross margin decreased.

This gross margin percentage of sales shown in a vertical analysis is the same as what you learned in Chapter 6 (page 342): Gross margin percentage = Gross margin ÷ Net sales revenue.

The vertical analysis of Winpak's balance sheet in Exhibit 18–5 shows that current assets decreased from 50.3 percent of total assets in 2013 to 49.6 percent of total assets in 2014. This might be a concern because it means relatively less money is available to pay short-term bills.

> Try It!

3. Refer to the Umoja Inc. information in Try It #1. Perform a vertical analysis of the comparative income statement. Was 2017 a good year or a bad year? Give your reasons.

Solutions appear at the end of this chapter and on MyAccountingLab

EXHIBIT 18–5 | **Comparative Balance Sheet—Vertical Analysis**

WINPAK LTD. Consolidated Balance Sheet (adapted) December 28, 2014, and December 29, 2013 (US dollar amounts in millions)				
	2014		**2013**	
	Amount	Percent*	Amount	Percent*
Assets				
Current assets:				
Cash and equivalents	$143.8	19.6%	$161.1	22.6%
Accounts receivable	112.5	15.3	98.4	13.8
Income taxes receivable	2.9	0.4	3.6	0.5
Inventory	100.6	13.7	92.3	12.9
Prepaid expenses	4.3	0.6	3.1	0.4
Total current assets	364.0	49.6	358.5	50.3
Property, plant, and equipment	348.0	47.4	329.7	46.2
Other assets, intangible assets, and goodwill	22.3	3.0	25.0	3.5
Total assets	$734.3	100.0%	$713.2	100.0%
Liabilities and Shareholders' Equity				
Current liabilities:				
Accounts payable and accrued liabilities	$ 70.4	9.6	$ 59.6	9.4
Income taxes payable	0.7	0.1	5.4	0.9
Total current liabilities	71.1	9.7	65.0	10.2
Non-current liabilities				
Employee benefit plan liabilities	7.7	1.1	3.4	0.5
Deferrals	47.6	6.5	44.1	6.2
Provisions	6.6	0.9	6.5	0.9
Total non-current liabilities	61.9	8.5	54	7.6
Total liabilities	132.9	18.1	120.6	16.9
Shareholders' equity:				
Common shares	29.2	4.0	29.2	4.1
Retained earnings	555.1	75.6	547.2	76.7
Non-controlling interests	17.1	2.3	16.2	2.3
Total shareholders' equity	601.4	81.9	592.6	83.1
Total liabilities and shareholders' equity	$734.3	100.0%	$713.2	100.0%

* Percentages may not add up due to rounding.

KEY POINTS

To show the *relative* importance of each item on a financial statement, vertical analysis presents everything on that statement as a percentage of one total amount. On an income statement, all amounts are presented as a percentage of net sales. On a balance sheet, all amounts are presented as a percentage of total assets.

COMMON-SIZE STATEMENTS

Horizontal analysis and vertical analysis provide useful data about a company. As we have seen, Winpak appears to be a successful company. But the Winpak data apply only to one business, so we might want to know—how do their results compare to other companies?

To compare one company to another we can use a common-size statement. A **common-size statement** reports only percentages—the same percentages that appear in a vertical analysis. For example, Winpak's common-size income statement could be created by removing the dollar amounts from Exhibit 18–4 and presenting just the percentages.

On a common-size income statement, each item is expressed as a percentage of the net sales (or revenues) amount. Net sales is the *common size* to which we relate the statement's other amounts. On the balance sheet, the *common size* is total assets *or* the sum of total liabilities and shareholders' equity.

Common-size statements provide information that is useful for analyzing the changes in account balances over time irrespective of the dollar amounts. For example, Winpak's total current assets increased from $358.5 million to

What are common-size financial statements, and how do we use them?

KEY POINTS

A common-size statement is a form of vertical analysis used to facilitate comparison between different companies by making all amounts relative to some base amount.

EXHIBIT 18-6 | Common-Size Analysis of Current Assets

WINPAK LTD. Partial Common-Size Balance Sheet December 28, 2014, and December 29, 2013		
	Percent of Total Assets	
	2014	**2013**
Current assets:		
Cash and equivalents	19.6%	22.6%
Accounts receivable	15.3	13.8
Income taxes receivable	0.4	0.5
Inventory	13.7	12.9
Prepaid expenses	0.6	0.4
Total current assets	49.6%	49.6%

$364 million, but percentage-wise it decreased from 50.3 percent of total assets in 2013 to 49.6 percent of total assets in 2014. If this decrease was not planned, this would be important information for management, telling them they have relatively less current assets.

A common-size statement also eases the comparison of different companies because their amounts are stated as percentages. If Winpak's competitors held inventory that was 17 percent of their total assets, then Winpak might be holding too little.

Benchmarking

Benchmarking is the practice of comparing any part of a company's performance with that of other leading companies. There are two main types of benchmarks in financial statement analysis: against another company and against an industry average.

Benchmarking Against Another Company A company's financial statements show past results and help investors predict future performance. Still, that knowledge may be limited to that one company. We may learn that gross margin and net income have increased. This information is helpful, but it does not consider how other companies in the same industry have fared over the same period. Have competitors profited even more? Is there an industry-wide increase in net income? Managers, investors, creditors, and other interested parties need to know how one company compares with other companies in the same line of business.

We can look at Alphabet Inc. (formerly Google Inc.) and Yahoo! Inc. as an example. They are competitors who could be compared to see which one is more profitable, but the different sizes of the companies would make a direct comparison very complex: Alphabet's revenues in 2014 were about $66 billion, while Yahoo!'s revenues were under $5 billion. So how does Alphabet's operating income of $16.5 billion compare to Yahoo!'s $142 million operating income? Exhibit 18–7 presents their common-size income statements. Alphabet's operating income is 25 percent of revenues while Yahoo!'s operating income is 3.1 percent of revenues. From this analysis, we can see that Yahoo! is less profitable than Alphabet when compared with the amount of revenues each earns.

When the same information—the common-size income statement data—is presented in a graph, we can also notice other differences in the companies, such as the fact that Yahoo! invests a greater percentage of its revenues into research and development than does Google.

Benchmarking Against the Industry Average The industry average can also serve as a useful benchmark for evaluating a company. An industry comparison would show how Google is performing compared with the industry. The *RMA Annual Statement Studies*, published by the Risk Management Association, provides common-size statements for most industries.

REAL WORLD EXAMPLE

Benchmarks can also be found in industry-specific publications. For example, the National Automobile Dealers Association provides some industry averages for car dealerships on its website.

	Alphabet Inc.	Yahoo! Inc.
Revenues	100.0%	100.0%
Cost of revenues	38.4	28.1
Gross margin	61.6	71.9
Selling, general, and administrative expense	21.2	39.2
Research and development expense	14.9	26.1
Other income/expenses	0.6	3.5
Operating income	25.0	3.1

Alphabet Inc.   **Yahoo! Inc.**

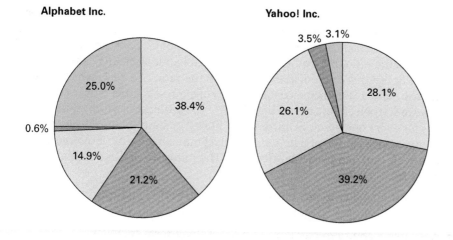

Information Sources

Financial analysts draw their information from various sources:

- Annual and quarterly reports offer readers a good look at an individual business's operations. The SEDAR website (www.sedar.com) provides access to annual reports and other financial information for Canadian corporations.

- Publicly held companies must submit annual and quarterly reports to the provincial securities commission in each province where they are listed on a

4. Refer to the vertical analysis of Umoja Inc. performed in Try It Question 3. Suppose Compet Ltd. is a competitor of Umoja Inc. in the same industry. Use the Compet Ltd. information given below to create its common-size income statement. How do the results of Umoja Inc. compare with those of Compet Ltd.?

COMPET LTD. Income Statement For the Year Ended December 31, 2017	
Net sales	$580,000
Expenses:	
Cost of goods sold	395,000
Engineering, selling, and administrative expenses	100,000
Interest expense	30,000
Income tax expense	23,000
Other expense (income)	1,800
Total expenses	549,800
Net income	$ 30,200

Solutions appear at the end of this chapter and on MyAccountingLab

stock exchange (e.g., the Ontario Securities Commission for the Toronto Stock Exchange).

- Business publications such as the *National Post* and the *Globe and Mail's Report on Business* carry information about individual companies and Canadian industries.
- Credit agencies, like Dun & Bradstreet Canada, for example, offer industry averages as part of their financial service.
- Online financial databases, such as LexisNexis, *Financial Post*, Market Data, and Globe Investor, offer quarterly financial figures for hundreds of public corporations going back as far as 10 years.

USING RATIOS TO MAKE DECISIONS

LO 4

How do we compute standard financial ratios, and what do they mean?

An important part of financial analysis is the calculation and interpretation of ratios. A ratio is a useful way to show the relationship of one number to another. For example, if the balance sheet shows current assets of $100,000 and current liabilities of $25,000, the ratio of current assets to current liabilities is $100,000 to $25,000. We could simplify this numerical expression to the ratio of 4 to 1, which may also be written 4:1 and 4/1. Other acceptable ways of expressing this ratio include "current assets are 400 percent of current liabilities," "the business has four dollars in current assets for every one dollar in current liabilities," or simply, "the current ratio is 4.0."

A manager, a lender, or a financial analyst may review any combination of ratios that are relevant to a particular decision. The ratios we discuss in this chapter may be classified as follows:

LEARNING TIPS

Notice that there are many different ways to say the same thing! Practise using each of the different ways. Also notice that the definition of liquidity in this context is different than the definition you have learned previously.

- Measuring ability to pay current liabilities (short-term **liquidity**)
- Measuring ability to sell inventory and collect receivables (efficiency)
- Measuring ability to pay long-term debt (long-term solvency)
- Measuring profitability
- Analyzing shares as an investment (value)

All the ratios discussed in this chapter are summarized on page 1084, after the Summary. You may want to tab the ratios summary page for easy reference.

Exhibits 18–8 and 18–9 give the comparative income statement and balance sheet, respectively, of Chairman Seating Inc. We will use this information to calculate several key ratios for the company.

EXHIBIT 18–8 | **Comparative Income Statement**

CHAIRMAN SEATING INC. Income Statement For the Years Ended December 31, 2017 and 2016		
	2017	**2016**
Net sales	$858,000	$803,000
Cost of goods sold	513,000	509,000
Gross margin	345,000	294,000
Operating expenses:		
Selling expenses	116,000	104,000
General expenses	118,000	123,000
Total operating expenses	234,000	227,000
Income from operations	111,000	67,000
Interest revenue	4,000	—
Less: interest expense	34,000	24,000
Income before income taxes	81,000	43,000
Income tax expense	33,000	17,000
Net income	$ 48,000	$ 26,000

EXHIBIT 18–9 | Comparative Balance Sheet

CHAIRMAN SEATING INC. Balance Sheet December 31, 2017 and 2016		
Assets	**2017**	**2016**
Current assets:		
Cash	$ 39,000	$ 42,000
Accounts receivable, net	114,000	85,000
Inventories	113,000	111,000
Prepaid expenses	6,000	8,000
Total current assets	272,000	246,000
Long-term investments	18,000	9,000
Property, plant, and equipment, net	507,000	399,000
Total assets	$797,000	$654,000
Liabilities		
Current liabilities:		
Notes payable	$ 42,000	$ 27,000
Accounts payable	83,000	78,000
Accrued liabilities	27,000	31,000
Total current liabilities	152,000	136,000
Long-term debt	289,00	198,000
Total liabilities	441,000	334,000
Shareholders' Equity		
Common shares	186,000	186,000
Retained earnings	170,000	134,000
Total shareholders' equity	356,000	320,000
Total liabilities and shareholders' equity	$797,000	$654,000

Measuring the Ability to Pay Current Liabilities

Working capital is calculated as:

$$\text{Working capital} = \text{Current assets} - \text{Current liabilities}$$

Working capital measures the company's ability to meet short-term obligations with current assets. The working capital amount considered alone, however, does not give a complete picture of the entity's working capital position. Consider two companies with equal working capital:

	Company A	**Company B**
Current assets	$100,000	$200,000
Less: current liabilities	50,000	150,000
Working capital	$ 50,000	$ 50,000
Working capital as a percent of current liabilities	100%	33%

Both companies have working capital of $50,000, but Company A's working capital is as large as its current liabilities. Company B's working capital, on the other hand, is only one-third as large as its current liabilities. Which business has a better level of working capital? Company A, because its working capital is a higher percentage of current assets and current liabilities. Two decision tools based on working capital data are the *current ratio* and the *acid-test ratio*.

Current Ratio The **current ratio** looks at total current assets compared to total current liabilities. We introduced the current ratio in Chapter 4 (p. 194).

The current ratio measures the company's ability to pay bills that are due to be paid in the coming year with items that can be turned into cash easily in the coming year. A high current ratio indicates a strong financial position and that the business has sufficient **liquid assets** to maintain normal business operations. Recall that:

- Current assets consist of cash, short-term investments, net receivables, inventory, and prepaid expenses.
- Current liabilities include accounts payable, short-term notes payable, unearned revenues, and all types of accrued liabilities.

$$\text{Current ratio} = \frac{\text{Current assets}}{\text{Current liabilities}}$$

	Chairman Seating Inc.		Industry Average
	2017	**2016**	
	$\frac{\$272,000}{\$152,000} = 1.79$	$\frac{\$246,000}{\$136,000} = 1.81$	1.68

> The current ratio measures the company's ability to pay current liabilities with current assets. So it should make sense that the result of the calculation of the current ratio should always be greater than 1. In other words, we need at least as much current assets as current liabilities, otherwise short-term payments cannot be made.

What is an acceptable current ratio? The answer to this question depends on the nature of the business. The current ratio should generally exceed 1.0, while the norm for companies is around 1.50. In many industries a current ratio of 2.0 is considered very good. Chairman Seating Inc.'s current ratio has declined from 2016 to 2017, but since it is still above the retail furniture industry average, the result is "good."

We can look at the ratios for some real companies from a variety of industries:

Company	Current Ratio
BlackBerry Limited (May 2014)	2.82
Canadian Tire Corporation, Limited (June 2014)	2.22
lululemon athletica inc. (August 2014)	5.95
Winpak Ltd.	5.71

Acid-Test Ratio? The **acid-test ratio** (or **quick ratio**) tells us whether the entity could pay all its current liabilities if they came due immediately. We saw in Chapter 9 (p. 524) that the higher the acid-test ratio, the better able the business is to pay its current liabilities. That is, *could the company pass this acid test*? To do so, the company would have to convert its most liquid assets to cash.

The acid-test ratio measures liquidity using fewer assets than the current ratio does. Inventory and prepaid expenses are *not* included in the acid-test computations because a business may not be able to convert them to cash immediately to pay current liabilities.

> Net current receivables includes accounts and notes receivable, net of allowances

$$\frac{\text{Acid-test}}{\text{ratio}} = \frac{\text{Cash + Short-term investment + Net current receivables}}{\text{Current liabilities}}$$

	Chairman Seating Inc.		Industry Average
	2017	**2016**	
	$\frac{\$39,000 + \$0 + \$114,000}{\$152,000} = 1.01$	$\frac{\$42,000 + \$0 + \$85,000}{\$136,000} = 0.93$	0.60

The company's acid-test ratio improved during 2017 and is better than the retail furniture industry average. An acid-test ratio of 0.90 to 1.00 is considered good in most industries. Note the range for the companies listed below is from a low of 1.77 to a high of 4.65.

Company	Acid-Test Ratio
BlackBerry Limited	2.82
Canadian Tire Corporation, Limited	1.77
lululemon athletica inc.	4.65
Winpak Ltd.	4.29

Measuring the Ability to Sell Inventory and Collect Receivables

The ability to sell inventory and collect receivables is fundamental to the business success of a merchandiser. (Recall the operating cycle: cash to inventory to receivables and back to cash in Chapter 5, p. 249). This section discusses three ratios that measure the ability to sell inventory and collect receivables.

Inventory Turnover   Companies generally seek to achieve the quickest possible return on their investments. A return on an investment in inventory is no exception, because inventory is often a large investment for the business. The faster inventory sells, the sooner the business creates accounts receivable, and the sooner it collects cash. In addition, companies make a profit each time they sell inventory. The more often they sell inventory, the greater the total amount of profit.

Inventory turnover measures the number of times a company sells its average level of inventory during a year. A turnover of 6 means that the company sold its average level of inventory six times during the year (or every two months). It is also used as a measure of the efficiency of a company in managing its inventory. A high rate of turnover indicates ease in selling inventory; a low turnover indicates slower sales and may indicate difficulty in selling. It could also indicate obsolete inventory or poor inventory management. We introduced inventory turnover in Chapter 5 (page 269).

Of course, there is a relationship between turnover and the product; Dollarama will have a higher rate of turnover than a company such as Finning International Inc. of Vancouver, which sells heavy equipment.

A business also strives for the *most profitable* rate of inventory turnover, not necessarily the *highest* rate. Selling for too low of a price just to move the product quickly may not be as profitable as keeping it a little longer and getting a better price for the product.

To compute inventory turnover, we divide cost of goods sold by the average inventory for the period. We use the cost of goods sold—not sales—because both cost of goods sold and inventory are stated *at cost*. Sales at *retail* are not comparable to inventory at *cost*.

REAL WORLD EXAMPLE

High turnover has been the recipe for success for companies like Walmart and Dollarama. Students who have taken a marketing course may recognize this pricing strategy—these are low-cost, high-volume retailers.

$$\text{Inventory turnover} = \frac{\text{Cost of goods sold}}{\text{Average inventory}}$$

Chairman Seating Inc. for 2017	Industry Average

From the income statement (Exhibit 18–8)

$$\frac{\$513,000}{(\$111,000 + \$113,000)/2} = 4.58 \text{ times} \qquad 2.70 \text{ times}$$

Beginning inventory of 2017 (which is the balance at the end of 2016)

Ending inventory of 2017 from Exhibit 18–9

If inventory levels vary greatly from month to month, compute the average by adding the 12 monthly balances and dividing this sum by 12.

Inventory turnover varies widely with the nature of the business. Companies that remove natural gas from the ground hold their inventory for a very short period of time and have an average turnover of 30. Chairman Seating Inc.'s turnover of 4.58 times a year is high for its industry, which has an average turnover of 2.70. Chairman Seating Inc.'s high inventory turnover results from its policy of keeping little inventory on hand. The company takes customer orders and has its suppliers ship directly to customers.

Another helpful way to analyze inventory is to compare the inventory turnover days. The calculation for Chairman Seating Inc. for 2017 would be:

$$\text{Inventory turnover in days} = \frac{\text{365 days}}{\text{Inventory turnover}} = \frac{\text{365 days}}{4.58} = 80 \text{ days}$$

It took the company approximately 80 days to sell all the items in inventory.

Accounts Receivable Turnover   **Accounts receivable turnover** measures the company's ability to collect cash from credit customers. It is also used as a measure of the efficiency of a company to manage its cash collections. The higher the ratio is, the faster are the cash collections. However, a receivable turnover that is too high may indicate that credit is too tight, causing the loss of sales to good customers.

Chairman Seating Inc. makes all sales on credit. (If a company makes both cash and credit sales, this ratio is best computed using only net *credit* sales. *Credit* means "on account"—it does not mean "using a credit card.")

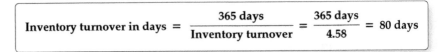

$$\text{Accounts receivable turnover} = \frac{\text{Net credit sales}}{\text{Average net accounts receivable}}$$

LEARNING TIPS

Recall that net accounts receivable is computed by subtracting the allowance for doubtful accounts from the accounts receivable total.

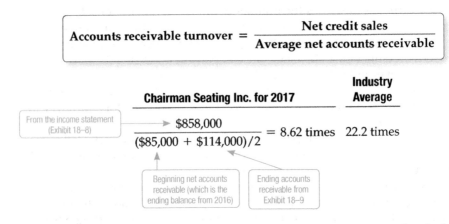

	Chairman Seating Inc. for 2017	Industry Average
From the income statement (Exhibit 18–8)	$\dfrac{\$858,000}{(\$85,000 + \$114,000)/2} = 8.62$ times	22.2 times

Beginning net accounts receivable (which is the ending balance from 2016)

Ending accounts receivable from Exhibit 18–9

REAL WORLD EXAMPLE

When a business's accounts receivable turnover is different from the industry average, look past the ratio before deciding if a result is "good" or "bad." In the case of Chairman, the industry average might be high due to the use of factors rather than faster collection. If this industry is dominated by large stores, then the industry average is not a reasonable benchmark for a smaller business like Chairman.

The result indicates how many times during the year the average level of receivables was turned into cash. Chairman Seating Inc.'s accounts receivable turnover of 8.62 times is much lower than the industry average. Why the difference? Chairman is a hometown store that sells to local people who tend to pay their bills over a period of time. Many larger furniture stores sell their receivables to other companies called **factors**. This practice keeps receivables low and receivable turnover high. In return for receiving the cash sooner, companies that factor (sell) their receivables receive less than face value for the receivables.

If accounts receivable balances exhibit a seasonal pattern, compute the average net receivable using the 12 monthly balances added together and divided by 12.

Days' Sales in Receivables   The **days' sales in receivables** ratio measures the ability to collect receivables. This ratio tells us how many days' credit sales remain in Accounts Receivable. Recall from Chapter 9 (p. 524) that days' sales in receivables indicates how many days it takes to collect the average level of receivables. To compute the ratio, we can follow a two-step process:

❶ Divide net credit sales by 365 days to calculate average sales for one day.

❷ Divide this average day's sales amount into the average net accounts receivable.

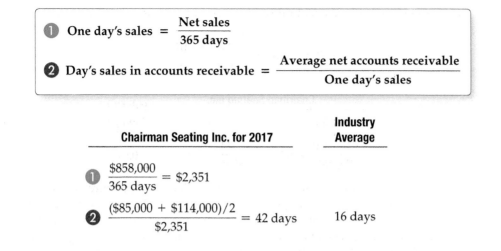

	Chairman Seating Inc. for 2017	Industry Average
①	$\dfrac{\$858{,}000}{365 \text{ days}} = \$2{,}351$	
②	$\dfrac{(\$85{,}000 + \$114{,}000)/2}{\$2{,}351} = 42 \text{ days}$	16 days

Days' sales in receivables can also be computed in a single step:

$$[(\$85{,}000 + \$114{,}000)/2] \div (\$858{,}000 \div 365 \text{ days}) = 42 \text{ days}$$

Chairman Seating Inc.'s ratio tells us that 42 days' sales remained in average accounts receivable during the year, or that it takes 42 days to collect receivables. The company will increase its cash inflow if it can decrease this ratio. Ways to do this include offering discounts for early payments, tightening credit policies to disallow slow-paying customers, using more aggressive collection procedures, and selling receivables to factors. The days' sales in receivables is higher (worse) than the industry average because the company collects its own receivables. Other furniture stores may sell their receivables or carry fewer days' sales in receivables. Chairman Seating Inc. remains competitive because of the personal relationship with customers. Without their good paying habits, the company's cash flow would suffer.

LEARNING TIPS

Days' sales in receivables and accounts receivables turnover are both "saying the same thing in a different way." Notice that when turnover is 8.62 times, that is $365 \div 8.62 = 42$ days!

Measuring the Ability to Pay Long-Term Debt (Solvency)

Debt Ratio   Suppose you are a loan officer at a bank and you are evaluating loan applications from two companies with equal sales and equal total assets of $1,000,000. Both A Co. and B Co. have asked to borrow $500,000 and have agreed to repay the loan over a five-year period. A Co. already owes $900,000 to another bank. B Co. owes only $250,000. Other things being equal, you would be more likely to lend money to B Co. because B Co. owes less money than A Co. owes. This relationship between total liabilities and total assets—called the **debt ratio**—shows the proportion of the company's assets that it has financed with debt. We introduced the debt ratio in Chapter 4 (pages 194–195).

If the debt ratio is 0.90, as shown in the margin for A Co., then debt has been used to finance most of the assets. A debt ratio of 0.25 for B Co. means that the company has borrowed to finance one-quarter of its assets; the owners have financed the other three-quarters of the assets. The higher the debt ratio is, the higher is the strain of paying interest each year and the principal amount at maturity, and the less likely a bank is to approve another loan.

What makes a corporation with a lot of debt a more risky loan prospect than one with a lot of equity? For a corporation with a lot of debt, interest on debt is contractual and must be paid. If interest on debt is not paid, creditors can force the company into bankruptcy. With equity, dividends are discretionary and do not have to be declared.

Creditors view a high debt ratio with caution. To help protect themselves, creditors generally charge higher interest rates on borrowings to companies with an already-high debt ratio.

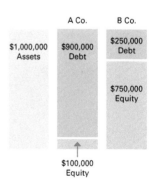

Chairman Seating Inc.'s debt ratios at the end of 2017 and 2016 are as follows:

$$\text{Debt ratio} = \frac{\text{Total liabilities}}{\text{Total assets}}$$

	Chairman Seating Inc.		Industry
	2017	2016	Average
	$\dfrac{\$441,000}{\$797,000} = 0.55$	$\dfrac{\$334,000}{\$654,000} = 0.51$	0.61

Chairman Seating Inc. expanded operations by financing the purchase of buildings and fixtures through borrowing, which is common. This expansion explains the company's increased debt ratio. Even after the increase in 2017, the company's debt is not very high. The average debt ratio for most industries ranges around 0.57 to 0.67, with relatively little variation from company to company. Chairman Seating Inc.'s 0.55 debt ratio indicates a fairly low-risk debt position in comparison with the retail furniture industry average of 0.61.

Times-Interest-Earned Ratio   The debt ratio indicates nothing about the ability to pay interest expense. Analysts use a second ratio—the **times-interest-earned ratio**—to relate income to interest expense. This ratio is sometimes called the *interest coverage ratio*. It measures the number of times that operating income can cover interest expense. A high times-interest-earned ratio indicates ease in paying interest expense; a low value suggests difficulty.

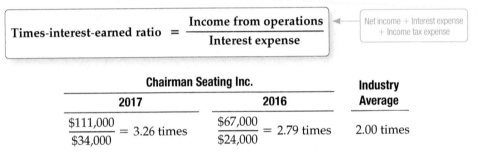

$$\text{Times-interest-earned ratio} = \frac{\text{Income from operations}}{\text{Interest expense}} \longleftarrow \begin{array}{c} \text{Net income} + \text{Interest expense} \\ + \text{Income tax expense} \end{array}$$

	Chairman Seating Inc.		Industry
	2017	2016	Average
	$\dfrac{\$111,000}{\$34,000} = 3.26$ times	$\dfrac{\$67,000}{\$24,000} = 2.79$ times	2.00 times

The company's times-interest-earned ratio increased in 2017. This is a favourable sign about the company, especially since the company's liabilities rose substantially during the year. We can conclude that Chairman Seating Inc.'s new buildings and fixtures have earned more in operating income than they have cost the business in interest expense. The company's times-interest-earned ratio of 3.26 is much better than the 2.00 average for furniture retailers. The norm for businesses falls in the range of 2.00 to 3.00 for many companies. Based on its debt ratio and times-interest-earned ratio, Chairman Seating Inc. appears to have little difficulty **servicing its debt**, that is, paying its liabilities.

Measuring Profitability

We often hear that the fundamental goal of business is to earn a profit. This is not the only objective of a business. Managers attempt to meet the needs of shareholders who require a sufficient return on their investment and to support other goals related to corporate social responsibility—to earn money to spend for the greater good (to support charities or environmental causes, for example). And yes, we do look to see if a company has made "enough" money! Ratios that measure profitability are reported in the business press, by investment services, and in annual reports. We examine four profitability measures.

Rate of Return on Net Sales   In business, the term *return* is used broadly as a measure of profitability. Consider a ratio called the **rate of return on net sales**, or **return on sales (ROS)**. (The word *net* is usually omitted for convenience, even though net sales is used to compute the ratio.) It is also called the *profit margin*. This ratio shows the percentage of each sales dollar earned as net income, or the amount of profit per dollar of sales.

$$\text{Rate of return on net sales} = \frac{\text{Net income}}{\text{Net sales}}$$

Chairman Seating Inc.		Industry Average
2017	**2016**	
$\frac{\$48,000}{\$858,000} = 0.56$ or 5.6%	$\frac{\$26,000}{\$803,000} = 0.032$ or 3.2%	0.008, or 0.8%

Companies strive for a high rate of return on sales. The higher the rate of return, the more sales dollars are providing profit. The increase in Chairman Seating Inc.'s return on sales is good. The company is more successful than the average furniture store.

Rate of Return on Total Assets The **rate of return on total assets**, or **return on assets (ROA)**, measures success in using assets to earn a profit. We first discussed rate of return on total assets in Chapter 13 (pages 748–749).

Two groups finance a company's assets. Creditors have lent money to the company, and they earn interest on this money. Shareholders have invested in shares, and their rate of return is the company's net income. The sum of interest expense and net income is thus the return to the two groups that have financed the company's assets.

$$\text{Rate of return on total assets} = \frac{\text{Net Income} + \text{Interest expense}}{\text{Average total assets}}$$

Chairman Seating Inc. for 2017	Industry Average
$\frac{\$48,000 + \$34,000}{(\$797,000 + \$654,000)/2} = 0.113$, or 11.3%	0.078, or 7.8%

From the income statement (Exhibit 18–8)

The average of beginning and ending total assets from the comparative balance sheet (Exhibit 18–9)

Compare Chairman Seating Inc.'s 11.3 percent rate of return on assets to the rates of some other Canadian companies, which range from –4.14 percent to 18.78 percent:

Company	Rate of Return on Assets
BlackBerry Ltd.	–0.0414, or –4.14%
Canadian Tire Corporation, Limited	0.0474, or 4.74%
lululemon athletica inc.	0.1878, or 18.78%
Winpak Ltd.	0.133, or 13.3%

Rate of Return on Common Shareholders' Equity A popular measure of profitability is the **rate of return on common shareholders' equity**, often shortened to **return on shareholders' equity** or **return on equity (ROE)**. We examined this ratio in Chapter 13 (page 749).

Return on shareholders' equity measures how much income is earned for every $1 invested by the *common* shareholders (both contributed capital and retained earnings).

$$\text{Rate of return on common shareholders' equity} = \frac{\text{Net income} - \text{Preferred dividends}}{\text{Average common shareholders' equity}}$$

	Chairman Seating Inc. for 2017	Industry Average
$\dfrac{\$48{,}000 - \$0}{(\$356{,}000 + \$320{,}000)/2} = 0.142\text{, or } 14.2\%$		0.121, or 12.1%

Observe that Chairman Seating Inc.'s return on equity, 14.2 percent, is higher than its return on assets, 11.3 percent. This difference results from borrowing from the bank and paying interest at a rate of 8 percent and then investing the funds to earn a higher rate, such as the firm's 14.2 percent return on shareholders' equity. This practice is called **trading on the equity**, or using **leverage**. It is directly related to the debt ratio. The higher the debt ratio, the higher the financial leverage. Companies that finance operations with debt are said to *leverage* their positions.

Leverage usually increases profitability because a company can earn more with the borrowed money than the interest it pays for the borrowed money. Leverage could have a negative impact on profitability. If revenues drop, debt and interest expense must still be paid. Therefore, leverage can have positive and negative effects on profits, increasing profits during good times but increasing risk during bad times because of higher fixed interest payments. Compare Chairman Seating Inc.'s rate of return on common shareholders' equity with rates of other companies:

Company	Rate of Return on Common Shareholders' Equity
BlackBerry Ltd.	−0.0825, or −8.25%
Canadian Tire Corporation, Limited	0.1191, or 11.91%
lululemon athletica inc.	0.2187, or 21.87%
Winpak Ltd.	0.165, or 16.5%

Chairman Seating Inc. is more profitable than two of these companies. A return on equity of 15 to 20 percent year after year is considered excellent in most industries.

Earnings per Common Share Earnings per common share, or **earnings per share (EPS)**, is perhaps the most widely quoted of all financial statistics. It was introduced in Chapter 14 (page 795). While Accounting Standards for Private Enterprises (ASPE) do not require that corporations disclose EPS figures on the income statement or in a note to the financial statements, many corporations do provide this information because investors and financial analysts use it to assess a corporation's profitability.

Earnings per share is computed by dividing net income available to common shareholders by the weighted average number of common shares outstanding during the year. Preferred dividends are subtracted from net income because the preferred shareholders have a prior claim to their dividends if they have been declared, or, if they have not been declared, if they are cumulative.

If the company has bonds or preferred shares that are convertible into common shares, the company must also disclose *fully diluted* earnings per share.

Chairman Seating Inc. has no preferred shares outstanding and so has no preferred dividends. It had 10,000 common shares outstanding throughout both years:

$$\text{Earnings per common share (EPS)} = \frac{\text{Net income} - \text{Preferred dividends}}{\text{Weighted average number of common shares outstanding}}$$

Chairman Seating Inc.

2017	2016
$\dfrac{\$48,000 - \$0}{10,000} = \$4.80$	$\dfrac{\$26,000 - \$0}{10,000} = \$2.60$

Chairman Seating Inc.'s EPS increased 85 percent from 2016 to 2017. (This is calculated as [$4.80 – $2.60] ÷ $2.60 = 85%). Its shareholders should not expect such a large increase in EPS every year. Most companies strive to increase EPS by 10 to 15 percent annually, and strong companies do so. However, even the most successful companies have an occasional bad year.

Analyzing Shares as an Investment

Investors purchase shares to earn a return on their investment from both gains from selling the shares at a price that is higher than the investors' purchase price, and dividends, the periodic distributions to shareholders. The ratios we examine in this section help analysts evaluate investments in shares.

Price–Earnings Ratio The **price–earnings (P/E) ratio** is the relationship between the market price of a common share and the company's earnings per share. The ratio plays an important part in evaluating decisions to buy, hold, and sell shares. It indicates the market price of $1.00 of earnings. The market price can be obtained online from financial websites, the company website, or other news outlets. If earnings are negative, the P/E ratio is not applicable.

We will assume that the market price of Chairman Seating's common shares were $50.00 at the end of 2017 and $35.00 at the end of 2016.

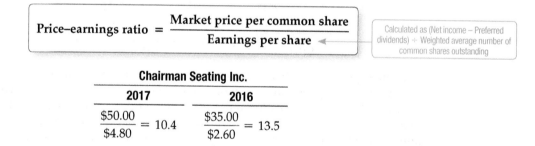

$$\text{Price–earnings ratio} = \frac{\text{Market price per common share}}{\text{Earnings per share}}$$

Calculated as (Net income – Preferred dividends) ÷ Weighted average number of common shares outstanding

Chairman Seating Inc.

2017	2016
$\dfrac{\$50.00}{\$4.80} = 10.4$	$\dfrac{\$35.00}{\$2.60} = 13.5$

Given Chairman Seating Inc.'s 2017 P/E ratio of 10.4, we would say that the company's shares are "selling at 10.4 times earnings." The decline from the 2016 P/E ratio of 13.5 is a concern but not a cause for alarm because the market price of the shares is not under Chairman Seating Inc.'s control. Net income is more controllable, and it increased during 2017.

Like most other ratios, P/E ratios vary from industry to industry. In October 2015, they range from 24.33 for Winpak Ltd. to 14.868 for Canadian Tire Corporation, to negative earnings for BlackBerry Limited.

The higher a share's P/E ratio, the higher its **downside risk**—the risk that the share's market price will fall. Some investors interpret a sharp increase in a share's P/E ratio as a signal to sell the shares.

Dividend Yield The **dividend yield** is the ratio of dividends per share to the share's market price. It may be calculated for both preferred shares and common shares. This ratio measures the percentage of a share's market value that is returned annually as dividends. Preferred shareholders, who invest primarily to receive dividends, pay special attention to this ratio.

REAL WORLD EXAMPLE

Check to see how these companies are doing now!

Chairman Seating Inc. paid annual cash dividends of $1.20 per share in 2017 and $1.00 in 2016 and market prices of the company's common shares were $50.00 in 2017 and $35.00 in 2016, so the yields are:

$$\text{Dividend yield on common shares} = \frac{\text{Dividend per common share}}{\text{Market price per common share}}$$

Chairman Seating Inc.

2017	2016
$\dfrac{\$1.20}{\$50.00} = 0.0.24$ or 2.4%	$\dfrac{\$1.00}{\$35.00} = 0.029$ or 2.9%

Investors who buy Chairman Seating Inc.'s common shares for $50.00 can expect to receive about 2.4 percent of their investment annually in the form of cash dividends. Dividend yields vary widely, from almost 5.0 percent for older, established firms (e.g., BCE Inc. at 4.88 percent) down to 0.41 percent for a growing company like Dollarama Inc. Chairman Seating Inc.'s dividend yield places the company somewhere in the middle.

Book Value per Common Share **Book value per common share** is simply common shareholders' equity divided by the number of common shares outstanding. Common shareholders' equity equals total shareholders' equity less preferred equity including cumulative preferred dividends.

Chairman Seating Inc. has no preferred shares outstanding. Recall that 10,000 common shares were outstanding throughout 2016 and 2017.

> Notice that the total of the numerator is common shareholders' equity.

$$\text{Book value per common share} = \frac{\text{Total shareholders' equity} - \text{Preferred equity}}{\text{Number of common shares outstanding}}$$

Chairman Seating Inc.

2017	2016
$\dfrac{\$356,000 - \$0}{\$10,000} = \$35.60$	$\dfrac{\$320,000 - \$0}{\$10,000} = \$32.00$

Some experts argue that book value is not useful for investment analysis. Recall from Chapter 13 (page 746) that book value depends on historical costs, while market value depends on investors' outlook for dividends and an increase in the share's market price. Book value bears no relationship to market value and provides little information beyond shareholders' equity reported on the balance sheet. However, some investors base their investment decisions on book value. For example, some investors rank shares on the basis of the ratio of market price to book value. To these investors, the lower the ratio, the lower the risk, and the more attractive the shares. These investors who focus on the balance sheet are called *value investors*, as contrasted with *growth investors*, who focus more on trends in a company's net income.

LIMITATIONS OF FINANCIAL ANALYSIS

Business decisions are made in a world of uncertainty. As useful as ratios may be, they do have limitations. When a physician reads a thermometer, 39°C indicates that something is wrong with the patient, but the temperature alone does not indicate what the problem is or how to cure it. The same is true of ratios.

In financial analysis, a sudden drop in a company's current ratio usually signals that *something* is wrong, but this change does not identify the problem or show how to correct it. The business manager and users of the financial statements must analyze the figures that go into the ratio to determine whether current assets have decreased, current liabilities have increased, or both. If current assets have dropped, is the problem a cash shortage? Are accounts receivable down? Are inventories too low? Is the condition temporary? This process can be shown in a figure:

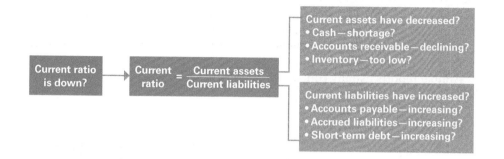

By analyzing the individual items that make up the ratio, managers can determine how to solve the problem and users of the financial statements can determine whether the company is a good investment or a credit risk. The managers and users of the financial statements must evaluate data on all ratios in the light of other information about the company and about its particular line of business, such as increased competition or seasonality or a slowdown in the economy.

Legislation, international affairs, competition, scandals, and many other factors can turn profits into losses, and vice versa. To be most useful, ratios should also be analyzed over a period of years to take into account a representative group of these factors. Any one year, or even any two years, may not be representative of the company's performance over the long term.

And finally, when comparing ratios across companies, remember to check how the ratio was calculated so you are sure you are actually comparing the same sort of information! There are no firm rules about what is included in a ratio nor how it is named. For example, the debt-to-equity ratio is another way to analyze solvency. In some companies, it is called the debt ratio even though the formula is different from what is shown in this book.

INVESTOR DECISIONS

An **efficient capital market** is one in which the market prices reflect the impact of all information available to the public. Market efficiency means that managers cannot fool the market with accounting gimmicks. If the information is available, the market as a whole can translate accounting data into a "fair" price for the company's shares.

Suppose you are the president of CompSys Ltd. Reported earnings per share are $4.00 and the share price is $40.00—so the P/E ratio is 10. You believe the corporation's shares are underpriced in comparison with other companies in your industry. What if you are considering changing from accelerated to straight-line amortization to give the market a more accurate reflection of the company's value? The accounting change will increase earnings per share to $5.00. Will the shares then rise to $50.00? Probably not. The share price will likely remain at $40.00 because the market can understand that the change in amortization method, not improved operations, caused earnings to increase.

In an efficient market, the search for "underpriced" shares is fruitless unless the investor has relevant private information. Moreover, it is unlawful to invest based on *insider* information—information that is available only to corporate management.

Users of financial statements should be aware of potential problems in companies they might want to invest in or lend money to. Users of a company's financial statements should also consider the following additional information found in annual reports and should look for red flags when evaluating the company.

Annual Reports

Annual reports are one key place to get information about a corporation beyond the figures used for horizontal and vertical analyses and computing the standard ratios. The non-quantitative parts of the annual report may hold more important information than the financial statements. For example, the president's letter may describe a turnover of top managers. The management's discussion and analysis will reveal management's opinion of the year's results.

Annual reports usually contain the following sections:

President's Letter to the Shareholders	The president of the company gives his or her view of the year's results and outlines the direction top management is charting for the company. A shift in top management or a major change in the company's direction is important to investors.
Management's Report to the Shareholders	There is a second letter written to the shareholders. Here management states that all information in the annual report is the responsibility of management and indicates which standards were followed in the preparation of the report. Winpak's report also addresses the topic of internal control and how the board of directors ensures that this is monitored.
Management's Discussion and Analysis (MD&A)	The people who know the most about a company are its executives. For this reason, the shareholders want to know what management thinks about the company's net income (or net loss), cash flows, and financial position. The MD&A section of the annual report discusses *why* net income was up or down, how the company invested the shareholders' money, and plans for future spending. Through the MD&A, investors may learn of the company's plan to discontinue a product line or to expand into new markets.
Auditor's Report	The president's letter, the management letter, and the MD&A express the views of corporate insiders. The financial statements are also produced by the management of the company. These people naturally want to describe the company in a favourable light. Therefore, all the information coming from the company could be slanted to make the company look good.
	Investors are aware of the possibility for management bias in the financial statements. For this reason, the various provincial securities acts require that all financial statements of public corporations be audited by independent accountants. The auditors are not employees of the companies they audit, so they can be objective. After auditing the Winpak Ltd. financial statements, KPMG LLP, an international accounting firm, issued its professional opinion on the Winpak statements. KPMG stated that the Winpak statements *present fairly* the financial position, financial performance, and cash flows in accordance with International Financial Reporting Standards. This is how investors in Canada and other developed countries gain *assurance* that they can rely on a company's financial statements.
The Financial Statements	The financial statements consist of the balance sheet, income statement, statement of retained earnings, cash flow statement, and the notes to the financial statements, including a statement of significant accounting policies. Comparative information is provided for at least two years.
Other Information	Other financial and non-financial information about the company, such as information related to environmental policies, are also included in the annual report.

Look for Red Flags When Analyzing Financial Statements

Recent accounting scandals highlight the importance of *red flags* that may signal financial trouble. Watch out for the following conditions:

- **Changes in sales, inventory, and receivables.** Sales, receivables, and inventory generally move together. Increased sales lead to higher receivables and require more inventory to meet demand. Unusual increases in receivables without an increase in sales may indicate trouble.

- **Earnings problems.** Has net income decreased significantly for several years in a row? Has income turned into a loss? Most companies cannot survive consecutive annual losses.

- **Decreased cash flow.** Is cash flow from operations consistently lower than net income? Are the sales of property, plant, and equipment assets a major source of cash? If so, the company may face a cash shortage.

- **Too much debt.** How does the company's debt ratio compare with that of major competitors and with the industry average? If the debt ratio is too high, the company may be unable to pay its debts.

- **Inability to collect receivables.** Are days' sales in receivables growing faster than for other companies in the industry? A cash shortage may be looming.

- **Buildup of inventories.** Is inventory turnover too slow? If so, the company may be unable to sell goods, or it may be overstating inventory. Recall from the discussion on cost of goods sold that one of the easiest ways to overstate net income is to overstate ending inventory.

Why It's Done This Way

Objective of Financial Reporting

This final chapter of the book discusses the many ways that a user of the financial statements can analyze results. As we have shown in the chapters prior to this one, the accounting framework has allowed us to develop financial statements that are *useful* to interested users.

For assessing the success of a company, however, the financial statements are a starting point. To evaluate the success of a company appropriately, we must perform a thorough analysis of the various aspects of the business. We also need to compare the performance of the company in the current year against the performance in previous years and against the performance of its competitors.

> Try It!

5. For each of the following ratios, indicate whether it is a liquidity, efficiency, solvency, or profitability ratio by checking off the appropriate column:

Ratio	Liquidity	Efficiency	Solvency	Profitability
Return on common shareholders' equity				
Inventory turnover				
Current ratio				
Debt ratio				
Acid-test ratio				
Accounts receivable turnover				
Return on net sales				

6. For each of the following unrelated situations, use a check mark to indicate whether the change is generally positive for the company or negative.

Situation	Positive change	Negative change
A decrease in return on equity		
A decrease in days' sales in inventory		
An increase in the debt ratio		
An increase in the acid-test ratio		
A decrease in receivables turnover		

7. Big Bend Picture Frames Inc. has asked you to determine whether the company's ability to pay its current liabilities and total liabilities has improved or deteriorated during 2017. To answer this question, you gather the following data:

	2017	2016
Cash	$ 50,000	$ 47,000
Short-term investments	27,000	—
Net receivables	128,000	124,000
Inventory	237,000	272,000
Total assets	480,000	490,000
Total current liabilities	295,000	202,000
Long-term note payable	44,000	56,000
Income from operations	170,000	168,000
Interest expense	46,000	33,000

Compute the following ratios for 2017 and 2016:

a) Current ratio

b) Acid-test ratio

c) Debt ratio

d) Times-interest-earned ratio

Solutions appear at the end of this chapter and on MyAccountingLab

THE IMPACT OF IFRS ON FINANCIAL STATEMENT ANALYSIS

LO 5

What is the impact of IFRS on financial statement analysis?

ASPE	IFRS
The procedures for performing financial analysis do not change because of the accounting standard being used. This is because financial analysis involves determining relationships between various components of the statements to assess the company's current position and to predict future performance.	
Dividend yield analysis may require an extra step because earnings per share is not required to be reported on the income statement and would need to be calculated before being used in the formula.	The calculation of dividend yield would be as shown in the chapter because earnings per share information must be reported on the income statement or statement of comprehensive income.
Accounting practices vary since some companies have choices about how to report information. Care must always be taken to read the notes to the financial statements.	

SUMMARY PROBLEM FOR YOUR REVIEW

Bazinga Inc., which operates a chain of clothing stores, reported these figures:

BAZINGA INC. Five-Year Selected Financial Data For the Years Ended January 31 (Dollar amounts in thousands)					
	2017	2016	2015	2014	2013
Operating Results					
Net sales	$2,960	$2,519	$1,934	$1,587	$1,252
Cost of goods sold	1,856	1,496	1,188	1,007	814
Interest expense (net)	4	4	1	3	3
Income from operations	340	371	237	163	126
Income taxes	129	141	92	65	52
Net income	211	230	145	98	74
Cash dividends	44	41	30	23	18
Financial Position					
Merchandise inventory	366	314	247	243	193
Total assets	1,379	1,147	777	579	481
Working capital	355	236	579	129	434
Shareholders' equity	888	678	466	338	276
Current ratio	2.06:1	1.71:1	1.39:1	1.69:1	1.70:1
Average number of common shares outstanding (in thousands)	144	142	142	141	145

Required

Refer to page 1084 for the ratios mentioned in this chapter and their formulas.

Compute the following ratios for 2014 through 2017, and evaluate Bazinga Inc.'s operating results. Are operating results strong or weak? Did they improve or deteriorate during the four-year period?

1. Gross margin percentage
2. Rate of return on net sales
3. Earnings per share
4. Inventory turnover
5. Times-interest-earned ratio
6. Rate of return on shareholders' equity

SOLUTION

For 1: Remember to add the previous year's ending inventory balance and the current year's ending balance and divide by two when calculating average inventory in the inventory turnover ratio.

For 2: Add the previous year's shareholders' equity and current year's shareholder's equity and divide by two when calculating average shareholders' equity in the rate of return on shareholders' equity.

	2017	2016	2015	2014
1. Gross margin percentage	$\dfrac{\$2,960 - \$1,856}{\$2,960}$ $= 37.3\%$	$\dfrac{\$2,519 - \$1,496}{\$2,519}$ $= 40.6\%$	$\dfrac{\$1,934 - \$1,188}{\$1,934}$ $= 38.6\%$	$\dfrac{\$1,587 - \$1,007}{\$1,587}$ $= 36.5\%$
2. Rate of return on net sales	$\dfrac{\$211}{\$2,960} = 7.1\%$	$\dfrac{\$230}{\$2,519} = 9.1\%$	$\dfrac{\$145}{\$1,934} = 7.5\%$	$\dfrac{\$98}{\$1,587} = 6.2\%$
3. Earnings per share	$\dfrac{\$211}{144} = \$1.47$	$\dfrac{\$230}{142} = \$1.62$	$\dfrac{\$145}{142} = \$1.02$	$\dfrac{\$98}{141} = \$0.70$
4. Inventory turnover	$\dfrac{\$1,856}{(\$366 + \$314)/2}$ $= 5.5 \text{ times}$	$\dfrac{\$1,496}{(\$314 + \$247)/2}$ $= 5.3 \text{ times}$	$\dfrac{\$1,188}{(\$247 + \$243)/2}$ $= 4.8 \text{ times}$	$\dfrac{\$1,007}{(\$243 + \$193)/2}$ $= 4.6 \text{ times}$
5. Times-interest-earned ratio	$\dfrac{\$340}{\$4} = 85 \text{ times}$	$\dfrac{\$371}{\$4} = 93 \text{ times}$	$\dfrac{\$237}{\$1} = 237 \text{ times}$	$\dfrac{\$163}{\$3} = 54 \text{ times}$
6. Rate of return on shareholders' equity	$\dfrac{\$211}{(\$888 + \$678)/2}$ $= 26.9\%$	$\dfrac{\$230}{(\$678 + \$466)/2}$ $= 40.2\%$	$\dfrac{\$145}{(\$466 + \$338)/2}$ $= 36.1\%$	$\dfrac{\$98}{(\$338 + \$276)/2}$ $= 31.9\%$

For the six ratios calculated, think of the results as "the higher the ratio, the better." When these ratios increase each year, it is a positive trend and indicates good news.

Evaluation: During the first three years, Bazinga Inc's operating results were outstanding: Operating results improved, with all ratio values higher. The most recent year might be a concern. Results are lower than the previous year. It is too soon to know if this is a downward trend or an isolated bad year. Lenders and investors might be cautious based on the most recent results, even though many results are better than the base year.

Remember to evaluate all ratios along with other information about the company. One ratio will not tell the complete story.

SUMMARY

LEARNING OBJECTIVE ① Perform a horizontal analysis of financial statements

How do we compare several years of financial information?   Pg. 1057

- *Horizontal analysis* is the study of percentage changes in financial statement items from one period to the next.
  - ① Calculate the dollar amount of the change from the base (earlier) period to the later period.
  - ② Divide the dollar amount of change by the base-period amount and multiply by 100.
- *Trend percentages* are a form of horizontal analysis.

LEARNING OBJECTIVE ② Perform a vertical analysis of financial statements

What is a vertical analysis, and how do we perform one?   Pg. 1061

- *Vertical analysis* shows the relationship of each statement item to a specified base, which is the 100 percent figure.
  - On an income statement, net sales (or revenues) is usually the base.
  - On a balance sheet, total assets is usually the base.

LEARNING OBJECTIVE ③ Prepare and use common-size financial statements

What are common-size financial statements, and how do we use them?   Pg. 1063

- Common-size financial statements:
  - Report only percentages, not dollar amounts
  - Ease the comparison of different companies
- *Benchmarking* is the practice of comparing a company's performance with that of other companies, usually in the same industry.

LEARNING OBJECTIVE ④ Compute the standard financial ratios

How do we compute standard financial ratios, and what do they mean?   Pg. 1066

- A ratio expresses the relationship of one item to another.
- The financial ratios we discussed measure:
  - **Liquidity:** a company's ability to pay current liabilities (current ratio, acid-test ratio)
  - **Efficiency:** its ability to sell inventory and collect receivables (inventory turnover, accounts receivable turnover, days' sales in receivables)
  - **Solvency:** its ability to pay long-term debt (debt ratio, times-interest-earned ratio)
  - **Profitability** (rate of return on net sales, rate of return on total assets, rate of return on common shareholders' equity, earnings per common share)
  - **Value as an investment** (price–earnings ratio, dividend yield, book value per common share)
- The formulas for these ratios are listed on the next page.

MyAccountingLab **Video:** Real World Accounting

LEARNING OBJECTIVE ⑤ Describe the impact of IFRS on financial statement analysis

What is the impact of IFRS on financial statement analysis?   Pg. 1081

The procedures for analyzing the relationships among the reported numbers are the same. Analysts must read the notes to the financial statements to understand the reporting *choices* made by each corporation.

Check **Accounting Vocabulary** on page 1085 for all key terms used in Chapter 18 and the Glossary at the back of the book for all key terms used in the textbook.

MORE CHAPTER REVIEW MATERIAL

MyAccountingLab

DemoDoc covering Financial Statement Analysis

Student PowerPoint Slides

Audio Chapter Summary

Note: All MyAccountingLab resources can be found in the Chapter Resources section and the Multimedia Library.

Ratios Used in Financial Statement Analysis

Name	Formula	Interpretation
Measuring the company's ability to pay current liabilities (liquidity):		
1. Current ratio	$\dfrac{\text{Current assets}}{\text{Current liabilities}}$	Measures ability to pay current liabilities with current assets.
2. Acid-test (quick) ratio	$\dfrac{\text{Cash} + \text{Short-term investments} + \text{Net current receivables}}{\text{Current liabilities}}$	Shows ability to pay all current liabilities if they come due immediately.
Measuring the company's ability to sell inventory and collect receivables (efficiency):		
3. Inventory turnover	$\dfrac{\text{Cost of goods sold}}{\text{Average inventory}}$	Indicates saleability of inventory—the number of times a company sells its average amount of inventory during a year.
4. Accounts receivable turnover	$\dfrac{\text{Net credit sales}}{\text{Average net accounts receivable}}$	Measures ability to collect cash from credit customers.
5. Days' sales in receivables	❶ One day's sales = Net sales/365 days ❷ $\dfrac{\text{Average net accounts receivable}}{\text{One day's sales}}$	Shows how many days' sales remain in Accounts Receivable—how many days it takes to collect the average level of receivables.
Measuring the company's ability to pay long-term debt (solvency):		
6. Debt ratio	$\dfrac{\text{Total liabilities}}{\text{Total assets}}$	Indicates the percentage of assets financed with debt.
7. Times-interest-earned ratio	$\dfrac{\text{Income from operations}}{\text{Interest expense}}$	Measures the number of times operating income can cover interest expense.
Measuring the company's profitability:		
8. Rate of return on net sales (profit margin)	$\dfrac{\text{Net income}}{\text{Net sales}}$	Shows the percentage of each sales dollar earned as net income.
9. Rate of return on total assets	$\dfrac{\text{Net income} + \text{Interest expense}}{\text{Average total assets}}$	Measures how profitably a company uses its assets.
10. Rate of return on common shareholders' equity	$\dfrac{\text{Net income} - \text{Preferred dividends}}{\text{Average common shareholders' equity}}$	Gauges how much income is earned for each dollar invested by common shareholders.
11. Earnings per common share	$\dfrac{\text{Net income} - \text{Preferred dividends}}{\text{Weighted average number of common shares outstanding}}$	Gives the amount of earnings earned for each of the company's common shares.
Analyzing the company's shares as an investment (value):		
12. Price–earnings ratio	$\dfrac{\text{Market price per common share}}{\text{Earnings per share}}$	Indicates the market price of $1 of earnings.
13. Dividend yield	$\dfrac{\text{Annual dividends per common (or preferred) share}}{\text{Market price per common (or preferred) share}}$	Shows the percentage of the market price of each share returned as dividends to shareholders each period.
14. Book value per common share	$\dfrac{\text{Total shareholders' equity} - \text{Preferred equity}}{\text{Number of common shares outstanding}}$	Indicates the recorded accounting amount for each common share outstanding.

ACCOUNTING VOCABULARY

Accounts receivable turnover Ratio of net credit sales to average net accounts receivable. Measures ability to collect cash from credit customers (p. 1070).

Acid-test ratio Ratio of the sum of cash plus short-term investments plus net current receivables to current liabilities. Tells whether the entity could pay all its current liabilities if they came due immediately. Also called the *quick ratio* (p. 1068).

Benchmarking Comparison of current performance with some standard. The standard often is the performance level of a leading outside organization or the industry average (p. 1064).

Book value per common share Common shareholders' equity divided by the number of common shares outstanding (p. 1076).

Common-size statement A financial statement that reports only percentages (no dollar amounts); a type of vertical analysis (p. 1063).

Current ratio Current assets divided by current liabilities. Measures the ability to pay current liabilities from current assets (p. 1068).

Days' sales in receivables Ratio of average net accounts receivable to one day's sales. Indicates how many days' sales remain in Accounts Receivable awaiting collection (p. 1070).

Debt ratio Ratio of total liabilities to total assets. Gives the proportion of a company's assets that it has financed with debt (p. 1071).

Dividend yield Ratio of dividends per share to the share's market price per share. Tells the percentage of a share's market value that the company pays to shareholders as dividends (p. 1075).

Downside risk An estimate of the potential loss from a change in market conditions (p. 1075).

Earnings per share (EPS) The amount of a company's net income per outstanding common share (p. 1074).

Efficient capital market A market in which the market prices fully reflect the impact of all information available to the public (p. 1077).

Factors Companies that purchase other firms' accounts receivable at a discount. Receivables are sold so that the cash can be received more quickly (p. 1070).

Horizontal analysis The calculation and use of percentage changes in comparative financial statements (p. 1057).

Inventory turnover The ratio of cost of goods sold to average inventory. Measures the number of times a company sells its average level of inventory during a year (p. 1069).

Leverage The use of financial instruments to increase the potential return on investment by earning more income on borrowed money than the related expense, thereby increasing the earnings for the owners of the business. Another name for *trading on the equity* (p. 1074).

Liquid assets Assets that can be converted to cash quickly. Often they are financial instruments that can be sold without a discount (p. 1068).

Liquidity A company's ability to meet current payments as they come due (p. 1066).

Long-term solvency The ability to generate enough cash to pay long-term debts as they mature (p. 1056).

Price–earnings (P/E) ratio The market price of a common share divided by the company's earnings per share. Measures the value that the stock market places on $1 of a company's earnings (p. 1075).

Quick ratio Another name for the *acid-test ratio* (p. 1068).

Rate of return on common shareholders' equity Net income minus preferred dividends divided by average common shareholders' equity. A measure of profitability. Also called *return on equity (ROE)* or *return on common shareholders' equity* (p. 1073).

Rate of return on net sales Ratio of net income to net sales. A measure of profitability. Also called *return on sales* (p. 1072).

Rate of return on total assets The sum of net income plus interest expense divided by average total assets. This ratio measures the success a company has in using its assets to earn income for the people who finance the business. Also called *return on assets (ROA)* (p. 1073).

Return on assets (ROA) Another name for *rate of return on total assets* (p. 1073).

Return on equity (ROE) Another name for *rate of return on common shareholders' equity* (p. 1073).

Return on sales (ROS) Another name for *rate of return on net sales* (p. 1072).

Return on shareholders' equity Another name for *rate of return on common shareholders' equity* (p. 1073).

Servicing its debt A phrase that means the repayment of principal and interest on loans or bonds (p. 1072).

Short-term liquidity Ability to meet current payments as they come due (p. 1056).

Times-interest-earned ratio Ratio of income from operations to interest expenses. Measures the number of times that operating income can cover interest expense. Also called the *interest coverage ratio* (p. 1072).

Trading on the equity Earning more income on borrowed money than the related expense, thereby increasing the earnings for the owners of the business. Also called *leverage* (p. 1074).

Vertical analysis Analysis of a financial statement that reveals the relationship of each statement item to a total, which is 100 percent (p. 1061).

Working capital Current assets minus current liabilities; measures a business's ability to meet its short-term obligations with its current assets (p. 1067).

SIMILAR ACCOUNTING TERMS

Acid-test ratio	Quick ratio
Current ratio	Working capital
EPS	Earnings per share
Leverage	Trading on the equity
P/E Ratio	Price–earnings ratio
Rate of return on common shareholders' equity	Return on common shareholders' equity; Return on equity; ROE
Rate of return on net sales	Return on sales; ROS; Profit margin
Rate of return on total assets	Return on assets; ROA
ROA	Return on assets
ROE	Return on equity
ROS	Return on sales
Solvency	Long-term solvency
Times-interest-earned ratio	Interest coverage ratio

SELF-STUDY QUESTIONS

Test your understanding of the chapter by marking the correct answer for each of the following questions:

1. Net income for PJ Ltd. was $240,000 in 2015, $210,000 in 2016, and $252,000 in 2017. The change from 2016 to 2017 is a(n) (*p. 1058*)
   a. Increase of 5 percent
   b. Increase of 20 percent
   c. Decrease of 10 percent
   d. Decrease of 12.5 percent

2. Vertical analysis of a financial statement shows (*p. 1061*)
   a. Trend percentages
   b. The percentage change in an item from period to period
   c. The relationship of an item to a base amount on the statement
   d. Net income expressed as a percentage of shareholders' equity

3. Common-size statements are useful for comparing (*p. 1063*)
   a. Changes in the makeup of assets from period to period
   b. Different companies
   c. A company to its industry
   d. All of the above

4. Benchmarking allows a user of the financial statements of a company to (*p. 1064*)
   a. Compare the performance of the company against that of its key competitors
   b. Compare the performance of the company against best practices
   c. Compare the performance of the company against average performance
   d. Do all of the above

5. The following figures were taken from the 2017 balance sheet of Plateau Golf Academy Ltd. Cash is $10,000, net accounts receivable amount to $22,000, inventory is $55,000, prepaid expenses total $3,000, and current liabilities are $40,000. What is the acid-test ratio? (*p. 1068*)
   a. 0.25   c. 2.18
   b. 0.80   d. 2.25

6. Inventory turnover is computed by dividing (*p. 1069*)
   a. Sales revenue by average inventory
   b. Cost of goods sold by average inventory
   c. Credit sales by average inventory
   d. Average inventory by cost of goods sold

7. Garnet Motors Ltd. is experiencing a severe cash shortage because of its inability to collect accounts receivable. The decision tool most likely to help identify the appropriate corrective action is the (*pp. 1070–1071*)
   a. Acid-test ratio
   b. Inventory turnover
   c. Times-interest-earned ratio
   d. Days' sales in receivables

8. Analysis of Sanjay Corp.'s financial statements over five years reveals that sales are growing steadily, the debt ratio is higher than the industry average and is increasing, interest coverage is decreasing, return on total assets is declining, and earnings per common share is decreasing. Considered together, these ratios suggest that (*p. 1079*)
   a. Sanjay Corp. should pursue collections of receivables more vigorously
   b. Competition is taking sales away from Sanjay Corp.
   c. Sanjay Corp. is in a declining industry
   d. The company's debt burden is hurting profitability

9. Which of the following is most likely to be true? (*pp. 1073–1074*)
   a. Return on common equity > return on total assets
   b. Return on total assets > return on common equity
   c. Return on total assets = return on common equity
   d. None of the above is true

10. How are financial ratios used in decision making? (*pp. 1066–1067*)
    a. They remove the uncertainty of the business environment.

b. They give clear signals about the appropriate action to take.

c. They can help identify the reasons for success and failure in business, but decision making requires information beyond the ratios.

d. They are not useful because decision making is too complex.

ASSIGNMENT MATERIAL

QUESTIONS

1. Identify three groups of users of accounting information and the decisions they base on accounting data.

2. Name the three broad categories of analytical tools that are based on accounting information.

3. Briefly describe horizontal analysis. How do decision makers use this analytical tool?

4. What is vertical analysis and what is its purpose?

5. What is the purpose of common-size statements?

6. What is benchmarking? Give an example of its use.

7. Why are ratios an important tool of financial analysis? Give an example of an important financial ratio.

8. Identify two ratios used to measure a company's ability to pay current liabilities. Show how they are computed.

9. Why is the acid-test ratio given that name?

10. What does the inventory turnover ratio measure?

11. Suppose the days' sales in receivables ratio of Peanuts Inc. increased from 33 days at January 1 to 45 days at December 31. Is this a good sign or a bad sign about the company? What might Peanut Inc.'s management do in response to this change?

12. Janner Inc.'s debt ratio has increased from 0.40 to 0.75. Identify a decision maker to whom this increase is important, and state how the increase affects this party's decisions about the company.

13. Which ratio measures the effect of debt on (a) financial position (the balance sheet) and (b) the company's ability to pay interest expense (the income statement)?

14. Freshie Ltd. is a chain of grocery stores, and Benjamin's Inc. is a furniture store. Which company is likely to have the higher (a) current ratio, (b) inventory turnover, (c) rate of return on sales? Give your reasons.

15. Identify four ratios used to measure a company's profitability. Show how to compute these ratios and state what information each ratio provides.

16. Recently, the price–earnings ratio of WestJet Airlines was 10.1, and the price–earnings ratio of the Bank of Nova Scotia was 11.4. Which company did the stock market favour? Explain.

17. Recently, TransCanada Corporation paid cash dividends of $0.42 per share when the market price of the company's shares was $41.00 per share. What was the dividend yield on TransCanada's shares? What does dividend yield measure?

18. Hold all other factors constant and indicate whether each of the following situations generally signals good or bad news about a company. Explain your answer.
    a. Increase in return on sales
    b. Decrease in earnings per share
    c. Increase in price–earnings ratio
    d. Increase in book value per share
    e. Increase in current ratio
    f. Decrease in inventory turnover
    g. Increase in debt ratio
    h. Decrease in interest coverage ratio

19. Explain how an investor might use book value per share in making an investment decision.

20. Describe how decision makers use ratio data. What are the limitations of ratios?

21. Are there procedural differences when analyzing financial statements prepared under ASPE and financial statements prepared under IFRS? Why or why not?

STARTERS

Horizontal analysis of revenues and gross margin
(1)
2013 net sales increased 12.1%

Starter 18–1 Gildan Activewear Inc. reported the following income statement information in its annual reports:

| | (in millions) | | |
	2013	2012	2011
Net sales	$2,184.3	$1,948.3	$1,725.7
Cost of sales	1,550.3	1,552.1	1,288.1

Perform a horizontal analysis of net sales, cost of sales, and gross margin, both in dollar amounts and in percentages, for 2013 and 2012.

Trend analysis of revenues and net income
(1)
1. 2013 net sales, 127%

Starter 18–2 Gildan Activewear Inc. reported the following net sales and net income amounts:

| | (in millions) | | |
	2013	2012	2011
Net sales	$2,184.3	$1,948.3	$1,725.7
Net income	320.2	148.4	234.1

1. Show Gildan's trend percentages for net sales and net income. Use 2011 as the base year.
2. Did sales and income grow or decline in unison?

Vertical analysis of income statement
(2)
Expenses, 34.5%

Starter 18–3

Use the following information to perform a vertical analysis and check if selling and general expenses are in line with the industry average of 37 percent.

BHAP MILLS CORP.	
Income Statement	
For the year ended November 30, 2017	
Net sales	$310,550
Cost of goods sold	148,800
Gross margin	161,750
Selling and general expenses	107,150
Income from operations	54,600
Income tax expense	20,725
Net income	$ 33,875

Sporting Apparel Inc. reported the following amounts on its balance sheet at December 31, 2017:

	2017
Cash and receivables	$24,000
Inventory	19,000
Property, plant, and equipment, net	48,000
Total assets	$91,000

Perform a vertical analysis of the company's assets at the end of 2017.

Compare HomePro Corp. and Away Inc. by converting their income statements to common size.

	(in thousands)	
	HomePro Corp.	Away Inc.
Net sales	$18,978	$39,072
Cost of goods sold	11,570	28,202
Other expenses	6,228	8,994
Net income	$ 1,180	$ 1,876

Which company earns more net income? Which company's net income is a higher percentage of its net sales?

Match each of the following terms with its description. Place the letter for the description in the blank beside the term.

Terms	Description
_____ 1. Horizontal analysis	a. Ability to meet current payments as they come due.
_____ 2. Quick ratio	b. Ratio of cost of goods sold to average inventory.
_____ 3. Vertical analysis	c. Ratio of total liabilities to total assets.
_____ 4. Debt ratio	d. Ratio of the sum of cash plus short-term investments plus net current receivables to current liabilities.
_____ 5. Inventory turnover	e. Analysis of a financial statement that reveals the relationship of each statement item to a total, which is 100 percent.
_____ 6. Liquidity	f. Earning more income on borrowed money than the related expense, thereby increasing the earnings for the owners of the business.
_____ 7. Leverage	g. The use of percentage changes in comparative financial statements.

For each of the following ratios, indicate with a check mark if a higher result is considered "good."

_____ Current ratio	_____ Debt ratio
_____ Inventory turnover	_____ Earnings per common share
_____ Return on total assets	_____ Return on net sales
_____ Book value per common share	_____ Days' sales in receivables

Use the following data for Starters 18–8 through 18–12. Jeryht Bakers Corp., a baking-supplies chain, reported these summarized figures (in millions):

JERYHT BAKERS CORP. Income Statement For the Year Ended December 31, 2017	
Net sales	$61.6
Cost of goods sold	42.4
Interest expense	0.6
All other expenses	15.0
Net income	$ 3.6

	JERYHT BAKERS CORP. **Balance Sheet** **December 31**					
	2017	**2016**		**2017**	**2016**
Cash	$ 2.8	$ 1.6	Total current liabilities	$ 8.8	$ 7.2
Short-term investments	0.4	0.5	Long-term liabilities	8.6	8.3
Accounts receivable	0.5	0.4	Total liabilities	17.4	15.5
Inventory	9.2	8.0	Common shares	5.2	4.8
Other current assets	0.8	0.6	Retained earnings	15.7	11.8
Total current assets	13.7	11.1	Total equity	20.9	16.6
All other assets	24.6	21.0	Total liabilities and equity	$38.3	$32.1
Total assets	$38.3	$32.1			

Evaluating a company's current ratio

④

1. 2017 current ratio, 1.56

Starter 18–8 Use the Jeryht Bakers Corp. balance sheet data given above.

1. Compute the company's current ratio at December 31, 2017 and 2016.
2. Did Jeryht Bakers Corp.'s current ratio value improve, deteriorate, or hold steady during 2017?

Computing inventory turnover and days' sales in receivables

④

a. 4.9 times

Starter 18–9 Use the Jeryht Bakers Corp. data to compute the following (amounts in millions):

a. The rate of inventory turnover for 2017.
b. Days' sales in receivables during 2017. All sales are made on account. Round dollar amounts to three decimal places.

Measuring ability to pay liabilities

④

Debt ratio, 0.45

Starter 18–10 Use the financial statements of Jeryht Bakers Corp.

1. Compute the debt ratio at December 31, 2017.
2. Is Jeryht Bakers Corp.'s ability to pay its liabilities strong or weak? Explain your reasoning.

Measuring profitability

④

a. ROS, 5.8%

Starter 18–11 Use the financial statements of Jeryht Bakers Corp.

1. Compute these profitability measures for 2017:
   a. Rate of return on net sales
   b. Rate of return on total assets; interest expense for 2017 was $0.6 million
   c. Rate of return on common shareholders' equity
2. Are these rates of return strong or weak? Explain.

Computing EPS and the price–earnings ratio

④

1. $4.50

Starter 18–12 Use the financial statements of Jeryht Bakers Corp., plus the following item (in millions):

Number of common shares outstanding 0.8

1. Compute earnings per share (EPS) for Jeryht Bakers Corp. Round to the nearest cent.
2. Compute Jeryht Bakers Corp.'s price–earnings ratio. The price of a Jeryht Bakers Corp. common share is $131.00.

A summary of Pasmore Ltd.'s income statement appears as follows:

Using ratio data to reconstruct
an income statement
④
Net income, $342

PASMORE LTD.	
Income Statement	
For the Year Ended March 31, 2016	
Net sales	$3,600
Cost of goods sold	(A)
Selling and administrative expenses	855
Interest expenses	(B)
Other expenses	75
Income before taxes	500
Income tax expenses	(C)
Net income	$ (D)

Use the following ratio data to complete Pasmore Ltd.'s income statement:

a. Inventory turnover was 5.50 (beginning inventory was $395, ending inventory was $375).

b. Rate of return on sales is 0.095, or 9.5 percent.

Starter 18–14 A summary of Pasmore Ltd.'s balance sheet appears as follows:

Using ratio data to reconstruct a
balance sheet
④
Total current assets, $735

PASMORE LTD.			
Balance Sheet			
March 31, 2016			
Cash	$ 25	Total current liabilities	$1,050
Receivables	(A)	Long-term note payable	(E)
Inventories	375	Other long-term liabilities	410
Prepaid expenses	(B)		
Total current assets	(C)		
Property, plant, and equipment, net	(D)		
Other assets	1,075	Shareholders' equity	1,200
Total assets	$3,400	Total liabilities and equity	$ (F)

Use the following ratio data to complete Pasmore Ltd.'s balance sheet:

a. Current ratio is 0.70.

b. Acid-test ratio is 0.30.

EXERCISES

MyAccountingLab

Exercise 18–1

Compute the dollar change and the percentage change in Navin Ltd.'s working capital each year during 2016 and 2017. Is this trend favourable or unfavourable?

Computing year-to-year changes
in working capital
①
2017 increase in working
capital, 5.4%

	2017	2016	2015
Total current assets	$92,250	$87,000	$78,750
Total current liabilities	37,200	34,750	42,500

Exercise 18–2

Prepare a horizontal analysis of the comparative income statement of Keesha Shoes Inc. (shown on the next page). Round percentage changes to the nearest one-tenth percent (three decimal places).

Why was the percentage increase in net income higher than that in total revenue during 2017?

Excel Spreadsheet
Template
Horizontal analysis of an
income statement
①
2017 net income increased
19.8%

KEESHA SHOES INC.
Income Statement
For the Years Ended December 31, 2017 and 2016

	2017	2016
Net sales	$533,000	$465,000
Expenses		
Cost of goods sold	235,000	202,000
Selling and general expenses	140,000	135,000
Interest expense	10,000	6,000
Wages expense	51,000	41,000
Total expenses	436,000	384,000
Net income	$ 97,000	$ 81,000

Exercise 18–3

Computing trend percentages

(1)

2017 net sales grew 24.6%

Compute trend percentages for Ceder Inc.'s net sales and net income for the following five-year period, using 2013 as the base year:

	2017	2016	2015	2014	2013
	(Amounts in thousands)				
Net sales	$1,625	$1,469	$1,375	$1,200	$1,304
Net income	149	131	100	82	105

Which measure grew more during the period, net sales or net income? By what percentage did net sales and net income grow from 2013 to 2017?

Exercise 18–4

Vertical analysis of a balance sheet

(2)

Total current assets are 41.6% of total assets

Purposeful Products Inc. has requested that you perform a vertical analysis of its balance sheet. Determine the component percentages of its assets, liabilities, and shareholders' equity.

PURPOSEFUL PRODUCTS INC.
Balance Sheet
December 31, 2017

Assets	
Total current assets	219,000
Property, plant, and equipment, net	267,000
Other assets	40,000
Total assets	$526,000
Liabilities	
Total current liabilities	$85,000
Long-term debt	156,000
Total liabilities	241,000
Shareholders' Equity	
Total shareholders' equity	285,000
Total liabilities and shareholders' equity	$526,000

Excel Spreadsheet
Template
Preparing a common-size
income statement

(3)

2017 net income is 18.2%
of net sales

Exercise 18–5

Prepare a comparative common-size income statement for Keesha Shoes Inc. using the 2017 and 2016 data found in Exercise 18–2 and rounding percentages to one-tenth of a percent (three decimal places).

Exercise 18–6

Prepare a common-size analysis to compare the asset composition of Bhagwan Inc. and Bigwig Ltd. (amounts in millions).

Common-size analysis of assets
(3)
Cash and equiv. as % of total assets: Bhagwan Inc. 4.1%; Bigwig Ltd. 2.4%

Assets	Bhagwan Inc.	Bigwig Ltd.
Current assets:		
Cash and equivalents	$ 462	$ 472
Short-term investments	—	804
Accounts receivable, net	2,898	882
Inventories	2,082	5,380
Other current assets	408	134
Total current assets	5,850	7,672
Property, plant, and equipment, net	4,960	11,280
Goodwill and other intangibles	206	226
Other assets	302	540
Total assets	$11,318	$19,718

To which company are *current assets* more important? Which company places more emphasis on its *property, plant, and equipment?*

Exercise 18–7

Compare the results of two years of ratios for Prince George Corp.

Interpreting ratio results
(4)
ROE: +, +

Ratio	2017	2016	Change + or –	Benchmark	Performance + or –
Current ratio	1.5	1.7		2:1	
Acid-test ratio	0.83	0.85		0.95	
Inventory turnover	8	7		10	
Accounts receivable turnover	12	14		13	
Debt ratio	0.3	0.2		0.7	
Times-interest-earned ratio	7	6		4	
Rate of return on total assets	0.06	0.04		0.05	
Rate of return on common shareholders' equity	0.24	0.23		0.14	

Required

1. Identify whether the change from 2016 to 2017 was good (+) or bad (−).
2. Assess whether the performance in 2017 is good (+) or bad (−) compared to the industry average presented in the benchmark column.

Exercise 18–8

The financial statements of Baca Bay Ltd. include the following items:

Excel Spreadsheet Template
Computing five ratios
(4)
c. 3.30 x

	2017	2016
Balance sheet		
Cash	$ 11,500	$ 14,500
Short-term investments	6,500	10,500
Net receivables	39,000	35,000
Inventory	45,500	38,500
Prepaid expenses	3,500	3,500
Total current assets	$106,000	$102,000
Total current liabilities	$ 69,000	$ 46,000
Income statement		
Net credit sales	$248,500	
Cost of goods sold	138,500	

Required Compute the following ratios for 2017: (a) current ratio, (b) acid-test ratio, (c) inventory turnover, (d) accounts receivable turnover, and (e) days' sales in receivables.

Exercise 18–9

Compute ratios and analyze a company

4

a. 2017, 2.04
2016, 1.78

Grewers Automotive Products Ltd. has requested that you determine whether the company's ability to pay its current liabilities and long-term debt has improved or deteriorated during 2017. To answer this question, compute the following ratios for 2017 and 2016: (a) current ratio, (b) acid-test ratio, (c) debt ratio, and (d) times-interest-earned ratio. Summarize the results of your analysis in a paragraph explaining what the results of the calculations mean.

	2017	2016
Cash	$ 13,000	$ 25,500
Short-term investments	15,000	—
Net receivables	59,500	65,500
Inventory	125,000	135,000
Prepaid expenses	9,000	5,500
Total assets	275,000	260,000
Total current liabilities	108,500	130,000
Total liabilities	137,000	143,000
Income from operations	99,000	82,500
Interest expense	22,500	21,000

Exercise 18–10

Analyzing profitability

4

EPS: 2017, $0.34
2016, $0.71

Compute four ratios that measure the ability to earn profits for Gardener Farm Supplies Ltd., whose comparative income statement appears below. Additional data follow.

GARDENER FARM SUPPLIES LTD. Income Statement For the Years Ended December 31, 2017 and 2016		
	2017	2016
Net sales	$195,000	$174,000
Cost of goods sold	101,500	91,750
Gross margin	93,500	82,250
Selling and general expenses	50,200	40,000
Income from operations	43,300	42,250
Interest expense	25,400	12,050
Income before income tax	17,900	30,200
Income tax expense	4,475	7,550
Net income	$ 13,425	$ 22,650

Additional data	2017	2016
a. Average total assets	$230,000	$222,000
b. Average common shareholders' equity	102,000	98,000
c. Preferred dividends	5,000	5,000
d. Number of common shares outstanding	25,000	25,000

Did the company's operating performance improve or deteriorate during 2017?

Exercise 18–11

Evaluate the common shares of Payment Software Inc. as an investment. Specifically, use the three share ratios to determine whether the shares have increased or decreased in attractiveness during the past year.

Evaluating shares as an investment
④
Dividend yield:
2017, 3.9%
2016, 3.3%

	2017	2016
Net income	$ 33,000	$ 27,000
Dividends (25% to preferred shareholders)	19,000	13,000
Common shareholders' equity at year end (75,000 shares)	275,000	250,000
Preferred shareholders' equity at year end	50,000	50,000
Market price per common share at year end	$4.83	$3.89

Exercise 18–12

Pria Developments Corp. is a Canadian real estate investment and development company looking to expand internationally. For the year ended December 31, 2016, Pria Developments prepared two sets of financial statements—one in accordance with ASPE, and the other in accordance with IFRS.

Excerpts from Pria Development's financial statements appear below and on the following pages.

Computing ratios under ASPE and IFRS
⑤
Current ratio:
1. (a) Under ASPE, 0.39
2. (a) Under IFRS, 0.62

ASPE-Based Financial Statements:

PRIA DEVELOPMENTS CORP. Consolidated Balance Sheet ($ amounts in thousands)		
	December 31, 2016	December 31, 2015
Assets		
Investment properties	$3,310,317	$2,939,960
Development properties	360,562	293,955
Long-term investments	40,086	39,562
Intangible assets	110,067	100,619
Goodwill		33,036
Restricted cash	25,969	27,704
Cash	16,359	17,927
Receivables and other	138,397	78,845
Currency guarantee receivable	28,165	
	$4,029,922	$3,531,608
Liabilities		
Long-term debt	$2,952,124	$2,094,122
Accounts payable and other liabilities	268,796	579,373
Construction financing	102,433	66,393
Future income taxes	129,097	110,578
Intangible liabilities	15,429	12,234
Liabilities of discontinued operations	28,903	28,903
Derivative instrument liability	19,427	
	3,516,209	2,891,603
Shareholders' equity	513,713	640,005
	$4,029,922	$3,531,608

PRIA DEVELOPMENTS CORP.
Consolidated Statement of Earnings (Loss)
For the Year Ended December 31
($ amounts in thousands)

	2016	2015
Property revenue	$309,579	$207,331
Sale of properties developed for resale	191,260	229,139
Dividend income and distributions	2,992	2,011
Gain on fair value increase in investments		938
Other income	1,849	3,857
Foreign exchange gain		18,305
Gain on derivative instrument		2,303
Gain on sale of assests	443	2,051
	506,123	465,935
Property operating expenses	84,421	45,173
Cost of sale of properties developed for resale	142,841	147,677
Interest on long-term debt	154,899	106,818
Interest and financing costs	11,916	13,053
Depreciation and amortization	62,860	39,278
General and administrative	23,956	11,051
Stock-based compensation	307	5,288
Foreign exchange loss	19,656	
Loss on derivative instruments	18,542	
Goodwill impairment loss	63,456	
Loss on fair value decrease in investments	23,133	
	605,987	368,338
Earnings (loss) before income taxes	(99,864)	97,597
Total income taxes (recovery)	(3,781)	16,270
Net earnings (loss) from continuing operations	(96,083)	81,327
Net loss from discontinued operations		(2,159)
Net earnings (loss)	$ (96,083)	$ 79,168

IFRS-Based Financial Statements:

PRIA DEVELOPMENTS CORP. Consolidated Balance Sheet ($ amounts in thousands)	December 31 2016	December 31 2015
Assets		
Non-current assets		
Investment properties	$ 3,549,744	$ 3,304,880
Development properties	224,285	126,522
Currency guarantee receivable	28,165	
Goodwill		48,594
Investments	40,086	39,562
Restricted cash	25,969	27,704
	3,868,249	3,547,262
Current assets		
Cash	16,359	17,927
Construction properties being developed for resale	194,638	225,596
Receivables and other	65,390	26,694
	276,387	270,217
Total assets	$ 4,144,636	$ 3,817,479
Equity and Liabilities		
Total equity	$ 606,768	$ 886,271
Non-current liabilities		
Long-term debt	2,901,348	1,910,668
Derivatives	19,427	
Deferred tax liabilities	143,930	145,559
Other liabilities	29,727	28,602
	3,094,432	2,084,829
Current liabilities		
Accounts payable and other	255,585	561,122
Income taxes payable	5,739	6,507
Liabilities of discontinued operations	28,903	28,903
Construction financing	102,433	66,393
Current portion of long-term debt	50,776	183,454
	443,436	846,379
Total liabilities	3,537,868	2,931,208
Total equity and liabilities	$ 4,144,636	$ 3,817,479

PRIA DEVELOPMENTS CORP.
Consolidated Income Statement
For the Year Ended December 31
($ amounts in thousands)

	2016	2015
Property revenue	$ 310,466	$ 211,025
Sales of properties developed for resale	186,350	191,139
Total revenues	496,816	402,164
Property operating expenses	88,414	51,854
Cost of sale of properties developed for resale	143,131	131,677
	231,545	183,531
Gross income from operations	265,271	218,633
General and administrative	(23,956)	(11,051)
Stock-based compensation	(307)	(5,288)
Other income, net	1,849	3,857
Dividend income and distributions	2,992	2,011
Net adjustment to fair value of investment properties	(286,060)	55,757
Gain on sale of investment properties	443	924
Goodwill impairment loss	(48,594)	
Net adjustment to fair value of held-for-trading financial assets	(23,133)	938
Net adjustment to fair value of derivative financial instruments	(18,542)	2,303
Interest expense	(166,815)	(119,871)
Exchange differences, net	(19,656)	18,305
Income (loss) before income taxes	(316,508)	166,518
Total income taxes (recovery)	(39,855)	23,864
Net income (loss) from continuing operations	(276,653)	142,654
Net loss from discontinued operations		(2,159)
Net income (loss)	$ (276,653)	$140,495

Notice that the presentation of the financial statements differs somewhat, as well as some of the recorded balances. These differences arise because ASPE and IFRS rules measure certain transactions differently. However, the focus of this question is the impact on ratios of using a different set of accounting rules. Investors need to understand that if two companies in the same industry are being compared, their results could be very different depending on whether IFRS or ASPE is used in the preparation of the financial information.

Required

1. Compute the following ratios for 2016 based on Pria Developments Corp.'s financial statements prepared in accordance with ASPE. For the purpose of this exercise, assume that "cash" and "receivables and other assets" are current assets, and that "accounts payable and other liabilities," "construction financing," and "liabilities of discontinued operations" are current liabilities. Include both "interest on long-term debt" and "interest and financing costs" in your computations for part (d).
   a. Current ratio
   b. Acid-test ratio
   c. Debt ratio
   d. Rate of return on total assets

2. Compute the same ratios in Requirement 1 for 2016 based on Pria Developments Corp.'s IFRS financial statements.

SERIAL EXERCISE

This exercise continues the Lee Consulting Corporation situation from Exercise 17–23 of Chapter 17. If you did not complete any Serial Exercises in earlier chapters, you can still complete Exercise 18–13 as it is presented.

Exercise 18–13

Suppose at January 31, 2018, Lee Consulting Corporation has the following balance sheet:

Computing six ratios

④

a. 2.67

LEE CONSULTING CORPORATION Balance Sheet January 31, 2018	
Assets	
Current assets:	
Cash	$ 5,000
Accounts receivable	2,200
Supplies	420
Total current assets	7,620
Equipment, net	15,150
Furniture, net	3,650
Building, net	52,227
Land	40,000
Total assets	$118,467
Liabilities and Shareholders' Equity	
Current liabilities:	
Accounts payable	$ 350
Salary payable	2,500
Total current liabilities	2,850
Long-term liabilities:	
Notes payable	40,000
Shareholders' equity:	
Common shares	45,000
Retained earnings	30,617
Total liabilities and shareholders' equity	$118,467

Additional information: Lee Consulting Corporation incurred interest expense of $2,400 during January. Net income for the month ended January 31, 2018, was $38,910. The market price of Lee Consulting Corporation's 1,500 common shares is $50.00 per share on January 31, 2018. Total shareholders' equity last year was $51,334.

Required Using this information, calculate the following ratios for Lee Consulting Corporation:

a. Current ratio

b. Debt ratio

c. Earnings per share

d. Price–earnings ratio

e. Rate of return on total assets

f. Rate of return on common shareholders' equity

Comment on each as to whether you feel the business is doing well or not and why you think so.

CHALLENGE EXERCISE

Exercise 18–14

Using ratio data to reconstruct a
company's balance sheet
② ③ ④
Current liabilities, $13,999

The following data (dollar amounts in thousands) are from the financial statements of Joachim's Equipment Manufacturing Ltd:

Total liabilities...	$29,204
Preferred shares..	0
Total current assets...	$24,498
Accumulated amortization...	$ 7,854
Debt ratio..	55.312%
Current ratio	1.75:1

Required   Complete the following condensed balance sheet. Report amounts to the nearest thousand dollars:

Current assets		$?
Property, plant, and equipment	$?	
Less accumulated amortization	_?_	_?_
Total assets...		$?
Current liabilities...		$?
Long-term liabilities...		?
Shareholders' equity		_?_
Total liabilities and shareholders' equity......................		$?

BEYOND THE NUMBERS

Beyond the Numbers 18–1

Understanding the components
of accounting ratios
④

Consider the following unrelated business situations:

1. Teresa Chan has asked you about the shares of a particular company. She finds them attractive because they have a high dividend yield relative to another company's shares that she is also considering. Explain to her the meaning of the ratio and the danger of making a decision based on it alone. Suggest other information (ratios) Teresa should consider as she makes the investment decision.

2. Saskatoon Plumbing Supplies Ltd.'s owners are concerned because the number of days' sales in receivables has increased over the previous two years. Explain why the ratio might have increased.

Beyond the Numbers 18–2

Taking unethical action to
improve accounting ratios
④

Moe Sahota is the controller of Forochar Ltd., whose year end is December 31. Sahota prepares cheques for suppliers in December and posts them to the appropriate accounts in that month. However, he holds on to the cheques and mails them to the suppliers in January. What financial ratio(s) are most affected by the action? What is Sahota's purpose in undertaking the activity?

ETHICAL ISSUE

Harrison Outfitters Inc.'s (HOI) long-term debt agreements make certain demands on the business. For example, HOI may not repurchase company shares in excess of the balance of Retained Earnings. Long-term debt may not exceed shareholders' equity, and the current ratio may not fall below 1.60. If HOI fails to meet these requirements, the company's lenders have the authority to take over management of the corporation.

Changes in consumer demand have made it hard for HOI to sell its products. Current liabilities have increased faster than current assets, causing the current ratio to fall to 1.45. Prior to releasing financial statements, HOI management is scrambling to improve the current ratio. The controller points out that an equity investment can be classified as either long term or short term, depending on management's intention. By deciding to convert an investment to cash within one year, HOI can classify the investment as short term (a current asset). On the controller's recommendation, HOI's board of directors votes to reclassify the long-term equity investments as short-term equity investments.

Required

1. What effect will reclassifying the investment have on the current ratio? Is Harrison Outfitters Inc.'s financial position stronger as a result of reclassifying the investment?

2. Shortly after releasing the financial statements, sales improve and so, then, does the current ratio. As a result, HOI management decides not to sell the investments it had reclassified as short term. Accordingly, the company reclassifies the investments as long term. Has management behaved unethically? Give your reason.

PROBLEMS (GROUP A)   MyAccountingLab

Problem 18–1A

Net sales, net income, and common shareholders' equity for Naturah Products Ltd. for a six-year period follow:

Trend percentages, return on common equity, and comparison with the industry

① ④

2. Return on common shareholders' equity 2017, 16.0%

	2017	2016	2015	2014	2013	2012
			(Amounts in thousands)			
Net sales	$1,806	$1,757	$1,606	$1,704	$1,638	$1,588
Net income	144	120	89	126	100	96
Ending common shareholders' equity	940	860	772	684	628	600

Required

1. Compute trend percentages for 2013 through 2017, using 2012 as the base year. Round to the nearest whole percentage.

2. Compute the rate of return on common shareholders' equity for 2013 through 2017, rounding to three decimal places. In this industry, rates of 12 percent are average, rates above 15 percent are considered good, and rates above 20 percent are viewed as outstanding.

3. How does Naturah Products Ltd.'s return on common shareholders' equity compare with the industry's?

Performing vertical analysis

(2)

1. Net income, 11.5%

The McConnell Department Stores, Inc. chief executive officer (CEO) has asked you to compare the company's profit performance and financial position with the averages for the industry. The CEO has given you the company's income statement and balance sheet, as well as the industry average data for retailers:

MCCONNELL DEPARTMENT STORES INC. Income Statement Compared with Industry Average For the Year Ended December 31, 2017		
	McConnell	Industry Average
Net sales	$778,000	100.0%
Cost of goods sold	522,816	65.8
Gross margin	255,184	34.2
Operating expenses	161,046	19.7
Operating income	94,138	14.5
Other expenses	4,668	0.4
Net income	$ 89,470	14.1%

MCCONNELL DEPARTMENT STORES INC. Balance Sheet Compared with Industry Average December 31, 2017		
	McConnell	Industry Average
Current assets	$325,440	70.9%
Property, plant, and equipment	120,960	23.6
Intangible assets, net	8,640	0.8
Other assets	24,960	4.7
Total assets	$480,000	100.0%
Current liabilities	$222,720	48.1%
Long-term liabilities	107,520	16.6
Total liabilities	330,240	64.7
Shareholders' equity	149,760	35.3
Total liabilities and shareholders' equity	$480,000	100.0%

Required

1. Prepare a vertical analysis for McConnell for both its income statement and balance sheet.

2. Compare the company's gross margin and profit margin ratios with the average for the industry. Comment on their investment in assets as well as their debt to assets compared to the industry information shown.

Common-size statements, analysis of profitability, and comparison with the industry

(2) (3) (4)

2017 current assets are 64.1% of total assets

Fixxit Ltd. has asked for your help in comparing the company's profit performance and financial position with the computer services industry average. The manager has given you the company's income statement and balance sheet, and also the following industry average data for computer services companies:

FIXXIT LTD. Income Statement For the Year Ended December 31, 2017		
	Fixxit Ltd.	Industry Average
Net sales	$425,625	100.0%
Cost of goods sold	250,375	53.2
Gross margin	175,250	46.8
Operating expenses	87,300	21.3
Operating income	87,950	25.5
Other expenses	20,500	5.2
Net income	$ 67,450	20.3%

FIXXIT LTD. Balance Sheet December 31, 2017		
	Fixxit Ltd.	Industry Average
Current assets	$162,750	62.5%
Property and equip., net	85,250	35.2
Other assets	6,000	2.3
Total assets	$254,000	100.0%
Current liabilities	$112,500	42.5%
Long-term liabilities	62,500	32.5
Shareholders' equity	79,000	25.0
Total liabilities and shareholders' equity	$254,000	100.0%

Required

1. Prepare a two-column common-size income statement and a two-column common-size balance sheet for Fixxit Ltd. The first column of each statement should present Fixxit Ltd.'s common-size statement, and the second column should show the industry averages.

2. For the profitability analysis, compute Fixxit Ltd.'s (a) ratio of gross margin to net sales, (b) ratio of operating income to net sales, and (c) ratio of net income to net sales. Compare these figures to the industry averages. Is Fixxit Ltd.'s profit performance better or worse than the industry average?

3. For the analysis of financial position, compute Fixxit Ltd.'s (a) ratio of current assets to total assets, and (b) ratio of shareholders' equity to total assets. Compare these ratios to the industry averages. Is Fixxit Ltd.'s financial position better or worse than the industry averages?

Problem 18–4A

Financial statement data of MKR Dealer Supplies Ltd. include the following items:

Effects of business transactions on selected ratios

④

1. Earnings per share, $2.70

Cash	$ 68,000
Accounts receivable, net	97,500
Inventories	129,000
Prepaid expenses	6,000
Total assets	625,000
Short-term notes payable	39,000
Accounts payable	109,500
Accrued liabilities	27,000
Long-term liabilities	204,000
Net income	108,000
Number of common shares outstanding	40,000 shares

Required

1. Compute MKR Dealer Supplies Ltd.'s current ratio, debt ratio, and earnings per share.

2. Compute each of the three ratios after evaluating the effect of each transaction that follows. Consider each transaction *separately*.

   a. Purchased merchandise of $43,000 on account, debiting Inventory.
   b. Paid long-term liabilities, $40,000.
   c. Declared, but did not pay, a $60,000 cash dividend on common shares.
   d. Borrowed $50,000 on a long-term note payable.
   e. Issued 10,000 common shares at the beginning of the year, receiving cash of $140,000.
   f. Received cash on account, $29,000.
   g. Paid short-term notes payable, $25,000.

Set up a table in the following format for your answers:

Transaction	Current Ratio	Debt Ratio	Earnings per Share

Problem 18–5A

Comparative financial statement data of Old Tyme Candies Corp. appear below:

OLD TYME CANDIES CORP. Income Statement For the Years Ended December 31, 2017 and 2016		
	2017	**2016**
Net sales	$311,850	$297,000
Cost of goods sold	148,850	147,000
Gross margin	163,000	150,000
Operating expenses	79,250	77,000
Income from operations	83,750	73,000
Interest expense	12,500	14,000
Income before income tax	71,250	59,000
Income tax expense	17,850	14,600
Net income	$ 53,400	$ 44,400

OLD TYME CANDIES CORP. Balance Sheet December 31, 2017 and 2016 (selected 2015 amounts given for computation of ratios)			
	2017	**2016**	**2015**
Current assets:			
Cash	$ 27,500	$ 25,000	
Current receivables, net	67,500	62,500	$ 52,500
Inventories	127,500	117,500	95,000
Prepaid expenses	5,000	4,000	
Total current assets	227,500	209,000	
Property, plant, and equipment, net	100,500	98,000	
Total assets	$328,000	$307,000	295,500
Total current liabilities	$ 93,000	$100,725	
Long-term liabilities	117,500	127,500	
Total liabilities	210,500	228,225	
Preferred shares, $1.25	5,000	5,000	
Common shares	50,000	37,500	17,500
Retained earnings	62,500	36,275	25,000
Total liabilities and shareholders' equity	$328,000	$307,000	

Other information:

- Market price of Old Tyme Candies Corp. common shares: $24.00 at December 31, 2017, and $12.00 at December 31, 2016.
- Common shares outstanding: 10,000 during 2017 and 7,500 during 2016. There are 1,000 preferred shares outstanding at December 31, 2017 and 2016.
- All sales are on credit.

Required

1. Compute the following ratios for 2017 and 2016:
   a. Current ratio
   b. Inventory turnover
   c. Accounts receivable turnover

d. Times-interest-earned ratio
e. Return on assets
f. Return on common shareholders' equity
g. Earnings per common share
h. Price–earnings ratio
i. Book value per common share at year end

2. Decide (a) whether Old Tyme Candies Corp.'s financial position improved or deteriorated during 2017, and (b) whether the investment attractiveness of its common shares appears to have increased or decreased.

3. How will what you have learned in this problem help you evaluate an investment?

Problem 18–6A

Incomplete and adapted versions of the comparative financial statements of Canadarch Ltd. follow (amounts in thousands):

Using ratio data to complete a set of financial statements

④

Net income, $4,954,000

CANADARCH LTD.
Income Statement
For the Year Ended May 31, 2017

Net sales	$ 30,718
Cost of goods sold	(a)
Gross margin	(b)
Selling and general expenses	9,654
Other expense (income)	1,130
Income before income tax	(c)
Income tax expense (25%)	(d)
Net income	$ (e)

CANADARCH LTD.
Balance Sheet
May 31, 2017 and 2016

Assets	2017	2016
Current assets:		
Cash	$ (f)	$ 300
Short-term investments	1,852	1,630
Receivables, net	4,224	3,726
Inventories	1,300	1,046
Prepaid expenses	(g)	168
Total current assets	(h)	6,870
Property, plant, and equipment, net	22,354	19,248
Total assets	$ (i)	$26,118
Liabilities		
Current liabilities	$ 9,270	$ 7,434
Long-term liabilities	(j)	15,964
Total liabilities	(k)	23,398
Shareholders' Equity		
Common shareholders' equity	(l)	2,720
Total liabilities and shareholders' equity	$ (m)	$26,118

CANADARCH LTD.	
Cash Flow Statement	
For the Year Ended May 31, 2017	
Net cash inflow from operating activities	$4,324
Net cash outflow from investing activities	(2,464)
Net cash outflow from financing activities	(1,130)
Net increase (decrease) in cash during 2017	$ (n)

Ratio data:

- Current ratio at May 31, 2017, is 0.9276, or 92.76 percent.
- Inventory turnover for the year ended May 31, 2017, is 11.362.
- Debt ratio at May 31, 2017, is 0.7521, or 75.21 percent.

Required Complete the financial statements. Start with the income statement, then go to the cash flow statement. Complete the balance sheet last.

Excel Spreadsheet
Template
Using ratios to decide between
two share investments
④

a. BildRite, 1.86; Highbuild, 2.56

Problem 18–7A

Assume you are purchasing an investment and have decided to invest in a company in the home renovation business. Suppose you have narrowed the choice to BildRite Ltd. and Highbuild Homes Ltd. You have assembled the following selected data:

Selected income statement data for current year:

	BildRite Ltd.	Highbuild Homes Ltd.
Net sales (all on credit)	$323,050	$231,875
Cost of goods sold	187,700	154,250
Income from operations	89,500	48,750
Interest expense	15,000	2,500
Net income	70,000	36,550

Selected balance sheet and market price data at end of current year:

	BildRite Ltd.	Highbuild Homes Ltd.
Current assets:		
Cash	$ 17,250	$ 18,500
Short-term investments	11,500	9,750
Current receivables, net	32,300	26,100
Inventories	60,950	55,775
Prepaid expenses	2,000	1,250
Total current assets	124,000	111,375
Total assets	225,000	169,000
Total current liabilities	66,750	43,500
Total liabilities	97,500	68,500
Preferred shares: $3.00 (250 shares)	12,500	
Common shares (4,000 shares)		15,000
Common shares (7,000 shares)	17,500	
Total shareholders' equity	127,500	100,500
Market price per common share	$10.00	$10.00

Selected balance sheet data at beginning of current year:

	BildRite Ltd.	Highbuild Homes Ltd.
Current receivables, net	$ 30,250	$ 16,000
Inventories	52,500	52,500
Total assets	240,000	192,500
Preferred shareholders' equity, $3.00 (250 shares)	12,500	—
Common shares (4,000 shares)		15,000
Common shares (7,000 shares)	17,500	
Total shareholders' equity	90,000	87,500

Your investment strategy is to purchase the shares of companies that have low price–earnings ratios but appear to be in good shape financially. Assume you have analyzed all other factors, and your decision depends on the results of the ratio analysis to be performed.

Required Compute the following ratios for both companies for the current year and decide which company's shares better fits your investment strategy:

a. Current ratio

b. Acid-test ratio

c. Inventory turnover

d. Days' sales in receivables

e. Debt ratio

f. Times-interest-earned ratio

g. Return on net sales

h. Return on total assets

i. Return on common shareholders' equity

j. Earnings per common share

k. Book value per common share

l. Price–earnings ratio

Problem 18–8A

Natural Microwave Products Ltd.'s financial statements for the year ended December 31, 2017, are shown below:

Preparing a horizontal and vertical analysis of a financial statement, computing the standard financial ratios used for decision making, using ratios in decision making

① ② ④

3. a. 8.64

NATURAL MICROWAVE PRODUCTS LTD. Income Statement For the Year Ended December 31, 2017	
Net sales	$945,000
Cost of goods sold	610,000
Gross margin	335,000
Operating expenses:	
Selling expenses	128,200
Administrative expenses	78,000
Interest expense	22,000
Total operating expenses	228,200
Operating income	106,800
Income taxes (25%)	26,700
Net income	$ 80,100

NATURAL MICROWAVE PRODUCTS LTD.
Statement of Retained Earnings
For the Year Ended December 31, 2017

Retained earnings, January 1, 2017		$162,000
Add net income for 2017		80,100
		242,100
Less dividends: Preferred	$25,000	
Common	9,000	34,000
Retained earnings, December 31, 2017		$208,100

NATURAL MICROWAVE PRODUCTS LTD.
Balance Sheet
December 31, 2017 and 2016

	2017	2016
Assets		
Cash	$ 92,000	$ 45,000
Accounts receivable	84,000	92,000
Merchandise inventory	102,000	118,000
Prepaid expenses	8,000	6,000
Property, plant, and equipment	498,000	474,000
Accumulated amortization	(106,000)	(70,000)
Goodwill	40,000	40,000
Total assets	$718,000	$705,000
Liabilities		
Accounts payable	$ 30,100	$ 43,000
Notes payable (due in 30 days)	3,000	10,000
Mortgage payable	68,800	130,000
Total liabilities	101,900	183,000
Shareholders' equity		
Preferred shares (1,250 shares, $20.00		
callable at $210.00 per share)	$240,000	$240,000
Common shares		
(2017—12,000 shares; 2016—6,000 shares)	168,000	120,000
Retained earnings	208,100	162,000
Total shareholders' equity	616,100	522,000
Total liabilities and shareholders' equity	$718,000	$705,000

Required

1. Perform a horizontal analysis of the comparative balance sheets. Comment on the analysis.

2. Perform a vertical analysis of the income statement. The industry standards are gross margin of 35 percent and net income of 12 percent. Comment on the results

3. Calculate each of the following ratios for the year ended December 31, 2017. The industry standards are provided in parentheses for some of the ratios.

   a. Current ratio (3:1)
   b. Acid-test ratio
   c. Inventory turnover
   d. Days' sales in receivables
   e. Debt ratio (0.50)
   f. Times-interest-earned ratio
   g. Rate of return on net sales

   h. Rate of return on total assets
   i. Rate of return on common shareholders' equity
   j. Price–earnings ratio—the market price per share is $30.00 at year end, when dividends were paid (5.0)
   k. Dividend yield (5%)

4. Comment on your calculations for Natural Microwave Products Ltd. in Requirement 3. Include comments for those ratios for which industry standards were provided.

PROBLEMS (GROUP B)

MyAccountingLab

Problem 18–1B

Net sales, net income, and total assets for River Holdings Ltd. for a six-year period follow:

Trend percentages, return on sales, and comparison with the industry
① ④

	2017	2016	2015	2014	2013	2012
			(Amounts in thousands)			
Net sales	$804	$912	$662	$714	$616	$604
Net income	112	92	65	82	68	58
Total assets	654	610	522	470	462	410

Required

1. Compute trend percentages for 2013 through 2017. Use 2012 as the base year. Round to the nearest whole percentage.

2. Compute the return on net sales for 2013 through 2017, rounding to three decimal places. In this industry, rates above 8 percent are considered good, and rates above 10 percent are viewed as outstanding.

3. How does River Holdings Ltd.'s return on net sales compare to the industry's?

Problem 18–2B

The Specialty Department Stores, Inc. chief executive officer (CEO) has asked you to compare the company's profit performance and financial position with the averages for the industry. The CEO has given you the company's income statement and balance sheet, as well as the industry average data for retailers:

Performing vertical analysis
②

SPECIALTY DEPARTMENT STORES INC.
Income Statement Compared with Industry Average
For the Year Ended December 31, 2017

	Specialty	Industry Average
Net sales	$782,000	100.0%
Cost of goods sold	528,632	65.8
Gross margin	253,368	34.2
Operating expenses	163,438	19.7
Operating income	89,930	14.5
Other expenses	4,692	0.4
Net income	$ 85,238	14.1%

SPECIALTY DEPARTMENT STORES INC.
Balance Sheet Compared with Industry Average
December 31, 2017

	Specialty	Industry Average
Current assets	$303,750	70.9%
Property, plant, and equipment	117,000	23.6
Intangible assets, net	5,850	0.8
Other assets	23,400	4.7
Total assets	$450,000	100.0%
Current liabilities	$208,800	48.1%
Long-term liabilities	102,600	16.6
Total liabilities	311,400	64.7
Shareholders' equity	138,600	35.3
Total liabilities and shareholders' equity	$450,000	100.0%

Required

1. Prepare a vertical analysis for Specialty for both its income statement and balance sheet.

2. Compare the company's gross margin and profit margin ratios with the average for the industry. Comment on their investment in assets as well as their debt to assets compared to the industry information shown.

Problem 18–3B

Common-size statements, analysis of profitability, and comparison with the industry

② ③ ④

Top managers of Bella Tiles Inc., a specialty fabricating company, have asked for your help in comparing the company's profit performance and financial position with the average for the tile-making industry. The accountant has given you the company's income statement and balance sheet, and also the average data for the tile-making industry (amounts in millions):

BELLA TILES INC. Income Statement For the Year Ended December 31, 2017	Bella Tiles Inc.	Industry Average
Net sales	$29.2	100.0%
Cost of goods sold	17.6	65.9
Gross margin	11.6	34.1
Operating expenses	8.4	28.1
Operating income	3.2	6.0
Other expenses	0.2	0.4
Net income	$ 3.0	5.6%

BELLA TILES INC. Balance Sheet December 31, 2017	Bella Tiles Inc.	Industry Average
Current assets	$10.4	66.6%
Property, plant, equip., net	8.0	32.3
Other assets	0.2	1.1
Total assets	$18.6	100.0%
Current liabilities	$ 6.2	35.6%
Long-term liabilities	5.2	19.0
Shareholders' equity	7.2	45.4
Total liabilities and shareholders' equity	$18.6	100.0%

Required

1. Prepare a two-column common-size income statement and a two-column common-size balance sheet for Bella Tiles Inc. The first column of each statement should present Bella Tiles Inc.'s common-size statement, and the second column should show the industry averages.

2. For the profitability analysis, compare Bella Tiles Inc.'s (a) ratio of gross margin to net sales, (b) ratio of operating income (loss) to net sales, and (c) ratio of net income (loss) to net sales. Compare these figures with the industry averages. Is Bella Tiles Inc.'s profit performance better or worse than the average for the industry?

3. For the analysis of financial position, compare Bella Tiles Inc.'s (a) ratio of current assets to total assets and (b) ratio of shareholders' equity to total assets. Compare these ratios with the industry averages. Is Bella Tiles Inc.'s financial position better or worse than the average for the industry?

Problem 18–4B

Effects of business transactions on selected ratios

④

Financial statement data of Xi Supplies Inc. as at December 31, 2017, include the following items:

Cash	$ 53,000
Accounts receivable, net	127,000
Inventories	251,000
Prepaid expenses	10,000
Total assets	922,000
Short-term notes payable	80,000
Accounts payable	91,000
Accrued liabilities	64,000
Long-term liabilities	248,000
Net income	147,000
Number of common shares outstanding	44,000 shares

Required

1. Compute Xi Supplies Inc.'s current ratio, debt ratio, and earnings per share. Round all ratios to two decimal places.

2. Compute each of the three ratios after evaluating the effect of each transaction that follows. Consider each transaction *separately*.

   a. Borrowed $100,000 on a long-term note payable.
   b. Issued 12,000 common shares on January 2, 2018, receiving cash of $180,000.
   c. Received cash on account, $29,000.
   d. Paid short-term notes payable, $50,000.
   e. Purchased merchandise costing $62,000 on account, debiting Inventory.
   f. Paid long-term liabilities, $15,000.
   g. Declared, but did not pay, a $40,000 cash dividend on the common shares.

Set up a table in the following format for your answers:

Transaction	Current Ratio	Debt Ratio	Earnings per Share

Problem 18–5B

Comparative financial statement data of Avenger Hardware Ltd. are as follows:

Using ratios to evaluate a share investment

④

AVENGER HARDWARE LTD.
Income Statement
For the Years Ended December 31, 2017 and 2016

	2017	2016
Net sales	$351,500	$310,000
Cost of goods sold	201,000	155,000
Gross margin	150,500	155,000
Operating expenses	65,000	71,000
Income from operations	85,500	84,000
Interest expense	26,000	20,000
Income before income tax	59,500	64,000
Income tax expense	19,000	22,500
Net income	$ 40,500	$ 41,500

AVENGER HARDWARE LTD.
Balance Sheet December 31, 2017 and 2016
(selected 2015 amounts given for computation of ratios)

	2017	2016	2015
Current assets:			
Cash	$ 21,000	$ 25,000	
Current receivables, net	116,000	80,500	$ 62,500
Inventories	149,000	137,000	86,000
Prepaid expenses	6,000	9,000	
Total current assets	292,000	251,500	
Property, plant, and equipment, net	154,500	143,500	
Total assets	$446,500	$395,000	351,500
Total current liabilities	$141,000	$138,500	
Long-term liabilities	114,500	121,000	
Total liabilities	255,500	259,500	
Preferred shares, $1.50	30,000	30,000	
Common shares	75,000	60,000	60,000
Retained earnings	86,000	45,500	19,000
Total liabilities and shareholders' equity	$446,500	$395,000	

Other information:

- Market price of Avenger Hardware Ltd. common shares: $19.00 at December 31, 2017, and $31.00 at December 31, 2016.

- Weighted-average number of common shares outstanding: 15,000 during 2017 and 12,000 during 2016.

- There are 2,000 preferred shares outstanding.

- All sales are on credit.

Required

1. Compute the following ratios for 2017 and 2016:

   a. Current ratio
   b. Inventory turnover
   c. Accounts receivable turnover
   d. Times-interest-earned ratio
   e. Return on assets

   f. Return on common shareholders' equity
   g. Earnings per common share
   h. Price–earnings ratio
   i. Book value per common share at year end

2. Decide (a) whether Avenger Hardware Ltd.'s ability to pay its debts and to sell inventory improved or deteriorated during 2017 and (b) whether the investment attractiveness of its common shares appears to have increased or decreased.

3. How will what you have learned in this problem help you evaluate an investment?

Problem 18–6B

Using ratio data to complete a set of financial statements
④

Incomplete and adapted versions of the financial statements of Beach Paradise Corp. follow (amounts in thousands).

Ratio data:

- Current ratio at December 31, 2017, is 0.7547.

- Inventory turnover for 2017 was 5.284.

- Debt ratio at December 31, 2017, is 0.5906.

BEACH PARADISE CORP. Income Statement For the Year Ended December 31, 2017	
Net sales	$32,548
Cost of goods sold	(a)
Gross margin	(b)
Selling and general expenses	13,624
Other expense (income)	480
Income before income tax	(c)
Income tax expense (35%)	(d)
Net income	$ (e)

BEACH PARADISE CORP. Cash Flow Statement For the Year Ended December 31, 2017	
Net cash inflow from operating activities	$ 6,640
Net cash outflow from investing activities	(2,420)
Net cash outflow from financing activities	(4,094)
Net increase (decrease) in cash during 2017	$ (n)

BEACH PARADISE CORP.
Balance Sheet
December 31, 2017 and 2016

	2017	2016
Assets		
Current assets:		
Cash	$ (f)	$ 2,528
Short-term investments	1,702	1,702
Receivables, net	3,600	2,984
Inventories	2,428	2,196
Prepaid expenses	(g)	204
Total current assets	(h)	9,614
Property, plant, and equipment, net	19,632	17,336
Total assets	$ (i)	$26,950
Liabilities		
Current liabilities	$14,204	$11,684
Long-term liabilities	(j)	4,416
Total liabilities	(k)	16,100
Shareholders' Equity		
Common shareholders' equity	(l)	10,850
Total liabilities and shareholders' equity	$ (m)	$26,950

Required   Complete the financial statements. Start with the income statement. Then go to the cash flow statement. Complete the balance sheet last.

Problem 18–7B

Excel Spreadsheet Template
Using ratios to decide between two share investments
④

Assume that you are purchasing shares in a company in the variety store and gas bar supply business. Suppose you have narrowed the choice to BFI Trading Ltd. and Lin Corp. and have assembled the following data:

Selected income statement data for the year ended December 31, 2017:

	BFI Trading Ltd.	Lin Corp.
Net sales (all on credit)	$1,060,000	$1,246,000
Cost of goods sold	602,000	722,000
Income from operations	186,000	202,000
Interest expense	40,000	10,000
Net income	82,000	124,000

Selected balance sheet and market price data for the year ended December 31, 2017:

	BFI Trading Ltd.	Lin Corp.
Current assets:		
Cash	$134,000	$110,000
Short-term investments	0	24,000
Current receivables, net	312,000	392,000
Inventories	424,000	448,000
Prepaid expenses	24,000	28,000
Total current assets	894,000	1,002,000
Total assets	2,070,000	2,344,000
Total current liabilities	748,000	800,000
Total liabilities	1,444,000	1,508,000
Preferred shares, $10.00 (300 shares)	60,000	
Common shares (75,000 shares)		450,000
Common shares (10,000 shares)	100,000	
Total shareholders' equity	626,000	836,000
Market price per common share	$84.00	$55.00

Selected balance sheet data at January 1, 2017:

	BFI Trading Ltd.	Lin Corp.
Current receivables, net	$ 330,000	$ 280,000
Inventories	448,000	470,000
Total assets	1,970,000	1,720,000
Preferred shareholders' equity, $10.00 (300 shares)	60,000	
Common shares (75,000 shares)		450,000
Common shares (10,000 shares)	100,000	
Total shareholders' equity	560,000	720,000

Your investment strategy is to purchase the shares of companies that have low price–earnings ratios but appear to be in good shape financially. Assume you have analyzed all other factors, and your decision depends on the results of the ratio analysis to be performed.

Required Compute the following ratios for both companies for the current year and decide which company's shares better fit your investment strategy:

a. Current ratio
b. Acid-test ratio
c. Inventory turnover
d. Days' sales in receivables
e. Debt ratio
f. Times-interest-earned ratio
g. Return on net sales

h. Return on total assets
i. Return on common shareholders' equity
j. Earnings per common share
k. Book value per common share
l. Price–earnings ratio

Problem 18–8B

Jens Hardware Inc.'s financial statements for the year ended December 31, 2017, are shown below:

Preparing a horizontal and vertical analysis of a financial statement, computing the standard financial ratios used for decision making, using ratios in decision making

① ② ④

JENS HARDWARE INC.
Balance Sheet
December 31, 2017 and 2016

	2017	2016
Assets		
Cash	$ 21,600	$ 15,600
Accounts receivable	33,050	21,000
Merchandise inventory	38,000	42,000
Prepaid expenses	1,000	1,500
Property, plant, and equipment	170,000	157,000
Accumulated amortization	(34,000)	(24,000)
Goodwill	15,000	15,000
Total assets	$244,650	$228,100
Liabilities		
Accounts payable	$ 15,000	$ 18,500
Notes payable (due in 30 days)	2,000	3,500
Mortgage payable	40,000	45,000
Total liabilities	57,000	67,000
Shareholders' equity		
Preferred shares (8,000 shares; $2.00, callable at $15.00 per share)	48,000	48,000
Common shares (2017—12,000 shares; 2016—8,000 shares)	81,000	65,000
Retained earnings	58,650	48,100
Total shareholders' equity	187,650	161,100
Total liabilities and shareholders' equity	$244,650	$228,100

JENS HARDWARE INC.
Income Statement
For the Year Ended December 31, 2017

Net sales	$330,000
Cost of goods sold	190,000
Gross margin	140,000
Operating expenses:	
Selling expenses	40,000
Administrative expenses	23,000
Interest expense	6,000
Total operating expenses	69,000
Operating income	71,000
Income taxes (30%)	21,300
Net income	$ 49,700

JENS HARDWARE INC.		
Statement of Retained Earnings		
For the Year Ended December 31, 2017		
Retained earnings, January 1, 2017		$48,100
Add net income for 2017		49,700
		97,800
Less dividends: Preferred	$16,000	
Common	23,150	39,150
Retained earnings, December 31, 2017		$58,650

Required

1. Perform a horizontal analysis of the comparative balance sheets. Comment on the analysis.

2. Perform a vertical analysis of the income statement. The industry standards are a gross margin of 45 percent and net income of 15 percent. Comment on the analysis.

3. Calculate each of the following ratios for the year ended December 31, 2017. The industry standards are provided in parentheses for some of the ratios.

   a. Current ratio (2:1)
   b. Acid-test ratio
   c. Inventory turnover
   d. Days' sales in receivables
   e. Debt ratio (0.47)
   f. Times-interest-earned ratio
   g. Rate of return on net sales

   h. Rate of return on total assets
   i. Rate of return on common shareholders' equity
   j. Price–earnings ratio—the market price per share is $9.00 at year end, when dividends were paid (14.0)
   k. Dividend yield (4%)

4. Comment on your calculations for Jens Hardware Inc. Include comments for those ratios for which industry standards were provided.

CHALLENGE PROBLEMS

Problem 18–1C

Using horizontal analysis to assess whether a company is using improper accounting practices

(1)

Recently, newspapers carried stories about a company that fired three top executives for management fraud. The three had been using dishonest accounting practices to overstate profits, including improperly recording assets on the company's balance sheet, overstating sales, and understating cost of goods sold by inflating inventory numbers. When inventory got out of line, the executives would debit property, plant, and equipment and credit inventory to further hide their fraud.

The company had been growing at a rapid pace, outdistancing its competitors. However, there were warning signals or "red flags" that revealed that all was not well with the company and that suggested that the books might have been "cooked" to report the rapid growth. For example, sales, which were almost all on credit, grew much faster than did accounts receivable when these balances on the company's financial statements were compared with industry data. Inventory turnover was lower than that of competitors, while sales were unusually low relative to property, plant, and equipment. A final "red flag" was that management bonuses were tied to sales increases.

Required

1. Which items would be misstated in a horizontal analysis of the company's income statement? Which items would be misstated in a horizontal analysis of the company's balance sheet? Indicate the direction of the misstatement.

2. Why do you think the issue of management bonuses is considered a "red flag"?

Problem 18–2C

You are a senior staff member of a public accounting firm, and you have been asked by one of the firm's partners to discuss the impact of improper accounting practices on the financial statements of a company to new junior staff accountants. Using the information given in Problem 18–1C, use the following questions to frame your comments to the new juniors.

Understanding the impact of improper accounting practices on the financial statements of a company
④

Required

1. Sales grew faster than receivables. Would this situation create an unusually high or unusually low accounts receivable turnover?

2. Why was the fact that sales grew faster than receivables relative to other companies in the industry a "red flag"?

3. Explain why inventory turnover was too low.

4. Why was the fact that inventory turnover was low relative to other companies a "red flag"?

5. Compare the company's receivables turnover with inventory turnover. Does the comparison suggest a "red flag"? If so, what is it?

EXTENDING YOUR KNOWLEDGE

DECISION PROBLEM

Suppose you manage WinterWorld Inc., a ski and snowboard store, which lost money during the past year. Before you can set the business on a successful course, you must first analyze the company and industry data for the current year in an effort to learn what is wrong. The data appear below.

Identifying action to cut losses and establish profitability
② ④

Required On the basis of your analysis of these figures, suggest three courses of action WinterWorld Inc. should take to reduce its losses and establish profitable operations. Give your reasons for each suggestion.

Income Statement Data		
	WinterWorld Inc.	**Industry Average**
Net sales	100.0%	100.0%
Cost of sales	(61.2)	(55.4)
Gross margin	38.8	44.6
Operating expense	(40.2)	(38.6)
Operating income (loss)	(1.4)	6.0
Interest expense	(3.1)	(1.2)
Other revenue	0.8	0.4
Income (loss) before income tax	(3.7)	5.2
Income tax (expense) saving	1.3	(1.8)
Net income (loss)	(2.4)%	3.4%

Balance Sheet Data		
	WinterWorld Inc.	Industry Average
Cash and short-term investments	0.2%	8.0%
Accounts receivable	20.0	15.5
Inventory	67.1	57.5
Prepaid expenses	0.5	0.6
Total current assets	87.8	81.6
Property, plant, and equipment, net	10.2	14.4
Other assets	2.0	4.0
Total assets	100.0%	100.0%
Bank loan, 6%	18.0%	14.0%
Notes payable, short-term, 8%	6.0	0.0
Accounts payable	18.2	22.3
Accrued liabilities	6.9	8.4
Total current liabilities	49.1	44.7
Long-term debt, 8%	16.0	14.0
Total liabilities	65.1	58.7
Common shareholders' equity	34.9	41.3
Total liabilities and shareholders' equity	100.0%	100.0%

FINANCIAL STATEMENT CASE

Measuring profitability and analyzing shares as an investment
(4)

Indigo Books & Music Inc.'s 2014 annual report included a Five Year Summary of Financial Information on page 58, with data for the fiscal years ended April 3, 2010, to March 29, 2014. Portions are reproduced below.

For the years ended (millions of Canadian dollars, except share and per share data)	IFRS				Canadian GAAP
	March 29, 2014	March 30, 2013	March 31, 2012	April 2, 2011	April 3, 2010
SELECTED STATEMENTS OF EARNINGS INFORMATION					
Revenues					
Superstores	617.8	626.6	656.5	667.6	670.5
Small format stores	127.4	137.6	145.2	149.4	159.3
Online	102.0	91.9	91.3	90.6	92.2
Other	20.5	22.7	27.2	33.9	46.1
Total revenues	867.7	878.8	920.2	941.5	968.1
Adjusted EBITDA[1]	0.1	28.5	25.0	54.8	76.1
Earnings (loss) before income taxes	(26.9)	4.2	(29.3)	25.8	49.8
Net earnings (loss) and comprehensive earnings (loss)	(31.0)	4.3	66.2	(19.4)	34.9
Dividends per share	$0.33	$0.44	$0.44	$0.44	$0.40
Net earnings (loss) per common share	$(1.21)	$0.17	$3.68	$(0.23)	$1.42
SELECTED BALANCE SHEET INFORMATION					
Working capital	189.7	224.3	223.7	101.1	106.4
Total assets	512.6	569.1	591.8	510.3	519.8
Long-term debt (including current portion)	0.8	1.5	2.2	3.3	3.0
Total equity	311.7	350.3	355.6	267.4	259.0
Weighted-average number of shares outstanding	25,601,260	25,529,035	25,201,127	24,874,199	24,549,622
Common shares outstanding at end of period	25,298,239	25,297,389	25,238,414	25,140,540	24,742,915

[1] Earnings before interest, taxes, depreciation, amortization, impairment, and equity investment. Also see "Non-IFRS Financial Measures."

Required

1. Using the Five Year Summary of Financial Information, perform a four-year trend analysis of
   a. Total revenues
   b. Net earnings (loss) before income taxes
   c. Net earnings (loss) per common share

   Start with 2011 and end with 2014; use 2010 as the base year. Do not calculate anything for losses.

2. Evaluate Indigo's profitability trend during this four-year period.

IFRS MINI-CASE

Blue Jay Metals Inc. is a small Canadian manufacturer of parts used in the construction of machinery. For the year ended December 31, 2017, Blue Jay Metals prepared two sets of financial statements—one in accordance with ASPE for its Canadian business associates, the other in accordance with IFRS, which it requires for doing business overseas. It is considering adopting IFRS as a one-time change so that it no longer has to prepare two sets of statements. Excerpts from Blue Jay Metals Inc.'s financial statements appear below.

ASPE-Based Financial Statements:

BLUE JAY METALS INC.		
Consolidated Balance Sheet		
December 31, 2017 and 2016		
($ amounts in thousands)	**December 31, 2017**	**December 31, 2016**
Assets		
Cash	$ 40,000	$ 30,000
Securities	85,000	85,000
Accounts receivable, net	100,000	95,000
Inventory	375,000	370,000
Total current assets	600,000	580,000
Plant and equipment, net	600,000	520,000
Total assets	$1,200,000	$1,100,000
Liabilities		
Accounts payable	$ 100,000	$ 110,000
Bank loans	125,000	135,000
Accrued expenses	25,000	25,000
Total current liabilities	250,000	250,000
Bonds payable	500,000	450,000
Total liabilities	750,000	700,000
Shareholders' equity		
Shareholders' equity	450,000	400,000
Total liabilities and shareholders' equity	$1,200,000	$1,100,000

Key information from the 2017 Consolidated Statement of Earnings:
Net income = $91,000
Interest expense = $94,000

IFRS-Based Financial Statements:

BLUE JAY METALS INC. Consolidated Statement of Financial Position December 31, 2017 and 2016		
($ amounts in thousands)	December 31, 2017	December 31, 2016
Assets		
Non-current assets		
Investments	$ 70,000	$ 85,000
Plant and equipment, net	850,000	750,000
Total non-current assets	920,000	835,000
Current assets		
Cash	40,000	30,000
Marketable securities	5,000	3,000
Receivables, net	100,000	95,000
Inventory	375,000	370,000
Total current assets	520,000	498,000
Total assets	$1,440,000	$1,333,000
Equity and Liabilities		
Total equity	$ 680,000	$ 505,000
Non-current liabilities		
Bonds payable	500,000	550,000
Current liabilities		
Accounts payable and other	100,000	110,000
Bank loans	125,000	135,000
Accrued expenses	35,000	33,000
Total current liabilities	260,000	278,000
Total liabilities	760,000	828,000
Total equity and liabilities	$1,440,000	$1,333,000

Key information from the 2017 Consolidated Statement of Comprehensive Income:
Net Income = $31,000
Interest expense = $94,000

Notice that the presentation of the financial statements differs somewhat, as well as some of the recorded balances. These differences arise because ASPE and IFRS rules measure certain transactions differently. However, the focus of this question is the impact on ratios of using a different set of accounting rules. Investors need to understand that if two companies in the same industry are being compared, their results could be very different depending on whether IFRS or ASPE is used in the preparation of the financial information.

Required

1. Compute the following ratios for 2017 based on Blue Jay Metals' financial statements prepared in accordance with ASPE:

   a. Current ratio   b. Acid-test ratio   c. Debt ratio   d. Rate of return on total assets

2. Compute the same ratios in Requirement 1 for 2017 based on Blue Jay Metals' IFRS financial statements.

3. What effect did the different standards have on the results? Should Blue Jay Metals switch to IFRS?

1. $ change = 2017 $ amount − 2016 $ amount
% change = $ change ÷ 2016 $ amount × 100
Large or unusual changes in $ or % should be investigated.

UMOJA INC.
Horizontal Analysis of Comparative Income Statement
For the Years Ended December 31, 2017 and 2016

			Increase (Decrease)	
	2017	2016	Amount	Percent
Net sales	$275,000	$225,000	$50,000	22.2%
Expenses: Cost of goods sold	$194,000	$165,000	$29,000	17.6
Engineering, selling, and administrative expenses	54,000	48,000	6,000	12.5
Interest expense	5,000	5,000	—	—
Income tax expense	9,000	3,000	6,000	200.0
Other expense (income)	1,000	(1,000)	2,000	—*
Total expenses	263,000	220,000	43,000	19.5
Net income	$ 12,000	$ 5,000	$ 7,000	140.0%

*Percentage changes are typically not computed for shifts from a negative amount to a positive amount, and vice versa.

The net earnings increase of 140 percent occurred because the dollar amounts are quite small. Income tax expense increased 200 percent, which should be investigated.
   The horizontal analysis shows that net sales increased 22.2 percent. This percentage increase was greater than the 19.5 percent increase in total expenses, resulting in a 140 percent increase in net income. This indicates 2017 was a good year.

2. a)

	(in thousands)			
	2017	2016	2015	2014
Net sales	138%	113%	105%	100%
Net income	400%	167%	200%	100%

   b) Net income increased faster than net sales.

3. % of net sales = Each expense $ (and net income $) ÷ Net sales $

UMOJA INC.
Vertical Analysis of Comparative Income Statement
For the Years Ended December 31, 2017 and 2016

	2017		2016	
	Amount	Percent	Amount	Percent
Net sales	$275,000	100.0%	$225,000	100.0%
Expenses: Cost of goods sold	$194,000	70.5	$165,000	73.3
Engineering, selling, and administrative expenses	54,000	19.6	48,000	21.3
Interest expense	5,000	1.8	5,000	2.2
Income tax expense	9,000	3.3	3,000	1.4*
Other expense (income)	1,000	0.4	(1,000)	(0.4)
Total expenses	263,000	95.6	220,000	97.8
Net income	$ 12,000	4.4%	$ 5,000	2.2%

*Number rounded up.

The vertical analysis shows decreases in the percentages of net sales consumed by
- Cost of goods sold (from 73.3 percent in 2016 to 70.5 percent in 2017)
- Engineering, selling, and administrative expenses (from 21.3 percent in 2016 to 19.6 percent in 2017).

These two items are Umoja Inc.'s largest dollar expenses, so their percentage decreases are important positive changes.

In addition, the 2017 net income rose to 4.4 percent of sales, compared with 2.2 percent the preceding year. The analysis shows that 2017 was significantly better than 2016.

4.

Common-Size Income Statement of Umoja Inc. and Compet Ltd. For the Year Ended December 31, 2017	UMOJA INC.	COMPET LTD.
Net sales	100.0%	100.0%
Expenses: Cost of goods sold	70.5	68.1
Engineering, selling, and administrative expenses	19.6	17.2
Interest expense	1.8	5.2
Income tax expense	3.3	4.0
Other expense (income)	0.4	0.3
Total expenses	95.6	94.8
Net income	4.4%	5.2%

Umoja Inc.'s results are similar to those of Compet Ltd., although they are, in general, not quite as good. Umoja's cost of goods sold and engineering, selling, and administrative expenses are slightly higher than Compet's, perhaps reflecting efficiencies that Compet might have from being a larger company (its sales are more than twice those of Umoja's). Except for interest expense, Compet's expenses as a proportion of net sales are not as great as Umoja's. Compet's net income percentage would have been almost double that of Umoja if Compet did not have such a high proportion of interest expenses. As a result of this benchmarking against a competitor, Umoja should explore ways to further reduce its cost of goods sold and engineering, selling, and administrative expenses to improve its future performance.

5.

Ratio	Liquidity	Efficiency	Solvency	Profitability
Return on common shareholders' equity				✓
Inventory turnover		✓		
Current ratio	✓			
Debt ratio			✓	
Acid-test ratio	✓			
Accounts receivable turnover		✓		
Return on net sales				✓

6.

Situation	Positive change	Negative change
A decrease in return on equity		✓
A decrease in days' sales in inventory	✓	
An increase in the debt ratio*		✓
An increase in acid-test ratio	✓	
A decrease in receivables turnover		✓

*This could also be a positive change depending on a company's situation. If there was too little debt then more might mean they can use leverage to their advantage.

7.
a) Current ratio:

$$2017: \frac{\$50,000 + \$27,000 + \$128,000 + \$237,000}{\$295,000} = 1.50$$

$$2016: \frac{\$47,000 + \$124,000 + \$272,000}{\$202,000} = 2.19$$

b) Acid-test ratio:

$$2017: \frac{\$50,000 + \$27,000 + \$128,000}{\$295,000} = 0.69$$

$$2016: \frac{\$47,000 + \$124,000}{\$202,000} = 0.85$$

c) Debt ratio:

$$2017: \frac{\$295,000 + \$44,000}{\$480,000} = 0.71$$

$$2016: \frac{\$202,000 + \$56,000}{\$490,000} = 0.53$$

d) Times-interest-earned ratio:

$$2017: \frac{\$170,000}{\$46,000} = 3.70 \text{ times}$$

$$2016: \frac{168,000}{33,000} = 5.09 \text{ times}$$

Summary: The company's ability to pay its current liabilities has deteriorated based on the comparison of the current and acid-test ratios from 2017 to 2016. The ability to cover long-term debt has also deteriorated, as evidenced by the higher debt ratio and the lower times-interest-earned ratio in 2017 compared to 2016.

COMPREHENSIVE PROBLEM FOR PART 4

ANALYZING A COMPANY FOR ITS INVESTMENT POTENTIAL

AltaGas Ltd., a Canadian energy infrastructure company, included a five-year summary of its operating and financial record highlights on its website (www.altagas.ca). Selected information is shown below.

Required

Analyze the company's Financial Highlights for the fiscal years 2009 to 2013. Include the following sections in your analysis and explain if you think this business is doing well or not:

- Trend analysis (use 2009 as the base year): Analyses for net revenue, net income, total assets, and shareholders' equity are suggested.

- Profitability analysis: Returns on sales, return on equity, and earnings per share would be key.

($ millions except per-share amounts)	2013	2012	2011	2010	2009
Income Statement[1]					
Net Revenue[2]	960.2	664.4	513.1	504.8	456.6
EBITDA[2]	538.9	319.4	257.2	234.9	251.5
EBITDA per basic share	$4.64	$3.36	$3.06	$2.88	$3.20
Operating income[2]	360.1	214.1	175.1	152.1	174.3
Net income	181.5	101.8	82.7	117.0	141.3
Net income per basic share	$1.56	$1.07	$0.98	$1.43	$1.80
Dividends declared per share	$1.50	$1.40	$1.34	$0.66	
Balance Sheet					
Capital assets	4,952.5	3,949.2	2,486.1	1,923.50	1,857.1
Intangible assets	195.3	189.8	177.5	80.0	128.9
Total assets	7,281.3	5,932.4	3,556.2	2,743.10	2,628.90
Short-term debt	84.4	66.9	16.8	9.5	14.5
Long-term debt	2,925.7	2,626.1	1,214.3	903.0	1,000.10
Shareholders' equity	2,791.7	1,959.8	1,355.4	1,209.90	1,048.90
Ratios (percent)					
Return on average equity	9.4	7.8	8.0	9.44	13.6
Return on average invested capital	8.5	7.7	8.5	8.23	10.0

Notes:

(1) Columns may not add due to rounding

(2) Non-GAAP financial measure. See discussion in previous public disclosures available on this website or our SEDAR profile page.

Portions of Indigo's 2014 Annual Report are reproduced here. The information here is needed to complete each chapter's Financial Statement Case 1. To download your own copy of the full annual report, please go to the Chapter Resources section of MyAccountingLab. In addition, the TELUS 2013 Annual Report is available there, which is needed to complete the Financial Statement Case 2 in each chapter.

ANNUAL REPORT
FOR THE 52-WEEK PERIOD ENDED MARCH 29, 2014

"We are what we repeatedly do. Excellence, then, is not an act, but a habit."

— *Aristotle*

Enrich your life™

Indigo   Chapters   Coles   indigo.ca

Report of the CEO

Dear Shareholder,

In this note last year, I confirmed that we were in the early stages of a journey that is taking us from our position as Canada's leading bookseller to our vision of becoming the world's first cultural department store. 2013/14 was the year in which we made a very meaningful financial commitment to accelerate our transformation, positioning ourselves for real growth in the years ahead.

Over the course of this year we launched 37 Indigotech™ shops and meaningfully enhanced the lifestyle merchandising in almost all of our large format stores. At the same time, we made effective advances in the merchandising of our book experience reinforcing our commitment to booklovers, writers and publishers who are, without doubt, at the very core of our business.

This was also the year in which we focused investment on the digital side of our business, expanding our digital marketing and merchandising capabilities and launching a five-star rated mobile app.

Finally, just after the end of the year, we launched our first two American Girl® shops within IndigoKids, reinforcing our commitment to being the leading specialty kids' book and toy retailer in the country.

Contrary to last year, when we had the benefit of the biggest blockbuster in book history as well as some very strong performing titles, this year was one in which we had no single breakout book. We also experienced some important learning curves in our lifestyle business which impacted margin in the second half of the year.

The combination of the very significant operating investments, the pressure on margin, and some non-cash accounting requirements impacting us, result in a challenged bottom line.

I want to highlight that we are focused and committed to returning to full growth and profitability; that said, I am fully convinced that both the decisions we made and the learning in the Company are key ingredients to achieve these objectives.

In a time of industry transformation, investing to reposition is the key to success. It is also satisfying to know that as we invest in our future, we have the strength on our balance sheet to comfortably support our efforts. Even with these significant operating investments Indigo remains in a very healthy financial position.

As the year came to a close and even more so now that we are into our new year – there are several key indicators that our strategy is gaining real traction. For the first time since the advent of eReading we are seeing growth in our core book business – and not driven by a big hit but rather by efforts from our book team to create a great experience for readers both in our stores and online. We are also seeing growth in every one of our lifestyle categories (gift, paper and toys) both in sales and in margin. It is truly energizing to see our customers responding so well to what we are doing.

That said, going through a transformation is no easy task. It requires a clear vision, tenacity, incredible dedication from everyone on the team, and the willingness to take risks, make mistakes, course correct and push forward. We are totally up to the challenge.

We have a clear path forward and firm conviction that we are on the right track – one which will see Indigo grow customer affection and deliver meaningfully to both our shareholders and our employees.

As always, we have, over the course of the year, continued to support the tremendous work of the Indigo Love of Reading Foundation. This year brings to over $15.5 million the amount we have invested in high needs schools across Canada. This is a very special initiative for us – and for those we touch. It is work in which we take great pride and to which we remain fully committed. I want to thank our customers who directly, and through their support of us, allow us to change forever the lives of the children we touch.

In closing, I want to take this opportunity to thank everyone on our team for the creativity and tremendous effort which you bring to work every day. I also want to thank our Directors and Shareholders for their continued support.

I look forward to reporting on our progress quarter-over-quarter and in this Letter next year.

Heather Reisman

Heather Reisman
Chair and Chief Executive Officer

Management's Responsibility for Financial Reporting

Management of Indigo Books & Music Inc. ("Indigo") is responsible for the preparation and integrity of the consolidated financial statements as well as the information contained in this report. The following consolidated financial statements of Indigo have been prepared in accordance with International Financial Reporting Standards, which involve management's best judgments and estimates based on available information.

Indigo's accounting procedures and related systems of internal control are designed to provide reasonable assurance that its assets are safeguarded and its financial records are reliable. In recognizing that the Company is responsible for both the integrity and objectivity of the consolidated financial statements, management is satisfied that the consolidated financial statements have been prepared according to and within reasonable limits of materiality and that the financial information throughout this report is consistent with these consolidated financial statements.

Ernst & Young LLP, Chartered Accountants, Licensed Public Accountants, serve as Indigo's auditors. Ernst & Young's report on the accompanying consolidated financial statements follows. Their report outlines the extent of their examination as well as an opinion on the consolidated financial statements. The Board of Directors of Indigo, along with the management team, have reviewed and approved the consolidated financial statements and information contained within this report.

Heather Reisman
Chair and Chief Executive Officer

Kay Brekken
Chief Financial Officer

Independent Auditors' Report

We have audited the accompanying consolidated financial statements of Indigo Books & Music Inc., which comprise the consolidated balance sheets as at March 29, 2014, March 30, 2013, and April 1, 2012, and the consolidated statements of earnings (loss) and comprehensive earnings (loss), changes in equity and cash flows for the 52 week periods then ended March 29, 2014 and March 30, 2013 and a summary of significant accounting policies and other explanatory information.

Management's responsibility for the consolidated financial statements

Management is responsible for the preparation and fair presentation of these consolidated financial statements in accordance with International Financial Reporting Standards, and for such internal control as management determines is necessary to enable the preparation of consolidated financial statements that are free from material misstatement, whether due to fraud or error.

Auditors' responsibility

Our responsibility is to express an opinion on these consolidated financial statements based on our audits. We conducted our audits in accordance with Canadian generally accepted auditing standards. Those standards require that we comply with ethical requirements and plan and perform the audit to obtain reasonable assurance about whether the consolidated financial statements are free from material misstatement.

An audit involves performing procedures to obtain audit evidence about the amounts and disclosures in the consolidated financial statements. The procedures selected depend on the auditors' judgment, including the assessment of the risks of material misstatement of the consolidated financial statements, whether due to fraud or error. In making those risk assessments, the auditors consider internal control relevant to the entity's preparation and fair presentation of the consolidated financial statements in order to design audit procedures that are appropriate in the circumstances, but not for the purpose of expressing an opinion on the effectiveness of the entity's internal control. An audit also includes evaluating the appropriateness of accounting policies used and the reasonableness of accounting estimates made by management, as well as evaluating the overall presentation of the consolidated financial statements.

We believe that the audit evidence we have obtained in our audits is sufficient and appropriate to provide a basis for our audit opinion.

Opinion

In our opinion, the consolidated financial statements present fairly, in all material respects, the financial position of Indigo Books & Music Inc. as at March 29, 2014, March 30, 2013 and April 1, 2012 and its financial performance and its cash flows for the 52 week periods then ended March 29, 2014 and March 30, 2013 in accordance with International Financial Reporting Standards.

Ernst & Young LLP

Toronto, Canada
May 27, 2014

Chartered Accountants
Licensed Public Accountants

Consolidated Balance Sheets

(thousands of Canadian dollars)	As at March 29, 2014	As at March 30, 2013 restated (notes 4 and 22)	As at April 1, 2012 restated (notes 4 and 22)
ASSETS			
Current			
Cash and cash equivalents (note 6)	157,578	210,562	206,718
Accounts receivable	5,582	7,126	12,810
Inventories (note 7)	218,979	216,533	229,199
Prepaid expenses	5,184	4,153	3,692
Total current assets	387,323	438,374	452,419
Property, plant and equipment (note 8)	58,476	58,903	66,928
Intangible assets (note 9)	21,587	22,164	22,810
Equity investment (note 20)	598	968	961
Deferred tax assets (note 10)	44,604	48,731	48,633
Total assets	512,588	569,140	591,751
LIABILITIES AND EQUITY			
Current			
Accounts payable and accrued liabilities (note 19)	136,428	150,177	173,416
Unredeemed gift card liability (note 19)	46,827	47,169	42,711
Provisions (note 11)	928	2,168	232
Deferred revenue	12,860	13,733	11,234
Income taxes payable	–	11	65
Current portion of long-term debt (notes 12 and 18)	584	773	1,060
Total current liabilities	197,627	214,031	228,718
Long-term accrued liabilities (note 19)	2,896	4,004	5,800
Long-term provisions (note 11)	164	78	460
Long-term debt (notes 12 and 18)	227	705	1,141
Total liabilities	200,914	218,818	236,119
Equity			
Share capital (note 13)	203,812	203,805	203,373
Contributed surplus (note 14)	8,820	8,128	7,039
Retained earnings	99,042	138,389	145,220
Total equity	311,674	350,322	355,632
Total liabilities and equity	512,588	569,140	591,751

See accompanying notes

On behalf of the Board:

Heather Reisman
Director

Michael Kirby
Director

Consolidated Statements of Earnings (Loss) and Comprehensive Earnings (Loss)

(thousands of Canadian dollars, except per share data)	52-week period ended March 29, 2014	52-week period ended March 30, 2013 restated (notes 4 and 22)
Revenues	867,668	878,785
Cost of sales	(493,955)	(495,099)
Gross profit	373,713	383,686
Operating, selling and administrative expenses (notes 8, 9 and 15)	(403,693)	(383,319)
Operating profit (loss)	(29,980)	367
Interest on long-term debt and financing charges	(95)	(101)
Interest income on cash and cash equivalents	2,377	2,609
Share of earnings from equity investment (note 20)	789	1,315
Earnings (loss) before income taxes	(26,909)	4,190
Income tax recovery (expense) (note 10)		
Current	37	–
Deferred	(4,127)	98
Net earnings (loss) and comprehensive earnings (loss) for the period	(30,999)	4,288
Net earnings (loss) per common share (note 16)		
Basic	$(1.21)	$0.17
Diluted	$(1.21)	$0.17

See accompanying notes

Consolidated Statements of Changes in Equity

(thousands of Canadian dollars)	Share Capital	Contributed Surplus	Retained Earnings	Total Equity
Balance, March 31, 2012	203,373	7,039	145,220	355,632
Earnings for the 52-week period ended March 30, 2013	–	–	4,288	4,288
Exercise of options (notes 13 and 14)	417	(85)	–	332
Directors' deferred share units converted (note 13)	15	(15)	–	–
Stock-based compensation (note 14)	–	743	–	743
Directors' compensation (note 14)	–	446	–	446
Dividends paid (note 13)	–	–	(11,119)	(11,119)
Balance, March 30, 2013	203,805	8,128	138,389	350,322
Balance, March 30, 2013	203,805	8,128	138,389	350,322
Loss for the 52-week period ended March 29, 2014	–	–	(30,999)	(30,999)
Exercise of options (notes 13 and 14)	7	–	–	7
Directors' deferred share units converted (note 13)	–	–	–	–
Stock-based compensation (note 14)	–	1,242	–	1,242
Directors' compensation (note 14)	–	425	–	425
Dividends paid (note 13)	–	–	(8,348)	(8,348)
Repurchase of options (note 14)	–	(975)	–	(975)
Balance, March 29, 2014	203,812	8,820	99,042	311,674

See accompanying notes

Consolidated Statements of Cash Flows

(thousands of Canadian dollars)	52-week period ended March 29, 2014	52-week period ended March 30, 2013 restated (notes 4 and 22)
CASH FLOWS FROM OPERATING ACTIVITIES		
Net earnings (loss) for the period	(30,999)	4,288
Add (deduct) items not affecting cash		
Depreciation of property, plant and equipment (note 8)	16,358	17,638
Amortization of intangible assets (note 9)	11,123	10,245
Net impairment of capital assets (note 8)	2,604	250
Loss on disposal of capital assets	302	65
Stock-based compensation (note 14)	1,242	743
Directors' compensation (note 14)	425	446
Deferred tax assets (note 10)	4,127	(98)
Other	(206)	(482)
Net change in non-cash working capital balances (note 17)	(19,196)	1,089
Interest on long-term debt and financing charges	95	101
Interest income on cash and cash equivalents	(2,377)	(2,609)
Income taxes received	26	32
Share of earnings from equity investment (note 20)	(789)	(1,315)
Cash flows from (used in) operating activities	(17,265)	30,393
CASH FLOWS FROM INVESTING ACTIVITIES		
Purchase of property, plant and equipment (note 8)	(18,700)	(9,441)
Addition of intangible assets (note 9)	(10,546)	(9,621)
Distributions from equity investment (note 20)	1,159	1,308
Interest received	2,463	2,691
Cash flows used in investing activities	(25,624)	(15,063)
CASH FLOWS FROM FINANCING ACTIVITIES		
Notes payable (note 21)	–	190
Repayment of long-term debt	(814)	(1,200)
Interest paid	(110)	(160)
Proceeds from share issuances (note 13)	7	332
Dividends paid (note 13)	(8,348)	(11,119)
Repurchase of options (note 14)	(975)	–
Cash flows used in financing activities	(10,240)	(11,957)
Effect of foreign currency exchange rate changes on cash and cash equivalents	145	471
Net increase (decrease) in cash and cash equivalents during the period	(52,984)	3,844
Cash and cash equivalents, beginning of period	210,562	206,718
Cash and cash equivalents, end of period	157,578	210,562

See accompanying notes

Notes to Consolidated Financial Statements

March 29, 2014

1. CORPORATE INFORMATION

Indigo Books & Music Inc. (the "Company" or "Indigo") is a corporation domiciled and incorporated under the laws of the Province of Ontario in Canada. The Company's registered office is located at 468 King Street West, Toronto, Ontario, M5V 1L8, Canada. The consolidated financial statements of the Company comprise the Company, its equity investment in Calendar Club of Canada Limited Partnership ("Calendar Club"), and its wholly-owned subsidiary, Soho Inc. The Company is the ultimate parent of the consolidated organization.

2. NATURE OF OPERATIONS

Indigo is Canada's largest book, gift and specialty toy retailer and was formed as a result of an amalgamation of Chapters Inc. and Indigo Books & Music, Inc. under the laws of the Province of Ontario, pursuant to a Certificate of Amalgamation dated August 16, 2001. The Company operates a chain of retail bookstores across all ten provinces and one territory in Canada, including 95 superstores (2013 – 97) under the *Chapters*, *Indigo* and the *World's Biggest Bookstore* names, as well as 131 small format stores (2013 – 134) under the banners *Coles*, *Indigo*, *Indigospirit*, *SmithBooks*, and *The Book Company*. Subsequent to year end, the Company closed the *World's Biggest Bookstore*. In addition, the Company operates *indigo.ca*, an e-commerce retail destination which sells books, gifts, toys, and paper products. The Company also operates seasonal kiosks and year-round stores in shopping malls across Canada through Calendar Club.

The Company's operations are focused on the merchandising of products and services in Canada. As such, the Company presents one operating segment in its consolidated financial statements.

Indigo also has a separate registered charity under the name Indigo Love of Reading Foundation (the "Foundation"). The Foundation provides new books and learning material to high-needs elementary schools across the country through donations from Indigo, its customers, suppliers, and employees.

3. BASIS OF PREPARATION

Statement of compliance

These consolidated financial statements have been prepared in accordance with International Financial Reporting Standards ("IFRS") as issued by the International Accounting Standards Board ("IASB") and using the accounting policies described herein.

These consolidated financial statements were approved by the Company's Board of Directors on May 27, 2014.

Use of judgment

The preparation of the consolidated financial statements in conformity with IFRS requires the Company to make judgments, apart from those involving estimation, in applying accounting policies that affect the recognition and measurement of assets, liabilities, revenues, and expenses. Actual results may differ from the judgments made by the Company. Information about judgments that have the most significant effect on recognition and measurement of assets, liabilities, revenues, and expenses are discussed below. Information about significant estimates is discussed in the following section.

Impairment

An impairment loss is recognized for the amount by which the carrying amount of an asset or a cash-generating unit ("CGU") exceeds its recoverable amount. The Company uses judgment when identifying CGUs and when assessing for indicators of impairment.

Intangible assets

Initial capitalization of intangible asset costs is based on the Company's judgment that technological and economic feasibility are confirmed and the project will generate future economic benefits by way of estimated future discounted cash flows that are being generated.

Leases

The Company uses judgment in determining whether a lease qualifies as a finance lease arrangement that transfers substantially all the risks and rewards incidental to ownership.

Deferred tax assets

The recognition of deferred tax assets is based on the Company's judgment. The assessment of the probability of future taxable income in which deferred tax assets can be utilized is based on management's best estimate of future taxable income that the Company expects to achieve from reviewing its latest forecast. This estimate is adjusted for significant non-taxable income and expenses and for specific limits to the use of any unused tax loss or credit. Deferred tax assets are recognized to the extent that it is probable that taxable profit will be available against which the deductible temporary differences and the carryforward of unused tax credits and unused tax losses can be utilized. Any difference between the gross deferred tax asset and the amount recognized is recorded on the balance sheet as a valuation allowance. If the valuation allowance decreases as the result of subsequent events, the previously recognized valuation allowance will be reversed. The recognition of deferred tax assets that are subject to certain legal or economic limits or uncertainties are assessed individually by the Company based on the specific facts and circumstances.

Use of estimates

The preparation of the consolidated financial statements in conformity with IFRS requires the Company to make estimates and assumptions in applying accounting policies that affect the recognition and measurement of assets, liabilities, revenues, and expenses. Actual results may differ from the estimates made by the Company, and actual results will seldom equal estimates. Information about estimates that have the most significant effect on the recognition and measurement of assets, liabilities, revenues, and expenses are discussed below.

Revenues

The Company recognizes revenue from unredeemed gift cards ("gift card breakage") if the likelihood of gift card redemption by the customer is considered to be remote. The Company estimates its average gift card breakage rate based on historical redemption rates. The resulting revenue is recognized over the estimated period of redemption based on historical redemption patterns commencing when the gift cards are sold.

The Indigo plum rewards program ("Plum") allows customers to earn points on their purchases. The fair value of Plum points is calculated by multiplying the number of points issued by the estimated cost per point. The estimated cost per point is based on many factors, including the expected future redemption patterns and associated costs. On an ongoing basis, the Company monitors trends in redemption patterns (redemption at each reward level), historical redemption rates (points redeemed as a percentage of points issued) and net cost per point redeemed, adjusting the estimated cost per point based upon expected future activity. Points revenue is included with total revenues in the Company's consolidated statements of earnings (loss) and comprehensive earnings (loss).

Inventories

The future realization of the carrying amount of inventory is affected by future sales demand, inventory levels, and product quality. At each balance sheet date, the Company reviews its on-hand inventory and uses historical trends and current inventory mix to determine a reserve for the impact of future markdowns which will take the net realizable value of inventory on-hand below cost. Inventory valuation also incorporates a write-down to reflect future losses on the disposition of obsolete merchandise. The Company reduces inventory for estimated shrinkage that has occurred between physical inventory counts and the end of the fiscal year based on historical experience as a percentage of sales. In addition, the Company records a vendor settlement accrual to cover any disputes between the Company and its vendors. The Company estimates this reserve based on historical experience of settlements with its vendors.

Share-based payments

The cost of equity-settled transactions with counterparties is based on the Company's estimate of the fair value of share-based instruments and the number of equity instruments that will eventually vest. The Company's estimated fair value of the share-based instruments is calculated using the following variables: risk-free interest rate; expected volatility; expected time until exercise; and expected dividend yield. Risk-free interest rate is based on Government of Canada bond yields, while all other variables are estimated based on the Company's historical experience with its share-based payments.

Impairment

To determine the recoverable amount of an impaired asset, the Company estimates expected future cash flows at the CGU level and determines a suitable discount rate in order to calculate the present value of those cash flows. In the process of measuring expected future cash flows, the Company makes assumptions about future sales, gross margin rates, expenses, capital expenditures, and working capital investments which are based upon past and expected future performance. Determining the applicable discount rate involves estimating appropriate adjustments to market risk and to Company-specific risk factors.

Property, plant and equipment and intangible assets (collectively, "capital assets")

Capital assets are depreciated over their useful lives, taking into account residual values where appropriate. Assessments of useful lives and residual values are performed annually and take into consideration factors such as technological innovation, maintenance programs, and relevant market information. In assessing residual values, the Company considers the remaining life of the asset, its projected disposal value, and future market conditions.

4. SIGNIFICANT ACCOUNTING POLICIES

The accounting policies set out below have been applied consistently to all periods presented in these consolidated financial statements.

Basis of measurement

The Company's consolidated financial statements are prepared on the historical cost basis of accounting, except as disclosed in the accounting policies set out below.

Basis of consolidation

The consolidated financial statements comprise the financial statements of the Company and entities controlled by the Company. Control exists when the Company is exposed to, or has the right to, variable returns from its involvement with the controlled entity and when the Company has the current ability to affect those returns through its power over the controlled entity. When the Company does not own all of the equity in a subsidiary, the non-controlling interest is disclosed as a separate line item in the consolidated balance sheets and the earnings accruing to non-controlling interest holders is disclosed as a separate line item in the consolidated statements of earnings (loss) and comprehensive earnings (loss).

The financial statements of the subsidiary are prepared for the same reporting period as the parent company, using consistent accounting policies. Subsidiaries are fully consolidated from the date of acquisition, being the date on which the Company obtains control, and continue to be consolidated until the date that such control ceases. All intercompany balances and transactions and any unrealized gains and losses arising from intercompany transactions are eliminated in preparing these consolidated financial statements.

Equity investment

The equity method of accounting is applied to investments in companies where Indigo has the ability to exert significant influence over the financial and operating policy decisions of the company but lacks control or joint control over those policies. Under the equity method, the Company's investment is initially recognized at cost and subsequently increased or decreased to recognize the Company's share of earnings and losses of the investment, and for impairment losses after the initial recognition date. The Company's share of losses that are in excess of its investment are recognized only to the extent that the Company has incurred legal or constructive obligations or made payments on behalf of the company. The Company's share of earnings and losses of its equity investment are recognized through profit or loss during the period. Cash distributions received from the investment are accounted for as a reduction in the carrying amount of the Company's equity investment.

Cash and cash equivalents

Cash and cash equivalents consist of cash on hand, balances with banks, and highly liquid investments that are readily convertible to known amounts of cash with maturities of three months or less at the date of acquisition. Cash is considered to be restricted when it is subject to contingent rights of a third-party customer, vendor, or government agency.

Inventories

Inventories are valued at the lower of cost, determined on a moving average cost basis, and market, being net realizable value. Costs include all direct and reasonable expenditures that are incurred in bringing inventories to their present location and condition. Net realizable value is the estimated selling price in the ordinary course of business. When the Company permanently reduces the retail price of an item and the markdown incurred brings the retail price below the cost of the item, there is a corresponding reduction in inventory recognized in the period. Vendor rebates are recorded as a reduction in the price of the products, and corresponding inventories are recorded net of vendor rebates.

Prepaid expenses

Prepaid expenses include store supplies, rent, license fees, maintenance contracts, and insurance. Store supplies are expensed as they are used while other costs are amortized over the term of the contract.

Income taxes

Current income taxes are the expected taxes payable or receivable on the taxable earnings or loss for the period. Current income taxes are payable on taxable earnings for the period as calculated under Canadian taxation guidelines, which differs from taxable earnings under IFRS. Calculation of current income taxes is based on tax rates and tax laws that have been enacted, or substantively enacted, by the end of the reporting period. Current income taxes relating to items recognized directly in equity are recognized in equity and not in the consolidated statements of earnings (loss) and comprehensive earnings (loss).

Deferred income taxes are calculated at the reporting date using the liability method based on temporary differences between the carrying amounts of assets and liabilities and their tax bases. However, deferred tax assets and liabilities on temporary differences arising from the initial recognition of goodwill, or of an asset or liability in a transaction that is not a business combination, will not be recognized when neither accounting nor taxable profit or loss are affected at the time of the transaction.

Deferred tax assets arising from temporary differences associated with investments in subsidiaries are provided for if it is probable that the differences will reverse in the foreseeable future and taxable profit will be available against which the tax assets may be utilized. Deferred tax assets on temporary differences associated with investments in subsidiaries are not provided for if the timing of the reversal of these temporary differences can be controlled by the Company and it is probable that reversal will not occur in the foreseeable future.

Deferred tax assets and liabilities are calculated, without discounting, at tax rates that are expected to apply to their respective periods of realization, provided they are enacted or substantively enacted by the end of the reporting period. Deferred tax assets and liabilities are offset only when the Company has the right and intention to set off current tax assets and liabilities from the same taxable entity and the same taxation authority.

Deferred tax assets are recognized to the extent that it is probable that taxable profit will be available against which the deductible temporary differences and the carryforward of unused tax credits and unused tax losses can be utilized. Any difference between the gross deferred tax asset and the amount recognized is recorded on the balance sheet as a valuation allowance. If the valuation allowance decreases as the result of subsequent events, the previously recognized valuation allowance will be reversed.

Property, plant and equipment

All items of property, plant and equipment are initially recognized at cost, which includes any costs directly attributable to bringing the asset to the location and condition necessary for it to be capable of operating in the manner intended by the Company. Subsequent to initial recognition, property, plant and equipment assets are shown at cost less accumulated depreciation and any accumulated impairment losses.

Depreciation of an asset begins once it becomes available for use. The depreciable amount of an asset, being the cost of an asset less the residual value, is allocated on a straight-line basis over the estimated useful life of the asset. Residual value is estimated to be zero unless the Company expects to dispose of the asset at a value that exceeds the estimated disposal costs. The residual values, useful lives, and depreciation methods applied to assets are reviewed annually based on relevant market information and management considerations.

The following useful lives are applied:

Furniture, fixtures and equipment	5 – 10 years
Computer equipment	3 – 5 years
Equipment under finance leases	3 – 5 years
Leasehold improvements	over the lease term and probable renewal periods to a maximum of 10 years

Items of property, plant and equipment are assessed for impairment as detailed in the accounting policy note on impairment and are derecognized either upon disposal or when no future economic benefits are expected from their use. Any gain or loss arising on derecognition is included in earnings when the asset is derecognized.

Leased assets

Leases are classified as finance leases when the terms of the lease transfer substantially all the risks and rewards related to ownership of the leased asset to the Company. At lease inception, the related asset is recognized at the lower of the fair value of the leased asset or the present value of the lease payments. The corresponding liability amount is recognized as long-term debt.

Depreciation methods and useful lives for assets held under finance lease agreements correspond to those applied to comparable assets which are legally owned by the Company. If there is no reasonable certainty that the Company will obtain ownership of the financed asset at the end of the lease term, the asset is depreciated over the shorter of its estimated useful life or the lease term. The corresponding long-term debt is reduced by lease payments less interest paid. Interest payments are expensed as part of interest on long-term debt and financing charges on the consolidated statements of earnings (loss) and comprehensive earnings (loss) over the period of the lease. As at March 29, 2014, computer equipment assets are the only type of asset leased under finance lease arrangements.

All other leases are treated as operating leases. Payments on operating lease agreements are recognized as an expense on a straight-line basis over the lease term. Associated costs, such as maintenance and insurance, are expensed as incurred.

The Company performs quarterly assessments of contracts which do not take the legal form of a lease to determine whether they convey the right to use an asset in return for a payment or series of payments and therefore need to be accounted for as leases. As at March 29, 2014, the Company had no such contracts.

Leased premises

The Company conducts all of its business from leased premises. Leasehold improvements are depreciated over the lesser of their economic life or the initial lease term plus renewal periods where renewal has been determined to be reasonably assured ("lease term"). Leasehold improvements are assessed for impairment as detailed in the accounting policy note on impairment. Leasehold improvement allowances are depreciated over the lease term. Other inducements, such as rent-free periods, are amortized into earnings over the lease term, with the unamortized portion recorded in current and long-term accounts payable and accrued liabilities. As at March 29, 2014, all of the Company's leases on premises were accounted for as operating leases. Expenses incurred for leased premises include base rent, taxes, and contingent rent based upon a percentage of sales.

Intangible assets

Intangible assets are initially recognized at cost, if acquired separately, or at fair value, if acquired as part of a business combination. After initial recognition, intangible assets are carried at cost less accumulated amortization and any accumulated impairment losses.

Amortization commences when the intangible assets are available for their intended use. The useful lives of intangible assets are assessed as either finite or indefinite. Intangible assets with finite lives are amortized over their useful economic life. Intangible assets with indefinite lives are not amortized but are reviewed at each reporting date to determine whether the indefinite life continues to be supportable. If not, the change in useful life from indefinite to finite is made on a prospective basis. Residual value is estimated to be zero unless the Company expects to dispose of the asset at a value that exceeds the estimated disposal costs. The residual values, useful lives and amortization methods applied to assets are reviewed annually based on relevant market information and management considerations.

The following useful lives are applied:

Computer application software	3 – 5 years
Internal development costs	3 years

Intangible assets are assessed for impairment as detailed in the accounting policy note on impairment. An intangible asset is derecognized either upon disposal or when no future economic benefit is expected from its use. Any gain or loss arising on derecognition is included in earnings when the asset is derecognized.

Computer application software

When computer application software is not an integral part of a related item of computer hardware, the software is treated as an intangible asset. Computer application software that is integral to the use of related computer hardware is recorded as property, plant and equipment.

Internal development costs

Costs that are directly attributable to internal development are recognized as intangible assets provided they meet the definition of an intangible asset. Development costs not meeting these criteria are expensed as incurred. Capitalized development costs include external direct costs of materials and services and the payroll and payroll-related costs for employees who are directly associated with the projects.

Impairment testing

Capital assets

For the purposes of assessing impairment, capital assets are grouped at the lowest levels for which there are largely independent cash inflows and for which a reasonable and consistent allocation basis can be identified. For capital assets which can be reasonably and consistently allocated to individual stores, the store level is used as the CGU for impairment testing. For all other capital assets, the corporate level is used as the group of CGUs. Capital assets and related CGUs or groups of CGUs are tested for impairment at each reporting date and whenever events or changes in circumstances indicate that the carrying amount may not be recoverable. Events or changes in circumstances which may indicate impairment include a significant change to the Company's operations, a significant decline in performance, or a change in market conditions which adversely affects the Company.

An impairment loss is recognized for the amount by which the carrying amount of a CGU or group of CGUs exceeds its recoverable amount. To determine the recoverable amount, management uses a value in use calculation to determine the present value of the expected future cash flows from each CGU or group of CGUs based on the CGU's estimated growth rate. The Company's growth rate and future cash flows are based on historical data and management's expectations. Impairment losses are charged pro rata to the capital assets in the CGU or group of CGUs. Capital assets and CGUs or groups of CGUs are subsequently reassessed for indicators that a previously recognized impairment loss may no longer exist. An impairment loss is reversed if the recoverable amount of the capital asset, CGU, or group of CGUs exceeds its carrying amount, but only to the extent that the carrying amount of the asset does not exceed the carrying amount that would have been determined, net of depreciation or amortization, if no impairment loss had been recognized.

Financial assets

Individually significant financial assets are tested for impairment on an individual basis. The remaining financial assets are assessed collectively in groups that share similar credit risk characteristics. Financial assets are tested for impairment at each reporting date and whenever events or changes in circumstances indicate that the carrying amount may not be recoverable. Evidence of impairment may include indications that a debtor or a group of debtors are experiencing significant financial difficulty, default or delinquency in interest or principal payments, and observable data indicating that there is a measurable decrease in the estimated future cash flows.

A financial asset is deemed to be impaired if there is objective evidence that one or more loss events having a negative effect on future cash flows of the financial asset occurs after initial recognition and the loss can be reliably measured. The impairment loss is measured as the difference between the carrying amount of the financial asset and the present value of the estimated future cash flows, discounted at the original effective interest rate. The impairment loss is recorded as an allowance and recognized in net earnings. If the impairment loss decreases as the result of subsequent events, the previously recognized impairment loss is reversed.

Provisions

Provisions are recognized when the Company has a present legal or constructive obligation as a result of past events, for which it is probable that the Company will be required to settle the obligation and a reliable estimate of the settlement can be made. The amount recognized as a provision is the best estimate of the consideration required to settle the present obligation at the end of the reporting period, taking into account risks and uncertainties of cash flow. Where the effect of discounting to present value is material, provisions are adjusted to reflect the time value of money. Examples of provisions include legal claims, onerous leases, and decommissioning liabilities.

Borrowing costs

Borrowing costs are primarily comprised of interest on the Company's long-term debt. Borrowing costs are capitalized using the effective interest rate method to the extent that they are directly attributable to the acquisition, production, or construction of qualifying assets that require a substantial period of time to get ready for their intended use or sale. All other borrowing costs are expensed as incurred and reported in the consolidated statements of earnings (loss) and comprehensive earnings (loss) as part of interest on long-term debt and finance charges.

Total equity

Share capital represents the nominal value of shares that have been issued. Retained earnings include all current and prior period retained profits. Dividend distributions payable to equity shareholders are recorded as dividends payable when the dividends have been approved by the Board of Directors prior to the reporting date.

Share-based awards

The Company has established an employee stock option plan for key employees. The fair value of each tranche of options granted is estimated on grant date using the Black-Scholes option pricing model. The Black-Scholes option pricing model is based on variables such as: risk-free interest rate; expected volatility; expected time until exercise; and expected dividend yield. Expected stock price volatility is based on the historical volatility of the Company's stock for a period approximating the expected life. The grant date fair value, net of estimated forfeitures, is recognized as an expense with a corresponding increase to contributed surplus over the vesting period. Estimates are subsequently revised if there is an indication that the number of stock options expected to vest differs from previous estimates. Any consideration paid by employees on exercise of stock options is credited to share capital with a corresponding reduction to contributed surplus.

Revenues

The Company recognizes revenue when the substantial risks and rewards of ownership pass to the customer. Revenue is measured at the fair value of consideration received or receivable by the Company for goods supplied, inclusive of amounts invoiced for shipping, and net of sales discounts, returns and amounts deferred related to the issuance of Plum points. Return allowances are estimated using historical experience. Revenue is recognized when the amount can be measured reliably, it is probable that economic benefits associated with the transaction will flow to the Company, the costs incurred or to be incurred can be measured reliably, and the criteria for each of the Company's activities (as described below) have been met.

Retail sales

Revenue for retail customers is recognized at the time of purchase.

Online sales

Revenue for online customers is recognized when the product is shipped.

Commission revenue

The Company earns commission revenue through partnerships with other companies and recognizes revenue once services have been rendered and the amount of revenue can be measured reliably.

Gift cards

The Company sells gift cards to its customers and recognizes the revenue as gift cards are redeemed. The Company also recognizes gift card breakage if the likelihood of gift card redemption by the customer is considered to be remote. The Company determines its average gift card breakage rate based on historical redemption rates. Once the breakage rate is determined, the resulting revenue is recognized over the estimated period of redemption based on historical redemption patterns, commencing when the gift cards are sold. Gift card breakage is included in revenues in the Company's consolidated statements of earnings (loss) and comprehensive earnings (loss).

Indigo irewards loyalty program

For an annual fee, the Company offers loyalty cards to customers that entitle the cardholder to receive discounts on purchases. Each card is issued with a 12-month expiry period. The fee revenue related to the issuance of a card is deferred and amortized into earnings over the expiry period, based upon historical sales volumes.

Indigo plum rewards program

Plum is a free program that allows members to earn points on their purchases in the Company's stores and enjoy member pricing at the Company's online website. Members can then redeem points for discounts on future purchases of store merchandise.

When a Plum member purchases merchandise, the Company allocates the payment received between the merchandise and the points. The payment is allocated based on the residual method, where the amount allocated to the merchandise is the total payment less the fair value of the points. The portion of revenue attributed to the merchandise is recognized at the time of purchase. Revenue attributed to the points is recorded as deferred revenue and recognized when points are redeemed.

The fair value of the points is calculated by multiplying the number of points issued by the estimated cost per point. The estimated cost per point is determined based on a number of factors, including the expected future redemption patterns and associated costs. On an ongoing basis, the Company monitors trends in redemption patterns (redemption at each reward level), historical redemption rates (points redeemed as a percentage of points issued) and net cost per point redeemed, adjusting the estimated cost per point based upon expected future activity. Points revenue is included with total revenues in the Company's consolidated statements of earnings (loss) and comprehensive earnings (loss).

Interest income

Interest income is reported on an accrual basis using the effective interest method.

Vendor rebates

The Company records cash consideration received from vendors as a reduction to the price of vendors' products. This is reflected as a reduction in cost of goods sold and related inventories when recognized in the consolidated financial statements. Certain exceptions apply where the cash consideration received is a reimbursement of incremental selling costs incurred by the Company, in which case the cash received is reflected as a reduction in operating and administrative expenses.

Earnings per share

Basic earnings per share is determined by dividing the net earnings attributable to common shareholders by the weighted average number of common shares outstanding during the period. Diluted earnings per share are calculated in accordance with the treasury stock method and are based on the weighted average number of common shares and dilutive common share equivalents outstanding during the period. The weighted average number of shares used in the computation of both basic and fully diluted earnings per share may be the same due to the anti-dilutive effect of securities.

Financial instruments

Financial assets and financial liabilities are recognized when the Company becomes a party to the contractual provisions of the financial instrument. Financial assets are derecognized when the contractual rights to the cash flows from the financial asset expire, or when the financial asset and all substantial risks and rewards are transferred. A financial liability is derecognized when it is extinguished, discharged, cancelled, or expires. Where a legally enforceable right to offset exists for recognized financial assets and financial liabilities and there is an intention to settle the liability and realize the asset simultaneously, or to settle on a net basis, such related financial assets and financial liabilities are offset.

For the purposes of ongoing measurement, financial assets and liabilities are classified according to their characteristics and management's intent. All financial instruments are initially recognized at fair value. The following methods and assumptions were used to estimate the initial fair value of each type of financial instrument by reference to market data and other valuation techniques, as appropriate:

 (i) The fair values of cash and cash equivalents, accounts receivable, and accounts payable and accrued liabilities approximate their carrying values given their short-term maturities; and

(ii) The fair value of long-term debt is estimated based on the discounted cash payments of the debt at the Company's estimated incremental borrowing rates for debt of the same remaining maturities. The fair value of long-term debt approximates its carrying value.

Embedded derivatives are separated and measured at fair value if certain criteria are met. Management has reviewed all material contracts and has determined that the Company does not currently have any significant embedded derivatives that require separate accounting and disclosure.

After initial recognition, financial instruments are subsequently measured as follows:

Financial assets

(i) Loans and receivables – These are non-derivative financial assets with fixed or determinable payments that are not quoted in an active market. These assets are measured at amortized cost, less impairment charges, using the effective interest method. Gains and losses are recognized in earnings through the amortization process or when the assets are derecognized.

(ii) Financial assets at fair value through profit or loss – These assets are held for trading if acquired for the purpose of selling in the near term or are designated to this category upon initial recognition. These assets are measured at fair value, with gains or losses recognized in earnings.

(iii) Held-to-maturity investments – These are non-derivative financial assets with fixed or determinable payments and fixed maturities which the Company intends, and is able, to hold until maturity. These assets are measured at amortized cost, less impairment charges, using the effective interest method. Gains and losses are recognized in earnings through the amortization process or when the assets are derecognized.

(iv) Available-for-sale financial assets – These are non-derivative financial assets that are either designated to this category upon initial recognition or do not qualify for inclusion in any of the other categories. These assets are measured at fair value, with unrealized gains and losses recognized in Other Comprehensive Income until the asset is derecognized or determined to be impaired. If the asset is derecognized or determined to be impaired, the cumulative gain or loss previously reported in Accumulated Other Comprehensive Income is included in earnings.

Financial liabilities

(i) Other liabilities – These liabilities are measured at amortized cost using the effective interest rate method. Gains and losses are recognized in earnings through the amortization process or when the liabilities are derecognized.

(ii) Financial liabilities at fair value through profit or loss – These liabilities are held for trading if acquired for the purpose of selling in the near term or are designated to this category upon initial recognition. These liabilities are measured at fair value, with gains or losses recognized in earnings.

The Company's financial assets and financial liabilities are generally classified and measured as follows:

Financial Asset/Liability	Category	Measurement
Cash and cash equivalents	Loans and receivables	Amortized cost
Accounts receivable	Loans and receivables	Amortized cost
Accounts payable and accrued liabilities	Other liabilities	Amortized cost
Long-term debt	Other liabilities	Amortized cost

All other balance sheet accounts are not considered financial instruments.

All financial instruments measured at fair value after initial recognition are categorized into one of three hierarchy levels for disclosure purposes. Each level reflects the significance of the inputs used in making the fair value measurements.

Level 1: Fair value is determined by reference to quoted prices in active markets.
Level 2: Valuations use inputs based on observable market data, either directly or indirectly, other than the quoted prices.
Level 3: Valuations are based on inputs that are not based on observable market data.

As at March 29, 2014, there are no financial instruments classified into these levels. The Company measures all financial instruments at amortized cost.

Retirement benefits

The Company provides retirement benefits through a defined contribution retirement plan. Under the defined contribution retirement plan, the Company pays fixed contributions to an independent entity. The Company has no legal or constructive obligations to pay further contributions after its payment of the fixed contribution. The costs of benefits under the defined contribution retirement plan are expensed as contributions are due and are reversed if employees leave before the vesting period.

Foreign currency translation

The consolidated financial statements are presented in Canadian dollars, which is the functional currency of the Company. Sales transacted in foreign currencies are aggregated monthly and translated using the average exchange rate. Transactions in foreign currencies are translated at rates of exchange at the time of the transaction. Monetary assets and liabilities denominated in foreign currencies which are held at the reporting date are translated at the closing consolidated balance sheet rate. Non-monetary items are measured at historical cost and are translated using the exchange rates at the date of the transaction. Non-monetary items measured at fair value are translated using exchange rates at the date when fair value was determined. The resulting exchange gains or losses are included in earnings.

Accounting Standards Implemented in Fiscal 2014

Adoption of these amendments and standards in fiscal 2014 impacted the Company's results of operations, financial position, and disclosures as follows:

• Joint Arrangements ("IFRS 11") replaces IAS 31, "Interests in Joint Ventures" ("IAS 31") and SIC-13, "Jointly-controlled Entities – Non-monetary Contributions by Venturers," and requires that a party in a joint arrangement assess its rights and obligations to determine the type of joint arrangement and account for those rights and obligations accordingly. Previously, the Company accounted for its interest in Calendar Club under IAS 31 using proportionate consolidation. However, the Company concluded that its interest in Calendar Club does not meet the definition of a joint arrangement under IFRS 11 and needs to be accounted for under "Investments in Associates and Joint Ventures" ("IAS 28") as a significant investment using the equity method. The Company has retrospectively restated its comparative financial statements to reclassify proportionately consolidated Calendar Club operating results into a single equity investment line. These restatements have no impact to the Company's total net earnings (loss) or cash flows. The impact of reclassification on the Company's financial statements is as follows:

(thousands of Canadian dollars)	52-week period ended March 30, 2013
Decrease in revenues	(15,272)
Decrease in expenses	(13,957)
Increase in equity investment	1,315

(thousands of Canadian dollars)	As at March 30, 2013	As at April 1, 2012
Decrease in assets	(2,074)	(1,746)
Increase in equity investment	968	961
Decrease in liabilities	(1,106)	(785)

- Amendments to Investments in Associates and Joint Ventures ("IAS 28") impact accounting for associates and joint ventures held for sale and changes in interests held in associates and joint ventures; and
- Disclosure of Interests in Other Entities ("IFRS 12") includes all of the disclosures that were previously in IAS 27, "Separate Financial Statements," IAS 31 and IAS 28, "Investments in Associates." These disclosures relate to an entity's interests in subsidiaries, joint arrangements, associates, and structured entities.

Adoption of the following amendments and standards in fiscal 2014 did not have an impact on the Company's results of operations, financial position, or disclosures:

- Amendments to Presentation of Financial Statements ("IAS 1") require companies to group together items within other comprehensive earnings which may be reclassified to net earnings. The amendments are effective for annual periods beginning on or after July 1, 2012 and were applied retrospectively;
- Amendments to Financial Instruments: Disclosures ("IFRS 7") regarding the offsetting of financial instruments. These amendments were applied retrospectively and are effective for annual periods beginning on or after January 1, 2013 and interim periods within those annual periods;
- Fair Value Measurement ("IFRS 13") provides guidance to improve consistency and comparability in fair value measurements and related disclosures through a fair value hierarchy. This standard was applied prospectively and is effective for annual periods beginning on or after January 1, 2013;
- Amendments to Separate Financial Statements ("IAS 27") remove all requirements relating to consolidated financial statements. This standard was applied retrospectively and is effective for annual periods beginning on or after January 1, 2013; and
- Consolidated Financial Statements ("IFRS 10") replaces portions of IAS 27, "Consolidated and Separate Financial Statements," supersedes SIC-12, "Consolidation – Special Purpose Entities," and establishes standards for the presentation and preparation of consolidated financial statements when an entity controls one or more entities. This standard was applied retrospectively and is effective for annual periods beginning on or after January 1, 2013.

5. NEW ACCOUNTING PRONOUNCEMENTS

Impairment of Assets ("IAS 36")

In May 2013, the IASB issued amendments to IAS 36 which require disclosures about assets or CGUs for which an impairment loss was recognized or reversed during the period. The Company will apply the amendments to IAS 36 as of the first quarter of its 2015 fiscal year. Additional information will be disclosed through notes to financial statements.

Levies ("IFRIC 21")

The IASB has issued IFRIC 21, an interpretation which provides guidance on when to recognize a liability for a levy imposed by a government, both for levies that are accounted for in accordance with IAS 37, "Provisions, Contingent Liabilities and Contingent Assets," and those where the timing and amount of the levy is certain. A levy is an outflow of resources embodying economic benefits that is imposed by governments on entities in accordance with legislation. This interpretation is applicable for annual periods beginning on or after January 1, 2014 and must be applied retrospectively. The Company will apply these amendments beginning in the first quarter of fiscal 2015. The Company is assessing the impact of the new interpretation on its consolidated financial statements.

Financial Instruments: Presentation ("IAS 32")

The IASB has issued amendments to IAS 32 that clarify its requirements for offsetting financial instruments. These amendments must be applied retrospectively and are effective for annual periods beginning on or after January 1, 2014. The Company will apply these amendments beginning in the first quarter of fiscal 2015. The Company does not expect implementation of these amendments to have a significant impact on its consolidated financial statements.

Financial Instruments ("IFRS 9")

The IASB has issued a new standard, IFRS 9, which will ultimately replace IAS 39, "Financial Instruments: Recognition and Measurement" ("IAS 39"). The replacement of IAS 39 is a multi-phase project with the objective of improving and simplifying the reporting for financial instruments. Issuance of IFRS 9 provides guidance on the classification and measurement of financial assets and financial liabilities. Due to the incomplete status of the project, the mandatory effective date of this standard has not been determined. The Company will evaluate the overall impact on its consolidated financial statements when the final standard, including all phases, is issued.

6. CASH AND CASH EQUIVALENTS

Cash and cash equivalents consist of the following:

(thousands of Canadian dollars)	March 29, 2014	March 30, 2013	April 1, 2012
Cash	57,098	88,268	86,199
Restricted cash	3,369	470	487
Cash equivalents	97,111	121,824	120,032
Cash and cash equivalents	157,578	210,562	206,718

Restricted cash represents cash pledged as collateral for letter of credit obligations issued to support the Company's purchases of offshore merchandise.

7. INVENTORIES

The cost of inventories recognized as an expense was $495.1 million in fiscal 2014 (2013 – $499.5 million). Inventories consist of the landed cost of goods sold and exclude online shipping costs, inventory shrink and damage reserve, and all vendor support programs. The amount of inventory write-downs as a result of net realizable value lower than cost was $8.6 million in fiscal 2014 (2013 – $3.9 million), and there were no reversals of inventory write-downs that were recognized in fiscal 2014 (2013 – nil). The amount of inventory with net realizable value equal to cost was $1.8 million as at March 29, 2014 (March 30, 2013 – $1.4 million; April 1, 2012 – $1.7 million).

(thousands of Canadian dollars)	Furniture, fixtures and equipment	Computer equipment	Leasehold improvements	Equipment under finance leases	Total
Gross carrying amount					
Balance, March 31, 2012	56,273	15,756	58,773	6,146	136,948
Additions	4,296	2,439	2,706	465	9,906
Transfers/reclassifications	(4)	(411)	415	–	–
Disposals	(161)	(20)	(110)	(2,976)	(3,267)
Assets with zero net book value	(5,113)	(3,279)	(5,015)	–	(13,407)
Balance, March 30, 2013	55,291	14,485	56,769	3,635	130,180
Additions	10,008	3,451	5,241	137	18,837
Transfers / reclassifications	16	(465)	449	–	–
Disposals	(478)	(217)	(208)	(948)	(1,851)
Assets with zero net book value	(2,719)	(6,174)	(7,922)	–	(16,815)
Balance, March 29, 2014	62,118	11,080	54,329	2,824	130,351
Accumulated depreciation and impairment					
Balance, March 31, 2012	25,953	8,895	31,240	3,932	70,020
Depreciation	5,208	3,092	8,129	1,209	17,638
Transfers/reclassifications	–	5	(5)	–	–
Disposals	(130)	(9)	(109)	(2,976)	(3,224)
Net impairment losses and reversals	–	–	250	–	250
Assets with zero net book value	(5,113)	(3,279)	(5,015)	–	(13,407)
Balance, March 30, 2013	25,918	8,704	34,490	2,165	71,277
Depreciation	5,422	2,631	7,495	810	16,358
Transfers / reclassifications	–	5	(5)	–	–
Disposals	(216)	(197)	(188)	(948)	(1,549)
Net impairment losses and reversals	1,007	60	1,537	–	2,604
Assets with zero net book value	(2,719)	(6,174)	(7,922)	–	(16,815)
Balance, March 29, 2014	29,412	5,029	35,407	2,027	71,875
Net carrying amount					
April 1, 2012	30,320	6,861	27,533	2,214	66,928
March 30, 2013	29,373	5,781	22,279	1,470	58,903
March 29, 2014	32,706	6,051	18,922	797	58,476

Capital assets are assessed for impairment at the CGU level, except for those capital assets which are considered to be corporate assets. As certain corporate assets cannot be allocated on a reasonable and consistent basis to individual CGUs, they are tested for impairment at the corporate level.

A CGU has been defined as an individual retail store, as each store generates cash flows that are largely independent from the cash flows of other stores. CGUs and groups of CGUs are tested for impairment if impairment indicators exist at the reporting date. Recoverable amounts for CGUs being tested are based on value in use, which is calculated from discounted cash flow projections over the remaining lease terms, plus any renewal options where renewal is likely. Corporate asset testing calculates discounted cash flow projections over a five-year period plus a terminal value.

The key assumptions from the value in use calculations are those regarding growth rates and discount rates. The cash flow projections are based on both past and forecasted performance and are extrapolated using long-term growth rates which are calculated separately for each CGU being tested. Average long-term growth rates for impairment testing ranged from 0.0% to 3.0% (2013 – 0.0% to 3.0%). Management's estimate of the discount rate reflects the current market assessment of the time value of money and the risks specific to the Company. The pre-tax and post-tax discount rates used to calculate value in use for store assets were 20.3% and 12.0%, respectively (2013 – 21.9% and 14.0%, respectively).

Impairment indicators were identified during fiscal 2014 for Indigo's retail stores and corporate assets. Accordingly, the Company performed impairment testing, which resulted in the recognition and reversal of impairment losses for Indigo's retail stores only. Impairment losses recognized were $2.6 million in fiscal 2014 (2013 – $1.3 million) and are spread across a number of CGUs. The impairment losses relate to CGUs whose carrying amounts exceed their recoverable amounts. In all cases, impairment losses arose due to stores performing at lower-than-expected profitability. There were no capital asset impairment reversals recognized in fiscal 2014 (2013 – $1.0 million). Impairment reversals arose due to improved store performance and the likelihood of lease term renewals.

9. INTANGIBLE ASSETS

(thousands of Canadian dollars)	Computer application software	Internal development costs	Total
Gross carrying amount			
Balance, March 31, 2012	23,929	12,078	36,007
Additions	5,936	3,685	9,621
Transfers / reclassifications	266	(266)	–
Disposals	(5)	(21)	(26)
Assets with zero net book value	(4,890)	(2,999)	(7,889)
Balance, March 30, 2013	25,236	12,477	37,713
Additions	6,609	3,937	10,546
Transfers / reclassifications	(203)	203	–
Disposals	–	–	–
Assets with zero net book value	(4,361)	(3,471)	(7,832)
Balance, March 29, 2014	27,281	13,146	40,427
Accumulated amortization and impairment			
Balance, March 31, 2012	8,408	4,789	13,197
Amortization	6,567	3,678	10,245
Disposals	(2)	(2)	(4)
Assets with zero net book value	(4,890)	(2,999)	(7,889)
Balance, March 30, 2013	10,083	5,466	15,549
Amortization	7,071	4,052	11,123
Disposals	–	–	–
Assets with zero net book value	(4,361)	(3,471)	(7,832)
Balance, March 29, 2014	12,793	6,047	18,840
Net carrying amount			
April 1, 2012	15,521	7,289	22,810
March 30, 2013	15,153	7,011	22,164
March 29, 2014	14,488	7,099	21,587

Impairment testing for intangible assets is performed using the same methodology, CGUs, and groups of CGUs as those used for property, plant and equipment. The key assumptions from the value in use calculations for intangible asset impairment testing are also identical to the key assumptions used for property, plant and equipment testing. Impairment and reversal indicators were identified during fiscal 2014 for Indigo's retail stores. Accordingly, the Company performed impairment and reversal testing but there were no intangible asset impairment losses or reversals in fiscal 2014 (2013 – no impairment losses or reversals).

10. INCOME TAXES

Deferred tax assets are recognized to the extent that it is probable that taxable profit will be available against which the deductible temporary differences and the carryforward of unused tax credits and unused tax losses can be utilized. As at March 29, 2014, the Company has recorded $56.2 million in gross value of deferred tax assets with a valuation allowance of $11.6 million based on management's best estimate of future taxable income that the Company expects to achieve from reviewing its latest forecast. If the valuation allowance decreases as the result of subsequent events, the previously recognized valuation allowance will be reversed.

Deferred income taxes reflect the net tax effects of temporary differences between the carrying amounts of assets and liabilities for financial reporting purposes and the amounts used for income tax purposes. Significant components of the Company's deferred tax assets are as follows:

(thousands of Canadian dollars)	March 29, 2014	March 30, 2013	April 1, 2012
Deferred tax assets			
Reserves and allowances	2,032	2,990	3,343
Tax loss carryforwards	23,562	22,648	25,620
Corporate minimum tax	1,354	1,354	1,354
Book amortization in excess of cumulative eligible capital deduction	249	267	285
Book amortization in excess of capital cost allowance	29,002	21,472	18,031
Deferred tax assets before valuation allowance	56,199	48,731	48,633
Valuation allowance	(11,595)	–	–
Net deferred tax assets	44,604	48,731	48,633

The Company has recorded deferred tax assets of $44.6 million pertaining to tax loss carryforwards and other deductible temporary differences based on the probable use of the deferred tax assets.

Significant components of income tax expense (recovery) are as follows:

(thousands of Canadian dollars)	52-week period ended March 29, 2014	52-week period ended March 30, 2013
Current income tax recovery		
Adjustment for prior periods	(37)	–
	(37)	–
Deferred income tax expense (recovery)		
Origination and reversal of temporary differences	(7,164)	(6,174)
Increase in valuation allowance	11,595	–
Deferred income tax expense relating to utilization of loss carryforwards	–	7,745
Adjustment to deferred tax assets resulting from increase in substantively enacted tax rate	(261)	(1,636)
Change in tax rates due to change in expected pattern of reversal	(44)	(32)
Other, net	1	(1)
	4,127	(98)
Total income tax expense (recovery)	4,090	(98)

The reconciliation of income taxes computed at statutory income tax rates to the effective income tax rates is as follows:

(thousands of Canadian dollars)	52-week period ended March 29, 2014	%	52-week period ended March 30, 2013	%
Earnings (loss) before income taxes	(26,909)		4,190	
Tax at combined federal and provincial tax rates	(7,110)	26.4%	1,102	26.3%
Tax effect of expenses not deductible for income tax purposes	246	(0.9%)	388	9.3%
Increase in valuation allowance	11,595	(43.1%)	–	–
Adjustment to deferred tax assets resulting from increase in substantively enacted tax rate	(261)	1.0%	(1,636)	(39.0%)
Change in tax rates due to change in expected pattern of reversal	(44)	0.2%	(32)	(0.8%)
Other, net	(336)	1.2%	80	1.9%
	4,090	(15.2%)	(98)	(2.3%)

The combined federal and provincial income tax rate used for fiscal 2014 is 26.4% (2013 – 26.3%). The rate has increased due to higher provincial income tax rates.

As at March 29, 2014, the Company has combined non-capital loss carryforwards of approximately $89.1 million for income tax purposes that expire in 2031 if not utilized.

11. PROVISIONS

Provisions consist primarily of amounts recorded in respect of decommissioning liabilities, onerous lease arrangements, and legal claims. Activity related to the Company's provisions is as follows:

(thousands of Canadian dollars)	52-week period ended March 29, 2014	52-week period ended March 30, 2013
Balance, beginning of period	2,246	692
Charged	230	1,814
Utilized / released	(1,384)	(260)
Balance, end of period	1,092	2,246

12. COMMITMENTS AND CONTINGENCIES

(a) Commitments

As at March 9, 2014, the Company had the following commitments:

(i) Operating lease obligations

The Company had operating lease commitments in respect of its stores, support office premises and certain equipment. The leases expire at various dates between 2014 and 2022, and may be subject to renewal options. Annual store rent consists of a base amount plus, in some cases, additional payments based on store sales. The Company expects to generate $10.9 million of revenues from subleases related to these operating leases over the next seven fiscal years.

(ii) Finance lease obligations

The Company entered into finance lease agreements for certain equipment. The obligations under these finance leases is $0.8 million as at March 29, 2014 (March 30, 2013 – $1.5 million; April 1, 2012 – $2.2 million), of which $0.6 million (March 30, 2013 – $0.8 million; April 1, 2012 – $1.1 million) is included in the current portion of long-term debt. The remainder of the finance lease obligations have been included in the non-current portion of long-term debt.

The Company's minimum contractual obligations due over the next five fiscal years and thereafter are summarized below:

(millions of Canadian dollars)	Operating leases	Finance leases	Total
2015	57.6	0.6	58.2
2016	49.6	0.2	49.8
2017	40.1	–	40.1
2018	31.8	–	31.8
2019	19.8	–	19.8
Thereafter	6.9	–	6.9
Total obligations	205.8	0.8	206.6

(b) Legal claims

In the normal course of business, the Company becomes involved in various claims and litigation. While the final outcome of such claims and litigation pending as at March 29, 2014 cannot be predicted with certainty, management believes that any such amount would not have a material impact on the Company's financial position or financial performance, except for those amounts which have been recorded as provisions on the Company's consolidated balance sheets.

13. SHARE CAPITAL

Share capital consists of the following:

Authorized

Unlimited Class A preference shares with no par value, voting, convertible into
  common shares on a one-for-one basis at the option of the shareholder

Unlimited common shares, voting

	52-week period ended March 29, 2014		52-week period ended March 30, 2013	
	Number of shares	Amount C$ (thousands)	Number of shares	Amount C$ (thousands)
Balance, beginning of period	25,297,389	203,805	25,238,414	203,373
Issued during the period				
Directors' deferred share units converted	–	–	1,075	15
Options exercised	850	7	57,900	417
Balance, end of period	25,298,239	203,812	25,297,389	203,805

During fiscal 2014, the Company did not issue any common shares (2013 – 1,075 common shares) in exchange for Directors' deferred share units ("DSUs").

During fiscal 2014, the Company distributed dividends per share of $0.33 (2013 – $0.44).

14. SHARE-BASED COMPENSATION

The Company has established an employee stock option plan (the "Plan") for key employees. The number of common shares reserved for issuance under the Plan is 3,294,736. Most options granted between May 21, 2002 and March 31, 2012 have a ten-year term and have one fifth of the options granted exercisable one year after the date of issue with the remainder exercisable in equal instalments on the anniversary date over the next four years. Subsequently, most options granted after April 1, 2012 have a five-year term and have one third of the options granted exercisable one year after the date of issue with the remainder exercisable in equal instalments on the anniversary date over the next two years. A small number of options have special vesting schedules that were approved by the Board. Each option is exercisable into one common share of the Company at the price specified in the terms of the option agreement.

During the first quarter of fiscal 2014, the Company offered a one-time cash repurchase to holders of stock options above a specified value. The repurchase was approved by the Board of Directors and by the Company's shareholders; repurchased options were subsequently cancelled by the Company. As part of this transaction, the Company immediately recorded the remaining unamortized expense of $0.5 million for repurchased options. The Company repurchased and cancelled 870,500 options and made a cash payment to option holders of $1.0 million.

The Company uses the fair value method of accounting for stock options, which estimates the fair value of the stock options granted on the date of grant, net of estimated forfeitures, and expenses this value over the vesting period. During fiscal 2014, the pre-forfeiture fair value of options granted was $2.8 million (2013 – $0.7 million). The weighted average fair value of options issued in fiscal 2014 was $1.97 per option (2013 – $1.54 per option).

The fair value of the employee stock options is estimated at the date of grant using the Black-Scholes option pricing model with the following weighted average assumptions during the periods presented:

	52-week period ended March 29, 2014	52-week period ended March 30, 2013
Black-Scholes option pricing assumptions		
Risk-free interest rate	1.3%	1.2%
Expected volatility	35.4%	37.1%
Expected time until exercise	3.0 years	3.0 years
Expected dividend yield	3.4%	5.0%
Other assumptions		
Forfeiture rate	26.7%	24.9%

A summary of the status of the Plan and changes during both periods is presented below:

	52-week period ended March 29, 2014		52-week period ended March 30, 2013	
	Number #	Weighted average exercise price C$	Number #	Weighted average exercise price C$
Outstanding options, beginning of period	1,627,000	12.64	1,372,400	13.64
Granted	1,401,000	10.25	430,000	8.63
Forfeited / repurchased	(1,347,000)	13.77	(117,500)	12.97
Expired	(4,000)	4.45	–	–
Exercised	(850)	8.00	(57,900)	5.74
Outstanding options, end of period	1,676,150	9.75	1,627,000	12.64
Options exercisable, end of period	245,900	8.88	722,500	14.52

Options outstanding and exercisable

	March 29, 2014				
	Outstanding			Exercisable	
Range of exercise prices C$	Number #	Weighted average exercise price C$	Weighted average remaining contractual life (in years)	Number #	Weighted average exercise price C$
7.20 – 8.06	313,650	7.74	3.1	143,700	7.61
8.07 – 9.72	366,500	8.36	4.3	43,900	8.66
9.73 – 10.80	910,000	10.70	4.3	23,800	10.70
10.81 – 14.05	78,500	12.79	6.9	30,000	12.88
14.06 – 15.21	7,500	15.21	6.6	4,500	15.21
7.20 – 15.21	1,676,150	9.75	4.2	245,900	8.88

Directors' compensation

The Company has established a Directors' Deferred Share Unit Plan ("DSU Plan"). Under the DSU Plan, Directors receive their annual retainer fees and other Board-related compensation in the form of deferred share units ("DSUs"). The number of shares reserved for issuance under this plan is 500,000. The Company issued 43,757 DSUs with a value of $0.4 million during fiscal 2014 (2013 – 46,409 DSUs with a value of $0.4 million). The number of DSUs to be issued to each Director is based on a set fee schedule. The grant date fair value of the outstanding DSUs as at March 29, 2014 was $3.3 million (March 30, 2013 – $2.9 million; April 1, 2012 – $2.5 million) and was recorded in contributed surplus. The fair value of DSUs is equal to the traded price of the Company's common shares on grant date.

15. SUPPLEMENTARY OPERATING INFORMATION

Supplemental product line revenue information:

	52-week period ended March 29, 2014	52-week period ended March 30, 2013
Print[1]	585,239	613,626
General merchandise[2]	240,237	207,520
eReading[3]	24,743	35,898
Other[4]	17,449	21,741
Total	867,668	878,785

1 Includes books, calendars, magazines, and newspapers.
2 Includes lifestyle, paper, toys, music, DVDs, and electronics.
3 Includes eReaders, eReader accessories, and Kobo revenue share.
4 Includes cafés, irewards, gift card breakage, and Plum breakage.

Supplemental operating and administrative expenses information:

(thousands of Canadian dollars)	52-week period ended March 29, 2014	52-week period ended March 30, 2013
Wages, salaries and bonuses	157,904	150,469
Short-term benefits expense	18,321	17,598
Termination benefits expense	4,945	3,482
Retirement benefits expense	1,286	1,224
Stock-based compensation	1,242	743
Total employee benefits expense	183,698	173,516

Termination benefits arise when the Company terminates certain employment agreements.

Minimum lease payments recognized as an expense during fiscal 2014 were $63.5 million (2013 – $62.7 million). Contingent rents recognized as an expense during fiscal 2014 were $1.0 million (2013 – $1.3 million).

16. EARNINGS PER SHARE

Earnings per share is calculated based on the weighted average number of common shares outstanding during the period. In calculating diluted earnings per share amounts under the treasury stock method, the numerator remains unchanged from the basic earnings per share calculations as the assumed exercise of the Company's stock options do not result in an adjustment to net earnings. The reconciliation of the denominator in calculating diluted earnings per share amounts for the periods presented is as follows:

(thousands of shares)	52-week period ended March 29, 2014	52-week period ended March 30, 2013
Weighted average number of common shares outstanding, basic	25,601	25,529
Effect of dilutive securities		
Stock options	47	34
Weighted average number of common shares outstanding, diluted	25,648	25,563

As at March 29, 2014, 1,246,000 (March 30, 2013 – 1,505,500; April 1, 2012 – 1,293,000) options could potentially dilute basic earnings per share in the future, but were excluded from the computation of diluted net earnings per common share in the current period as they were anti-dilutive.

17. STATEMENTS OF CASH FLOWS

Supplemental cash flow information:

(thousands of Canadian dollars)	52-week period ended March 29, 2014	52-week period ended March 30, 2013
Net change in non-cash working capital balances:		
Accounts receivable	1,544	5,494
Inventories	(2,446)	12,666
Income taxes recoverable	(37)	(86)
Prepaid expenses	(1,031)	(461)
Accounts payable and accrued liabilities	(14,857)	(25,035)
Unredeemed gift card liability	(342)	4,458
Provisions	(1,154)	1,554
Deferred revenue	(873)	2,499
	(19,196)	1,089
Assets acquired under finance leases	137	465

18. CAPITAL MANAGEMENT

The Company's main objectives when managing capital are to safeguard its ability to continue as a going concern while maintaining adequate financial flexibility to invest in new business opportunities that will provide attractive returns to shareholders. The primary activities engaged by the Company to generate attractive returns include construction and related leasehold improvements of stores, the development of new business concepts, and investment in information technology and distribution capacity to support the online and retail networks. The Company's main sources of capital are its current cash position, cash flows generated from operations, and long-term debt. On June 12, 2013, the Company cancelled its revolving line of credit. Cash flow is used to fund working capital needs, capital expenditures and debt service requirements.

In order to maintain sufficient capital resources to fund the Company's transformation, management and the Company's Board of Directors decided to suspend quarterly dividend payments beyond December 3, 2013. The Company primarily manages its capital by monitoring its available cash balance to ensure that sufficient funds are available for long-term debt and interest payments over the next year.

The following table summarizes selected capital structure information for the Company:

(thousands of Canadian dollars)	March 29, 2014	March 30, 2013	April 1, 2012
Current portion of long-term debt	584	773	1,060
Long-term debt	227	705	1,141
Total debt	811	1,478	2,201
Total equity	311,674	350,322	355,632
Total capital under management	312,485	351,800	357,833

19. FINANCIAL RISK MANAGEMENT

The Company's activities expose it to a variety of financial risks, including risks related to foreign exchange, interest rate, credit, and liquidity.

Foreign exchange risk

The Company's foreign exchange risk is largely limited to currency fluctuations between the Canadian and U.S. dollars. Decreases in the value of the Canadian dollar relative to the U.S. dollar could negatively impact net earnings since the purchase price of some of the Company's products are negotiated with vendors in U.S. dollars, while the retail price to customers is set in Canadian dollars. The Company did not use any forward contracts to manage foreign exchange risk in fiscal 2014 (2013 – no forward contracts).

As the Company expands its product selection to include a greater number of non-book items, foreign exchange risk has increased due to more purchases being denominated in U.S. dollars. A 10% appreciation or depreciation in the U.S. and Canadian dollar exchange rates during fiscal 2014 would have had an impact of $3.9 million (2013 – $3.9 million) on net earnings (loss) and comprehensive earnings (loss).

In fiscal 2014, the effect of foreign currency translation on net earnings (loss) and comprehensive earnings (loss) was a loss of $0.4 million (2013 – gain of $0.2 million).

Interest rate risk

On June 12, 2013, the Company cancelled its revolving line of credit. As such, the Company's interest rate risk is largely limited to its long-term debt, for which interest rates are fixed at the time a contract is finalized. The Company's interest income is also sensitive to fluctuations in Canadian interest rates, which affect the interest earned on the Company's cash and cash equivalents. The Company has minimal interest rate risk and does not use any interest rate swaps to manage its risk.

Credit risk

The Company is exposed to credit risk resulting from the possibility that counterparties may default on their financial obligations to the Company. The Company's maximum exposure to credit risk at the reporting date is equal to the carrying value of accounts receivable. Accounts receivable primarily consists of receivables from retail customers who pay by credit card, recoveries of credits from suppliers for returned or damaged products, and receivables from other companies for sales of products, gift cards and other services. Credit card payments have minimal credit risk and the limited number of corporate receivables is closely monitored.

Liquidity risk

Liquidity risk is the risk that the Company will be unable to meet its obligations relating to its financial liabilities. The Company manages liquidity risk by preparing and monitoring cash flow budgets and forecasts to ensure that the Company has sufficient funds to meet its financial obligations and fund new business opportunities or other unanticipated requirements as they arise.

The contractual maturities of the Company's current and long-term liabilities as at March 29, 2014 are as follows:

(thousands of Canadian dollars)	Payments due in the next 90 days	Payments due between 90 days and less than a year	Payments due after 1 year	Total
Accounts payable and accrued liabilities	109,671	26,757	–	136,428
Unredeemed gift card liability	46,827	–	–	46,827
Provisions	–	928	–	928
Current portion of long-term debt	–	584	–	584
Long-term accrued liabilities	–	–	2,896	2,896
Long-term provisions	–	–	164	164
Long-term debt	–	–	227	227
Total	156,498	28,269	3,287	188,054

20. EQUITY INVESTMENT

The Company holds a 50% equity ownership in its associate, Calendar Club, to sell calendars, games, and gifts through seasonal kiosks and year-round stores in Canada. The Company uses the equity method of accounting to record Calendar Club results. In fiscal 2014, the Company received $1.2 million (2013 – $1.3 million) of distributions from Calendar Club.

The following tables represent financial information for Calendar Club along with the Company's share therein:

(thousands of Canadian dollars)	Total			Company's share		
	March 29, 2014	March 30, 2013	April 1, 2012	March 29, 2014	March 30, 2013	April 1, 2012
Cash and cash equivalents	1,185	2,278	1,766	593	1,139	883
Total current assets	2,565	3,316	2,798	1,283	1,658	1,399
Total long-term assets	658	831	1,071	329	416	536
Total current liabilities	2,027	2,212	1,948	1,014	1,106	974

(thousands of Canadian dollars)	Total		Company's share	
	52-week period ended March 29, 2014	52-week period ended March 30, 2013	52-week period ended March 29, 2014	52-week period ended March 30, 2013
Revenue	31,003	30,543	15,502	15,272
Expenses	(29,425)	(27,914)	(14,713)	(13,957)
Net earnings	1,578	2,629	789	1,315

Changes in the carrying amount of the investment were as follows:

(thousands of Canadian dollars)	Carrying value
Balance, March 31, 2012	961
Equity income from Calendar Club	1,315
Distributions from Calendar Club	(1,308)
Balance, March 30, 2013	968
Equity income from Calendar Club	789
Distributions from Calendar Club	(1,159)
Balance, March 29, 2014	598

21. RELATED PARTY TRANSACTIONS

The Company's related parties include its key management personnel, shareholders, defined contribution retirement plan, equity investment in Calendar Club, and subsidiary. Unless otherwise stated, none of the transactions incorporate special terms and conditions and no guarantees were given or received. Outstanding balances are usually settled in cash.

Transactions with key management personnel

Key management of the Company includes members of the Board of Directors as well as members of the Executive Committee. Key management personnel remuneration includes the following expenses:

(thousands of Canadian dollars)	52-week period ended March 29, 2014	52-week period ended March 30, 2013
Wages, salaries, bonus and consulting	4,654	4,085
Short-term benefits expense	242	246
Termination benefits expense	457	450
Retirement benefits expense	60	66
Stock-based compensation	789	443
Directors' compensation	425	446
Total remuneration	6,627	5,736

Transactions with shareholders

During fiscal 2014, Indigo purchased goods and services from companies in which Mr. Gerald W. Schwartz, who is the controlling shareholder of Indigo, holds a controlling or significant interest. In fiscal 2014, Indigo paid $5.3 million for these goods and services (2013 – $0.2 million). As at March 29, 2014, Indigo had less than $0.1 million payable to these companies under standard payment terms and $2.8 million of restricted cash pledged as collateral for letter of credit obligations issued to support the Company's purchases of merchandise from these companies (March 30, 2013 and April 1, 2012 – no amounts payable and no restricted cash). All transactions were in the normal course of business for both Indigo and the related companies.

Transactions with defined contribution retirement plan

The Company's transactions with the defined contribution retirement plan include contributions paid to the retirement plan as disclosed in note 15. The Company has not entered into other transactions with the retirement plan.

Transactions with associate

The Company's associate, Calendar Club, is a seasonal operation which is dependent on the December holiday sales season to generate revenues. During the year, the Company loans cash to Calendar Club for working capital requirements and Calendar Club repays the loans once profits are generated in the third quarter. The net amount of these transactions for fiscal 2014 was nil (2013 – nil), as Calendar Club has repaid all loans as at March 29, 2014. In fiscal 2013, Calendar Club repaid an outstanding $0.2 million note payable to Indigo.

22. COMPARATIVE CONSOLIDATED FINANCIAL STATEMENTS

The comparative consolidated financial statements have been reclassified from statements previously presented to conform to the presentation of the current year audited consolidated financial statements.

Five Year Summary of Financial Information

| For the years ended | IFRS | | | | Canadian GAAP |
| | March 29, | March 30, | March 31, | April 2, | April 3, |
(millions of Canadian dollars, except share and per share data)	2014	2013	2012	2011	2010
SELECTED STATEMENTS OF EARNINGS					
INFORMATION					
Revenues					
Superstores	617.8	626.6	656.5	667.6	670.5
Small format stores	127.4	137.6	145.2	149.4	159.3
Online	102.0	91.9	91.3	90.6	92.2
Other	20.5	22.7	27.2	33.9	46.1
Total revenues	867.7	878.8	920.2	941.5	968.1
Adjusted EBITDA[1]	0.1	28.5	25.0	54.8	76.1
Earnings (loss) before income taxes	(26.9)	4.2	(29.3)	25.8	49.8
Net earnings (loss) and comprehensive					
earnings (loss)	(31.0)	4.3	66.2	(19.4)	34.9
Dividends per share	$0.33	$0.44	$0.44	$0.44	$0.40
Net earnings (loss) per common share	$(1.21)	$0.17	$3.68	$(0.23)	$1.42
SELECTED BALANCE SHEET INFORMATION					
Working capital	189.7	224.3	223.7	101.1	106.4
Total assets	512.6	569.1	591.8	510.3	519.8
Long-term debt (including current portion)	0.8	1.5	2.2	3.3	3.0
Total equity	311.7	350.3	355.6	267.4	259.0
Weighted average number of shares outstanding	25,601,260	25,529,035	25,201,127	24,874,199	24,549,622
Common shares outstanding at end of period	25,298,239	25,297,389	25,238,414	25,140,540	24,742,915
STORE OPERATING STATISTICS					
Number of stores at end of period					
Superstores	95	97	97	97	96
Small format stores	131	134	143	150	151
Selling square footage at end of period					
(in thousands)					
Superstores	2,200	2,235	2,235	2,235	2,217
Small format stores	370	379	400	413	417
Comparable store sales					
Superstores	(0.9%)	(4.6%)	(1.9%)	(0.3%)	0.6%
Small format stores	(5.0%)	(2.4%)	(0.8%)	(3.2%)	(2.2%)
Sales per selling square foot					
Superstores	281	280	294	299	302
Small format stores	344	362	363	362	382

1 Earnings before interest, taxes, depreciation, amortization, impairment, and equity investment. Also see "Non-IFRS Financial Measures".

TYPICAL CHART OF ACCOUNTS FOR SERVICE PROPRIETORSHIPS AND SERVICE PARTNERSHIPS (ASPE)

ASSETS	LIABILITIES	OWNER'S EQUITY
Cash	Accounts Payable	Owner, Capital
Petty Cash	Notes Payable, Short-Term	Owner, Withdrawals
Accounts Receivable	Salaries Payable	
Allowance for Doubtful Accounts	Wages Payable	**Revenues and Gains**
Notes Receivable, Short-Term	Goods and Services Tax Payable	Service Revenue
Goods and Services Tax Recoverable	Harmonized Sales Tax Payable	Interest Revenue
Harmonized Sales Tax Recoverable	Employee Income Tax Payable	Gain on Sale of Land (or Furniture,
Interest Receivable	Employment Insurance Payable	Equipment, or Building)
Supplies	Canada Pension Plan Payable	
Prepaid Rent	Quebec Pension Plan Payable	**Expenses and Losses**
Prepaid Insurance	Employee Benefits Payable	Amortization Expense—Furniture
	Interest Payable	Amortization Expense—Equipment
Furniture	Unearned Service Revenue	Amortization Expense—Building
Accumulated Amortization—	Estimated Warranty Payable	Amortization Expense—Land
Furniture	Estimated Vacation Pay Liability	Improvements
Equipment	Current Portion of Long-Term Debt	Bad Debt Expense
Accumulated Amortization—		Bank Charge Expense
Equipment		Cash Short & Over
Building	Notes Payable, Long-Term	Credit Card Discount Expense
Accumulated Amortization—		Debit Card Service Fee
Building		Delivery Expense
Land Improvements		Employee Benefits Expense
Accumulated Amortization—Land		Interest Expense
Improvements		Insurance Expense
Leasehold Improvements		Miscellaneous Expense
Land		Property Tax Expense
Notes Receivable, Long-Term		Rent Expense
Patents		Supplies Expense
Goodwill		Utilities Expense
		Vacation Pay Expense
		Warranty Expense
		Loss on Sale (or Exchange) of Land
		(or Furniture, Equipment, or
		Buildings)

SERVICE PARTNERSHIP
Same as Service Proprietorship, except for Owners' Equity:
OWNERS' EQUITY
Partner 1, Capital
Partner 2, Capital
Partner N, Capital
Partner 1, Withdrawals
Partner 2, Withdrawals
Partner N, Withdrawals

MERCHANDISING CORPORATION

ASSETS	LIABILITIES	SHAREHOLDERS' EQUITY	
Cash	Accounts Payable	Common Shares	**Expenses and Losses**
Short-Term Investments	Notes Payable, Short-Term	Contributed Surplus	Cost of Goods Sold
Fair-Value Valuation	Current Portion of Bonds	Accumulated Other	Salaries Expense
Allowance	Payable	Comprehensive Loss	Wages Expense
Accounts Receivable	Salaries Payable	Retained Earnings	Commission Expense
Allowance for Doubtful	Wages Payable	Dividends	Payroll Benefits Expense
Accounts	Goods and Services Tax Payable		Insurance Expense for
Notes Receivable, Short-Term	Harmonized Sales Tax Payable	**Revenues and Gains**	Employees
Goods and Services Tax	Employee Income Tax Payable	Sales Revenue	Rent Expense
Recoverable	Employment Insurance Payable	Interest Revenue	Insurance Expense
Harmonized Sales Tax	Canada Pension Plan Payable	Dividend Revenue	Supplies Expense
Recoverable	Quebec Pension Plan Payable	Equity-Method Investment	Amortization Expense—
Interest Receivable	Employee Benefits Payable	Revenue	Land Improvements
Inventory	Interest Payable	Gain on Sale of Investments	Amortization Expense—
Supplies	Income Tax Payable	Unrealized Gain on	Furniture and Fixtures
Prepaid Rent	Provisions	Short-Term Investments	Amortization Expense—
Prepaid Insurance	Unearned Service Revenue	Gain on Sale of Land	Equipment
Notes Receivable, Long-Term	Deferred Tax	(or Furniture and	Amortization Expense—
Deferred Tax	Notes Payable, Long-Term	Fixtures, Equipment, or	Buildings
Investment Subject to	Bonds Payable	Building)	Amortization Expense—
Significant Influence	Lease Liability	Discontinued	Franchises
Long-Term Investments	Non-controlling Interest	Operations—Gain	Amortization Expense—
Other Receivables, Long-Term			Leaseholds
Land			Incorporation Expense
Land Improvements			Income Tax Expense
Accumulated Amortization—			Loss on Write-down of
Land Improvements			Goodwill
Furniture and Fixtures			Loss on Sale of Investments
Accumulated Amortization—			Unrealized Loss on
Furniture and Fixtures			Short-Term Investments
Equipment			Loss on Sale (or Exchange)
Accumulated Amortization—			of Land (or Furniture and
Buildings			Fixtures, Equipment, or
Organization Cost			Buildings)
Franchises			Discontinued
Patents			Operations—Loss
Leaseholds			
Goodwill			

GLOSSARY

Accounts receivable turnover Ratio of net credit sales to average net accounts receivable. Measures ability to collect cash from credit customers (p. 1070).

Acid-test ratio Ratio of the sum of cash plus short-term investments plus net current receivables to current liabilities. Tells whether the entity could pay all its current liabilities if they came due immediately. Also called the *quick ratio* (p. 1068).

Actively traded Financial instruments that are easily bought or sold because there are a lot of them in the market and it is easy to find someone who is willing to engage in a transaction (p. 913).

Affiliated company An investment in a company in which there is significant influence and 20 to 50 percent ownership. These investments are accounted for using the equity method (p. 922).

Amortized cost method To account for long-term bond investments, the discount or premium is amortized to more accurately reflect the interest revenue. These bonds are reported at their amortized cost (p. 932).

Appropriations Restriction of retained earnings that is recorded by a formal journal entry (p. 802).

Arrears To be behind or overdue in a debt payment (p. 745).

Articles of incorporation The document issued by the federal or provincial government giving the incorporators permission to form a corporation (p. 730).

Asset revaluation Adjusting asset values to reflect current market values, usually based on an independent appraisal of the assets (p. 693).

Authorization of shares A provision in a corporation's articles of incorporation that permits a corporation to sell a certain number of shares of stock (p. 732).

Authorized shares The number of shares a corporation is allowed to sell according to the articles of incorporation (p. 736).

Basic EPS Earnings per share calculated using the number of outstanding common shares (p. 797).

Bearer bonds Bonds payable to the person that has possession of them. Also called *unregistered bonds* (p. 840).

Benchmarking Comparison of current performance with some standard. The standard often is the performance level of a leading outside organization or the industry average (p. 1064).

Bid price The highest price that a buyer is willing to pay for a bond (p. 841).

Blended payments Payments that are a constant amount, and the amount of interest and principal that are applied to the loan change with each payment (p. 862).

Board of directors A group elected by the shareholders to set policy for a corporation and to appoint its officers (p. 732).

Bond A formal agreement in which a lender loans money to a borrower who agrees to repay the money loaned at a future date and agrees to pay interest regularly over the life of the bond (p. 838).

Bond indenture The contract that specifies the maturity value of the bonds, the stated (contract) interest rate, and the dates for paying interest and principal (p. 838).

Bonds payable Groups of notes payable (bonds) issued to multiple lenders called bondholders (p. 838).

Book value The amount of shareholders' equity on the company's books for each of its shares (p. 746).

Book value per common share Common shareholders' equity divided by the number of common shares outstanding (p. 1076).

Bylaws The constitution for governing a corporation (p. 732).

Callable bond Bonds that the issuer may call or pay off at a specified price whenever the issuer wants (p. 858).

Capital deficiency A partnership's claim against a partner. Occurs when a partner's Capital account has a debit balance (p. 699).

Capitalized retained earnings Retained earnings that are not available for distribution. Stock dividends result in retained earnings being moved to contributed capital (p. 783).

Capital lease A lease agreement that substantially transfers all the benefits and risks of ownership from the lessor to the lessee (p. 864).

Carrying value The amount at which an asset is reported on the balance sheet (p. 915).

Cash equivalents Highly liquid short-term investments that can be converted into cash with little delay (p. 980).

Cash flows Cash receipts and cash payments (disbursements) (p. 978).

Cash flow statement Reports cash receipts and cash payments classified according to the entity's major activities: operating, investing, and financing (p. 978).

Certificate of deposit A secure form of investment with a fixed interest rate and term. Unlike a bank account, they must be held to maturity (p. 913).

Chairperson (of board) An elected person on a corporation's board of directors; usually the most powerful person in the corporation (p. 732).

Closely held Describes a corporation with only a few shareholders (p. 748).

Common shares The most basic form of share capital. In describing a corporation, the common shareholders are the owners of the business (p. 734).

Common-size statement A financial statement that reports only percentages (no dollar amounts); a type of vertical analysis (p. 1063).

Companion account An account that is typically paired up with another account (p. 915).

Consolidated financial statements Financial statements of the parent company plus those of majority-owned subsidiaries as if the combination were a single legal entity (p. 923).

Consolidation A decrease in the number of shares outstanding by a fixed ratio. Also called a *reverse split* (p. 786).

Contract interest rate The interest rate that determines the amount of cash interest the borrower pays and the investor receives each year. Also called the *stated interest rate* (p. 842).

Contributed capital A corporation's capital from investments by the shareholders. Also called *share capital* or *capital stock* (p. 733).

Controlling interest Ownership of more than 50 percent of an investee company's voting shares. Also called *majority interest* (p. 923).

Conversion privileges Shareholders with this right may exchange specified bonds or shares into a stated number of common shares (p. 797).

Convertible bond Bonds that may be converted into the common shares of the issuing company at the option of the investor (p. 859).

Convertible note Notes that may be converted into the common shares of the issuing company at the option of the investor (p. 859).

Convertible preferred shares Preferred shares that may be exchanged by the preferred shareholders, if they choose, for another class of shares in the corporation (p. 741).

Counterbalancing transaction Engaging in a second transaction to offset the risk of the first transaction (p. 939).

Coupon rate The contractual rate of interest that the issuer must pay the bondholders (p. 839).

Cumulative preferred shares Preferred shares whose owners must receive all dividends in arrears before the corporation pays dividends to the common shareholders (p. 745).

Currency options A contract that can be purchased to guarantee the right to a future exchange rate (p. 939).

Current ratio Current assets divided by current liabilities. Measures the ability to pay current liabilities from current assets (p. 1068).

Date of record On this date, which is a few weeks after the declaration of the dividend, the list of shareholders who will receive the dividend is compiled (p. 743).

Days' sales in receivables Ratio of average net accounts receivable to one day's sales. Indicates how many days' sales remain in Accounts Receivable awaiting collection (p. 1070).

Debenture An unsecured bond, backed only by the good faith of the issuer (p. 840).

Debt ratio Ratio of total liabilities to total assets. Gives the proportion of a company's assets that it has financed with debt (p. 1071).

Declaration date The date on which the board of directors announces the dividend. There is a liability created on this date (p. 743).

Deficit A debit balance in the Retained Earnings account (p. 735).

Direct method The format of the operating activities section of the cash flow statement that shows cash receipts from and cash payments for operating activities (p. 985).

Discount The amount of a bond's issue price under its maturity (par) value; also called bond discount (p. 841).

Dissolution Ending a partnership (p. 675).

Dividends Distributions by a corporation to its shareholders (p. 735).

Dividend yield Ratio of dividends per share to the share's market price per share. Tells the percentage of a share's market value that the company pays to shareholders as dividends (p. 1075).

Double taxation Corporations pay their own income taxes on corporate income. Then, the shareholders pay personal income tax on the cash dividends that they receive from corporations (p. 731).

Downside risk An estimate of the potential loss from a change in market conditions (p. 1075).

Earnings per share (EPS) The amount of a company's net income per outstanding common share (pp. 795, 1074).

Effective-interest amortization An amortization method in which a different amount of bond discount or premium is written off through interest expense each year (or period) of the bond's life. The amount of amortization expense is the same percentage of a bond's carrying value for every period over a bond's life (p. 851).

Effective interest rate The interest rate that investors demand in order to loan their money. Also called the *market interest rate* (p. 843).

Efficient capital market A market in which the market prices fully reflect the impact of all information available to the public (p. 1077).

Equity method for investments The method used to account for investments in which the investor generally has 20 to 50 percent of the investor's voting shares and can significantly influence the decisions of the investee. The investment account is debited for ownership in the investee's net income and credited for ownership in the investee's dividends (p. 920).

Face value Another name for the principal or maturity value of a bond (p. 839).

Factors Companies that purchase other firms' accounts receivable at a discount. Receivables are sold so that the cash can be received more quickly (p. 1070).

Fair value method The method of accounting for shares held as short-term investments that values them at their fair, or market, value on the year-end balance sheet date. Any gain or loss resulting from the change in fair value is recognized in net income for the period in which it arises, and fair value becomes the new carrying value of the shares. Also called the *market value method* (p. 914).

Financial instrument A contract that creates an asset for one party and a liability or equity for another (p. 940).

Financing activity An activity that obtains the funds from investors and creditors needed to launch and sustain the business; a section of the cash flow statement (p. 981).

Foreign-currency exchange rate The measure of one currency against another currency (p. 935).

Foreign-currency transaction gain The gain that occurs when a cash payment is less than the related account payable or a cash receipt is greater than the related account receivable due to a change in exchange rate between the transaction date and the payment date (p. 937).

Foreign-currency transaction loss The loss that occurs when a cash payment is greater than the related account payable or a cash receipt is less than the related account receivable due to a change in exchange rate between the transaction date and the payment date (p. 937).

Forward contract An agreement to purchase at a specified future date and price (p. 939).

Free cash flow The amount of cash available from operations after paying for planned investments in plant, equipment, and other long-term assets (p. 984).

Fully diluted EPS Earnings per share calculated using the number of outstanding common shares plus the number of additional common shares that would arise from conversion of convertible bonds and convertible preferred shares into common shares (p. 798).

Futures contract A contract that can be purchased to guarantee the right to a product at a specified price in the future (p. 939).

General partnership A form of partnership in which each partner is an owner of the business, with all the privileges and risks of ownership (p. 677).

Hedging A way to protect oneself from losing money in a foreign-currency transaction by engaging in a counterbalancing foreign-currency transaction (p. 939).

Horizontal analysis The calculation and use of percentage changes in comparative financial statements (p. 1057).

Indirect method The format of the operating activities section of the cash flow statement that starts with net income and shows the reconciliation from net income to operating cash flows. Also called the *reconciliation method* (p. 985).

Initial public offering (IPO) The first time a particular class of a corporation's shares are sold to investors (p. 736).

Insider trading According to the Canada Business Corporations Act, the purchase/sale of a security by someone who knows information not known by the general public that might affect the price of that security (p. 792).

Interest allowance An interest component that rewards a partner with an allocation because of his or her investment in the business. This is not the same as interest expense paid on a loan (p. 684).

Inventory turnover The ratio of cost of goods sold to average inventory. Measures the number of times a company sells its average level of inventory during a year (p. 1069).

Investing activity An activity that increases and decreases the long-term assets available to the business; a section of the cash flow statement (p. 981).

Issued shares Shares that are offered for sale to investors (p. 737).

Issue price The price at which shareholders first purchase shares from the corporation (p. 737).

Joint venture When two or more businesses enter into a contractual arrangement to own a separate entity or project. In 2016 this term will change to *joint arrangement*. (p. 922).

Lease An agreement in which the tenant (lessee) agrees to make rent payments to the property owner (lessor) in exchange for the exclusive use of the asset (p. 863).

Lessee The tenant, or user of the asset, in a lease agreement (p. 863).

Lessor The property owner in a lease agreement (p. 863).

Leverage The use of financial instruments to increase the potential return on investment by earning more income on borrowed money than the related expense, thereby increasing the earnings for the owners of the business. Another name for *trading on the equity* (pp. 750, 1074).

Limited liability No personal obligation of a shareholder for corporation debts. The most that a shareholder can lose on an investment in a corporation's shares is the cost of the investment (p. 731).

Limited liability partnership (LLP) A partnership in which each partner's personal liability for the business's debts is limited to a certain dollar amount (p. 678).

Limited partnership A partnership with at least two classes of partners: a general partner and limited partners (p. 677).

Liquid assets Assets that can be converted to cash quickly. Often they are financial instruments that can be sold without a discount (p. 1068).

Liquidation The process of going out of business by selling the entity's assets and paying its liabilities. The final step in liquidation of a business is the distribution of any remaining cash to the owners (p. 696).

Liquidation value (redemption value or call value) The amount of capital that a preferred shareholder would receive per preferred share upon liquidation of the corporation (p. 747).

Liquidity A company's ability to meet current payments as they come due (p. 1066).

Long-term investments Investments that a company intends to hold for more than one year (p. 913).

Long-term liabilities Debts due to be paid in more than a year or more than one of the entity's operating cycles if an operating cycle is greater than one year (p. 838).

Long-term solvency The ability to generate enough cash to pay long-term debts as they mature (p. 1056).

Majority interest Another name for *controlling interest* (p. 923).

Market interest rate The interest rate that investors demand in order to loan their money. Also called the *effective interest rate* (p. 843).

Market value The price for which a person could buy or sell a share (p. 746).

Market value method Another name for the *fair value method* of accounting for short-term investments in shares (p. 914).

Maturity date The date on which the borrower must pay the principal amount to the lender (p. 839).

Maturity value A bond issued at par that has no discount or premium. Also another name for a bond's principal value (p. 839).

Memorandum entry A journal entry without debits and credits (p. 786).

Minority interest Another name for *non-controlling interest* (p. 928).

Money market fund An investment product generally considered safe because it invests in short-term debt securities, such as certificates of deposit (p. 913).

Mortgage The borrower's promise to transfer the legal title to certain assets to the lender if the debt is not paid on schedule. A mortgage is a special type of *secured bond* (p. 862).

Mutual agency Every partner/owner can bind the business to a contract within the scope of the business's regular operations (pp. 675, 731).

Non-controlling interest A subsidiary company's equity that is held by shareholders other than the parent company. Also called *minority interest* (p. 928).

No-par-value shares Shares that do not have a value assigned to them by the articles of incorporation (p. 738).

Operating activity An activity that creates revenue or expense in the entity's major line of business; a section of the cash flow statement. Operating activities affect the income statement (p. 981).

Operating lease Usually a short-term or cancellable rental agreement (p. 864).

Organization costs The costs of organizing a corporation, including legal fees and charges by promoters for selling the shares. Organization costs are an intangible asset under ASPE but are written off as an expense under IFRS (p. 742).

Other comprehensive income Income that arises from a number of sources, including unrealized gains and losses on certain classes of investment securities due in part to the use of fair value measurement (p. 804).

Outstanding shares Shares in the hands of shareholders (p. 737).

Over-the-counter (OTC) market The decentralized market where bonds are traded between dealers. Unlike the stock market, there isn't a central bond exchange where transaction prices are posted for all to see (p. 841).

Par value An arbitrary value assigned when certain shares are initially offered to the public; these types of shares are not common in Canada; another name for the principal or maturity value of a bond (pp. 738, 839).

Parent company An investor company that generally owns more than 50 percent of the voting shares of a subsidiary company (p. 923).

Partnership An unincorporated business with two or more owners (p. 674).

Partnership agreement An agreement that is the contract between partners specifying such items as the name, location, and nature of the business; the name, capital investment, and duties of each partner; and the method of sharing profits and losses by the partners (p. 675).

Preemptive right Existing shareholders are given the right to purchase additional shares of the company before the shares are offered to others. This would give existing shareholders the opportunity to maintain the same percentage of ownership as they would have had before the new shares were issued (p. 736).

Preferred shares Shares of stock that give their owners certain advantages over common shareholders, such as the priority to receive dividends before the common shareholders and the priority to receive assets before the common shareholders if the corporation liquidates (p. 739).

Premium The excess of a bond's issue price over its maturity (par) value; also called bond premium (p. 841).

Present value The amount a person would invest now to receive a greater amount at a future date (p. 842).

President The chief operating officer in charge of managing the day-to-day operations of a corporation (p. 732).

Price–earnings (P/E) ratio The market price of a common share divided by the company's earnings per share. Measures the value that the stock market places on $1 of a company's earnings (pp. 798, 1075).

Principal value The amount a company borrows from a bondholder. Also called the bond's *maturity value*, *par value*, or *face value* (p. 839).

Private corporation A corporation that does not issue shares that are traded on a stock exchange (p. 730).

Proportionate consolidation The venturer combines its share of the interest in the assets, liabilities, revenues, and expenses of a joint venture with its own assets, liabilities, revenues, and expenses in its consolidated financial statements (p. 922).

Proportionate share The same amount of shares in relation to others before and after an event such as a new issue of shares (p. 736).

Prospective In the future. For example, changes in accounting estimates are reflected in future financial statements, *not* in past financial statements (p. 802).

Prospectus A mandatory legal document that describes an investment to potential purchasers (p. 736).

Provision An account that represents a liability of one entity to another entity (p. 864).

Proxy A formal appointment of one person to cast a vote for another person (p. 733).

Public corporation A corporation that issues shares that are traded on a stock exchange (p. 730).

Quick ratio Another name for the *acid-test ratio* (p. 1068).

Rate of return on common shareholders' equity Net income minus preferred dividends divided by average common shareholders' equity. A measure of profitability. Also called *return on equity (ROE)* or *return on common shareholders' equity* (pp. 749, 1073).

Rate of return on net sales Ratio of net income to net sales. A measure of profitability. Also called *return on sales* (p. 1072).

Rate of return on total assets The sum of net income plus interest expense divided by average total assets. This ratio measures the success a company has in using its assets to earn income for the people who finance the business. Also called *return on assets (ROA)* (pp. 748, 1073).

Rebuttable assumption A conclusion that something is true unless proven that it isn't (p. 940).

Reconciliation method Another name for the *indirect method* of formatting the operating activities section of the cash flow statement (p. 985).

Redeemable bonds Bonds that give the purchaser the option of retiring them at a stated dollar amount prior to maturity (p. 858).

Repurchase shares When a corporation purchases its own shares that it issued previously (p. 788).

Retained earnings A corporation's capital that is earned through profitable operation of the business (p. 733).

Retrospective In the past. For example, changes in accounting policies are reflected in past financial statement figures as if those policies had always been in place (p. 801).

Return on assets (ROA) Another name for *rate of return on total assets* (pp. 748, 1073).

Return on equity (ROE) Another name for *rate of return on common shareholders' equity* (pp. 749, 1073).

Return on sales (ROS) Another name for *rate of return on net sales* (p. 1072).

Return on shareholders' equity Another name for *rate of return on common shareholders' equity* (p. 1073).

Reverse split Another name for a share *consolidation* (p. 786).

Salary allowance Another term for *service* (p. 683).

Secured bond A bond that gives the bondholder the right to take specified assets of the issuer if the issuer fails to pay principal or interest (p. 840).

Segmented information Financial information presented in the notes to the financial statements either by industry or by geography (p. 930).

Segment of the business A significant part of a company (p. 794).

Serial bond A bond that matures in instalments over a period of time (p. 840).

Service An allocation to a partner based on his or her service to the partnership. This is not the same as salary expense for an employee (p. 683).

Servicing its debt A phrase that means the repayment of principal and interest on loans or bonds (p. 1072).

Share dividend Another name for a *stock dividend* (p. 783).

Shareholder A person or a company that owns shares in a corporation (p. 730).

Shareholder loan A loan that is obtained from the owner either in the form of cash or in kind. This amount can be shown as a liability or as a receivable on the balance sheet, depending on whether the balance is a debit or credit (p. 863).

Shareholders' equity Owners' equity of a corporation (p. 733).

Shares Units into which the owners' equity of a corporation is divided (p. 731).

Short-term investments Investments that management intends to hold for less than one year (p. 913).

Short-term liquidity Ability to meet current payments as they come due (p. 1056).

Significant influence When a company participates in the decision making of another company without having full control over it (p. 913).

Stated interest rate The interest rate that determines the amount of cash interest the borrower pays and the investor receives each year. Also called the *contract interest rate* (p. 842).

Stated value An arbitrary amount assigned to a share of stock when it is issued (p. 738).

Statement of equity Another name for *statement of shareholders' equity* (p. 799).

Statement of shareholders' equity Presents changes in all components of equity. Also called *statement of equity* (p. 799).

Stock Shares into which the owners' equity of a corporation is divided (p. 731).

Stock dividend A proportional distribution by a corporation of its own shares to its shareholders. Also called a *share dividend* (p. 783).

Stock split An increase in the number of authorized and outstanding shares coupled with a proportionate reduction in the book value of each share (p. 785).

Straight-line amortization Allocating a bond discount or a bond premium to expense by dividing the discount or premium into equal amounts for each interest period (p. 849).

Strong currency A currency that is rising relative to other nations' currencies (p. 936).

Subsidiary An investee company in which a parent company owns more than 50 percent of the voting shares (p. 923).

Term bond Bonds that all mature at the same time for a particular issue (p. 840).

Times-interest-earned ratio Ratio of income from operations to interest expenses. Measures the number of times that operating income can cover interest expense. Also called the interest coverage ratio (p. 1072).

Trading on the equity Earning more income on borrowed money than the related expense, thereby increasing the earnings for the owners of the business (pp. 861, 1074).

Translation Another term for a currency conversion or foreign-currency exchange (p. 936).

Treasury bills A short-term debt obligation issued by a government (p. 913).

Treasury shares When a corporation repurchases its own shares and holds the shares in its treasury for resale (p. 788).

Underwriter An independent firm that is hired to sell shares on a corporation's behalf (p. 736).

Unlimited personal liability When a partnership (or a proprietorship) cannot pay its debts with business assets, the partners (or the proprietor) must use personal assets to meet the debt (p. 676).

Unregistered bonds Another name for *bearer bonds* (p. 840).

Vertical analysis Analysis of a financial statement that reveals the relationship of each statement item to a total, which is 100 percent (p. 1061).

Weak currency A currency that is falling relative to other nations' currencies (p. 936).

Working capital Current assets minus current liabilities; measures a business's ability to meet its short-term obligations with its current assets (p. 1067).

Write-down An accounting entry to recognize the decrease in the value of an asset by debiting an expense account and crediting the asset account (p. 922).

Yield The interest rate that an investor will receive based on a compounding period of one year (p. 841).

INDEX

A

accounting firms, largest, 674
accounting framework, 801, 867, 930, 986
accounting policy changes, 801
accounting standards. *See* Accounting Standards for Private Enterprises (ASPE); International Financial Reporting Standards (IFRS)
Accounting Standards Board, 985
Accounting Standards for Private Enterprises (ASPE), 730, 782
  see also ASPE-IFRS comparisons
  accrual-basis accounting, 985
  amortization methods, 851, 867
  capital lease, 864
  cash flow statement, 977, 1005
  earnings per share (EPS), 795, 1074
  financial statement analysis, 1081
  income statement, 803–804
  international transactions, 940–941
  investments, 924, 940–941
  investments and accounting methods, 918
  long-term liabilities, 867
  share capital, 750
  short-term investments, 915
  statement of shareholders' equity, 799, 803–804
  subsidiaries, accounting for, 923
accounts receivable turnover, 1070
accrual-basis accounting, 985
ACE Bakery, 923
acid-test ratio, 1068–1069
actively traded, 913
adjusting entries
  effective-interest method, 857–858
  interest expense, 855–858
  straight-line method, 856
admission of a partner, 688–692
  by investment in partnership, 689–692
  by investment in partnership, bonus to new partner, 691–692
  by investment in partnership, bonus to old partners, 690–691
  by investment in partnership at book value, no bonus, 689–690
  by purchase of partner's interest, 688–689
affiliated company, 922
Agnico Eagle Mines Ltd., 792
Allowance for Doubtful Accounts, 915

Alphabet Inc., 1064
amortization
  bond discount or bond premium, 849–855, 932
  effective-interest amortization, 851–855, 857–858, 867
  mortgage amortization schedule, 862
  partial-period amortization, 858
  straight-line amortization, 849–851, 856, 867
amortization expense, 989, 1002
amortized cost method, 932
annual reports, 1065, 1078
annuity
  future value of, 899–901
  present value of, 903–904
appropriations, 802
arrears, 745, 797
articles of incorporation, 730, 736
ASPE. *See* Accounting Standards for Private Enterprises (ASPE)
ASPE-IFRS comparisons
  amortization methods, 867
  bonds, investments in, 941
  cash flow statement, 1005
  equity investments, 940
  financial statement analysis, 1081
  foreign-currency transactions, 941
  hedging, 941
  income statement, 803–804
  investments in debt instruments, 941
  joint ventures, 940
  long-term liabilities, 867
  majority interest, 940–941
  non-strategic investments, 940
  other comprehensive income, 804
  share capital, 750
  statement of shareholders' equity, 803–804
  strategic investments, 940
asset revaluation, 693
assets
  current assets, 1004, 1064
  intangible assets, 742, 989–990, 997
  overstating assets, 742
  personal assets, and partnerships, 679
  rate of return on total assets, 748–749
  return on assets (ROA), 748–749

  sale of assets at a gain, on liquidation, 697–699
  sale of assets at a loss, on liquidation, 699
  tangible assets, 997
  understating assets, 742
auditor's report, 1078
authorization of shares, 732, 736
authorized shares, 736–737

B

balance sheet, 992, 1003
  cash flows and, 981
  comparative balance sheet, 1067
  consolidated balance sheet, 925–929
  elimination entry, 926, 928
  horizontal analysis, 1059
  investments, 913
  mortgage loans, 862–863
  note disclosure of cumulative preferred dividends, 745
  partnership, 678, 680
  shareholders' equity section, 741
  sole proprietorship, 678
  vertical analysis, 1063
basic EPS, 795, 797
BDO Canada LLP, 674
bearer bonds, 840
Bell Canada Enterprises (BCE), 785
benchmarking, 1064–1065
  against another company, 1064
  against industry average, 1064
bid price, 841
blended payments, 862
board of directors, 731, 732
Bombardier Aerospace (BA), 937
Bombardier Inc., 740, 935, 937
bond certificate, 839
bond discount. *See* discount
bond indenture, 838
bond investments, 917
bond premium. *See* premium
bond prices, 841–843
  bid price, 841
  bond interest rates, 842–843
  discount. *See* discount
  premium. *See* premium
  present value, 842
  yield, 841
bonds, 838–839, 867
  advantages of issuing bonds, 860

bonds (*Cont.*)
  amortization of bond discount or bond premium, 849–855
  amortized cost method, 932
  bearer bonds, 840
  bond certificate, 839
  bond prices, 841–843
  callable bonds, 858
  carrying amount, 853, 855
  conversion privileges, 797
  convertible bonds, 859–860
  coupon rate, 839
  debentures, 840, 859
  disclosure, 867
  face value, 839
  interest expense, bonds issued at a discount, 846–847
  interest expense, bonds issued at a premium, 848
  investments in, 931–935, 941
  issuing bonds and notes between interest dates, 844–845
  issuing bonds at a discount, 845–847
  issuing bonds at a premium, 847–848
  issuing bonds at par value, 843–844
  issuing bonds to borrow money, 843–848
  long-term investments, 932–935, 941
  maturity date, 839, 841
  maturity value, 839
  par value, 839, 843–844
  principal value, 839
  redeemable bonds, 858
  retirement of bonds, 858–859
  secured bonds, 840
  serial bonds, 840
  short-term investments, 932, 941
  sweeteners or incentives, 859
  term bonds, 840
  types of bonds, 840
  unregistered bonds, 840
  vs. shares, 840, 860–861
bonds payable, 838, 855, 904–905
book value, 746, 998
  book value per common share, 746–747, 1076
  book value per preferred share, 747
  in decision making, 748
  investment in partnership, 689–690
  of a share, 746–748
  withdrawal at, 693–695
book value per common share, 746–747, 1076
book value per preferred share, 747

borrowing, 860–861
Boston Pizza Royalties Income Fund, 740
Brazil, 922
BRIC countries, 922
business publications, 1066
bylaws, 732

C
call value, 747
callable bonds, 858
Canada
  largest accounting firms, 674
  stock market performance (TSX Composite), 738
Canada Business Corporations Act (CBCA)
  no-par-value shares, 738
  sale of repurchased shares, 791
  share repurchase, 788
  shareholders' rights, 735
  stated capital, 733
  stock dividends, and market value of shares issued, 784
Canada Revenue Agency, 676
Canada Savings Bonds, 859
Canadian dollar, 936
Canadian National Railway Company (CN), 838
Canadian Securities Administrators, 736
Canadian Tire Corporation, Limited, 730, 800
Capital balances, 698
capital deficiency, 699–700
capital investments, 682–684
capital lease, 863, 864–866
capitalized retained earnings, 783
carrying value, 915
cash, 743, 782, 980
  collection of cash in foreign currency, 938–939
  collections, 987, 988, 992–994
  measurement of cash adequacy, 984–985
  paying cash in a foreign currency, 937–938
Cash account, 978
cash-basis accounting, 985
cash dividends, 743–745, 782, 784, 787, 914, 919, 990
cash equivalents, 980
cash flow statement, 976–977, 978
  ability to pay dividends and debts, 979
  basic concepts, 978
  Cash account, transactions affecting, 978

cash and cash equivalents, 980
cash receipts and payments, 983
computation of individual amounts, 991–999
direct method, 982, 985, 986–990
discontinued operations, 983
evaluation of management decisions, 979
financing activities. *See* financing activities
format, 985
free cash flow, 984–985
indirect method, 985, 1000–1004
investing activities. *See* investing activities
net income-cash flow relationship, 979
operating activities. *See* operating activities
prediction of future cash flows, 979
purpose of, 979–980
cash flows, 978
  decreased cash flow, 1079
  from financing activities, 990
  free cash flow, 984–985
  future cash flows, prediction of, 979
  from investing activities, 989–990
  net income-cash flow relationship, 979
  from operating activities, 987–989
cash payments, 983
  see also cash flows
cash receipts, 983
  see also cash receipts
cash receipts of dividends, 988
CBCA. *See* Canada Business Corporations Act (CBCA)
certificates of deposit, 913
chairperson (of board), 732
change
  in accounting policy, 801
  in circumstances, 802
chief executive officer (CEO), 732
China, 922
CIBC Investor Services Inc., 912
circumstances, change in, 802
classes of preferred shares, 739–740
closely held, 748
co-ownership of property, 676
Collins Barrow, 674
common shares, 734, 737–739
  book value per common share, 746–747
  investors, 738
  issued at stated value, 739
  issued for assets other than cash, 739

no-par-value shares, 738

par value, 738

rights attached to, 735–736

stated value, 738–739

weighted average number of common shares outstanding, 796

common-size statements, 1063–1064, 1065

companion account, 915

comparability, 805

compound interest, 897–898

consistency principle, 800, 801

consolidated financial statements, 923, 925–930

consolidated balance sheet, 925–929

income of consolidated entity, 930

parent buys subsidiary's shares and pays for goodwill, 926–928

parent owns all subsidiary's shares, 925–926

parent owns less than 100 percent of subsidiary's shares, 928–929

consolidated statement of earnings and comprehensive income, 804–805

consolidation, 786

consolidation accounting, 923

consolidation method, 923

continuing operations, 793–794

continuous life of corporations, 731

contract interest rate, 842–843

contributed capital, 733, 734

controlling interest, 923

see also majority interest

conversion privileges, 797

convertible bonds, 859–860

convertible notes, 859–860

convertible preferred shares, 741

corporations, 730

advantages, 732

articles of incorporation, 730, 736

board of directors, 731, 732

characteristics, 730–732

closely held, 748

continuous life, 731

contributed capital, 733, 734

corporate taxation, 731

disadvantages, 732

dividends, 735, 743–745

evaluation of operations, 748–750

government regulation, 731

income statement, 792–798

issuing shares, 736–741

limited liability, 731

no mutual agency, 731

organization costs, 742

organization of a corporation, 732–733

owners' equity, 731

owner's investment, recording of, 733

private corporation, 730

proxy, 733

public corporation, 730, 1065

retained earnings, 733, 734–735, 782–783

rights of, 730–731

separate legal entity, 730–731

separation of ownership and management, 731

share capital, 733

share repurchase, 788–792

shareholders, 730

shareholders' equity, 733–736

shareholders' rights, 735–736

shares. See shares

statement of income and retained earnings, 798–799

statement of retained earnings, 798

statement of shareholders' equity, 799–800

transferability of ownership, 731

typical authority structure, 732

unique costs, 731–732

vs. partnership, 677

counterbalancing transaction, 939

coupon rate, 839

CPA Canada Handbook, 923, 928

capital lease, 864

consolidation, 923

financial instruments, 931 n

joint venture, 922

non-cash investing and financing activities, 984

organization costs, 742

proportionate consolidation, 922

retroactive restatement of financial information, 804

share investments, 914

share repurchase, 789

credit, 1070

credit agencies, 1066

creditors, 749, 1056, 1071

Criminal Code, 792

cumulative preferred shares, 745

currency options, 939

current assets, 1004, 1064

current liabilities, 1004, 1067–1069

current ratio, 1068

D

date of record, 743

days' sales in receivables, 1070–1071

death of a partner, 696

debentures, 840, 859

debt

cash received from, 990

collection of loans, 989–990

loans to other companies, 989

long-term debt, 854, 998–999, 1071–1072

long-term loans, 998

payment of, 990

servicing its debt, 1072

shareholder loans, 863

too much debt, 1079

vs. equity, 740

debt investments, 917

debt ratio, 1071–1072

declaration date, 743

declaration of dividends, 744

deficit, 734, 735, 782

Deloitte Canada's 50 Best Managed Companies, 729

Deloitte LLP, 674

direct financing leases, 863

direct method, 982, 985, 986–990, 996

directors' liability, 731–732

DIRTT Environmental Solutions Ltd., 729, 730, 731, 736, 737, 738–739, 739, 746, 748, 792

disclosure

bond issue details, 867

earnings per share (EPS), 1074

EPS information, 804

non-cash investing and financing activities, 984

discontinued operations, 794–795, 983

discount, 841, 843

amortization of bond discount, 849–855, 932

effective-interest method, 851–853

interest expense, bond issued at a discount, 845–847

straight-line amortization, 849–850

discounting, 901

dissolution, 675

dividend announcements or notices, 743

dividend dates, 743

dividend yield, 1075–1076, 1081

dividends, 735, 743–745

arrears, 745, 797

cash dividends, 743–745, 782, 784, 787, 914, 919, 990

cash receipts, 988

cumulative preferred shares, 745

date of record, 743

dividends (*Cont.*)

declaration date, 743

declaration of dividends, 744

dividend announcements or notices, 743

dividend dates, 743

division of dividends, 744

effects of, 787

financing activity, 999

limits on, 802–803

noncumulative preferred shares, 745

as operating activities, 983

payment of dividends, 744

preferred dividends, 797

proportionate share, 736

and retained earnings, 782

share dividend, 783–785

stock dividends. *See* stock dividends

Dollarama Inc., 781, 784, 788, 912

double taxation, 731

downside risk, 1075

drawings, 686–687

Dun & Bradstreet Canada, 1066

E

earnings per share (EPS), 795–798, 804, 1074–1075

basic EPS, 795, 797

borrowing, advantages of, 860–861

disclosure of, 1074

fully diluted EPS, 797–798, 1074

preferred dividends, 797

price-earnings ratio, 798

stock dividends, 796–797

stock splits, 796–797

weighted average number of common shares outstanding, 796

earnings problems, 1079

economic entity assumption, 930

effective-interest amortization, 851–855, 857–858, 867

effective interest rate, 843

efficient capital market, 1077

elimination entry, 926, 928

Emera Inc., 838

employees, payments to, 988, 994–995

EnCana Corporation, 730, 748

EPS. *See* earnings per share (EPS)

equity

return on equity (ROE), 749

shareholders' equity, 733–736

vs. debt, 740

equity investments. *See* share investments

equity method for investments, 920–922, 925

Ernst & Young LLP, 674

errors, 800–801

ethical considerations

issuance of shares, 742

share repurchase, 791–792

evaluation of operations, 748–750

Excel, 1058

F

face value, 839

factors, 1070

fair value method, 914, 917, 918

Fair Value Valuation Allowance, 915

financial analysis. *See* financial statement analysis; ratios

financial instruments, 931 *n*, 940

Financial Post, 1066

financial statement analysis

annual reports, 1078

benchmarking, 1064–1065

common-size statements, 1063–1064, 1065

horizontal analysis, 1057–1060, 1061

information sources, 1065–1066

investor decisions, 1077–1079

limitations of financial analysis, 1076–1077

methods of analysis, 1057

objectives of, 1056–1057

ratios. *See* ratios

red flags, 1079

trend percentages, 1060

vertical analysis, 1061–1062

financial statements, 1078

see also specific financial statements

common-size statements, 1063–1064

consolidated financial statements, 923, 925–930

partnership, 678–679

sole proprietorship, 678–679

timing of, 978

useful, 1079

financing activities, 981–982, 984

cash dividends, payment of, 990

cash flows from, 990

computation of cash amounts of, 998–999

debt, cash received from, 990

debt, payment of, 990

direct method, 988, 1004

dividend payments, 999

long-term debt, issuances and payments of, 998–999

share issuance, 990, 999

share repurchases, 990, 999

foreign-currency conversion. *See* translation

foreign-currency exchange rate, 935–936, 937

foreign-currency transaction gain, 937, 939

foreign-currency transaction loss, 937, 939

foreign-currency transactions, 935–939, 936–937

ASPE-IFRS comparison, 941

collection of cash in foreign currency, 938–939

counterbalancing transaction, 939

foreign-currency exchange rate, 935–936, 937

foreign-currency transaction gain, 937, 939

foreign-currency transaction loss, 937, 939

hedging, 939

paying cash in a foreign currency, 937–938

risk minimization, 939

strong currency, 936

translation, 936

weak currency, 936

forward contracts, 939

free cash flow, 984–985

Fruita de Norte (FDN) project, 922

fully diluted EPS, 797–798, 1074

future value, 897–901

of an annuity, 899–901

formula for, 898

tables, 898–899

futures contracts, 939

G

GAAP. *See* generally accepted accounting principles (GAAP)

gains

foreign-currency transaction gain, 937, 939

realized gain, 919

sale of assets, 1002–1003

sale of assets at a gain, on liquidation, 697–699

on sale of equity method investment, 921–922

on sale prior to adjustments to fair value, 915

unrealized, 915

general partner, 677

general partnership, 677

generally accepted accounting principles (GAAP), 730, 782

George Weston Limited, 923, 925

Globe and Mail's Report on Business, 798, 1066
Globe Investor, 1066
going concern, 979
going out of business. *See* liquidation
Goldman Sachs Group, 838
Google Inc., 1064
government regulation, 731
Grant Thornton Canada, 674

H

hedging, 939, 941
Heenan Blaikie, 697
High Liner Foods Inc., 1055
horizontal analysis, 1057–1060, 1061

I

IFRS. *See* International Financial Reporting Standards (IFRS)
Imperial Oil Limited, 731
income statement, 991, 1002
   ASPE, 803–804
   common-size income statement, 1065
   comparative income statement, 1066
   continuing operations, 793–794
   corporations, 792–798
   discontinued operations, 794–795
   earnings per share (EPS), 795–798
   horizontal analysis, 1058
   IFRS, 803–804
   multi-step income statement approach, 805
   net income, 792
   partnership, 678
   single-step income statement, 793
   sole proprietorship, 678
   vertical analysis, 1062
income tax expense, 794, 988–989
income trust, 740
incorporators, 732
India, 922
Indigo Books & Music Inc., 730, 980
indirect method, 985, 1000–1004
industry average, 1064
industry-specific publications, 1064
information sources, 1065–1066
initial public offering (IPO), 729, 736
insider information, 1077
insider trading, 792
insiders, 792
intangible assets, 742, 989–990, 997
interest, 983, 988
interest allowance, 684
interest coverage ratio, 1072
interest expense, 851

adjusting entries, 855–858
bonds issued at a discount, 846–847, 853
bonds issued at a premium, 848, 855
cash payments, 988–989
interest rate
   bond interest rates, 842–843
   contract interest rate, 842–843
   effective interest rate, 843
   market interest rate, 843
   stated interest rate, 842–843, 843
international accounting, 935
   see also foreign-currency transactions
International Accounting Standard (IAS) 8, 804
International Financial Reporting Standards (IFRS), 730, 782
   see also ASPE-IFRS comparisons
   amortization methods, 851, 867
   cash flow statement, 1005
   effective-interest method, 851, 867
   financial statement analysis, 1081
   income statement, 803–804
   international transactions, 940–941
   investments, 940–941
   long-term liabilities, 867
   share capital, 750
   statement of shareholders' equity, 803–804
inventory
   buildup of, 1079
   changes in, 1079
   sale of, 1069–1071
inventory turnover, 1069–1070
investees, 912–913
investing activities, 981–982, 984
   cash flows from, 989–990
   collection of loans, 989–990
   computation of cash amounts of, 997–998
   intangible assets, acquisitions of, 997
   intangible assets, payments for, 989
   intangible assets, sale of, 989–990, 997
   investments, payments for, 989
   investments, sale of, 989–990
   loan collections, acquisitions and sales of, 998
   loans to other companies, 989
   long-term investments, acquisitions and sales of, 998
   long-term loans, acquisitions and sales of, 998

property, plant, and equipment, payments for, 989
property, plant, and equipment, sale of, 989–990
tangible assets, acquisitions and sales of, 997
investment trust, 740
investments
   analysis of shares as an investment, 1075–1076
   under ASPE, 918
   on balance sheet, 913
   in bonds, 931–935
   capital investments, 682–684
   cash payments for, 989
   cash receipts from sale of, 989–990
   classification of, 913
   equity investments. *See* share investments
   equity method for investments, 920–922
   long-term investments, 913, 917–924
   non-strategic investments, 940
   in partnership, 689–692
   share investments. *See* share investments
   short-term investments, 913, 914–917
   strategic investments, 940
   summary of accounting for investments under ASPE, 924
investor decisions, 1077–1079
investor in a joint arrangement, 922 *n*
investors, 738, 740, 912–913, 1056
IPO. *See* initial public offering (IPO)
issue price, 737
issued shares, 737
issuing shares. *See* share issuance

J

The Jean Coutu Group (PJC) Inc., 730
Jim Pattison Group, 730, 794
joint arrangement, 922*n*
joint venture, 922, 940

K

Kinross Gold Corporation, 736, 911, 912–913, 922, 935
KPMG LLP, 674

L

Landen, Barry, 792
lease, 863–866
   capital lease, 863, 864–866
   direct financing leases, 863
   operating leases, 864, 866
   provisions, 864
   sales-type leases, 863

lessee, 863
lessor, 863
leverage, 750, 1074
Levi Strauss & Co., 988
LexisNexis, 1066
liability (personal)
    directors' liability, 731–732
    limited liability, 731
    unlimited personal liability, 676
life insurance, 696
limited liability, 731
limited liability partnerships (LLPs), 678, 731
limited life of partnership, 675
limited partners, 677–678
limited partnership, 677–678
liquid assets, 1068
liquidation, 696
    capital deficiency, 699–700
    of a partnership, 696–700
    sale of assets at a gain, 697–699
    sale of assets at a loss, 699
liquidation value, 747
liquidity, 1066
loan collections, 998
loans to other companies, 989
Loblaw Companies Limited, 730, 785, 923, 925
long-term debt, 998–999, 1071–1072
long-term investments, 913
    acquisitions and sales of, 998
    amortized cost method, 932
    in bonds, 932–935
    long-term share investments, 917–924
long-term liabilities, 838
    bonds. See bonds
    IFRS, 867
    mortgages, 862–863
    reporting, 855
    shareholder loans, 863
long-term loans, 998
long-term share investments
    consolidation method, 923
    controlling interest, 923
    equity method for investments, 920–922
    at fair value, 919
    fair value method, 918
    gain or loss on sale of equity method investment, 921–922
    recording share of dividends, 921
    recording share of income/loss, 920–921
    sale of, where no significant influence, 919
    ...nificant influence, 920–922

summary of accounting for investments under ASPE, 924
without significant influence, 918–919
long-term solvency, 1056
loss
    foreign-currency transaction loss, 937, 939
    realized loss, 919
    sale of assets, 1002–1003
    sale of assets at a loss, on liquidation, 699
    on sale of equity method investment, 921–922
    on sale of partnership interest, 689
    on sale prior to adjustments to fair value, 915
    sharing partnership losses, 681–686
    unrealized, 915
lotteries, 903
Lululemon Athletica Inc., 785
Lune Gold Corporation, 786

M
Magna International Inc., 737
majority interest, 923, 940–941
Mallette, 674
management intent, 911, 913
management's discussion and analysis (MD&A), 1078
management's report to the shareholders, 1078
Maple Leaf Foods Inc., 1055
Market Data, 1066
market efficiency, 1077
market interest rate, 843
market price, 746
market value, 746, 748, 784
market value method, 914, 918
    see also fair value method
marketable securities. See short-term investments
maturity date, 839, 841
maturity value, 839
McCain Foods Limited, 1055
McDonald's Corporation, 838
measurement, 867
memorandum entry, 786
minority interest, 928
MNP LLP, 674
money market funds, 913
mortgage amortization schedule, 862
mortgage instalment payment schedule, 862
mortgage note, 862
mortgages, 862–863

multi-step income statement approach, 805
Muskrat Falls energy project, 838
mutual agency, 675–676, 731

N
Nalcor Energy, 838
National Automobile Dealers Association, 1064
National Post, 1066
negative retained earnings, 735, 782
Neilson Dairy, 923
net income, 792
net income-cash flow relationship, 979
Newfoundland and Labrador, 838
no-par-value shares, 738
non-controlling interest, 928
non-strategic investments, 940
noncumulative preferred shares, 745
Nygård International, 988

O
online financial databases, 1066
Ontario Securities Commission, 1066
operating activities, 981–983
    amortization expense, 989
    cash collections from customers, 988, 992–994
    cash flows from, 987–989
    computation of cash amounts of, 992–996
    direct method, 996
    dividends, receipt of, 988
    employees, payments to, 988, 994–995
    income tax expense, 988–989
    income tax payments, 996
    indirect method, 1001, 1004
    interest, receipts of, 988
    interest expense, 988–989
    interest payments, 996
    operating expenses, payments for, 995–996
    suppliers, payments to, 988, 994
operating leases, 864, 866
operations, 981
organization costs, 742
organization of a corporation, 732–733
other comprehensive income, 804
outstanding shares, 737, 746, 789
over-the-counter (OTC) market, 841

P
P/E ratio. See price-earnings (P/E) ratio
par value, 738, 839, 843–844
parent company, 923

parent buys subsidiary's shares and pays for goodwill, 926–928

parent owns all subsidiary's shares, 925–926

parent owns less than 100 percent of subsidiary's shares, 928–929

partial-period amortization, 858

partnership, 674

admission of a partner, 688–692

advantages, 677

balance sheet, 680

capital deficiency, 699–700

characteristics, 675–677

co-ownership of property, 676

death of a partner, 696

disadvantages, 677

dissolution, 675

financial statements, 678–679

formation of, 679–680

general partner, 677

general partnership, 677

life insurance, 696

limited liability partnerships (LLPs), 678, 731

limited life, 675

limited partners, 677–678

limited partnership, 677–678

liquidation, 696–700

mutual agency, 675–676

partnership agreement, 675

personal assets, use of, 679

sale of assets at a gain, on liquidation, 697–699

sale of assets at a loss, on liquidation, 699

sharing partnership profits and losses. See partnership profits and losses

taxation of, 676

types of, 677–678

unlimited personal liability, 676

vs. corporations, 677

vs. sole proprietorships, 677

withdrawal of partner from the business, 693–696

withdrawals (drawings), 686–687

partnership agreement, 675

partnership profits and losses

allocation of negative remainder, 685

allocation of net loss, 686

allocation of profit, 684–685

interest allowance, 684

sharing based on a stated fraction, 681–682

sharing based on capital investments, 682–683

sharing based on capital investments and on service, 683–684

sharing based on service and interest, 684–685

PepsiCo Inc., 984

percentage change in net revenues, 1057

personal liability. See liability (personal)

"plus accrued interest," 844, 845

Ponzi schemes, 977

preemptive right, 736

preferred dividends, 797

preferred shares, 739–741

book value per preferred share, 747

classes, 739–740

conversion privileges, 797

convertible preferred shares, 741

cumulative preferred shares, 745

debt vs. equity, 740

investors, 740

issuing preferred shares, 740

liquidation value, 747

noncumulative preferred shares, 745

premium, 841, 843

amortization of bond premium, 849–855, 932

effective-interest method, 853–855

interest expense, bond issued at a premium, 848

straight-line amortization, 850–851

present value, 842, 865, 901–905

of an annuity, 903–904

bonds payable, 904–905

discounting, 901

formula for, 901

tables, 902–903

president, 732

president's letter to the shareholders, 1078

price-earnings (P/E) ratio, 798, 1075

PricewaterhouseCoopers LLP, 674, 675, 688

principal, 842

principal value, 839

private corporation, 730

see also Accounting Standards for Private Enterprises (ASPE)

proceeds, 998

Proctor & Gamble, 1055

profit

on sale of partnership interest, 689

sharing partnership profits, 681–686

profit-and-loss ratio, 698

property, plant, and equipment, 989–990

proportionate consolidation, 922

proportionate share, 736

proprietorship. See sole proprietorship

prospective treatment, 802

prospectus, 736

provincial securities commission, 1065–1066

provisions, 864

proxy, 733

public corporation, 730, 1065

see also International Financial Reporting Standards (IFRS)

pyramid schemes, 977

Q

quarterly reports, 1065

quick ratio, 1068–1069

R

rate of return on common shareholders' equity, 749, 1073–1074

rate of return on net sales, 1072–1073

rate of return on total assets, 748–749, 1073

ratios, 1066

ability to collect receivables, 1069–1071

ability to pay current liabilities, 1067–1069

ability to pay long-term debt, 1071–1072

ability to sell inventory, 1069–1071

accounts receivable turnover, 1070

acid-test ratio, 1068–1069

analysis of shares as an investment, 1075–1076

book value per common share, 1076

current ratio, 1068

days' sales in receivables, 1070–1071

debt ratio, 1071–1072

dividend yield, 1075–1076, 1081

earnings per share (EPS), 1074–1075

inventory turnover, 1069–1070

price-earnings (P/E) ratio, 1075

profitability, 1072–1075

quick ratio, 1068–1069

rate of return on common shareholders' equity, 1073–1074

rate of return on net sales, 1072–1073

rate of return on total assets, 1073

return on assets (ROA), 1073

return on equity (ROE), 1073–1074

return on sales (ROS), 1072–1073

return on shareholders' equity, 1073–1074

solvency, 1071–1072

times-interest-earned ratio, 1072

working capital, 1067

RBC Dominion Securities, 736, 912
rebuttable presumption, 940
receivables
    changes in, 1079
    collection of, 1069–1071
    inability to collect, 1079
recognition, 867
reconciliation method, 985
    see also indirect method
red flags, 1079
redeemable bonds, 858
redemption value, 747
relevance, 804, 805, 867, 986
reliability, 804, 867, 986
repurchase shares, 788
    see also share repurchase
retained earnings, 733, 734–735,
        782–783
    appropriations, 802
    capitalized retained earnings, 783
    and dividends, 782, 783–784
    dividends, declaration of, 743
    ending balance, 783
    limits on dividends and share
        repurchases, 802–803
    negative retained earnings, 735, 782
    restrictions on, 802–803
    statement of income and retained
        earnings, 798–799
    statement of retained earnings, 798
retirement of bonds, 858–859
retroactive restatement of financial
        information, 804
retrospective treatment, 801
return on assets (ROA), 748–749,
        1073
return on equity (ROE), 749,
        1073–1074
return on sales (ROS), 1072–1073
return on shareholders' equity,
        1073–1074
reverse split, 786
Richter, 674
Risk Management Association, 1064
RMA Annual Statement Studies, 1064
ROA. See return on assets (ROA)
ROE. See return on equity (ROE)
Rogers Communications Inc., 737
RONA Inc., 975, 976–977
ROS. See return on sales (ROS)
Russia, 922

S
salary allowance, 683
sales, changes in, 1079
sales-type leases, 863
Saputo Inc., 923

Scotiabank, 785
secured bonds, 840
SEDAR (System for Electronic
        Document Analysis and Retrieval),
        736, 1065
segment of the business, 794
segmented information, 930
separate legal entity, 730–731
separation of ownership and
        management, 731
serial bonds, 840
service, 683
servicing its debt, 1072
share capital, 733, 734, 750
    see also share issuance; shares
share certificates, 733
share dividend, 783
    see also stock dividends
share investments, 912–913
    accounting for, 914–917
    carrying value, 915
    cost per share, 914
    gain or loss on sale prior to
        adjustments to fair value, 915
    investors and investees, 912–913
    long-term share investments,
        917–924
    sale of, 916–917
    share prices, 912
    significant influence, 913
share issuance, 736–741
    advantages, 860
    authorized shares, 736–737
    common shares, 737–739
    ethical considerations, 742
    financing activity, 990, 999
    initial public offering (IPO), 736
    issue price, 737
    issued shares, 737
    number of shares, 736–737
    outstanding shares, 737
    preferred shares, 739–741
    prospectus, 736
    SEDAR (System for Electronic
        Document Analysis and Retrieval),
        736
    underwriter, 736
share prices, 912
share repurchase, 788–792
    above average issue price, 790
    at average issue price, 788–789
    below average issue price, 789
    ethical issues, 791–792
    financing activity, 990, 999
    journal entries, summary of, 791
    legal issues, 791–792
    limits on, 802–803

no balance in Contributed Surplus-
        Share Repurchase account, 790
    recording, 788–791
    sale of repurchased shares, 791
    treasury shares, 788
shareholder loans, 863
shareholders, 730, 749
shareholders' equity, 733–736, 747
    on balance sheet, 741
    common shareholders' equity, 749
    contributed capital, 733, 734, 782
    negative retained earnings, 735
    rate of return on common
        shareholders' equity, 749,
        1073–1074
    reporting formats, 800
    retained earnings, 733, 734–735,
        782
    statement of shareholders' equity,
        799–800, 803–804
    variations in reporting shareholders'
        equity, 800
shareholders' rights, 735–736
shares, 731, 733
    advantages of issuing shares, 860
    analysis of shares as an investment,
        1075–1076
    authorization of shares, 732, 736
    authorized shares, 736–737
    book value, 746–748
    common shares. See common shares
    different values of, 746–748
    issued shares, 737
    issuing shares. See share issuance
    market value, 746, 748
    no-par-value shares, 738
    outstanding shares, 737, 746, 789
    par value, 738
    preferred shares. See preferred
        shares
    share repurchase. See share
        repurchase
    stated value, 738–739
    underpriced shares, 748
    vs. bonds, 840, 860–861
short-term investments, 913
    accounting for, 914–917
    bond investments, 917
    in bonds, 932
    fair value method, 914, 917
    market value method, 914
    reporting, 915–916
    sale of, 916–917
    share investments, 914–917
    summary of accounting for
        investments under ASPE, 924
short-term liquidity, 1056

shutting down the business. *See* liquidation

significant influence, 913, 920–922, 940

single-step income statement, 793

Sleeman Breweries Ltd., 748

sole proprietorship
  financial statements, 678–679
  owner's investment, recording of, 733, 782
  vs. partnership, 677

solvency, 1071–1072

spreadsheets, 861, 1058

Stanfield's Ltd., 988

stated capital, 733–734
  see also share capital

stated interest rate, 842–843, 843

stated value, 738–739

statement of changes in equity. *See* statement of shareholders' equity

statement of comprehensive income, 804–805

statement of earnings. *See* income statement

statement of equity, 799–800

statement of income and retained earnings, 798–799

statement of owner's equity, 678

statement of partners' equity, 678

statement of retained earnings, 798

statement of shareholders' equity, 799–800, 803–804

stewardship, 806

stock, 731

stock dividends, 783–785
  amount of retained earnings transferred, 783–784
  earnings per share (EPS), 796–797
  effects of, 783, 787
  reasons for, 784
  receipt of, 914–915
  recording, 784–785
  and taxable income, 787
  vs. stock splits, 785, 786–787

stock exchanges, 912

stock splits, 785–787

consolidation, 786

earnings per share (EPS), 796–797

effects of, 787

memorandum entry, 786

reverse split, 786

and taxable income, 787

2-for-1 stock split, 786

vs. stock dividends, 785, 786–787

stockholders' equity. *See* shareholders' equity

straight-line amortization, 849–851, 856, 867

strategic investments, 940

strong currency, 936

subsidiary, 923, 925–930
  financial statements in foreign currency, 939
  parent buys subsidiary's shares and pays for goodwill, 926–928
  parent owns all subsidiary's shares, 925–926
  parent owns less than 100 percent of subsidiary's shares, 928–929

suppliers, payments to, 988, 994

T

T-account approach, 991

tangible assets, 997

taxation
  corporations, 731
  double taxation, 731
  of partnerships, 676

TD Securities Inc., 736

TELUS Corporation Inc., 730, 748, 749, 750, 838, 841, 912

temporary investments. *See* short-term investments

term bonds, 840

Tim Hortons Inc., 730, 731, 736

time value of money, 842, 897
  see also future value; present value

times-interest-earned ratio, 1072

Toronto-Dominion Bank, 838

Toronto Stock Exchange (TSX), 729, 738, 912, 1066

trading on the equity, 861, 1074

transferability of ownership, 731

translation, 936

treasury bills, 913, 980

treasury shares, 788

trend percentages, 1060

TSX Venture Exchange, 912

2-for-1 stock split, 786

U

understandability, 930

Underworld Resources Inc., 912–913

underwriter, 736

unlimited personal liability, 676

unregistered bonds, 840

US dollar, 936

useful information, 930

V

venturer, 922 *n*

vertical analysis, 1061–1062

vice-president, 732

W

weak currency, 936

weighted average number of common shares outstanding, 796

WestJet Airlines Ltd., 838, 912

"what if" analysis, 861

Winpak Ltd., 1055, 1056, 1058, 1060, 1062

withdrawal of partner from the business, 693–696
  asset revaluation, 693
  at book value, 693–695
  close the books, 693
  death of a partner, 696
  identification of amount owed to withdrawing partner, 693
  at less than book value, 695
  at more than book value, 695

withdrawals, 686–687

working capital, 1067

write-downs, 922, 934

written partnership agreement, 675

Y

Yahoo! Inc., 1064

yield, 841